GENERAL INTRODUCTION 4

PART ONE: PARAPSYCHOLOGICAL AND PSYCHIC SOURCES
   INTRODUCTION 5
     Societies, Organizations And General Guides 6
     Journals, Periodicals, Magazines And Newspapers 23
     Books And Bookstores 33

PART TWO: ENERGIES
   INTRODUCTION 53
     Fields Of Life And Cosmic Influences 54
     The Aura And Out-Of-Body Experiences (O.O.B.E.) 59
     Plants And Pyramids 74

PART THREE: METHODS OF PSYCHIC AND SPIRITUAL DEVELOPMENT
   INTRODUCTION 85
     Divination, Mediums And Psychics 86
     Altered States Of Consciousness And Extended Sensory Awareness 124
     Personal Paths And Teachers 163

PART FOUR: DIMENSIONS OF HEALING
   INTRODUCTION 205
     Roads To Health 205
     Spiritual Healing 224
     Radionics And Medical Radiesthesia 228

PART FIVE: MYSTERIES OF TIME AND SPACE
   INTRODUCTION 239
     Time And The Multi-Dimensional Self 239
     Ancient Mysteries 254
     Strange Sightings And Extraterrestrials 266

Diligent effort has been made to locate and secure permission for the inclusion of all copyrighted material in this book. If any such acknowledgments have been inadvertently omitted, the editor and the publisher would appreciate receiving full information so that proper credit may be given in future editions.

Copyright © 1974 by June and Nicholas Regush

All rights reserved. This book, or parts thereof, must not be reproduced in any form without permission. Published simultaneously in Canada by Longman Canada Limited, Toronto.

SBN: 399-11475-0
Library of Congress Catalog Card Number: 74-16613
PRINTED IN THE UNITED STATES OF AMERICA

ACKNOWLEDGEMENTS

We would like to acknowledge the cooperation of the following: Academy Of Parapsychology And Medicine, American Society For Psychical Research, Aquarian Research Foundation, Arica Institute, Association For Humanistic Psychology, Association For Research And Enlightenment, Association For The Understanding Of Man, Astara, Aum Esoteric Study Center, Baywood Publishing Company, Beyond Reality, Biofeedback Instrument Company, Biofeedback Instruments, Bio Scan Corporation, Borderland Sciences Research Foundation, Burchette Brothers Productions, Canadian Institute Of Psychosynthesis, Church Of All Worlds, College Of Psychic Studies, Delawarr Laboratories, Dialogue House Associates, Dr. Stanley Dean, Dr. Milan Ryzl, El Cariso Publications, Fate Magazine And Venture Bookshop, Fields Within Fields, Foundation For Research On The Nature Of Man, F.S.R. Publications, General Educational Media, Gordon And Breach, Health Research, Hippocrates Health Institute, Inner-Space Interpreters Services, Institute Of Psychic Science, International Imports, Linear And Circular Permutations, Llewellyn Publications, Markham House Press, Marlar Publishing Company, Matagiri, New Horizons Research Foundation, New York Astrology Center, Oriental Institute Of Chinese Studies, Parapsychology Foundation, Psychic News, Psychical Research Foundation, Psychic Spectrum, Psychic Tapestry, Rolling Stone, Scarecrow Press, Schneider Instrument Company, Silva Mind Control International, Sivananda Yoga Vedanta Centre, Southern California Society For Psychical Research, Spaceview, Spiritual Frontiers Fellowship, Sri Aurobindo International Center, The American Society Of Dowsers, The A.R.E. Clinic, The Associated Readers Of Tarot, International, The Church Of Scientology Of California, The Dowsing Supply Company, The Findhorn Community, The Institute For Psychoenergetics, The Institute For Religious Psychology, The Institute Of Mentalphysics, The Love Project, The Movement Of Spiritual Inner Awareness, The R.M. Bucke Memorial Society, The Society For Psychical Research, The Spiritualist Association Of Great Britain, The Summit Lighthouse, The Theosophical Publishing House, Toth Pyramid Company, The Triune Science Of Being Awareness Center, Yes Bookstore.

•

Extra special thanks goes to The International Cooperation Council, Fate Magazine, and the staff of Weiser's Bookstore in New York, to Mankind Research Unlimited and to Bruce Sullivan whose suggestions were extremely helpful.

We would also like to thank our editor at G.P. Putnam's Sons, Walter Betkowski, the people at Twin Arts, Inc. in New York who designed the book and our secretary Norah Lloyd-Jones.

AN IMPORTANT NOTE

We have tried to take into account as many price changes as possible before this book went to press. Books listed as clothbound may already be in paper editions. Product prices as well may have gone up since publication. In writing for any catalogue, we ask that at least one dollar be enclosed due to spiralling handling costs. This will greatly help smaller organizations in answering requests. A self-addressed envelope with postage would in most cases be a kind consideration.

ABOUT THE EDITORS

June and Nicholas Regush have been actively involved in the psychic field for the last four years and are presently working together on two new books. They are currently living in Montreal.

June Regush has a degree in visual arts and is presently involved in art history studies at McGill University with a special focus on the metaphysical impulse in art. She is also a sculptress and is involved in dream research.

Nicholas Regush has written widely in the social sciences and political affairs. He is also the co-author of Open Reality and Ic (with Richard Altschuler) and has edited The Human Aura. In 1975, his latest books, Parapsychology; The Dimensions Of Medicine; Exploring The Human Aura — A New Way of Viewing and Investigating Psychic Phenomena (in collaboration with Jan Merta); Facing The Challenge—An Introduction To Sociology and The Hieronymous Machine And Other Devices will be published.

This book is dedicated to Tam Mossman for the many insights.

The Western world has in recent years experienced an explosion of public interest in a wide range of human behavior which does not fit into the more conventional and routinized sensory expectations of everyday life. PSI, the twenty-third letter of the Greek alphabet, has become a popular symbol of the human mind's unlimited possibilities and points to THE OTHER WORLD in which barriers to realizng our human potential are being transcended by a broad spectrum of ideas and methods of extending sensory awareness derived from ancient and modern systems of experiencing reality.

This book catalogues and documents the OTHER WORLD in the hope that more people will discover that interest in PSI is not a whirlwind fad but reflects a wide-scale conscientious human effort to examine how man, society and nature are intimately related. At a time when the increasing global violations of our resources and spirit enmesh us in a web of planetary anguish and alienation, the need for alternative ways of living and relating to one another has never been quite so urgent.

While there is less resistance to a wide range of unexplained behavior, unusual human experiences continue to be denigrated by those who remain arrogantly addicted to one way of experiencing "reality." If interest in PSI is to fulfill its promise to offer humanity a more comprehensive appreciation of the diversity of human experience, it will be necessary to explore the possibility that there is a meaningful continuity to all mental states. We therefore must rid ourselves of the habitual tendency to create imaginary lines between what is real and what is not. This requires the ability and desire to better understand how each of us creates our own everyday beliefs. For this reason, we would like to stress that the information in this book be viewed *in terms of your own evolving beliefs and values* and that it would be wise to be wary of any system of experiencing reality which calls for blind acceptance.

We have attempted to provide a large representative sample of information from what we call THE OTHER WORLD—those states of mind that lie at the periphery of our consciousness and are increasingly being integrated into the more dominant behavioral patterns of everyday life. While many worthwhile organizations, products and services have been excluded due to space limitations, we have also omitted anything we believe to be exploitive. The emphasis throughout is on those ideas and techniques which can be used as points of departure for the on-going process of increasing self-awareness.

PART ONE: PARAPSYCHOLOGICAL AND PSYCHIC SOURCES

After a long, difficult struggle for scientific recognition, psychical research made great strides in the last decade. In 1969, the Parapsychological Association was granted affiliation with the American Association for the Advancement of Science. Anthropologist Margaret Mead had argued in favor of acceptance, stating that "the whole history of scientific advance is full of scientists investigating phenomena that the establishment did not believe were there." She might have added that what is called today's science and dominant world view often resembles nineteenth century scientific thinking and certainly is not congruous with advances in physics. With the arrival of quantum physics and the theory of relativity, in Sir James Jeans' words, "the universe began to look more like a great thought than like a great machine." A smoothly functioning clock-like mechanical universe was conceptually destroyed by the "hidden environments" of the atom and intergalactic space. According to quantum physicist, Wolfgang Pauli, mind and body were "complementary aspects of the same reality." Others, including Albert Einstein and Werner Heisenberg, introduced a new world of non-mechanical reality placing man at the very centre. The observer could not be separated from the observed. Probability replaced certainty. Chance replaced determinism.
Parapsychology fits well with these developments. According to psychologist Gardner Murphy, "It is the physics of the nineteenth century . . . that makes the phenomena impossible. As long as the reality described by (recent) advances is overshadowed by older models of the universe, we can hardly expect any psychic phenomena, no matter how well researched and documented, to receive the scientific attention it merits."

Societies, Organizations And General Guides

Numerous psychic research organizations have been founded which add to the work being done by the older professional societies, and growing networks of information exchange have been established. In the process, a multidimensional approach to PSI is emerging which incorporates basic discoveries from all the sciences with a greater understanding and respect for cross-cultural systems of experiencing the world.

THE GUIDE BOOK FOR THE STUDY OF PSYCHICAL RESEARCH
Robert H. Ashby
Weiser, 1972

Includes annotated and unannotated bibliographies for the beginning and advanced student, as well as procedures for locating and arranging a sitting with a medium. Also lists research organizations in the United Kingdom and the United States, libraries, publications and organizations, important figures in psychical research, and a glossary of terms.

INSTITUT FUR GRENZGEBIETE DER PSYCHOLOGIE
(Institute for Border Areas of Psychology)
78 Freiburg im Bresgau,
Eichhalde 12, West Germany

Dr. Hans Bender and colleagues are involved in many phases of parapsychological research. The institute publishes a semi-annual bulletin and occasional monographs.

TV SERIES ON PARAPSYCHOLOGY

The 26-program TV series on parapsychology, "WHO IS MAN?", featuring Herbert B. Puryear, Director of Education of the Association for Research and Enlightenment, has recently been made a part of the Public Television Library Catalog used by station managers and program directors. If you would like these programs to be seen in your own area, you can contact the manager of your local Public Television station and request it.

Using a basically conversational format, the programs are designed to give insights into the general field of parapsychological research, and explore the relevance of such research for man's understanding of himself.

PURPOSE OF THE WORLD UNIVERSITY

The highest purposes of man are served by pursuing the ways of peace and discovering the nature of life. His claims to greatness are embodied in his dreams, his visions, and his ideals. The World University seeks to build upon this divine creative urge and to apply itself to the common cause of discovery and interpretation.

• To prepare the peoples of the world for the planetary age of intercultural cooperation and international citizenship is the aim of the World University. Its purpose is to inspire men and women of goodwill to place their humanity above their nationality, to elevate their faith above their creed, and to reconcile the many diverse cultural and ideological expressions into a synthesis of understanding, capable of laying foundations ultimately for a world order under world law.

• To channel human energies into a major assault on the principal enemies of man: poverty, hunger, ignorance, and war.

• To lift education into a new spiritual dimension by shifting the learning process from mind training to soul cognition.

• To demonstrate Twenty–First Century living in a Twentieth Century environment.

You Are Cordially Invited

• To send for our latest free literature on the formation of the World University and the current operation of its world program.

• To inquire without obligation about faculty opportunities and student enrollment.

• To assist with the further development of the World University by becoming a member of the prestigious WU Roundtable now extant in more than sixty nations.

Write the World University, International Administration, Tucson, Arizona 85717 for membership, employment, and enrollment information. Interested educators please send resume with inquiry.

"From sheer psychological and philosophical necessity, traditional common-sense philosophy from the earliest Greeks to Aquinas accepted the existence in man of an essential immaterial element . . . setting him above the merely animal. This element they called psyche, enelechy, anima or soul.

"It has also to be recognized that for the soul's functioning as an essential element in the hylomorphic human person, it needs sense data, of which the brain is the collecting, integrating and distributing mechanism. Yet it would be quite childish to identify the insturment with its user, even though the user be dependent upon the instrument for operating. . . . We shall have to accept the ancient concept of the soul again: as an immaterial, noncorporeal part of the human person, and yet an integral part of his nature, not just some concomitant aspect of man, but something without which he is not a human person. . . .

"There is a sense in which the present is an age of which a characteristic is its failure to understand the status of its own abstractions, and this, perhaps, is the inevitable fruit of the divorce of natural science from metaphysics, to have achieved which was the empty triumph of the nineteenth century. . . . For me, the chill physico-mathematical concept of the human mind is a muddy vesture of decay in which I am not willing to be enfolded. It is unworthy of the dignity of Man. And if any say that this is not a scientific attitude I am unmoved by the irrelevance, for, outside its proper field of discourse, the word 'science' does not intimidate me. Man was not made for science, but science by man, who remains more and greater than his creations."

SIR FRANCIS WALSHE, Neurologist,
Thoughts upon the Equation of Mind with Brain,
Brain—A Journal of Neurology, March 1953

"In the same way that our misconception of the solar system had to be freed from prejudice by Copernicus, the most strenuous efforts of a well-nigh revolutionary nature were needed to free psychology . . . from the prejudice that the psyche is, on the one hand, a mere epiphenomenon of a biochemical process in the brain or, on the other hand, a wholly unapproachable and recondite matter. The connection with the brain does not in itself prove that the psyche is an epiphenomomen, a secondary function causally dependent on biochemical processes. . . .

"The phenomena of parapsychology . . . warns us to be careful for they point to a relativization of space and time through psychic factors which casts doubt on our naive and overhasty explanation of the parallels between the psychic and the physical. For the sake of this explanation people deny the findings of parapsychology outright, either for philosophical reasons or from intellectual laziness. This can hardly be considered a scientifically responsible attitude, even though it is a popular way out of a quite extraordinary intellectual difficulty. To assess the psychic phenomenon, we have to take account of all the other phenomena that come with it, and accordingly we can no longer practice any psychology that ignores the existence of the unconscious or of parapsychology. "The structure and physiology of the brain furnish no explanation of the psychic process. The psyche has a peculiar nature which cannot be reduced to anything else."

CARL G. JUNG, *Undiscovered Self*

THE HUMAN DIMENSIONS INSTITUTE

The Institute has undertaken to help individuals of all ages to understand themselves more fully and to relate more healthfully, creatively and cooperatively with the total environment — physical, emotional, mental and spiritual. Its program includes public lectures, seminars, workshops and experience groups. The Institute also conducts its own scientific research program, book sale and library service. It is sending speakers and workshop leaders throughout the country and abroad.

Beginning as a lecture series in 1967, the Program's rapid success and the increasing demand of the public for more in-depth understanding of human potentials resulted in establishment of the Institute as a separate entity. It is housed at and uses the facilities of Rosary Hill College, but is separately incorporated and financed.

Unique in its total ecological approach to the human condition, HDI's discriminative investigation of human capabilities heralds a new potential for education by means of experience-giving as well as fact-finding. The Institute also publishes *Human Dimensions Magazine*, a quarterly which members receive free; subscription for non-members, $3.50 a year.

Inquiries welcomed.

President and Executive Director:
Jeanne Pontius Rindge
4380 Main Street
Buffalo, New York 14226
U.S.A.

The Parapsychology Foundation was founded in 1951 by Eileen J. Garrett as a nonprofit organization to encourage research, study and experiment in those areas of the paranormal which include extrasensory perception, psychokinesis, telepathy, clairvoyance, precognition and related phenomena.

The Foundation works closely with scholars and scientists, in universities and laboratories everywhere in the world, who wish to study those aspects of the human mind which seem to fall beyond the hitherto accepted provinces of conventional psychology, the other behavioral sciences, and the exact sciences.

While maintaining an objective view, the Foundation seeks to advance a better understanding of the psychical manifestations in man through research in psychology, chemistry, biology, physics, mathematics, philosophy, anthropology, and related disciplines in which there are widely varying viewpoints.

The Foundation does not maintain its own research division or conduct public lecture programs, and it is not a membership organization.

LIBRARY

The Eileen J. Garrett Library of the Parapsychology Foundation is a research library comprising a collection of books and journals concentrated in the area of parapsychology.

No materials may be borrowed.

The library, at the Foundation offices in New York, is open Monday through Friday, 9:30 a.m. to 4:30 p.m.

CONFERENCES

Domestic and international conferences have been held since 1953, in Holland, England, France and the U.S.A. Parapsychologists and other scientists are invited to present papers addressed to specific areas of study. The proceedings and discussions of these conferences are recorded, transcribed and published by the Foundation.

PUBLICATIONS

Parapsychological Monographs, a continuing series of research studies issued by the Foundation.

Parapsychology Review, the official journal of the Foundation, issued six times a year, publishes international news, current events, educational notes, book reviews and articles.

YEAR ONE CATALOGUE: A SPIRITUAL DICTIONARY FOR THE NEW AGE
Ira Friedlander, ed. and introduction by Pir Dilayatniayat Khan, Harper & Row, 1972
$1.95

JAPANESE SOCIETY FOR PARAPSYCHOLOGY
26-14 Chou 4
Nakamo, Tokyo

Founded in 1963, many of the Society's members are psychologists who meet monthly to discuss experimental data. The Society publishes *Parapsychology News* (in Japanese).

PARAPSYCHOLOGICAL MONOGRAPHS

No. 1 A Review of Published Research on the Relationship of Some Personality Variables to ESP Scoring Level, by Gordon L. Mangan. 62 pages. $1.75.

No. 2 ESP in Relation to Rorschach Test Evaluation, by Gertrude Schmeidler. 89 pages. $1.75.

No. 3 Deathbed Observations by Physicians and Nurses, by Karlis Osis. 113 pages. $1.75.

No. 4 New Directions in Parapsychological Research, by Joseph H. Rush. 61 pages. $1.75.

No. 5 ESP Experiments with LSD 25 and Psilocybin, by Roberto Cavanna and Emilio Servadio. 123 pages. $2.50.

No. 6 Toward a New Philosophical Basis for Parapsychological Phenomena, by Hornell Hart. 68 pages. $1.75.

No. 7 Psychophysical Elements in Parapsychological Traditions, by A. Tanagras. 151 pages. $3.00.

No. 8 Paranormal Phenomena, Science, and Life After Death, by C. J. Ducasse. 63 pages. $1.75.

No. 9 Toward a General Theory of the Paranormal, by Lawrence LeShan. 112 pages. $3.00.

No. 10 On the Evaluation of Verbal Material in Parapsychology, by J. G. Pratt. 78 pages. $2.00.

No. 11 Mind, Matter, and Gravitation, by Haakon Forwald. 72 pages. $3.00.

No. 12 Dream Studies and Telepathy, by Montague Ullman and Stanley Krippner. 119 pages. $3.00.

PARAPSYCHOLOGY REVIEW
Published six times a year. Subscription: $4 for one year; $7 for two years; single copies 85¢.

PARAPSYCHOLOGY FOUNDATION, INc.
29 West 57th Street
New York, N.Y. 10019

FOUNDATION FOR PARASENSORY INVESTIGATION
1 West 81st Street
New York, N.Y.

Sponsors research and conferences

ABSTRACTS
505 items in parapsychology and psychic phenomena
Write to:
National Institute of Mental Health, National Clearinghouse for Mental Health Information
5600 Fishers Lane
Rockville, Md. 20852

Free for mental health workers and researchers.

INNER-SPACE INTERPRETERS SERVICES
P.O. Box 1133, Magnolia Park Station
Burbank. Calif. 91507

The 1974 Inner-Space Interpreters Directory for Southern California gives you the names, addresses and telephone numbers of organizations and individual counselors established in these fields and others. It lists types of classes, locations, schedules and other information the individual who wants to broaden his understanding of other dimensions—personal and cosmic—will find invaluable.

$2.00 per copy

Also available:
  1974 Guide to Occult Periodicals
  A Directory of nearly 100 newspapers, magazines and journals. $2.00

International Co-operation Council
17819 Roscoe Boulevard   Northridge, Calif. 91324

The International Cooperation Council (ICC) is a coordinating body composed of educational, scientific, cultural, and religious organizations which in their own ways "foster the emergence of a new universal man and civilization based on unity in diversity among all peoples." It also provides for individuals having similar concerns. ICC was originally formed to continue the ideals and activities undertaken by six of these organizations during International Cooperation Year voted into being for 1965 by the General Assembly of the United Nations. It believes in utilizing the methods and discoveries of modern science coupled with the deepest insights of religion, philosophy, and the arts.

The Council is constantly taking steps to contact organizations in the United States and around the world which share its goals. Activities of the Council are aimed at making the work and ideas of these humanitarian groups better known to the public, and at facilitating the exchange of information and ideas between the groups themselves in order to bring about greater cooperation in areas of common concern. The Council hopes to provide a framework within which the efforts of all groups becomes highly significant in helping to bring about a new world civilization.

The eighth edition of the ICC Directory which follows is an attempt to provide current information about organizations working in this worldwide endeavor. Full-page statements are provided for groups participating in ICC activities; two or three line listings of organizations having similar purposes and of importance in the fields mentioned appear at the end of the book. A new edition of the Directory is issued each year, and it is hoped to make subsequent editions increasingly comprehensive.

ICC does not necessarily endorse all of the organizations listed, though each has been checked for its suitability to ICC work, nor do the editors agree with all their ideas and claims.

It is hoped that the Directory will serve a useful purpose for the many worthy individuals and groups around the globe who are dedicated to aiding the emergence of the new age.

ICC ACTIVITIES IN BRIEF

Area Centers

The Los Angeles Area Center has existed since the beginning of ICC in 1965. During that time a continuing program of Sunday meetings consisting of growth groups, experiential services, and workshops has developed, with frequent weekend workshops and classes as well. More recently a training program for young adults in various new counselling techniques has emerged. Other long range programs are likewise coming into being. About two years ago an ICC intergroup center began in San Francisco, which now has an office and program facility. Within the last year centers have begun in Santa Barbara, San Diego, Las Vegas, Colorado, Kansas City, Chicago, Boston and New York. Others will be coming about in the near future.

International Cooperation Festival

A central part of ICC work revolves around the annual Festival held each January in or near Los Angeles. More than half of the cooperating organizations participate in the weekend event through displays, dialogue sessions, interest groups, and in other ways. The Festival provides an excellent opportunity not only to hear leading specialists related to ICC work, but also to keep abreast of the many new developments that are pointed toward the new universal man and civilization.

Action Projects

The beginning of ICC work is in helping to bring about the convergence of new consciousness organizations to discover each other and to exchange information. The next vital step in the process of convergence is to find areas of concern where much better results can be obtained by working together. ICC has come to know several of these areas already and others are emerging. The Council then acts as a facilitator for effective intergroup dialogue and action in any of these areas as they become felt needs. To date these include (1) new consciousness education, (2) healing of the whole person, (3) public awareness, and (4) spiritual convergence.

Worldview Exploration Seminar

The Worldview Exploration Seminar was formed in the spring of 1969 as an outgrowth of the Fifth Annual International Cooperation Festival. Composed primarily of professional people with diverse backgrounds including science, religion, art, education, and philosophy, it meets monthly on the campus of the California State College at Los Angeles, exploring the meaning of universal man and the new civilization. Four books have been compiled from papers presented during the first to fourth phase of the seminar and are available from ICC.

Spectrum

The newsletter from ICC's World Headquarters, which presently is also located at the Los Angeles Area Center in Northridge, is mailed out monthly free of charge and contains information as to activities taking place and materials that are available. Greater Los Angeles area residents receive announcements of ICC at the Northridge center and elsewhere, as well as listings of major events sponsored by cooperating organizations.

The Cooperator

ICC is now in its third year of publishing "The Cooperator" magazine, which is the successor to "Challenge" dating back to 1958. It lists the cooperating organizations and publishes outstanding articles, art work, poetry, and other materials that forward its work and that of the organizations. Subscriptions are $3.50 for two years. ICC membership includes "The Cooperator" without additional charge. Write for details.

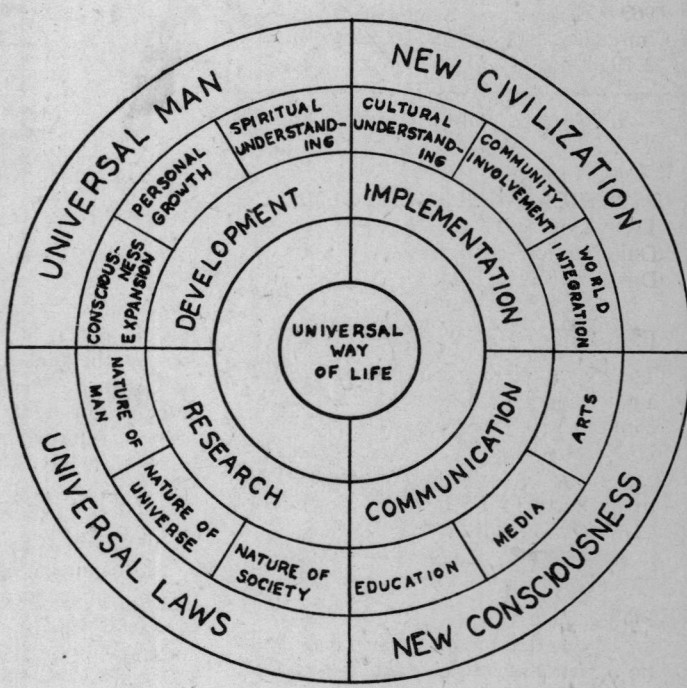

THETA
Annual subscription is $3.50 in the United States; $3.60 in Canada and 1.60 in the United Kingdom. A special bound edition of *Theta*'s 1–38, 1963–1973, is available at $4.50 in the United States; $4.60 in Canada; and 2.10 in the U.K.

PSYCHICAL RESEARCH FOUNDATION INC.
Duke Station
Durham, N.C. 27706

EXPLORING THE UNKNOWN

The Psychical Research Foundation is a parapsychological research center located on the West Campus of Duke University. It is an independent organization created in 1960 to conduct scientific studies on the question of whether man survives the death of his body. It is the only such organization in the world.

PRF research has ranged over many areas which touch on the survival question, including studies of the brainwaves of mediums, out-of-body experiences, transpersonal consciousness, ESP, and cases of haunting and poltergeist activity. Summaries of this work are presented regularly at scientific meetings including the annual conventions of the Parapsychological Association and the American Association for the Advancement of Science. Research papers and reviews by the PRF research staff can be found in the *Journal of the American Society for Psychical Research*, the *Journal of Parapsychology* and other professional publications.

The PRF does not hold any beliefs about survival. It is committed only to the conviction that the survival question can be investigated by the methods of science.

WHY SURVIVAL?

Why investigate post-mortem survival while we are besieged by gargantuan problems of the living? Throughout every age, culture, religion and philosophy, the question of mortality vs. immortality has been a central factor in the development of codes of living. Among our own modern people, psychologists have shown that one's attitude toward death plays a large part in the ways in which he lives.

In our time, science has developed tools and methods sufficient to probe this dark question with the same bright and critical light which has unmasked other secrets of the universe.

We may be a long way from final answers, but we are gathering information which will enable us to move beyond speculation to scientific understanding. Investigation of the question of death is presently a vital pursuit to deal with our problems of living.

EDUCATION AND INFORMATION

THETA

THETA is a quarterly bulletin published by THE PRF, and is available to the public by subscription. *THETA* highlights recent research at the PRF and elsewhere dealing with the survival issue. It also has reviews of books and articles as well as general news concerning our field.

LIBRARY

The PRF library contains a wide variety of parapsychological and other works relevant to the survival question. It is open to the public.

SEMINARS

The PRF staff conducts biweekly seminars which are open to the public. Students from Duke, North Carolina Central University and the University of North Carolina, as well as members of the research community, attend and contribute to the discussions.

FUNDING

The PRF is a non-profit and non-private foundation. Its financial mainstay is its original endowment, contributed by the late Charles E. Ozanne. This provides approximately $34,000 annually in perpetuity. The balance of an average annual budget of $80,000 must be raised through grants and contributions. The PRF is presently seeking other endowments in perpetuity in order to guarantee a further portion of its yearly research. Persons who may wish to contribute funds to our program are urged to write for more information.

MEDITATION CENTER

The PRF maintains a Meditation Center adjacent to its other facilities on Duke's West Campus. The Center affords a small library on meditation and yoga systems as well as offering opportunities for meditation-related research, meetings and seminars, group meditation and yoga sessions, and individual exploration.

CORRESPONDENCE

In addition to *THETA*, the PRF makes available to those interested summaries and reprints of PRF research projects and proposals. We welcome interactions with those who have an interest in this work.

STUDENTSHIPS AND ASSISTANTSHIPS

Qualified individuals may be able to arrange a work-study period at the PRF, depending on the availability of funds for that purpose.

FOUNDATION FOR RESEARCH ON THE NATURE OF MAN (FRNM)
Box 6847, N.C. 27708

FRMN has succeeded the Duke University Parapsychology Lab and continues to promote parapsychology. The Institute for Parapsychology, the research arm, has also become an information center on parapsychological research. The Parapsychology Press publishes the *Journal of Parapsychology*.

From the *JOURNAL OF PARAOSYCHOLOGY*
Vol. 38, No. 1   March, 1974

A description of the basic experimental methods, of the findings, and of the statistical procedures for evaluating ESP and PK results may be found in *Parapsychology, Frontier Science of the Mind* by J. B. Rhine and J. G. Pratt (Published by Charles C Thomas, Springfield, Illinois, U. S. A., Blackwell Scientific Publications, Ltd., Oxford, England, and The Ryerson Press, Toronto, Canada).

The Journal of Parapsychology

Volume 38, No. 1, March 1974

The Journal of Parapsychology

The *Journal of Parapsychology* is published quarterly in March, June, September, and December by the Parapsychology Press, a subsidiary of the Foundation for Research on the Nature of Man. The *Journal* is devoted mainly to original reports of experimental research in parapsychology. It also publishes research reviews, theoretical and methodological articles that are closely linked to the empirical findings in the field, book reviews, news, comments, letters, and abstracts.

The subscription price to individual subscribers is $10.00 for one year; $10.50 for countries outside the U.S. Single current numbers are $2.50. Subscriptions, changes of address, and other business communications should be sent to Mrs. Anne Carroll, *Journal of Parapsychology*, Box 6847, College Station, Durham, N.C. 27708. Checks should be made payable to the *Journal of Parapsychology*. Copies lost in the mail will be replaced free of charge if written notice is given within one month of the date of issue.

Some back numbers, beginning with Volume 13 up to the present, are still in print. These are available at $3.00 a copy from the *Journal*. For information about Volumes 1–12, write to Walter J. Johnson, Inc., 111 Fifth Avenue, New York, N.Y. 10003. Xerox, microfilm, and microfiche copies can be obtained from University Microfilms, Ann Arbor, Mich. 48106. Microfiche is also available from Johnson Associates Inc., 175 Fifth Ave., New York, N.Y. 10010.

GLOSSARY

AGENT: The "sender" in tests for telepathy, the person whose mental states are to be apprehended by the percipient. In GESP tests, the person who looks at the target object.

BT (Basic Technique): The clairvoyance technique in which each card is laid aside by the experimenter as it is called by the subject. The check-up is made at the end of the run.

CALL: The subject's guess (or cognitive response) in trying to identify the target in an ESP test.

CHANCE: The complex of undefined casual factors irrelevant to the purpose at hand.

Mean Chance Expectation (also *Chance Expectation* and *Chance Average*): The most likely score if only chance is involved.

CHI-SQUARE: A sum of quantities, each of which is a deviation squared divided by an expected value. Also a sum of the squares of CR's.

CLAIRVOYANCE: Extrasensory perception of objects or objective events.

CR (Critical Ratio): A measure to determine whether or not the observed deviation is significantly greater than the expected random fluctuation about the average. The CR is obtained by dividing the observed deviation by the standard deviation. (The probability of a given CR may be obtained by consulting tables of the probability integral, such as Pearson's.)

CR (Critical Ratio of the Difference): The observed difference between the average scores of two samples of data divided by the standard deviation of the difference.

DEVIATION: The amount an observed number of hits or an average score varies (either above or below) from mean chance expectation of a run or series or other units of trials.

DIFFERENTIAL EFFECT: Significant difference between scoring rates when subjects are participating in an experiment in which two procedural conditions (such as two types of targets or two modes of response) are compared.

DISPLACEMENT: ESP responses to targets other than those for which the calls were intended.

Backward Displacement: ESP responses to targets preceding the in-

tended targets. Displacement to the targets one, two, three, etc. places preceding the intended target are designated as (−1), (−2), (−3), etc.
Forward Displacement: ESP responses to targets coming later than the intended targets. Displacement to the targets one, two, three, etc., places after the intended target are designated as (+1), (+2), (+3), etc.

DT (Down Through): The clairvoyance technique in which the cards are called down through the pack before any are removed or checked.

ESP (Extrasensory Perception): Experience of, or response to, a target object, state, event, or influence without sensory contact.

ESP CARDS: Cards, each bearing one of the following five symbols: star, circle, square, cross, and waves (three parallel wavy wavy lines). A standard pack has 25 cards.
Closed Pack: An ESP pack composed of five each of the five symbols.
Open Pack: An ESP pack made up of the ESP symbols selected in random order.

EXPECTATION: See *Chance*.

EXTRACHANCE: Not due to chance alone.

GESP (General Extrasensory Perception): ESP which could be either telepathy or clairvoyance or both.

MCE (Mean Chance Expectation): See *Chance*.

P (Probability): The fraction of times that in a great number of chance repetitions the observed result will be equalled or exceeded.

p (Probability): The number which the fraction of successes approaches the limit with a sufficiently large succession of chance trials; e.g., in chance matchings with five targets, $p=1/5$, or one success in five trials.

PARAPSYCHICAL (Parapsychological): Attributable to psi.

PARAPSYCHOLOGY: The branch of science that deals with psi communication, i.e., behavioral or personal exchanges with the environment which are extrasensorimotor—not dependent on the senses and muscles.

PERCIPIENT: The person experiencing ESP; also, one who is tested for ESP ability.

PK (Psychokinesis The extramotor aspect of psi; a direct (i.e., mental but nonmuscular) influence exerted by the subject on an external physical process, condition, or object.

PLACEMENT TEST: A PK technique in which the aim of the subject is to try to influence falling objects to come to rest in a designated area of the throwing surface.

PQ (Psi Quotient): A measure of psi efficiency in a given test of performance. $PQ = 1000\,(CR^2/n)$ where n is the number of trials. (See *Journal of Parapsychology*, Volume 34, 1970, pp. 210–14.)

PRECOGNITION: Prediction of random future events the occurrence of which cannot be inferred from present knowledge.

PREFERENTIAL MATCHING: A method of scoring responses to free material. A judge ranks the stimulus objects (usually pictures in sets of four) with respect to their similarity to, or association with, each response; and/or he ranks the responses with respect to their similarity to, or association with, each stimulus object.

PSI: A general term to identify a person's extrasensorimotor communication with the environment. Psi includes ESP and PK.

PSI-DIFFERENTIAL EFFECT: See *Differential Effect*.

PSI-MISSING: Exercise of psi ability in a way that avoids the target the subject is attempting to hit.

PSI PHENOMENA: Occurrences which result from the operation of psi. They include the phenomena of both ESP (including precognition) and PK.

PSYCHICAL RESEARCH: Older term used for parapsychology.

RUN: A group of trials, usually the successive calling of a deck of 25 ESP cards or symbols. In PK tests, 24 single die-throws regardless of the number of dice thrown at the same time.

SCORE: The number of hits made in any given unit of trials, usually a run.
Total score: Pooled scores of all runs.
Average score: Total score divided by number of runs.

SD (Standard Deviation): Usually the theoretical root mean square of the deviations. It is obtained from the formula $\sqrt{npq}$ in which n is the number of single trials, p the probability of success per trial, and q the probability of failure.

SERIES: Several runs of experimental sessions that are grouped in accordance with the stated purpose and design of the experiment.

SET: A subdivision of the record page serving as a scoring unit for a consecutive group of trials, usually for the same target.

SIGNIFICANCE: A numerical result is significant when it equals or surpasses some criterion of degree of chance improbability. The criterion commonly used in parapsychology today is a probability value of .02 (odds of 50 to 1 against chance) or less, or a deviation in either direction such that the CR is 2.33 or greater. Odds of 20 to 1 (probability of .05) are regarded as strongly suggestive.

SINGLES TEST: A PK technique in which the aim of the subject is to try to influence dice to fall with a specified face up.

SPONTANEOUS PSY EXPERIENCE Natural, unplanned occurrence of an event or experience that seems to involve parapsychical ability.

STM (Screened Touch Matching): An ESP card-testing technique in which the subjects indicates in each trial (by pointing to one of five key positions) what he thinks the top card is in the inverted pack held by the experimenter behind a screen. The card is then laid opposite that position.

SUBJECT: The person who is tested in an experiment.

TARGET: In ESP tests, the objective or mental events to which the subject is attempting to respond; in PK tests, the objective process or object which the subject tries to influence (such as the face or location of a die).
Target Card: The face of the falling die which the subject tries to make turn up by PK.
Target Pack: The pack of cards the order of which the subject is attempting to identify.

TELEPATHY: Extrasensory perception of the mental state or activity of another person.

TRIAL: In ESP tests, a single attempt to identify a target object; in PK tests, a single unit of effect to be measured in the evaluation of results.

VARIANCE, THEORETICAL: A measure of the dispersal of a group of scores about their theoretical mean (see *MCE*, or *Mean Chance Expectation*).
High Variance: Fluctuation of scores beyond mean chance variance.
Low Variance: Fluctuation of scores below mean chance variance.
Mean Variance (theoretical): The expected variance of the theoretical mean score.
Run-Score Variance: The fluctuation of the scores of individual runs around the theoretical mean.
Subject Variance: The fluctuation of a subject's total score from the theoretical mean of his series.
Variance-Differential Effect: Significant difference between variances of run scores (or other units) in two experimental series designed to affect results differentially.

THE COLLEGE OF PSYCHIC STUDIES
16 Queensberry Place
South Kensington
London, S.W. 7. 2

* The College of Studies exists to foster a spirit of free inquiry into the psychical field. The word "College" is used in its original meaning of a society of persons engaged in a study of common interest, however varied its aspects. It does not set out to be a formal educational institution, conducting examinations or conferring certificates. The field it studies is a complex one; after a hundred years of investigation a very great deal within its still lies outside our present understanding.
* The College endeavors to maintain an outlook upon the subject which any reasonable person could respect. Its purpose is not to commit its members to any particular belief. Each must be left to form his own views.
* It is not a religious organization.
* It is a non-profit-making body with charitable status.
* Its objects are to offer both to newcomers and to seasoned investigators the opportunity for experience, experiment and intelligent discussion in the field of psychical phenomena, with particular reference to the evidence for survival of death and for communication from the dead, and to examine its relationship to existing philosophical and scientific opinion.
* It recognizes that there is an accumulation of evidence which, although it does not yet amount to scientific proof, justifies belief in survival. It therefore sets up a working hypothesis of survival, while leaving every member entirely free to accept or reject it.
* A good deal of evidence also exists for the operation of extrasensory perception between minds on earth. This needs to be studied as a human faculty; it is also a factor which must always be taken into account in assessing the evidence for survival.
* The College endeavors to work in this difficult and complex field with integrity.
* The College attempts, so far as it can, to raise and refine the quality of the material received in the psyochical field. For those who accept

survival, whether as a working hypothesis or on a basis of conviction, the personal need often arises to discover what function and value can exist in human relationships between the living and the discarnate. Can these be so extended in depth as to bear spiritual fruit for the individual and possibly throw light on some of the great world problems? Nobody yet knows how far such relationships can be developed and their partial limitations overcome.

* The ultimate aim of the College is thus the legitimate exploration of evidence of an objective spiritual world, and of the possibility of ordinary men and women reaching an inner knowledge of its existence and forming a working rapport with it.
* The College helps its members to approach the more esoteric side of the subject, through meditation and otherwise.
* As a Society which holds no corporate opinion, and therefore exclude no views, it provides a valuable service to all serious searchers.
* Guest lecturers and experts in specialized fields are given the opportunity for free expression of views to members and the public. Distinguished lecturers have included: Sir William Barrett, F.R.S., Algernon Blackwood, Geraldine Cummins, Sir Ronald Fraser, K.B.E., C.M.G., Sir Victor Goddard, K.C.B., C.B.E., Sir Alister Hardy, F.R.S., Dr. Martin Israel, M.B., M.R.C.P., Elizabeth Jenkins, Dr. Raynor Johnson, Prof. G. Wilson Knight, C.B.E., Rosamond Lehmann, Sir Oliver Lodge, F.R.S., P. W. Martin, The Worshipful Chancellor The Rev. E. Garth Moore, M.A., J.P., Prof. H. H. Price, Kathleen Raine, Dr. Hugh Schonfield, Sir Kelvin Spencer, Dr. R. H. Thouless, Sir George Trevelyan, Bt., W. B. Yeats, and many others.

HOW
WE CAN HELP *YOU*

* Membership, which may be taken up at any time, is open to all, whether as inquirers, students or observers.
* Weekly lectures covering a very wide sphere in psychical and associated fields are held for members and non-members during the greater part of the year. Seats may be reserved.
* Evening courses of study, one-day conferences, and annual residential conferences (in provinces).
* The College endeavors to demonstrate mediumship of good standard and provides private, group and open sessions. It must be appreciated that the psychic faculty fluctuates and must always be regarded as having an experimental aspect. Guaranteed results are therefore impossible, and members should retain an open mind and independent judgment at all times.
* Lecturers are available to students, professional bodies and other organizations by arrangement.
* The College Library, comprising around 10,000 volumes on psychical research, the esoteric and allied subjects, is the most comprehensive of its kind in Great Britain. Three books at a time may be borrowed, personally or by post. Catalogues are available. Additionally, a reference library of rare books can be consulted on the College premises.
* Confidential and sympathetic guidance in individual study, experiments, psychic development and related problems.
* Groups for meditation are held regularly.
* A form of healing for assisting in the overcoming of physical and psychologogical illness.
* *LIGHT*, the quarterly College journal, founded in 1881, is the oldest publication in the psychic field. It has a world-wide circulation. The journal contains articles by well-known writers, book reviews, and discussion of psychical and spiritual matters. Members receive LIGHT *Light* free.
* College papers, average length 10,000, are printed twice yearly, and sent free to members. Additional copies may be purchased at 28p., inc. post and packing.

RECOMMENDED READING LIST AND COLLEGE PROGRAM AVAILABLE ON REQUEST

MEMBERSHIP

Fellows, Full Members, Associate Members and Junior Members (under 25) are entitled to full use of all College services, including the Library; free receipt of *Light* and COLLEGE PAPERS; and a Guest Card.

Fellows and Full Members are entitled, in addition, to reduced fees for private and group sessions by mediums, and for most meetings.

Fellows are also admitted free to Tuesday lectures and Sunday meetings (with tea).

Associate and Junior Members are entitled to reduced fees for meetings. Junior Members are required to pay a deposit of 1 if using the Library.

FEES PER ANNUM
FELLOWSHIP 5.50
FULL MEMBERS 4.50
ASSOCIATES 3.40
JUNIOR MEMBERS 1.15
JOINT MEMBERS 6.80

A subscription to *Light* is $3.20 postpaid. Write for a free sample copy.

BIBLLIOGRAPHIES ON PARAPSYCHOLOGY (PSYCHOENERGETICS) AND RELATED SUBJECTS—USSR.
$6.00
Available from:
National Technical Information Service
Springfield, Va. 22151

COURSES AND OTHER OPPORTUNITIES IN PARAPSYCHOLOGY.
A ten-page directory. Write: The American Society for Psychical Research, 5 West 73rd Street, New York, 10023, C/O Education Department. $1.00 with self-addressed 10 envelope.

EVENTS IN CALIFORNIA
Write to:
P.O. Box 3051
San Jose, Calif. 95116
ESP ORBIT $4.00 Monthly

THERE IS NO ABSOLUTE KNOWLEDGE. And those who claim it, whether they are scientists or dogmatists, open the door to tragedy." J.
—BRONOWSKI

THE SUPERNATURAL
Douglas Hill and Pat Williams
New American Library, 1965.
$6.95

This fascinating and comprehensive guide to the occult pursues the quest of the supernatural into mysterious cults: the worship of voodoo's Baron Samedi, the covert celebration of the satanic Black Mass. Stories of hauntings, werewolves, witches, vampires, ghosts and poltergeists are meticulously examined, as are the findings of modern scientific investigators around the world today.

AMERICAN SOCIETY FOR PSYCHICAL RESEARCH, INC.

5 West 73 Street

New York, N. Y. 10023

212-799-5050

Purpose of the American Society for Psychical Research

The ASPR is a non-profit organization whose purpose is to advance the understanding of phenomena alleged to be paranormal: telepathy, clairvoyance, precognition, psychokinesis and related occurrences that at present are not thought to be explicable in terms of physical, psychological and biological theories. The Society approaches the problem on two broad fronts—research and educational.

Research Activities

The Society brings the resources of modern scientific and statistical techniques to the study of such paranormal phenomena as extrasensory perception (ESP) and psychokinesis (PK) as they occur under controlled conditions in the laboratory setting. It investigates reports of spontaneous occurrences—telepathic or precognitive dreams, apparitions, poltergeists, hauntings and the like. The study of special sensitives or mediums is a third area of investigation. Work by the Society's staff and members in recent years has included surveys and detailed study of spontaneous cases; the role of subject and experimenter attitudes in ESP testing; ESP tests with school children; physical and physiological correlates of ESP; the telepathic influencing of dreams; object-reading tests (psychometry) with special sensitives; ESP and creativity during altered states of consciousness; and deathbed observations by physicians and nurses.

General Educational Activities

The ASPR believes that information about psychical research must be made available to scientists and to the general public. This is being done by means of its publications, which are received by individual members, by libraries, and other educational institutions all over the world. The quarterly *Journal* publishes reports of experimental work, case reports and discussions, articles dealing with relevant trends in other disciplines and reviews of current books and periodicals in the field. *Proceedings*, issued from time to time, contain contributions which are too long for inclusion in the *Journal*.

The Society also disseminates information by means of its lecture series; by forums, seminars and workshops; and by counsel to researchers, writers, students and educators. Upon request, students and others are supplied with background information and materials for term papers, theses and research projects.

Membership

There are no special requirements for membership in the ASPR. It welcomes members of the general public and of the professions, as well as active researchers and students. (Fulltime students are eligible for membership with reduced annual dues.) Membership does not imply acceptance either of the factuality of paranormal phenomena or of any particular explanation of such phenomena. (The various classes of individual membership are listed at the end of this leaflet.)

Other Membership Opportunities

Opportunities are provided for members with a general interest in psychical research to meet with others having kindred concerns. The ASPR's publications, lectures and seminars keep them in touch with current work and thinking in the field. Members are encouraged to bring guests to the lectures. Members with special research interest and training can meet with colleagues at informal gatherings. Here also students have an opportunity to talk with senior researchers and visiting scientists about specific research problems and other matters of mutual interest.

Members are urged to use, either directly or by mail, the ASPR library, which contains a wide selection of classic and current books on psychical research and related topics as well as publications from research centers in various parts of the world.

A Brief History of the ASPR

The ASPR, first organized in 1885 with Simon Newcomb, the astronomer, as president, later became a branch of the (British) Society for Psychical Research (founded in 1882) and functioned in Boston under the guidance of Richard Hodgson, formerly of Cambridge University, until his death in December, 1905. A newly-organized and independent ASPR was soon thereafter established in New York with James H. Hyslop, formerly Professor of Logic and Ethics at Columbia University, as its secretary and treasurer. During the years between 1906 and his death in 1920, Professor Hyslop greatly expanded the scope of the Society's work and built up its endowment fund. Publication of the *Journal* and *Proceedings* was initiated in 1907 and has continued uninterruptedly to the present. A vast amount of valuable scientific data has thus been recorded over the years.

The closeness of the bearing of paranormal phenomena on important scientific and philosophic issues is testified to by the fact that the investigation of such phenomena has enlisted the interest and active participation of a number of outstanding scientists and philosophers. Among the distinguished contributors of the past may be mentioned the physicists Sir William Barrett, Sir Oliver Lodge and Lord Rayleigh; the physiologist Charles Richet; the biologist Hans Driesch; the psychologists William James (who was active in the formation of the ASPR) and William McDougall; and the philosophers Henri Bergson and Henry Sidgwick. The contemporary scene in psychical research includes, among the philosophers, C. D. Broad, C. J. Ducasse and H. H. Price; among the biologists, Sir Alister Hardy; and among the psychologists, Gardner Murphy and R. H. Thouless.

Future Perspectives

In recent years developments in both psychical research and the larger body of the behavioral and physical sciences have made it increasingly apparent that paranormal phenomena will have to be integrated with our theoretical conceptions of the world we live in. This integration will probably demand major revisions of our present theoretical constructs, though the direction these will take is at present uncertain. With this task before us, the ASPR's investigations must be expanded with the initiative and energy which their importance calls for. Necessary for this increased effort are (1) a substantial growth in the size of the Society's membership and (2) an enlargement of its existing endowment fund.

Membership Privileges

Journal: Issued quarterly.

Newsletter: Issued quarterly.

Proceedings: Issued occasionally, but not every year.

Library: Access to the circulating library, a specialized collection of current and classic books on psychical research and related subjects. Periodicals, world-wide publications, on file.

Lectures: A spring and fall series is presented: outstanding speakers report on their own and others' work.

Membership Participation: Social events and certain types of research at 5 W. 73 St.

Classes of Membership and Annual Dues

Member: $20. All membership privileges.

Member & Spouse: $25. Includes only one copy of each publication, but all other membership privileges for both.

Fellow: $35. Includes all regular privileges, plus the special privilege of borrowing books by mail.

Student: $10. Special rate includes all membership privileges. (Only full-time students enrolled at accredited secondary schools, colleges or universities are eligible.)

Library: $12.50. For libraries only. Includes all publications.

Sustaining Patron: $100 per year. Includes all membership privileges.

For those who wish to make larger contributions to the Society's work, Life Fellowship, Patrons and Founders classes are open at $500, $1000, and $5000. Such contributions may be earmarked for specific research projects. Gifts and membership dues are deductible for income tax purposes.

PARAPSYCHOLOGY: A SCIENTIFIC APPROACH
Milan Ryzl
Hawthorn
$7.95

PARAPSYCHOLOGY: SOURCES OF INFORMATION
Compiled under the auspices of the American Society for Psychical Research by Rhea A. White, Director of Information, A.S.P.R., and Assistant Reference Librarian, East Meadow Public Library, and Laura A. Dale, editor, journal and proceedings, A.S.P.R. 1973 Available from:
The Scarecrow Press, Inc.
Metuchen, N.J.

The editors present carefully selected annotated book lists and a guide to encyclopedias, parapsychological organizations, periodicals and a section on scientific recognition of parapsychology, as well as a glossary of terms. A must book for the introductory student of parapsychology.

THE DIRECTORY OF THE OCCULT
Hans Holzer
Henry Regnery Company, 1974.
$3.95

The Journal of the American Society for Psychical Research

JANUARY 1974   Volume 68   Number 1

A Case of RSPK Involving a Ten-Year-Old Boy:
   The Powhatan Poltergeist .... *John Palmer*   1
An Experimentally Testable Model for Spontaneous Psi Events.
   I. Extrasensory Events .... *Rex G. Stanford*   34
Some New Cases Suggestive of Reincarnation.
   V. The Case of Indika Guneratne .... *Ian Stevenson*   58
The Raudive Voices—Objective or Subjective?
   A Discussion .... *E. Lester Smith*   91

Reviews:
   The Poltergeist by William G. Roll
                             Gertrude R. Schmeidler   101
   Experimental Studies of the Differential Effect in Life Setting by P. Sailaja and K. R. Rao ...... *John Palmer*   104
   Methods and Models for Education in Parapsychology by D. S. Rogo .... *Alan D. Price*   110
   On the Psychology of Meditation by Claudio Naranjo and Robert E. Ornstein .... *Rex G. Stanford*   113
   The Occult Sciences in the Renaissance: A Study in Intellectual Patterns by Wayne Shumaker ...... *Joseph M. Backus*   121
   Consciousness and Reality: The Human Pivot Point by Charles Muses and Arthur M. Young (Eds.) ... *Rhea A. White*   128

THE AMERICAN SOCIETY FOR PSYCHICAL RESEARCH, Inc.

5 West 73rd Street, New York, N.Y. 10023

Published Quarterly

the UNI-COM GUIDE
Unique — Different!
Nothing else like it!

DO YOU KNOW WHAT'S HAPPENING IN CALIFORNIA?
The Uni-Com Guide will tell you everything that's going on in Metaphysics!

THE *UNI-COM* GUIDE
Monthly Calendar of Metaphysical or Parapsychological Events for California
$5.00 per year, $8.00 two years
(listings invited by all groups)

UNI-COM Foundation
P.O. Box 11716
Palo Alto, Calif. 94306

The Society for Psychical Research
1 Adam & Eve Mews
Kensington, London, W8 6UQ
Telephone: 01-937 8984

OBJECTS AND ACTIVITIES
origin and purpose

The Society for Psychical Research was founded in 1882, by a group of scholars and scientists which included Professor Henry Sidgwick, Sir William Barrett, F.R.S., Frederic W. H. Myers, and Edmund Gurney. Its purpose was to make a systematic investigation of certain phenomena which appeared to be inexplicable on any generally recognized hypothesis. As a result of much painstaking inquiry, some of these contested matters have already been brought into the general scheme of organized knowledge. By investigation and experiment the Society continues to add to a wealth of data unique in its field. The Society's method has always been to approach its problems in a scientific manner, without prejudice or prepossession of any kind. It does not hold or express corporate views; any opinions expressed in its publications are those of the authors alone.

FIELD OF WORK

The Society's work falls under the following main headings:

Inquiry into the reality and nature of telepathy and all forms of paranormal cognition, by means of experiments and by collecting and analyzing accounts of spontaneous cases which appear to be of this nature.

Examination of the phenomena of mediumship, e.g. automatic writing, trance-speaking, alleged spirit communications, alleged movement of objects without contact, and other physical effects.

Investigation of reports of any other phenomena which appear to be paranormal.

Inquiry into both the theoretical and psychological aspects of the phenomena.

The collection and dissemination of information and evidence bearing on these subjects.

ACTIVITIES

Meetings of the Society, for the reading and discussion of papers, are held at frequent intervals. Most meetings are open only to Members and their guests, but occasionally public ("General") meetings are held. The latter include the Myers Memorial Lectures which are delivered, usually biennially, by speakers who have made notable contributions to thought or knowledge in psychical research.

The Society's *Journal*, now published quarterly, contains reports of spontaneous cases and experiments, special articles, the texts of summaries of some of the papers read at meetings of the Society, reviews of books and periodicals, and correspondence. The *Proceedings*, published in Parts as and when suitable material becomes available, are devoted to major pieces of research, presidential addresses, and papers of a theoretical or analytical nature. Other publications include the Myers Memorial Lectures, a series of introductory booklets on various aspects of psychical research, reading lists of publications on psychical research, etc.

The Society maintains a Library of books, pamphlets, and periodicals relating not only to psychical research but also to psychology, philosophy, mysticism, hypnotism, and other subjects bearing on the Society's field of work. Many books and periodicals in foreign languages are included.

The Society is always glad to receive reports of investigations and experiments from Members or from persons unconnected with the Society. These, if considered of sufficient interest and of adequate scientific standard, may be printed in the *Proceedings* or *Journal*. Grants are available in order to facilitate research. The Society's officers also welcome information about cases which seem to call for investigation and, if asked, are glad to give advice or assistance.

MEMBERSHIP

The Council thinks it desirable to quote a Note which appeared on the first page of the original Constitution of the Society, and still holds good: "To prevent misconception, it is here expressly stated that membership of the Society does not imply the acceptance of any particular explanation of the phenomena investigated, or any belief as to the operation, in the physical world, of forces other than those recognized by physical science."

All Members are elected by the Council. Every candidate is required *either* (a) to be proposed and seconded by two Members, *or* (b) to supply the names and address of two responsible persons willing to support his application.

Subscriptions

Members subscribe four pounds (in the United States 12 dollars) annually. Students at universities or other persons between the ages of eighteen and twenty-five may become Student Associates.[1] A Student Associate subscribes two pounds (in the United States, seven dollars) annually. Husband and Wife joint membership, six pounds.

These subscriptions have been kept as low as possible in order that membership may be within reach of all who are able to contribute to the Society's work. They are, however, regarded as *minimum* subscriptions, and all who can do so are asked to make an additional annual donation of one guinea or more towards the furtherance of the Society's objects.

All subscriptions become payable immediately upon election, and subsequently on the first day of January in each year. The subscription for a Member elected on or after 1 October is accepted as for the following year. a Member may cease to be a Member by sending written notice to the Secretary that he is desirous of resigning. Notice of resignation must be sent before the end of any current year.

On reaching the age of 25 Student Associates may become Members without further formality, on paying the appropriate subscription.

Rights of Members and Student Associates

Members are eligible to any of the offices of the Society, and are entitled to vote in the election of the Council and at all meetings of the Society. Student Associates are eligible to any of the offices of the Society, including the Council, and may attend all meetings of the Society except Annual and Extraordinary General meetings. Both Members and Student Associates may (on application to the Secretary) bring one guest to each meeting.

Under the existing arrangements, and until the Council otherwise decide, *Journal* and *Proceedings* are issued to Members and Student Associates free of charge, and they may purchase issues published during the last ten years, or additional copies of the current number, at half the price at which they are sold to the public. Early issues of *Proceedings* and *Journal* can be purchased at the same price as issues of comparable size published to-day. They may use the Library and borrow Library books, by post if necessary, while living in Great Britain. A member wishing to carry out research, whether on his own or in a groups, will receive every encouragement from the officers of the Society, and can obtain gratis, on application, three pamphlets intended to assist him in his researches, namely: *Tests for Extrasensory Perception: an introductory guide* by Dr. D. J. West, *Hints on Sitting with Mediums*, and *Notes for Investigators of Spontaneous Cases*.

NOTE

While the Society stands in special relationship with the American Society for Psychical Research and with undergraduate societies in certain universities in Great Britain, the Council feel it advisable to state that the S.P.R. is in no way connected with any other societies with titles similar to its own.

MANKIND RESEARCH UNLIMITED, INC.

MANKIND RESEARCH UNLIMITED
1143 New Hampshire Avenue, N.W.
Washington, D.C. 20037

Mankind Research Unlimited, Inc. (MRU) was established in early 1972 to provide an organization for the scientific development and application of biocommunications, biocybernetics, bionics, biophysics, pschophysiology and other activities which have an impact on the welfare of mankind.

Mankind Research Unlimited was organized to collect, study, develop and apply extensive and proliferating data on what may be called the "frontiers of science." This data has come into being as a result of the close cross-fertilization of various scientific fields which long had little or nor direct contact with one another, and the re-examination of research areas which were previously ignored by academe as unorthodox.

Mankind Research Unlimited has unique capabilities for collecting, analyzing and evaluating scientific and technological data (both U.S. and foreign) to assist customers in determining the impact of bio-sensory, human engineering, and behavioral science applications in their area of control, interest or responsiblilty.

In addition, MRU has, and is acquiring on a regular basis, a large amount of unique biocybernetic data from the USSR and Eastern Europe, which is otherwise unavailable in the United States. MRU will make this unique date available for analysis and evaluation for customers with an interest in Soviet and Eastern European biocybernetics and human engineering state-of-the-art applications. Supplementing this data will be information collected from sources in Western Europe, including leading research centers located in France, Germany, England and Switzerland.

MRU ASSOCIATE MEMBER PRO GRAM

MEMBERSHIP

Each member receives

A vital monthly newsletter comprised of unique parapsychological and parascientific inputs from around the world, including a feature article by prominent "frontiers of science" researchers . . . a comprehensive calendar of events and activities plus other information to keep you well informed. Our objective is to open all communication channels, thus keeping you apprised of the ever-broadening spectrum of happenings and their impace upon the future health, education and well-being of mankind.

A quarterly magazine including information on parascience personnel, research programs, biotechnology devices and techniques, plus research and development projects accompanied by illustrations and photographs with global significance. This publication will make an ideal vehicle for your own research endeavors including a forum for your own products, services, educational seminars and publications.

As an MRU Associate Member you will also be entitled to attend, and participate in, MRU special events and metaphysical activities, plus instant referral services when you desire special information which focuses on yor own sphere of interest. Associate members are also accorded discounted advertising rates in all MRU publications.

The newsletter and quarterly are to be crative, open and unrestricted exchanges for ideas and information, as "channel outlets" channel outles" for frontiers of science data. Much of the information collected, processed and translated from MRU's unique worldwide sources has not been published in the Western Hemisphere and will be condensed and published here along with MRU's own research results. A good example is our detailed feature article in Vol. 1, No. 1 on the "Telepathic Ability of Tofik Dadashev of the USSR."

Cost: $915.00

WRITE FOR INFORMATION ON WIDE RANGE OF MRU ACTIVITIES

New Research Aids

Mankind Research Unlimited, Inc., and ESPress, Inc. of Washington, D.C., are entering a cooperative publishing venture to bring out two important bibliographies in the fields of plant sensitivity and psychoenergetics Comprehensive annotations cover research highlights and experimental methodologies utilized by leading researchers in the the field.

1 Evoked Biological Responses of Plants: Annotated Bibliography.
Compiled by Skaidrite Maliks Fallah.
$3.95

(August 1974)

2 Psychoenergetics: Annotated Bibliography.
Compiled by Skaidrite Maliks Fallah.
$5.50

(September 1974)

- Completely current sources, including Russian, German, French and Czechoslovakian, up to January, 1974
- Indispensable tool to the researcher and serious student in each field.
- A noteworthy addition to the reference shelves of universities, high schools and public libraries.
- Foreword by Dr. Stanley Krippner, Western Hemisphere Chairman of the International Association of Psychotronics Research and well known for his work at the Maimonides Hospital Dream Laboratory in Brooklyn, N.Y., and the Humanistic Psychology Institute of San Francisco, Calif.

Order now to reserve a copy of each book from this limited printing.

SOUTHERN CALIFORNIA SOCIETY FOR PSYCHICAL RESEARCH

170 South Beverly Drive
Beverley Hills
Room 314
California 90212
Regular Membership Dues
$20 per year

Contributing Member: $100.00

OUR PURPOSE—EXPLORING NEW DIMENSIONS

The basic purpose of the Southern California Society for Psychical Research is to promote scientific psychical research and to transmit reliable information about it to the interested public. An additional function is that of directly presenting phenomena, unevaluated and untested, for the enjoyment of our members and the interested public. It is in this spirit of adventure into new ways of perceiving our world that we present our various lectures and study group programs.

CONFERENCES PRESENTED BY SOUTHERN CALIFORNIA SOCIETY FOR PSYCHICAL RESEARCH, INC.

Listed below are lectures on Psychic Phenomena recorded during this and other conferences and available at an individual price per cassette of $4.25 (Add cents to orders not purchased at conferences or lectures.)

These recordings are available on standard autio cassettes and also in a revolutionary format called Speech Compression you can literally listen to to a one-hour compressed program in 1/3 to 1/2 of the original time with perfect comprehension and with the original voice quality.

MR. MARCEL VOGEL—"Bioenergetics responses between man and plant forms" 165

DR. STANLEY KRIPPNER—"ESP and the Soviet Union" 166

MR. KENDALL L. JOHNSON—"Photographing the transfer of bioenergy at a distance" 167

DR. JAMES FADIMAN—"The transcendent human potential 168

DR. MELVYN R. WERBACH—"The promise of biofeedback" 169

MISS LOUISE LUDWIG—"Haunted houses: are the spirits real?" 170

PROFESSOR E. DOUGLAS DEAN—"1st report on the international conference at Prague" 272

REV. HOWARD CAREY—"Dreams, psychic and symbolic—key to self" 172

MR. DAVID ST. CLAIR—"Psychometry, the how and value of" 173

MR. HOWARD THRASHER—"The science of hand prints" 174

MRS. M. AHSER—"Atlantis—revolution or evolution" 175

REV. DOUGLAS JOHNSON—"The gift of healing" 176

MR. PAUL HARRIS—"Conversation with a psychic" 177

Academic psychology, trying to imitate the natural sciences and laboratory methods of weighing and counting, dealt with everything except the soul. It tried to understand those aspects of man which can be examined in the laboratory and claimed that conscience, value judgements, the knowledge of good and evil are metaphysical concepts outside the problems of psychology; it was more often concerned with insignificant problems which fitted an alleged scientific method than with devising new methods to study the significant problems of man. Psychology thus became a science lacking its main subject matter, the soul. . . . (In) Egypt the priests were the "physicians of the soul," in—
. . . Greece this function was at least partly assumed by philosophers—
. . . Because the word soul has associations which include these higher human powers (of love, reason, conscience, values) I use it here and throughout these chapters rather than the words "psyche" or "mind."
—Erich Fromm, *Psychoanalysis and Religion*

THE INSTITUTE OF NOETIC SCIENCES

The Institute of Noetic Sciences was founded in early 1973 by Edgar D. Mitchell, Sc.D., Apollo 14 astronaut and sixth man on the moon.

Dr. Mitchell believes that civilization is in a critical state and mankind is at an evolutionary crossroad. On one hand, problems and conflicts have arisen which are global in scale and have brought society to a condition of escalating planetary crises. On the other hand, man's potential for creative change, fulfillment and control of his environment has never been greater. Dr. Mitchell believes that both the problems and the potentialities are ultimately a function of human consciousness—i.e., "there will never be a better world until there are better people in it." The most efficient and enduring way to resolve the problem and realize the potentialities is through the enlightenment of individuals.

The Institute is therefore dedicated to research and education in the processes of human consciousness. To help achieve a new understanding and expanded consciousness among all people, it has five main functions:

1. Performing basic research in the nature of consciousness and the body-mind relationship.
2. Offering educational activities to expand human awareness and release human potential.
3. Informing society about activities, developments and trends in the areas of personal and cultural transformation through all channels of communication.
4. Advising and consulting with governments, industry, science, education and other areas of society on planetary problems and their solution.
5. Consulting, supporting and coordinating with those individuals and organizations working for the transformation of human consciousness and culture in ways that are compatible with the philosophy and pruposes of the Institute.

Membership in the Institute is open to the public. For details, write to the Institute.

575 Middlefield Road
Palo Alto, Calif. 94301
Telephone: (415) 328-2340

Aquarian Research Foundation

SUPPLEMENTARY LITERATURE LIST: OCTOBER, 1973.

IS A RESEARCH PROJECT SEEKING WAYS TO OVERCOME SOCIETY"S RESISTANCE TO THE CHANGES THAT A NEW AGE OF PEACE AND LOVE REQUIRES:

We want to help the new age come quickly and peacefully by opening people's minds to new possibilities.

For over three years we have been publishing a newsletter which is sent out to people who help with the work. There is no fixed donation, but $10 per year, more or less, according to ability is suggested. Suggested books and subjects of previous newsletters can be found in our 1972 literature list. Since then we have published the following:

#24 on Cancer and the Laetrile Therapy: DID GOVERNMENT OUTLAW CANCER CURE? & a poem about school by a schoolboy. #25; Visitor's impression of ARF. Also natural cures for infections, Experiment in Psychokinesis and an article on the Ovulation Method (of birth control).

#26 is about scientific research in prayer healing & bio-feedback as a possible way to learn it: Also effect of prayer on plants (a scientific article from PSYCHIC MAGAZINE, March-April, 1972.) #27: Jose Silva comes to Philadelphia, ARF gets Chart Recorder, Getting a message to the president: Human Dimensions Institute - introduction. #28: A visit to the Human Dimensions Institute, an Eckankar Conference & a visit to the ZBS Media Commune in N.Y. State. #29 suggests using psychic methods to unveil secret talks of Nixon with China and Russia.

#30 reports on new types of healing; Jimmie Scribner's "Solarama Therapy" & visit to Willard Fuller who is credited with healing teeth through prayer. Working for McGovern; War in VietNam.

#31 reports meeting with Dr. Ernst T. Krebs, co-developer of Laetrile therapy for cancer; also a report on BREAKTHROUGH, a book about the tape recording of spirit voices (aparently real)., report on "Solarama" board; Relationship of Psychic and Political concerns.

#32 Full instructions for the tape recording of voices from the spirit world. #33: War in the Philippines & news of Psychic Surgery there: also a fable describing the history and role of Banking in our system. Further details on Cancer, including excerpts of letter from Dr. Dean Burke of the National Cancer Institute & Ralph Nader's efforts with FDA in favor of new tests for Laetrile (which is now legal in 22 countries). #34 gives full report, with pictures, of Psychic Surgery in the Philippines with information supplied by Doug Voeks, an American psychologist apprenticed to one of their best psychic surgeons. Also gives information on Philippine political situation including letter from mother of girl who spent two years there; was arrested, but is now on speaking tour in U.S. Also reports on psychic prophecies of possible third world war, and supplies names of top people in international finance who need to be turned on to new insights to prevent it. #35 tells about the Youth Liberation in the words of the young people themselves, giving most of their concerns and program. Also tells about the TRAVELER'S DIRECTORY and how it has been allowed to fall apart by an embezzler.

#36 tells of experiments in Kirlian Photography (photographs of the Aura), the new parapsychological novel, 2150, A Macro Love Story by Don & Thea Plym; The question of reincarnation, and it's reality.; more on scientific research in the field of spirit voice recording; possible experimental class in mental control of conception; 2nd Western Hemisphere Conference on Auras, Accupuncture & Kirlian Photography; Research into transmutation of elements; Report on Pyramid experiments; Hippocrates Health Institute - healing through natural & raw food diets costing only pennies a day; Nuclear Power Plants and their detrimental effect on the health and survival of infants. #37; More on Hippocrates Inst., Transmutation, ESP & Astrology, Suggested Silva Mind Control school. & 38 Breaking the News Blackout over Wounded Knee; Report on the medical underground and the Int. Assoc. of Cancer Victims & Friends Convention in NY

5620 Morton Street
Philadelphia, Pa. 19144

Journals, Periodicals, Magazines, And Newspapers

Numerous PSI research organizations publish their own journals or newsletters. These range from the very scientific in tone and content to more popular appraisals of the field. While magazines and newspapers still tend to be sensationalistic in their coverage of PSI, this appears to be slowly changing in response to a burgeoning demand for greater sophistication and editorial discrimination. A scan of social science, psychiatric, medical and general scientific publications will often turn up articles on PSI written from new perspectives. As research on PSI accelerates and an awareness of relevant conceptual schema from metaphysical publications develops, the character of journals, newspapers and magazines oriented toward specific audiences may achieve a much broader base and lose the "psychic" label.

NEW HORIZONS RESEARCH FOUNDATION
P.O. Box 427, Station F
Toronto 5, Ontario, Canada

The foundation is a nonprofit organization whose purpose is to promote research on the frontiers of science and disseminate information. Publishes a journal occasionally incorporating the Transactions of the Toronto Society for Psychical Research.
Individual copies are $3.50 U.S. or $3.00 Canadian.

New Horizons

Journal of the New Horizons Research Foundation

incorporating

Transactions of the Toronto Society for Psychical Research

Vol. 1, Number 2	Summer 1973
Editorial	
Objective Events in the Brain Correlating with Psychic Phenomena	D. H. Lloyd
Experiments on ESP in relation to (a) distance, and (b) mood and subject matter	A. R. G. Owen
An Experiment with Mr. James Wilkie involving handwriting samples	A. R. G. Owen and I. M. Owen
The Pyramid and Food Dehydration	Allen Alter
Experiments on the Alleged Sharpening of Razor Blades and the Preservation of Flowers by Pyramids	Dale Simmons
The Shapes of Egyptian Pyramids	A. R. G. Owen

NEW HORIZONS RESEARCH FOUNDATION
P.O. Box 427, Station F, Toronto 5, Ontario, Canada

Published occasionally. Copyright 1973 by New Horizons.

Zygon: Journal of Religion and Science
University of Chicago Press,
5801 Ellis Ave.,
Chicago, Ill. 60637
$12/quarterly.

FIELDS WITHIN FIELDS
A Publication of World Institute Council
777 United Nations Plaza
New York, N.Y. 10017
A subscription in the U.S. and Canada
is $10.00. Add $2.00 for subscriptions
outside U.S., its possessions and Canada.

FIELDS WITHIN FIELDS...

Its Philosophy, Contents and Long Range Goals

WE KNOW SO MUCH and make sense of so little.

As we rush to apply new knowledge (though at times we delay incredibly), we find again and again that we have compounded our problems and created new difficulties even as we thought we were overcoming the old ones.

Again and again we show that we do not have an adequate methodology for dealing with change, for assimilating the new information, that we really do not grasp the meaning of the changes that are upon us, that we do not understand the implications of the knowledge that we have acquired, and even that we really do not understand very well the processes by which we acquire knowledge.

In the past we relied on the insights of brilliant individuals to show us the path toward progress. But today the interrelations and complexities attending every problem are so numerous that it is impossible for any one person to gain complete understanding of even one field of inquiry.

In short, under our present system we are dealing largely in ignorance. We fail to see how to organize our intellectual, material and spiritual resources in such a manner as to facilitate the flow of change toward the most constructive human development. We fail to see that the human search at its deeper level is for some process for integrating what we know and do into meaningful metamorphosis through which man can become more truly human and whole. We fail to see that the changes of our age and the processes by which ever more changes are coming about are transforming man and society in ways and to degrees never before experienced.

What is called for is an awakening to new beginning points, a new methodology for thinking, one that leads us from the simple viewpoint to a system of thinking, from system to an organization of systems to synthesis, and from synthesis ultimately into metamorphosis. In other words, a methodology in which there is a continuing feedback and flow forward that brings constant and continual change to all parts of the system.

Above all, what is called for is the understanding that man is part of the system of the movement itself ... that man himself is a multiple within the interplay of multiple systems.

To assist and promote that understanding, to provide a forum in which relevant proposals and discussions may be heard, to help advance the catalyzation of creative powers in order for all men to grow beyond their present expectations — these are the purposes and long range goals of FIELDS WITHIN FIELDS...

INSIGHT

A Magazine exploring the Occult in depth from the Intuitive angle.

Contents include:
- Psychic Research
- Spiritualism
- Comparative Religion
- Witchcraft
- Occult Fraternities
- The Tarot
- Ancient British Mysteries
- Readers' Letters

For all enquiries write to:
The Editor, 'Insight,'
118 Windham Road,
Springbourne,
Bournemouth,
Hants. England.

PRICE 25p. ($1) Post and Packing included

Subscription Rate: L1.00 ($4 a year (4 issues).

EVERY THREE MONTHS (ILLUSTRATED)

Please notify the Editor if you require a copy.

THE SCIENCES
Published by the New York Academy of Sciences
2 East 63rd Street
New York, 10021
Ten times a year. $6.50 U.S.; $7.50 foreign.
Ocassionally publishes articles directly related to interests in the psychic field. Example, Vol. 14, No. 5, June, 1974, has an article called "Measuring Meditation."

SPECTRUM: JOURNAL OF THE OCCULT
Edited by Joan O'Connell
Subscriptions $4.00 yearly
Foreign subscriptions $5.00
Sample copy 25 cents
Available from Barbara Lucas
6290 34th Avenue North
St. Petersburg, Fla. 33710

BEYOND REALITY: THE LATEST DISCOVERIES IN ESP
the Occult and Psychic Phenomena
303 West 42 Street
New York 10036, N.Y.
Bimonthy $6.00.
Back issues at $1.00.

THE OCCULT TRADE JOURNAL
International occult—metaphysical news
Published 10 times a year by The Awareness Publishing Co. Inc.
2274 Como Avenue
St. Paul, Minn. 55108
U.S. and Canada subscriptions $12.00; $14.00 elsewhere.
The subscription is solicited only from individuals actively involved in research organizations, businesses, societies and teachers supporting occult metaphysical studies and parapsychology.

NEW AWARENESS MAGAZINE
(encompassing the Occult Commentary)
Write for details to:
2274 Como Avenue,
St. Paul, Minn. 55108

OCCULT—AMERICANA: OCCULTISM IN AMERICA
A bimonthly mini-magazine
Subscription $3.00.
Available from Occult-Americana,
3686 Ludgate Road
Cleveland, Ohio 44120

PROBE THE UNKNOWN
Order from rainbow Publications, Inc.
5650 West Washington Boulevard
Los Angeles, Calif. 90016
Quarterly $2.50.

OCCULT: NEW DIMENSIONS OF LIFE IN THE FIELD OF PSYCHIC PHENOMENA
Order from Popular Library Publishers, Publishers 600 Third Avenue
New York, N.Y. 10016
quarterly $3.00.
Add 50 cents for foreign and Candian postage.

PSYCHIC DIMENSIONS
order from Charlton Publications, Inc.
Division Street
Derby, Conn. 06418
Bi-monthly $3.75

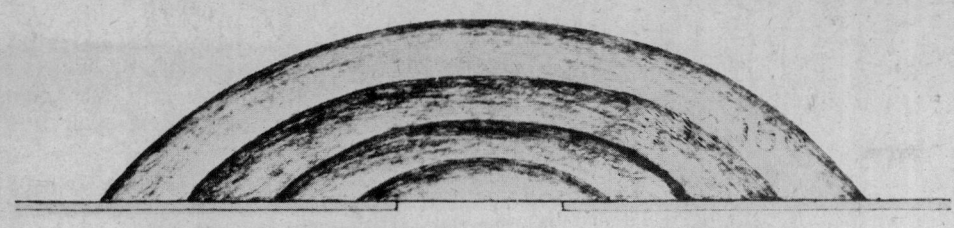

EDITORIAL AURA

PSYCHIC SPECTRUM
Published by P.S. Foundation
P.O. Box 3-562
Anchorage, Alaska, 99501
Subscription $5.00

"Welcome to *Psychic Spectrum*, a Journal that will give expression to the vast range of psychic activity throughout the 586,400 square miles of the Great Land. Its purpose will be to inform, to educate and to provide a place of discussion for the host of Alaskans interested in this sometimes puzzling phenomena.

"The *Spectrum* will strive for quality in appearance as well as in content. We want our readers to be proud to place the Journal in the hands of those who know little or nothing about psychic phenomena, but who are openly curious. Summing it up, we intend to be a responsible medium of communication.

"We intend to be very zealous in doing something about the inflammatory credibility gap that fans the fires of anger and disgust among those who decry the psychic. This is especially true of many church men and women. Repeatedly we hear the paranormal castigated and called satanic; a thing of the devil. The editors of *Psychic Spectrum* feel that the paranormal is integral to God's sublime and eternal truth; a facet of his enormous spectrum of love. Thus, *P.S.* trusts it may, even in a minuscule way, help to close that credibility gap and to awaken the churches to a new era of spiritual responsibility.

"*P.S.* accepts its obligation to inform; to educate. It can serve as a channel through which information can be disseminated concerning the various State-wide groups and organizations. This alone can serve as a unifying factor and will help to pull us together. We need to know what is going on and *P.S.* is making this one of its primary objectives. Some of the space within its pages, such as 'Psychic Notebook,' will be intended as a primer so that we will always be on the growing edge. We will endeavor to inform and to educate, not in high-falutin pompous jargon, but in language that makes sense and is readable.

"It is our design and desire to publish without advertising, so subscriptions will provide our life's blood. You have an enormous stake in our longevity, and the promotion of *P.S.* among your friends and neighbors will give us needed nourishment.

"This inaugural issue concentrates on psychic activities in the Greater Anchorage Area; however, our responsibility will be to the entire State of Alaska. Contact will be made as quickly as possible with reliable reporters representing the different groups and organizations. Your editors need to be kept fully informed about the activities of your groups. What is your reason for being? What are your plans for the future? What is the format of your regular meetings? Informative bits concerning people doing things, going places would be especially welcome for 'Psychic Patter.' This will be a gossipy type column and will always be fascinating to read. Jot down on a card, or in a letter, the information you have, and send it to *Psychic Spectrum*, P.O. Box 3-3798, Anchorage, Alaska 99501. Remember, in preparing your copy, the 'who,' 'what,' 'why,' 'when,' 'where.'

"The mission of *P.S.* takes the form of personal ministry. This is a Greek word which means to serve. This is the purpose of our Journal—to serve you well and faithfully; to honestly report what you are doing, planning and thinking. Ambitious? Yes, but we are thinking positively."

PSYCHIC NEWS

The only weekly newspaper in the world covering the psychic field.

6p.   By post 8½p (27 cents)

AND ALSO

TWO WORLDS

A monthly magazine featuring all aspects of the supernormal; it appeals to thinkers who are concerned with life's deeper issues.

18p.   By post 20½p (65 cents)

Back number of either or both will be sent free on request.

PSYCHIC PRESS LTD.,
23 GREAT QUEEN STREET, LONDON, WC2B 5BB

Our Bookshop will send you a free list of titles that we recommend.

OUR BOOKSHELF Fate Mail Order

FATE ANNUAL 1974	25p
FATE SUBSCRIPTIONS 1 YEAR	£2.90
THE NUMBERS BOOK by Sepharial	90p
THE KEY AND GUIDE TO ASTROLOGY by Rapheal	50p
TEACUP FORTUNE TELLING	20p
CARD FORTUNE TELLING	20p
DREAMS & OMENS	40p

Mark X against books required. Cheques and P.O.'s made out to FATE and addressed to: FATE, Offshore House, Loch Promenade, Douglas, Isle of Man. Please include 5p p. & p. for each Book ordered.

NEWS RELEASE... from gordon and breach

Psychoenergetic Systems

Edited by Stanley Krippner,
Director, Dream Laboratory,
Maimonides Medical Center,
New York

EDITORIAL BOARD: V. G. Adamenko, Jerome D. Frank, Arthur Hastings, Gladys McGarey, Brendan O'Regan
ADVISORY BOARD: Ankisola Akowowo, Joel Elkes, Françoise Gauguelin, Jean Houston, S D Kirlian, Hilton Lopez, Gardner Murphy, Soji Otani, Zdenek Rejdak, Salvador Roquet, Charles T Tart, Montague Ullman.

PSYCHOENERGETIC SYSTEMS is a quarterly journal devoted to the publication of papers regarding consciousness, matter, and energy interactions, with those relations treated as systems, rather than as isolated characteristics. Experimental, clinical and theoretical articles, book reviews, research reports, and critiques are to be included. Examples of topics which can contribute relevant data are acupuncture, alterations of consciousness, bioelectric fields, brain research, Kirlian photography, psychokinetic effects. quasisensory communication, and unorthodox healing. The journal emphasizes holistic approaches; the contributions from many cultures and specialties will enable the creation of alternative scientific paradigms and knowledge processes, potentially of a transdisciplinary and transcultural nature.

Gordon and Breach Science Publishers
1 Park Avenue, New York, NY 10016
42 William IV Street, London WC2
7-9 rue Emile Dubois, Paris 14e

NOUS LETTER
Studies in Noetics
Linear and circular permutations
924 Garden Street
Santa Barbara, Calif. 93101
$3.00 a year, semi-annual

The **NOUS LETTER** is a review, communications, and explorations exchange for the study of Noetics, the science of the nature of consciousness and altered states. We believe there are profound parallels between disciplines which, when found and clarified afford valuable insights into the nature of reality.

Areas of interest include psychology, astrology, sociology, philosophy, religion, cosmology, mathematics, personal poetic insight and other reflections of Mind. (chemistry, physics, biology, ecology, topology, music, literature, and art.) The NOUS LETTER recognizes that the communication of consciousness doesn't depend on the sheath which carries it.

We hope to maintain a depth, continuity, and clarity of thought which affords intellectual integrity, and to interpret the findings of divergent disciplines in a form aimed at building interdisciplinary bridges. Maps of consciousness, diagrams, essays, letters, book reviews, and information about individuals and groups involved in noetic pursuits will be the basic presentational matrix. Condensed quanta of information about consciousness and altered states will be put forth with the goal of kindling and igniting depths of intuitive knowledge. We believe that knowledge is primarily a recognition of truth, and less a process of adding more and more information.

ASTROLOGICA
$8.00 a year
A semi-annual companion journal to the *Nous Letter*.

Knowing at last that the goal revealed long ago—to establish peace and joy on Earth—is brought about by establishing peace and joy within each individual being, we dedicate ourselves and guide the journal *Astrologia* with that same purpose. Furthering us in carrying out our goal are three focal categories: Time, Consciousness, and Liberation.

Peak experiences occur when the environment, other people, and the prevailing climate of purpose, effort, and goals are felt as unified by a sense of integration and attunement. That is, at higher levels one's own rhythms are synchronized perfectly with the cosmic rhythms of ongoing creation.

A realization and acknowledgment of this essential unity is one of the cornerstones of developing more awareness. In *Astrologia*, it is our hope to reinstate the ancient (and modernly abused) time-based science of astrology in its legitimate and essential position as a means of self-development through attunement with natural law. Mutual growth and benefit will be the outcome of the addition of this study of time to the closely interrelated disciplines of psychiatry, humanistic psychology, philosophy, and theology.

Again, the possibilities of an individual's conscious liberation from those states of nonacceptance of a truly cosmic role will be presented. Then our task continues: each of us opening to the influx from higher inspirational energies, so that we may effectively order and sustain ourselves together with our precious interdependent Earth.

And yet, when the present moment holds the promise of little that is discernible, where lies the way then? Here must open the threshold of consciousness itself. The 20th-century methodology for inquiry into the nature of alterable states of consciousness is called Noetics (Gr. "Mind"). *Astrologia* will extensively investigate the hierarchical and dimensional qualities of consciousness, as well as call attention to the evolutionary precipice we find ourselves on as we approach the 1980's.

PSYCHIC: EXPLORING THE EXTENDED NATURE OF MAN AND THE UNIVERSE
P.O. Box 26289 Custom House,
San Francisco, Calif. 94126
Bimonthly $5.00.
Back issues available at $1.00.

THE CHURCHES' FELLOWSHIP FOR PSYCHICAL AND SPIRITUAL STUDIES QUARTERLY REVIEW
Order From:
St. Mary's Abchurch
Abchurch Lane
London, England EC4N 7BA

4 issues per year. One pound.
Deals with religious viewpoint of paranormal.

PSYCHIC OBSERVER AND CHIMES
Published by ESPress, Inc.
Box 8606
Washington, D.C. 20011
Monthly. Subscription is $7.50 for 1 year.

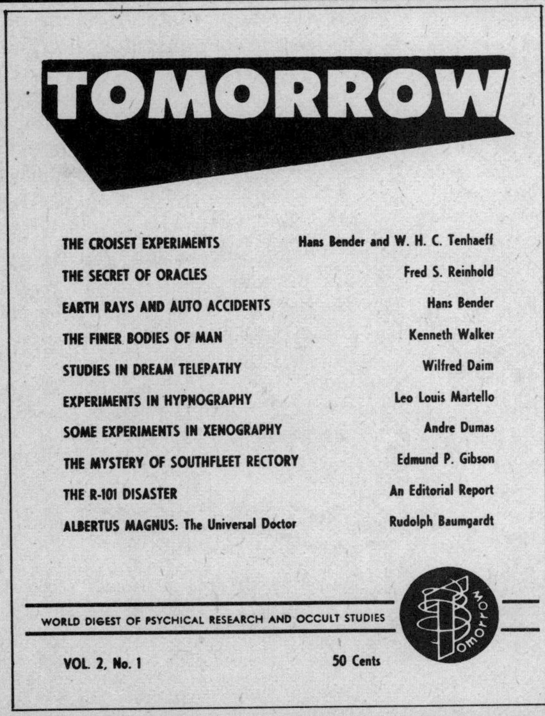

REVUE METAPSYCHIQUE PARAPSYCHOLOGIE
Order From:
Institut Métapsychique International
1 — Place Wagram
Paris, France 75017

Irregular Publication.
Write for details.

THE JOURNAL OF PARAPHYSICS, INTERNATIONAL
Published by Paraphysical Laboratory
Downton, Wiltshire
England
6 issues per year. $15.00

Reports on activities of the laboratory and on Russian and Eastern European research.

TOMORROW
No longer published by Garret publications, but back issues are still available in numerous occult bookshops.

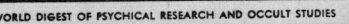
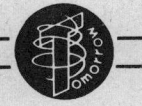

31

 **Psychic Tapestry**

MUSIC-MEDIA CONCERT

114 MAINE STREET　　BRUNSWICK, MAINE 04011

Seminar
PSYCHIC SCIENCE
EVE WEIR
Phone: 207-725-2838

Seminar
MUSIC & MIND EXPANSION
NAN PULSIFER
Phone: 207-725-2620

The TRAVELING SOUND TO SOUND

learning program consists of five full-color filmstrips, accompanying audio cassettes, and a Sound Book. Each filmstrip introduces several different sound and music experiences, their applications in the realms of art and science, and the primary concepts which may be drawn from other curriculum areas. The Sound Books contain the music in each program, which is accompanied by illustrations and literature that relate to the filmstrip presentations. These books provide the basis for class participation in a rich and exciting music program.

Included with the series is an extensive Teacher's Guide, *Sound Ideas*, which fully defines the concepts and objectives of the program, and offers supplementary enrichment activities that are coordinated with the five filmstrips.

TRAVELING SOUND TO SOUND, produced by Psychic Tapestry, Inc., owes its success to its creators, Eve Weir and Nan Pulsifer. Both are renowned as authors, composers, teachers, and lecturers on music in education.
TRAVELING SOUND TO SOUND is the unique result of their combined talents, a program that captures the imagination and takes unexpected musical routes. A program they describe as "A Tapestry of Association which crosses curriculum lines . . . frees the mind and lets it reach for new horizons of thought . . . new awareness."

Darshana International: An International Quarterly of Philosophy, Psychology, Psychical Research, Religion, Mysticism & Sociology.
Moradabad, INDIA. $7.50/quarterly.

"Its only aim is discovery, propagation and popularization of Truth. Darshana is a Sanskrit word, which, among other things, means seeing, insight, outlook or philosophy of life. The name . . . is meant to arouse and awaken humanity to build a new civilization and culture . . ."

WRITE FOR DETAILS AND ORDER FROM:
General Educational Media, Inc.
350 Northern Boulevard,
Great Neck, N.Y. 11021

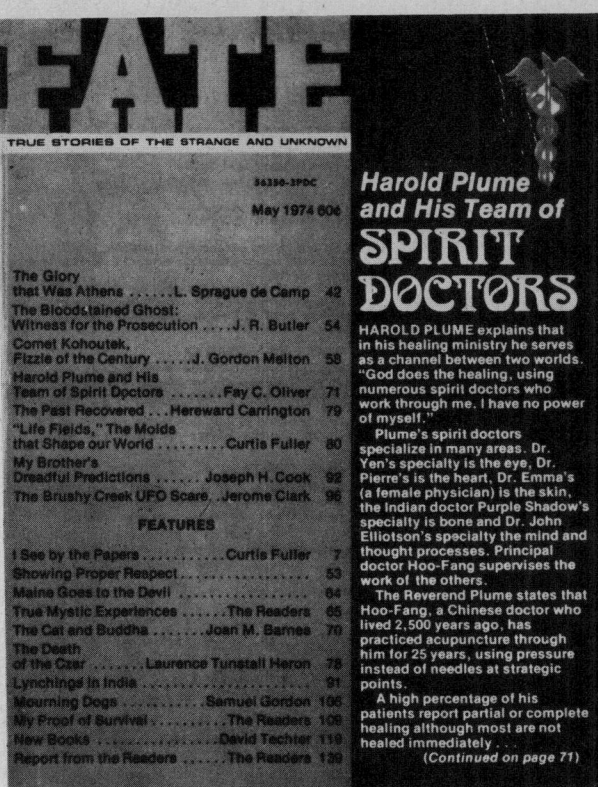

FATE
Order from Clark Publishing Co.
500 Hyacinth Place
Highland Park, Ill. 60035
Monthly, for one year $4.95; Foreign $5.45.
Popular scientific articles, book reviews, personal testimonies and the largest forum for personal ads and mass advertising for products and services in the psychic field.

BACK ISSUES OF FATE

Looking for a hard-to-find back issue of FATE? Or a story of particular interest that appeared months or even years ago?

Anything that ever appeared in FATE since the very first issue back in Spring, 1948, can be yours — accurately reproduced from the newly created microfilm library of FATE.

University Microfilms, with the cooperation of FATE Magazine, is offering xerographic reproductions of FATE made from microfilm.

Issues may be purchased at 8c per page, at a minimum of $3.00 per issue. A complete article or a portion is available for $3.00, with additional copies of the same article 50c each.

FATE on Microfilm reels, too

For libraries, bookstores and ambitious collectors of past issues of FATE Magazine, microfilm reels of up to 12 issues of FATE are now available at $12.60 per reel.

Reel	Volume From	Volume To
1	1 (Spring 1948)	3 (December 1950)
2	4 (January 1951)	5 (December 1952)
3	6 (January 1953)	6 (December 1953)
4	7 (January 1954)	7 (December 1954)
5	8 (January 1955)	8 (December 1955)
6	9 (January 1956)	9 (December 1956)
7	10 (January 1957)	10 (December 1957)
8	11 (January 1958)	11 (December 1958)
9	12 (January 1959)	12 (December 1959)
10	13 (January 1960)	13 (December 1960)
11	14 (January 1961)	14 (December 1961)
12	15 (January 1962)	15 (December 1962)
13	16 (January 1963)	16 (December 1963)
14	17 (January 1964)	17 (December 1964)
15	18 (January 1965)	18 (December 1965)
16	19 (January 1966)	19 (December 1966)
17	20 (January 1967)	20 (December 1967)
18	21 (January 1968)	21 (December 1968)
19	22 (January 1969)	22 (December 1969)

Complete Backfile: Volume 1 (Spring 1948) to Volume 22 (December 1969) — 19 reels — is $214.00. Volume 23 (1970) and subsequent volumes may be purchased at $8.80 per volume.

For specific information and order form write to:
FATE #5876
Periodicals, Order Entry
University Microfilms
300 North Zeeb Road
Ann Arbor, MI 48106

Books And Bookstores

Books dealing with psychic phenomena have frequently offered testimonies by uncredentialled mediums and psychics about unusual human behavior and events with very little attempt to provide a theoretical perspective. These testimonies are now being re-evaluated in the context of recent theoretical developments. While old books, long out of print, featuring psychic testimony are now being revived, newer more scientifically-oriented books are increasingly employing a technical language which incorporates basic concepts from all sciences. Investing in a good dictionary of technical terms is well worthwhile to assist you in following these more scholarly arguments. Better bookstores as a rule employ an experienced sales staff capable of helping you to discover a book geared to your own level of involvement with PSI.

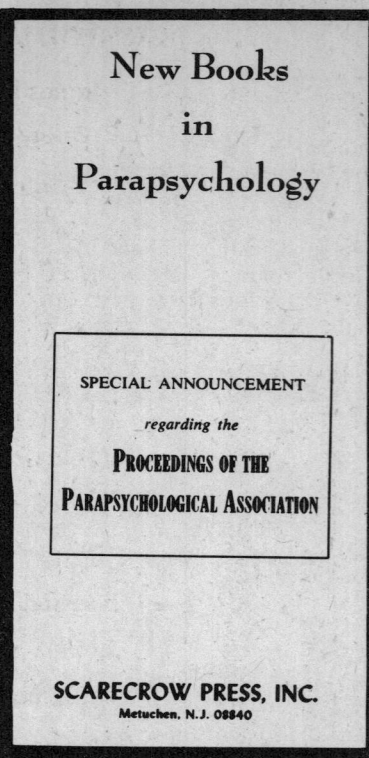

RESEARCH IN PARAPSYCHOLOGY 1972: Abstracts and Papers from the Fifteenth Annual Convention of the Parapsychological Association, 1972

Parapsychological Association
W. G. Roll, R. L. Morris and J. D. Morris, Editors

249 pages 1973 LC: 66-28580 ISBN 0-8108-0666-5 $6.50

This volume continues the published series of Proceedings of the Parapsychological Association, Numbers 1 (1957-1964) through 8 (1971). It contains up to date research briefs reporting the details of experiments performed primarily in 1972 on a wide variety of current parapsychological subjects. Also included, among other presentations, are reports on experiments with animals, and symposia on the potential use of space vehicles in parapsychological research, on the ramifications of "PSI, Science and Society," and on what evidence is needed for survival (reincarnation) to be scientifically convincing.

Highlights of this volume include the Invited Address delivered by Arthur Koestler ("Out on a Tightrope: Parapsychology and Physics") and John Beloff's Presidential Address on "Belief and Doubt."

SPECIAL ANNOUNCEMENT

Commencing with this volume the *Proceedings of the Parapsychological Association* will be published by Scarecrow Press, Inc., under the title *Research in Parapsychology*.

ESP RESEARCH TODAY: A Study of Developments in Parapsychology Since 1960

by J. Gaither Pratt

195 pages 1973 LC: 73-3098 ISBN: 0-8108-0609-6 $6.00

Satisfying the need for an authoritative, comprehensive view of modern parapsychology, ESP RESEARCH TODAY outlines the current status of parapsychology research, covering special areas of research in depth. Written by an Associate Professor of Psychiatry at the University of Virginia School of Medicine who is on the research staff of the Division of Parapsychology, it is aimed for the general reader and offers anyone seeking further information the opportunity to expand his knowledge intelligently as far as he might wish to advance.

The introductory chapters demonstrate how parapsychology is grounded in everyday psychical experiences and provide an overview of current research. Following are chapters covering ESP research in Russia; work with a special ESP subject in Prague; tests of a South African man with a built-in ESP alarm clock; Ted Serios and his "psychic photography"; investigations of poltergeists; studies of cases of the reincarnation type; and an evaluation of parapsychology as a new and emerging field of science.

Detailed literature notes and a long list of suggested further readings are included.

PARAPSYCHOLOGY: Sources of Information

Compiled under the auspices of the American Society for Psychical Research by Rhea A. White and Laura A. Dale

303 pages 1973 LC: 73-4853 ISBN 0-8108-0617-7 $7.50

This annotated bibliography, the first comprehensive guide to information sources on parapsychology, identifies 282 of the best books in the field arranged within 24 subject categories. White and Dale, long associated with parapsychology as researchers and later as librarian and editor respectively, have provided a lengthy annotation for each book, with reading level rating, types of libraries for which it is suited and book review citations.

There is a chapter evaluating and describing coverage of parapsychology in 30 general and specialized encyclopedias. Other sections provide detailed descriptions of major parapsychological research organizations and periodicals (including availability of back issues, information on indexing and a list of libraries with complete runs); information on academic and scientific acceptance of parapsychology with a list of advanced degrees granted for work in parapsychology; a glossary; and detailed appendices and indexes with keys to further information.

NEW CASSETTE!
TAKE A TRIP WITH THE ASTRONAUT
Available from:
Science of Mind publications
3251 West Sixth Street
P.O. Box 75127
Los Angeles Ca. 90075

Join with Astronaut Edgar D. Mitchell in finding a new perspective on life. Learn how to develop the understanding, trust and love necessary to function as an elite team, the crew of spaceship Earth. $4.95

Contributors

James B. Beal
E. Douglas Dean
Martin Ebon
Jule Eisenbud
Gerald Feinberg
Willis W. Harman
Charles Honorton
Jean Houston
Stanley Krippner
Lawrence L. LeShan
Robert Masters
Edgar D. Mitchell
Robert L. Morris
Thelma Moss
Brendan O'Regan
Henry K. Puharich
Harold Puthoff
D. Scott Rogo
William G. Roll
Gertrude Schmeidler
Helmut Schmidt
Rex G. Stanford
Russell Targ
Charles T. Tart
William A. Tiller
Montague Ullman
Robert L. Van De Castle
Alan Vaughan
Marcel Vogel
Evan Harris Walker
Rhea A. White

PSYCHIC EXPLORATION: A CHALLENGE FOR SCIENCE
Edgar D. Mitchell and John White, eds.,
Putnam, 1974
$17.50

BIOGRAPHICAL DICTIONARY OF PARAPSYCHOLOGY—WITH DIRECTORY AND GLOSSARY
1964–1966
Garrett Publications, 1964
$9.00

BIOGRAPHICAL DICTIONARY OF PARAPSYCHOLOGY

A COMPREHENSIVE INTERNATIONAL WHO'S WHO OF MEN AND WOMEN WHO INVESTIGATE CLAIRVOYANCE, TELEPATHY, "GHOSTS," MEDIUMS, SURVIVAL AFTER DEATH, AND OTHER TYPES OF PSYCHIC PHENOMENA

THE HIDDEN SPRINGS: AN ENQUIRY INTO EXTRA-SENSORY PERCEPTION
Renee Haynes
Little, Brown, 1972
(revised edition).
$7.95

THE PSYCHIC FORCE: EXCURSIONS IN PARAPSYCHOLOGY—
The International Journal of Parapsychology
Allan Angoff, ed.
Putnam, 1970
$7.95

For scholar and layman alike, the *Biographical Dictionary of Parapsychology* brings together in one volume 467 sketches of men and women who have interested themselves in the study of telepathy, clairvoyance, mediumship, "apparitions," and many other apparently supernormal phenomena, including the question of life after death.

This study was once known as "psychic research," and it attracted men of both attainment and imagination. Studies of the so-called occult, of witchcraft, yoga, alchemy and the folklore of the supernatural occupied isolated scholars for centuries. But it was not until 1882 that an effort was made to document and to correlate material relating to seemingly inexplicable manifestations of the human mind. In that year the Society for Psychical Research was founded in England with the stated purpose of making "an organized attempt to investigate that large group of debatable phenomena designated by such terms as mesmeric, psychical and spiritualistic."

It is appropriate that a physicist, Sir William Barrett, joined with a classical scholar, Frederic W. H. Myers, a philosopher, Henry Sidgwick, and a specialist on hypnotism, Edmund Gurney, to form the SPR. For psychic research has always attracted a wide spectrum of disciplines, and with the advent of its more statistically based successor, parapsychology, that spectrum has continued to widen. The question, "Do ghosts exist?" has been succeeded—but not supplanted—by the question, "If ghosts do *not* exist, why do some people believe they see them?" The question, "Can some people read minds?" has given way to further questions: "*How* does telepathy operate? Is it the manifestation of a sense that we haven't yet given a name to? Or is it an 'extrasensory' operation? And what, exactly, does 'extrasensory' mean?"

The Biographical Dictionary of Parapsychology is devoted to information about the backgrounds and contributions of people who sought in the past and who are seeking today to answer all these questions, and many more besides.

THE PROBABILITY OF THE IMPOSSIBLE:
Scientific Discoveries and Explorations in the Psychic World
Thelma Moss
J. P. Tarcher, 1974.
$10.00

THE REIGN OF QUANTITY AND THE SIGNS OF THE TIMES
Rene Guenon
Penguin, 1972
$2.65

The Reign of Quantity is an attack on the scientism of the modern world. In these beautiful and profound pages, Rene Guenon looks back to an ancient wisdom, once common to both East and West, but now almost entirely lost. Contemporary civilization itself—with its industrial societies and illusory notions of progress—is his target. In particular, he shows that today's sciences and social sciences are dominated by a quantitative approach, that they neglect the idea of quality. To this "reign of quantity" he opposes the sacred metaphysics of the ancients, which he sees as rooted in Divine Truth. His book is ultimately a warning against the real danger that humanity faces today—a warning all the more urgent because that danger is unperceived by those from whom guidance is sought and expected.

TEST YOUR ESP
Martin Ebon, ed.
Signet, 1970
95 cents

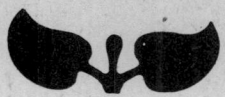

ESP: THE SEARCH BEYOND THE SENSES
Daniel Cohen
Harcourt Brace Jovanovich, 1973
$5.95

PUT YOUR PSYCHIC POWERS TO WORK: A PRACTICAL GUIDE TO PARAPSYCHOLOGY
Evelyn M. Monahan with Terry Bakken
Nelson-Hall Co., 1973
$6.95

MIND OVER MATTER
Glen Barclay
Bobbs-Merrill, 1973
$5.95

A GEOGRAPHY OF CONSCIOUSNESS
William Arkle
Neville Spearman, 1974
$7.00

"We receive experience of events as a package of signals. These signals are valued and responded to from the 'inner' worlds of consciousness which are multi-dimensional and multi-temporal. They are discreet worlds, while functioning in a related way, to which a scale of attitudes can be attached. The main theory of this description of the condition of man is built on the strong basis it has in a Masculine-Feminine, Father-Mother current which is concerned chiefly with the creative act of evolving 'children' in order that they should mature into 'friends'. The vectors describe this structure within the field of consciousness or awareness. The third vector shows the scale of evolving attitudes. A scale of matter is also proposed which goes 'beyond' the conditions of matter which we can observe at this time. Matter and consciousness are then tied together as matter-consciousness. A series of bodies are proposed which belong to each level of matter-consciousness and which are a proper part of the whole man. These are called bodies of communication, and we should use them for this purpose rather than identify with them. Successful evolution is thus seen to be a very complicated process which requires great balance and the best of our attention and effort. Fortunately our real nature is so much more able than we give it credit for that the situation is still an optimistic one."

PSYCHIC DISCOVERIES BEHIND THE IRON CURTAIN,
Sheila Ostrander and Lynn Schroeder
Bantam, 1971
$1.25

The publication of this book by Prentice-Hall in 1970 (hardback edition) greatly influenced the development of interest in psychic phenomena in North America. While focusing on Soviet and Eastern European psychic research, Ostrander and Schroeder throughout attempted to introduce comparable American work in this field, much of it previously being conducted in private and in underground fashion. While American response to psychic research was extremely cautious this book emphasized that Iron Curtain countries had accepted the reality of psychic phenomena and were already exploring its practical application.

PSYCHICAL PHENOMENA AND THE PSYCHICAL WORLD
Charles McCreery
Ballantine, 1973
$1.25

AN ENCYCLOPAEDIA OF PSYCHIC SCIENCE
Nandor Fodor
Citadel Press, 1974
$5.95

An extensive survey of the entire field by an early pioneer.

LLEWELLYN PUBLICATIONS
P.O. Box 3383
St. Paul, Minn. 55165

Serving the Occult Community for over 70 Years

The occult boom that swept Europe during the last of the nineteenth century made its way to the west coast of the United States by 1905, spawning with its passage a generation of truly great American astrologers. Among them were Marc Edmund Jones, Donald Bradley, Grant Lewi, and Llewellyn George. The occult had been an unquestionably dynamic force in American history long before this, but here at last was a group of seriously dedicated men—writers, mystics, and astrologers—who could open our occult heritage to public view. Out of this beginning one publishing company has carried the initial thrust of these men into the present and has expanded to meet the growing diversity of interest outside the astrological field, all the while maintaining standards of scholarship, professionalism, and respectability. **Llewellyn Publications** is that company.

Llewellyn Publications was founded in 1905 with the first publication of the **Moon Sign Book,** an annual astrological almanac. The immediate success of this guide to lunar gardening and astrological prediction led to the writing and publication of Llewellyn George's astrological classic, **The A to Z Horoscope Maker and Delineator,** and a variety of smaller astrological handbooks. Through the depression years, the company continued to grow, adding to the work of George the scholarship of Donald Bradley, **Solar and Lunar Returns,** and the innovative and modern approach of Grant Lewi, **Astrology for the Millions** and **Heaven Knows What.**

With the death of Llewellyn George in the early 1950s, Llewellyn Publications faced a decade of changing leadership and a succession of editors, including Sydney Omarr, for the **Moon Sign Book.** By 1961, because of decaying leadership, the company went up for sale and was purchased by Carl L. Weschcke, who was able to provide a focal point through which the original astrological base of Llewellyn was maintained and from which a dynamic program of expansion was initiated.

The occult explosion into public consciousness coincided synchronistically with Llewellyn's move from Los Angeles to St. Paul and the leadership of Mr. Weschcke. With a staff of five, immediate efforts went into the republication of the astrological texts which were the foundation of the original company. With these in print and selling at phenomenal rates, the way was open to explore the newly blossoming occult market. The renaissance in occult thinking implied more than the onset of a new American fad. For Mr. Weschcke, and interwoven through him into the basic philosophy of the company, this renaissance was the dawning of the Aquarian Age, the first indication of a new humanitarian philosophy, the frontier of a psychological awakening that would change the course of human history.

To meet the challenge of a vision so all-encompassing meant more than republication of the classics in various fields. It meant that within the context of each occult endeavor Llewellyn had to meet the demands of a twentieth century society with twenty-first century minds. The work of Israel Regardie on the hermetic orders flourishing at the turn of the century and, specifically, the phenomenon of Aleister Crowley, became Llewellyn's first venture outside the astrological field and was an immediate success. The republication of **The Golden Dawn,** an encyclopedia of ceremonial magic, the publication of **The Eye in the Triangle,** a first-hand view of the "Great Beast," Aleister Crowley followed by five new Regardie titles put Llewellyn into the forefront of the occult renaissance.

As the 1960s came to a close, the occult movement was beginning to organize itself. That organization found its focus in the Pagan and Witchcraft groups that were rapidly forming across the country and proving to be by far the most vocal of those upholding the aquarian philosophy. Llewellyn Publications, through the work of Lady Sheba, was the first to open the doors of secrecy which had surrounded the Wiccan movement by the first publication of an authentic **Book of Shadows,** traditionally containing the Witch's spells, the laws of the craft, rituals and herbal remedies. This book met with acceptance and approval from an extremely diverse audience of Pagans and Witches of varying traditions and essentially made way for a variety of similar publications from other companies.

Mr. Weschcke himself received initiation from Lady Sheba and has since been in the forefront of the movement, organizing the Council of American Witches, which has been instrumental in achieving a sense of unity within the movement hitherto unknown, and founding the First Wiccan Church of Minnesota.

Throughout, the original astrological orientation of Llewellyn has been maintained and recently reemphasized with the publication of **The Principles and Practice of Astrology,** a twelve-volume series of astrological texts by Noel Tyl, which approach the subject with a twenty-first century emphasis on communication, not only teaching astrological mechanics in a systematic, simplified manner, but also communicating the art of interpretation in a wholly new and dynamic way. First response from such noted figures in the field as Marc Jones and Dorothy Hughes indicates that this series is, in fact, going to be the standard for the twenty-first century, emphasizing the scholarship and professionalism that has been the backbone of Llewellyn.

As we move into our seventieth year of operation, Llewellyn continues its search for original work in all occult fields. This autumn will see the publication of the first of five volumes in the **Magical Philosophy** series by Denning and Phillips, dealing with the Order of the Sacred Word, a fully functioning hermetic order similar to the nineteenth century Golden Dawn, as well as a new work by Noel Tyl focusing on the psychological approach to astrology, **The Horoscope as Identity.** We are continuing to reprint our older titles which remain authoritative in their fields.
At Llewellyn we do not look on astrology or any of the occult sciences and arts as entertainment, but we seek to provide the means for each person to become an expert in applying these systems to improve his own life. We make no effort to cater to the whims of popular fads. Our emphasis which has grown out of the 1960s has been upon the sensational destruction of the Piscean Age, rather than upon the discipline which is essential if we are to move into the Aquarian Age and see the successful realization of that humanitarian vision. It is that discipline which Llewellyn has been promoting for nearly three quarters of a century. It is that discipline under which our authors work and which ultimately gives continuity and dependability to all of Llewellyn's titles—**Heaven Knows What** by Gfant Lewi has sold over 300,000 copies; **The A to Z Horoscope Maker** by Llewellyn George and **Astrology for the Millions** by Grant Lewi, over 75,000 copies each; and the **Moon Sign Book,** which has over the course of its 70 years sold more than 2 million copies!

AN ENCYCLOPAEDIA OF OCCULTISM: A COMPENDIUM OF INFORMATION ON THE OCCULT SCIENCES, OCCULT PERSONALITIES, PSYCHIC SCIENCES, MAGIC, DEMONOLOGY, SPIRITISM, MYSTICISM AND METAPHYSICS
Lewis Spence
Citadel Press, 1974
$5.95

The Comprehensive Illustrated Treasury of Occult Knowledge from All Times and Places
More Than 2,500 Entries and Articles

YES INC.
1039 31st. Street, N.W.,
Washington, D.C. 20007
This comprehensive catalog with over 3,000 listings is annotated. The best available source of available spiritual, metaphysical and psychic books.

For those of you who are new to YES!, let us introduce ourselves. We are providers of food for the spirit, mind and body. We are a bookstore, a foodstore selling pure, natural food, and a small self-service restaurant serving natural, vegetarian food. We occupy three old buildings and a lovely garden in Georgetown.

A society mirrors the people who comprise it. We see the necessity for many changes in our political and social system, but believe that it will not be changed for the better until we—its members—change ourselves for the better. Thus the books we sell are generally concerned with the "inner" revolution in our minds, rather than the "outer" revolution of political activism. To quote a line from our poster "All of the significant battles are waged within the self."

We feel that the spiritual path has many branches—all leading to the same ultimate goal. We at Yes! follow many paths, harmonized by our efforts to, as Ram Dass says, "Love, Serve, Remember." Our eclectic approach is reflected in the content of our catalog. Our aim is to be as comprehensive as possible within the subjects we cover, eliminating only those books that we feel don't make a worthwhile contribution to the topics they discuss (such as most of the mass market astrology books). We import many of our titles from England, India, and other countries.

We realize how hard it is to order from a catalog where you cannot see and scan the books. For this reason we have tried to be as helpful as possible, within our space limitations, to give you a feel for each book so that you can decide whether it is right for you. This second edition of our catalog has three times as many books as the first one, many more categories, and more descriptive and biographical material. If you are overwhelmed by the large selection of books, relax and browse through the catalog at random; letting your eyes and attention focus where they will. In this way you can put your unconscious mind to work. Hopefully, the right books for you will speak to you.

Our division of the books into categories is inevitably arbitrary. If you don't find what you are looking for where you think it ought to be, try a related category.

In our bookshop we also have a comprehensive selection of books on health and nutrition, cookbooks, and books on organic gardening and country living. If you are interested in titles in these areas, write and ask us for them, or tell us your interests and we'll make suggestions. The best way we have found to find new sources for books is by talking with our customers. If you have any suggestions please write to us, giving all the information you have on the books as well as a short description if possible.

A catalog is not a very personal way of communicating. You'll probably get some feel of what we are like from reading it, and we'll get some feel of what you are like from the books you order. But we'd rather have you visit us when you come to Washington. We're open from 11 AM to 9 PM, 7 days a week. We've met many wonderful people who have been attracted by what we have to offer. We'd like to meet you too.

Ordering Information
All prices are net—we are a retail, not a wholesale operation. We do, however, offer a 5% reduction on orders over $50.000. (We also solicit orders from libraries.). . . .

Our postage and handling charge is 35 cents for the first book and 30 cents for each additional book. For overseas orders the cost is 50 cents for the first and 30 cents for each additional book. Send us a check or money order payable to Yes! Inc. Overseas orders please send us a bank check or money order payable in dollars; we cannot accept personal checks from overseas. D.C. residents add 5% sales tax. We send our books by surface mail. Airmail is very costly—frequently to overseas destinations it equals the cost of the book, or more. If you wish your order sent airmail, send us amount for postage equal to the cost of the book. We will refund any unused money or bill you for the difference.

MIND OVER MATTER
Louisa E. Rhine
Collier Books, 1972
$1.95

A comprehensive inquiry into the phenomenon of psychokinesis. This book also provides an intimate account of early parapsychological research problems and aims.

ESP IN LIFE AND LAB: TRACING HIDDEN CHANNELS
Louisa E. Rhine
Collier, 1969
$1.50

THE COMPLETE ILLUSTRATED BOOK OF THE PSYCHIC SCIENCES
Walter B. Gibson and Litzka R. Gilson
Pocket Books, 1974
$1.50

THE PSYCHIC SCENE
Martin Ebon, ed.
Signet, 1974
$1.25

WILLIAM JAMES ON PSYCHICAL RESEARCH
Gardner Muphy and Robert O. Ballou, eds.
Viking Press, 1960
$1.95

FROM THE AUTHORS OF *PSYCHIC DISCOVERIES BEHIND THE IRON CURTAIN.*

THE RESEARCH THAT PROVES THAT EXECS OF TOP COMPANIES OFTEN KNOWINGLY RELY ON ESP.

EXECUTIVE ESP
by DOUGLAS DEAN and JOHN MIHALASKY and SHEILA OSTRANDER and LYNN SCHROEDER

Why do some people rise to the top of the business ladder? Partly brains and hard work and, as ten years' research proves, partly ESP. Here's the first definitive report of that trailblazing project, proof that "a valid and logical link beween ESP and decision-making exists." *International Business Digest*) It's also a guidebook to letting your own hunches pay off for you in every area of life. Illustrated
$7.95

At your bookseller or direct from:

PRENTICE HALL
ATT: Addison Tredd
Englewood Cliffs, N.J. 07632

Please send me _____ copies of *Executive ESP* @ $7.95 ea. I enclose ☐ check ☐ money order for $_____ total. (Please add 50¢ postage and handling plus sales tax where applicable.)

Name _____
Address _____
City _____ State _____ Zip _____

SAMUEL WEISER, INC.

Back in 1926, Samuel Weiser opened his first shop on Fourth Avenue in the Greenwich Village Book District. It was not the greatest occult bookstore then, but rather a small shop stocked with general titles, patronized by random customers. However, there were a few shelves of books loosely classified under "occult."

Through the years Mr. Weiser moved several times. Each move saw an enlargement of his specialized collection, until in 1960 the store took larger quarters at 845 Broadway, just below Fourteenth Street. While the street floor of this vast store was liberally stocked with general titles, the magnet was the downstairs shop of occult books, both new and antiquarian.

The store had literally come into its own. The young came eagerly, and the conventional old-time customer came confidently. There was no generation gap here, for everyone found his "thing." Here were all occult topics from Astrology to Zen. Here, too, were popular books in paperback for the slim purse, as well as rare, obscure titles in fine bindings for the bibliophile or collector.

The secret of the store's success was the attitude of its owner. Mr. Weiser was always the interested mentor. He never hurried a customer, treating him as if he were the only person in the store. Many of the customers of those early days continue to go or call or write to Weiser's rather than purchase a book elsewhere. It is something more than sentiment—it is nostalgic loyalty.

Before another move became necessary, Samuel Weiser had turned the store over to his son, Donald, who carries on in the same characteristic manner. When the move was finally made in 1968, the general titles were abandoned. The store not only has specialized, but has covered every phase of occultism, until today it is the largest occult bookstore in the world. The store has a highly trained staff of clerks, each having an honest interest in varied areas of occult subjects, who are able to carry on the tradition begun by Samuel Weiser and give customers the personal attention they have come to expect.

Besides the many people who call daily at the store to shop, there are thousands of mail-order customers. Weiser's publishes a circular which covers recent books, giving a brief description of each title. The circular literally encircles the globe, and may be had upon request.

**CONSCIOUSNESS AND REALITY:
THE HUMAN PIVOT POINT**
Charles Muses and Arthur M. Young
Outerbridge & Lazard, Inc.
(distributed by Dutton),
1972

Also available in paperback edition:
Avon, 1974
$2.45.

THE WORLD OF TED SERIOS
Jule Eisenbud, M.D.
Pocket Books, 1968
95 cents

Ted Serios had the amazing ability, through intense concentration, to imprint a mental image on Polaroid negatives. Effective controls eliminated any possibility of fraud, and he consistently baffled scientists. An illuminating insight into the massive obstacles confronting psychics whose abilities transcend known scientific laws.

THE MEDIUM, THE MYSTIC AND THE PHYSICIST: TOWARD A GENERAL THEORY OF THE PARANORMAL
Lawrence Le Shan,
Viking Press, 1974
$8.95

". . . Try to determine which of the following quotations (taken from the experiment) were written by mystics and which by physicists.

"1. 'The stuff of the world is mind-stuff.'

"2. 'The reason why our sentient, percipient, and thinking ego is met nowhere in our world picture can easily be indicated in seven words: because it is ITSELF that world picture. It is identical with the whole and therefore cannot be contained in it.'

"3. 'It is the mind which gives to things their quality, their foundation, their being.'

"4. 'It is necessary, therefore, that advancing knowledge should base herself on a clear, pure and disciplined intellect. It is necessary, too, that she should correct her errors, sometimes by a return to the restraint of sensible fact, the concrete realities of the physical world. The touch of Earth is always reinvigorating to the Sons of Earth. . . . It may even be said that the superphysical can only be really mastered in its fullness . . . when we keep our feet firmly on the physical.'

"5. 'Thus the material world . . . constitutes the whole world of appearance, but not the whole world of reality; we may think of it as forming a cross section of the world of reality.'

"6. 'As far as the laws of mathematics refer to reality, they are not certain, and as far as they are certain, they do not refer to reality.'

"7. 'Pure logical thinking cannot yield us any knowledge of the empirical world; all knowledge of reality starts from experience and ends in it. Propositions arrived at by pure logical means are completely empty.'

"The important thing about a game like this is not how many one guesses correctly (turns of phrases and ways of verbalizing, for example, will often point to the persuasion of the author), but that it was *difficult* to guess correctly. The similarity in viewpoints is so great, the conclusions about the nature of reality so identical, that in a specific situation it is very hard to know whether the author is a medium, a mystic, or a physicist." *No. of Quotation Source*

1. Physicist—Sir Arthur Eddington
2. Physicist—Erwin Schrodinger
3. Mystical Document—The Dhammapada
4. Mystic—Sri Aurobindo
5. Physicist—Sir James Jeans
6. Physicist—Albert Einstein
7. Physicist—Albert Einstein

KINSHIP WITH ALL LIFE
J. Allen Boone
Harper & Row, 1954
$3.95

THE LANGUAGE OF SILENCE
J. Allen Boone
Harper & Row, 1970
$3.95

THE DOLPHIN, COUSIN TO MAN
Robert Stenuit
Bantam, 1972
95 cents

THE MIND OF THE DOLPHIN
John C. Lilly
Avon, 1967
95 cents

MAN AND DOLPHIN
John C. Lilly
Pyramid, 1961
95 cents

THE STRANGE WORLD OF ANIMALS AND PETS
Vincent and Margaret Gaddis
Pocket Books, 1971
95 cents

THE OCCULT
Colin Wilson
Vintage, 1973
$3.95

"A single obsessional idea runs through all my work: the paradoxical nature of freedom. When the German tanks rolled into Warsaw, or the Russians into Budapest, it seemed perfectly obvious what we meant by freedom; it was something solid and definite that was being stolen, as a burglar might steal the silver. But when a civil servant retires after forty years, and finds himself curiously bored and miserable, the idea of freedom becomes blurred and indefinite; it seems to shimmer like a mirage. When I am confronted by danger or crisis, I see it as a threat to freedom, and my freedom suddenly becomes positive and self-evident—as enormous and obvious as a sunset. Similarly, a man who is violently in love feels that if he could possess the girl, his freedom would be infinite; the delight of union would make him undefeatable. When he gets her, the whole thing seems an illusion; she is just a girl. . . .

"I have always accepted the fundamental reality of freedom. The vision is *not* an illusion or a mirage. In that case, what goes wrong?

"The trouble is *the narrowness of consciousness*. It is as if you tried to see a panoramic scene through cracks in a high fence, but were never allowed to look *over* the fence and see it as a whole. And the narrowness lulls us into a state of permanent drowsiness, like being half anaesthetised, so that we never attempt to stretch our powers to their limits. With the consequence that we never discover their limits. William James stated, after he had breathed nitrous oxide, 'our normal waking consciousness . . . is but one special type of consciousness, whilst all about it, parted from it by the filmiest of screens, there lie potential forms of consciousness entirely different.''

CREATIVITY AND INTUITION: A PHYSICIST LOOKS AT East and WEST
Hiedeki Ukawa
Kodansha International Ltd., 1973
$8.95

PSYCHIC DISCOVERIES BY THE RUSSIANS
Martin Ebon, ed.
Signet, 1971
95 cents

PROBING THE UNEXPLAINED: STARTLING NEW EVIDENCE ABOUT ESP, PSYCHIC HEALING, LIFE AFTER DEATH AND OTHER AMAZING PHENOMENA
Allen Spraggett
Signet, 1973
$1.25

ADVENTURES INTO THE PSYCHIC
Jess Stearn
Signet, 1971
$1.25

THE OCCULT EXPLOSION
Nat Freeland
Berkley, 1972
95 cents

FILMS FOR A NEW AGE

ON THE NEW CONSCIOUSNESS OF THE WEST:

PSYCHICS, SAINTS, AND SCIENTISTS—Leading scientists explore parapsychology... telepathy... faith-healing... religious experience. 33 Min. COLOR

POTENTIALLY YOURS: Techniques For Growth—Humanistic Psychology... lively techniques for developing human potential. 31 Min. COLOR

THE EXPANDING UNIVERSE OF SCULPTURE—Avant-garde artists demonstrate new approaches to creativity. 14 Min. COLOR

ON THE ANCIENT WISDOM OF THE EAST:

EVOLUTION OF A YOGI—Baba Ram Dass, from LSD at Harvard to Raja Yoga and beyond. 28 Min. COLOR

THE ILLUSION OF SEPARATNESS—Ram Das lectures on universal oneness. Companion to the above. 28 Min. B & W

Islamic Mysticism: THE SUFI WAY—With Prof. Huston Smith from Morrocco to India to study Muslim ritual and Sufism. 28 Min. COLOR

REQUIEM FOR A FAITH—Award-winning classic with Prof. Huston Smith on Tibetan Buddhism. 28 Min. COLOR

MEDITATION CRYSTALLIZED: Lama Govinda on Tibetan Art—Mandalas and paintings as a guide to meditation. 14 Min. COLOR

SACRED ART OF TIBET—Larry Jordan's prize-winning photography interprets Tibetan dieties. 31 Min. COLOR

THE ART OF MEDITATION—Alan Watts is our guide... an audience-participation film. 28 Min. COLOR

Four Films on Zen with Alan Watts:
MOOD OF ZEN—intro to Zen... shot in Japan
BUDDHISM, MAN, AND NATURE—Zen ecology
ZEN AND NOW—on living in the eternal NOW
FLOW OF ZEN—the fluid rhythm of life   Each 14 Min. COLOR

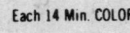

LATEST RELEASES:

INNER SPACES—Capt. Edgar D. Mitchell, Apollo 14 Astronaut, sixth man to set foot on the moon, conducted telepathy experiments from outer space and is now exploring the "Inner Spaces" of the mind. 28 Min. COLOR

THE ULTIMATE MYSTERY—Astronaut Edgar D. Mitchell presents remarkable scientific data supporting the claims of mystics through the ages that there is a oneness to all living things. 40 Min. COLOR

FLOWING WITH THE TAO—Alan Watts, America's foremost interpreter of Eastern thought, explores the nature of reality as illustrated in the flowing forms of water. 14 Min. COLOR

STAIRWAYS TO THE MAYAN GODS—Prof. Joseph Campbell, author of "Masks of the Gods," explores the mythology and spectacular cities of the ancient Maya of Mexico and Central America. 28 Min. COLOR

14 Minute Films $200 Rental $25 • 28 Minute Films $300 Rental $35
31-35 Minute Films $350 Rental $40 • 40 Minute Films $400 Rental $45
B&W Films $200 Rental $25

HARTLEY PRODUCTIONS, INC.
CAT ROCK ROAD • COS COB, CONN. 06807 • (203) 869-1818

SUPERNATURE
Lyall Watson
Anchor Press, 1973
$7.95

A biologist demonstrates that paranormal phenomena need not be clouded in a fog of mysticism. Instead, he provides a natural history of the supernatural, which "is an attempt to fit all of nature, the known and the unknown, into the body of Supernature and to show that, of all the faculties we possess, none is more important at this time than a wide-eyed sense of wonder."

"Supernature knows no bounds. Too often we see only what we expect to see: our view of the world is restricted by the blinkers of our limited experience, but it need not be this way. Supernature is nature with all its flavours intact waiting to be tasted. I offer it as a logical extension of the present state of science as a solution to some of the problems with which traditional science cannot cope and as an analgesic to modern man.

"I hope that it will prove to be more than that. Few aspects of human behaviour are so persistent as our need to believe in things unseen—and as a biologist, I find it hard to accept that this is purely fortuitous. The belief, or the strange things to which this belief is so stubbornly attached, must have real survival value and I think that we are rapidly approaching a situation in which this value will become apparent. As man uses up the resources of the world, he is going to have to rely more and more on his own. Many of these are at the moment concealed in the occult—a word that simply means 'secret knowledge' and is a very good description of something that we have known all along but have been hiding from ourselves."

HEALTH RESEARCH
Box 70
Mokelumne Hill, Calif. 95245

We have no store. We operate a mail-order publishing business. We have no display rooms. Our prices & information are based on serving you via mail. We cover many subjects but do not have a specific catalogue on each subject (which is not feasible).

If you are interested in the following—we can serve you: Alchemy; Aluminum; Anthropology; Apocrypha; Apollonius; Astral Projection; Astrology; Aum; Aura; Beauty; Bible; Bio-Chemistry; Book of Dead; Breathing; Clairvoyance; Chiromancy; Cosmic Science; Chemicals; Catastrophism & Earth History; Crystal Gazing; Chromotherapy & Colors; Comparative Religion; Character Analysis, Cell Salts; Concentration Divination; Chiropractic; Diagnosis; Doctor's Books; Demonology; Devil; Dowsing; Economics; Eyes; ESP; Dreams; Egyptology; Fortune Telling; Fluoridation; Freemasonry; Financial Success; Fasting; Flying Saucers; Food Combinations; Graphology; Garlic; Hex; Hollow Earth; Health; Herbals; Homeopathy; Hypnotism; Hydrotherapy; Inspirational; Isometrics; Irisdiagnosis; Kabbalah (Cabala, Qabalah); Karma; Lost Continents (Atlantis, Lemuria, Mu); Law of Compensation; Longevity; Massage; Magnetic Healing; Masonry; Magnetism; Mental Healing; Magic; Memory; Metaphysics; Mediumship; Mysticism; Mystic & Occult Novels; Numerology; Natural Hygiene; Nutrition; Od Force; Organic Foods & Gardening; Palmistry; Prophecy; Psychometry; Pyramids; Psychic Phenomena; Pendulum; Practitioner's Books; Political; Personal Power; Psychic Power; Psychokinesis; Precognition; Parapsychology; Religion; Rosicrucianism; Radiesthesia; Regeneration; Rejuvenation; Reincarnation; Reflexology; Raw Foods; Sex; Spiritualism; Sun Bathing; Sphinx; Symbology; Suggestion; Spiritual Healing; Tarot; Telepathy; Theosophy; UFO; Vibration; Voodoo; Vampirism; Witchcraft; Water Cure; Yogi; Zone Therapy—we can help you.

Make your wants known by mail. Often we have the very title & author you are seeking. Or if it is a issued out-of-print book we'll attempt to locate it for you. (We do not attempt to locate current new books, but often have many new titles of other publishers—especially on the occult.) These are listed at the back of our 1971 Catalogue #4-A. This makes this one of the largest selections of occult titles available anywhere.

Our terms are Cash With Order. Airmail postage (runs .90 per book in U.S.) must be paid in advance. We sell herbals, but do not sell herbs per se. We sell health books but do not sell health products or health foods. *Please do not send us money for items we do not list.* It costs us over $1.00 just to fill out the papers for a refund. We'll locate out-of-print books at $5.00 Minimum (SEND NO DEPOSIT).

Our line of publications encompasses over 900 titles in facsimile (usually offset—which is lithography and not mimeographing as many believe). This is an actual photographic process which reproduces the same size of print as the original book from which our books are taken. They are not condensed, but word for word of the original. Some of our publications have an I.B.M. typewritten format—so stated and some are mimeographed and so stated. These books usually have light cardboard covers, plastic spiral binding. *These are always in stock.* Cloth bound books of other publishers may be temporarily out of stock—if so these will be backordered and sent later. If out-of-print as many may be later—a refund check is sent promptly. We will not enter into correspondence regarding books of other publishers and listed by author and title without a detailed description. Know exactly what you want—no exchanges or refunds. California residents please add 5% sales tax. Postage is 15 cents per book. Insurance is 20 cents per order. These prices prevail within the U.S. and its possessions. Foreign postage varies—airmail and insurance are expensive. Be specific—give author & title and advise if you wish insured. I If you move, send us the old mailing envelope *from us* which has our key for your name plate—otherwise we lose contact.

All of our books are in English language with a very few exceptions which are noted in the listing.

Help us give you the best possible service—follow our few simple instructions: (1) Print name & address on envelope & order, including zip code. (2) State correct title, price & author. (3) Send correct amount including postage, insurance and sales tax where applicable. (4) Do not order books we do not advertise. (5) If discount is earned, deduct it at the time of order or if Budget Answers are wanted, request them by number at the time of order.

THE IMPRISONED SPLENDOUR
Raynor C. Johnson
Quest, 1971
$2.95

A comprehensive survey of the data of psychical research, mystical experience, and the implications of both.

HANDBOOK OF PSI DISCOVERIES
Sheila Ostrander and Lynn Schroeder
Putnam, 1974
$8.95

"The gist of this handbook is experience, explore, demonstrate, innovate, communicate. Where all the accelerating probing of psi may lead in a hundred years is probably as hard for us to project as it would have been for Graham Bell and his friends to quite imagine the content and feeling of life today. But they did have a feeling for what was happening in their own time. You can read, you can argue, you can say yes, never, maybe; but no matter what the subject, experience gives you an expanded view. It does make a difference if it's *your* telepathic experience or the picture *you* made of a sparkling corona around a leaf. It makes a difference too if you try out a claim and find it doesn't work for you.

"We've tried to answer many how-to questions that people often ask us and, where possible, to supply fresh information, updating in areas that currently seem to be of cardinal interest to ad hoc experimenters. Some of the psi phenomena included, such as telepathy and PK, are well established. Others are highly controversial. Is a pyramid an energy generator? Is there truth to the claim that you can pick up paranormal voices during ordinary tape-recording? Yet every subject does have some basis in scientific work, a takeoff point, a certain measure of assurance that something unusual seems to be happening. And all are highly open ended, with much room for exploration. Recently the field has become so rich that we have only been able to cover some of the current routes to investigation. There are many more.

THE BRAIN REVOLUTION: the frontiers of mind research
Marilyn Ferguson
Taplinger, 1973
$7.95

"FOR PERHAPS TWO HUNDRED YEARS RATIONAL SCIENCE PAINSTAKINGLY CLEANSED THE CIVILIZED WORLD OF MAGIC AND SUPERSTITION. For a time it seemed well on its way to reducing a mechanistic universe to an understandable equation. Then came Einstein, with his 'holy curiosity,' and physicists began talking about curved space, antimatter, relative time, and the nonreal world. More recently the discoveries in other branches of science are contributing to a composite picture of man more startling, more miraculous, than science fiction.

"The most astonishing reality of all appears to be the potential of the human brain. Science and the humanities have converged in the most unexpected way. In order to describe the wonders they have come upon, brain researchers have begun quoting Buddha and William Blake. And poets and mystics, long fearful of the dehumanizing aspects of science, now cite laboratory reports to verify what they had long held as intuitive knowledge.

"Although the great change under way has been called the consciousness movement, the term consciousness has been much abused, and movement is inadequate to describe the impact of a scientific revolution.

"This book will emphasize the findings of the laboratory and their implications. As Abraham Maslow observed, although our visionary artists and mystics may be correct in their insights they can never make the whole of mankind sure. 'Science,' he wrote, 'is the only way we having of shoving truth down the reluctant throat.'

"The findings of brain research and allied disciplines are revolutionizing scientific theory and society. They are setting off chain reactions in medicine, psychiatry, and education. Theories of the nature of intelligence are being turned upside down. There is an enormous groundswell of scientific interest in practices considered quackery a brief decade ago, in altered states of consciousness, unorthodox healing, and parapsychology. And so many improbable theories have proved to be genuine insights that one noted scientist said of a colleague's purported conclusion, 'It isn't crazy enough to be ture.'"

WHERE THE WASTELAND ENDS: POLITICS AND TRANSCENDENCE IN POSTINDUSTRIAL SOCIETY
Theodore Roszak
Doubleday, 1972

In this study of the "religious dimension of political life," Theodore Roszak examines the ways in which the transcendent energies of the human personality have been denatured in Western culture and how this process of psychic deprivation has contributed to the artificial environment and technocratic politics of an urban-industrial society. He argues that "we are long past the time for pretending that the death of God is not a political fact. The repression of the religious sensibilities in our culture over the past few centuries has been as much an adjunct of social and economic necessity as any act of class oppression or physical exploitation; it has been as mandatory for urban-industrial development as the accumulation of capital or the inculcation of factory discipline upon the working millions. It has been achieved with as much ruthlessness."

CHALLENGING PSI DISCOVERIES
Throughout its historical development psychic research has been severely critiqued, by both those who desire to create better and more rigid scientific guidelines as well as those who wish to simply deny the possibility of psi phenomena. These three books are representative of the kinds of criticism researchers and theoreticians have faced.

Martin Gardner, *Fads and Fallacies in the Name of Science*, Dover, 1957, $2.00.

C. M. Hansel, *ESP: A Scientific Evaluation*, Charles Scribner's Sons, 196 $2.45.

D. H. Rawcliffe, *Illusions and Delusions of the Supernatural and the Occult*, Dover, 1969, $2.00.

INSIGHTS FOR THE AGE OF AQUARIUS
Gina Cerminara
Prentice-Hall, 1973
$7.95

"Earth people needed to see the validity of three propositions:

"1. *It is just as proper, and just necessary, to apply scientific methods to religion as to anything else.*

"2. *Religious knowledge, like a other knowledge, must be examin for the authenticity of its origins.*

"3. *Religious knowledge, like oth knowledge, is dependent upon communication process, and the fore the reliability of that proc must be carefully scrutinized.*

". . . Because General Semantics h no religious presuppositions, it does not tend to antagonize non-religious people or to alienate people of any pa ticular religious persuasion. Since its formulations are scientifically groun ed, it has a potentially universal appe Like the axioms of algebra or geometry, the formulations of GS can be agreed on by persons of every countr and from every religious background They can therefore be of inestimable value in establishing the sound and amicable foundations for a planetary culture.

"The system concerns itself with thr major areas: 1) the nature of the universe; 2) the nature of the knowing process; and 3) the nature of the com municating process. It does not deal with any of these three topics exhaus tively, but it does deal with *crucial fa tors* in each one."

MUSIC of the SPHERES: The Material Universe—From Atom to Quassar Simply Explained: Vol. I *The Macrocosm:* Planets, Stars, Galaxies, Cosmology; **Vol. II.** *The Microcosm:* Matter, Atoms, Waves, Radiation, Relativity.
Guy Murchie
Dover, 1967,
$2.50 and $3.00

At a time when psychic research is making tremendous inroads there is a growing need to acquire an understanding of developments in the physical sciences. Those interested in the scientific investigation of psi phenomena therefore must make a concerted attempt to deal with a wide panorama of scientific findings. These two volumes present an excellent introduction.

Also highly recommended: Lincoln Barnett, *The Universe and Dr. Einstein,* Bantam 1968. $.75.

While not directly related to the study of psychic phenomena, the following two books are required reading for those who wish to explore the societal changes which are ushering in the new age.

THE NATURAL DEPTH IN MAN
Wilson Van Dusen
Perennial Library, 1971
$1.75

AWARENESS
Eileen J. Garrett
Berkley, 1968
75 cents

THE MEANING OF PERSONAL EXISTENCE: IN THE LIGHT OF PARANORMAL PHENOMENA, REINCARNATION AND MYSTICAL EXPERIENCE
Arthur W. Osborn
Theosophical Publishing House, 1968
$1.50

THE PSYCHIC WORLD OF CALIFORNIA
David St. Clair
Bantam, 1973
$1.50

THE SIXTH SENSE
Rosalind Heywood
Pan Books, 1971
$1.25

PSYCHOLOGY AND EXTRASENSORY PERCEPTION
Raymond Van Over, ed.
Mentor, 1972
$1.95

"One of the most distinctive aspects of ESP has always been its elusive, sporadic sporadic nature. The problem early researchers faced was unlike that encountered in any other science. The elusiveness of ESP was recognized eventually as the result of subtle psychological elements which began to appear in experiments. Questions relating to personality types, the interaction between subject and experimenter, motivation, the effect of the atmosphere and experimental 'setting,' and numerous other influences began to draw the attention of a growing number of professional people, many of whom were psychologists. The close relationship between ESP phenomena and psychological factors in a subject's personality became clearer as research progressed. In fact, it became rapidly evident—as Myers said quite early—that the source and medium of the psi process was the unconscious.

"As Louisa Rhine points out in her article in this anthology and in several places in her writings, 'A big step forward in understanding was made when it came to be fully realized that the psi process is one that goes on unconsciously. It seems now that about ninety-nine per cent of the difficulties of parapsychological experimentation are the result of the fact that the process is not consciously controlled. Unconscious mental processes are still largely uncharted ones, and those involved here have never studied in depth sufficiently for the needs of parapsychology.' Dr. Rhine rightly emphasizes that this leaves parapsychology with much the same problem as psychology."

ENCYCLOPAEDIA OF THE UNEXPLAINED: MAGIC, OCCULTISM AND PARAPSYCHOLOGY Parapsychology,
Richard Cavendish, ed.
and J. B. Rhine—Consultant
McGraw Hill $17.95

PARAPSYCHOLOGY

"Parapsychology is the science of 'psychic' abilities. Parapsychologists, the people who study these abilities, prefer the Greek letter *psi* to the popular word 'psychic', but the two terms have the same meaning. People in different countries also have different names for this branch of study. The term 'psychical research' originated in England. The word 'parapsychology' comes from *Parapsychologie* in German. In France the term *metapsychique* is used. 'Parapsychical' as an adjective goes better with parapsychology than do 'super-normal' and 'paranormal', which imply a wrong assumption of 'normality'. But psi has for the present taken over this adjectival usage.

"Whatever name is applied to this relatively new branch of study, the abilities themselves can be clearly described. They enable a person to make contact with the world around him without the aid of his senses and muscles. On the receiving side, he obtains knowledge by extrasensory means, which is called extrasensory perception (ESP). On the outgoing side, the ability is known as 'mind over matter', or psychokinesis (PK). PK ability allows a person to influence his physical environment without the use of the motor system of his body, his muscles and glands.

"The two main types of psi interaction, ESP and PK, make up the entire field covered by parapsychology thus far. The two-way communication may be called 'extrasensorimotor' to distinguish it from the sensorimotor interaction on which we mainly rely. To distinguish the varieties of psi phenomena that occur, each of the main types of psi is subdivided into three more specific groups, as follows.

CLAIRVOYANCE, PRECOGNITION, TELEPATHY,

Extrasensory perception has been found to consist of three kinds of phenomena—clairvoyance, precognition, and telepathy. Clairvoyance is the awareness of things of objective events that is acquired without sensory means. The individual who has such an experience may know of the presence of a hidden object that he could not perceive in any sensorial way and that could not be identified by reasoning, or he may be aware of a physical process or action, such as the distant sinking of a ship.

"In a precognitive experience the person knows of something that is going to happen at some future time. Of course no sensory ability can tell him that, and no way is known to predict a specific chance event by purely rational means. This is what is meant by prophecy—foreknowledge of an occurrence such as cannot reliably be inferred from present knowledge (as, of course, a great deal can be).

"Telepathy is still more distinctive. The general idea is that one person makes direct mental contact with another without the sensorimotor mediation of language, code, clue, or other physical signalling. In other words, the communication is assumed to occur as a pure transfer of a mental message; hence the descriptive synonym 'thought-transference'. "These three inclusive categories of possible extrasensory exchange, although extremely different in the kinds of knowledge they convey, all have a common feature in addition to being extrasensory: the knowledge they bring shows intelligent purpose, often of great importance. For example, the message may concern a crisis occurring to a friend far enough away to exclude any possible sensory cues. Or ESP may occur to a person who falls asleep with an anxious concern over a lost object; he may dream of its location and find on waking that his clairvoyant awareness has solved the problem in his sleep. The experience of spontaneous precognition is probably familiar to most people. With this subtype, too, the dream is a frequent conveyor of information. The dreamer may see a vivid picture of an accident that is actually experienced days afterwards, and perhaps hundreds of miles away. He may visit in his dreams a new scene at which, days later, he unexpectedly finds himself (see also DREAMS).

"Telepathy seems to be the most familiar kind of psi experience for most people, and sometimes seems almost to be a dependable method of exchange between two persons accustomed to close contact with each other. When it involves the sharing of a completely accidental experience occurring to one of the pair when the two are separated, it is most impressive; for example, a mother may feel much the same discomfort as her daughter while the latter (at an unexpected time) is giving birth to a child.

"It is well to remember that in all such cases as these other explanations are possible, and it is best to be slow in reaching conclusions as to the psi interpretation. Although the science of parapsychology begins with cases like these because they suggest a possibility that calls for investigation, the more definite conclusions must be left for the more careful examination that is possible in experiments.

PSYCHOKINESIS

"PSYCHOKINESIS, TOO, FALLS INTO THREE SUBDIVISIONS AND, AS WITH ESP, natural branches. Because PK is the direct influence of mind on matter, it is classified according to the three states of matter on which it can take effect. These are not, however, the three categories of solid, liquid, and gaseous known to every beginning student of physics, nor are they those of animal, vegetable, or mineral from the old guessing game. Rather, for the PK student, the material world is divided into moving, living, and static matter.

'THESE THREE DIVISIONS ARE OBVIOUSLY LOOSE CLASSIFICATIONS OF MATTER, BUT THEY ARE PARTICULARLY SUITED TO THE TESTING OF PK. For example, many more individuals have thought they could mentally influence rolling dice or an arrow in flight than have believed they could make a stationary body move. This tendency to believe in the ability to exert PK on a moving target object made it easier to get subjects to try to demonstrate the suspected ability. In the form of dice-throwing, it became a gamelike test of PK, just as the guessing of cards has made ESP tests essentially a kind of contest with chance.

"AS YET THERE IS NO NAME IN PARAPSYCHOLOGY FOR THE DEMONSTRATION OF PK on moving targets because it is still too new, but it is commonly referred to by the abbreviation PK—MT. This, of course, draws attention by contrast to the PK of static targets, which is called PK—ST. As will be seen later, our knowledge of this subtype from careful research still lags behind, but a growing number of persons believe they have observed stationary objects spontaneously moved by human agency without direct or indirect muscular effort. In other words, they have been convinced that they have witnessed PK—ST.

"REGARDLESS OF HOW THE PHYSICIST MAY CLASSIFY MATTER FOR HIS OWN PURPOSES, THERE IS A DISTINCTLY DIFFERENT CATEGORY WHICH HE USUALLY OMITS, NAMELY, LIVING MATTER. This type of matter is, as everyone knows, different from inanimate substances, whether static or moving. Yet some people believe they have mentally influenced living matter in both plants and animals, in its special functions of growth, healing, and the like. This would be PK—LT. Fortunately, this is a phenomenon that can be studied by means of controlled experiments; therefore, it is not necessary to try to decide whether these reports of personal experience provide acceptable evidence in themselves.

"IT SHOULD BE REMEMBERED THAT IT IS NOT NECESSARY TO MAKE UP ONE'S MIND CONCLUSIVELY ABOUT THE OCCURRENCE OF EACH SUBTYPE OR TO TRY TO DECIDE WHETHER EACH KIND OF PSI PHENOMENON IS INDEPENDENT OF THE OTHER SUBTYPES. More final decisions can be made at a later stage, at least in most cases, and one can study the evidence for certain aspects while making only tentative judgments as to its firmness and finality. It will be seen later that as a result of the more controlled experimental studies, clairvoyance and precognition are the more conclusively established subtypes of ESP; telepathy is still inconclusive (in its mind-to-mind interpretation). With regard to mind over matter, the PK of moving targets is very well established, but the PK of living targets is only moderately well established. The case for the PK of static targets should still be considered to belong in the inconclusive stage, even more so than telepathy, although it may not remain so for very long. In this way we can keep the question open and continue investigation. Although it is not as hazardous to accept a claim prematurely as to reject it, it is still a dangerous decision because it tends to stop the investigation.

"WHILE WE SUSPEND JUDGMENT ABOUT THE ACCEPTABILITY OF TELEPATHY AND OF PK—ST, we can tentatively consider them possible and keep them in the tentative chart of the territory claimed by the science of parapsychology. The following outline of this territory will help keep these subtypes in mind:

Psi ('Psychic') or Parapsychical Ability
Extrasensory Perception
Clairvoyance (conclusive)
Precognition (conclusive)
Telepathy (inconclusive)

Psychokinesis
PK—MT (conclusive)
PK—LT (marginal)
PK—ST (inconclusive)"

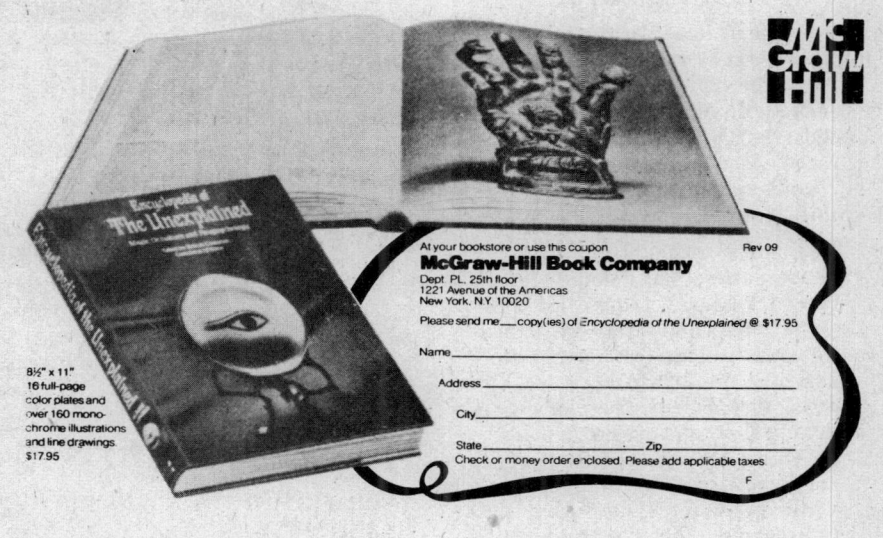

THE CRACK IN THE COSMIC EGG: CHALLENGING CONSTRUCTS OF MIND AND REALITY
Joseph Chilton Pearce
Pocket Books, 1973
$1.25.

Truly a breakthrough book which provides an in-depth philosophical and scientific appreciation of how we create our realities. While many books may provide more specific data on psychic phenomena, Pearce has given us an invaluable primer on how we must learn continuously to reevaluate what we believe to be real.

"Our cosmic egg is the sum total of our notions of what the world is, notions which define what reality can be for us. The crack, then, is a mode of thinking through which imagination can escape the mundane shell and create a new cosmic egg. The crack is that 'twilight between the worlds' found by the young anthropologist, Carlos Castaneda, in his study of the Yaqui Indian sorcerer, don Juan, and his 'Way of Knowledge.' The crack is found as well in that 'narrow gate' of Jesus' Way of Truth. The crack is an open end, going beyond the broad, statistical way of the world. . . .

"The Platonists and Stoics have always assumed the forest to be ready planted. Corresponding ideas of what was 'out there' were planted also in our minds, leading us by heuristic devices until we finally stumbled our way to various discoveries and conclusions. The gods and fates looked on, rather as we would watch rats in a maze.

"Consider, however, that the kind of trees we succeed in felling at the clearing's edge need not have always *been*. Indeed, there may be no trees at all in the depths of that dark. Rather, the forest may shape, the trees may grow, according to the kind of light our reason throws.

"Scientists speak of the dark forest of nature as essentially simple. Nature is a category, however, a label, a concept shot through and through with man's thought. And man's thought is designed to simplify from an endless possibility. Scientists are never really talking about the unknown nature of the forest beyond their circle of reason and logic. They talk about their garden within it, the forest converted, the trees labeled, the plants and shrubs cataloged, selected, arranged in orderly patterns. When the scientists look at the forest, they look for additions to their garden, and they look with a gardener's eye.

HIAWATHA PUBLISHING CO.
P.O. Box 400
Perry, Iowa 50220
Write for catalog of metaphysical and self-help books.

JACOB'S LADDER BOOK STORE
P.O. Box 20082, Montclair Station
Denver, Colo. 80220
Write for catalog.

POINT DAWN BOOKS
Route 1, Box 244-B
Oroville, Calif. 95965
Write for circular.

CITYLIGHTS BOOKSTORE
261 Columbus Ave.,
San Francisco, Calif. 94133.
Carries a selection of books dealing with psychic and related phenomena.

"The nature 'discovered' is determined, to an indeterminable degree, by the mind that sets out to discover. We can never know the full extent we play in this reality formation. It will never be computable or reducible to formula. An ultimately serious commitment of mind, however, can be the determinate in any issue, overriding randomness and chance. . . ."

DICTIONARY OF ALL SCRIPTURES AND MYTHS
G. A. Gaskell
Julian Press, 1973
$13.00

EXPLORING THE CRACK IN THE COSMIC EGG
Split-minds & Meta-realities
Joseph Chilton Pearce
The Julian Press, 1974.
$6.95

This book is a sequel to Mr. Pearce's uniquely challenging *The Crack in the Cosmic Egg*. In *Exploring the Crack,* Mr. Pearce deals with the despair, anxieties, and confusion modern man suffers. He identifies this dilemma as an attempt to live according to the imposed abstract programming that allows thinking and living only in culturally evaluated terms of reality.

Culture's limited and mechanical focus has brought about a split in man's functioning, distorting and lessening the larger, symbiotic relationship to life. While man can create and use abstractions, and has great adaptability, humanity is more than that, and needs more than the sum total and potential the culture allows.

Pearce presents other viable approaches emerging out of man's history and evolution, demonstrating that man has found and can achieve wholeness and a more expansive and fulfilling existence. Reuniting the self is the issue.

'Pearce also explores the "non-ordinary" and paranormal, but these phenomena are seen as a natural expression of man's logical possibilities, a biological norm totally disacknowledged by cultural rules.

In *Exploring the Crack in the Cosmic Egg,* the deeper meaning of don Juan's way of life (Carlos Castaneda) becomes clear, as do the concepts of individuals, philosophers, and poets who break with the rigid rules of a limited, quasi-scientific establishment.

For those seeking a way through the maze of contemporary education, politics, mysticism, and psychology, this is an indispensable book.

PASSAGES ABOUT EARTH: AN EXPLORATION OF THE NEW PLANETARY CULTURE
William Irwin Thompson
Harper & Row, 1974.
$6.95.

"Consciousness is like an FM radio band: as long as one is locked into one station, all he receives is the information of one reality; but if, through the transformation of the sexual energy that holds him into the physical plane of Eros and Thanatos, he is able to move his consciousness to a different station on the FM band, then he discovers universes beyond matter in the cosmic reaches of spirit. In Yoga, the spinal column is the FM band and the chakras along the spine represent the various stations of cosmic information. After one has gone through these universes, he returns to the body, but now the body has been altered by the process and a new nervous system develops in preparation for the continued evolution of man. . . .

"Now the yogis would claim that just as there is a negative feedback of consciousness to nature and culture, so, in terms of the laws of symmetry, is there a positive feedback. But before we can observe the positive feedback of consciousness to the body of the planet, we must first observe it in our own bodies. When a yogi stops his heart or alters other physical conditions hitherto thought to be part of the involuntary nervous system, he demonstrates that 'matter' is subordinate to 'mind.' When a devout Christian develops the stigmata on Good Friday, he demonstrates the same priority of consciousness. Symbol is clearly dominant, for how is it that the devotee selects the right cells in the right symbolic spots, and does not miss and bleed from the cheek or forearm? When Swami Rama stopped his heart for seventeen seconds at the Menninger Institute under conditions of precise scientific observation, he closed a chapter of Western medicine and showed that the old Cartesian split between the *res extensa* and the *res cogitans* had been carried over into our medical textbooks in terms of the autonomic and voluntary nervous systems. . . .

"The 'feedback' of consciousness to nature is called culture; when culture reaches nature. We can see this effect in the earth's ecosytem, for our culture is changing the earth's atmosphere and weather. The point of maximum information, or maximum civilization, will correspond with entropy, and we will reach the end of history—which is precisely what the ecologists and the mystics have been prophesying. If the mind is, therefore, an energy state in which the increase of information is generating an increase in entropy in the surrounding system, then, for all practical purposes, the mind has to be looked upon as a very real event in the physical system. . . .

"If mathematical form becomes more basic than matter itself, then it follows that science, the cultural process in which the mind develops *modes* for the knowing of *forms*, is an inseparable part of nature. The subjective-objective distinction collapses. It does little good, then, to talk confidently of 'facts' when you do not understand the *structure* of consciousness through which one can entertain the *content* of facts.

"The difficulty always arises when one confidently thinks in terms of a subjective 'inside' world and an objective 'outside' world. We are not standing outside nature and observing it through a window. We ourselves are a part of the nature we seek to describe, and through what Whitehead calls 'the witness of the body' we can discover the correspondence between neurons and neutrinos. . . .

LINDISFARNE

50 Fishcove Road
Southampton, New York 11968

Write for information about this New Age community, founded by William Irwin Thompson.

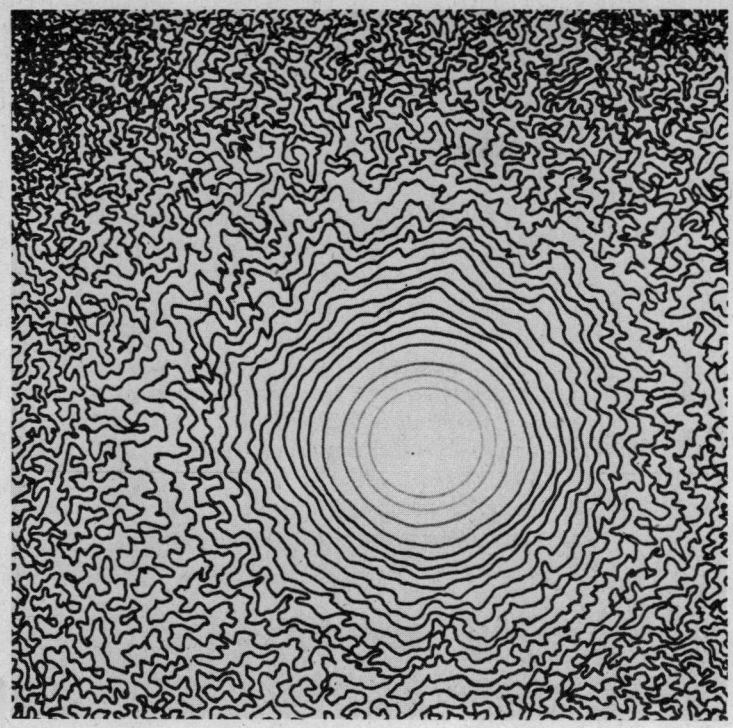

PART TWO: ENERGIES

PSI literature offers a great number of references to a mysterious luminous emanation or "aura" which sensitives claim to be capable of perceiving around human beings. Until recently, scientists have refused to see such claims as evidence of anything other than hallucination or deliberate fraud, demanding scientific evidence. When news reached this continent of a technique of photographing these emanations, perfected by Semyon Kirlian, a Soviet electrician, a large-scale scientific effort was generated to make sense of the visible energy patterns of leaves, human fingertips and even coins.
It is hoped that correct interpretations of these emanations will provide significant break-throughs in our understanding of the intimate relationship between man and universe. Present research suggests the existence of a prephysical body serving as a buffer zone between cosmic environmental forces and the physical body and that the "aura" may be part of a wider energy matrix which governs bodily organization. These speculations have laid the groundwork for a wide-scale re-examination of beliefs in the existence of life energies and "fields of life," described in metaphysical and spiritual teachings and in the work of unorthodox scientists. While much of the experimentation in Kirlian photography itself is being carefully reassessed in the light of recent criticisms, the next phase in the story of the aura suggests that more scientists may be willing to re-examine enigmas of human existence in far more comprehensive, scientific and metaphysical terms.

Fields Of Life, And Cosmic Influences

The idea that our physical body is a by-product of a matrix of swirling energies challenges many of our root assumptions about life. It implies that all aspects of human existence are intimately related to environmental forces. Revived interest in the electrodynamic theory of life proposed in 1935 by Harold Saxton Burr and F.S.C. Northrup and in the attempt to systematize explanations of how celestial bodies influence daily activity, signals a growing tendency to ask new questions about the origins of life, and to consider the possibility of vital life energies interpenetrating everything, everywhere.

THE THEORY OF CELESTIAL INFLUENCE
Rodney Collin
Samuel Weiser, 1973
$5.00

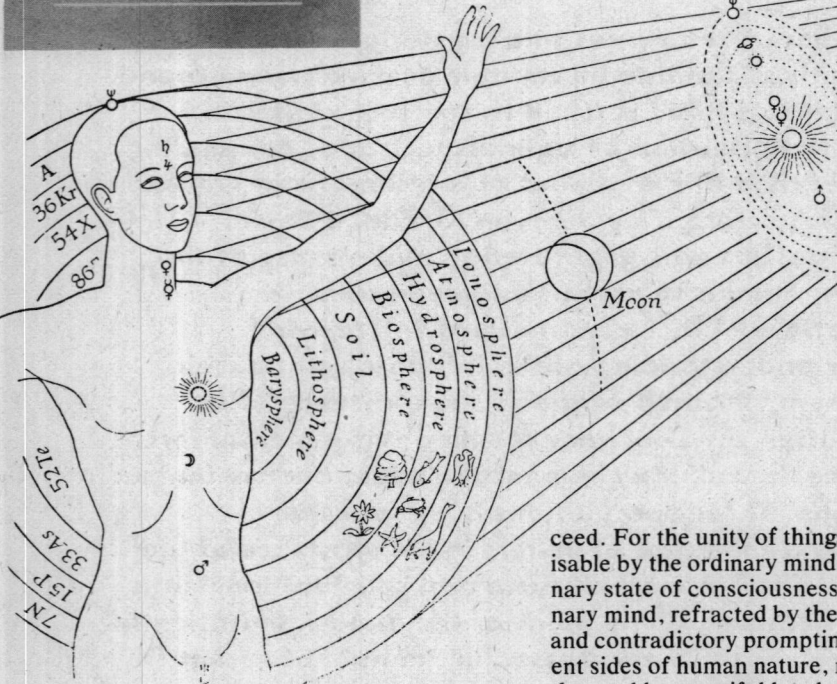

"In every age men have tried to assemble all the knowledge and experience of their day into a single whole which would explain their relation to the universe and their possibilities in it. In the ordinary way they could never succeed. For the unity of things is not realisable by the ordinary mind, in an ordinary state of consciousness. The ordinary mind, refracted by the countless and contradictory promptings of different sides of human nature, must reflect the world as manifold and confused as is man himself. A unity, a pattern, an all-embracing meaning—if it exists—could only be discerned or experienced by a different kind of mind, in a different state of consciousness. It would only be realisable by a mind which had itself become unified. . . .

"Philosophically, man can suppose an Absolute. Such an Absolute would include all possible dimensions both of time and space. That is to say:

"It would include not only the whole universe which man can perceive or imagine, but all other such universes which may lie beyond the power of his perception.

"It would include not only the present moment of all such universes, but also their past and their future, whatever past and future may mean on their scale.

"It would include not only everything actualised in all the past, present and future of all universes, but also everything that potentially could be actualised in them.

"It would include not only all possibilities for all existing universes, but also all potential universes, even though they do not exist, nor ever have.

"Such a conception is philosophical for us. Logically, it must be like that, but our mind is unable to come to grips with the formula or make any sense of it."

Remarkable New Scientific Discoveries That Can Change Your Life!

Body Time

Gay Gaer Luce
Bantam, 1973
$1.50

"Deep within us, the seething commotion of our cells is organized. Intermeshed cycles of timing may be the glue that holds us together.

"This is a book about the role of biological time cycles in our health and enjoyment of life. It is an admittedly crude and early look at a most overlooked dimension of our lives—time.

". . . Time is the most intimate and pervasive aspect of our lives, yet the language of our self-expectations is static. We traverse the life cycle from birth to maturity, aging, and death. We observe the round of seasons, the ceaseless alternation of day and night. We are touched by inner cycles of sleepiness and hunger, yet our self-image is as fixed as a photograph. We expect consistent feeling and behavior in family and friends. We aspire to undeviating performance at work, and measure our state of health against some static norm. Our habitual language imposes the expectations of a steady state. All of this hinders us from feeling our rhythmic nature. Indeed, cyclic change is so unexpected even among medical doctors and scientists that it is often mistaken for abnormality."

NATURAL BIRTH CONTROL
Sheila Ostrander and Lynn Schroeder
Bantam, 1972
$1.25

"According to Dr. Eugen Jonas, *astrological birth control* is a natural form of birth control based on the idea that a woman has *two* fertility cycles per month: the regular, monthly ovulation cycle, *plus* a second fertility cycle which can be precisely calculated from the time of her birth. Jonas postulates a *biological rhythm* involved with both fertility and sex determination.

". . . His three rules are: (which will be discussed in detail later)

"1. The time of a woman's fertility depends on the recurrence of the angle of the sun and moon that occurred at the woman's own birth.

"2. The sex of the child depends on the position of the moon at conception.

"3. Certain configurations of the nearer celestial bodies at the time of conception can affect the viability of the embryo."

ENERGIES: MATERIAL, VITAL, COSMIC
J. G. Bennett
Coombe Springs Press, 1964
$3.50

THE LIVING CLOCKS
Ritchie R. Ward
Mentor, 1971
$1.95

"No single idea of the twentieth century has contributed more broadly to today's understanding of the life sciences than that organisms—from one-celled plants to man—either are endowed with, or perhaps *are*, living clocks.

"And certainly no idea of such far-reaching consequences has been less accessible to the general reader. The biologists who write of biochronometry, as they call it, have a specialized language of their own within the special language of biology itself, and it is hardly surprising that a cultural gap has separated the intelligent man from the momentous discoveries in this field. In this book I have tried to tell the story of living clocks for readers who have no special background in science, but with such attention to accuracy that no scientist will take offense. . . ."

COSMIC INFLUENCES ON HUMAN BEHAVIOR
Michel Gauquelin
Stein and Day, 1973
$7.95

This book is a major attempt to examine astrology from a strictly scientific point of view. Michel Gauquelin, whose work at the Sorbonne was in psychology and statistics, has devoted more than twenty years' research to the question of astrology. In *Cosmic Influences on Human Behavior*, he reveals the startling results of his research.

Is our universe astrological? Does time of birth affect temperament? Do planetary types correspond to personality types? Gauquelin's answers to these and other questions may surprise many readers—including the experts. For the statistical correlations he has discovered in thousands of case histories cannot be explained by the laws of chance.

"A whole new train of thought has spread like wildfire throughout the world."

"No one should regard it as impossible that, from the follies and blasphemies of astrologers, may emerge a sound and useful body of knowledge."—Johannes Kepler.

GOETHE'S THEORY OF COLOUR APPLIED BY MARIA SCHINDLER
New Knowledge Book, 1964
$8.00

Specifications of Hewlett-Packard D.C. Vacuum Tube Voltmeter Model 412A recommended by Dr. Burr to measure electrodynamic fields."

MIND AND MATTER
Cecil J. Schneer
Grove Press, 1969
$2.95

MUSIC: ITS SECRET INFLUENCE THROUGHOUT THE AGES
Cyril Scott
Weiser, 1958
$5.00

THE PSYCHIC STUDY OF "MUSIC OF THE SPHERES"
D. Scott Rogo
University Books, 1972
$6.95 each (Vols. I and II)

COLOR AND MUSIC IN THE NEW AGE
Corinne Heline
New Age Press, 1969
$2.50

"Perhaps the most deeply mystic definition of color is the one given by Goethe in these words: 'Colors are the sufferings of light.' As the vibratory rhythms of pure white light—which contains all colors within itself—is lowered, colors become manifest. Thus it is definitely a fact that colors are born through the sufferings of light.

• • •

"*Red*

"Reddish-brown indicates avarice, greed, selfishness.

"Bright brick-red: anger.

"Deep dark red: sensuality.

"Scarlet reveals an overabundance of personal pride.

"Carmine—a clear pure red—denotes strength, endurance and a high state of physical perfection.

"Clear, bright pink bespeaks human affection that has been softened by sorrow."

THE ROOTS OF PEACE
Viva Emmons
Quest, 1969
$1.75

"It has often been said that our bodies begin to die as soon as we are born. In this sense, our existence on earth is as precarious as that of a man walking a tight rope, one who must constantly balance himself skillfully between forces that would destroy him. Yet he is born, and must live and die in accordance with some irrevocable timeplan, a life span. Therefore he has only a limited period of time in each life, a duration between birth and death, to exercise such powers as he can command to maintain his life in whatever measure of peaceful existence he can employ for his survival."

THE PLANETARIZATION OF CONSCIOUSNESS
Dane Rudyhar
Harper Colophon, 1972
$2.95

"Mind is the capacity to hold images of existence in a coherently interrelated, consistent and formal state of consciousness. The character of a mind depends therefore on the nature of the images which it is its function to interrelate and more or less formally to integrate into a system. It is at some level of existence a system of concepts; but we should be able to think of a mind which operates at a level at which we can no longer speak precisely of concepts, but rather of 'Images.'

". . . Many modern psychologists of the academic type are bent upon proving that mind can be entirely reduced to the activities of the nerves and particularly of the brain of the physical body. That such activities, explainable in electrical and chemical terms, exist is evident. The question is whether they may not be the end-results of the operation of a formative principle inhering in the total field-of-existence which constitutes a human person.

". . . This Ideity-field, or 'Auric Egg,' is the limited and apparently ovoidal 'space' within which the Soul-to-person relationship has to work out. The relationship operates on an active basis as long as the human person lives, exceptions notwithstanding. When the man or woman dies the Ideity-field becomes inactive. It enters into a condition of 'obscuration' or latency. When a new human being is conceived or born with whom the Soul enters into relationship, the field is reactivated. But the person who had previously died and the new one are not the same person. The Ideity-field and thus the monad are the same; the Soul-field is also the same—but a new human organism is drawn into the Ideity-field, and the social-cultural environment of the new birth differs in most cases from the one in which the first person was born."

THE SEARCHERS
Gustaf Stromberg
Science of Mind Publications, 3251 West 6th Street, Los Angeles, Calif. 90005 1967
$3.00

THE SOUL OF THE UNIVERSE
Gustaf Stromberg
Educational Research Institute, 1973
$4.00

"From the turmoil caused by the great discoveries in the science of physics during the last decades two outstanding new principles have emerged. The first is contained in the Quantum Theory and explains the strange fact that both matter and light appear sometimes as particles and sometimes as waves. The second has evolved from the Theory of Relativity and has resulted in a realization that the material universe is a uniform and interrelated whole, that it is a special aspect of a rational Cosmos. These two new principles have in this book been applied to the field of biology and have been found extremely useful in explaining the marvelous structures and the purposeful organization in the living world. We can then understand how an egg cell can develop into an animal, and a larva into a butterfly, new light is thrown on the origin and the development of life on the earth, and as in a flash we realize the meaning and nature of death.

"The two principles have also been applied to the age-old problem of the relationship between mind and matter. We can then understand the connection between the chemical and electric processes in the nervous system and the corresponding sensations and feelings. The most startling results of this study are that the individual memory is probably indestructible and that the essence of all living elements is probably immortal. The study leads to the inevitable conclusion that there exists a World Soul or God."

DESIGN FOR DESTINY
Edward W. Russell
Ballantine, 1971
$1.25

"It is true that DNA-fans credit molecules with anthropomorphic powers, in much the same way as primitive tribes attribute human attributes to idols of stone or wood. They solemnly assure us that Molecule A has all the information needed for heredity, that Molecule B passes this on to the cells while Molecule C assesses the needs of the cells and restrains A and B from getting too enthusiastic. But nobody has so far explained *how* Molecule A got the information in the first place, *how* Molecule B distributes it and *how* Molecule C can judge anything, let alone check A and B. . . .

". . . Field physics recognizes that there are many fields in nature—with their associated particles—which interact with one another. These range from tiny fields within the atom to vast gravitational and other fields of stars and planets which can exert their influence across great distances. The moon, for instance, produces tides within the field of the earth.

"Is there any reason to suppose that the human body is a miraculous exception to the universal rule of fields and is organized by some mystical, unexplained chemistry? Surely it is more reasonable to suppose that genes and DNA produce their effects by means of their inherent fields? For fields cannot be affected by chemical changes and can, in fact, control them."

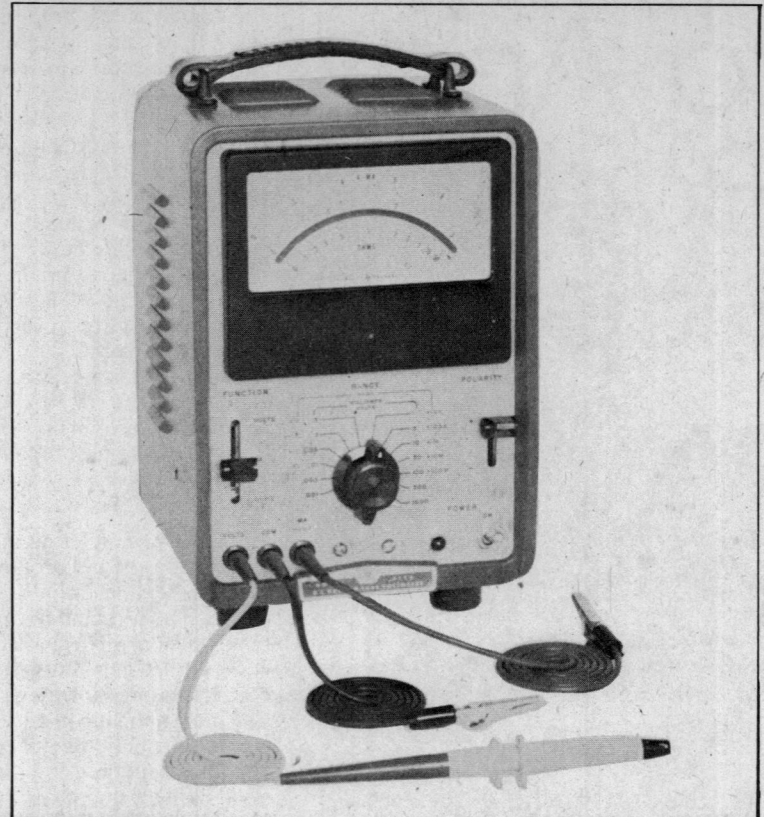

Specifications of Hewlett-Packard D.C. Vacuum Tube Voltmeter Model 412A recommended by Dr. Burr to measure electrodynamic fields.

Voltmeter
Voltage Range: Positive and negative voltages from 1 millivolt full scale to 1,000 volts full scale in thirteen ranges.
Accuracy: ±1% of full scale on any range.
Input Resistance:
10 megohms ±1% on 1 mV, 3 mV, and 10 mV ranges.
30 megohms ±1% on 30 mV range.
100 megohms ±1% on 100 mV range.
200 megohms ±1% on 300 mV range and above.
AC Rejection: A voltage at power line or twice power line frequency 40 dB greater than full scale affects reading less than 1%. Peak voltage must not exceed 1,500 volts.
Voltages and Currents:

Range	Open Circuit Volts	Short Circuit Current
X1	10 mV	10 mA
X10	100 mV	10 mA
X100	1 V	10 mA
X1000	1 V	1 mA
X10K	1 V	100 µA
X100K	1 V	10 µA
X1M	1 V	1 µA
X10M	1 V	0.1 µA
X100M	1 V	0.01 µA

General
Meter: Individually calibrated.
Isolation Resistance: At least 100 megohms shunted by 0.01 µF between common terminal and case (power line) ground.
Isolation: May be operated up to 500 V dc or 130 V ac from ground.
Power: 115 or 230 volts ± 10%, 50 to 60 Hz, 35 watts.
Dimensions:
Cabinet Mount: 11½" high, 7½" wide, 10" deep (292 x 191 x 254 mm).
Weight:
Cabinet Mount: Net, 12 lbs. (5.5 kg). Shipping, 14 lbs. (6.4 kg).
Rack Mount: Net, 12 lbs. (5.5 kg.). Shipping, 20 lbs. (9.0 kg).

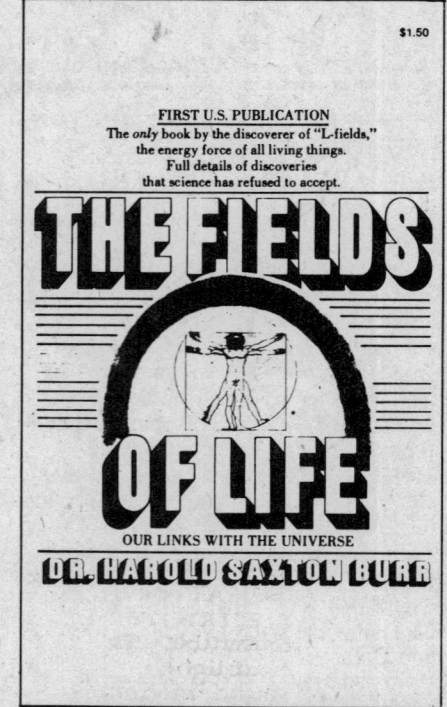

THE FIELDS OF LIFE: OUR LINKS WITH THE UNIVERSE
Dr. Harold Saxon Burr
Ballantine, 1973
$1.50

"The Universe in which we find ourselves and from which we can not be separated is a place of Law and Order. It is not an accident, nor chaos. It is organized and maintained by an Electrodynamic Field capable of determining the position and movement of all charged particles.

"For nearly half a century the logical consequences of this theory have been subjected to rigorously controlled experimental conditions and met with no contradictions.

"... *The following theory may then be formulated. The pattern or organization of any biological system is established by a complex electro-dynamic field which is in part determined by its atomic physio-chemical components and which in part determines the behaviour and orientation of those components. This field is electrical in the physical sense and by its properties relates the entities of the biological system in a characteristic pattern and is itself, in part, a result of the existence of those entities. It determines and is determined by the components.*

"*More than establishing pattern, it must maintain pattern in the midst of a physio-chemical flux. Therefore, it must regulate and control living things. It must be the mechanism, the outcome of whose activity is wholeness, organization, and continuity.* . . .

". . . L-fields are detected and examined by measuring the difference in voltage between two points on—or close to—the surface of the living form. In men and women L-field voltages can be measured by placing one electrode on the forehead and the other on the chest or the hand. Alternatively, the index finger of each hand is dipped into bowls of saline solution connected to the voltmeter In special cases voltage readings may be taken by applying the electrodes to some specific organ or part of the body.

". . . Dr. Ravitz has discovered that the voltages of the L-fields of healthy people are not constant but vary in steady rhythms over periods of weeks—whatever the cause may be. From plotting over 50,000 measurements on 500 human subjects he has found that these rhythms show how the subjects feel. When they feel 'on top of the world' their voltages are high; when they feel 'below par' their voltages are low.

The Aura And Out Of Body Experiences

Is the "aura" the key to understanding all paranormal behavior? Investigation of the aura necessitates the possibility that there are more subtle planes of existence. Some investigators lean more toward viewing the aura as a buffer zone reflecting the nature of the information being exchanged between the physical body and the environment and that it is possible to master techniques which alter the nature of this exchange and produce "paranormal effects."

THE ETHERIC DOUBLE
Arthur E. Powell

The Theosophical Publishing House, 1969
$3.95

"The occultist finds that physical matter exists in seven grades or orders of density, viz.:

Atomic.
Sub-Atomic.
Super-Etheric.
Etheric.
Gaseous.
Liquid.
Solid.

". . . It is known to occultists that there are at least three separate and distinct forces which emanate from the sun and reach our planet. There may be countless other forces, for all we know to the contrary, but at any rate we know of these three. They are:—

1. Fohat, or Electricity.
2. Prana, or Vitality.
3. Kundalini, or Serpent-Fire."

PRÂNA, OR VITALITY

DIAGRAM 1
SOLAR FORCES

SUN

FOHAT OR ELECTRICITY convertible into heat, light, sound, motion etc.

PRANA OR VITALITY

KUNDALINI OR SERPENT-FIRE

Each of these manifests on all planes of the Solar System.

THE ETHERIC DOUBLE
TABULAR STATEMENT

NO.	PLACE.	SPOKES.	APPEARANCE.	VITALITY RECEIVED.	VITALITY SENT OUT.
1	Base of Spine.	4	Fiery orange-red.	Orange and red, from Spleen Centre: also some dark purple.	..
2	Navel.	10	Various shades of red, with much green.	Green, from Spleen Centre.	..
3	Spleen.	6	Radiant and sun-like.	..	(1) Violet-blue, to Throat. (2) Yellow, to Heart. (3) Green, to Solar Plexus. (4) Rose, to Nervous System. (5) Orange-red, to Base of Spine, with some dark purple.
4	Heart.	12	Glowing golden.	Yellow, from Spleen Centre.	Yellow, to Blood, Brain and middle of Top of Head Centre.
5	Throat.	16	Silvery and gleaming with much blue.	Violet-blue, from Spleen Centre.	Dark blue, to Lower and Central Brain. Violet, to Upper Brain and outer part of Top of Head Centre.
6	Between Eyebrows.	96	Half: Rose, with much yellow. Half: Purplish-blue.	?	..
7	Top of Head.	12 / 960	Centre: gleaming white and gold. Outer part: full of indescribable chromatic effects.	Yellow, from Heart Centre. Violet, from Throat Centre.	..
8 9 10	Not used in "white magic."			..	..
1	In Developed Person. Base of Spine.	4	Fiery orange-red.	Orange and red, from Spleen Centre, and some dark purple.	..

TABULATION OF RESULTS
OF CENTRES, ETC.

NO.	REGION VITALISED.	FUNCTION OF ASTRAL CENTRE.	FUNCTION OF ETHERIC CENTRE.
1	Sex organs. Blood, for heat of body.	Seat of Kundalini. Kundalini goes to each Centre in turn and vivifies it.	Seat of Kundalini. Kundalini goes to each Centre in turn and vivifies it.
2	Solar plexus, Liver, Kidneys, Intestines and Abdomen generally.	Feeling: general sensitiveness.	Feeling astral influences.
3	..	Vitalises Astral Body. Power to travel consciously.	Vitalises Physical Body. Memory of astral journeys.
4	Heart.	Comprehension of Astral Vibrations.	Consciousness of feelings of others.
5	..	Hearing.	Etheric and Astral hearing.
6	..	Sight.	Clairvoyance. Magnification.
7	..	Perfects and completes faculties.	Continuity of consciousness.
8 9 10	..	..	..
1	Orange, through Spinal Column, to Brain: becomes yellow and stimulates intellect. Dark red, through Spinal Column, to Brain: becomes crimson and stimulates affection. Dark purple, through Spinal Column, to Brain: becomes pale violet and stimulates spirituality.		..

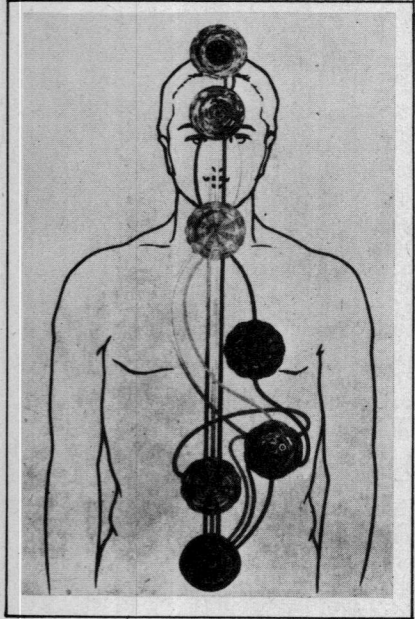

THE CHAKRAS
C.W. Leadbeater
Quest, 1972
$3.75

According to ancient Hindu philosophy and yoga teachings, there are subtle psychic sense organs in man's body which channel psychic energies and vital forces and are related to the glandular and nervous systems. They are also said to serve as a link between physical, psychic and superphysical states of consciousness. These centers are called *chakras*, a Sanskrit term meaning wheels or disks.

The chakras have been seen and described by clairvoyant investigators as wheel-like vortices which appear in vivid colors like blazing coruscating whirlpools. In Oriental books they have also been likened to flowers with many petals.

C.W. Leadbeater (1847–1934), regarded by many as a highly developed clairvoyant, was the author of more than 30 books concerning the psychic nature of man and the spiritual life. He has described his research into the nature and functions of the chakras in this book, which was first published in 1927. It has since been through several printings and has become a classic in its field. The work is handsomely illustrated with ten color plates and nine drawings.

THOUGHT-FORMS
Annie Besant and C.W. Leadbeater
Quest, 1969
$3.45

"Each definite thought produces a double effect—a radiating vibration and a floating form. The thought itself appears first to clairvoyant sight as a vibration in the mental body, and this may be either simple or complex. If the thought itself is absolutely simple, there is only the one rate of vibration, and only one type of mental matter will be strongly affected. The mental body is composed of matter of several degrees of density, which we commonly arrange in classes according to the subplanes. Of each of these we have many sub-divisions. . . .

". . . These radiating vibrations, like all others in nature, become less powerful in proportion to the distance from their source, though it is probable that the variation is in proportion to the cube of the distance instead of to the square, because of the additional dimension involved. Again, like all other vibrations, these tend to reproduce themselves whenever opportunity is offered to them; and so whenever they strike upon another mental body they tend to provoke in it their own rate of motion. That is—from the point of view of the man whose mental body is touched by these waves—they tend to produce in his mind thoughts of the same type as that which had previously arisen in the mind of the thinker who sent forth the waves.

". . . Three general principles underlie the production of all thought-forms:

1. Quality of thought determines color.
2. Nature of thought determines form.
3. Definiteness of thought determines clearness of outline."

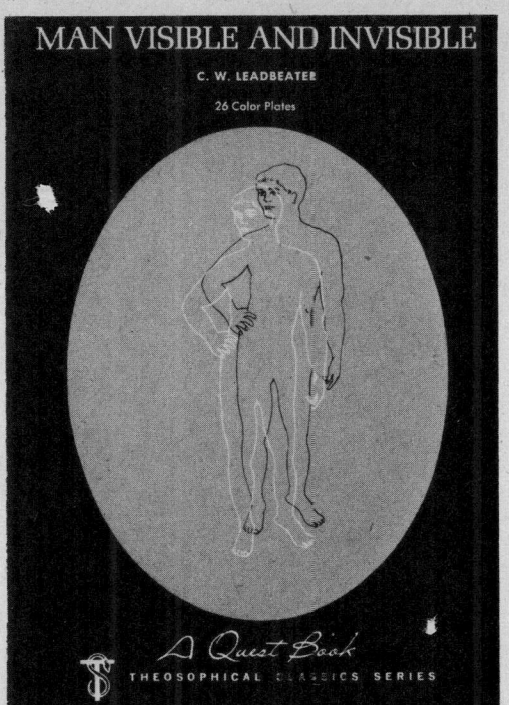

MAN VISIBLE AND INVISIBLE
C.W. Leadbeater
Quest, 1971
$3.75

"We are all aware that matter exists in different conditions, and that it may be made to change its conditions by variation of pressure and temperature. We have the three well-known states of matter, the solid, the liquid, and the gaseous, and it is the theory of science that all substances can, under proper variation of temperature and pressure, exist in all these conditions.

"Occult chemistry shows us another and higher condition than the gaseous, into which also all substances known to us can be translated or transmuted; and to that condition we have given the name of etheric. . . .

". . . Once again we find matter existing in definitely marked conditions corresponding at that much higher level to the states with which we are familiar; and the result of our investigations brings us once again to a unit—the unit of this third great realm of nature, which in Theosophy we call the mental world. So far as we know, there is no limit to this possibility of subdivision, but there is a very distinct limit to our capability of observing it. However, we can see enough to be certain of the existence of a considerable number of these different realms, each of which is in one sense a world in itself, though in another and wider sense all are parts of one stupendous whole."

FROM: THE ETHERIC DOUBLE

KUNDALINI: THE EVOLUTIONARY ENERGY IN MAN
Gopi Krishna
Shambala, 1970
$2.95

"One morning during the Christmas of 1937 I sat cross-legged in a small room in a little house on the outskirts of the town of Jammu, the winter capital of the Jammu and Kashmir State in northern India. I was meditating with my face towards the window on the east through which the first grey streaks of the slowly brightening dawn fell into the room. Long practice had accustomed me to sit in the same posture for hours at a time without the least discomfort, and I sat breathing slowly and rhythmically, my attention drawn towards the crown of my head, contemplating an imaginary lotus in full bloom, radiating light.

"I sat steadily, unmoving and erect, my thoughts uninterruptedly centered on the shining lotus, intent on keeping my attention from wandering and bringing it back again and again whenever it moved in any other direction. The intensity of concentration interrupted my breathing; gradually it slowed down to such an extent that at times it was barely perceptible. My whole being was so engrossed in the contemplation of the lotus that for several minutes at a time I lost touch with my body and surroundings. During such intervals I used to feel as if I were poised in mid-air, without any feeling of a body around me. The only object of which I was aware was a lotus of

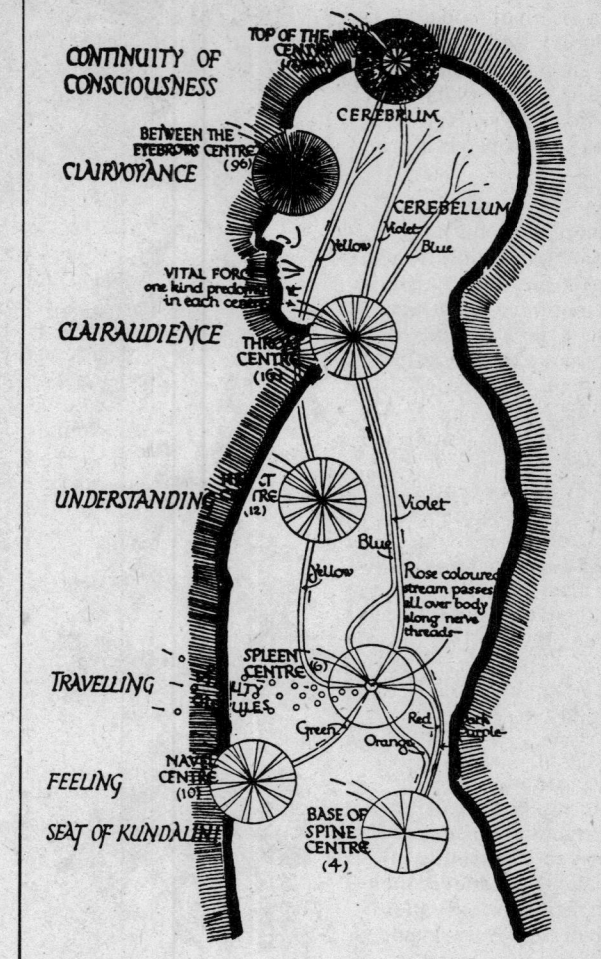

brilliant colour, emitting rays of light. This experience has happened to many people who practise meditation in any form regularly for a sufficient length of time, but what followed on that fateful morning in my case, changing the whole course of my life and outlook, has happened to few.

"During one such spell of intense concentration I suddenly felt a strange sensation below the base of the spine, at the place touching the seat, while I sat cross-legged on a folded blanket spread on the floor. The sensation was so extraordinary and so pleasing that my attention was forcibly drawn towards it. . . .

". . . What had happened to me? Was I the victim of a hallucination? Or had I by some strange vagary of fate succeeded in experiencing the Transcendental? Had I really succeeded where millions of others had failed? Was there, after all, really some truth in the oft-repeated claim of the sages and ascetics of India, made for thousands of years and verified and repeated generation after generation, that it was possible to apprehend reality in this life if one followed certain rules of conduct and practised meditation in a certain way? My thoughts were in a daze. I could hardly believe that I had a vision of divinity. There had been an expansion of my own self, my own consciousness, and the transformation had been brought about by the vital current that had started from below the spine and found access to my brain through the backbone. I recalled that I had read long ago in books on Yoga of a certain vital mechanism called Kundalini, connected with the lower end of the spine, which becomes active by means of certain exercises, and when once roused carries the limited human consciousness to transcendental heights, endowing the individual with incredible psychic and mental powers."

KUNDALINI RESEARCH FOUNDATION

"The enterprise of Yoga (or any other spiritual discipline) is not aimed merely to procure peace of mind for the aspirants or merely a vision of God and psychic gifts, but it is designed to raise one to the lofty stature of an intellectual prodigy, blessed with Vaikhari—that is spontaneous flow of words, whether in poetry or prose—full of wisdom and worth.

"Dispassionately considered, can psychic gifts and miraculous powers bear comparison with genius? Do we need greater testimony to prove the incalculable worth of properly directed intellect than the amazing transformation that has occurred in the world?

"In our time can there be any other branch of knowledge as deserving of serious attention as that which can show the way to the cultivation of this one of the most precious ornaments of the human mind?

"So strong is the force of habit, however, that even after knowing of this possibility—with all the authentic evidence that has been cited in its support*—even the erudite and the intelligent may be assailed by doubts and refuse to believe until the truth of this great discovery of the ancient Indian savants is empirically demonstrated.

"So far as I can see, nothing can halt the growing tide of skepticism about not only God and the Divine, but also about the great founders of religions—Christ, Buddha, Mohammad and others—as effectively as the doctrine of Kundalini.

"By no means whatsoever can we arrest the advance of the materialistic forces in the light of the present tendencies of science except by the empirical demonstration of the psychosomatic Divine power-center in man by which every prophet and seer attained to his extraordinary stature and became instrumental in guiding mankind rightly on the spiritual path.

"Once the existence of this Power-Reservoir is empirically demonstrated, its impact, even on skeptics and atheists, would be irresistible, resulting in a tremendous revival of interest in spiritual matters.

"I think that such an eventuality should be dear to every lover of mankind and every spiritual-minded man or woman of our day."

*From *The Secret of Yoga*, by Gopi Krishna. Published 1972 by Harper & Row.

10 East 39th Street
New York, N.Y. 10016

1. SEVEN SPINAL CHAKRAS, Hall, Manly
   Beautifully illustrated in full and exploding color. The radiant, human-energy centers and surrounding spiritual emanations powerfully dramatize the subtle beckoning in our higher selves.
2. THIRD EYE
   Startling reproduction of a rare painting, depicting the star-form profile. Illustration shows the outline and location of the mysterious pituitary and resonating spiritual pineal glands.

$1.25 (includes postage & handling)

$1.25 (includes postage & handling)

CALIFORNIANS PLEASE ADD SALES TAX

ORDER FROM: EL CARISO PUBLICATIONS, P.O. Box 176, Elsinore, Calif. 92330

THE SCIENCE OF THE AURA S. G. J. Ouseley
L. N. Fowler, 1970

"With most people auric vision does not come in a few days or even months. It is a life-time study and one's life and habits must be on a high plane to get good results. The finer forces are not discernible to the eyes of the gross materialist or the seeker after wonders and sensations. It is not to be considered that 'having eyes they see not.' The study and practice of seeing the aura is not to be lightly entered upon. It is a serious and priceless power and should be utilized for the upliftment and betterment of humanity."

THE HUMAN AURA AND THE SIGNIFICANCE OF COLOR
W. J. Colville
Health Research, 1970
$1.50

THE MYSTERY OF THE HUMAN AURA
Ursula Roberts
The Spiritualist Association of Great Britain, 1972
$1.00

"Just as your physical skin both *protects* and *receives*, so the human aura *protects* and *receives* likewise. Both sympathy and antipathy are sensed through the aura. Personal magnetism and the human aura are close companions. As control over our vehicles increases, personal magnetism has greater facility for expression and the human aura increases its power of extension and influence.

". . . It is the aura that makes people appear to you as they do. There are phrases to fit this fact. 'How I wish I could get under his skin,' or 'I wish I could break through the barrier he keeps about himself and contact the real person.' What you really mean is that you wish you could break through an unusually hard aura and reach the other person's emotional nature. Then, some people have a spongy aura and when you are with them even though you like them immensely, you feel devitalized. Such persons are almost vampires but know it not, because the spongy or porous aura they have developed *absorbs yours* and you feel a sense of loss. . . .

". . . There are persons who have a very exhausting aura. They are unintentional vampires and have given rise to many legends. They have a porous or spongy aura and they unconsciously absorb and draw vitality from those around them. At first you cannot help them as easily as you *can protect yourself*. Visualize yourself bathed in Light and protected by this Light. If your visualization is intense enough the Light will effectually shut out your aura from all that surrounds it. This is why some teachers refer to this Light as a 'Wall of Protection.'

SPIRITUAL VIRTUES IN THE AURA: RAMADAHN THROUGH THE MEDIUMSHIP OF URSULA ROBERTS
$1.00
Obtainable from:
The Secretary of Ursula Roberts
South 7, Sunny Gardens Road
Hendon, London, N.W. 4. England

TO BE PUBLISHED!
EXPLORING THE HUMAN AURA: A NEW WAY OF VIEWING—AND INVESTIGATING PSYCHIC PHENOMENON
Nicholas M. Regush, in colloboration with Jan Merta
Prentice-Hall (Spring 1975)
$7.95

This book suggests the "aura" is in fact a living computer, processing and transmitting raw information from the Universe to the conscious mind. In this context, it provides a radical and complete revaluation of psi research data.

THE HUMAN AURA
Edited by Nicholas M. Regush
Berkley, 1974
$1.25

The Human Aura

Develop your PSYCHIC POWER OF ATTRACTION

What strange forces pull you toward another? Why do you at times experience uneasiness in the presence of some person ... without any apparent cause? The human organism radiates psychic energy. This is an aura — a field of supersensitivity surrounding the body. Our thoughts and emotions continually vary the vibratory nature of this psychic aura. This aura can and does impinge upon the inner self of others. The auras of others also can and do react upon your aura.

You are subject to such psychic radiations of persons daily. It can account for your moods — even your intuitive impressions. This is a natural phenomenon — it is part of the subliminal, mysterious inner powers of self which everyone has, but few understand. Learn to master this phenomenon. The full application of your natural powers can provide a greater personal achievement and happiness in life.

FREE BOOK

The Rosicrucians, a worldwide cultural fraternity, have for centuries taught men and women to understand and utilize fully all the faculties of self. The Rosicrucians are not a religious sect. No creeds or dogmas are offered but factual information on man and his cosmic relationship. Write today for the free booklet, the Mastery of Life, that tells how you may use and share this workable knowledge.

Please use this coupon or write to:
SCRIBE: G.H.D.
The ROSICRUCIANS (AMORC)
San Jose, California 95114, U.S.A.

Scribe G.H.D.
THE ROSICRUCIANS (AMORC)
San Jose, California 95114, U.S.A.

Gentlemen:
In sincere interest, not out of curiosity, I ask for a free copy of THE MASTERY OF LIFE.

Name..
Address...
City.................... State............. Zip..........

THE MYSTERY OF THE HUMAN AURA
Rosicrucian Wisdom Teachings
Society of Rosicrucians Inc., 1950

"To clairvoyant vision the aura appears as a mass of palpitant colour which differs in colouring and size with each individual. It betrays with unerring accuracy the habits, thoughts and diseases of each person. The generous person has an expansive, softly coloured aura. The miser has a murky, contracted aura. The sensualist has a scarlet and crimson field of radiation; the business man, with no thought above worldly success, has an aura of orange tint. The devotee has one of mauve or blue and the saint a dazzling mother-of-pearl light which radiates to a distance of several feet around him. The ordinary person, who is neither very good nor very bad, has an aura of medium size, radiating to a distance of about two feet and showing colouring that is sometimes radiant, sometimes murky, according to their mood.

". . . It would appear that the aura gives a true picture of every element which is in the human organism. If the food, as it is assimilated into the various centres, radiates its particular magnetic power into the aura, correspondingly a lack of certain substances will betray a weakening of this same aura, so that a person suffering from nervous debility will show an aura pale in colouring and tinged with grey. A cancerous person betrays an excess of vibration in the region of the cancer, since the growth itself is composed of organic matter which has its own individual field of vibration. The ills of man are too numerous to mention and the cures for the ills of man are almost as numerous. Which of the cures are the best? We can only think that the cure which gives the best and the most lasting result is the best cure. We should become like the Chinese, and keep our healers for the prevention of our ailments, not for the cure of them."

AURAS
Edgar Cayce
A.R.E. Press, 1970
50 cents

"Ever since I can remember I have seen colors in connection with people. I do not remember a time when the human beings I encountered did not register on my retina with blues and greens and reds gently pouring from their heads and shoulders. It was a long time before I realized that other people did not see these colors; it was a long time before I heard the word aura, and learned to apply it to this phenomenon which to me was commonplace. I do not ever think of people except in connection with their auras; I see them change in my friends and loved ones as time goes by—sickness, dejection, love, fulfillment—these are all reflected in the aura, and for me the aura is the weathervane of the soul. It shows which way the winds of destiny are blowing."

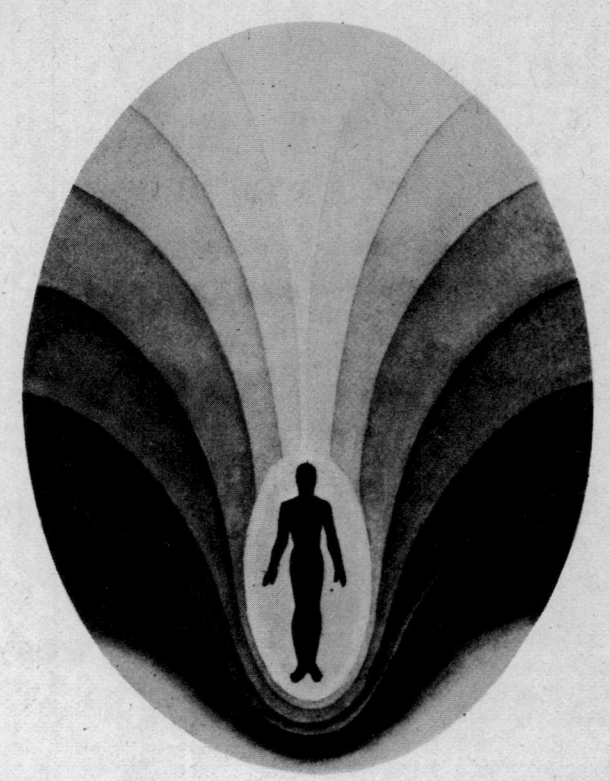

THE STORY OF THE HUMAN AURA
George Starr White
Health Research, 1969
$7.00

ISIS AURA-VISION TRAINER
Model 1204
Write to:
Aletheia Products and Publishing Corp.
1015 S.W. Yamhill
Portland, Ore. 97205.

THE ODIC FORCE: LETTERS ON OD AND MAGNETISM
Karl Von Reichenbach
University Books, 1968
$5.00

"Have you never in your life, dear reader, come across people with the strange fancy of disliking everything yellow, and yellow itself as a colour? . . .

". . . No doubt you have often travelled; and so it cannot but be that you have come across people in the mail coach, omnibus or railway-carriage, who with the most aggressive selfishness, wherever they may be, insist on throwing open the carriage windows. Be the weather as bad as may be, blowing a hurricane or as cold as ice, they will show no consideration for their fellow-travellers' rheumatism, but conduct themselves insufferably. You have regarded this as bad form; but I ask you to postpone your judgment a little—at any rate until a few more of my letters have come into your hands. They will succeed, perhaps, in convincing you that, within the confined limits of a 'present company,' things whose nature is still unrecognized are wont to happen, things strong enough to be quite irresistible to many of the persons who form that company, while others have not the faintest sense of their existence.

"Is it possible that among all your friends you have none whose crank it is never to sit between others in a row, be it at table, in the theatre, in society, or in church, but who always wants the corner-seat for himself, always elects to be fugleman of the file? Take note of him; he is our man; we shall soon come to closer acquaintance with him.

". . . How many people are there who cannot suppress a feeling of disgust when they make use of a fork of German silver at table, or a fork made of argentan, 'new silver,' Chinese silver, or whatever else such compositions may be called, while others cannot imagine why the compositions should make such a difference from genuine silver as not to be fitted for use on ordinary occasions? How many persons are to be met with who simply could not endure coffee, tea, or chocolate made in a brass kitchen utensil, while most other people would never notice the difference?

". . . There are some people who simply will not endure having anyone else standing close behind them; they avoid popular gatherings of all sorts, crowds, and markets. Others find it disagreeable to take another by the hand, and absolutely unbearable for anyone else to retain for any length of time the hand they themselves proffer; if they cannot get it free otherwise, they will wrench it away. Then how many people are there not who cannot bear the heat from an iron stove, but feel quite comfortable when it proceeds from one of stonework?

". . . When you trouble to investigate, you find most, and frequently all of the peculiarities mentioned in one and the same individual; but never, not one single time, do you find one only by itself. The foe to yellow shuns the looking-glass; it is the man in the corner-seat who flings the window open; the right-side sleeper is the one who gets faint in church; the people who are disgusted by brass and German silver like cold and simple eatables and are fastidious over fat and sweets; it is they who are fond of salad and so on; in every case the whole unbroken series of likes and dislikes is to be found down to disinclination for sugar, and from fondness for blue down to keen appetite for salad. There is a *solidarity* uniting all these wonderful peculiarities in their possessor; experience shows this on all sides; whoever has one of the list has, as a rule, all the others too.

". . . The latter class may be called 'Sensitives'; for they are, in fact, frequently more sensitive than a mimosa. They are so in the very depths of their nature, a nature they can neither lay aside nor treat with arbitrary violence; and whenever their peculiarities have been taken for cranks and contrariness their feelings have always been hurt by the fact. They have quite enough to suffer without that from our everyday world, which has never hitherto taken any account of them. Their sufferings are the consequence of their hitherto unrecognized peculiarity in the sensory faculty, and they are entitled to more consideration than has hitherto been accorded them. Their number is not small, and we shall soon see how deeply human life is penetrated by these peculiar factors, of which I have now given you only the most elementary and superficial sketch.

". . . First and foremost I shall take you to the stars, and, in fact, to the sun itself. Post a sensitive person in the shade, give him an ordinary unfilled barometer-tube, or any other sort of glass rod, or evern a wooden stick, in his left hand, and let him hold the rod in the sunshine, while his person and hand remain in the shade. You will shortly learn something from this simple experiment that will surprise you. You naturally expect that the person experimenting will perhaps feel the rod getting warm; the most that can happen will surely be that the sunshine will warm it up."

THE ORIGIN AND PROPERTIES OF THE HUMAN AURA
Oscar Bagnall
University Books, 1970
$5.00

"*Retina*

"Inner lining sensitized by the optic nerve, which carries impulses of sight from the retina to the brain. Consists of nerve endings:

1. *Cones:* most plentiful in the *fovea centralis*. Functions: clear vision and color appreciation.
2. *Rods:* most plentiful in the periphery. Function only in dim light when all objects appear blue-gray.

"The cones and rods will be fully dealt with in another chapter, so there is no need to discuss them further here.

". . . *In my opinion, we see the body's aura with the rods, or principally with the rods.*

"The aura is always gray or blue. It is never visible in a strong light. It is not visible in broad daylight.

"Although this view has never been previously expressed, I have often wondered whether Kilner made the same discovery—if discovery it be—but did not realize the cause of it. It must be remembered that Kilner did his experiments some fifty years earlier.

"He advised one never to strain the eyes by staring hard at the outline of a body. Since the rods lie to the *side* of the center part of the retina, which is lined solely by cones and which receives the direct image of the object being viewed, it would (if I am right) clearly be an advantage to look at the object, if not out of the corner of one's eye, at least not by peering hard and directly at it. . . .

". . . Kilner also said that the aura does not always appear at once. *The rods function more slowly than the cones do, in any case, and especially when they have been exhausted by the presence of a bright light. When one goes out into the night from a brightly lit room, one can see nothing at first. The reason is that the cones will not be stimulated by the dim light, and the rods, which have been exhausted by the bright one, recover but slowly.*"

THE AURA
J. W. Kilner
Weiser, 1973
$1.95

"Hardly one person in ten thousand is aware that he or she is surrounded by a haze intimately connected with the body, whether asleep or awake, whether hot or cold, which, although invisible under ordinary circumstances, can be seen when conditions are favourable. This mist, the prototype of the halo or nimbus constantly depicted around the saints, has been manifested to certain individuals possessing a specially gifted sight, who have received the title of 'Clairvoyants,' and until quite recently, to no one else. . . .

". . . It may as well be stated at once that we make not the slightest claim to clairvoyancy; nor are we occultists; and we especially desire to impress on our readers that our researches have been entirely physical, and can be repeated by any one who takes sufficient interest in the subject.

". . . The discovery of a *screen* capable of making the Aura visible was by no means accidental. After reading about the actions of the "N" Rays upon phosphorescent sulphide of calcium, we were for some time experimenting on the mechanical force of certain emanations from the body, and had come to the conclusion, whether rightly or wrongly, that we had detected two forces besides heat that could act upon our needles, and that these forces were situated in the ultra red portion of the spectrum.

". . . First, there is a narrow transparent portion appearing as a dark space, which is very often obliterated by the second portion of the Aura. When visible it looks like a dark band, not exceeding a quarter of an inch, surrounding and adjacent to the body, without any alteration in size at any part. This will be called the *Etheric Double*.

THE AURA OF HEALTHY PERSONS

Granular Aura by head and trunk of a woman. Light coloured patch over the left breast and lower part of thorax. A small darker spot near umbilicus.

"The second constituent is the *Inner Aura*. It is the densest portion and varies comparatively little, or even not at all, in width, either at the back, front, or sides, and both in the male and the female follows the contour of the body. It arises just outside the Etheric Double, but very frequently it looks as if it touched the body itself.

"The third portion, or the *Outer Aura*, commences at the outer edge of the Inner Aura, and is very variable in size. It is the extreme outer margin of this that has been taken for depicting the outline of the Aura hitherto."

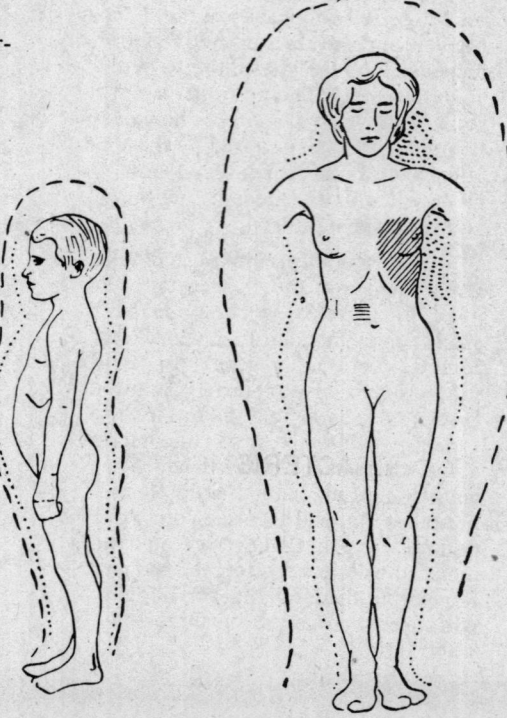

THE AURA AND WHAT IT MEANS TO YOU: A COMPILATION FROM MANY AUTHORITIES
Health Research, 1955
$4.00

RESEARCHES ON THE AURA PHENOMENA
Borderline Science Series No. 6
Mahmoud K. Muftic, M.D.
The Society of Metaphysics, 1970
$2.00

BREAKTHROUGH TO CREATIVITY
Shafica Karagulla, M.D.
De Vorss, 1973
$5.95

"It is the other things that Diane 'sees' which continue to fascinate me. She observes a 'vital or energy body or field' which sub-stands the dense physical body, interpenetrating it like a sparkling web of light beams. This web of light frequencies is in constant movement and apparently looks somewhat like the lines of light on a television screen when a picture is not in focus. This energy body extends in and through the dense physical body and for an inch or two beyond the body and is a replica of the physical body. She insists that any disturbance in the physical structure itself is preceded and later accompanied by disturbances in this energy body or field. Within this energy body or pattern of frequencies she observes eight major vortices of force and many smaller vortices. As she describes it, energy moves in and out of these vortices, which look like spiral cones. Seven of these major vortices are directly related to the different glands of the body. . . .

". . . The sensitive describes the sappers as having closed-in energy fields. Such individuals may be totally unaware of their energy pull on other people. They simply feel better when they are in the company of more vital people. Any individual who remains in the vicinity of the sapper for too long begins to feel desperately exhausted for no reason that he can understand. This baffles and bewilders him. Eventually a deep instinct of self-preservation causes the victim of the sapper to feel an irresistible desire to get away. He may attribute this to nay one of a number of reasons. By the time this happens he is usually feeling an unreasoning irritation with the sapper."

THE KIRLIAN AURA: PHOTOGRAPHING THE GALAZIES OF LIFE
Edited by Stanley Krippner and Daniel Rubin
Anchor Press, 1974
$3.95
28 linecuts, 62 black-and-white halftones

A breakthrough book, which *Psychic Magazine* magazine calls "the harbinger of a new era in scientific research." It relates the now familiar subject of acupuncture to the remarkable new process called Kirlian photography in which scientists can record the brightly colored "auras" that emanate from all living things. Human auras seem to be as individual as fingerprints and can be altered by the use of drugs or by induced emotional stress.

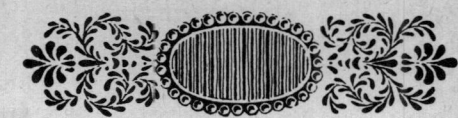

BOOKS ON: NIKOLA TESLA
Forerunner of Kirlian Photography
Write to:
Health Research
Box 70
Mokelumne Hill, Calif. 95245

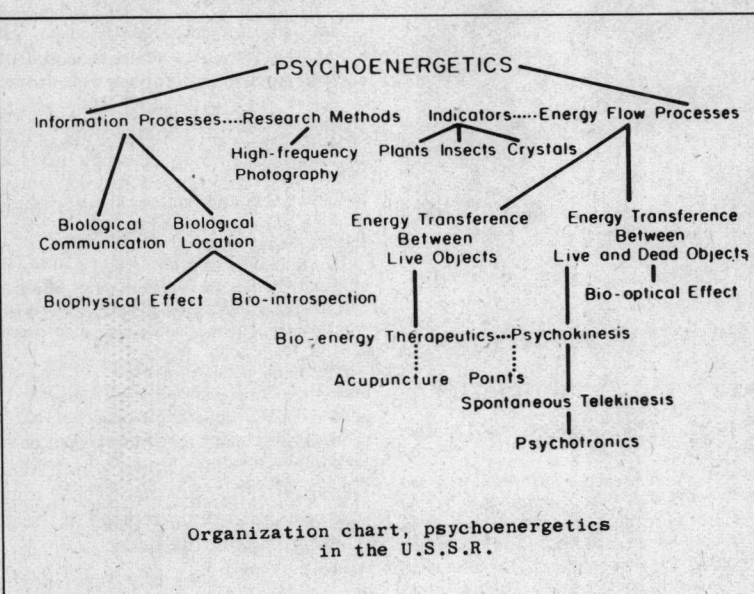

Organization chart, psychoenergetics in the U.S.S.R.

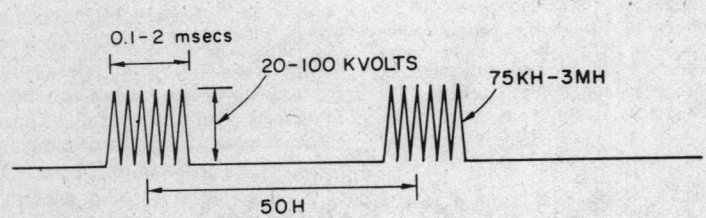

KIRLIAN POWER SUPPLY CHARACTERISTICS
Electrical output properties of the energy source

HIGH VOLTAGE PHOTOGRAPHY
H.S. Dakin, 1974
$5.00
Write to:
H. S. Dakin
3456 Jackson Street
San Francisco, Calif. 94118

THE CAMERON AURAMETER
Governor Brown and Verne Cameron, 1970
$3.95
Write to:
Borderland Sciences Research Foundation
P.O. Box 548
Vista, Calif. 92083

BIOENERGETIC QUESTIONS, MATERIAL OF THE SCIENTIFIC METHODOLOGICAL SEMINAR IN ALMA-ATA, 1969
Available for $9.00 from:
The Southern California Society for Psychical Research
170 South Beverly Drive
Beverly Hills, Calif. 90212

Aura Seen With Kirlian Photography Is Called Diagnostic of Disease

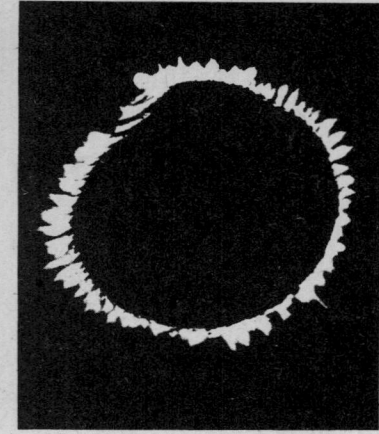
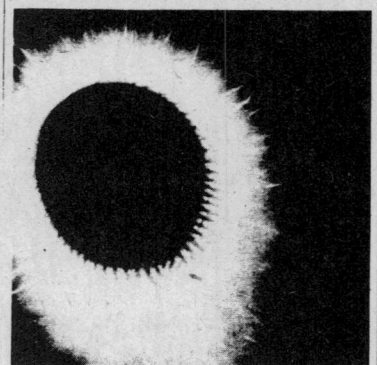

Electrophotographs of leaf (above) and fingertip (top right) show the typical corona energy discharge patterns of Kirlian photography. A fingertip of a person in the alpha meditation state is seen (right) as measured by electroencephalography. The soft, even, diffuse pattern of the corona is characteristic of the super state of awareness and relaxation associated with alpha wave production. Electrophotographs can be made with 35 mm Kodachrome II standard daylight film. A high AC frequency electrostatic field power supply attached to a nonferrous plate serves as a light source for the object to be photographed. (Photographs courtesy Mankind Research Unlimited, Washington, D.C.)

RESEARCH OPPORTUNITIES IN ELECTROPSYCHOGRAPHY
Mankind Research Unlimited, Inc. MRU), through its government and privately-funded life-energy research programs, has confirmed the feasibility of the applications cited in the article, and the remarks made by David Sheinkin. MRU is now broadening its research program in this area, now termed "electropsychography (EPG)" and hopes that, by adding "bioholograms (BHG)", a new dimension and useful tool will be added for diagnosticians— whether they be scientific or psychic.

To conduct your own "EPG's" and to photograph the apparent aura phenomena we offer the following services:

(A) Method and Procedure Book containing data Package for making Kirlian electrophotographs .... $ 5.00

(B) TESLA Power Supply (Light-Duty) .... $ 42.00

(C) TELSLA Power Supply (Heavy-Duty) .... $ 73.00

(D) Ten High Quality Color Kirlian Slides .... $ 7.50

Above pricing is all-inclusive and all orders are to be PREPAID.

Detection of Disease May Be Assisted by Kirlian Photo's Aura

Internal Medicine News Service
NEW YORK — Kirlian photography, a technique of picturing an unexplained aura surrounding animate objects, may provide a tool for the early detection of disease, Dr. David Sheinkin said at a symposium on new dimensions of healing presented by the Foundation for Parasensory Investigation.

Changes of the extent and density of the flared corona, seen only in Kirlian photographs, may herald the onset of illness before any physical symptoms develop, said Dr. Sheinkin, of the Institute for Bioenergetic Analysis and director of adult services at the Rockland County Community Mental Health Center, New York.

In normal individuals, the corona is full and completely surrounds the image of a fingertip or hand photographed with this technique. During illness, the corona is faded and incomplete.

A blank space on the corona indicates that the individual may develop symptoms. This interruption of the flared ring grows in size as the disease progresses and gradually closes again during recovery, Dr. Sheinkin said.

However, these findings are "speculative at this point," he said.

Dr. Sheinkin could not explain the connection between pathology and the coronas seen on Kirlian photographs. Others attending the conference explained the auras as manifestations of human energy fields.

Kirlian photography does not make use of a camera or a lens. Rather, an electric current is run through an object placed on film.

The high-voltage radiation field produces a flared corona on Kirlian photographs of some living objects, such as leaves or body parts. A less pronounced corona is seen surrounding inanimate objects.

The technique was developed in Russia in 1939 by Semyon Kirlian, who reported that photographs of his own hand changed in quality shortly before he developed physical symptoms of a disease, Dr. Sheinkin said.

Dr. Sheinkin and his associates have studied whether the coronas seen in Kirlian photographs change during illness and whether the changes are specific or nonspecific for a given illness.

Photographs taken of the same patient during the course of an illness were compared, as well as photographs taken on the same day of patients and normal controls.

Alcohol consumption causes the corona to flare noticeably, Dr. Sheinkin said.

In manic psychosis, a partial corona surrounding the fingertip, and a "speckling effect" on the image of the finger where the finger touches the film have been noted.

The incomplete corona fills out as the patient improves, he said.

In one patient with pneumonia, neither the fingertip nor the corona were visible on a Kirlian photograph.

In other illnesses, the normally distinct borderline between the physical image and the aura surrounding it becomes fuzzy, Dr. Sheinkin said.

MANKIND RESEARCH UNLIMITED INC.

1143 New Hampshire Avenue, N.W.
Washington, D.C. 20037
Telephone: (202) 785-1237

NOW

YOUR OWN KIRLIAN ELECTROPHOTOGRAPH!

(on Polaroid color film)

See your own ENERGY CORONA IN COLOR for only $1 and a few minutes of your time. Receive a high-quality photograph developed while you wait.

It's a unique and fascinating "portrait" of your fingertip, showing energy patterns now being tested at MRU for their diagnostic significance.

NO CAMERA OR LENS is employed in Kirlian Photography.

The image is produced when a weak electric current is run through an object or body-part resting lightly on unexposed film.

Aura, ion discharge, or maybe something else...a fascinating area of exploration.

SEE FOR YOURSELF!

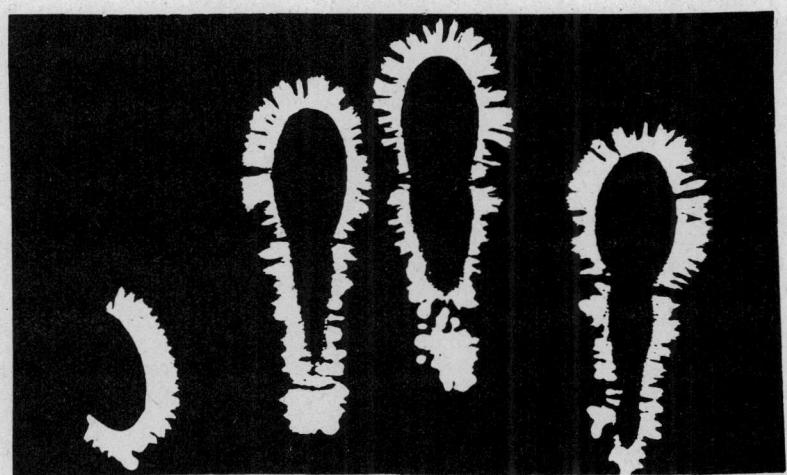

Kirlian photograph of fingertips show a typical corona energy discharge pattern.
Note: Although sample shown is black-and-white, all MRU Kirlian electrophotographs are made in color using high-quality Polaroid film.

SCIENTIFIC INVESTIGATIONS are being conducted throughout the world in efforts to understand this dramatic photographic technique. Subscribe to MRU's Associate Membership Program and receive monthly research reports.

DR. SEMYON KIRLIAN developed this technique in 1939 in Russia. He noted that electrophotographs of his own hand changed in quality shortly before he developed the physical symptoms of disease.

Your Kirlian Photograph--only $1.

Mankind Research Unlimited also provides Kirlian electrophotography kits, how-to-do-it experimental books, illustrative Kirlian color slides, and sponsors periodic Kirlian electrophotography workshops. Inquire for these and other MRU frontiers of science research services

THE DOCTRINE OF THE SUBTLE BODY IN WESTERN TRADITION
G. R. S. Mead
Quest, 1967
$1.65

CASE-BOOK OF ASTRAL PROJECTION, 545–746
Robert Crookall
University Books, 1972
$7.95

THE PHENOMENA OF ASTRAL PROJECTION
Sylvan Muldoon and Hereward Carrington
Weiser, 1969
$3.00

"Among students of the occult it is generally held that man, in addition to his physical body, possesses also another, more subtle body, normally coinciding with the physical, which is the body he inhabits after death, and which he is capable of detaching from his physical body at will, under certain circumstances, or which spontaneously leaves the physical body, more or less completely, in sleep, trance, coma, or under the influence of an anaesthetic. It is the body of desire, emotion and feeling, and is the vehicle of consciousness. It is normally invisible, intangible, impalpable to the senses, and hence cannot be discovered upon the operating table! It constitutes the human 'double', and is some form of subtle body, which we normally inhabit and utilize. It is the 'spiritual body' of St. Paul.

"Proofs of the existence of such a body have admittedly been difficult to obtain. However, there are many persons who assert that they have, on certain occasions, found themselves inhabiting such a body and, on looking back, seen their own physical body asleep upon the bed. They are convinced that they are possessed of such a body because they can see and feel and handle it. Moreover, they are fully conscious at the time, and realize that they are no longer functioning in the material body, but in this more subtle duplicate."

JOURNEYS OUT OF THE BODY
Robert A. Monroe
Anchor Books, 1973
$2.95

". . . We can formally define an OOBE as an event in which the experiencer (1) seems to perceive some portion of some environment which could not possibly be perceived from where his physical body is known to be at the time; and (2) knows *at the time* that he is not dreaming or fantasizing. The experiencer seems to possess his normal consciousness at the time, and even though he may reason that this cannot be happening, he will feel all his normal critical faculties to be present, and so knows he is not dreaming. Further, he will not decide after awakening that this was a dream. How, then, do we understand this strange phenomenon? . . ."

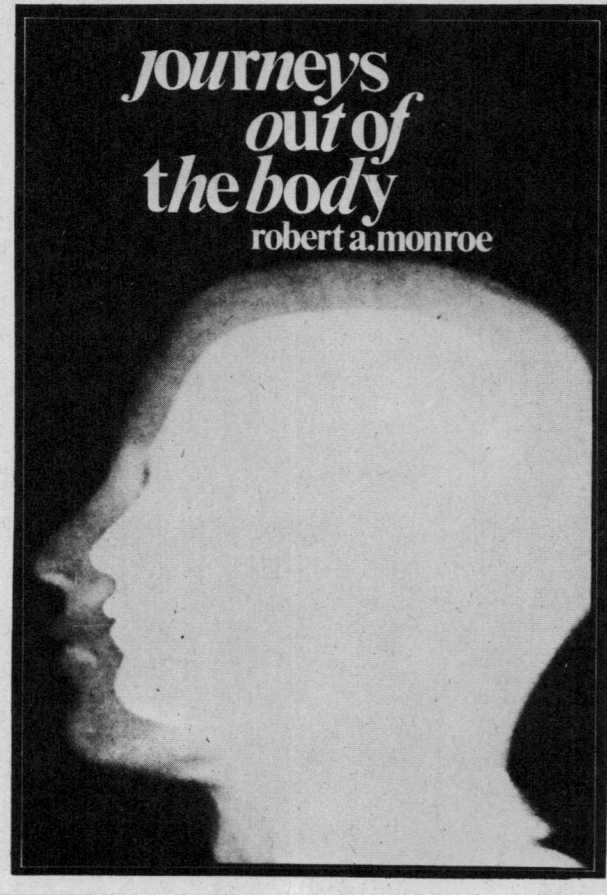

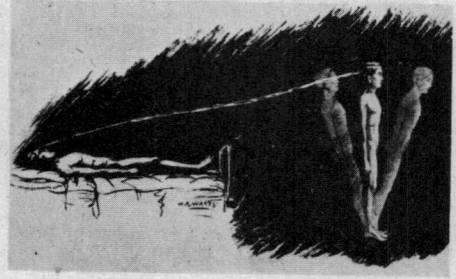 

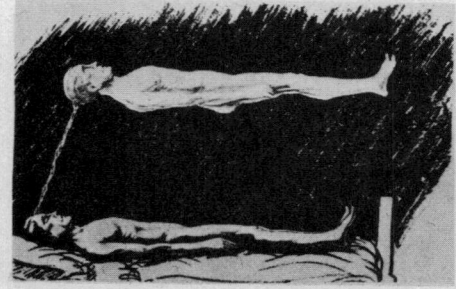 

DURING SLEEP: THE POSSIBILITY OF "CO-OPERATION" BETWEEN THE LIVING AND THE DEAD
Robert Crookall
University Books, 1974
$5.95

THE ASTRAL WORLD: ITS SCENES, DWELLERS AND PHENOMENA
Swami Panchadasi
Wehman Bros. Publishers
$1.00

THE HUMAN AURA—ASTRAL COLORS AND THOUGHT-FORMS
Swami Panchadasi
Yoga Publication Society, 1940
$1.00

THE ASTRAL BODY
A. E. Powell
Quest, 1972
$3.50

"The purpose of this book is to present to the student of Theosophy a condensed synthesis of the information at present available concerning the Astral Body of man, together with a description and explanation of the astral world and its phenomena. . . .

". . . the astral body of man is a vehicle, to clairvoyant sight not unlike the physical body, surrounded by an aura of flashing colours, composed of matter of an order of fineness higher than that of physical matter, in which feelings, passions, desires and emotions are expressed and which acts as a bridge or medium of transmission between the physical brain and the mind, the latter operating in the still higher vehicle—the mind-body. . . .

"A clear understanding of the structure and nature of the astral body, of its possibilities and its limitations, is essential to a comprehension of the life into which men pass after physical death. The many kinds of 'heavens,' 'hells' and purgatorial existences believed in by followers of innumerable religions, all fall naturally into place and become intelligible as soon as we understand the nature of the astral body and of the astral world."

THE Society of Astral Projectionists. Spiritual knowledge and development through Astral Travel. Meetings in central London. Details of guaranteed correspondence courses on request. Please forward S.A.E. to: BCM-Box 330, Monomark House, London W.C.1

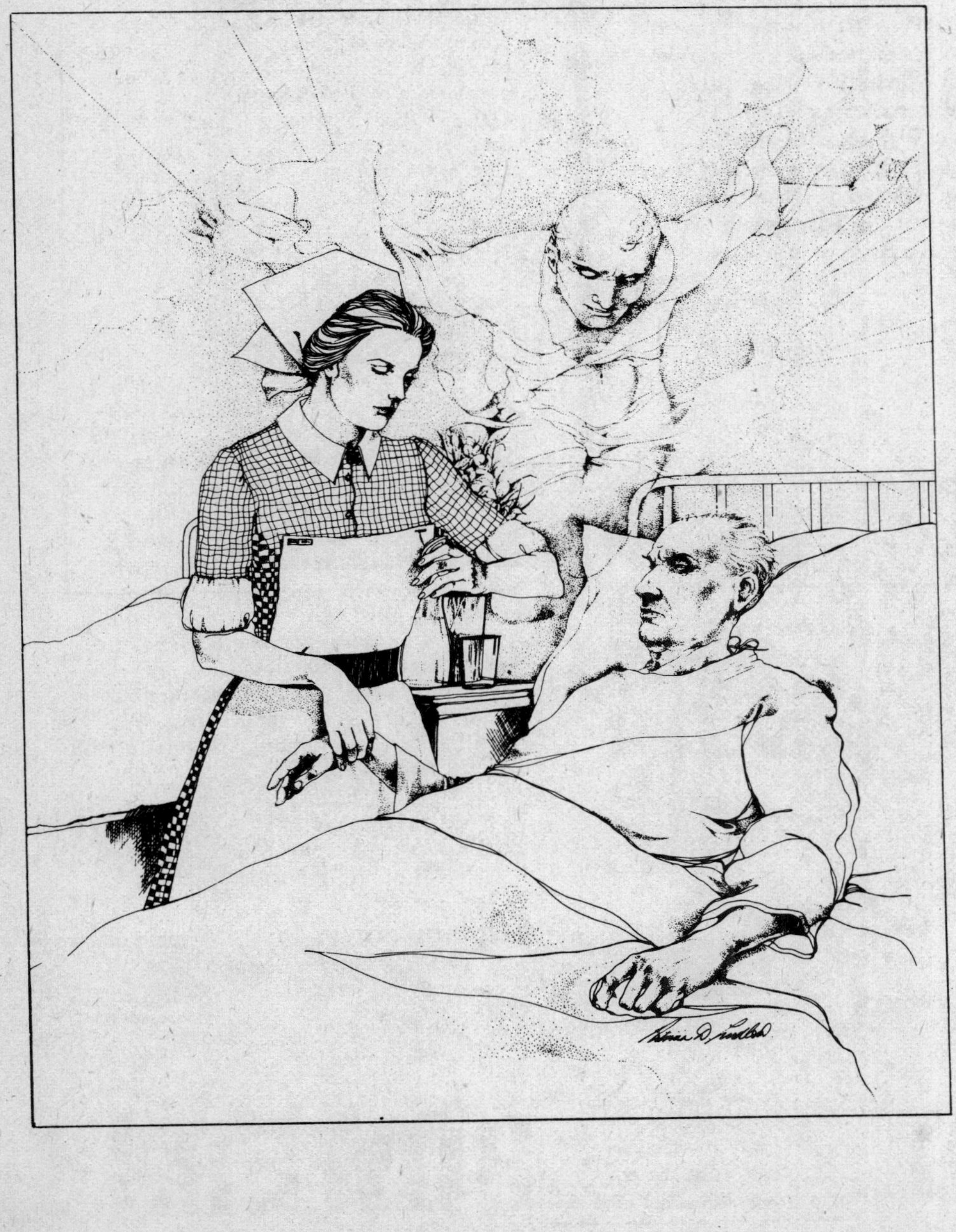

THE MECHANISMS OF ASTRAL PROJECTION: DENOUEMENT AFTER 70 YEARS
Robert Crookall
Darshana International, 1968
$5.00

"Certain medical psychologists, however, regard astral projections as mere dreams; they consider that the 'astral' or 'etheric' body is nothing but the mental image that we form of the physical body. We all form mental images of our own bodies and they suggest that a sick man may imagine that he sees his own mental image of his own body. If this interpretation of the phenomena is correct, if the 'astral' or 'etheric' body is purely subjective, then these matters have no bearing on survival whatever.

". . . Medical psychologists in general have failed to realise that the two hypothesis concerning 'doubles,' the first that they are real and objective bodies and the second that they are merely subjective hallucinations, are not mutually exclusive many tend to say (or to imply even when they do not explicitly say) that if some 'doubles' are imaginary, then all are imaginary. It is our contention that the evidence shows that while some are imaginary, others are objective, that each hypothesis has its own area of application."

THE TECHNIQUES OF ASTRAL PROJECTION
Douglas M. Baker
Regency Press
$5.50

Pyramids And Plants,

Are plants sensitive to human behavior? Do pyramid-like structures shapen razor blades? Can objects embody the thoughts of whomever handles them? Questions of this kind are generating considerable excitement in psychical research circles and while it may be necessary for subsequent research to seriously re-evaluate the inexact nature of many claims, there is little doubt that these issues are worthy of serious investigation.

experimental **CHEOPS PYRAMID TENT** $30.00
People using the Pyramid tent claim they are surrounded with energy. Those using meditation such as; Transcendential Meditation, Biofeedback, Alpha, Yoga, etc., report the Pyramid increases the ability to achieve the desired state. The Cheops Pyramid is made of wood legs and an opaque Vinyl cover. It is six feet square by fifty inches tall and will accommodate a full grown person. Boxed and assembled.

experimental **PYRAMID ENERGY PLATE: PEP**
A pocket companion to PEG. Duplicates most everything that PEG does. These plates are made from a gold colored aluminum and are charged with the same energy that exists in the pyramid. Plates lose their energy in 18 to 24 months.
3×5" pocket size .... $ 3.00
8×10" .. Try these under your pillow .. $10.00

COMBINATION OFFER
Keep the plate up to full energy by placing it on the Generator overnight every third or fourth night.
One 3 × 5" Pyramid Energy Plate (pocket size) and
One 3 × 5" Pyramid Energy Generator
.... $ 7.50

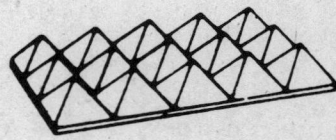

experimental **PYRAMID ENERGY GENERATOR: PEG** $5.00
The generator is composed of fifteen 1" pyramids on a 3" × 5" base. Containing it's own magnetic field source in the plastic base, the generator has a CONSTANT source of pyramid energy. It will work in any position and within any structure. This remarkable device will sharpen razor blades, remove bitterness from liquids, improves taste of cheap wines and liquors, drastically changes instant coffee, keep carrot juice from lumping, mummifies organic matter, etc.

PYRAMID PRODUCTS
PRICE LIST   Box 6386
Glendale, Ca. 91205

PYRAMID POWER
Max Toth and Greg Nielsen
Freeway Press, 1974
$1.75

PYRAMID POWER!!

TOTH PYRAMID COMPANY
81-60 248th St. Bellerose, N.Y. 11426

SOME MEASUREMENTS OF THE GREAT PYRAMID

Height to imaginary topstone's apex: .... 5,813"
Base measurement of one face: .... 9131.06"
Actual height, consequence of destruction .... 5,496"
Edge (face) Corner to Apex: .... 8,687.88"
Apothem center of base face to apex: .... 7,391.56"
Base angle, base to level ground .... 51° 51' 14.3"
Apex interfacial angle: .... 76° 17' 32"
Edge to level ground: .... 41° 59' 50"
Dihedral angle, face to face edge: .... 112° 25' 38.88"
Apex, edge to edge: .... 96°
Circuit of the base .... 36,524.24"
One terrestrial year equals 365.24 days!
Sum of base diagonals .... 25,826.5"
Precession of our equinox is 25,827 years!
Volume of Pyramid .... 90,000,000 ft^3
Area covered .... 54,000 square meters (13+ Acres)
Weight .... 5,955,000 TONS
Difference between English and Pyramid Inch 0.0011"

The number five appears throughout the Pyramid. Five sides, five corners. The temperature inside the King's Chamber is 68° Fahrenheit. This is exactly one fifth the distance mercury is raised in a tube between freezing and the boiling point of water at Sea Level. This is also the optimum temperature for health and long life.

One half the base of the Pyramid divided into the apothem is equal to φ   For example:

$$9131/2 = 4565.5; \quad 7387.15/4565.5 = 1.6180374$$

Compared to the base, the edge length of the face of the Pyramid is 4.9% less: 8683.58/9131=0.9509998.

The height of the Pyramid is 36.4% less than the base: base=9131, height=5813; 5813/9131=0.6366224.

Relation of golden section in Great Pyramid

Side of Great Pyramid
Measurements in pyramid inches

THE PYRAMID AND IT'S RELATION TO BIOCOSMIC ENERGY
by G. Patrick Flanagan, Ph.D.
This short but fact filled Essay is a distillation of over 300 books read by Dr. Flanagan. In it you will find scores of fascinating facts about the Cheops Pyramid. Here are exact measurements on how to build your pyramid. Additionally, this Essay describes many experiments Dr. Flanagan had performed which the reader can also try with the small pyramid included in the Essay Package. $3.00

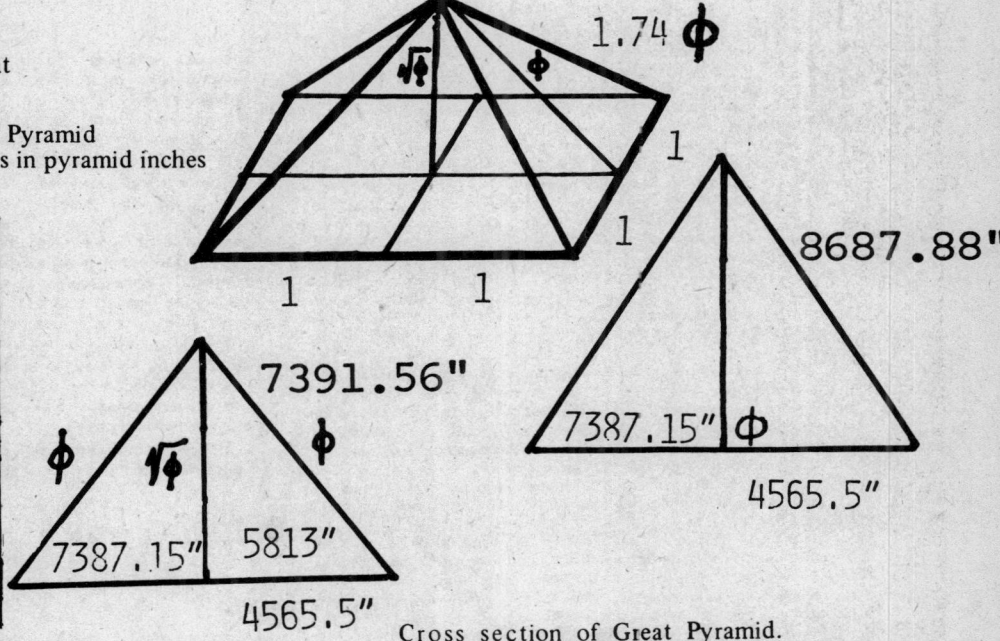

Cross section of Great Pyramid.
Measurements in pyramid inches.

Write to:
P.O. Box 6839
Glendale, CA. 91204

the PYRAMID Guide

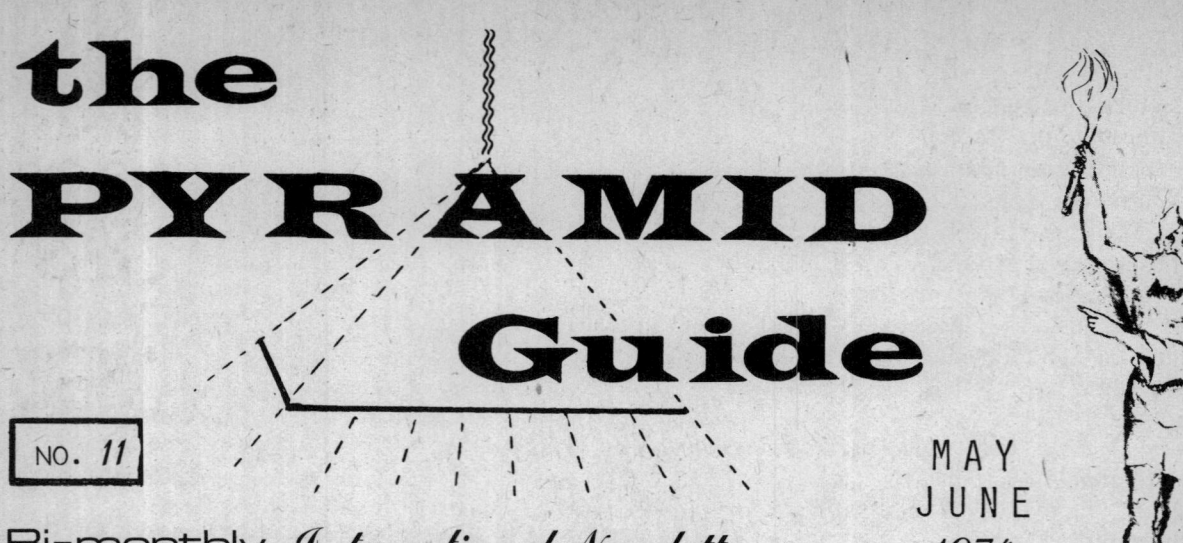

NO. 11

Bi-monthly *International Newsletter*
Single Copy 50¢   Yearly Pre-Paid $3.00   Foreign $3.75

MAY JUNE 1974

ALFRED DUNNING'S MUSICAL PYRAMID PRODUCES HAUNTING SOUNDS

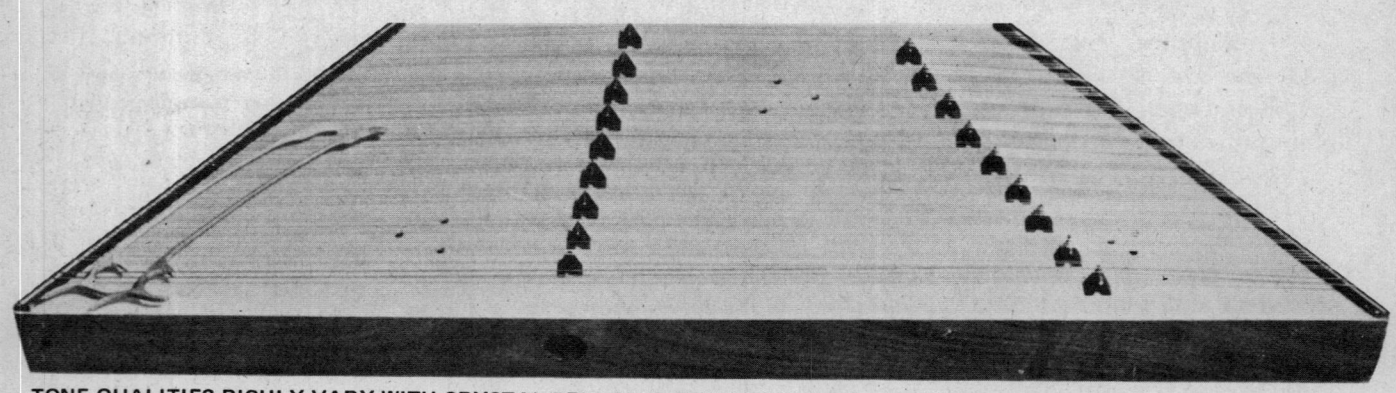

TONE QUALITIES RICHLY VARY WITH CRYSTAL BELL-LIKE TREBLES AND RESONATING BASS TONES.

MUSIC FROM THE PYRAMID

Dear Pyramid Guide Editors: I became interested in the history and construction of an obscure musical instrument at the same time a fascination for the pyramid awakened. I realized a hammer-struck stringed instrument close to the known design of the ancient Santur must have existed within the cultural fabric of the people who designed and built the pyramids on the Giza plateau.

Using the measurements and harmonic geometric proportions encapsulated in the monumental structure of the Cheops Pyramid, I designed an instrument essentially based on a meridian cross-section of the pyramid with height of one royal cubit and a base of one mega-lithic yard. The angle of the base to side is 51° 51', and the small pyramid is in exact scale or proportion to the Cheops.

The height is bi-sected to form a truncated pyramid of 1/2 royal cubit and a top of 1/2 mega-lithic yard. There are 72 strings (360 ÷ 5) arranged in 18 courses of four strings each. The moveable pyramid bridges are placed at intervals of 3/5 to 2/5 and 4/5 to 1/5. For materials I chose Indian Rosewood and vertical-grain spruce with brass and steel strings.

The sound quality of the finished instrument, greatly enhanced by the harmonic internal angles of the sound-box, gives haunting and sustained echoes produced at the slightest string vibration. The volume capacities are impressive – filling a room with music. Tone qualities are richly varied with crystal, bell-like trebles and resounding bass tones.

I am currently experimenting with the infinite tuning possibilities and would be interested if any readers have ideas or theories on ancient scales or modes. The instrument has a four octave range with intervals of natural fifths.

It is fairly clear now that megalithics sites such as Woodhenge were originally used as musical instruments which brought Celestial harmonies to the Terrestial realm. If any readers have ideas along this line, I would be pleased to communicate with them. Alfred Dunning, 20001 Grandview, Topanga Canyon, CA. 90290.

SUFI BUILDS ENERGIES

You must participate completely or nothing happens. First, shoeless, invited to share prayers, you become part of a great forming circle on the floor and silently meditate. A soft voice intones a lovely incantation. Then, on your feet, follow a graceful, sari-clad, barefoot young woman in hand-joined circles through simple, varied routines, accompanied by a monotone drum beat—mostly by your own chanting.

The mystical gazes from Indian Sufi Masters' candle-lit portraits appear to change with your every motion. "Toward THE ONE—in harmony, beauty, and balance", the theme is chanted as dancers relinquish individuality and feel the rising unity. New-found energies discharge from hearts, throats, and temples. Glances soften as eye contacts eye, and smiles are exchanged easily. Indefinable warmth and impersonal love move through the circles as expanding vibrations are shared.

The dances become more complex, but you are unaware as by then you are caught in their rythmic patterns and moving in spellbound communion. Accelerating energies now fuse into one great ego-less vortex as you experience a growing sense of timeless dimension!

Invited to Hollywood one recent evening to SEE it, Pyramid Guide editors found to our surprise we WERE Sufi dancers...!

Order from:
El Cariso Publications
P.O. Box 176
Elsinore, CA. 92330

Write For Catalogue

THE PYRAMID GUIDE
BACK ISSUES STILL AVAILABLE
50c EACH

ALL NEW ... Illuminating, profound, worldwide experiments, reports ... Cardboard replicas of *Great Pyramid* as forms accumulate free energy, cause levitation, tactile sensations ... Influence meditation, radio, television reception, PK, and Dowsing phenomena ... Induces dreams, clairvoyance, visions ... Makes wire rods cross, gyrate above ... Alters sound, time flow, consciousness, energy patterns, plant growth, auras ... Produces dehydration, mummification, preserves perishables, sharpens cutlery, etheric vibrations, crystal effects, symbolic emanations ... New light on Pyramidology, psychotronic generators, Hieonymus Box ... Diagrams, make your own replicas, cones, free energy accumulators ... This extraordinary Bi-Monthly features twenty-five years of comprehensive research by the late Dowsing mentor, Verne L. Cameron. ... Articles appearing as follows:

No. 1 September-October '72 ... The Pendulum & the Pyramid, The Amazing Cameron Cone & Pyramid Effects, Verne Cameron's Great Discovery, The Legendary Gold Ben Ben, Divining the Aura, Capstones, Orienting the Replica, Pyramids of the Mind, Tape Recorded Interview with Cameron.

No. 2 ... The Astonishing Cameron Cones, Energy of Form Explained, Preserving Perishables, Ra Worship & The Perfect Pyramid, Dowsing Thought Forms, Diagram for Making your Own Pyramid Replica.

No. 3 ... The Merrigan Clock Mystery, Pyramid - Cone Differential, Conic Energy Behavior, Great Pyramid - The Third Theory, A Haunting Paradox, Brainwave Patterns, Dowsing & The Body Aura, Diagram for Making Your Own Cone, Orienting the Replica, The Bishop's Rule, Rate Photo Of Hieronymus Box.

No. 4 ... Psychotronic Generators, The Pyramid Angle & Diagram, Comments From Readers On: Electroculture, Fourth Dimensional Wave-meter, Zero Gravity, Space Needles & Etheric Power, The Pyramid As A Form, Replica Affecting Television Reception and The Replica Inducing Dreams.

No. 5 ... Hand Levitation ... De-Levitation inside the Pyramid replica, Defying Gravity, Meditation Pyramid with Diagram for Constructing Your Own, Computerized Pi Formulas. Mathematical Guide to Making Pyramid Models of Any Size. The Great Pyramid Decoded, The Cameron Cones, Local Apparent Noon, The Pyramid Shadow and Orientation.

No. 6 ... Fourth Dimension Wave-meter, Dowsing Response From Two-dimensional *Symbolic* Patterns, Thoughts On Symbols, The Last Wonder, Replicap, History of Levitation, Auric Shift, Mind to Matter, Pyramids in Series, Dehydration Tests, Simplified Pyramid Simension Formula, Strange Forms From Signature Emanations, Has Verne Cameron Found the Ether?

No. 7 — Replica Turns Milk into Cheese, High Magic, Emanations from Crystal Forms, Wood Into Stone, Dowsing Auric Emanations, The Energy of Crystals and Stones, The Lodestone, Re-locating the Great Pyramid, Hidden Chambers, The Wire Pyramid, Audible Hums & Strange Sounds, Cone & Coil Rays Alike. Banjo Device, In and Out of Pyramid Parallels, The Symbolic Pattern, A Cone Cyclotron, Verne Cameron's Notebook.

No. 8 — Sharpening the Razor Blade, People in Pyramid Structures, Perforated Pyramids Change Energy Patterns, All Granite Replica, Replica Alters Aura, Light From Darkness, The Vortex and Weightlessness, Turks Who Live in Stone Cones, A Fifth Form of Energy, Feeling Emanations with the Aurameter, Kirlian Photography, The Human Pyramid, House & Meditation Pyramids.

No. 9 — The Pyramid's Power Range, Replica Charges Batteries, Time Warps, Lights to Remember, Pyramids as Living Monuments, Rays from Blessed Objects, Pyramid Food Tastes Better, Viewing Phenomena Through Prisms, Dowsing Into the Past, Perpetuum Mobile, Clunker-mid, Dowsing Doodlebug, Do-it-yourself Replicas, The Tetrahedron, Mechanics of Crystal Gazing, Panel-less Pyramid, Dowsing the Whirling Chakras.

No. 10 — Generator Time Shift, Hemisphere Conserving Energy, Living Legends, Stonehenge, Pyramid Traps, Untraps Light, Magnetic Field Changes, Dowsing Pyramids, Mental Beams and Cone-Rays, the Maltese Cross, Chalice Well, Replica Reducing Rust, Letters, Comments on Orgone Energy.

No. 11 — Musical Pyramid, Sufi Builds Energies, Glastonbury Modern Miracles, Music of the Spheres, Super Laser, Perpetual Motion, Gravity Waves, Voices in Stone, Message of the Great Pyramid, Earth Energy, Spectrone Color Pyramid Lamp, The Hieronymus Machine, Pyramid Designs in Astral Consciousness, Heavy Psi in Russia, Pyrameditation.

No. 12 — Pyramid Stimulates Plant Growth, GENESA, Living Geometry, The Psychic Musician, A Pro Explains Dowsing, On Magnetic North, Thoughts on Color, Measuring the Non-material World, Capstones, Letters, Worldwide Reports from Form-energy Researchers and a Great Deal More ...

PYRAMID PRODUCTS INCORPORATED
P.O. Box 5551
Fresno, Calif. 93755

"THE BACKGROUND

"Much has been said and written in recent years and months about the phenomenon called 'pyramid energy,' its effects and its potential. But only recently has the scientific community opened its eyes to the qualities contained within the pyramid form, which is one of the most basic in nature. The awareness is spreading like wildfire, however, among curious individuals intrigued more by results than 'reasons why?''.

"The energy contained within the pyramid form relies on the builder's true degree and angle with relation to the great pyramid of Egypt, and on the user's preciseness in directional orientation. The energy is said to increase as the size of the pyramid increases, but even the tiniest replicas are said to possess a mysterious self-contained energy capable of preserving perishables and sharpening cutlery. Persons spending time within the pyramid form report increased relaxation, a deepening of meditation, an increase in self-awareness and inner peace, among other exciting experiences.

"Researchers probing these and other 'pyramid mysteries' are producing important new effects every day—without actually understanding the origin or cause involved.

"Pyramid Products, Inc., has developed a variable size replica of the great pyramid, which allows the user to explore this exciting field in the comfort of his or her own home or environment, with a minimum of effort or technical knowledge.

"THE CONCEPT

"A patent is now pending on a unique new concept consisting of four corner pieces and an apex or capstone (a small but functional pyramid in itself) which have been engineered to reproduce the specific angles of the great pyramid. . . .

"The five components, made of cast aluminum, are then connected by aluminum tubing or whatever ¾" round material the user prefers, to erect any size pyramid form desired. With the angles remaining constant, the size is governed by the length of the connectors, which can be purchased pre-cut with the components, or purchased from a local merchant. This allows the user to erect a smaller pyramid for use indoors, or a larger one for the out of doors, utilizing the same set of corner pieces and capstone.

SECRETS OF THE GREAT PYRAMID
Peter Tompkins
Harper & Row, 1971
$12.50

"For a thousand years men from many occupations and many stations have labored to establish the true purpose of the Pyramid. Each in his own way has discovered some facet, each in its own way valid. Like Stonehenge and other megalithic calendars, the Pyramid has been shown to be an almanac by means of which the length of the year including its awkward .2422 fraction of a day could be measured as accurately as with a modern telescope. It has been shown to be a theodolite, or instrument for the surveyor, of great precision and simplicity, virtually indestructible. It is still a compass so finely oriented that modern compasses are adjusted to it, not vice versa.

"It has also been established that the Great Pyramid is a carefully located geodetic marker, or fixed landmark, on which the geography of the ancient world was brilliantly constructed; that it served as a celestial observatory from which maps and tables of the stellar hemisphere could be accurately drawn; and that it incorporates in its sides and angles the means for creating a highly sophisticated map projection of the northern hemisphere. It is, in fact, a scale model of the hemisphere, correctly incorporating the geographical degrees of latitude and longitude.

"The Pyramid may well be the repository of an ancient and possibly universal system of weights and measures, the model for the most sensible system of linear and temporal measurements available on earth, based on the polar axis of rotation, a system first postulated in modern times a century ago by the British astronomer Sir John Herschel, whose accuracy is now confirmed by the mensuration of orbiting satellites.

"Whoever built the Great Pyramid, it is now quite clear, knew the precise circumference of the planet, and the length of the year to several decimals—data which were not rediscovered till the seventeenth century. Its architects may well have known the mean length of the earth's orbit round the sun, the specific density of the planet, the 26,000-year cycle of the equinoxes, the acceleration of gravity and the speed of light."

PYRAMID AND RAZOR BLADES
From: "Experiments on the Alleged Sharpening of Razor Blades and the Preservation of Flowers by Pyramids," by Dale Simmons
New Horizons, Summer, 1973, Vol. 1, No. 2.

"Conclusions concerning razor blades

"Any changes in the blades which were under pyramids were mimicked in type by the control blade, the one kept in the open air. This would leave an impartial commentator to believe that the discernible changes in the blades were not caused by the pyramids. All the instructions prescribed for the use of pyramids were followed to the letter in the conduct of the experiment. As an overall conclusion the writer feels he must say that the pyramids did not affect the blades in any physical way and as such were a failure.

"In all the literature which the writer has encountered described the capacities of pyramids to preserve meat, resharpen razor blades, etc. no statistics or circumstantial data concerning experiments, or examples of control experiments have been cited. The writer therefore feels it legitimate to draw attention to two important aspects of the pyramid fad.

Subjectivity; the psychological aspect. How dull is dull when a person considers a blade too dull to shave with? Also, how does one tell whether a blade is really sharper or not after it has been in a pyramid for restoration? Judgment on either of these points is inevitable highly subjective, and liable to manipulation by underlying wishes, desires and expectations, so that it cannot be equated in any way to an assay made by a scientifically based objective method. In addition, these subjective tests of sharpness are rendered imprecise by the unquantifiable factor of acuteness of memory, because the 'before' and 'after' tests are separated by a considerable lapse of time.

"(b) Natural equilibrium; the homeostatic aspect. There is a tendency in Nature which though not universal is widespread, for things when disturbed to return to the previous state of equilibrium. In physics this is exemplified by Le Chatelier's Principle, in biology by homeostasis. It has long been known that a razor blade tends to feel sharper if it is used after a period of rest. This can be ascribed to the motion of the air molecules around and against the blade which helps to wear down the weakest parts (which are, in fact, the jagged peaks or points). Also when a blade is used the stress upon its cells is changed, some being compressed and others stretched. During a period of disuse the forces of compression and tension will tend to restore the internal stresses to an equilibrium state.

"Since, so far as the writer is aware, not a single scientific experiment on pyramids and razor blades has ever been published, he feels it is a legitimate inference that pyramid enthusiasts when testing their hypothesis have neglected to take adequate account of facts (a) and (b) or to do parallel control experiments.

THE GREAT PYRAMID IN FACT AND IN THEORY
William Kingsland
Health Research
$.00

HEALTH RESEARCH: The great pyram i construction, symbolism and chronology
Basil Stewart
$1.50

THE PYRAMIDS OF EGYPT
I.E.S. Edwards
Penguin, 1961
$1.95

THE RIDDLE OF THE PYRAMIDS
Kurt mendelsohn
Thames and Hudson, 1974

HEALTH RESEARCH: THE GREAT PYRAMID OF EGYPT' THE HISTORIC, GEOGRAPHIC, SCIENTIFIC, PROPHETIC AND ESCANTOLOGIC DISCLOSURES OF THE OLDEST AND MOST GIGANTIC OF ALL THE WORKS OF MAN
S.H. Ford
$4.00

For devices for experiments with plants, write to:

EDMUND SCIENTIFIC
300 Edscorp Building
Great Barrington N.J. 08007
Ask for catalog

THE SECRET LIFE OF PLANTS
Peter Tompkins and Christopher Bird
Harper & Row, 1973
$8.95   also available in paperback
Bantam $1.95

This book explores the world of plants and their relation to mankind as revealed by the latest discoveries of scientists of many disciplines. It includes remarkable information about plants as lie detectors and plants as ecological sentinels; it describes their ability to adapt to human wishes, their response to music, their curative powers and their ability to communicate with man. It analyzes experiments in theories from the past, many of them ignored or ridiculed, and it makes the startling suggestion that the most far-reaching revolution of the 20th century—one that may save or destroy the planet—may come from the bottom of your garden. . . .

"The dust-grimed window of the office building facing New York's Times Square reflected, as through a looking glass, an extraordinary corner of Wonderland. There was no White Rabbit with waistcoat and watch chain, only an elfin-eared fellow called Backster with a galvanometer and a house plant called *Dracaena massangeana*. The galvanometer was there because Cleve Backster was America's foremost lie-detector examiner; the dracaena because Backster's secretary felt the bare office should have a touch of green; Backster was there because of a fatal step taken in the 1960s which radically affected his life, and may equally affect the planet. . . .

"The adventure started in 1966. Backster had been up all night in his school for polygraph examiners, where he teaches the art of lie detection to policemen and security agents from around the world. On impulse he decided to attach the electrodes of one of his lie detectors to the leaf of his dracaena. The dracaena is a tropical plant similar to a palm tree, with large leaves and a dense cluster of small flowers; it is known as the dragon tree (Latin *draco*) because of the popular myth that its resin yields dragon blood. Backster was curious to see if the leaf would be affected by water poured on its roots, and if so, how, and how soon.

"As the plant thirstily sucked water up its stem, the galvanometer, to Backster's surprise, did not indicate less resistance, as might have been expected by the greater electrical conductivity of the moister plant. The pen on the graph paper, instead of trending upward, was trending downward, with a lot of sawtooth motion on the tracing. . . .

"When Backster left the room and returned with some matches, he found another sudden surge had registered on the chart, evidently caused by his determination to carry out the threat. Reluctantly he set about burning the leaf. This time there was a lower peak of reaction on the graph. Later, as he went through the motions of pretending he would burn the leaf, there was no reaction whatsoever. The plant appeared to be able to differentiate between real and pretended intent.

"Backster felt like running into the street and shouting to the world, 'Plants can think!' Instead he plunged into the most meticulous investigation of the phenomena in order to establish just how the plant was reacting to his thoughts, and through what medium. . . ."

79

From: FRONTIERS OF SCIENCE, August, Vol. 1, No. 12, Mankind Research Unlimited.

BREAKTHROUGH IN PLANT WORK

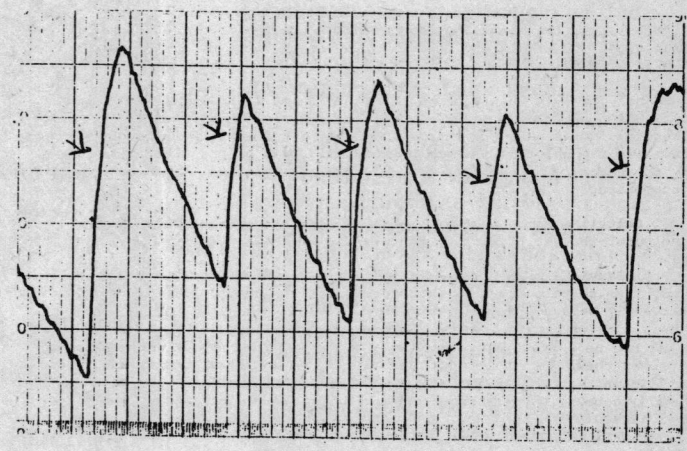

A most unusual triangle pattern send on demand.

Independent confirmation of evoked biological responses between plants and man has been accomplished by staff members of Mankind Research Unlimited, which could lead to a major breakthrough in technological applications. Positively identified and repeatable thought patterns sent over a distance of several miles have been detected using simple galvanic skin response equipment and a strip chart recorder, connected to a philodendron plant. Specific thoughts produce a specific, repeatable graph pattern. The technology exists to decode these patterns and to apply them to activate switches for electrical devices. Using this type of "thought activated switch" system, a psychic has opened up miniature garage doors, through plant response, when he was 20 miles away, and performed the operation several times on demand.

This series of experiments, based on the initial discovery of Cleve Backster in February of 1966, was conducted by Paul Sauvin, a long-time researcher in the field, who believes this "repeatable transmission of specific information opens a whole new area of practical applications for plant research, and supports other major findings that psychic energy can be transmitted, with control, over a distance and irrespective of so-called 'space barriers'."

Out of this series of experiments came a strong warning that negative stimulus should not be used on plants or oneself, because the sensitive participating in the energy transfer may receive severe shock to the nervous system from such stimulus. These dangers have been encountered by Paul Sauvin, Marcel Vogel and other researchers and caused them to stop further research along this line. The demonstration of a safe approach that yields positive, repeatable results will make it possible to proceed rapidly with experiments that do not have a detrimental effect on either the plant or the operator.

Though still in the early stages of development, the demonstration has been witnessed several times by non-partisan parties, and recorded on video tape and a three-track strip chart recorder.

Establishing initial biological response with the plant to be used in the experiment is of utmost importance to the test subject who will be transmitting the information. There is a special technique involved called "sensitizing the plant" and only when this first step has been successfully accomplished can the plant be expected to respond. Each test subject seems to develop a sensitizing technique that works best for him. Our test subject, Mr. "G.," sensitizes the plants by "projecting my consciousness into the plant until I become one with it. I water it, fondle the leaves, exchange love with it, until I can actually feel the water coming up the roots to the leaves," he said.

This type of rapport in which one receives the sensations of merging consciousness with the plant caused Paul Sauvin much consternation on one occasion. Mr. "G" was transmitting thought to the plant but not receiving satisfactory responses on the graph recorder. He claimed immediately after watering the plant, that he "just couldn't feel the water coming up." This made for a very perplexing situation. Paul checked the equipment, recalibrated it, rechecked the connections of the electrodes attached to the plant leaf and then checked the whole system, and verified that it was in good working condition. Much later in the day, after an only partially successful experiment with a group of philodendron vines all in one large pot, it was discovered that in the process of moving the plant some of the main vine stems were fractured and in one case actually broken. The damage occurred under the soil and was so severe that the broken stem was barely connected to it's roots. Emergency "surgery" was quickly performed, and in a few weeks the plant became a star performer. (Different plants have been used successfully besides the philodendron, including an unknown variety of Ivy which responds particulary well to Mr. "G".)

Early in his research with plants, Cleve Backster reported that once a plant was attuned to a person it would be possible to make a graph recording of the emotional response of that person over a distance. After lengthy plant experiments one day with Mr. "G," Paul observed that the plant was electrically responding as if it were still responding to Mr. "G's" emotions. He carefully checked the equipment again so that he might be able to obtain a quiet, non-evoked response reading. However, the graph was recording signals just as if it were responding to Mr. "G's" emotions.

Finally at almost one l'clock in the morning, Paul telephoned Mr. "G" and sought his advice on what could possibly be going wrong with the plant. Mr. "G" then explained that he was describing the day's experiments in great detail to his wife, and apparently was closely tied into the plant during the retelling.

Paul asked Mr. "G" to quiet the plant down and see if he could send information at a distance from his home in Alexandria, Va. The phone line was kept open and Mr. "G" sent his first transmission without telling Paul what it would be about. In this case it was the phrase "God is divine and the creator of us all." The plant immediately responded with a high peak that almost went off the graph paper!

The transmission was then repeated at 10 second intervals, with Mr. "G" not saying beforehand what he would send, only that it would be a specific thought at a specific time. These came out exactly as predicted with the graph peaks having definite wave patterns similar enough to be decoded and then applied to triggering "thought controlled" switches near the plant and over a distance of several miles from the subject.

Since this first successful experiment at a distance, Mr. "G's" learning curve continues to improve and tighter controls are being established for more accurate replication of transmission.

Up to this time inexpensive equipment had been used of a type that is readily available for other researchers who may wish to duplicate the experiment. Now it was time to set up tighter controls and formalize procedures so that they would conform to more rigorous laboratory tests. A six-channel strip chart recorder was used to successfully record the transmissions of Mr. "G" from a nearby location, and the real-time plant responses were video taped.

Another psychic was present in the laboratory who provided a running commentary to describe the thought patterns that were being sent by Mr. "G". These were written down at the time on the graph and when later compared with the actual thought form patterns that were sent, were found to be essentially correct.

The most interesting test pattern recorded on the graph was a series of 10 triangle-shaped thought patterns which were amazingly similar. This is an unusual pattern that Paul Sauvin had never seen before in all of his work with plants, and the "regularity was outstanding" he exclaimed.

Mr. "G" discussed the most interesting parts of his plant experiments in great detail and gave a warning about further tests involving himself and any plant he was attuned to during the transmission time. "I projected my consciousness into the plant and had a sense of knowing exactly how it felt. It was surprising that the plant seemed to meet me half way and for a time there was a feeling that we exchanged consciousness and I felt that my consciousness was at one with all plants."

"It was a beautiful experience, but I knew then that if anyone had pulled the plant out by the roots while this exchange was happening, that I would have died on the spot, " he claimed.

"Never hurt the plant, or even think of hurting it or sending it pain at that time," he warned the others in the room, "because I will surely feel it," Mr. "G" said.

Marcel Vogel experienced a similar sensation with almost disastrous results while performing plant experiments in California recently. During the session, he asked a psychologist in attendance to send a thought to the plant. The psychologist thought of cutting a leaf on the plant. As he did this, Mr. Vogel fell over into a deep state of shock and had to be hospitalized to recuperate.

"I felt like someone had put a rapier through my stomach when the psychologist thought of cutting the plant," Vogel said latter.

Paul Sauvin also notes that it "is very dangerous to the psychic to use negative stimulus just to get a response from the plant which can be consistently measured above a certain line."

He had been stymied by this problem for a number of years. He could always get the plant to respond, but not on cue, at a distance, and in measurable fashion, without using negative influence on himself. The pain was just too much to bear, so he stopped trying to get plants to operate other technological equipment this way, and continued searching for a clue to separate out low-level responses which could be replicated with a definite pattern on demand.

Now, through this series of experiments, he believes it is possible to demonstrate that psychics do have the ability to transmit specific energy patterns at a distance which can be directed and recorded. The ability to throw a switch by particular code, through a plant, is just one example of this type of transmission.

"We don't understand the mechanism involved with the sending of the energy, or how the plant responds, but we are sure there is a demonstrable transmission which has measurable effect," he claimed.

"Even non-living matter can be affected this way," he said in broadening the scope of possibilities. He referred to a tightly controlled experiment conducted by the Ernest Holmes Research Foundation at Agnes Scott College in Atlanta, Ga., in March of this year.

The experiment involved the sending of healing energy by Dr. Olga Worrall, a spiritual healer who has worked in Baltimore, Md., for many years. At the first session, a Wilson cloud chamber was used under proper laboratory conditions to measure healing energy coming from Dr. Worrall's hands.

She was able to cause a definite wave pattern in the cloud chamber when she placed her hands around it, and then changed direction of the pattern by 90 degrees as she moved her hands to different positions around the chamber.

Camera were not set up for the first experiment to record this, but during the second experiment, when Dr. Worrall was 600 miles away and sending energy, it was recorded on film. They had asked her to cause a second change of direction during this experiment, but she didn't do it, which created consternation in those attending at the time. However, later phone confirmation revealed that she deliberately didn't change direction of the energy just to throw them off. It was felt that this double-blind aspect made the experiment even more creditable.

Other members of the investigating team could get no results when they placed their hands around the cloud chamber, nor could they affect it in any other way. The experiments were limited, and there could be extraneous influences, but the possibility of "thought influencing matter at a distance" is worth serious consideration as its effects are being ever more precisely measured under strict laboratory control in a variety of situations.

The present thesis that MRU staff and other researchers are working on is that this "life energy" or "thought form energy" is not random, that it can be focused, directed, and sent over a distance.

By refining testing methods, it is hoped that psychic ability can be validated further to open up new fields of inquiry by scientists into energy states not too well understood at this time.

As these plant response tests continue to yield satisfactory results, it is hoped that a codified language will be developed for "particular bits of information" to be sent to a plant for basic computer-type programming.

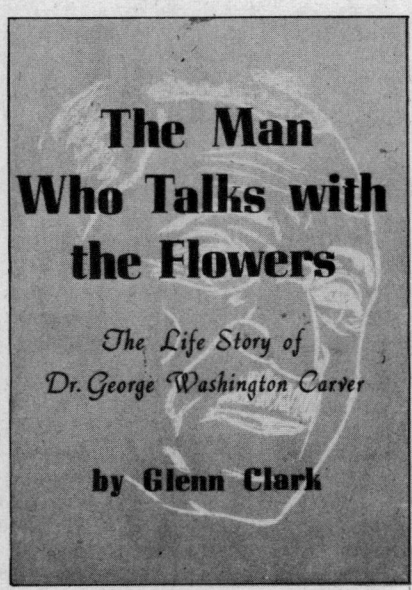

THE MAN WHO TALKS WITH FLOWERS: THE LIFE STORY OF DR. GEORGE WASHINGTON CARVER
Glenn Clark
Macalester Park Publishing Co., 1939
65 cents

THE SECRET POWERS OF PLANTS
Brett L. Bolton
Berkley, 1974
$1.25

For centuries, man has attributed strange and mysterious powers to plants. Now, some men have begun to prove in experiments — under controlled, scientific conditions — that plants do have almost incredible faculties, powers we are only just beginning to understand.

Tracing our knowledge of plants from ancient history to the present, this clear, concise and fascinating book explores the remarkable research being done, and details, among other topics:

- **How plants feel**
- **How plants react to good and evil**
- **How plants might actually someday help solve crimes**
- **How prayer affects plants**
- **How plants express love, fear, hate**
- **The mental links between man and plants**
- **Plants and ESP**

Complete with plant cures, and a special chapter on plants and astrology, THE SECRET POWERS OF PLANTS is a challenging book that opens the door on one of the unknown aspects of life.

THE VISION OF FINDHORN IN WORLD TRANSFORMATION

We are living in a time of world transformation. However one examines world affairs, whether from a scientific, a technological, an economic, a political, a cultural or a religious viewpoint, accelerated change is upon us and a new world is emerging. In places, this emergence follows smoothly along the lines of development established in the past; in other places, transformation is characterized by conflict between the old and the new. Revolution and evolution now march side by side through human affairs as mankind enters what many philosophers, scientists and social thinkers are calling the most significant and radical change in the human condition since the development of agriculture and civilization in the Late Stone Age. Whether this change can be accomplished in relative peace and creativity or whether it plunges us into increasing confusion and chaos depends on how clearly we can unfold from within ourselves the wisdom, the stability, the harmony and the vision to cope with the new age that is upon us. We can retreat from the future in fear and resistance or we can rise to meet it with understanding and become its master by mastering ourselves, releasing the best within us in creative blending with the present moment.

Man has always grown and unfolded the best within him when he has been inspired by noble vision, particularly when that vision has clarified his own nature and its relationship with the rest of creation. When such vision has been lost, then chaos, confusion, fear and lack of direction result and truly, as it is written, "the people perish." Yet visions and ideals alone are not sufficient. They must show the way to concrete action and that action must then be followed. They must be put into practice and shown to be realistic, attainable visions and ideals which assist man practically and creatively to embrace and use wisely the processes of growth and change.

To embody a vision and give it meaningful substance is an invaluable service in the world today. This is the service being provided by the Findhorn Trust community in northern Scotland. It is a centre where the vision of the future into which man is rapidly advancing is very real, where the vision is held of what man is unfolding into and of what he must do to make that unfoldment a balanced and creative one. It is a centre highly attuned to the principles underlying the transformation of the world into a new age of consciousness and expression. Although many centres have this vision of a new age and of the change in man's consciousness now being revealed, the primary role of Findhorn is to prove the reality of this vision. It is a centre where principles are lived and shown to be workable and practical through daily demonstration in the lives and affairs of the people of the community.

The major difficulty in the world today is that each individual tends to follow and manifest his own personal will (and consequently, each nation its national will), often irrespective of the good of the whole, the result being conflict and disharmony. Yet, the universe is essentially a wholeness, infilled by the one life and harmony of God, His will being the spirit of that wholeness in action. That life and will live in each of us; if we attune to them and unveil them in our actions, then harmony and wholeness are created within us and about us. That is the principle. Findhorn is founded on the demonstration of the reality and practicality of that principle. All that Findhorn has achieved and manifested first comes from the process of becoming still, going within and attuning to the inner centre of being where God's will and life are known and then implementing God's will through outer action. In fact, all that is done at Findhorn is ultimately intended to demonstrate the power, the beauty, the abundance and the freedom of a life that is lived in harmony and oneness with God within the individual and within all things.

The idea of the wholeness of all life is an important spiritual principle. At Findhorn, it is demonstrated through the co-operation with the nature forces and the creation of a garden of exceptional beauty and productivity growing in an otherwise inhospitable oceanside climate of sandy, gravelly soil and harsh, drying winds. This principle of wholeness and the communion of all life is also manifested in the human kingdom by the fact that this centre is a community. People from many varied backgrounds are living and working together in love, co-operation and blending, like many instruments contributing their individual and unique sounds to the harmonious wholeness of an orchestra. The interrelating of the human and nature kingdoms enriches both as well, creating a greater sense of community and oneness with all life, of ecological responsibility and joy; for man, though seemingly separate within his culture and civilization, is still a child of Nature and attuned to its rhythms. He cannot escape being part of Earth's ecology.

Another principle upon which Findhorn is based is the realization that man is entering a new age, a new cycle of creative expression and growth of consciousness. The institutions and life styles of the past often do not provide sufficiently creative and progressive solutions to the increasing problems of modern society. New life styles, new consciousness, new patterns of problem-solving and creativity must be pioneered and developed, especially to help the young, who are seeking new directions. The spirit of the new is seeking expression; where it is denied or distorted, revolution and conflict erupt, as they do where the new is feared simply because it is unknown. In some fashion, the consciousness that is creating the changes and unfolding the new age must be given expression within balanced and creative centres so that the frightening aura of the unknown is stripped from it and man can see the emergence of new forms and structures of manifestation on which he can base his hopes and dreams for the future. In other words, the vision must be clarified and brought into reality through living demonstration.

At Findhorn, this is being brought about by providing opportunities and outlets for the unfoldment and delineation of the new vision and consciousness through community living, through work in arts and crafts, in drama, music, dance, education and other activities. In realization that the new age of man represents the release of hidden inner potentials and an expansion of consciousness, the development of the individual and the heightening of his talents and abilities are encouraged. All of these activities are followed, not for their own sake alone, but as channels through which the expanding spirit of man can express itself and unfold directions of growth for the new culture and new civilization, directions that can be helpful and practical to men everywhere in adjusting positively and progressively to the changes of world transformation.

The essence of this transformation is seen as being a spiritual one, as the word "spiritual" implies the whole nature of man's consciousness and being as an expression of a universal life. This entails a fundamental alteration of man's definition of his own nature and the nature of creation, in order to allow for the recognition of laws of being, action and creativity transcending material limitations. Findhorn is a centre for demonstrating, in concrete and practical form, the reality, the nature and the outworking of these spiritual laws and principles. It is not primarily a garden or agricultural centre, nor a community nor an arts and crafts centre nor a place for the development of the performing arts. These are the secondary manifestations that derive from the primary purpose. It is a centre where vision inspires action and action is based upon inner attunement to God, to His life and will, and to the dynamic motion of His spirit and wholeness which, as it breaks through into greater creative manifestation throughout the world, reveals a new age, a new world for man in harmony with all life.

It is important that the proper perspective be gained of the role and value of Findhorn and its work in assisting world transformation, for Findhorn and its work do not stand alone. This community is not an isolated expression, a minor quest for utopia amidst turmoil and confusion. To understand Findhorn and why it has come into being, as well as the vision that it seeks to make plain through its manifestations, is to understand the nature, the extent and the power of the movement of expanded human consciousness, a movement into a new age, now active throughout the world. Findhorn is a particular expression of a universal unfoldment of unprecedented significance, for all over the world there are centres and individuals working to bring down into demonstration the powerful and positive creativity of man's higher spiritual consciousness, seeing in that consciousness and its oneness with the universal life of God, the only source of creative solutions to pressing human problems.

This is a planetary movement of consciousness, inspiring a universal outlook both horizontally in promoting the realization of the brotherhood and oneness of all humanity, and vertically in proving that *spiritual consciousness* is not a synonym for vague, imprecise and impractical thinking. Rather it is an indication of man's next leap of evolution into a level of thought and awareness filled with the power and creativity of the wholeness of life and therefore fully capable of handling the complexities of modern life through its own integrated harmony and wisdom. This movement is the consciousness of universal world harmony active within individuals and between individuals, within nations and between nations, within humanity and Nature and between humanity and Nature, within matter and spirit and between matter and spirit.

For years, the centres and individuals which have spearheaded this birth of new consciousness amongst humanity have often been isolated. Now they are increasingly linking up and sharing their strengths, aided by the growth of modern technology in rapid travel and global communications. Centres such as Findhorn, which are attuned to universality, become points of focus around which these links can coalesce and become stabilized. Individuals who visit Findhorn or receive its literature become tuned in to this broadening vision and work. Through these links and the vision of the whole plan of revelation and transformation active upon the planet which the individual thus receives, he is made more encouragingly aware of how this new consciousness is unfolding about him and how he can live that unfoldment within himself. He is aided in adding his own contribution of co-operation and harmony to the whole by transforming his own consciousness, the primary level on which world transformation and renewal must be accomplished.

From the life of the individual arises the life of the group and the nation; therefore, the work must be done on the fundamental level of individual vision, understanding and action. Then, through the linking of such integrated and transformed individuals, a universal foundation of shared inspired consciousness is formed, a movement that unveils itself as an organic expression of expanding human life, not as a political program conceived by governments. Such a movement, born of the very essence of being human and hence needing to unfold greater rhythms of life and fulfilment, has the power of evolution, not revolution, behind it. By adding the power of a demonstrated vision, the power of achievement and tangible manifestation of the reality and effectiveness of living in harmony with spiritual law, Findhorn strengthens this movement, sometimes called the "New Age movement", and becomes a cornerstone of the universal foundation of new, inspired consciousness.

The community at Findhorn is based on the principle of following God's guidance and demonstrating the abundance, beauty and harmony that result when this is done—but God is not seen as a force outside of man, a separated supernatural agent acting on the perimeters of human evolution to be supplicated and worshipped. He is seen as the spirit and reality of the inner and outer wholeness, the essence of life in all forms of creation, the pressure of that life toward greater and greater revelation and expression of itself from within outward; He is seen as the Beloved seeking union and oneness with mankind. The emphasis at Findhorn is on being and living the will and guidance of God; it is on breaking down barriers of intellectual and emotional separation, feelings of guilt and unworthiness, and images of the Divine that keep man from realizing his inherent divine potential. The vision is of man and God united in a oneness of will and action and love; through various activities, Findhorn seeks to promote this—to reveal and fulfil the godliness of the individual and the divinity of wholeness within group action and creativity.

Seeing the worship of God as being the very act of *being* His spirit in loving, practical, harmonious and creative action through work, art, education, self-fulfilment and community activity, there is nothing unbalanced, pious or mystically superior in this quest for godliness within the community. Action is the keyword. The balance must be demonstrated, the principles lived, the visions given substance; God is revealed through applying the qualities of His life within us to daily problems. Findhorn is definitely a working community. All who come add the contribution of their time and energy to community tasks that need to be done. There is time for meditation, for lectures and discussions, but the fruits of these periods must show forth in the quality of the life and its achievements. Work is seen as meditation in expression, a key to personal development and the liberation of inner potential. Work is the gift of the individual's uniqueness to the rhythms of life, the opening of the doors of himself in giving that he might also receive.

Seen in this light, work at Findhorn takes on a wider meaning than is normally given to that word. Everything that reveals the divinity of the individual in action is work and at the same time is play and fun. It may be working in the garden, in the office, in the kitchen or the publishing department, or it may be creating in the fields of arts and crafts, drama, music, dance, writing, child care and education. Each individual is generally asked to do what he can do best or what he wishes to do within the needs of the community at that time. He is asked to infil his work with a sense of joy and harmony through realizing that his work is the outward revelation of his relationship of love and oneness with the rest of creation. Out of this spirit of work comes a spirit of fun, laughter and abundance, a realization of the inner festival of living, which often results in the celebration of day-long festivals of music, dance, drama and artistic displays, as well as occasional evenings of entertainment in the community centre.

The vision Findhorn holds of man's new estate of being is that man does not need to suffer, for he lives in the midst of God's abundance. He can receive this abundance when he makes of himself a clear channel through which life can flow without restriction, freely being received and freely being given. All his needs, on all levels from material to spiritual, are perfectly met each moment when he has proven his ability to release what he has back to the whole when his need for it is fulfilled. Findhorn is not a commune where joint ownership is practised; God, the wholeness of life, is the only owner in creation. The consciousness which Findhorn seeks to demonstrate is that of the community and each individual who comprises it being a steward of abundance, rather than an owner, for to hold on and try to possess indicates a lack of trust that one's needs will continue to be met perfectly in the future. If one truly lives in the consciousness of abundance, then there is no need to try to possess and accumulate. One treats the materials one is given by life with respect, love and understanding, as any steward would care for what is under his charge, ready to release them freely if need be; then one is open to manifesting abundance in one's life.

This principle is well demonstrated at Findhorn. All that the community has in the way of buildings, equipment and land has been manifested through faith and through being open to God's guidance and abundance. The community has little money in the bank at any given time, yet it freely and in full faith initiates building programs, purchases equipment and living accommodation and goes about its activities of feeding and caring for the hundreds of visitors who come each year. Always needs are met. When a bill comes due or an expenditure arises, the money is there; it may come from donations for literature, from guests who have stayed for awhile or "out of the blue" from anonymous donors. Materials may be given at a time when they are needed, and when certain skills or talents are required, the right personnel arrive as well. The members of the community do the work necessary both physically and spiritually to keep the doors of manifestation open; there is no sitting back and letting God do it all. Yet, as it is written, to those who are willing to give all in loving service to the whole, all is returned in increased abundance. To those who can put God—His life within us, the consciousness and action of His wholeness—above all else, then all else is added in overflowing measure. The vision of Jesus's promise that man might have more abundant life is daily given reality at Findhorn.

Furthermore, what manifests does so in beauty and perfection, for this is also the vision that Findhorn holds out for the new age of mankind's fulfilment: it is an age of order, beauty and perfection on all levels. Therefore, the community strives for spiritual and material perfection, which finds expression in the beauty of the garden and the comfort of the surroundings in which the people live and work. This is a far cry from the public stereotype of a spiritual centre as a place of austerity and privation and of the spiritual life as a path of suffering, sackcloth and hairshirts. All true spiritual centres and teachings proclaim the order, beauty and perfection of the universe and, obeying the maxim, "As above, so below," seek to manifest that perfection on Earth. At Findhorn, appreciation and right use of material things is an important part of its vision and the lessons it teaches; in this centre, it is demonstrated that man's consciousness must change and be willing to accept both the joy and responsibility of abundance and beauty, not to seek to possess things or to allow one's consciousness to be possessed by them, but to unfold the inner spirit of divine artistry in order to use the best of the physical, emotional and mental worlds to reveal the perfection inherent in material and earthly forms and expressions.

These, then, are some of the visions which Findhorn is offering through living demonstration to the world in this time of planetary transformation. They are visions of man's inner splendour, of his potential for love and creativity beyond the scope of his past consciousness, limited as it has been by emotional and mental turmoil and conflict. It is, in its wholeness, a vision of a new age dawning for man, as this splendour and these potentials are brought forward into expression. It is a vision of a world united in harmony and blessed with abundance, a world resting on a foundation of universal individual fulfilment and crowned with a humanity united in love and understanding with the wholeness of life, one with God.

Such a vision is neither the product nor the possession of any one centre or individual. It has been man's dream for ages. Now we stand on the brink of that dream's fulfilment. Findhorn is a centre where that dream is even now being given tangible manifestation in form, a place where people can come and experience for themselves the reality of the new age. That is its value, its significance, its contribution to world transformation. Those who do come and stay, especially the young people, will one day go forth as emissaries of this new age and new consciousness, spreading the reality of this vision over the earth and linking with people from other centres who are doing the same thing.

This vision is not a static program. Those who leave Findhorn to take what they have unfolded from themselves for application in other centres or in the starting of new communities do not carry with them a carefully worked out manifesto for change. They will be the embodiment of a new consciousness through which the individual can fulfil each moment of his life wherever he is and bring out of that moment its inherent perfection. They will have learned at Findhorn of the existence and application of certain spiritual laws which underlie that consciousness and give it substance and strength. They will not be mouthpieces for a new revelation; they will BE the new revelation in service, in action, in life.

There are visions but there are no blueprints for the new age; there are the spiritual laws and states of consciousness which create the transformations when they are attuned to and practised. Thus, Findhorn is not establishing blueprints for new age forms nor training people to represent a particular dogma. It is pioneering the revelation and demonstration of the laws and consciousnesses from which the new will organically unfold itself. It is helping people to realize within themselves the new age consciousness and to find oneness with God through their own actions and unique rhythms of life, that they may contribute their uniqueness to the building of a new world. In this fashion, the universal foundation of inspired individual consciousness is brought ever more into reality as the base on which is being built, from the transformations of the old world, a new culture of universal world harmony, a new civilization and a renewed humanity.

David Spangler

THE POWER OF PRAYER ON PLANTS
Rev. Franklin Loehr
Signet, 1959
$1.25

"The discovery that prayer can measurably, consistently, affect plant growth, which is the discovery scientifically established by the prayer-plant research told of in this book, is now recognized as a major breakthrough for both science and religion. Powers hitherto considered occult, extrasensory, or just plain magic, were given scientific proof by the three-year laboratory research here related. Man *does* have spiritual powers beyond his physical being. . . .

". . . Beginners in this field are apt to consider prayer a form of *willing* something into being; advanced students

   come to see their prayers as definite, conscious ideas set in motion in the subjective world which surrounds and includes us all, and which accepts ideas at their face value and proceeds to act upon them. The power of a prayer is thus thought of as limited only by the prayer-maker's ability to embody an idea mentally, and the prayer-receiver's ability and willingness to receive it mentally."

FINDHORN—A CENTER OF LIGHT
Paul Hawken, 1974
$1.25
Write to:
East West Journal, Tao Publications
31 Farnsworth Street
Boston, Mass. 02210

"There have been stories in the press and other media about a small community of people in the north of Scotland who talk to plants with amazing results; stories of vegetable and flower gardens animated by angelic forms where Pan's pipes are heard in the wind through the leaves; stories of plants performing incredible feats of growth and endurance: 40 lb. heads of cabbage, eight-foot delphiniums, and roses blooming in the snow, all a short distance from the Arctic circle; Don Juan and Tolkien combined where the elemental world of plants and animals cooperate with fairies, elves and gnomes in creating a land where nothing is impossible and legends are reborn; people heard talking to plants and angels in a casual and informal way creating a Garden of Eden where only gorse bushes and spiky grass grew before; a cold, windblown peninsula jutting into the North Sea with soil as sandy and worthless as your local beach. With those sketchy and incredible tales I left for Scotland to search out Findhorn Gardens. What I found instead was something infinitely larger than 40 lb. cabbages and equally more incredible. Fairies and elves seem tame compared to what is happening here. Findhorn may very well be a manifestation of a light and a power which is so strong and divine that it could very well transform the planet we inhabit—within our lifetime. Born a skeptic, I can well appreciate that some of what I will write here will seem incredible. Neither the people of Findhorn or myself ask that you believe this account. As Peter Caddy, the founder and custodian of Findhorn, has said: 'You cannot really describe Findhorn; people must experience it themselves in order to understand it.'

THE FINDHORN FOUNDATION

The Findhorn Community consists of some 150 people of all ages and many different nationalities living and working together. The Center is situated on the Moray Firth far up the Eastern coast of Scotland, 30 miles East of Inverness.

"The Community came into being under Divine guidance as an experiment in pioneering a way of life for the New Age. Many young people are drawn to Findhorn, and in recent years great emphasis has been laid on the training and educational aspect of community life. Work is often spoken of as 'Love in Action'. It is through working and sharing together that the individual not only grows in self-knowledge and spiritual understanding, but learns the meaning and joy of Group Consciousness, and so fits himself to take his place in the great body of World Servers.

"Peter Caddy, Founder
The Park—Findhorn Bay—Forres
Moray—Scotland—IV36 QTY
Telephone: Findhorn 311''

PART THREE:

METHODS OF PSYCHIC AND SPIRITUAL DEVELOPMENT

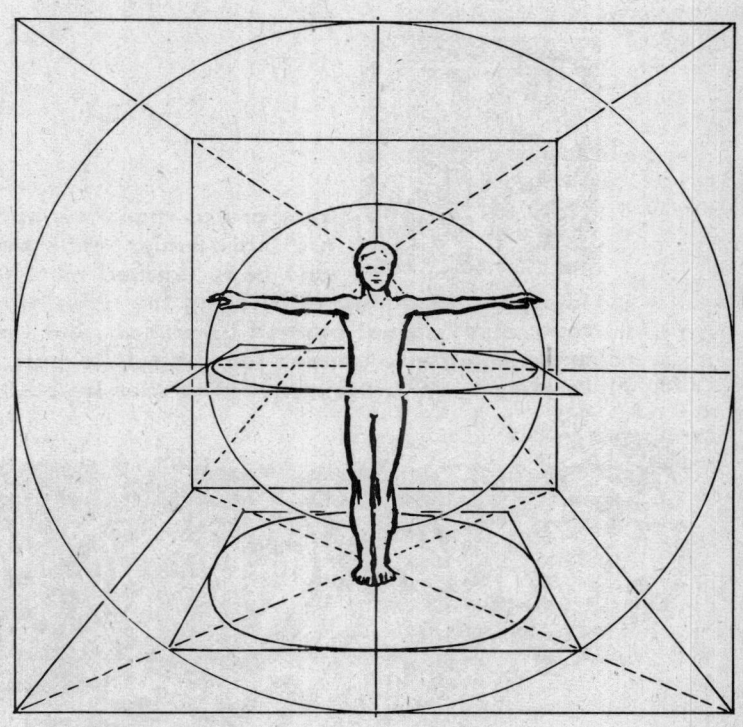

One of the unfortunately prevalent assumptions of numerous individuals who are motivated by a sincere desire to realize and utilize their untapped potential, is that an imaginary line separating "normal" and "psychic" consciousness can be crossed by a total immersion in a crash course promising instant psychic development. Rooted in the very real hope and need to become suddenly equipped to meet the demands of a jumbled complexity of pressing personal and planetary problems, this approach can result in the unexpected confrontation of an unprepared mind with potentially dangerous, alarming crises.

While most of these programs have implicit value, it must be remembered that the techniques taught may be built on scientific and metaphysical foundations that can be differentially interpreted and which may have to be altered in response to new information. They should therefore be seen essentially as "maps" or "paths" serving as places to start.

Divination, Mediums And Psychics

here are as many methods to begin extending awareness as there are individuals. While divination techniques abound, many people who have learned to focus on specific instruments have developed idiosyncratic methods of facing the unknown. Instruments used for divination in themselves do not expand awareness, but instead help to focus attention on tasks that might otherwise appear too difficult to perform. They also serve to amplify personal responses which might not otherwise be easily detected by the conscious mind.

The divinatory arts

From: WITCHCRAFT, Erich Maple.

1 *Catoptromancy. In ancient times the outcome of an illness was foretold by the appearance of the sick person's face on a plate of burnished metal, which had been suspended over a sacred stream.*

2 *Hydromancy. Symbols in a pool or stream suggested future events.*

3 *Smoke-reading. Smoke rising from a sacrifice was a good or bad omen: good if it rose vertically, bad if it was thick and slow to disperse.*

4 *Involuntary omens. It was believed that sneezing, trembling and other involuntary actions betrayed the future.*

5 *Astrology. The future was determined according to the movements of the planets through the twelve signs of the Zodiac.*

6 *Chiromancy. The lines and other configurations of the human palm were consulted for signs of events to come.*

7 *Necromancy. The future was disclosed through contact with the dead.*

8 *Alectryomancy. A cockerel was set down in a circle divided into twenty-four sections, each containing a letter of the Greek alphabet and a seed. As it ate the grains the pattern of the future was revealed.*

9 *Dice-throwing. This was a well-tried method among Greek magicians.*

10 *Bird flight. Patterns of take-off, flight, etc., were interpreted.*

11 *Entrail-reading. The innards of a fowl were thought portentous.*

12 *The sound of thunder. Each burst and interval had its meaning.*

13 *Spiders' webs. The design of each revealed a different future.*

14 *Onirocriticism. This was the art of interpreting dreams.*

MAPS OF CONSCIOUSNESS
ralph Metzner
Collier, 1971
$3.95

"If we use the analogy of a journey or path to consider the process of psychological transformation to the level of individuality, we can perhaps arrive at some conclusions as to the requirements for such a process. The best way of proceeding on a long and difficult journey into unknown territory is with a guide. Claudio Naranjo has written: 'The teacher-therapist-guide is the person who, by virtue of his own individual understanding of a system, may help another individual in the process of creative translation of the general into the particular, of the way into a given, unique way. Each individual is, as it were, a variation on a universal theme, and a teacher is one with enough insight into the theme to know how the idea may become flesh and deed.' Genuine teachers however are hard to find and there is a phase where the individual is probing, testing, and experimenting with different ways and means in order to find the one that works for him. During this stage maps are useful, and that is why in recent years there has been such an upsurge of interest in the old maps of evolutionary development.

"There is an important difference between a map and a model or theory. A model or theory states that 'Man is like this, he learns this way, perceives like this, and thinks and acts according to these laws.' All Western psychology, insofar as it has theories at all, is of this type. A map on the other hand is pragmatic, it is designed to help us find our way. It says: 'Look at it this way and observe the results'; or 'Try this procedure and the following experiences will occur.' Much oriental psychology and esoteric systems such as those of Gurdjieff are of this type. They imply a model of man oriented toward this goal. Often they include instructions for the practice of certain psychological techniques. However, since the techniques are generally held to be learnable only directly from a teacher, the technical indications are usually coded in a language accessible only to those who have, through a teacher, already had practical experience of the technique. They serve therefore more as reminders. It is a characteristic of such systems that they are written on many levels, and each student will derive from them what information he can assimilate according to his level of understanding.

THE SECRETS OF NUMBERS
Vera Scott Johnson and Thomas Wommach
Berkley, 1973
95 cents

"The science of Numerology assumes that the mind or the central core of intelligence of man is infinite but ever changing. The eternal plane on which all life exists and evolves is called the cosmic plane. A lifetime or life on a physical plane is just one cycle or incarnation through which each man's infinite intelligence passes in its continual search for perfection and balance with the universe. That mind is constantly evolving, registering, evaluating, incorporating or discarding outside influences. What we are is the total of what has happened to us and, more importantly, of how we have reacted to it. Each physical incarnation adds new experiences. We have been through many before and have more to come. The infinite mind keeps a constant record of all that has happened to it, although it may not be readily seen by the conscious mind.

"Numerology focuses on this metaphysical premise in the following manner. First it breaks down man's two basic tools of communication—letters and numbers—into a simplified system of numbers. Then the numbers of an individual's name are used to analyze the past experiences of the individual on the cosmic plane and to indicate predisposition of character in his present physical plane, and the numbers in an individual's birthdate are used to predict the destiny of that individual in his present physical plane."

NEW YORK INSTITUTE OF NUMEROLOGY AND PSYCHIC POTENTIAL
136 Lexington Ave.
New York, N.Y. 10016
Write for information on seminars, workshops and classes

✶✶✶✶✶

NUMBERS: THEIR MEANING AND MAGIC
Isidore Kozminsky
Weiser, 1972
$2.00

I CHING
3419 Main Highway
Coconut Grove, Florida
New Age books

✶ ✶ ✶

SYBIL LEEK BOOK OF FORTUNE-TELLING
Sybil Leek
Collier, 1969
$2.95

Deals with tarot I Ching, I-Ching, palmistry, crystal gazing, tea leaves and candle imagery, cards, dice and dominoes and their ancient variations

COMPUTERIZED I-CHING HOROSCOPE

NOW A CHINESE Horoscope for the FIRST time! A 10-Page individualized I-CHING prediction – INCLUDING:
 a. 2 Destiny Hexagrams
 b. 1 Hexagram for the Current Year
 c. 12 Hexagrams for Each Month of the Current Year

The I-CHING (Book of Changes): 4000 Year Old Book of Wisdom and Divination. I-CHING text translated and interpreted by DA LIU, whom the Boston Globe calls "sage and master of the Book of Changes" and author of T'AI CHI CH'UAN AND I CHING (A Choreography of Body and Mind) Harper & Row, 1972 – now in its 2nd printing.

BIRTH DATA
SEX _____
TIME _____ A.M. _____ P.M.
DAY _____ MONTH _____ YEAR _____

(Note: If exact birth time is not known, an approximate time is necessary for preparing your horoscope.)
PRINT NAME _____
ADDRESS _____
City _____ State _____ Zip _____

Mail check or money order of $10.00 to:

COMPUTERIZED I CHING HOROSCOPE, INC.
Pan Am Building – Suite 303 East
200 Park Avenue, New York, N.Y. 10017

E/W

HANDS and Handwriting

1824 – CHEIRO'S COMPLETE PALMISTRY 7.95
A 301-page, one-volume edition which merges all significant material scattered in Cheiro's many palmistry books.

1410 – COMPLETE HAND READING – Edith Niles . . 2.50
Shows you how to take accurate "readings" from the human hand after a few short hours. 191 pages.

1412 – HANDWRITING ANALYSIS – Dorothy Sara 2.50
An easy-to-follow approach to graphology. 160 pages.

137 – HANDWRITING ANALYSIS – M. N. Bunker 5.00
230 pages, 14 full and complete chapter-lessons, with check-up questions at the end of each. Shows how to understand others, as well as yourself, from letters, signatures, notes, doodles.

832 – KEY TO PALMISTRY – Leona Lehman 2.00
Learn to read palms for pleasure and profit.

1456 – GYPSY SORCERY & FORTUNE TELLING – Charles Leland – 271 pages 4.95
A delightful grab-bag of spells, customs, incantations, love philtres, superstitions, and fetishes garnered from Europe, the East, and America.

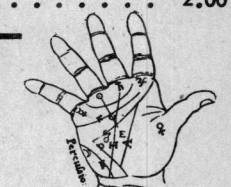

THE SEXUAL KEY TO THE TAROT
Theodore Laurence
Signet
$1.25

MASTERING THE TAROT: BASIC LESSONS ON AN ANCIENT MYSTIC ART
Eden Gray
Signet
$1.50

TAROT CARDS
Write for catalogue to:
U.S. Games Systems Inc.
Dept. ERN
468 Park Avenue South
New York, N.Y., 10016

YOUR PRACTICAL GUIDE TO FORTUNE-TELLING
Rod Davies
Zebra Books, 1974
$1.25

ASTRO-TAROT MEDITATION
A method of uniting the Tarot with Astrology in the attainment of serpent power, through one simple daily practice. Method sent for 50p to those writing for information about the Cult of Ishtar. Temple of Ishtar, 93 Clifden Road, London, E.5.

Order From:
International Imports
Box 2010
Toluca Lake
California 91602

TAROT CARDS

Tarot playing cards are believed to have originated in Italy in the 14th century. The original purpose of the cards was severalfold — to provide a pictorial presentation of the times, to play a game involving suit trumps, and to read the future.

1706 – AQUARIAN TAROT CARDS – Full 78-card deck in full color . . $ 6.50
Authentic interpretation of the medieval tarot.

1765 – COMPLETE TAROT DECK – 78 cards with directions 4.00
Deck is in full color, and meaning is printed on each card. Large how to spread the cards chart included with instructions. Great beginners deck.

1766 – CROWLEY TAROT CARDS – 78 cards in color 10.00

1704 – GRAND ETTEILLA, Egyptian Gypsies Tarot 7.50
78 full-color cards, plus 118-page instruction booklet.

778 – THE NEW TAROT 8.00
Complete kit includes 78-card deck in full color, three instruction booklets, and a vinyl game map to assist in specific problem areas.

1767 – RIDER TAROT DECK – 78 color cards, 15 pg. explicative booklet . 6.50

1544 – SWISS TAROT DECK – 78 cards in color, 10 pg. instruction booklet 5.00

1705 – TAROT OF MARSEILLES – One of the oldest known decks 7.50
Ancient 78-card deck with 48-page instruction booklet.

1992 – TINY TAROT DECK – Full 78 card deck, in full color 1.50
3/4 x 1 1/2" cards, with instructions.

TAROT BOOKS

339 – THE TAROT REVEALED – Eden Gray . . $ 3.00
A modern guide to reading the cards. The ancient lore of the Tarot in a form that beginners can use and understand. 120 pages, all cards illustrated.

741 – PICTORIAL KEY TO THE TAROT – Arthur E. Waite . . . . . $ 7.50
An occult authority explains the Tarot. 344 pages, hard cover.

1423 – TAROT FOR THE MILLIONS – Sidney Bennett 2.50
Excellent introduction to one of the most famous, ancient, and accurate methods of fortune telling through cards. 157 pages, soft cover.

1440 – UNDERSTANDING THE TAROT – Dr. Leo Martello 1.50
192 pages.. how to read the future, destiny, and fortune. Illustrated.

1415 – MORE TAROT SECRETS – Sidney Bennett 2.50
New techniques for reading, and astrological interpretations. 149 pages.

MYSTICISM & OCCULT

World's Largest CRYSTAL BALL Selection
Glowing pools of light... Flawlessly beautiful

When you look into the unfathomable depths of a flawless crystal ball, what do you see? A point of light on which to meditate? Psychic images? A dark nothingness? Or do you seek a self-hypnotic experience, a light trance state, a transcendental insight?

F. W. H. MYERS, the famed psychic researcher, wrote: "Few phenomena are more fantastic than true crystal vision. Perhaps one man or woman in 20 will experience it. The vision often begins with a milky clouding of the ball, coming at the beginning of a series of pictures...."

Perfection Quality balls in 4-inch, 3-inch, 2½-inch, and 2-inch sizes are now in stock for immediate delivery from the Venture Bookshop. Each ball is guaranteed free of any flaw, bubble, mold mark or cloudiness — and each ball is the finest now available anywhere at any price!

These Optical Acrylic Plexiglas crystal balls are the result of years of searching for a method of manufacturing flawless balls, and we believe they are exactly what is needed by the occult student. Order the ball that best meets your needs and begin your adventures in the age-old science of Visualization today.

A At $9.95 this 2-inch ball with an unusual spiral stand of crystal-clear Acrylic represents an outstanding value for the new student.

B For $15.95 this impressive 2½-inch ball with square-based stand will effectively meet average requirements and provide beauty with pride of ownership.

C This 3-inch ball at $21.95 is suitable for almost all occult work and cannot be matched for quality at twice the price. Conical stand included.

D The 4-inch ball at $45.95 is one of the largest and finest crystal balls available in the world today. It is unconditionally guaranteed.

Please add 50c for postage and handling. Each ball is exactly as shown in these unretouched photos, and comes complete with a sculpted stand and authentic instructions.

THE VENTURE BOOKSHOP P.O. Box 249, Highland Park, IL 60035

RARE...GENUINE ROCK CRYSTAL BALLS

The Venture Bookshop has contracted with the Bodoh Lapidary for its entire production of rock crystal balls. The Lapidary has been grinding exquisite flawless balls of genuine rock crystal for a number of years — the only manufacturer of quartz crystal balls known to us in the United States. Production is limited and slow — no more than a dozen or so crystal balls are produced for sale each year.

Each ball is a flawless gem — hand-cut and polished from the largest and best quartz crystal available to the Lapidary. World supplies of crystal quartz are diminishing. Prices are rising and values increasing rapidly. We can guarantee these prices only for a brief time. ORDER TODAY to get a rare and glowing jewel you'll prize for your entire life. Complete with handsome stand.

Rock Crystal Balls available only as shown:

Only 4, 1¾-inch	$165.00	each
Only 4, 2-inch	$215.00	each
Only 1, 2¼-inch	$290.00	each
Only 1, 2½-inch	$435.00	each
Only 1, 2¾-inch	$500.00	each

VENTURE BOOKSHOP, P.O. Box 249, Highland Park, IL 60035

CRYSTAL-GAZING
Theodore Besterman
University Books, 1965
$5.00

PALMISTRY MADE PRACTICAL
Elizabeth Daniel Squire
Wilshire Book Co., 1966
$1.50

PALMISTRY—SECRETS REVEALED
Henry Frith
Wilshire Book Co., 1971
$2.00

FASTER THAN OUIJA BOARD!

Smooth-rolling ball bearings speed flow of automatic writing—without awkward pauses.

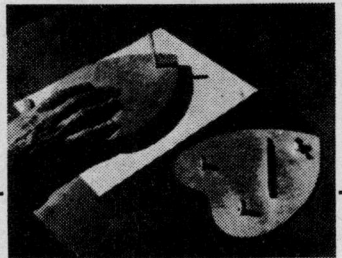

THE PLANCHETTE
Beautifully hand-crafted of smooth wood. Wood-resin polish gives high lustre.

Many experienced automatic writers learned with a planchette, and still find it the only way to obtain manifestations. Once you have acquired the gift, you will agree that the planchette is far superior to the Ouija Board. It is particularly favored by those who prefer to work in meditative solitude.

HOW THE PLANCHETTE WORKS:
Specially-fitted pencil forms one leg of planchette, the other two rolling free on ball bearings. These ball bearings permit the slightest indication of movement to take effect, the tiniest wisp of pressure transmitted through your hand. Only a superior product, an authentic psychic appliance, could have this expensive ballbearing feature. Complete instructions for use of the planchette, as well as for its care and protection, are included with this advanced psychic instrument.

ORDER YOURS TODAY! ONLY $5.95
Please add 50c postage and handling.

```
VENTURE BOOKSHOP
P.O. Box 249, Highland Park, Ill. 60035
Please send me ............ planchettes at
only $5.95 each, plus 50c postage and
handling.
I enclose check............, or money order
............ for $............
Name............................................
Address........................................
City............. State............. Zip.........
```

- Money lines.
- Lines of opposition—just that.
- Line of intuition—gives insight.
- Lines of influence—predictors of events.
- Family lines—show how your family influences you in present, past, future.
- Sister lines—these can accompany any of the major or minor lines and reinforce the meaning of the line.

THE LINES
(illustrated)

1. LIFE
2. HEAD
3. HEART
4. HEALTH
5. FATE
6. FAME
7. MARRIAGE
8. CHILDREN
9. MONEY
10. SEX
11. SPIRIT
12. TRAVEL
13. LUCK

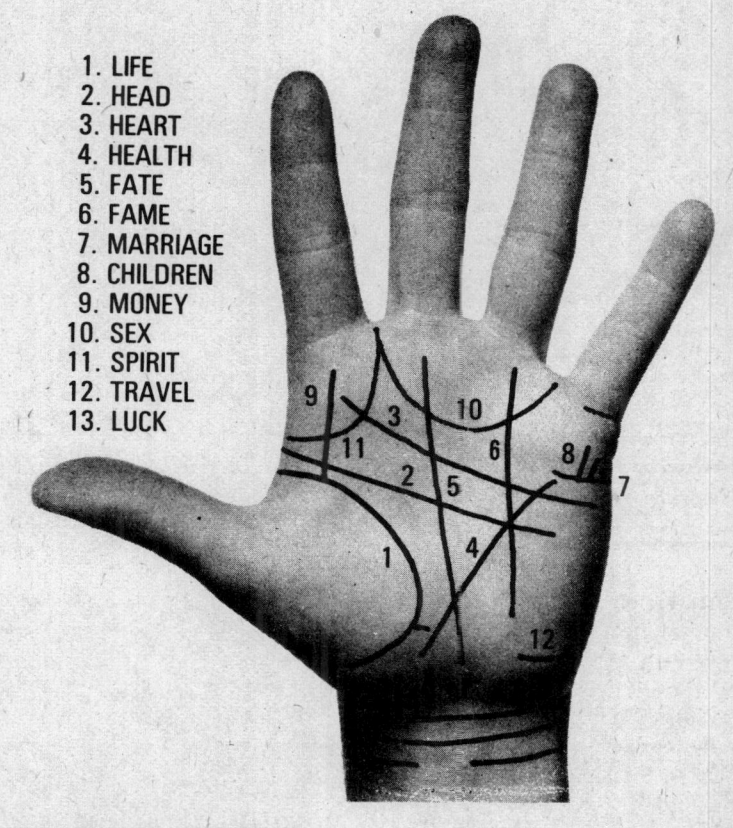

THE COMPLETE BOOK OF PALMISTRY
Joyce Wilson
Bantam, 1971
$1.00

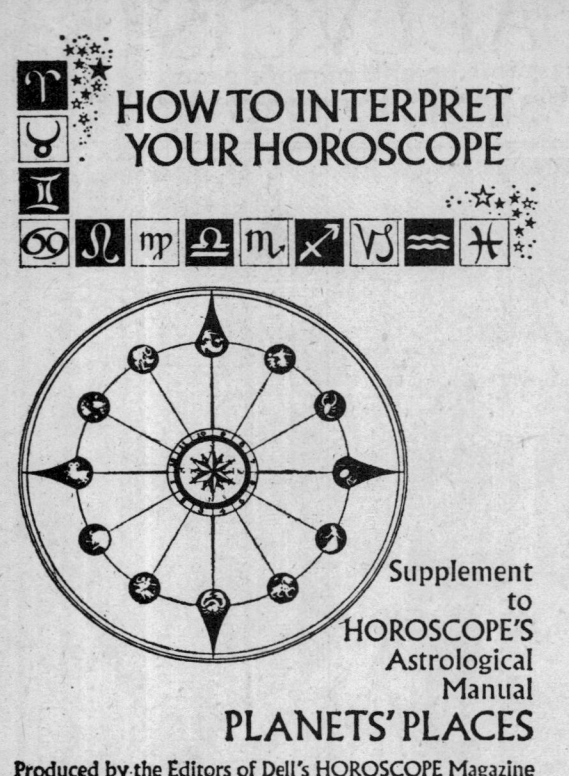

HOW TO INTERPRET YOUR HOROSCOPE

Supplement to HOROSCOPE'S Astrological Manual
PLANETS' PLACES
Produced by the Editors of Dell's HOROSCOPE Magazine

This supplement of 42 pages contains key words to planetary positions and aspects. It also includes a Pluto ephemeris for the years 1880-1980.

Price: $1.50
Order from:
Dell Publishing Co., Inc.,
Box 3000, Pinebrook,
N.J. 07058
(Sorry no C.O.D.)

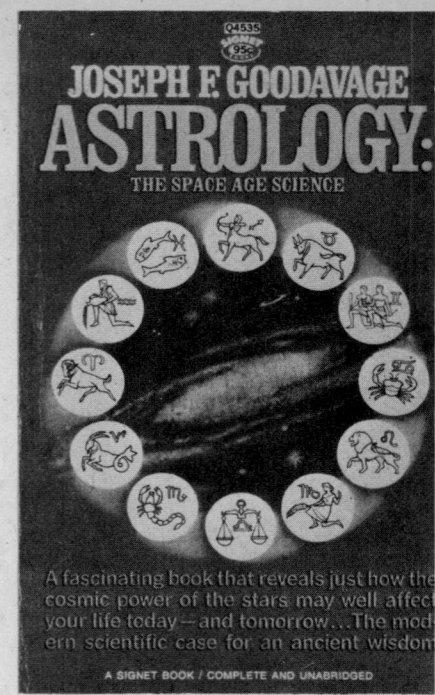

ASTROLOGY: THE SPACE AGE SCIENCE
Joseph F. Goodavage
Signet, 1966
95 cents

"Let's see if we can build a case, based on factual data, step by step. Let's try to determine, logically, whether the planets *could* have some unknown effect upon human beings.

"1—Sunspots and solar flares have a powerful effect on the Earth's weather, particularly on the ion concentration in the atmosphere.

"2—Electrical atmospheric charges, geomagnetism, and electromagnetism all affect plant, animal, and human health and disease conditions.

"3—It has been proven that positive and negative ions in the atmosphere definitely affect the way we think, feel, and behave.

"4—Lunar influence has an important direct effect on climate, atmospheric moisture, plants, animals, and humans.

"5—Oxygen has certain magnetic properties, so solar magnetic fields and sunspots can affect the Earth's atmosphere magnetically as well as thermally.

"6—Geomagnetism affects animal and human organisms, which respond to geomagnetic changes.

"7—Cosmic radiation is known to alter DNA and RNA, the nucleic acids in all living things.

"8—The ever-changing angles formed by the planets trigger solar flares and spots. There is some evidence that they are also responsible for seismic and volcanic disturbances due to the shifting center of gravity of the solar system.

PREDICTION
Incorporating Weekly
Horoscope and Fantasy
Link House,
Dingwall Avenue
Croydon, Surrey,
CR9 2TA, England
Subscription 2.70
Monthly

ASTROLOGY GUIDE
Star Guidance
75 Rockefeller Plaza,
New York, 10019.
$3.00, Canada $4.00.
Foreign $5.00, bi-monthly.

GAMES
I-Ching, numerology,
ESP and astrology in game format.
Write to:
Dynamic Games
Midwest Merchandise Mart,
800 North Washington,
Minneapolis,
Minnesota 55401.

ASTROLOGY: THE CELESTIAL MIRROR
Warren Kenton
Themes and Hudson, 1974
$5.85

This diagram designed by the author is a synthesis of astrological principles. Beginning with the rim, it edges our relative view of the world with the fixed stars, one half in night, the other (above the horizon of the ascendant and descendant) in day. This is the stellar background to our existence, and represents in the inner universe the spirit. Next comes the zodiac, arranged with Aries the spring sign coinciding with the dawn of a perfect equinox day of twelve hours light and dark. The winter solstice represents the noon of the spiritual year, the sun being in man the essential point of contact. The next thin band outlines the hours of a classical day with the decans or ten-degree sections and their rulers. Inside this are the mundane houses and key words which enclose a band describing the status of the planets in each sign. The four triangles of the elements, and the three crosses, come next, with the planetary rulers in their active and passive roles; this is the level of the soul. Inside these come the luminaries and planets with their gods, metals, ages of man and psychological key words: finally the elements and the three organic kingdoms. The whole sets out the interacting sets of laws that govern our psyche. Study of its dynamics in conjunction with self-examination illuminates it as a working system and philosophy of cosmic knowledge.

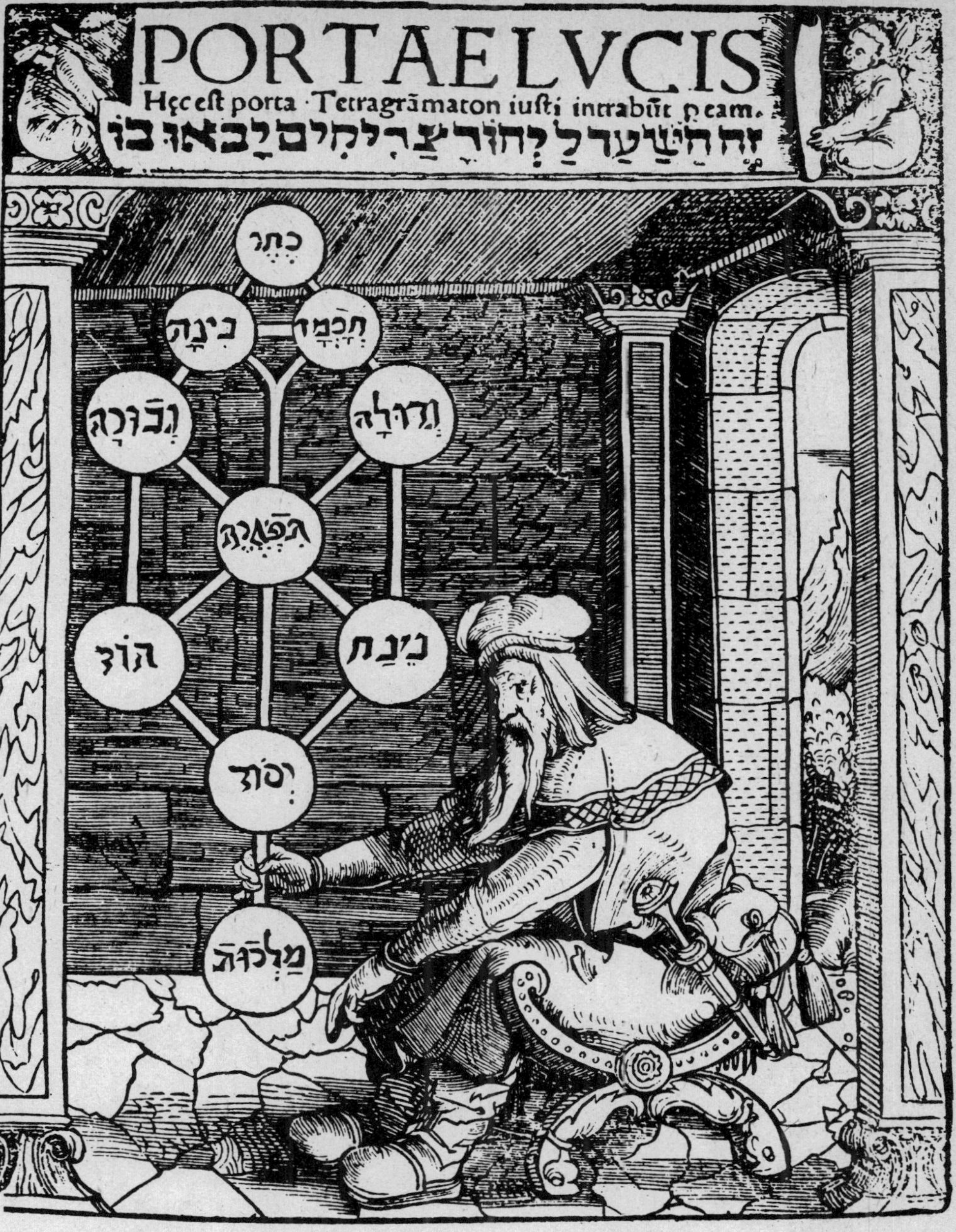

Jewish interest in astrology is evident in the Talmud and Kabbalah. Indeed, Kabbalists placed the planetary gods on the diagram of the Tree of Life, saying that they expressed in mythological and astronomical parallel the qualities of the Divine emanations or Sephiroth whose relationships the Tree defines. In this presentation, the active (right) and passive (left) roles of the planets are defined, as is the central line of consciousness in the luminaries (sun and moon). (Tree of Life, engraving from Ricius' *Portae Lucis*, 1516.)

The Wheel of Fortune was a common astrological theme of medieval times. In this print Mars has his moment of ascendancy, but this will give way to the sun, followed by Venus. The wax and wane of planetary influence was fully appreciated in the tides of fortune for mankind, the wise and the enterprising catching and using the period of each god. For ordinary men there was little choice, because without real knowledge or a flair for timing they were subject to the mass ebb and flow that governs world affairs. Escape was possible from these events, but only if an individual really wanted to choose it. The same situation occurs today. (Wheel of Fortune, page from MS., German, c. 1490.)

MYTHOLOGICAL STAR GLOBE

Printed in 3 colors this transparent star globe shows the 44 ancient or original constellations with drawings of the mythological figures much as the ancient Greeks visualized them in the sky. The drawings are based on the poem, "Phenomena," written by the Greek poet Aratus about 270 B.C. A copy of the poem is included with globe. The 44 "modern" constellations are also named but are without drawings. The present day boundaries of all 88 constellations are shown. Approximately 1100 stars are shown with names of the brighter stars given. By looking through the globe to the concave far side you see the stars (and read their names) as you would see them in a planetarium or in the night sky. An adjustable Sun pointer is provided which shows the apparent positions of the Sun against the stars and it can be set to the current date along the ecliptic circle. The unit provides your personal, local horizon plane which can be rotated by a knob at the south celestial pole. The horizon plane can also be tilted to correspond to your latitude. This is done through a hand hole in the star globe. Miniature human figures are provided and can be affixed at the center of the horizon plane. Degrees of the compass are shown on the horizon plane. A time disc is also provided enabling the globe to exactly correspond to the real sky for the current time. The globe rests on a cradle base which has a magnetic compass to assist in orienting the device to true north.

(without mythological figures) at same price

MS 14H	14" Diameter	$ 89.50
MS 20H	20" Diameter	$140.00

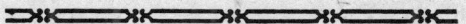

TRANSPARENT CELESTIAL GLOBE

The transparent star globe can be set to show star, sun, and planet positions at any time and place to demonstrate basic earth-space relationships. The star map shows principal stars to the 5th magnitude, names major stars and constellations, and includes the ecliptic, right ascension and declination scales. Mounted within the 12-in. diameter transparent star sphere is an adjustable sun and a new geo-physical Earth Globe that rotates independently. Full horizon mounting included. Study Guide.

300 Size: 16" x 14" x 14" **$55.00**

BASIC TRANSPARENT CELESTIAL GLOBE

The economical Basic Transparent Celestial Globe with new geo-physical Earth Globe has been designed to teach earth-space relationships at the beginning level of astronomy. This simplified teaching aid features a 4-inch diameter terrestrial globe mounted within a 12-inch diameter star globe, plus adjustable sun model. Both globes and the sun may be easily set to show the positions of the stars and planets for any time and place. Study Guide.

310 Size: 12" x 12" x 14" **$40.00**

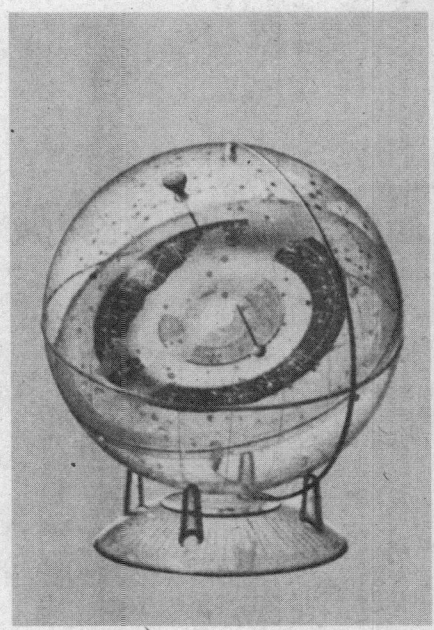

PLANETARY CELESTIAL GLOBE

A model of the inner planet orbits has been mounted within the celestial sphere enabling positions of Mercury, Venus, Earth and Mars to be plotted without the use of planetary tables. Earth model may be positioned from outside the sphere, and the planets may be marked through the year 2000. Developed by Herbert R. Baerg at the Jet Propulsion Laboratory for NASA. Study Guide.

305 12" diameter **$50.00**

NATIONAL ASTROLOGICAL SOCIETY

The National Astrological Society (NASO) is a non-profit tax exempt organization formed in 1969. NASO's goals are to promote high standards of practice and instruction, facilitate communication among Astrologers through meetings and publications, and to foster cooperation among persons and organizations interested in the study of Astrology.

Activities of the Association

Annual Meetings NASO holds an annual Spring Conference in various cities throughout North America. These meetings consist of discussions, talks, and seminars on various aspects of Astrological teaching and research.

Journal of the National Astrological Society Subscription to NASO Journal is included in NASO membership. The Journal has 2 aims: (1) to act as an information bulletin of current events in Astrology and related fields providing listings of study programs, current research, international visitors, news of members, and other conferences. (2) to include the publication of scholarly articles in all disciplines concerned with astrological studies.

Placement Service. NASO provides interested persons and organizations with the names of specialists in astrological studies. A special lecture bureau has been established to engage speakers for Astrology and college groups.

Research and Education. The NASO School of Astrology is an educational institution for the training of Astrologers and also offers a program of professional level seminars. A resident Library has been established. Members who wish to donate their publications will help to promote the growth of a complete resource library.

Computer Oriented Research Access to IBM computing facilities is available at minimal costs for members with high level projects.

Qualified Astrologers are eligible to become professional members (voting). The other category of membership (non-voting) is Associate. Annual dues are $10.00 for professional and Associate Members. Life Membership is $100.00.

Groups who wish to be affiliated with NASO must (1) hold regularly scheduled lectures; (2) provide classes; and (3) possess a reference library. Membership is $10.00 annually.

YOUR PERSONAL ASTROLOGY
Published by Star Guidance, Inc.
315 Park Avenue South, New York, N.Y. 10010.
Quarterly $2.00, Canada $2.50
$3.00 Foreign.

AMERICAN ASTROLOGY
Clancy Publications,
2505 N. Alvernon Way,
Tucson, Arizona, 85712,
$7.00. Monthly.

HOROSCOPE
Subscription Department,
Box 4800
Marion, Ohio 43302.

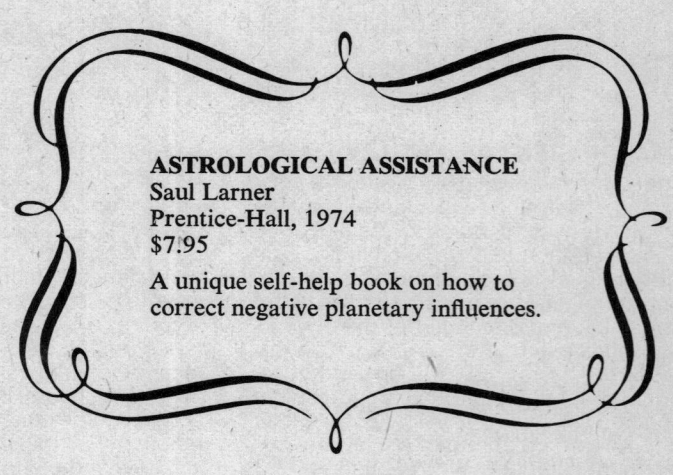

ASTROLOGICAL ASSISTANCE
Saul Larner
Prentice-Hall, 1974
$7.95

A unique self-help book on how to correct negative planetary influences.

AQUARIAN AGENT
Distributed and published bimonthly by
Astrology Services International, Inc.
127 Madison Ave., N.Y., N.Y. 10016

Subscription is $11 for 12 issues
(2 years), $20 for 24 issues (4 years).

NATIONAL ASTROLOGICAL SOCIETY
127 Madison Ave.
New York, N.Y. 10016

THE ASTROLOGY NEWSPAPER: RISING SUN
P.O. box 4868
North Hollywood, Calif. 91607
$5.00 per year; outside U.S. $5.50
Monthly

FACULTY OF ASTROLOGICAL STUDIES LONDON SCHOOL OF ASTROLOGY (EVENING CLASSES)

A Certificate Course course designed especially for beginners is now available. The Faculty also offers a correspondence course. For either course apply for prospectus and full details to: The Registrar, G. M. Hayward, B.A., Hook Cottage, Vines Cross, Heathfield, Sussex.

A HANDBOOK FOR THE HUMANISTIC ASTROLOGER
Michael R. Meyer
Anchor, 1974
$4.50

SKY DIAMONDS: THE NEW ASTROLOGY
Owen S. Rachleff
Hawthorn, 1973
$7.95

ASTRAL CONSULTANTS
Horoscope charts and interpretations
box 5651, Columbia, S.C. 9205

AN ASTROLOGICAL MANDALA: THE CYCLE OF TRANSFORMATIONS AND ITS 360 SYMBOLIC PHASES
Dane Rudhyar
Vintage, 1974
$2.45

ASTROLOGY AND PSYCHOLOGICAL WARFARE DURING WWII
Ellie Howe
Rider, 1972
$6.25

A TIME FOR ASTROLOGY
Jess Stearn
Signet, 1972
$1.50

THE CASE FOR ASTROLOGY
John Anthony West and Jan Gerhard Toonder
Penguin, 1973
$2.15

ASTROLOGY: A FASCINATING HISTORY
P. I. H. naylor
Wilshire Book Co., 1967
$2.00

ASTROLOGICAL ORIGINS
Cyril Fagan
Llewllyn Publications, 1973
$2.95

ASTROLOGY AND RELIGION AMONG THE GREEKS AND ROMANS
Franz Cumont
Dover, 1960
$1.35

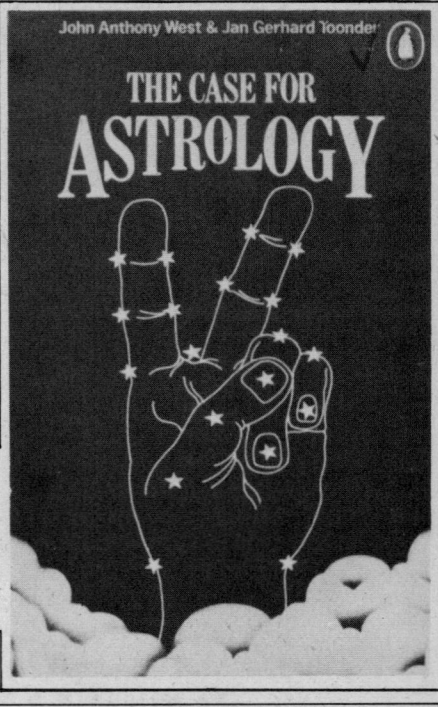

Published by ASTROLOGERS' GUILD of AMERICA, Inc.
520 Fifth Avenue, New York, New York 10036

The Astrological Review

FOUNDED 1929

PUBLISHED QUARTERLY
Subscribers in Pan-American Postal Union countries add $1 per year. Other countries add $2 per year.

One Year $8
Two years $15
Three years $21

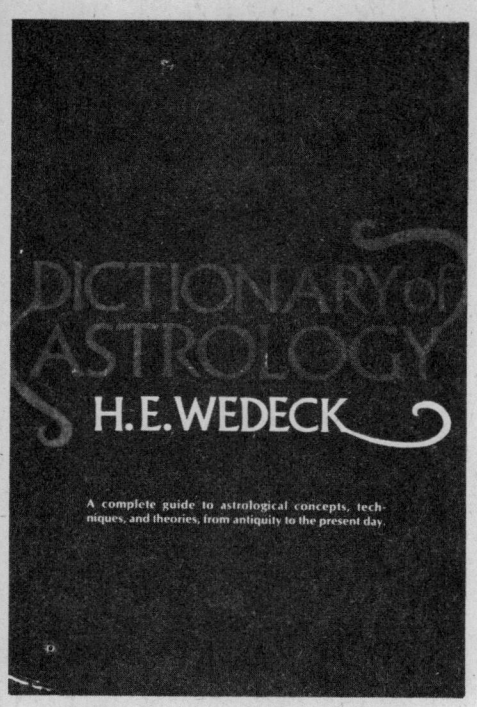

DICTIONARY OF ASTROLOGY
H. E. wedeck
The Citadel Press, 1973
$3.95

EGYPT

Ancient Egypt had the most profound knowledge and interest in astrology. One of the most eminent authorities on Egyptian astrology was Franz Cumont (1868–1947), Professor at the University of Ghent, in Belgium. He is the author of a study entitled *L'Egypte des Astrologues*.

It was anciently believed, on the other hand, that the Egyptians acquired their astrological knowledge from the Ethiopians.

EGYPTIAN AFTERLIFE

In the tombs of Egyptian kings papyri have been found inscribed with astronomical and astrological information as guides in the journey through the afterlife.

EGYPTIAN ASTROLOGY

In ancient Egypt Virgo, the zodiacal sign, represented the goddess Isis. It was also a hermaphroditic symbol.

EGYPTIAN CALENDER

In 4241 B.C. the Egyptian calendar was introduced. It consisted of twelve months of thirty days each, plus five feast days.

THE MAYO SCHOOL OF ASTROLOGY
Principal: Jeff Mayo, D.F.Astrol.S., F.R. Met.S.
(formerly the Course for External students of the Faculty of Astrological Studies)

Correspondence course in astrology. U.S. and overseas. Basic and Advanced Courses leading to Diploma. Up-to-date comprehensive study by means of textbook, instruction letters, test papers, individual advice and correction from qualified, experienced tutors. Jeff Mayo has personally taught students for 16 years in over 80 countries. Send stamp for Prospectus to The Mayo School of Astrology)dept. P) "Piper's Wood", Slackhead, Beetham, Milnthorpe, Westmorland.

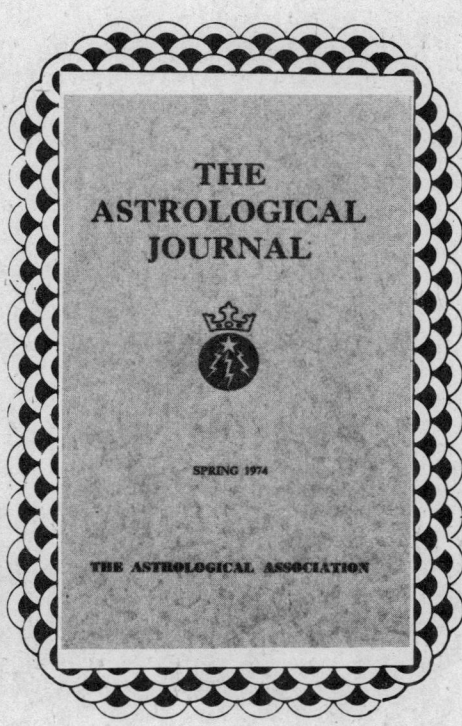

ASTROLOGICAL Lodge of THE Theosophical Society.

Membership which is open to all seriously interested in the study of Astrology, confers benefits of Quarterly Magazine, Library, Discussion Group, Beginners Class 6:15 p.m., Public Lectures on Mondays at 7 p.m.—50 Gloucester Place, W.I. Refreshments served. For prospectus send S.A.E. to the Hon. Sec. at above address.

THE ASTROLOGICAL JOURNAL
Publications Department
5 Alyth Road,
Talbot Woods,
Bournemouth BH3 7DF, England.
Issued quarterly by:
The Astrological Association
membership fees 3 per annum

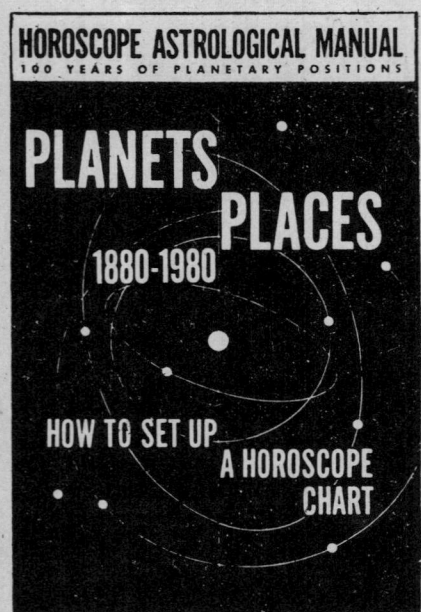

NEW, REVISED, ENLARGED EDITION NOW AVAILABLE!

HOROSCOPE ASTROLOGICAL MANUAL
100 YEARS OF PLANETARY POSITIONS

PLANETS PLACES 1880-1980

HOW TO SET UP A HOROSCOPE CHART

HOROSCOPE MAGAZINE has prepared a booklet, containing the tables that show the sign position of the planets for any date from 1880 to 1980 inclusive—Neptune, Uranus, Saturn, Jupiter, Mars, Venus, and Mercury—also the Moon's place, by sign and degree, for any date during these years. This booklet also contains directions for setting up your own horoscope chart; we have reprinted in this handy booklet the articles that gave these instructions in the magazine some years ago. The entire booklet, with directions for erecting an individual chart and the sign positions of all planets, will be sent you postage prepaid. Send only $1.00 to

PLANETS' PLACES
Dell Publishing Co., Inc.
Post Office Box 3000
Pinebrook, N.J. 07058

ASSOCIATION OF ASTROLOGY, METAPHYSICS, AND PSYCHIC SCIENCES
(AMPS)
P.O. Box 6045 HD
Toledo, Ohio 43614

Aims and Objectives

1. To organize members into small groups for the purpose of discussion and study.
2. To promote interest in the study of metaphysical and occult subjects.
3. To unite members into a firm purpose of helping each other to become more proficient in their particular occult interest.
4. To organize seminars in various cities throughout the states.
5. To promote fellowship through public lectures and exchange of knowledge.
6. To open occult centers for the study and promotion of astrology, metaphysics, and psychic sciences.
7. To inspire the membership to promote and raise funds for an occult center in their city.

Until the funds become available for a center, AMPS will continue to organize and promote interest in these subjects. We will do this through various lectures and regular meetings at different locations.

●

SIMPLIFIED SCIENTIFIC ASTROLOGY: HOW TO CHART YOUR HOROSCOPE
Max Heindel,
Wilshire Book Co., 1974
$2.00

●

ZODIAC AND SWASTIKA: HOW ASTROLOGY GUIDED HITLER'S GERMANY
Wilhelm Wulff
Coward, McCann & Geoghegan, 1973
$5.95

ASTROLOGY
Aleister Crowley
Weiser, 1974
$7.95

●

ASTROLOGY FOR EVERYONE
Edward Lindoe
Dutton, 1970
$5.95

●

ESSAYS ON THE FOUNDATIONS OF ASTROLOGY
C. E. O. carter
$5.00
Dorothy B. Hughes
1833 Queen Anne Avenue
North Seattle, Wash. 98109.

●

THE ASTROLOGER'S HANDBOOK
Frances Sakoian and Louis S. Acker
Harper & Row, 1973
$9.95

●

THE ASTROLOGER'S GUIDE
fi$—%
$3.75
The American Federation of Astrologers
6 Library Court, S.E.,
Washington D.C. 20003

●

ENCYCLOPAEDIA OF MEDICAL ASTROLOGY H. L. cornell
Weiser, 1972
$15.00

PRACTICAL DOWSING—A SYMPOSIUM
A.H. Bell, ed.,
G. Bell and Sons Ltd., 1965
$5.00

SOCIETY FOR THE APPLICATION OF FREE ENERGY (SAFE)

The Society for the Application of Free Energy (SAFE) was formed in the Fall of 1972, and was incorporated in the District of Columbia as a non-profit educational and scientific organization.

The purpose and objectives of SAFE are to study, research, use and seek practical applications of the disciplines of dowsing, radionics, radiesthesia, and healing to meeting and serving the needs of mankind.

The founders of SAFE have recognized the need for an organization which can now focus on, and develop the "life energy" bioscience areas, and thus transfer any potential benefits derived to various human problem areas. It has been noted that this can best be achieved in a scientific, impartial, creative, and open-minded atmosphere.

Although the initial SAFE Chapter was set up in the nation's capital, Washington, D.C., SAFE is organized to be a truly national organization and responsive to the needs of all of its members and associates. It is strongly desired to set up SAFE chapters in other areas, and full support will be given to sponsors of these new chapters. Current plans call for a national convention to be held in 1974 to emphasize these bioscience areas. This convention will be the first of its kind to be held in North America, and is a pioneering effort, as are all SAFE activities.

The by-laws and articles of SAFE have been written to ensure that the Society's actions will be guided by the highest standards of morality, honesty, and integrity. All SAFE activities are, and shall be, carried out within the framework of established law; no encouragement or support shall be given to those who depart from established legal or moral standards. Equal rights are guaranteed to members of all geographic areas of the North American continent.

Some special areas of SAFE interest include:
DOWSING—Use as an exploratory tool in natural resource development and in archaeology.
RADIONICS—Use in insect control to neutralize harmful pests through non-chemical means and to enhance crop growth and yield.
HEALING—Study of those with this paranormal ability and investigating the L-fields ("life energy fields", as denoted by Dr. H. S. Burr and E. W. Russell) so that this human potential can be better understood and applied.
RADIESTHESIA—Investigation of human sensitivity to the vibratory effects created by living organisms as well as those effects inherent in inanimate objects.

Annual membership in SAFE can be obtained by sending $10.00, payable to SAFE, to Mrs. Edith Serbin at 1036 Ruatan Street, Silver Spring, Maryland 20903.

Details on setting up SAFE Chapters, research projects, etc., can be received by writing to Ms. Susan J. Rice, National Secretary of S.A.F.E. 1143 New Hampshire Avenue, N.W., Washington, D.C. 20037.

An independent, non-profit organization devoted to applying dowsing, radionics, radiesthesia, and healing to meeting and serving the needs of mankind.

Chamber in Handle Holds Materials to be Dowsed

Sensitive spring amplifies and focuses signals

Vibroscopic DIVINING ROD

The Vibroscopic Divining Rod is like no other dowsing instrument we know. It is used by professional dowsers when they search for water, oil, valuable metals, lost jewelry. Parapsychology views dowsing as a natural talent latent in many persons. Instruments such as the Vibroscopic Divining Rod are used merely to manifest or focus it.

Even dowsers don't agree whether vibrations are received from the object or whether dowsing is a kind of psychic ability akin to clairvoyance. Skeptics deny it exists at all — yet there are thousands of dowsers in the U.S. and a national association to which many of them belong. Perhaps you have this controversial ability. Using the Vibroscopic Divining Rod is fun as a parlor game, too!

Price $5.95
Complete instructions for use included
Please add 50c postage and handling.

VENTURE BOOKSHOP
P.O. Box 249, Highland Park, Ill. 60035

From *De Re Metallica*, by G. Agricola, 1556

WELCOME ASD
TO
DANVILLE
HOME OF THE
DOWSERS

103

We want you to learn about the AMERICAN SOCIETY OF DOWSERS, INC. We want to provide you with a capsule acquaintance with dowsing, one of the few areas of human experience that tunes man in with the unknown.

Dowsing is the name given to a human capability that allows one to obtain practical information either to help you personally or to serve the general needs of our culture. Such information comes to the dowser in some manner beyond the operation of the standard human senses. Intelligent use of dowsing as a searching tool is possible in spite of the obvious mystery about how dowsing operates.

How and Why the Society was Formed

In the fall of 1958 about 50 persons were drawn to Danville, Vermont for a one-day meeting which was advertised as a *"National Dowsing Convention."* This meeting was sponsored by a local committee as a feature of Fall Foliage Week observance in a three-county region to attract tourists. The newspaper wire services picked up the item as an oddity and gave the meeting wide publicity. The 50 who were attracted by this news item came from eight states. Most were dowsers. We had to make our own program for the day. And we realized that probably never before had so many individuals met in this country just to talk about dowsing. To our pleased surprise, talking freely and exchanging ideas and demonstrating individual techniques created a common bond of interest. In 1959 and 1960 the meeting again was advertised. Many there in 1958 returned and others appeared. We still had to arrange an informal program for the day.

In 1960 we chose a steering committee to assure a better format for future meetings. By the spring of 1961 an application for a charter as a non-profit corporation in the State of Vermont was prepared. Eleven of the steering committee met and signed the charter application, and, in a few weeks received the charter,

A general membership meeting was called for the fall of 1961, again at Danville during Fall Foliage Week. A simple informational program was presented. Nearly 100 attended and became charter members of the AMERICAN SOCIETY OF DOWSERS, INC.

Our Goal

The 11 who signed the application for the charter were mature business and professional men. Most could dowse and had varying amounts of experience in finding water for others. And they had been subject to skepticism and ridicule for believing in dowsing. They knew that dowsing had helped and could continue to help many people with many kinds of needs.

The motivation for the formation of our Society was accepted at the time of founding as obvious. The objectives of this motivation were spelled out thus:

1. To give dowsing a stature of dignity and authority.
2. To win for dowsing prestige and respectful recognition for its great worth.
3. To help members in their dowsing problems.
4. To give assistance, guidance and encouragement to beginners.
5. To disseminate dowsing knowledge and information to as large a group as possible.

Later our Society added the initiation of research and the co-ordination of research by others, has moved to interest our Federal government in making use of dowsing to develop natural resources, and to build up a source of information about dowsing, including a library.

A Brief History of Dowsing

In the caves of Tassili, in the Atlas Mountains of North Africa, is a huge wall drawing of a dowser at work surrounded by onlookers. It has been dated by the Carbon 14 technique as at least 8,000 years of age. This is the first knowledge of dowsing which can be proved.

Dowsing was well accepted in Europe when this country was discovered. While this country was being colonized there was an imperative need for water and the colonists transferred their dowsing skill from the old world to the new. The dowser was a respected member of the community and it was commonly said that a man undertaking to dig a well without consulting a dowser was a fool. It is estimated that our colonial forebears developed several hundred thousand wells by depending on the advice of dowsers.

The consistent use of dowsing persisted until about the end of the last century. About that time scientific technology began to exert its influence on our culture and since dowsing proved to be outside the understanding of science it was by-passed by orthodox scholarship. More communities were served by municipal water systems although dowsing continued in a lessened degree, particularly in rural areas.

Recent Developments

Some 25 years ago a sudden expansion in suburban building brought urgent calls for dowsing. The quiet, competent country dowser again received attention, often after a land owner had paid a driller heavily for unsuccessful attempts to obtain water.

Other factors set the stage for new and perceptive uses of dowsing. Knowledge spread that this human searching tool could be applied to a tremendous range of needs. Dowsing was used, first in Europe, for prospecting for mineral deposits.

Currently, through dowsing, lost articles are found, archaeological sites unearthed, criminals tracked, missing persons found, downed aircraft located, malfunctions in home appliances pinpointed, etc.

Modern Dowsing Methods

The traditional method finds the dowser walking over a field, his instrument in position, watching for the moment when it starts to respond. Today the skilled dowser stands at the edge of the field and determines, from a distance, exactly where the water vein is located. Or, if particularly skilled, the modern dowser zeroes in on his target from a map with equal accuracy. And distance is no barrier to map dowsing. He can dowse across the street or across the ocean with equal facility.

Who Can Dowse?

Everyone is born with this capability and children up to the age of 15 or 16 are almost universally sensitive. However, it has been established that in any group of 25 adults between two and five will obtain the dowsing reaction immediately when properly instructed. Others may have to practice for a while.

Those who discover they can dowse stand on the threshold of fascinating and challenging experiences. Practice searches normally should be for water sources. Once the interest really gets to you, you will find yourself putting in many hours of practice. Membership in the Society will lead you to answers to the questions which will arise. Our quarterly, THE AMERICAN DOWSER, has instructions for beginners and more technical material for advanced dowsers.

In its pages you will find activities of other dowsers with whom you may correspond. You learn about new techniques and new uses of dowsing. Everyone is welcome at our annual convention held in mid-September at Danville, Vt. You will listen to speakers of world renown and receive individual and group coaching. You see manufactured dowsing devices on display. You meet with those active in dowsing in this country and abroad.

Using Dowsing Skills

When you find that you can get a response from whichever dowsing instrument you use you may feel that you are ready to carry on all kinds of searches. You may be fortunate and make some successful searches with very little experience and preparation. You will soon find, however, that very much practice is necessary if you wish to become consistently successful. Our Society very frankly calls attention to this fact. Membership in the Society will help you to attain a high standard in your work.

The Mystery of Dowsing

You will find many ideas presented on what makes dowsing work. The Society believes that much study still remains to be done before all the facets of the dowsing process can be explained in terms of what is already known in the scientific field and in the field of human behavior and functioning. Your interest in dowsing may turn in the direction of the study of this mystery. There is opportunity for you to contribute to man's knowledge. You will find the study of dowsing a true pioneering venture.

How to Join the Society

An application may be mailed directly to the *American Society of Dowsers, Inc.*, Danville, Vt. 05828, with the annual dues. The fiscal year starts October 1. Whenever you join you are assured of receiving all four copies of the quarterly, THE AMERICAN DOWSER, for that year.

 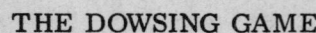 

INSTRUCTIONS FOR THE DOWSING GAME

Introduction

This fascinating game can be played anywhere with two to two hundred people, and is suitable for ages from 10 years upward. The game can make an instant success out of a cocktail party or make an exciting classroom demonstration of the science of parapsychology (ESP or extra sensory perception).

Outline of Game

The game basically is a demonstration of how ESP can be used to locate hidden objects. Starting with a group of people (from 2 upward), one person is chosen (or volunteers) to be the "finder". The "finder" should have an open or positive attitude toward ESP, since his chance of success will be greatly enhanced if this is the case. With the "finder" in the room, the group chooses an object to be hidden. It is preferable that a personal object be chosen. These should be in pairs or should be two objects which have some connection with one another. For example, a pair of gloves may be used, two matching coins from a person's pocket, two rings from someone's hand, etc., are other examples. If personal objects cannot be found, impersonal items such as two halves of a piece of paper, two like pieces of fruit from a fruit bowl, etc. can be used. When the object to be hidden is chosen, the "finder" is sent out of the room, preferably in the presence of another person, to guard against peeking. He takes along with him the dowsing pendulum in order to familiarize himself with its operation (see following section). At the same time, he takes along ONE of the chosen items.

While the "finder" is out of the room, the remaining group hides the SECOND ITEM somewhere within the room. When this is done, the "finder" (and his escort) are brought back and the search begins.

The search is made in a systematic fashion by the "finder", using the lucite dowsing pendulum. First a rough outline of the room is made on a piece of paper by a member of the group (see diagram).

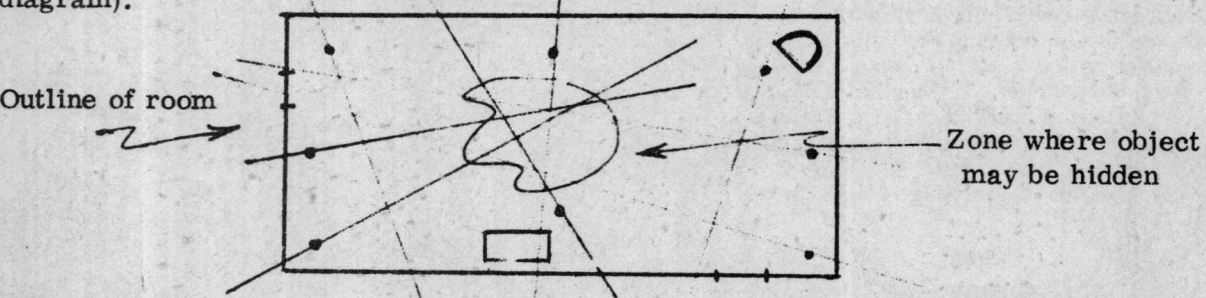

The "finder" then proceeds to any corner (CR) or any wall center (CT) of the room and stands facing into the room as close to the wall as possible.

The approximate position of the "finder" is marked on the diagram with a dot. If a piece of furniture is in the way, the "finder" may stand in front of it. His position is marked as shown in the lower right corner of the diagram. Holding the pendulum in one hand and the "mate" object in the other, the "finder" asks mentally for the pendulum to swing in the direction of the hidden object. He should take care to hold his hand with the pendulum as still as possible and concentrate on having the pendulum swing in the unknown direction. Within 10 to 15 seconds, the pendulum should start swinging. A member of the group should record the direction of swing on the diagram, starting at the point representing the "finder" (see lines drawn on diagram). After recording, the "finder" moves to a second position and the entire procedure is repeated. The "finder" thus continues until all eight points in the room are recorded, providing a map which should reveal the location of the missing "mate". During this procedure, the finder should not be allowed to see the map in the making, since seeing it may subconsciously effect his performance.

Finally, the "finder" takes the map and observes whether a majority of the lines pass through any given area. If this is the case, the hidden object is usually to be located in that zone. It is fascinating to find how often the lines converge exactly on the area in which the hidden object is located.

Further Sophistication

In some cases, two areas may be found where a large number of lines cross. If this occurs, the "finder" may hold his pendulum over one area of the map (or, if he prefers, go to that area of the room). He then asks the pendulum to rotate in a clockwise fashion, if the hidden object is in that zone. He then does the same thing for the other zone. The pendulum will usually show, by rotating strongly in one place or the other, which area contains the hidden object.

In many cases, there may be many places within the zone where the object may be hidden. The "finder" may wish to "ask" the pendulum to rotate in a clockwise manner when it is held over each place in question. The pendulum will usually rotate strongly when held over or near the missing object.

The pendulum used in this game is identical to those used by professional dowsers to locate oil, water, minerals, hidden treasure, missing persons, downed airplanes, lost ships at sea, etc., etc.

DOWSING SUPPLY COMPANY

"DOWSING SUPPLY COMPANY"
of North America
P. O. Box 28
St. Bruno, Quebec, Canada
J3V 4P8

Established 1961
(Formerly of East
Kingston, N. H.)

The complete catalogue for books and supplies on Dowsing and Radiesthesia.

The complete catalogue for books and supplies on Dowsing and Radiesthesia.

General Books on Dowsing

"Dowsing, An Introduction to an Ancient Practice", Gordon MacLean, Sr. A brand new edition of the already famous book on how to dowse. A must for all beginning and serious dowsers.
(soft cover) $2.00

"The Diving Rod", Barrett and Besterman. Probably the best known book ever written on dowsing. First published in 1926, it has now become the "bible" of dowsing. $7.50

"The Pendulum and Possession", William Finch. A complete kit including book, pendulum and pad of charts. The book contains complete instructions on the theory and use of the pendulum in all fields. Special emphasis is placed on human personality and health. (kit) $4.00

"Resonating Reflex", Rev. John Rudd. An excellent book for beginner and experienced dowser explaining the use and theories of the angle rods. Undoubtedly the best book on the angle rods yet written. A "lucid and factual monograph" — J. Cecil Maby. $7.00

"Aquavideo", V. Cameron. A good book for beginners which introduces them to a wide range of dowsing techniques. Clear and well illustrated. (soft cover) $4.95

"Map Dowsing", V. Cameron (Dowser's Handbook Series No. 1). An excellent guide in the use of the pendulum for map dowsing. (soft cover) $2.75

"Oil Locating", Verne Cameron (Dowser's Handbook No. 2). Complete instructions on locating oil using pendulum techniques. (soft cover) $2.75

"Elementary Radiesthesia", F. A. Archdale. An introduction to the use of the pendulum, including applications in health, food and agriculture. $1.95

"The Science of Water-Witching", Karl George. The observations, experiences and research of many years of dowsing. $3.95

"Practical Dowsing", A. H. Bell. An excellent symposium on dowsing of every kind by dowsing experts. $6.50

"Principles and Practice of Radiesthesia", Abbe Mermet. A translation of the work of the world's most famous pendulum dowser. Describes techniques for near and far dowsing. $6.50

"The Elements of Dowsing", Henry DeFrance. An elementary and practical guide for the beginner. $2.95

"Ghost and Divining Rod", T. C. Lethbridge. A controversial but delightful book linking the mechanisms of dowsing to ghosts. Considerable instructions on the use of the pendulum are given. $4.95

"Introduction to Medical Radiesthesia", V. D. Wethered. A description of the use of the pendulum for diagnosis and treatment by radionic methods. $6.00

"The Practice of Medical Radiesthesia", V. D. Wethered. Further practical applications of the radionic method. $6.00

"The Cameron Aurameter", Borderline Science Foundation. This is an excellent review of the work of the famous Vernon Cameron. $5.00

"The Eyes, Brain and Nerve System an relation to the Earths Magnetism", H. St. L. Cookes. This is an extensive study on just why people are able to dowse and the influences that cause a dowsing reaction. $7.00

"Water Witching U.S.A.", Vogt & Hyman. A negative scientific analysis of dowsing. $7.00

"The Divining Rod", A. J. Ellis. The only official publication of the U.S. Government on the subject of dowsing. Published in 1917 by the U.S. Geological Survey, the book gives a negative account of dowsing. A good study for the serious minded student, since it contains over 500 references. $2.50

"Radiation, Magnetism, and Living Things", Daniel S. Halacy, Jr. A clear and well written scientific work describing just about every physical environmental factor which can interact with living organisms and human beings. Discusses possible dowsing mechanisms, telepathy, biological clocks, hypnotism, etc. $4.95

"Possible Physiological Causes of Dowsing", S. W. Tromp. Scientific theories and experiments showing mechanisms for dowsing. (Article in Internation Journal of Parapsychology). This journal also contains article describing Cleve Baxter's work in communicating with plants.) $2.00

"Biological Effects of Magnetic Fields", M. Barnothy, editor. Two collections of research papers by the foremost researchers in the field of biomagnetics on the effects of magnetic fields on humans and living organisms.
Volume I 324 pages $20.00
Volume II 306 pages $17.50

Books of General Interest

"The Brain Revolution", Marilyn Ferguson. Every important area of current research is covered from parapsychological phenomena to electronic stimulation of the brain. This book is called the "Future Shock" of mind science. $9.95

"Biological Rhythms in Human and Animal Physiology", Gay G. Luce of the National Institute of Mental Health. The complete guide to the role of biological rhythms and their influence upon us both physically and mentally. $3.50

"Report on Radonics", Edward W. Russell. A very recent insight into Radonics which is sometimes called "The science of the future which can cure where orthodox medicine fails". $10.00

"Magnets and Magnetic Fields or Healing by Magnets", Davis & Bhattacharyya. This book takes a look at the research done in India probing the many hidden secrets in magnetic fields. $6.50

"Gem Therapy", A. K. Bhattacharyya D. M. S. (revised and enlarged edition). Gems have been used in India as medicine from time immemorial. This is an excellent look into this very interesting area of research in India and their reasons why gem therapy should have a place among the numerous medical systems of the world. $6.50

"Passages" The delightful guide for the pilgrims of the mind. $5.00

"Pyramid Power" Dr. Pat Flanagan. The first modern study of Pyramids and their role in the bio-energy; this is a must for those doing Pyramid research. $7.00

"Wishcraft", Helen Hadsell. The name it and claim it game with wineuvers for wishcraft by the woman who wins every contest she enters — Great book! $3.00

"The Human Aura", Dr. Walter J. Kilner. Considered the most comprehensive studies on the Human Aura by medical science. $7.50

"The Secret Science Behind Miracles", Max Freedom Long — The Study of the Kahunas and their magic and philosophy. $6.50

"The Seth Material", Jane Roberts — The extraordinary time story of a "personality who has dictated over 5,000 pages on reincarnation, clairvoyance and the universe beyond the five senses. $3.95

Supplies

All articles sold by the Dowsing Supply Company are supplied with complete instructions. The material is sufficient to provide both lay person and researchers complete background for further study of the phenomenon of dowsing. The Dowsing Supply Company assumes no responsibility for, nor makes any claims to the accuracy of effectiveness of the materials supplied. We do however select are books and materials with great care with the idea that they are sold for information and experimental purposes only.

Beginners "Y" Rod Kit — These rods are similar to the classic "forked sticks" used by dowsers for centuries. They were originally made from wood, however, modern professional dowsers usually use synthetic materials, such as the rod included in the kit. This beginners' kit includes a professional but inexpensive plastic Y rod, complete with instructions. $3.50

Beginners' Pendulum Kit — This beginners' kit features a handsome plastic ball pendulum used by most dowsers in Europe. Can be used for water, mineral or oil dowsing, as well as map, missing persons, treasure dowsing, etc. 1¼" Clear acrylic ball $5.00

"The Dowsing Game" — This fascinating game can be played with two to two hundred people and is suitable for ages from 10 years old. The game consists of sending someone out of the room with the pendulum. An object is hidden, and the person reenters the room and attempts to find the hidden object with the dowsing pendulum. The pendulum itself consists of a beautiful clear 1½ inch diameter lucite ball on a gold chain. This pendulum is a professional model and is used by many dowsers throughout the country. $5.00

Angle Rods — 3/16 inch diameter cold rolled steel angle (or L) rods with plastic handles. Excellent for professional or intermediate dowser who wants to try new techniques. $5.00

Pendulums — Flawless Clear Solid Acrylic Plastic Spheres with Gold Chain — Can be used as crystal ball.
2 inch diameter $10.00
1¾ inch diameter $ 7.50
1½ inch diameter* $ 5.00
1¼ inch diameter $ 3.50
*Standard professional model.

Hollow Conical Pendulum. Clear with screw cap for inserting "witness". 1 inch diameter by 1½ in. long with nylon monofiliment. $8.00

Hollow Conical Pendulum. Same as above except black. $7.50

"Torpedo" Pendulum. Simulated ivory pendulum with screw cap for "witness". ¾ in. diameter by 1¼ in. long with nylon monofilament. $8.00

Natural Wood Pendulum. 1½ in. diameter (solid). $2.00

Cylindrical "Tantalum" Pendulum with pointer. Excellent for chart work. ¼ in. dia. by 1 in. long. $3.50

MAGER ROSETTE—A brilliant 2½ inch diameter disc divided into eight colored segments. Excellent for use with pendulum. $5.00

"Y" Rod Standard — This is the standard 18" size professional model made of special plastic for good reaction and sensitivity. $6.00

"The Water Dowsers" A delightful western style song about water dowsers on 45 rpm record. A conversation piece which is a must for all dowsers. $1.00

"AURAMETER" This incredibly sensitive dowsing instrument was designed and used by Vernon Cameron to great success. We recommend it only to experienced dowsers. $49.50

For our complete catalogue on Dowsing and Radiesthesia plus our new catalogue of books (and many other things of interest) on "Concepts, Sciences and the Philosophy of the New Age" send $1.00 to:

DOWSING SUPPLY COMPANY Reg'd
P. O. Box 28
St. Bruno, Quebec, Canada
J3V 4P8

Ordering instructions: Please send certified check or money order for the total amount plus 10% to cover postage and handling. We ship all orders (with very few exceptions) by first class mail because of favorable Canadian postal rates. Full refund given on all items returned within 10 days.

THE ELEMENTS OF DOWSING
Henry DeFrance
translated by A. H. Bell
G. Bell & Sons, 1971
$2.50

DOWSING: AN INTRODUCTION TO AN ANCIENT PRACTICE
Gordon MacLean, Sr.
Write to: Gordon MacLean, Sr.,
30 Day Street,
South Portland, Maine 04106

MAP DOWSING—THE DOWSER'S HANDBOOK SERIES, no. 1
Verne L. Cameron, edited and prepared by Bill Cox and Georgiana Teeple
El Cariso Publications, 1971
$2.75

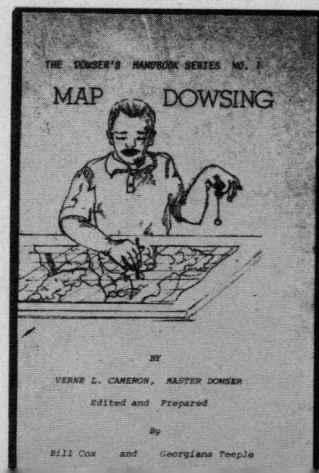

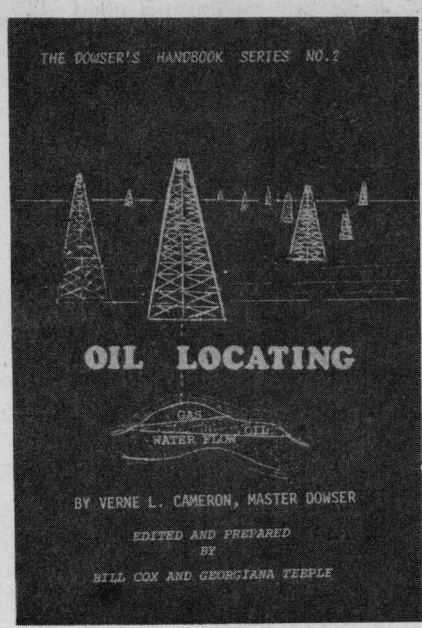

OIL LOCATING: THE DOWSER'S HANDBOOK
Series No. 2
Verne L. Cameron, edited and prepared by Bill Cox and Georgiana Teeple
El Cariso Publication, 1971
$2.75

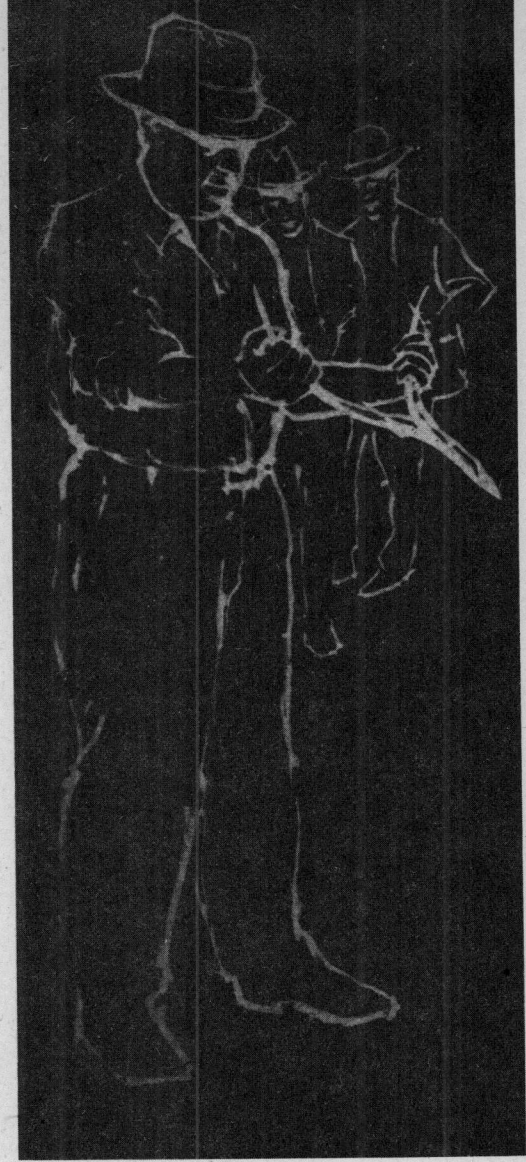

"AQUAVIDEO"

AQUA: Latin for WATER
VIDEO: I SEE

The name, AQUAVIDEO, coined and conceived by Verne L. Cameron is an exciting, profusely illustrated account of the Old Master's highly developed *"Sensory - eye"* technique for SEEING into the underground to locate the UNSEEN, "Virgin" (Primary) water flowing in substrata stream beds.

Cameron shows how one without previous knowledge of Dowsing - and using only a crude, forked-switch - can immediately attain a surprising degree of dowsing skill.

AQUAVIDEO explores the myths of so-called WATER WITCHING and unlocks the deep mysteries of DIVINING. It reveals an accumulation of knowledge gained in a lifetime of enthusiastic study and experimentation in the Dowsing science, spanning nearly a half-century, by the greatest Master of them all.

Here he clearly explains the three powers so essential to successful Dowsing: The PHYSICAL, METAPHYSICAL, and *DIVINE PRESENCE*.

In the third stage one senses the location of underground water through intuition or a state of knowing-"the POWER", says Cameron, "that puts the DIVINE in DIVINING."

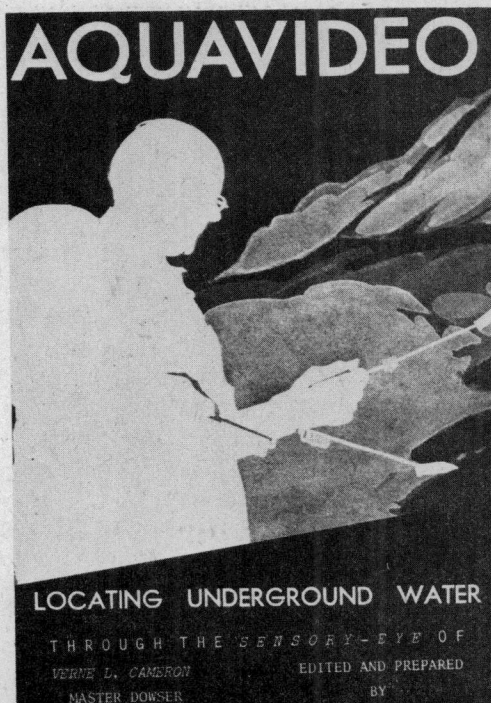

AQUAVIDEO—LOCATING UNDERGROUND WATER
Verne L. Cameron and Bill Cox
El Cariso Publications, 1970
$4.95

Instructions for handling and use of
The CAMERON AURAMETER
(Manufactured and exclusively distributed by: El Cariso Publications P.O. Box 176, Elsinore, Ca-92330 --)

1. The instrument can be held in either hand, with the palm facing upward, or down. But once decided, stick with one hand and method selected. Alternating styles generally causes confusion in seeking intuitional response.

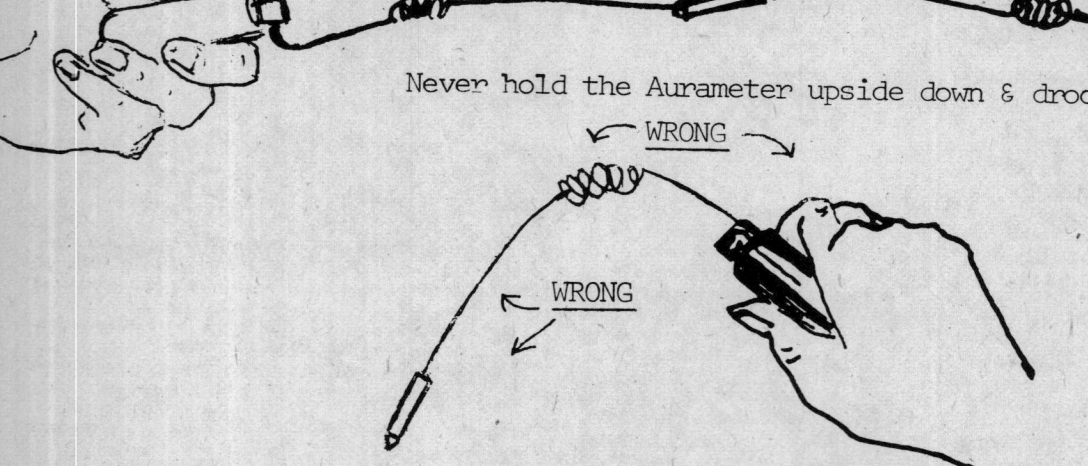

Never hold the Aurameter upside down & drooping
WRONG
WRONG

2. Be sure to hold the handle half-way back. If held forward the index finger invariably makes contact with the stem, frequently placing a drag on free movement of the spring wire going through the bearing and nullifying the activity of the tiny spring inside the handle. It is the interplay between the wire's flexibility and coil action counterbalanced against this little spring that places the Aurameter among the most sensitive dowsing devices ever invented.
3. Begin by bringing the Aurameter into position with the tip pointing straight out in front of you.
4. Keep its length parallel with the floor (a droop or slanting its length downward tends to reduce the Aurameter's sensitivity.
5. Once the instrument's poised, as described in #3, gradually arch the wrist so that your grip hand tilts slowly upward.
6. When the Aurameter reaches a position with the top of your hand on a line lower than the tip, it will prove more difficult to hold the instrument in balance. The higher you raise the tip, the greater this sensitivity. Herein lies the key to delicate response. Sometimes, when movement-directed from the sub, unconscious,

and superconscious levels of mind, is not forthcoming, you can stimulate the device to respond using this simple method.

7. Allow for a time-lapse - frequently from a few seconds to a half-minute or more - after the question is posed in your mind, to permit time for your Aurameter to respond. The time delay is usually caused by one or more of the following reasons:
   a. too much external stimuli through one or more of your five senses. Get into a more subjective (intuitional) state. Try shutting your eyes. Feel the interplay between the handle and the floating tip, as if there is no connecting stem and coil between the two.
   b. your question is unclear, or too abstract. Be specific.
   c. asking more than one question at a time tends to confuse the deeper levels of mind.
   d. re-check your code, or convention. For example, a right-swing can mean "yes"; a left swing "no"; short oscillation between left and right swings can mean "maybe", "don't know", "question unclear", or "info not available at this time", or the tip may bob up and down instead. Experiment with the device to develop your code.
   e. You can work with numbers and letters of the alphabet with swings or dips. When in doubt as to the precise moment the Aurameter stops on a letter or number, question by seeking "yes" and/or "no" answers for confirmation.
8. Remember, the Aurameter is a combination "water-compass", allowing right and left swings, a "weighing-device", dipping down and up for information, and an "upright pendulum", with gyrating and rotating movements possible.

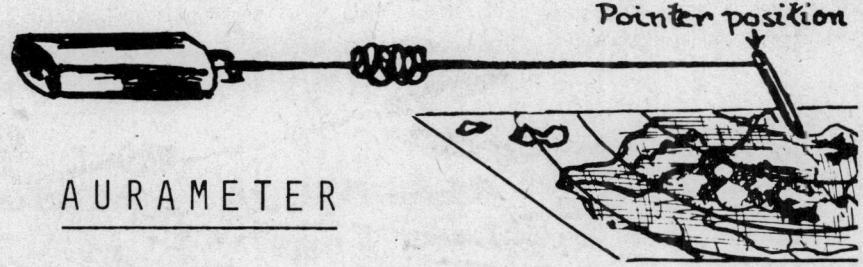

AURAMETER

9. The tip may be adjusted down for map dowsing, or up as desired. (see illus. above)

THE AURAMETER

The Cameron <u>AURAMETER</u> as depicted here, has been extremely useful in the research and testing of the Great Pyramid replicas and other free-energy accumulators. In addition, the AURAMETER, so named by the late Max Freedom Long, author of *The Secret Science Behind Miracles, Psychometric Analysis*, and Editor of "The Huna Research Bulletin," when he and Verne L. Cameron, inventor of the unique instrument, demonstrated Cameron's ability to delineate the human auras of several people in Long's study in 1952.

This ingenious device in the dowsing master's hand seemingly became an extension of the invisible, neumonal world, coupling the extra-dimensional properties of the Aurameter in powerful attunement with Cameron's psyche. The instrument also outlined numerous other related energies.

A hinged, floating pointer, poised at one end of two straight wires, joined by a coil-spring, counterbalances against the pull of a tiny spring mounted inside the hollow handle. The assembly amplifies the most delicate action physically prompted by the nervous system through super-intelligent information originating in the subconscious, unconscious, and superconscious levels of mind.

"It is an upright pendulum, combination weighing device, water compass, and vibrating four-dimensional wave-meter in my hand," said the late Verne L. Cameron. The Aurameter, tested by competent engineers with ultra-sensitive equipment indicates down into the mili-ounces of response.

"What seems so fantastic," said Long, "so difficult to accept, is that spirit forces, the human aura, the astral or etheric body — a blending of AKA bodies of the low and middle selves — produces long, triangular-like extensions out from the shoulder-blades resembling wings."

Verne Cameron and Max Long found the Aurameter picked up a beam projecting from the left eye, "like a ray of light," some twenty-two inches. Similar shafts of energy emitted from one or both temples believed to be associated with the direct telepathic sending apparatus. A triangular shaped fin at the back of the head, was calculated by both men to be the concentrated receptor for telepathic messages.

Many other force-fields around magnets, jewels, stones, etc., were measured, also emotional beams from the chest or solar plexus areas, rays and rods from religious objects, (particularly after prayer) and blessing.

Cameron originally designed the Aurameter after some twenty-five years of trial and error, to improve his ability to Divine underground water, oil, ore, and other buried objects or substances. He also used the instrument to map-dowse (locate at a distance) missing persons, animals, lost articles, and other valuables.

In the early stages, the dowsing mentor noted the power-beams from his hands caused the Aurameter to respond with a push away from his approaching palm similar to the repelling force of two positive ends of a magnet. "Thought energy alters readings," Cameron noted; "the sensation can be described as though the pointer is touched by a delicate brush of air from a distance, unfocused source. It can also have a levitory, lifting action," Cameron added. "We had only Cameron's word for it," said Long; "however several successful tests proved his ability to sense tactile forces from other dimensions."

For more information about the Cameron *Aurameter*, (now in production), write to "The Pyramid Guide."

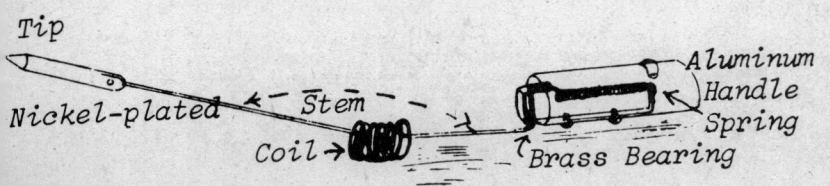

For more and complete details on dowsing with the Aurameter, Verne Cameron's master work, AQUAVIDEO, Locating Underground Water, @ $4.95 Soft cover, and MAP DOWSING, Handbook #1 @ $2.75, available El Cariso Pubs.

THE DIVINING ROD
Sir William Barrett and Theodore Besterman
University Books, 1968
$7.50

"There are in many parts of the world certain persons who profess to be able to discover, without the aid of any known means of investigation, the exact location of underground water. For this purpose they usually employ a Y-shaped twig of hazel or some other wood; this so-called divining-rod is held in the hand and the diviner then traverses the ground. When supposed to be approaching the hidden water the rod is seen to move, sometimes with such vigour as to forcibly strike the holder's body, although he claims to make considerable efforts to restrain it—a fact which seems to be proved by one limb of the twig being often snapped across under the strain of the opposing forces.

. . .The historical evidence adduced in the next chapters renders it practically certain that the birthplace of the modern use of the dowsing-rod is in the mining districts of Germany, probably the Harz Mountains. It was probably introduced into England in the latter part of the 16th century by the German miners brought into this country to work the Cornish mines. . . .

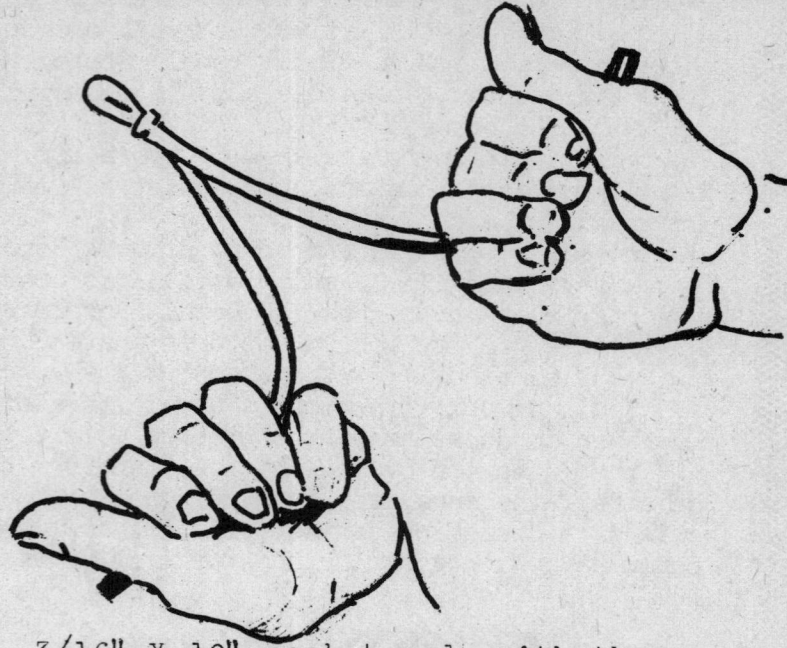

3/16" X 10" pocket rods with the short hold.

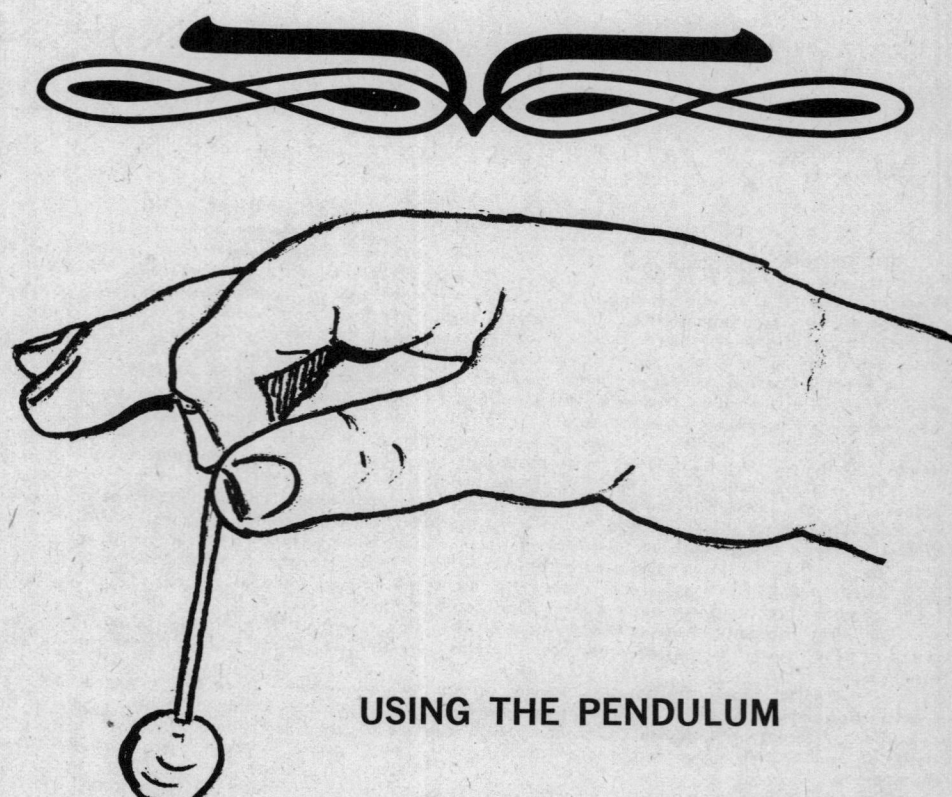

USING THE PENDULUM

Ruth Montgomery

Best selling author of A World Beyond

Companions Along The Way

An extraordinary account, dictated from the other side, of Group Karma and of incarnations shared with the world-famous medium, Arthur Ford —including the Palestinian incarnation in the time of Jesus

COMPANIONS ALONG THE WAY
Ruth Montgomery
Coward, McCann & Geoghegan, 1974
$6.95

HOW TO DEVELOP YOUR ESP POWER
Jane Roberts
Frederick Fell Publishers
1974—$2.95

"You may be able to predict the future. You may speak to distant friends without using a telephone, act on the message, and never know that you received it to begin with. You may be warned of disasters before they occur, change your plans, and never be consciously aware of the warning itself. You may visit with relatives and friends who are no longer alive in our terms. They may visit you, and you may not even be aware of their presence. You may do one or all of these things, without ever knowing it.

"Impossible? Unbelievable? Not at all. Your conscious mind knows only what you permit it to know. Everything else is hidden in your subconscious mind. Often you lose important data simply because you are afraid of it. But no impression is ever really lost. We never really forget. Often we act on information from the subconscious, while refusing to admit its existence with the conscious ego."

"Your own inner capabilities and potentials are more varied and powerful than you realize. The purpose of this book is to enable you to recognize and use them in daily life. You use them now, but in a subdued and inefficient manner. They work in spite of you."

THE SETH MATERIAL
Jane Roberts
Prentice-Hall, 1970
$2.95

Late in 1963, Jane Roberts and her husband were experimenting with a Ouija board when a personality calling himself "Seth" began forming messages. Soon, Miss Roberts began passing easily into trance—her gestures, her eyes, her voice "borrowed" by Seth himself.

The Seth Material is the documented story of how a woman who balked at the idea of life after death was confronted with overwhelming proof. Seth has diagnosed illnesses, correctly described the contents of sealed envelopes (and buildings thousands of miles away), and give life readings. He has materialized apparitions in a well-lit living room, and continues to amaze students of the occult and professionals alike. And from the very beginning, the text of each semi-weekly session has been recorded in full.

Here is the best from an ongoing series of remarkable "lectures" on health, dreams, astral projection, God, reincarnation, and the mechanisms of man's subconscious. As Raymond Van Over says in his Introduction, "Seth, I believe, has a great talent for introducing complex and often difficult subjects simply and clearly. . . . Philosophically, the Seth material is some of the best of its type I have ever read." Often picking up a topic exactly where he left off six months before, Seth brilliantly explains many of the problems and paradoxes of the occult, and gives numerous instructions for developing ESP that any reader can test for himself. Illustrated with striking photographs taken during an actual session, *The Seth Material* THE SETH MATERIAL offers absorbing and convincing evidence of one of the most extraordinary psychic "teachers" of the century. . . .

"action is action whether or not you perceive it, and probable events are events whether or not you perceive them. Thoughts are also events, as are wishes and desires. The human system responds as fully to these as it does to physical events. In dreams, often portions of probable events are experienced in a semiconscious manner. This amounts to a bleed-through, and I use the term purposely, for your tape recorder can be used an an analogy.

"Imagine the whole self as composed of some master tape. Your recorder has four channels. We will give your recorder numberless channels. Each one represents a portion of the whole self, each existing in a different dimension, yet all a part of the whole self or tape. You see it would be ridiculous to say that Mono One on your tape was any more or less valid than Mono Two. Mono One could be compared to your present ego. . . ."

SETH SPEAKS: THE ETERNAL VALIDITY OF THE SOUL
Jane Roberts
Prentice-Hall, 1972
$7.95

"('Good evening, Seth.')

"We will begin Part Two, Chapter Nine, and we will title this, 'The Death Experience.'

What happens at the point of death? The question is much more easily asked than answered. Basically there is not any particular *point* of death in those terms, even in the case of a sudden accident. I will attempt to give you a practical answer to what you think of as this practical question, however. What the question really means to most people is this: What will happen when I am not alive in physical terms any longer? What will I feel? Will I still be myself? Will the emotions that propelled me in life continue to do so? Is there a heaven or a hell? Will I be greeted by gods or demons, enemies, or beloved ones? Most of all the question means: When I am dead, will I still be who I am now, and will I remember those who are dear to me now?

"I will answer the questions in those terms also, then; but before I do so, there are several seemingly impractical considerations concerning the nature of life and death, with which we must deal.

"First of all, let us consider the fact just mentioned. There is no separate, indivisible, specific point of death. Life is a state of becoming, and death is a part of this process of becoming. You are alive now, a consciousness knowing itself, sparkling with cognition amid a debris of dead and dying cells; alive while the atoms and molecules of your body die and are reborn. You are alive, therefore, in the midst of small deaths; portions of your own image crumble away moment by moment and are replaced, and you scarcely give the matter a thought. So you are to some extent now alive in the midst of the death of yourself—alive despite, and yet because of, the multitudinous deaths and rebirths that occur within your body in physical terms.

"If the cells did not die and were not replenished, the physical image would not continue to exist, so now in the present, as you know it, your consciousness flickers about your ever-changing corporeal image."

ADVENTURES IN CONSCIOUSNESS: AN INTRODUCTION TO ASPECT PSYCHOLOGY
Jane Roberts
Prentice-Hall (Fall 1975)
$7.95
AND
DIALOGUES OF THE SOUL AND MORTAL SELF
Jane Roberts
Prentice-Hall (Fall 1975)
$6.95

Seth, the "multi-person" who's lived more than one life, now shows you how to live yours.

the nature of personal reality
A SETH BOOK
by Jane Roberts

When a personality called Seth started imparting messages through Jane Roberts, late in 1963, the result was *The Seth Material* and later *Seth Speaks*. Now, Seth has dictated a new book which gives you specific, practical techniques for solving everyday problems and "enriching the life you know." It's a book that shows you your own reality and how to improve it.
$7.95

At your bookseller or direct from:

PRENTICE-HALL
Att: Addison Tredd
Englewood Cliffs, N.J. 07632

Please send me _____ copies of *The Nature of Personal Reality* @ $7.95 ea. I enclose ☐ check ☐ money order for $_____ total. (Please add 50¢ postage and handling plus sales tax where applicable.)

Name_____
Address_____
City_____ State_____ Zip_____

EDGAR CAYCE

ASSOCIATION FOR RESEARCH AND ENLIGHTENMENT, INC.
Atlantic Avenue and 67th Street, Virginia Beach, Va.
Write for comprehensive brochure on all programs and publications.

The A.R.E. received its charter in 1931 replacing an earlier group, the Association of National Investigators, Inc. The group's need for expanded quarters led in 1956 to the repurchase of the buildings and grounds of the Edgar Cayce Hospital. Since the Association's return to the old hospital building, further expansion needs have been met through the construction of an additional structure to house the A.R.E. Press and the business offices of the Association and the Edgar Cayce Foundation. The Foundation, established in 1947, is custodian of the original copies of the readings, all of which are stored in a fireproof vault in the basement of the original building. Duplicates of this material have been presented to the A.R.E. In addition it serves the function of dealing with other foundations and research groups interested in working with the Edgar Cayce material. . . .

One of the major purposes of the A.R.E. is dissemination of information on the readings. To this end, it has for many years maintained a broad program of lectures at National Headquarters in Virginia Beach, and at symposiums throughout the country. In addition, small organized groups throughout the world study certain topics for which specific groups of readings were given.

Research into the readings is another key role of the A.R.E. In internal projects and in conjunction with organizations and individuals throughout the world, continuing probes into the information provided by the readings are going on.

To help in this work, the readings have been indexed, and, along with other pertinent material, filed in the Association's library, where they are available to the public. In addition, the library contains one of the country's largest collections of books, magazines and papers on psychical material.

Although Edgar Cayce's dream of a hospital has not been revitalized, a great portion of the research work being done on the readings deals with the healing sciences. While the Association itself is no longer directly involved, it works to furnish private doctors of all types with information as they seek to explore, in private practice and in clinical study, concepts brought out in the readings.

1969 marked the beginning of a concept which is a part of the long-range ideal of the A.R.E., an extension, perhaps, of the hospital which had its tenure in the 20's. The A.R.E. Clinic, operative in January of 1970, was brought into being the prior June by the Board of Trustees of the Association, at their annual meeting.

The Edgar Cayce readings were given from 1901 until 1944, shortly before Edgar Cayce's death. It is estimated that he entered his sleep-like state at least 16,000 times during those years, although there is no way of definitely knowing the total. The earliest reading in the files dates back to 1909, but regular records were not kept on a systematic basis until Cayce's lifelong secretary, Gladys Davis, joined him in September, 1923.

With but few exceptions all the readings given from that time on, a total of 14,249, are on file along with related correspondence and reports. The great majority of this has been carefully cross-indexed, and a compilation of over 200,000 file cards makes location of a given reading or topic mentioned in a reading possible at the Virginia Beach Headquarters library.

The records defy easy precise categorization, since each one may deal with many topics, and the range of material, when viewed as a whole, is as broad as man's history and man himself. For the purpose of explanation, though, rough categories are traditional.

Of the entire number by far the largest section, totaling 8,985, is concerned with the mind and the body. This group, popularly known as the "physical readings," deals with diagnosis of a specific individual's problems in this area, and a specialized recommendation for his treatment.

The next largest group is generally known as the "life readings." These 2,500 readings deal with vocational, psychological, and human-relations problems. It was in this group, which Cayce only began giving many years after he had started the "physical readings," that the concept of reincarnation was introduced.

There are also 667 readings dealing with dream interpretation. The information indicated that dreams were powerful tools for man to use in his search for inner knowledge, and that interpretation of the symbols contained in the dreams was the key to understanding their content.

Of the remaining 2,097 a rough breakdown would yield almost as many categories as there are readings. This miscellaneous group covers a diverse field ranging from comments on geology to organizational advice on the A.R.E. itself.

Perhaps the most generally applicable information given by the sleeping Cayce is contained in the thousands of references to the Bible and the message it carries to all men. These references suffuse the readings in all categories, and serve to point up the unifying principle that underlies all the Cayce material. While advocating no specific philosophy, religion or ism, it expresses a deep belief in a Divine Creator of whose plan man is a part. The readings make it clear that if man would know himself, he must seek to live in harmony with his Creator's plan.

MEMBERSHIP

The A.R.E. is an open membership, non-profit association. Interested persons have a choice of three ways in which they may join.

All three forms of membership share in common certain features:
1. Use of the library facilities.
2. Receipt monthly of the *A.R.E. News*, and bimonthly (six issues per year) of *The A.R.E. Journal*.
3. Notification of programs at Virginia Beach and in members' locales.
4. A loan service program through which members may receive tape-recorded lectures given at A.R.E. programs throughout the country; circulating files of extracts from the readings; books and periodicals from the library.
5. Access to information on the Cooperating Doctor's Program.
6. An opportunity to send children to the A.R.E. summer camp or use of the facilities by the entire family during certain periods of the summer.

7. Use of A.R.E. Clinic, Phoenix, Arizona.

SPONSORING MEMBERSHIP This basic membership is offered at $35.00 annually. In addition to privileges already listed, members in this category receive a free copy of all new booklets produced by the A.R.E. Press, and complimentary copies of selected books on the readings or related fields of psychical research. They also receive the Individual Reference File ("the black book"), and ten circulating files on loan at no cost.

ASSOCIATE MEMBERSHIP This membership is offered at $15.00 to introduce individuals to the A.R.E. at a nominal cost. Members in this category have privileges numbered one through six listed above. Three circulating files are loaned at no cost; additional files may be borrowed at $1.00 apiece.

LIFE MEMBERSHIP This membership is offered at $15.00 to introduce individuals to the A.R.E. at a nominal cost. Members in this category have privileges numbered one through six listed above. Three circulating files are loaned at no cost; additional files may be borrowed at $1.00 apiece.

LIFE MEMBERSHIP This membership at $800 gives the subscriber Sponsoring Membership privileges for life. An Installment Plan is available.

It should be noted that all forms of membership are open on a family basis. Both the husband and wife and any children under eighteen can be included under a single membership application. Children over eighteen must apply for membership in their own right.

REPRESENTATION Regional representatives, council chairmen, and elected membership delegates compose a Board of Advisors who act as liason between membership, the Board of Trustees, and management during June A.R.E. Congress Week (at Virginia Beach) by making recommendations of the conduct of Association activities.

THE A.R.E. JOURNAL

The bi-monthly journal includes articles on a wide range of subjects from the readings or parallel fields by many noted authorities and a regular book review feature.

A.R.E. NEWS

All members receive a monthly newspaper pertaining to A.R.E. activities throughout the world—conferences, programs, group news and announcements. All members are urged to send in material for the *A.R.E. News*.

EDGAR CAYCE ON PROPHECY
Mary Ellen Carter
Paperback Library, 1970
75 cents

EDGAR CAYCE'S STORY OF KARMA
Mary Ann Woodward, ed.
Berkley, 1971
95 cents

EDGAR CAYCE ON ATLANTIS
Edgar Evans Cayce
Paperback Library, 1971
75 cents

VENTURE INWARD
High Lynn Cayce
Paperback Library, 1969
75 cents

EDGAR CAYCE ON DREAMS
Harmon H. Bro
Paperback Library, 1968
75 cents

DREAMS: YOUR MAGIC MIRROR—WITH INTERPRETATIONS OF EDGAR CAYCE
Elsie Sechrist
Dell, 1971
95 cents

HERITAGE STORE INCORPORATED
204-22nd Street
P.O. Box 444
Virginia Beach, Va. 23458
Specializing in Edgar Cayce Items.

A PROPHET IN HIS OWN COUNTRY, THE STORY OF A YOUNG Edgar Cayce
Jess Stearn
Morrow, 1974
$7.95

EDGAR CAYCE'S STORY OF JESUS
Jeffrey Furst, ed.
Berkley, 1970
95 cents

THE OUTER LIMITS OF EDGAR CAYCE'S POWER
Edgar Evans Cayce and Hugh Lynn Cayce
Perennial Library, 1973
$1.25

EDGAR CAYCE ON RELIGION AND PSYCHIC EXPERIENCE
Harmon H. Bro, Ph.D.
Paperback Library, 1970
95 cents

EDGAR CAYCE: MYSTERY MAN OF MIRACLES
Joseph Millard
Fawcett, 1956
60 cents

EDGAR CAYCE: THE SLEEPING PROPHET
Jess Stearn
Bantam, 1969
95 cents

EDGAR CAYCE'S STORY OF THE ORIGIN AND DESTINY OF MAN
Lytle W. Robinson
Coward, McCann & Geoghegan, Inc., 1972
$5.95

BEAUTY THROUGH HEALTH FROM THE EDGAR CAYCE READINGS
Laurence M. Steinhart, ed.
Argor House, 1974
$7.95

EDGAR CAYCE'S STORY OF ATTITUDES AND EMOTIONS
Jeffrey Furst, ed.
Coward, McCann & Geoghegan, 1972
$6.95

STRANGER IN THE EARTH
Thomas Sugrue
Paperback Library, 1971
95 cents

THE MEANING OF THE DEAD SEA SCROLLS
A. powell Davies
Mentor, 1956
95 cents

EDGAR CAYCE ON THE DEAD SEA SCROLLS
Glenn D. Kittler
Paperback Library, 1970
95 cents

HIGH PLAY: TURNING ON WITHOUT DRUGS
Harmon Hartzell Bro
Paperback Library, 1971
$1.25

EDGAR CAYCE ON HEALING
Mary Ellen Carter and William A. McGarey, M.D.
95 cents

EDGAR CAYCE ON REINCARNATION
Noel Langley
Paperback Library, 1969
75 cents

EDGAR CAYCE ON ESP
Doris Agee
Paperback Library, 1971
75 cents

THERE IS A RIVER: THE STORY OF EDGAR CAYCE
Thomas Surgue
Dell, 1972
95 cents

MY LIFE WITH EDGAR CAYCE
David E. Kahn as told to Will Oursler
Fawcett, 1971
75 cents

THE PSYCHIC WORLD OF PETER HURKOS
Norma Lee Browning
Signet, 1971
$1.25

MARGERY: AN ENTERTAINING AND INTRIGUING STORY OF ONE OF MOST CONTROVERSIAL PSYCHICS OF THE CENTURY
Thomas Barr Tietze
Harper & Row, 1973

The medium's name was Mina S. Crandon and she was known as Margery (in Boston). She was the center of an international set of admirers that included Sir Arthur Conan Doyle, William Butler Yeats and others.

THEY KNEW THE UNKNOWN
Martin Ebon
World, 1971
$6.95

Martin Ebon recounts the psychic experiences of prominent philosophers, authors, statesmen and scientists from the time of Socrates to the present.

PSYCHIC JOURNEY: THE MAKING OF A SEER:

$1.95
c/o Arthur J. Burks
Tarnhelm Press
Lakemont, Ga. 30552

THE BOOK OF MEDIUMS
Allan Kardec
Weiser, 1970
$7.50

NOTHING SO STRANGE: THE AUTOBIOGRAPHY OF ARTHUR FORD
Arthur Ford with Margueritte Harmon Bro
Paperback Library, 1968
75 cents

THE MIDDLE OF SILENCE GALLERY
65 Carmine Street
New York, N.Y. 10014

this gallery has been included primarily to indicate the constructive inspirational influence generated by a thoughtful reading of various Seth Books by Jane Roberts.

A new gallery, THE MIDDLE OF SILENCE, will open to inhabitants of the planet on the 242nd anniversary of the birth of George Washington whose mystical vision at Valley Forge presaged the physical and spiritual union of this country.

The primary purpose of this gallery will be to raise a hue and cry for the promulgation of a rational set of principles, an ethic of creativity that will go beyond Washington's vision to encompass the spiritual potential of all physical reality.

Physical reality is sustained by an inner reality. Thus, we feel that it is important to bring into existence the inner reality, the america (a/miracle) that resides within each one of us. That is why the standard we bear aloft reads, *"To bring into existence those untold creations that are within us."* The way we intend to achieve this end is through the creation of a shared spirituality (in which the one becomes many). We know that the more we discover in common, the less fear we will have in creating the uncommon.

We hope that the *middle of silence* gallery will emerge as a vital model for these ideals.

Our fate is to create. Our souls, utilizing vast resources of cosmic energy, create, by thought projection, physical reality as we know it. As the physical world was created by thought, and is maintained by thought, so it is changed by thought. Therefore we cannot blame fate or others for the outcome of our lives. We create a positive reality for ourselves or a negative one. We create a positive reality when we share our thoughts with others, and are open to the largest truths. On the other hand, if we keep our thoughts, feelings, and beliefs hidden from others and thereby refuse to take responsibility for them, we are bound to create a negative reality. When we do not admit our complicity in the creation of a negative reality, we invariably find ourselves trapped within it. The negative reality of a dog eat dog world is largely the result of our subconscious expectations and beliefs about the world. If we face up to these attitudes, we realize that they are destructive and must be changed. Changing these attitudes also changes how we experience the world. And conversely, examining how we experience the world helps us discover the nature of our inner reality. An analogy for this process can be found in the arts. The inner feelings and beliefs of the artist create the visual reality of his painting or sculpture. Because his work of art is open to public scrutiny and critical comment, the artist is forced to examine the relationship between his inner world and his external creations. He cannot escape questioning the validity of his art, nor avoid the challenge of larger concepts. If his feelings and beliefs fail to expand and grow as a result of this process, then his vision stagnates and he dies as an artist. We each have that same responsibility for the conduct of our lives. We must strive to create lives that are perfect works of art, open for all to share, and simultaneously help others, who are only aspects of our total self, to do the same.

Basic to an understanding of this quest is the knowledge disseminated by a multi-dimensional spiritual teacher, named Seth, whose personality, as an energy essence, is no longer focused in the physical world. In the book, *Seth Speaks, The Eternal Validity of the Soul*, he has said: "If you sell yourselves short, you will say, 'I am a physical organism and live within the boundaries cast upon me by space and time. I am at the mercy of my environment.' If you do not sell yourselves short, you will say, 'I am an individual. I form my physical environment. I change and make my world. I am free of space and time. I am a part of all that is. There is no place within me that creativity does not exist.'"

We believe that no one should sell his spiritual and physical heritage short. This gallery and its members are dedicated to helping all those who want to develop and nurture their creative powers of consciousness, and who will pledge to use this knowledge for the benefit and celebration of all that is.

A positive creativity demands that we learn to embrace the obligations and responsibilities involved in the creation of our fate. Essential to the accomplishment of this goal is fidelity to the inner voices that speak to us from the *middle of silence*.

IRENE HUGHES ON PSYCHIC SAFARI
Brad Steiger
Warner Paperback Library, 1972
95 cents

FIFTY YEARS A MEDIUM
Estelle Roberts
Avon, 1972
95 cents

THE PSYCHIC FEATS OF OF OLOF JONSSON
Brad Steiger
Popular Library, 1973
95 cents

Known and celebrated for years in his native Sweden, Jonsson was catapulted to world-wide fame after his astonishing telepathic experiments with Apollo astronaut Edgar Mitchell while Mitchell was in flight to the moon. Now recognized as the possessor of astonishing extrasensory powers, Jonsson is the man who:
Solved thirteen baffling murders only after visiting the scenes of the crimes;
Located three young women who had disappeared without a trace;
Accurately predicted the time and place of death of Nasser and De Gaulle.

SINGER IN THE SHADOWS: THE STRANGE STORY OF PATIENCE WORTH
Irving Litvay
Popular Library, 1972
95 cents

"Many moons ago I lived. . . . Again I come—Patience Worth my name." With these words, recorded on Mrs. Pearl Curran's ouija board on a hot summer night in 1913, began the most astonishing case of psychic communication in our century. Claiming to be the spirit of a 17th-Century Englishwoman, Patience Worth dictated seven full-length books, thousands of poems and carried on a bizarre and caustic dialogue with the living for over twenty-four years. Acclaimed by the critics, studied by puzzled scientists and psychic investigators, she was the literary rage of her day—and remains the greatest psychic riddle of our times.

THE POEMS OF ST. JOHN OF THE CROSS
English Versions And Introductions
By Willis Barnstone
New Directions, 1972
$1.95

Many critics regard the work of Saint John of the Cross, the 16th century mystic, to be among the finest poetry Spain has produced. His poetry of love and joy describes the soul's passage through dark light to final illumination in mystical union with Absolute Being.

LEARNING CLAIRVOYANCE AND PERCEPTION WITH AN EXTRASENSORY PERCEPTION TEACHING MACHINE*

By Russell Targ and David B. Hurt

The research reported here demonstrates the feasibility of increasing the extrasensory perception (ESP) of some subjects by means of an ESP teaching machine. At the present time, there is a substantial body of literature describing carefully conducted experiments to demonstrate the existence of ESP.[1-3] It is not our purpose to add another demonstration of the statistical appearance of ESP, but rather to demonstrate that learning can take place.

The teaching machine used in this work was designed with the goal of enhancing the ESP ability which we believe to be a latent capacity to some extent in all people.[4] Our hypothesis is that enhancement can be accomplished by allowing the user of the machine to become consciously aware of his own mental state at those times when he is most successfully employing his extrasensory faculties. With increased conscious awareness of this mental state, we believe that he is then able to bring his otherwise intermittent faculties under his volitional control.

The teaching machine we used generates four random targets for the user to choose. These targets are generated by the machine and are not presented until the user has indicated to the machine what he believes the target to be. The targets are 35 mm color transparencies and the user's task is to select the one the machine has chosen by means of its random target generator.

An important feature of the machine is that the choice per se of a target is not forced. That is, the subject may press a PASS button on the machine when he wishes not to guess. Thus, with practice the user can learn to recognize those states of mind in which he can correctly choose the target. He does not have to guess at

Fig. 1. *ESP Teaching Machine used in this experiment, with two of the four "encouragement lights" illuminated.*

targets when he truly does not feel he "knows" which to choose.

When the PASS button is pushed the machine indicates what its choice was, and neither a hit nor a trial is scored by the machine, which then goes on to make its next selection. We consider this elimination of forced choice to be a significant condition for learning ESP.

When the user of the machine indicates his choice to the machine, he is immediately and automatically informed of the correct answer. The machine described here is being used to enhance clairvoyant perception in which experimenter and the subject remain ignorant of the machine's state until the subject has made his choice.

Because the user obtains immediate information feedback as to the correct answer, he is able to recognize his mental state at those times when he has made a correct response. If the information feedback to the user were not immediate, we believe as much learning would not take place and less or no enhancement would be achieved. The machine used in this work is shown in Figure 1.

The machine has the following properties:

It generates random targets automatically and rapidly, with the rate

---

* Invited paper presented at the Institute of Electrical and Electronic Engineers International Symposium on Information Theory, January, 1972. Russell Targ is a physicist working with lasers and optics at GTE Sylvania; he is a senior member of the IEEE and is President of the Parapsychology Research Group, Palo Alto, California. David Hurt is a senior applications engineer with Fairchild Microwaves and Opto Electronics; he has been working in the field of ESP electronics for over fifteen years.

determined by the user. It automatically records and scores both the user's responses and the targets generated. The machine provides no sensory cue to the user as to its internal state, and its randomness has been carefully investigated. The distribution of targets with regard to singles, doubles and triples was analyzed for 2,400 trials, and was found to lie within one standard deviation of the expected value. The machine has four stable internal states. A 1.0 MHz square-wave oscillator sends pulses to an electronic counter that counts from "one" to "four." On the fifth pulse, the counter returns to "one." This is called a "scale of four counter." The machine therefore passes through each of its four states at a rate of 250,000 times per second. The state in which the scale of four counter resides is determined by the length of time the 1 MHz oscillator runs. Once the machine is in a fixed state (not scaling), the user indicates his choice as to which state he thinks the machine is in by pressing a button on the machine under the color slide of his choice. The correct slide will then light up. The correct answer for the next choice is determined by the length of time the choice button was held down in making the selection. Since the scaling rate is 250 KHz, there is no way for the user to control the final state of the machine since his reaction time is four orders of magnitude too slow for this. In addition to the reward of having pushed the button under the slide which lights, a bell rings to indicate that a correct choice was made, and four lights carrying messages of encouragement are lit sequentially as the subject obtains 8, 10, 12 and 14 hits.

In the course of this work we have encountered three general classes of subjects. The majority of the 12 subjects working with the machine in this study did not show any significant improvement in their ESP ability. Three of the subjects gave indirect evidence of increased ESP by guessing at targets in a manner to cause their scores to become bi-modal. Whereas chance scores should give a skewed binominal distribution, with the probability of a "hit" at each trial equal to $1/4$, we observe that several subjects show an increasing deviation from this distribution. That is, they generate a disproportionate number of high and low scores. This variance of scoring patterns has been noted in the ESP literature.[5,6] Among these subjects a particularly high score such as 12 out of 24 is often followed by a particularly low score such as 2 out of 24. We interpret this variance pattern as an indication of ESP although it is not an effect which we set out to cultivate.

In the group indicating some improvement, one subject has shown an exceptional increase in ESP scores through more than 1,600 trials. This subject has apparently learned to clairvoyantly perceive the state of the machine to an extent providing a significant deviation from chance expectation.

The protocol for the experiment was for the subject to make four runs of 24 trials ($P=1/4$). This was followed by a rest period, and four more runs of 24.

The most successful subject in this experiment reached a scoring level where on three occasions she scored more than 40 hits out of 96 trials in one of these sets of four runs, where only 24 hits would be expected. From the null hypothesis, the probability of 40 hits out of 96 trials is less than 10^{-3} (CR=3.77). This subject made a total of 64 runs of 24 trials with a mean score of 8.6 hits per run (CR=9.81, P for the whole series $< 19^{-15}$).

Based on the outcome of this work, we sought to determine if other phenomena in the ESP realm could be similarly enhanced.

The machine was altered so that the target was not chosen by the machine until after the subject indicated his choice. The time delay was approximately 0.2 second, which is to say that subjects were asked to make a perception of an event which was to occur 0.2 second in the future.

The single subject graduated to the precognitive experiment reported at the beginning of her first run, "I don't feel anything any more," about which picture would light, and moreover that she was "just guessing." This was borne out in her early scores in the precognition experiment. However, in the course of 672 trials, her performance increased to a level approaching her scores in the clairvoyant test; e.g., she obtained 19 hits out of her first 96 trials and 38 hits out of her last 96 trials. The results of the 28 precognitive runs of 24 trials each were subjected to a linear regression analysis in blocks of 96, corresponding to experimental protocol. The data are shown in Figure 2, and give a best fit to a

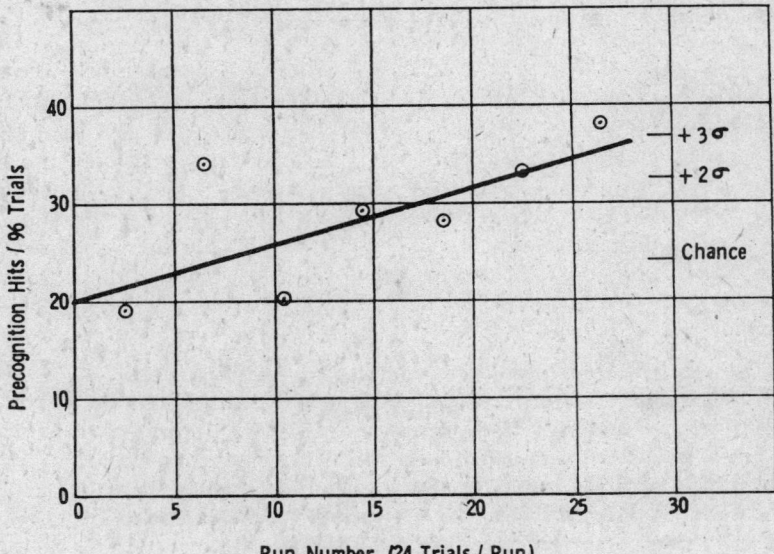

Fig. 2. *Precognition experiment showing number of hits/run of 96 trials vs. average trial number. Linear regression analysis of the data is also shown. Correlation coefficient = 0.68, P <0.01.*

line with positive slope 0.56 per run of 96, and a Y intercept of 20.0. The correlation coefficient was 0.68 (P <0.01). This is a clear indication that learning has taken place.

We conclude from this work that it may be possible to teach and enhance ESP phenomena through techniques of feedback and reward in much the same way as visceral and glandular functions are brought under volitional control.[7] Additional experiments will shortly be undertaken to find the relationship between accuracy of precognition and the temporal distance from the event.* Our overall goal is to achieve an understanding of the functional relationship of ESP to the various physical and psychological variables which control it.

---

* We hypothesize that significant events create a perturbation in the space-time in which they occur, and that this disturbance propagates forward, and to a small degree, backward in time. Since precognitive phenomena are quite rare, the disturbance evidently dies out extremely rapidly in the -t direction.

(This work was supported by a grant from the Parapsychology Foundation.)

REFERENCES

1. Pratt, J. G.; Rhine, J. B.; Stuart, C. E.; Smith, B. M.; and Greenwood, J.: *Extra-Sensory Perception after Sixty Years* (New York: Henry Holt, 1940).
2. Soal, S. G., and Bateman, F.: *Modern Experiments in Telepathy* (London: Faber and Faber, 1954).
3. Vasiliev, L. L.: *Experiments in Mental Suggestion* (Church Crookham, Hampshire, England: Institute for the Study of Mental Images, 1963).
4. Tart, C. C.: "Card Guessing Tests: Learning Paradigm or Extinction Paradigm?" *J. Amer. Soc. Psych. Res.* 60 (1966): 46-55.
5. Rogers, D. P.: "Negative and Positive Affect and ESP Run-Score Variance," *J. Parapsychol.* 30 (1966): 151-159.
6. Carpenter, J. C. "Scoring Effects within the Run," *J. Parapsychol.* 30 (1966): 73-83.
7. Miller, N. E.: "Learning of Visceral and Glandular Responses," *Science* 163 (1969): 434-445.

Altered States Of Consciousness And Sensory Awareness

ncreasing numbers of scientific systems, professional growth centers and spiritual and metaphysical organizations exist which can assist an individual in developing increased self-awareness and sensitivity to others. Many of these programs encourage personal approaches while others tend to be more standardized and impersonal. Both orientations can stimulate valuable experiences if the student views his immersion in eclectic and flexible terms. An honest confrontation with one's basic beliefs and motives is essential prior to reaching any decision to experiment with methods of developing extended sensory perception.

When life seems grim and you feel you want no part of it, do you sometimes find yourself fancying 'another place'? Most of us do at some time or other, and most of us are aware deep down inside that somewhere there exists such a place. The knowledge is often no more than a vague feeling, however. There is no way of expressing it adequately in words.

Awareness that such a place exists, and that we have a right of entry, can arouse frustration or fear depending upon the individual. Fear is the safer of the two reactions in our present society. The 'I don't know, I don't want to know, I'll face it when I must' type of attitude retards spiritual growth, but does not warp or destroy one's spirituality. Such a person avoids risking his soul and sanity on the off-chance of satisfying his pleasure-principle.

Frustration produces different responses in different intellects. The intelligent, clear-sighted and stable individual seeks an answer to his frustration in training. The muddled, inadequate person may turn to drugs, thinking of them as a short-cut. There are, I am afraid, no short-cuts in mysticism. You cannot step from reality to super-reality on the back of LSD and expect to come back refreshed and better equipped to control your development in this world. That expectation is the prerogative of the genuine mystic, the well-disciplined soul.

Exactly what are the mystic and the 'tripper' aiming for? The answer is ecstasy.

After a 'trip' on drugs a person may describe colours unknown to artists, scents beyond the perfumes of Grasse, and fluidity of shape and form that makes an object more easily understood. It is all very colourful. It is also superficial. The description, 'tripper', is a well chosen one for such people. Like the coachloads of tourists who rush frantically from one tourist attraction to another and then retire exhausted, they know as much about the soul of a place at the end of the trip as they did at the beginning—nothing.

The mystic, however, looks at a tree—and looks at a tree. He concentrates all his attention upon that tree until his soul has transcended his body, reality has been superseded and the mystic has become the tree. The common life force of mystic and tree are then combined for a certain degree of time. At the end of the experience the mystic knows the tree, and the tree knows the mystic. With each such experience the mystic grows spiritually. His understanding of why he exists here deepens: his knowledge of where he is going becomes more certain. As he becomes more and more attuned to the 'oneness' of the universe, so he also becomes more and more sure of himself, calmer, stronger, more likeable and, sadly, more envied.

Yes, you may say, but does the tripper not achieve the same knowledge and understanding without undertaking all that prolonged training and rigorous self-discipline? Does he not understand the divinity of things while still managing to avoid self-denial?

The answer is: 'No, he does not'.

Drugs are no new invention. The ancient Greeks, Egyptians and Assyrians knew of hallucinogenic drugs. The Celts were, and still are, past masters of herbal lore. If ecstasy is so simple a climax to reach, why have responsible people tried to keep hallucinogens hidden from mankind for so long? Spite? A desire for power? If you believe that you will believe anything. Hallucinogenic drugs will release the psyche—that no one will deny. Unfortunately, they also release the soul into uncharted territory, unarmed and totally unprepared for what it will meet there.

It must be understood that it is not a simple question of transition from 'here' to 'there'. There are many states of being, and moving from the state in which you are now could land you in any one of them. Using the terms 'up' and 'down' is as misleading as describing the Holy Trinity as one third of God at the top and two at the bottom.

Depending upon your mental state, your physical health and, above all, your spiritual stature at any given time, you may enter one of the spheres of the enlightened and beautiful, or one of the spheres of darkness and terror. It is tragic but true that all trippers will visit the spheres of darkness sooner or later: they have no way of controlling the trip upon which they so lightly embark. The dangers are cumulative as their minds open more and more, becoming susceptible to infiltration from the dark spheres. Depression is commonplace. It deepens with each trip, and leads to more trips seeking the spiritual solace and beauty they may have experienced initially.

There are physiological as well as psychological reasons for this tragedy. All hallucinogens—the best known and documented is LSD—change cellular structure in the cerebral cortex. The cortical changes produced by LSD are, so far as can be ascertained, permanent. So the fortunate few who take that drug once, have a good trip and never touch it again, may always have an inner vision of the world that is pleasant. For the great and unfortunate majority, the reverse is true. They will be forever tormented by a vision of dark horror.

I have contact with a wide variety of young people from all walks of life. Within my own circle I have seen the result of the careless use of hallucinogenic drugs. One young man who we shall call John, discovered that one of the toadstools growing wild in the south of England could produce similar results to LSD without the risk of lawbreaking. Not long afterwards he began to be noted for his silence, his withdrawn abstraction at inappropriate times. He has grown more dependent upon the drug as time has passed. Today, for him, there is no reality, no beauty, no truth. He lives in a solitary world no man can see. Everyday life is impossible for him. He can no longer exert any influence on it. He is not capable of using his widened psychological aspect to his advantage. He has become a passive observer watching his life drip uselessly away. Soon he will lose even that power. Then society will step in and try to repair the damage. Probably, it will only succeed in returning sufficient consciousness to make John bitterly unhappy at his wasted life. It is extremely unlikely that anyone can do anything to return him to a condition where he would be capable of influencing his own destiny. As pointed out, the cerebral changes are permanent...

Peter was 20 years old, tall, handsome, intelligent — and emotionally unstable. He sought the simple way out of his troubles: using the same toadstools as John, twice, and only twice. The effect was dramatic and appears to be permanent. The first time he had a 'bad trip'. Next time would be better, he thought. But next time was final. He opened his mind to influences he was not equipped to manage. Within six months he had been diagnosed a schizophrenic. Still under treatment, he lives in constant fear of voices that urge his self destruction.

Think hard before trying an instant trip into ecstasy. The old and tried method may be long but it is certain and its rewards are guaranteed. You will not find it simple, for great gifts require great minds to control them.

"PITFALLS: BEWARE THE PSYCHEDELIC SHORT CUT"
Mary-Jane Gethyn
Prediction, Vol. 40, No. 6,
June, 1974

ALTERED STATES OF AWARENESS: READINGS FROM SCIENTIFIC AMERICAN WITH INTRODUCTION
Timothy T. Taylor
w.h. freeman and Co., 1971
$2.95

"For any given individual, his normal state of consciousness is the one in which he spends the major part of his waking hours. That your normal state of consciousness and mine are quite similar and are similar to that of all other normal men is an almost universal assumption, albeit one of questionable validity. An altered state of consciousness for a given individual is one in which he clearly feels a *qualitative* shift in his pattern of mental functioning, that is, he feels not just a quantitative shift (more or less alert, more or less visual imagery, sharper or duller, etc.), but also that some quality or qualities of his mental processes are *different*. Mental functions operate that do not operate at all ordinarily, perceptual qualities appear that have no normal counterparts, and so forth. There are numerous borderline cases in which the individual cannot clearly distinguish just how his state of consciousness is different from normal, where quantitative changes in mental functioning are very marked, etc., but the existence of borderline states and difficult-to-describe effects does not negate the existence of feelings of clear, qualitative changes in mental functioning that are the criterion of ASCs.

"This book is concerned with those states of consciousness in which the individual feels one or more qualitative (and possibly one or more quantitative) shifts in mental functioning, so that he believes himself to be in an ASC.

"Persons interested in the biology of behavior are acutely alert to the fact that our awareness of the world about us is not constant—rather, we constantly fluctuate from one state of awareness to another. Indeed, some states of awareness are hardly what the layman would refer to as 'being aware' at all: while we are sleeping, for instance, we are certainly not cognizant of what is happening around us. Dreams are also perceived as being special or different from the perceptions and experiences of wakefulness. It can be argued, however, that sleeping and dreaming are merely different kinds or states of awareness. That is, they are *altered* states of awareness."

THE PSYCHOLOGY OF CONSCIOUSNESS
Robert Ornstein,
Viking Press, 1972
$8.95

By pushing beyond the limits of a purely logical, scientific approach to understandin conscious experience, Professor Robert E. Ornstein here attempts to reconcile the two basic streams of knowledge—the rational, or analytic, or intuitive, or esoteric. "Our highest creative achievements are the products of the complementary functioning of the two modes," he writes, a synthesis of which current psychology is now undergoing, and which "may form a more complete science of human consciousness with an extended conception of our own capabilities."

Modern psychological and physiological research has already indicated that there are significant differences in the functioning of the two hemispheres of the brain. In the left hemispheres of most human brains seem to be placed the functions of language, rational cognition and at times sense-functions Ornstein describes as "linear." It is the right hemisphere, in most cases, that seems to be responsible for "non-linear" (or non-verbal) thinking-intuition, spatial relationships and the direction of many bodily activities (including painting and sculpture).

Professor Ornstein analyzes Western thought as left-hemisphere dominated, oriented toward verbal mathematical rationality; Eastern thought, particularly as manifested in yoga and Zen, is seen as primarily influenced by the right hemisphere. Through research and allegories, through discussions of personal experience and questioning the reader, Ornstein uses his theme of right/left brain along with the new tools of scientific inquiry that have been developed during the past century to provoke a basic re-examination of, and provide a new perspective on, what we know (and feel) about the psychology of consciousness today.

THE BOOK OF HIGHS: 250 WAYS TO ALTER CONSCIOUSNESS WITHOUT DRUGS
Edward Rosenfeld
Quadrangle, 1973
$4.95

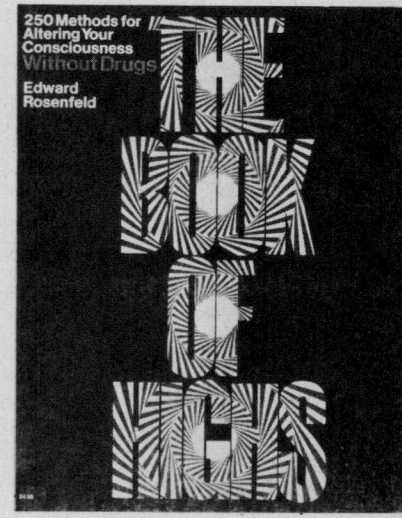

THE HIGHEST STATE OF CONSCIOUSNESS
John White, ed.
Anchor, 1972
$2.95

ALTERED STATES OF CONSCIOUSNESS
Charles T. Tart, ed.
Doubleday-Anchor Book, 1972
$4.95

FOUNDATION FOR MIND RESEARCH, INC.
315 E. 86th Street
New York, N.Y.
Main concern is investigation of non-drug transcendent experiences.

NATURE OF HUMAN CONSCIOUSNESS: A BOOK OF READINGS
Robert E. Ornstein, ed.
W.H. Freeman & Co.
$5.95

THE SACRED MUSHROOM: KEY TO THE DOOR OF ETERNITY
Andrija Puharich
Doubleday, 1974
$2.95

Since the dawn of history, civilizations have revered the famed "sacred mushroom"—known to botanists as Amanita Muscaria—with its mystical, mind-expanding properties. Written by one of America's leading authorities on parapsychology and extrasensory perception, *The Sacred Mushroom* is the fascinating account of Dr. Puharich's own investigation of the *Amanita muscaria*.

The book describes in vivid detail Puharich's extraordinary association with Harry Stone, a young sculptor of unusually acute extrasensory perception, who on a number of occasions spontaneously went into a deep trance state and then began to speak and write in the ancient Egyptian language. Identifying himself as Ra Ho Tep, a highborn Egyptian who lived 4,600 years ago, he defined the long-lost ritual of the sacred mushroom and its astonishing effects upon the human consciousness. . . .

"The world view we inherit has been built up by putting things into objective pigeonholes . . . categories that can be shared. The psychedelic may fracture these structures. Under LSD, for instance, the categories of color, by which we help organize our field of visual possibility, may be dissolved. Then colors may emerge, flow together, and not stay put. Faces may suddenly 'drip and run across the floor.' Shapes may become fluid and mixing.

"However to shatter our working models of the universe does not lead to *truth*, any kind of new data, or, above all, a 'true picture' of the universe. The universe, like nature, is a conceptual framework that changes from culture to culture and age to age. Our concepts are to some extent arbitrary constructs but to disrupt or dissolve them with drugs does not free us into some universal knowledge 'out there' in the great beyond. There is, instead, the loss of meaningful structures of agreement needed for communion with others. This can lead to the loss of personality definition itself, that which don Juan meant by 'loss of soul,' or Jesus meant by the 'outer darkness.'

"This 'freedom from false concepts' notion is but a recurrence of the old Garden of Eden myth, the 'noble savage,' return-to-nature nonsense of the romantics. Any world view is a creative tension between possibility and choice. This is the tension that holds community and 'real' world together. This is the Cohesive force of our own center of awareness, the thin line between loss of self to autistic dissolution on the one hand, or slavery to the broad statistics of the world on the other. Perceptions relieved of this natural tension, through drugs or the various occult religious techniques, may well be profound or rightfully chaotic."

eeeeeeeeeeeeeeeeeeeeeeee

THE NATURAL MIND: A NEW WAY OF LOOKING AT DRUGS AND THE HIGHER CONSCIOUSNESS
Andrew Weil
Houghton Mifflin, 1973
$2.95

"It is my belief that the desire to alter consciousness periodically is an innate, normal drive analogous to hunger or the sexual drive. Note that I do not say 'desire to alter consciousness by means of chemical agents.' Drugs are merely one means of satisfying this drive; there are many others, and I will discuss them in due course. In postulating an inborn drive of this sort, I am not advancing a proposition to be proved or disproved but simply a model to be tried out for usefulness in simplifying our understanding of our observations. The model I propose is consistent with observable evidence. In particular, the omnipresence of the phenomenon argues that we are dealing not with something socially or culturally based but rather with a biological characteristic of the species. Furthermore, the need for periods of nonordinary consciousness begins to be expressed at ages far too young for it to have much to do with social conditioning. Anyone who watches very young children without revealing his presence will find them regularly practicing techniques that induce striking changes in mental states. Three- and four-year-olds, for example, commonly whirl themselves into vertiginous stupors. They hyperventilate and have other children squeeze them around the chest until they faint. They also choke each other to produce loss of consciousness.

"Primarily, we need more information about altered states of consciousness. Altered from what? is a good first question. The answer is: from ordinary waking consciousness, which is 'normal' only in the strict sense of 'statistically most frequent'; there is no connotation of 'good,' 'worthwhile,' or 'healthy.' Sleep and daydreaming are examples of altered states of consciousness, as are trance, hypnosis, meditation, general anesthesia, delirium, psychosis, mystic rapture, and the various chemical 'highs.' If we turn to psychology or medicine for an understanding of these states, we encounter a curious problem. Western scientists who study the mind tend to study the objective correlates of consciousness rather than consciousness itself. In fact, because consciousness is nonmaterial, there has been great reluctance to accord it the reality of a laboratory phenomenon; psychologists, therefore, do not study consciousness directly, only indirectly, as by monitoring the physiological responses or brain waves of a person in a hypnotic trance or in meditation. Nonmaterial things are considered inaccessible to direct investigation if not altogether unreal. Consequently, there has been no serious attempt to study altered states of consciousness as such."

WHAT IS MEDITATION?
John White, ed.
Anchor, 1974
$2.75

"Meditation is a means of growth, both personal and transpersonal. This will never be a better world until there are better people in it, and meditators claim that the best way—indeed, the only way—for people to change is by 'working on yourself' from within, through meditation.

"The highest goal of meditation is enlightenment. Spiritual teachers of all ages have been unanimous in declaring that we can come to know God through meditation. Through direct experience—not through bookish learning or intellectual conceptualization—we may reach a state of conscious union with the ultimate reality and divine dimension of the universe. In that state all the long-sought answers are given, along with peace of mind and heart. There are other paths to God-knowledge, of course, but this is one path easily available to many and the chief reason for the worldwide interest and enduring value placed on meditation.

". . . In physiological terms meditation induces a fourth major state of consciousness. Neither waking, sleeping, nor dreaming, the meditation state has been described as a 'wakeful hypometabolic condition.' Brain waves, heartbeat, blood pressure, breathing, galvanic skin resistance, and many other factors are altered in meditation. Bodily functions slow to the point achieved in deep sleep, and sometimes beyond, yet the meditator remains awake and emerges from meditation with a feeling of rest and loss of stress or tension. (Here it should be understood that similarity or control of physiological processes—the art of the fakir—does not automatically grant spiritual growth and psychological maturity—the way of the yogi. Claims to the contrary, as seen in some advertisements for biofeedback devices and mind development courses, are highly misleading. Physiological control of nonconscious functions is often a byproduct of meditation, but it certainly is not the goal of meditation.)"

ELYSIAN TREE METAPHYSICAL BOOKSTORE
Box 463
1105½ W. Main Street
Urbana, Ill.

JOURNAL OF ALTERED STATES OF CONSCIOUSNESS
Order from:
Baywood Publishing Company, Inc.
43 Central Drive
Farmingdale, N.Y. 11735
Volume One (two issues) is $15.00

EXCERPTS:
Andrew Weil: "All of us experience states of consciousness different from our ordinary waking state. Sleep is such a state. Less obviously, perhaps, are daydreaming and movie watching unusual modes of awareness. Other distinct varieties of conscious states are trance, hypnosis, psychosis, general anaesthesia, delirium, meditation, and mystic rapture. Most societies, like our own, are uncomfortable about having people go off into trances, mystic raptures, and hallucinatory intoxications. Indeed the reason we have laws against possession of drugs in the first place is to discourage people from getting high."

Charles Tart: "An altered state of consciousness may be defined as a qualitative alteration in the overall pattern of mental functioning, such that the experiencer feels his consciousness is radically different from the way it functions ordinarily. . . . I propose that state-specific sciences be developed. Investigators of ASC's would certainly encounter an immense variety of phenomena labeled religious experience or mystical revelation during the development of state-specific sciences, but they would have to remain committed to examining these phenomena more carefully, and subjecting the beliefs (hypotheses, theories) that result from such experiences to the requirement of leading to testable predictions. In practice, because we are aware of the immense emotional power of mystical experiences, this would be a difficult task, but it is one that will have to be undertaken by disciplined investigators if we are to understand various altered states of consciousness."

Gardner Murphy: "There are psychological states for which there are no good names, including feeling states, cognitive states, and volitional states, upon which human destiny almost literally may depend, (involving) profound alterations in states of consciousness, well known in the East, regarding which Western man usually has expressed doubt or scorn."

THE JOURNAL OF TRANS PERSONAL PSYCHOLOGY
P.O. Box 4437
Stanford, California Calif. 94305
Semi-annually $7.50

. . . is concerned with the publication of theoretical and applied research, original contributions, empirical papers, articles, and studies in meta-needs, ultimate values, unitive consciousness, peak experiences, ecstasy, mystical experience, B. values, essence, bliss, awe, wonder, self-actualization, ultimate meaning, transcendence of the self, spirit, sacralization of everyday life, oneness, cosmic awareness, cosmic play, individual and species-wide synergy, transcendental paths, responsiveness, compassion; and related concepts, experiences and activities.

THE TRIUNE SCIENCE OF BEING AWARENESS CENTER
3497 Cahuenga Boulevard W.
Los Angeles, Calif. 90068
Write for information on classes dedicated to the total development of mind, body and spirit.

BIG SUR RECORDINGS
117 Mitchell Blvd.
San Rafael, Calif. 94903

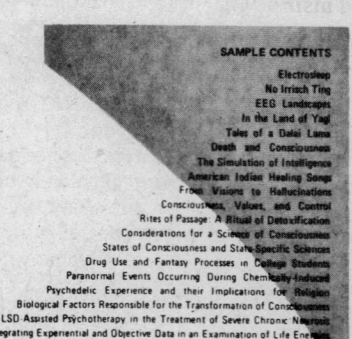

THE ASSOCIATION FOR HUMANISTIC PSYCHOLOGY:

A world-wide network formed in 1962 for the development of the human sciences in ways which recognize our distinctively human qualities and which work toward the fulfillment of the innate capacities of people—individually and in society.

Humanistic psychology is a name applied to a broad spectrum of approaches to human experience and behavior, all of which focus on:
—the fundamental uniqueness and importance of human life
—the conviction that all people have the potential for being creative
—an emphasis on what is characteristically human, as opposed to thinking about people in mechanistic and reductionistic terms. Humanistic psychology therefore encourages attention to topics having little place in most systems, such as choice, self-realization, spontaneity, love, creativity, valuing, responsibility, authenticity, meaning, transcendental experience, and courage.
—a centering of attention on the experiencing person, and thus on experiencing as primary in the understanding of people
—a belief that intentionality and values are crucial in determining human action
—a broad conception of the scientific method, with stress on the significance of the phenomena studied
—a fundamental commitment to psychology as an art and a science, rejecting only those assumptions which restrict inquiry and interfere with a total view of human experience. Humanistic psychology transcends the usual academic boundaries to include any of the disciplines which seek to understand human behavior and experience.
—an emphasis on the integration of the whole person—feelings and intellect, body and soul
—an interest in exploring synergistic relationships in groups, communities and institutions

With this orientation the Association encourages systematic study of the genuine problems of life and creative practice toward their solution.

To generate and foster these visions, to encourage the exchange of ideas and experiences, to aid in enriching society and its institutions as a field in which people can grow toward their potentials, as well as to serve the needs of its members, AHP offers these services:
—a quarterly *Journal of Humanistic Psychology*
—a monthly *Newsletter*
—an annual meeting featuring both the theory and the practice of humanistic psychology
—regional meetings throughout North America and increasingly in Europe and Asia
—international meetings
—local chapters and groups around the world
—communication networks among people working at humanizing various professions such as teaching and the ministry
—published information about colleges offering humanistically oriented programs, about growth centers, and other related activities
—an extensive bibliography of books in the field, and a discount book-ordering service
—*The Paper Dragon*, which circulates papers of interest at cost to members, upon request
—committees set up to foster communication and to encourage and coordinate activity in various aspects of humanistic psychology, currently:
  Human Policies Committee
  Theory Committee
  Research Committee
  Task Force for the Future
—the Humanistic Psychology Institute, an experiment in graduate education in psychology
—topical conferences on such subjects as humanistic politics, psychic healing, and alternative life styles
—liaison with organizations in related fields

The Association is in a state of continuing growth and change as it works toward its own actualization. AHP seeks to be an open, responsive forum and welcomes as members people of all backgrounds and vocations who share these values and who wish to support and participate in these activities. Membership rates: $29.00 regular membership; $50.00 2-year membership for new members; $19.00 student, retired or outside North America; $45.00 couple.

CYBERNETICS, LOGIC, ROBOTICS, AUTOMATA, COMPUTERS, ARTIFICIAL INTELLIGENCE

THE LOGIC PRESS©

CATALOG $1.00
260 GODWIN AVE.
WYCKOFF, N.J. 07481

ASSOCIATION FOR HUMANISTIC PSYCHOLOGY
325 Ninth Street,
San Francisco, Calif. 94103
Subscription rates: $10/yr individual; $14/yr institutional; $3.50 single issue
Frequency: quarterly—January, April, July, October
Editor: Thomas Greening, 1314 Westwood Blvd., Los Angeles, Calif. 90024
Index Information: Loose index supplied free upon request

Descriptive Data: The *Journal of Humanistic Psychology* began publication in 1961 and is the journal of the Association for Humanistic Psychology. It publishes experiential reports, theoretical papers, research studies, applications of humanistic psychology, and humanistic analyses of contemporary culture. Topics of special interest are authenticity, encounter, self-actualization, search for meaning, creativity, intentionality, psychological health, being motivation, values, love, identity and commitment.

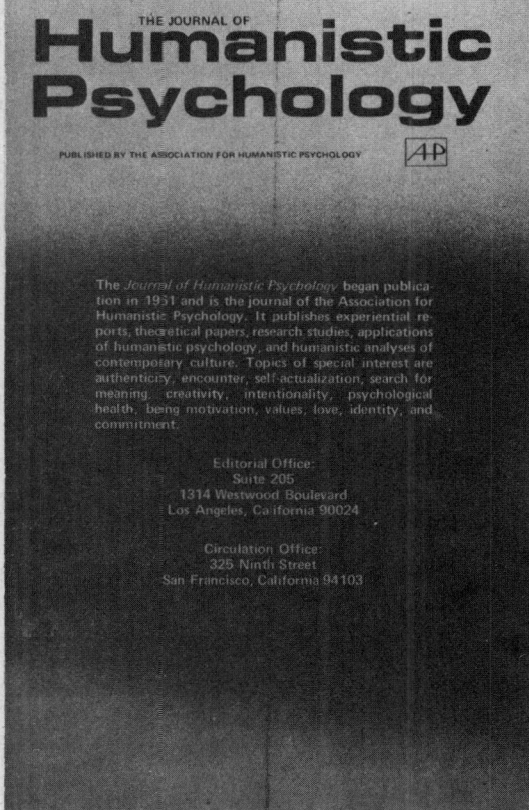

HALLUCINOGENS AND SHAMANISM
Michael J. Harner. ed.
Oxford University Press, 1972
$2.95

"The use of hallucinogenic agents to achieve trance states for perceiving and contacting the supernatural world is evidently an ancient and widespread human practice. In using a powerful hallucinogen, an individual is brought face to face with visions and experiences of an overwhelming nature, tending strongly to reinforce his beliefs in the reality of the supernatural world. We of a literate civilization may get both our religion and our religious proofs from books; persons in non-literate societies often rely upon direct confrontation with the supernatural for evidence of religious reality.

"In non-literate societies, the experts who directly confront the supernatural are called 'shamans' by anthropologists. Shaman, a term preferred in anthropology partially because it lacks the sensational or negative connotation of 'witch' or 'witch-doctor,' is a word from the language of the Tungus tribe of Siberia. A shaman may be defined as a man or woman who is in direct contact with the spirit world through a trance state and has one or more spirits at his command to carry out his bidding for good or evil. Typically shamans bewitch persons with the aid of spirits or cure persons made ill by other spirits, whether sent by another shaman or simply acting on their own volition. Depending on his traditions and beliefs, a shaman may also influence the course of events, find lost or stolen objects, divine the identity of persons who have committed crimes, communicate with the spirits of dead relatives and friends of clients, foretell the future, and practice clairvoyance. Contemporary anthropology tends to view the shaman as a psychotherapist, but the people of the cultures in which he operates believe him to be able to contact and deal with an invisible spirit world. In most non-literate societies the shaman is accorded considerable respect."

MEDITATION IN THE SILENCE
E.V. Ingraham
$1.00
Write to:
Unity School of Christianity
Lee's Summit, Missouri

The effectiveness of prayer does not depend on the form followed, but on the spirit involved. The monotonous beat of the Indian medicine man upon his tom-tom, as an appeal to the Great Spirit, has worked relatively as many miracles for the red man as has the well-thought-out and scientific prayer of the modern metaphysician. If one discerns the purpose of the form, and receives the thing for which it was designed, that is well; but if through following the form one loses sight of its purpose, it were better that the form did not exist.

". . . The silence is not in any sense the discovery of a new process of mind, but is a practice known very well to every genius, every inventor, every philosopher, and in fact every individual who has in any degree outstripped his fellow men and brought back to the world some new idea or invention from beyond the range of habitual thought and experience. The silence is clearly taught in the Scriptures, and is one of the most vital aspects of prayer. 'Be still, and know' is a clear command to let the mind rest from its own activities and record knowledge that the Infinite waits to reveal."

SHAMANISM
Mircea Eliade
Princeton University Press—Bollingen Series, 1964
$3.95

AVAILABLE FROM: BURCHETTE
BROTHERS PRODUCTIONS
P.O. Box 1363
Spring Valley, Calif. 92077
$6.98 plus 42 cents sales tax for California
Outside U.S. add $1.00

THE NEW WORLD OF DREAMS AN ANTHOLOGY
Ralph L. Woods and
Herbert B. Greenhouse
Macmillan, 1974
$12.95

A comprehensive and definitive collection.

THE COLLECTIVE DREAM IN ART
Walter Abell
Schocken, 1966
$2.95

A psycho-historical theory of culture. The arts are to society what dreams are to the individual.

THE R. M. BUCKE MEMORIAL SOCIETY
4453 De Maisonneuve Boulevard
Montreal 215, Quebec
Canada

NEWSLETTER-REVIEW

The Newsletter-Review is published by the R. M. bucke Memorial Society for the Study of Religious Experience. The Society commemorates a distinguished 19th-century Canadian psychiatrist, Richard Maurice Bucke, author of the well-known *Cosmic Consciousness*. Our area of interest includes not only states of mystical illumination such as those studied by Bucke, but more broadly all forms of human experience which seem of "absolute" or "ultimate" significance to the individual.

Though our frame of reference is multidisciplinary (drawing on the fields of anthropology, comparative religion, theology, biology, philosophy, psychology and psychiatry), our basic aim is the psychological understanding, both theoretical and empirical, of such phenomena. It is our goal in the *Newsletter-Review* to provide a forum for exchange of views among scholars in this field.

$2.50 an issue. Write for back issue information and film rental.

This classic study in the evolution of the human mind is a pioneering work as valuable today as when it was first published in 1901. At that time it was enthusiastically acclaimed by both William James and P. D. Ouspensky. It has long been accepted as a landmark in the field of mysticism.

In reviewing the mental and spiritual activity of the human race, Dr. Bucke discovers that at intervals certain individuals have appeared who are gifted with the power of transcendent realization—or illumination. Their experiences constitute a definite advance in man's relation with the Infinite. Moreover, the author shows from available records that this transfiguring endowment of illumination is on the increase, and he gives full details of practically all the cases on record up to the time when the book was written. . . .'

COSMIC CONSCIOUSNESS: A STUDY IN THE EVOLUTION OF THE HUMAN MIND
Richard Maurice Bucke, M.D.
Dutton, 1969
$2.95

DREAM POWER
Dr. Ann Faraday
Berkley, 1972
$1.50

SLEEP
Gay Gaer Luce and Julius Segal
Lancer, 1966
75 cents

DREAMS AND NIGHTMARES
J. A. hadfield
Penguin, 1961
$1.25

Price $1.95 each

Your dreams and what they mean is a new Special to answer most of the questions you can ask about the fascinating study of one of man's oldest preoccupations. History, scientific future, importance of dreams are all discussed, and you get a beautiful full-colour poster of dream images and what they mean, plus a collection of real dreams to compare with your own.

The other Specials in this series are *Fortune Telling* and *Handwriting*. These titles should be available from your magazine dealer, but if you have difficulty finding them, send a check or money order for $2.00 each made payable to Man, Myth and Magic, 6 Commercial Street, Hicksville, NY 11801.

SACRED DANCE

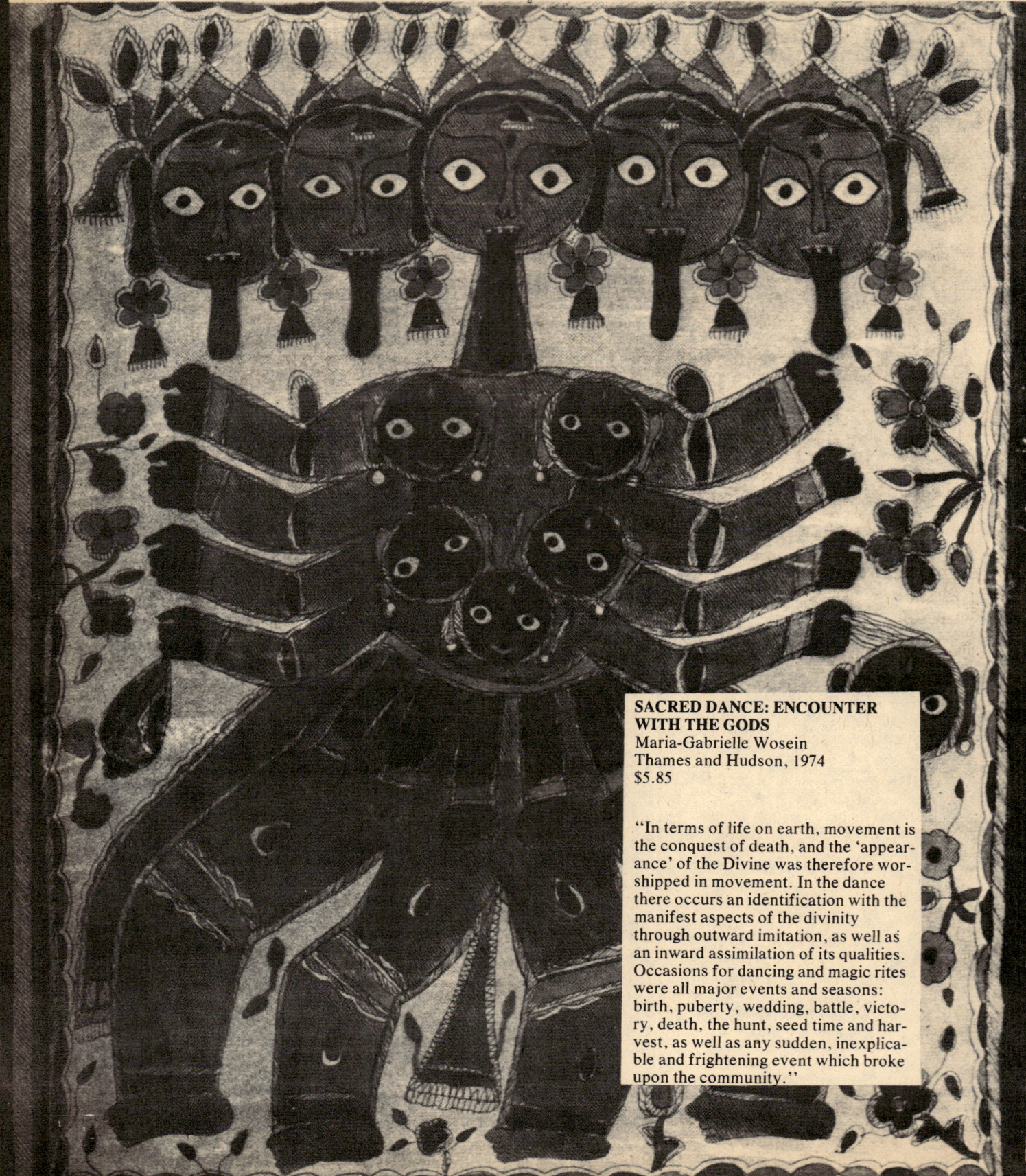

SACRED DANCE: ENCOUNTER WITH THE GODS
Maria-Gabrielle Wosein
Thames and Hudson, 1974
$5.85

"In terms of life on earth, movement is the conquest of death, and the 'appearance' of the Divine was therefore worshipped in movement. In the dance there occurs an identification with the manifest aspects of the divinity through outward imitation, as well as an inward assimilation of its qualities. Occasions for dancing and magic rites were all major events and seasons: birth, puberty, wedding, battle, victory, death, the hunt, seed time and harvest, as well as any sudden, inexplicable and frightening event which broke upon the community."

ALCHEMY
Titus Burckhardt
Penguin, 1972
$1.95

"Just as the outward work of the metallurgist with ore and fire has something violent about it, so also the influences which bear back on the spirit and the soul—and which are inescapable in this calling—must be of a dangerous and two-sided nature. In particular, the extraction of the noble metals from impure ores by means of solvent and purifying agents such as mercury and antimony and in conjunction with fire, is inevitably carried out against the resistance of the darksome and chaotic forces of nature, just as the achievement of 'inward silver' or 'inward gold'—in their immutable purity and luminosity—demands the conquest of all the dark and irrational impulses of the soul.

". . . That there is an inward gold, or rather, that gold has an inward as well as an outward reality, was only logical for the contemplative way of looking at things, which spontaneously recognized the same 'essence' in both gold and the sun. It is here, and nowhere else, that the root of alchemy lies. Alchemy traces its descent back to a priestly art of the ancient Egyptians; the alchemical tradition which spread all over Europe and the Near East, and which perhaps even influenced Indian alchemy, recognizes as its founder Hermes Trismegistos, the 'thrice-great Hermes', who is identifiable with the ancient Egyptian God Thoth, the God who presides over all priestly arts and sciences, rather like Ganesha in Hinduism."

The cross of Christ growing as a blue lily out of the Holy Virgin, who kneels on the crescent moon. The lily with five petals corresponds to the Quintessence, and the Mother of God corresponds to materia prima. From a miniature in the alchemical Book of the Holy Trinity *in the Staatsbibliothek, Munich.*

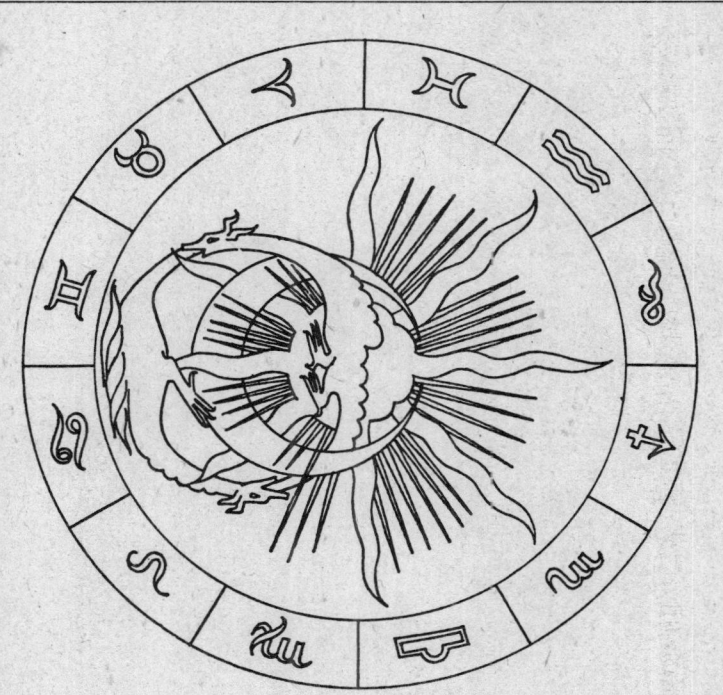

'Finis corruptionis et principio generationis' (The end of corruption and the beginning of generation). The struggle of the two primordial forces sun and moon, Sulphur and Quicksilver in the heavenly circle. – From the so-called 'Ripley Scrowle' in the British Museum Library.

A STRANGE STORY: AN ALCHEMICAL NOVEL
Edward Bulwer-Lytton
Shambala Publications, 1973
$3.95

THE SECRET TRADITION IN ALCHEMY
A. E. Waite
Weiser, 1969
$25.00

ALCHEMY, THE SECRET ART
Stanislas Klessowski de Rola
Thames and Hudson, 1973
$5.85

Early Egyptian "puffers" practicing their ancient version of alchemy which was full of carefully guarded secret rites.

Nature, as woman and tree, comes out rejuvenated from the two distilling retorts sun and moon. The birds are the 'seed' of gold and silver. The two directions of their flight represent respectively 'solution' and 'coagulation'. — From the 'Alchemical Manuscript' of 1550 in Basle University Library.

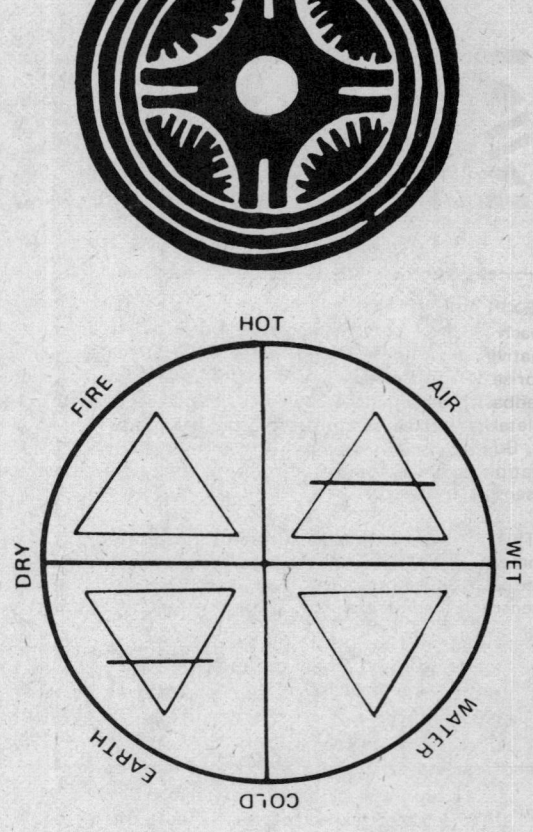

Illustration shows the ancient theory that all things are made of the same mixture of the four basic elements, fire, air, earth and water

THE FORGE AND THE CRUCIBLE: THE ORIGINS AND STRUCTURES OF ALCHEMY
Mircea Eliade
Harper Torchbooks, 1971
$1.95

"To collaborate in the work of Nature, to help her to produce at an ever-increasing tempo, to change the modalities of matter—here, in our view, lies one of the key sources of alchemical ideology. We do not, of course, claim that there is an unbroken continuity between the mental world of the alchemist and that of the miner, metal-worker and smith (although, indeed, the initiation rites and mysteries of the Chinese smiths form an integral part of the traditions later inherited by Chinese Taoism and alchemy). But what the smelter, smith and alchemist have in common is that all three lay claim to a particular magico-religious experience in their relations with matter; this experience is their monopoly and its secret is transmitted through the initiatory rites of their trades. All three work on a Matter which they hold to be at once alive and sacred, and in their labours they pursue the transformation of matter, its perfection and its transmutation.

". . . The history of science recognizes no absolute break between alchemy and chemistry; the one, like the other, works on the same mineral substances, uses the same apparatus and, generally speaking, applies itself to the same experiments. In so far as one acknowledges the validity of the investigations into the origins of science and technology, the perspective of the historian of chemistry is perfectly defensible: chemistry was born from alchemy, or, more precisely, it was born from the disintegration of the ideology of alchemy. But if we view it from the standpoint of the history of the human spirit we see the matter quite differently. Alchemy posed as a sacred science, whereas chemistry came into its own when substances had shed their sacred attributes. Now there must, of necessity, be a break of continuity between the sacred and the profane plane of experience."

ALPHA BRAIN WAVES
Jodi Laurence
Avon, 1972
$1.25

In "In York City, an epileptic learned to spot the abnormal brain wave that precedes an epileptic seizure, and turned off impending epileptic attacks at will through biofeedback training.

"In Baltimore, men and women trained in biofeedback were able to slow the rate of their heartbeats and smooth out dangerous cardiac irregularities.

"In Berkeley, slow readers suddenly learned to read well after only one session of feedback training.

"In San Francisco, a sixteen-year-old student reached a satorilike mystical experience by letting his alpha brain waves flow after only one feedback training session.

"In Topeka, an uptight housewife learned to turn on her alpha brain waves and relax away migraine headaches, without drugs.

"In Los Angeles, a young artist gave up LSD for self-controlled highs with alpha feedback.

". . . The four kinds of brain waves—alpha, beta, theta, and delta—are really descriptive tags for different wave speeds. Brain waves are measured in Hertz units (numbers of cycles per second), Delta brain waves are the slowest of all, 0 to 4 cycles per second, and are most prominent when you're so deeply asleep as not to be dreaming. Theta brain waves, 4 to 8 cycles per second, seem to be related to drowsiness, creativity, and the dream portion of the sleep cycle. Alpha brain waves run 8 to 13 cycles per second, and are generally connected with a relaxed, yet alert, mental state, or shifting consciousness. Alpha brain waves are often seen in profusion in the EEG's (electroencephalograms) of the brain patterns of skilled Zen monks and other Eastern mediators. Beta brain waves are the fastest, running 13 to 26 cycles per seconds, and even faster in cases of schizophrenia and other related mental disorders. Beta is linked to mental concentration, anxiety, certain kinds of problem solving, attention, orienting, and the jangled state most people feel from coping with the concerns of the everyday world."

EXPLORING YOUR INNER SPACE: Learn to meditate with the most talked about new approach — BIOFEEDBACK! Biofeedback is the highly efficient tool employed by those seeking alternatives or by those exploring the nature of individual consciousness as a serious and responsible enterprise. The Galvanic Skin Response monitor is the least-expensive, most straightforward biofeedback instrument available. All you do is attach the electrodes to two fingers, turn-on the completely transistorized unit and listen to the sound emitted. The more you relax, the more the pitch drops. But when worrisome thoughts intrude, the pitch goes up. You can actually hear your powers of meditation and relaxation. Also hear your emotional responses to various stimuli around you, even the most sensual and sexual.

This solid-state, reliable, compact Biofeedback Instrument Company unit is already in use & recommended by The Stress Transformation Center, NY Cyborgs, the Rama Society and the Biofeedback Educational Teaching Company, as well as many growth centers. With full range control, high sensitivity, complete instructions, it's scientific, fully safe and fun! Just $55.00 **complete** from

BIOFEEDBACK INSTRUMENT CO.
DEPT. P
255 W. 98 St., Suite 3D
NY, NY 10025
(212) 850–2156

INSTITUTE FOR PSYCHOENERGETICS
7 Harvard Square
Brookline, Mass. 02146

In experimenting with my biofeedback instruments, I have found that I can detect two different kinds, or aspects, of life energies. One kind apparently emanates from one person's palm, passing to another person, and the other kind appears to be transmitted via the emotional center of one person to another person. For labeling convenience, I am referring to one of these effects as "Bioenergy" and the other effect as "Psychoenergy."

Bioenergy effects were discovered in experimenting with heart beat synchronization of two or more persons. To observe this effect, I used the Biofeedback Monitor described on the accompanying sheet. I used the sensors for detecting heart beat, connecting one sensor to the wrist of one person, and one sensor to the wrist of another person, and then asking the person to moisten palms of free hands and hold hands. Their heart signals are connected in series and indicated by the biofeedback monitor as a series of beeps. Two or more persons can be connected in series.

After the people have been sitting a while, I ask them to gently separate their palms. The instrument sometimes registers heart beat signals when the palms are separate, by as much as 10 cm. The effect is not present with everyone and I do not know what factors are important in producing this effect. I have clearly observed the effect between myself and another person after first synchronizing heart beats. Heart beats were synchronized by making the effort to do so, by breathing together for a while, by chanting, and by tuning into the other person.

So far, I have observed the effect in about 6 persons out of approximately 50 tested. Measurements show that the heart signals are not transmitted between the palms if the resistance is greater than 220K or the capacitance is smaller than .1 microfarad. The impedance of air between palms separated by one or more centimeters is far greater than these values.

The second type of life energy, which I have called Psychoenergy, was observed by using the Biofeedback Monitor in the GSR mode of operation, or using the Relaxometer, Audible Psychogalvanometer, or BioSensor. Any GSR instrument would work.

I connected the instrument to the fingers of the subject and seated him or her ten or fifteen feet apart from a small group facing away from the group. The GSR instruments provide audible output which could be heard by everyone in the room. By prearranged hand signals, I directed the group to attempt to send either emotions of hate or anger towards the subject, or emotions of love or tranquility, for approximately five seconds. The subject did not know when he was the target, nor what emotion he was being bombarded with. No formal statistics were kept, but some subjects clearly showed large reactions (decreased skin resistance) when hate was directed towards them and moderate converse reactions (of increased skin resistance) when love was directed towards them. A few persons showed decreased skin resistance when either hate or love emotions were directed towards them.

Only about one person in ten seemed to be reactive in these preliminary experiments. After the tests, subjects talked about their inner sensations and, in some cases, they reported very strong sensations, such as prickling all over at the time when (unknown to the subject) hate emotions were being directed towards them.

All inferences regarding the nature, propagation, or even the objective reality of the effects described above are jut that—inferences.

Alternate inferences are welcome and attempts to replicate the effects would be appreciated, as would be references, contacts, or sources of potential funding for solid research.

Two references which touch this area are: *The Fields of Life*, by Harold Saxton Burr, Ballantine Books, 1972. *Orgone, Reich and eros*, by W. Edward Mann, Simon and Schuster, 1973.

James Beal at Marshall Space Flight Center in Alabama has written papers which also touch on this subject

BURYL PAYNE, PAYNE, PHD
DIRECTOR

WRITE FOR INFORMATION ON EQUIPMENT AND ON COURSES IN PSYCHIC DEVELOPMENT, UTILIZING HYPNOSIS AND BIOFEEDBACK. DIRECTOR BURYL PAYNE HAS WRITTEN *Getting There Without Drugs*)ballantine). It will soon be reprinted as *Fifth Dimensional Consciousness*

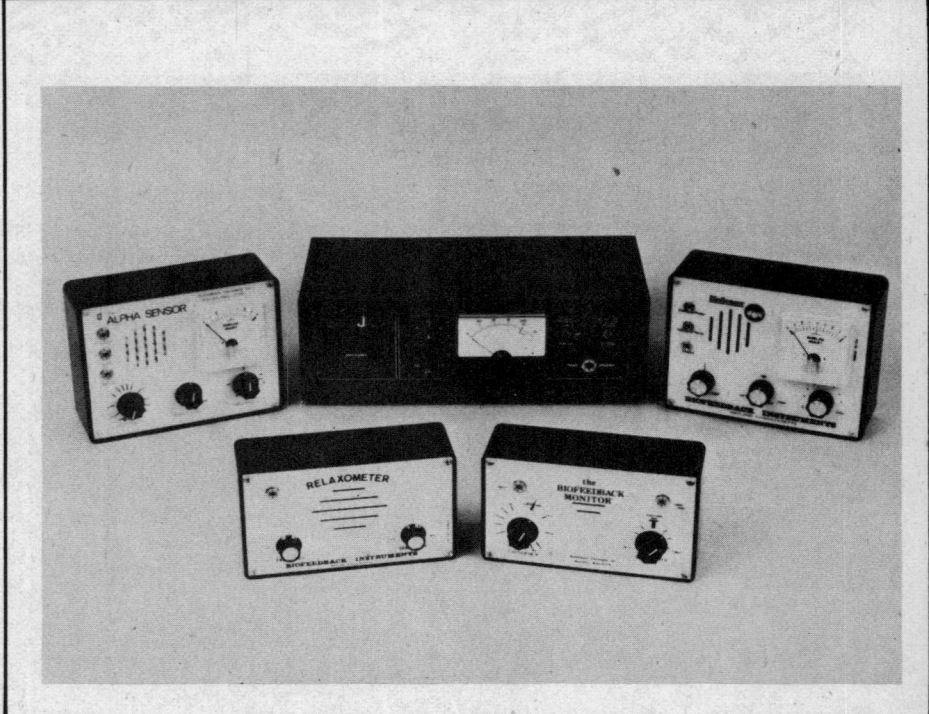

BIOFEEDBACK INSTRUMENTS

213 W. PLAIN ST.
WAYLAND,
MASSACHUSETTS 01778

617·653·6022

THE BIOFEEDBACK MONITOR

Five years of evolution in the design of portable EEG instruments has produced this versatile, compact, high quality instrument. Ideal for laboratory or home use, the Biofeedback Monitor is rugged, reliable, and completely safe.

Specifications and Features

Sensitivity	Nominally set for 5 microvolts at 10 Hz. May be increased or decreased by a simple internal adjustment.*
Input	A.C. differential input provides the advantages of three lead differential input with high common mode rejection, but requires only two sensors for the head. Input impedance set to 10,000 ohms to match the impedance of the head for optimum power transfer and minimum noise.
Filter	New compact filter design combines high gain with high rejection of unwanted frequencies. At 5 microvolts the filter will pass brain waves between 9 and 11 Hz. Sharper rejection for frequencies greater than 10 Hz. Filter range may be extended up or down by a simple internal adjustment for special measurements.*
Sensors	Two sturdy head sensors are moistened with salt water-alcohol mixture and may be applied anywhere on the head with velcro headband. Wrist and finger sensors for heart beat and GSR need only be moistened with tap water or may be used dry. Pastes, goos, and corrosive creams should not be used.
Batteries	One heavy duty nine volt, one size C flashlight. Over two hundred hours intermittent use.
Price	Basic unit with batteries, head sensors $140 post paid Finger sensors $ 5 Heart beat sensors $ 5

---

* We do not recommend fiddling with our internal adjustments unless you own our calibrated signal generator so you can know what's happening.
Signal Generator: variable from 2 to 20 Hz., 0-100 Microvolts $45

Write for complete catalog of hardware and books.

SCHNEIDER INSTRUMENT CO.
Grosse Point Medical Center
963 Grosse Point Road
Skokie, Ill. 60076

Write for further information.

"In an experiment by Simonov and Velueva in 1956 in Russia, subjects learned to control their GSR feedback and sent Morse code messages to each other with GSR responses.

"There are a number of physical changes that seem to occur along with alpha brain waves. During alpha-training control experiments at the University of Pennsylvania. Dr. David Paskewitz rigged up elaborate electrodes and machinery to record heart rate, GSR (Galvanic Skin Response), respiration, and eye movements. (Galvanic Skin Response measures the change in the skin resistance in response to an outside stimulus.) He was curious to learn if actual differences did occur as alpha waves were produced, and his findings were surprising. The brain waves and the rest of the bodily responses were linked together in a circle of response and feeling. Time after time, as he watched, Dr. Paskewitz saw heart rate increase in a pattern opposite to the rising alpha amplitude zigzagging across the graph-paper records. Then, after a short rest period, heart rates began to drop off gradually and return to the original states at the beginning of the experiment.

"The degree of tension spotted in the GSR records also changed. At first, substantial reactions occurred as each volunteer shifted the feedback control light from red to green, indicating that he had moved from beta brain waves to alpha brain waves. But, after awhile, the GSR recording began to drop in each case. As each volunteer drifted into long-controlled bursts of alpha brain waves, the GSR records dropped to highly relaxed levels.

"Can I increase my creative powers with biofeedback?

"The chemist, Kekule, devised a famous theory of molecular construction and advised his colleagues, 'Let us learn to dream, gentlemen,' in reference to his own dreamlike experience in conceptualizing his theoretical insight. Dr. Green uses biofeedback training to enhance the individual's imagery and reminds us of Robert Louis Stevenson's ability to dream publishable plots by commanding the 'brownies' of his mind to furnish him with a story. Poincare also described how mathematical ideas rose in clouds, dancing before him and colliding and combining into the first Fuschian functions, as he lay in bed awaiting sleep.

In the voluntary controls program of the Greens' laboratory, people learn how to free their thoughts, emotions, and attention, to reach creative reveries and enhanced hypnagogiclike imagery. Both alpha and theta waves are associated with creativity in different dimensions. To date, the Greens' sessions for self-enhanced imagery indicate that average people can be trained to turn on such skills.

The Alpha-Theta Brain Wave Sensor

For Feedback Training

The brain, composed of some ten billion nerve cells, is a highly developed biochemical factory, humming ceaselessly with activity. There is evidence that each state of consciousness is represented by a unique brain wave pattern. Many of these patterns have been recorded and classified by their shapes and rhythms. The most common of these are: *Delta Waves,* found in infants and sleeping adults; *Alpha Waves,* representing tranquility with eyes closed and a lack of visual imagery; *Theta Waves,* showing creative moods, fantasy and daydreaming; and *Beta Waves,* produced during daily activity and at times of tension, anxiety and intense concentration. All of these wave forms can be detected through the use of sensitive electronic equipment which picks up signals from the brain and relays them to the subject by means of audio and visual feedback.

The Brain Wave Sensor is a biofeedback instrument, designed for home and professional use, that picks up Alpha and Theta rhythms and allows the user to hear them. Instant continuous feedback of a recognizable signal tells the subject when he is proceeding in the desired direction to an Alpha state. Gradually he learns how to reach the tranquil state on his own and how to avoid high anxiety states. Complete instructions are included with your Brain Wave Sensor.

By closing the eyelids, most of us can slip in and out of Alpha a few times a minute. The key lies in recognizing the Alpha rhythm at the moment it is produced, and in learning to sustain and enhance its production. (8-12 hours with the sensor in most cases). The body then attains a state of relaxation which leads to greater control over the various states of consciousness. Alpha is the starting point for further progress.

Alpha biofeedback training has lasting effects. Subjects who have mastered Alpha production report a sense of relaxed wakefulness, with increased memory ability and dramatically improved concentration.

Various states such as yoga, meditation and hypnosis are characterized by high Alpha. Students of the above will find the Brain Wave Sensor especially helpful to shorten the training period.

Feedback that makes this possible occurs as you consciously adjust your response to the brain signals fed to the built-in speaker. The SENSOR tells if you are directing your response properly. There is no guesswork. You know when you have achieved the state of mind you are looking for.

The Brain Wave Sensor has some very innovative features. It is a lightweight, portable, compact instrument that is safe, operating on two 9 volt transistor batteries. The unique headband and electrode design allows the user the flexibility to slip it on and off within seconds without the use of electrode cream to establish contact with the skin.

NOTE: The Brain Wave Sensor is designed for use as a research instrument. No therapeutic claim is made for it.

RELAX LEARN

compact　　　efficient　　　reliable

BIOFEEDBACK INSTRUMENTS

GSR TYPE UNITS/ /DESIGN BREAKTHROUGH
Praised CLINICALLY and PROFESSIONALLY
Miniaturized, Sensitive, Solid-State, Easy to Operate

SAFE　　Powered by 9v Energy Cell　　SIMPLE
(Included, Easily Replaceable)
All units include fingertip electrodes, manufacturer's warranty
Ready to Operate　　Prices Start at $57.00

Free Information, Write: BIOFLUX Distributors
Box 8470, Portland, OR 97207

BIOFEEDBACK IS FOR EVERYONE

Biofeedback instruments have come out of the labs. People all over the country are using them daily. Experimental applications include relaxation training. Self-hypnosis. Nurturing of creative processes. And exciting new uses are constantly being discovered. The Institute for PsychoEnergetics in Brookline, Ma. uses the RELAXOMETER and BIOFEEDBACK MONITOR for developing psychic abilities and to monitor psychic energy and bioenergy.

The RELAXOMETER is part of a new generation of lab-quality instruments. Designed for general use. Built to be rugged and completely safe with easy-to-understand controls. The RELAXOMETER measures skin resistance and provides audio feedback. Its pitch varies in response to emotional changes. The only sensors are two cloth electrodes that wrap around any two fingers. No messy creams are necessary. A comprehensive manual of experiments written by Dr. Buryl Payne tells you how to get the most from training. *A good way to learn more about yourself.*

$49.50

The BIOFEEDBACK MONITOR is the only professional quality instrument with brainwave, skin resistance, and heartbeat monitoring capabilities in one package. In the EEG mode, the MONITOR produces a tone burst when brainwaves are within the selected frequencies. Since the frequency threshold is variable from 5.5-16 hz, any part of the ALPHA or THETA bands can be selected. Alpha training is related to relaxation. Theta has been associated with creative processes and "psychic experiences." The MONITOR has the same GSR capability as the RELAXOMETER and also features heartbeat monitoring. Synchronization of heartbeats between persons has been related to a new kind of energy. Write for details.

The BIOFEEDBACK MONITOR come complete with　$140
EEG/head electrodes and exercise manuals.

Optional: Heartbeat/wrist electrodes $5.00
Optional: GSR/ finger electrodes $5.00

FOR FREE LITERATURE ON THESE AND OTHER INSTRUMENTS
WRITE TO:

BIOFEEDBACK INSTRUMENTS, INC.

223 Crescent Street, Waltham, Mass. 02154 Tel. (617) 891-4800

DISTRIBUTED BY:
Lawson Electronics
P.O. Box 711
Poteet, Texas 78065

Whether for private, professional, or research applications one of the AlphaScan instruments should fill all requirements for high quality, portable and inexpensive EEG feedback instruments. All instruments come complete with built-in feedback indicators, electrode assembly, electrode cream, and instruction manual. All BioScan instruments are fully tested before delivery and are covered by a two year warranty. Complete technical data available free.

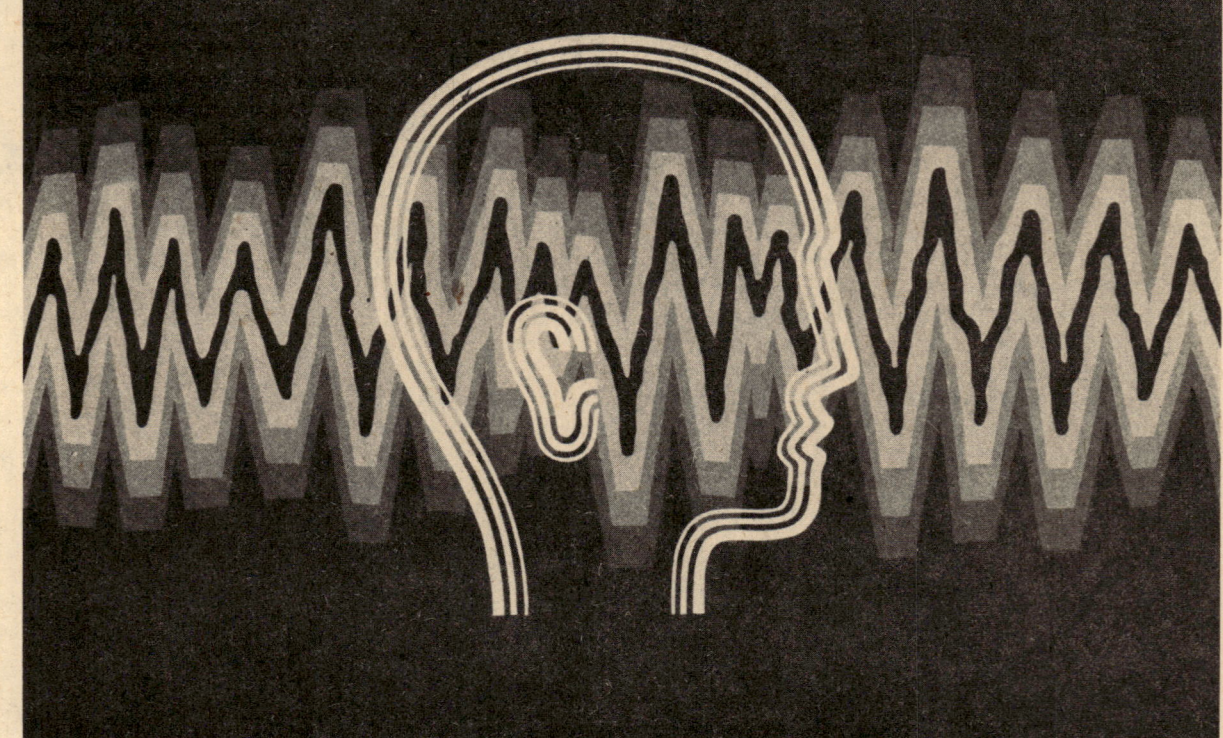

**NEW MIND, NEW BODY,
BIO-FEEDBACK: NEW DIRECTIONS
FOR THE MIND**
Barbara B. Brown
Harper & Row, 1974 $9.95

ALPHASCORER
Digital Percent-Time Computer

- Accuracy of ± one digit
- Completely digital integrated circuitry
- Solid state LED displays
- Optically coupled input for safety
- Four time spans
- Completely processed data

The AlphaScorer can be used with either the AlphaScan 400 or 600 to provide an accurate quantitative measure of EEG activity. The AlphaScorer will indicate the percent of time that feedback is produced in the corresponding AlphaScan instrument; i.e., the percent of time that the EEG signal meets the selected amplitude, frequency, and continuity criteria. Since the AlphaScorer reading is determined by the combinations of settings on the AlphaScan instrument an almost unlimited number of parameters can be scored.

OPERATION

One of four time spans (50, 100, 200, or 500 seconds) is selected. The start switch will begin the time span and the AlphaScorer will begin accepting data from the AlphaScan instrument. The Count light flashes to indicate when data is being transferred to the AlphaScorer. At the end of the selected time span a 1 kHz. tone will sound and the display will indicate the percent of time that the user successfully met the criteria selected on the AlphaScan 400 or 600.

The display will automatically be blanked after approximately fifteen seconds and may be recalled from memory at any time for an additional fifteen seconds by the recall switch. When the delay is switched on the AlphaScorer will wait approximately twenty seconds after being started before the time span is actually begun. This is particularly useful when the person using the AlphaScan instrument also must operate the AlphaScorer since it allows some time to return to the previous state of mind after operating the AlphaScorer controls.

The AlphaScorer is usually connected to the digital filter output on the AlphaScan 400 or the continuity output on the AlphaScan 600 to indicate the percent of time feedback is on. By connecting to other digital outputs an even wider range of measurements is possible. For example, on the AlphaScan 600 a reading may be taken directly from the digital filter and the continuity function will not affect the AlphaScorer reading while still providing feedback with continuity. On both the AlphaScan 400 and 600 the AlphaScorer can also measure the percent of time that the EEG signal exceeds the amplitude threshold without regard to the digital filter settings or continuity control.

The data obtained from the AlphaScorer serves several useful purposes. Studies have shown that biofeedback training is enhanced when the user is given periodic scores of his progress as well as receiving immediate feedback. The AlphaScorer also provides the hard data necessary to objectively evaluate any experiment or training program.

PROFESSIONAL BIO FEEDBACK EQUIPMENT

Bio Scan Corporation
POST OFFICE BOX 14168 • HOUSTON, TEXAS 77021

The Autogen™ 120 Encephalograph Analyser.
SETTING NEW STANDARDS IN FLEXIBILITY AND ACCURACY.

The AUTOGEN 120 Encephalograph Analyser has been designed to meet the basic requirements of biofeedback oriented researchers and clinicians. The 120 also provides the serious trainer with a comprehensive training tool.

As a major feature, the AUTOGEN 120 incorporates Hybrid Spectrum Analysis, our radically new approach to feedback encephalography. Hybrid Spectrum Analysis—unlike conventional analysis approaches incorporated in "competitive" units—assures the subject of a nearly perfect systems response. The 120 features a dual range Hybrid Spectrum Analyser, each range containing an upper and a lower calibrated frequency threshold control. The second range also contains the audio feedback, as well as calibrated upper and lower amplitude threshold controls. While audio feedback is initiated over the second range, instrumentation and analysis can be performed on the first (or either) range. This unique flexibility enables the subject's EEG response to be monitored over a broader or narrower spectrum than the feedback range.

The AUTOGEN 120 also offers the choice of two audio feedback modes. The first is Spectrum Modulation, a broadband sound energy standard on all ASI feedback encephalographs; the second is Tone Modulation, a musical audio signal. Both feedback modes function in the same manner: audio feedback is initiated when the subject's EEG frequency passes below the calibrated setting of the upper frequency threshold control, and his amplitude is equal to or greater than the amplitude threshold setting. Either signal shifts from the treble to bass regions as the EEG lowers in frequency below the calibrated threshold setting. Additionally, the loudness of either signal is proportional to the amplitude of the EEG. With Spectrum Modulation Feedback, as well as Tone Modulation, small changes in amplitude and/or frequency are easily, vividly, and immediately displayed. As a result, the subject is able to continuously correlate, both consciously and subliminally, shifts in EEG with discernible mental and physiological states. Since the 120 provides greater and more accurate feedback information, it maximizes the learning process. As a result, it is the most effective and versatile encephalograph analyser on the market today.

Additional features of the AUTOGEN 120 include instantaneous metered readouts of both frequency and amplitude. Furthermore, both amplitude and frequency can be stored in memory circuits and averaged for the frequency and amplitude parameters covered by either range, over a variety of selectable time intervals (up to 2000 seconds). At the end of a session, these averaging memories provide concrete data for both the analysis of the EEG and the appraisal of training progress. To enable readouts of both the averaging and instantaneous functions, amplitude and frequency meters may be repeatedly switched between their averaging and instantaneous modes without any interruption of memory processes.

The AUTOGEN 120 also incorporates a percent time meter which has its own time interval selector. Both range one and two have memory circuits which simultaneously record the percentage of time spent in their respective frequency spectra. The percent time meter may be repeatedly switched between these two memories with no loss of accuracy or data.

The AUTOGEN 120 also offers a six position switch which allows the selection of a variety of degrees of amplitude integration of the feedback signal. We provide this feature because some subjects feel that cycle per cycle amplitude modulation (found in a significant number of contemporary biofeedback trainers) tends to be subjectively distracting. As an alternative, one setting of the integration control offers complete amplitude integration, while lesser degrees of integration are available for those who desire some cycle per cycle modulation.

As a further feature, the 120 offers a drowsiness alarm. Its circuit is coupled to the lower frequency control of the audio feedback range (Range 2). When the circuit is turned on (it has an associated off/on/volume control), it monitors EEG activity and sounds a mild alarm when the subject's brainwave frequency falls 1 Hz. below the lower frequency threshold setting. This feature is particularly useful for theta training, since some individuals experience drowsiness—and a concurrent drop in EEG frequency—during their initial training efforts in this range. Drowsiness is not desired, since it usually leads to sleep (termination of the training session).

The AUTOGEN 120 is an exceptionally accurate and flexible EEG analyser and feedback system. We feel that it sets new standards that enable trainers, researchers, and clinicians to more fully explore and utilize brainwave feedback.

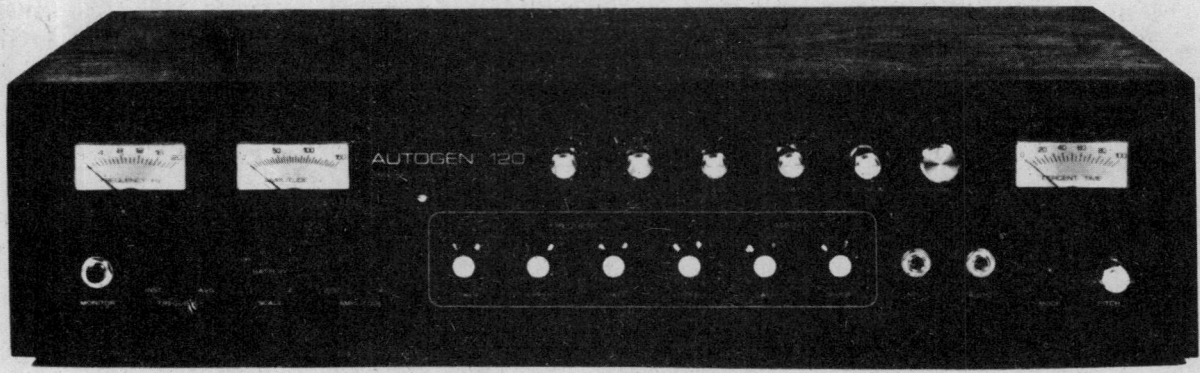

809 Allston Way   Berkeley, California 94710   Telephone (415) 548-6056

You are Psychic!

Learn to use _all_ your potential with these _proven_ techniques.

Yes, you really are psychic. We all are. It's simply a matter of being trained how to develop your natural ability—an ability which everyone has.

Alex Merklingar, founder of Mind Development, Inc. has taught thousands of people in classes all over the country how to realize and develop their psychic potential. Now he has created a Personal Program of Self-Development which enables YOU to learn and develop using the same growth techniques—in your own home.

Maybe being psychic isn't your first goal. What do you want—to lose weight? Quit smoking? Make more money? More friends? Attain greater spiritual enlightenment? It's all part of the program. There are no limits to what you can do.

Graduates of our Mind Development courses have discovered inner creative talents and resources, eliminated bad habits, developed ESP and clairvoyance, gained greater vitality and energy and solved their personal problems by applying the techniques that they learned.

You also can bring exciting changes into your life by using the home study program. Take it alone — or take it with family or friends and watch each other develop.

This remarkable home study program consists of lectures and exercises presented on six 90-minute tapes plus a fascinating, comprehensive instructional manual.

The cost is $150, all mailing and packaging charges included. For immediate delivery send a money order or certified cheque.

☐ Please send me the Mind Development, Inc. Personal Program of Self-Development. I enclose $150 in full payment.

☐ Please send me more information on the Personal Program of Self-Development.

☐ I am interested in purchasing the course on an installment plan. Please send the first of 10 segments. I enclose $20.

Mail to:
Mind Development, Inc.
P.O. Box 16037
Portland, Oregon 97216

NAME
ADDRESS
CITY
STATE   ZIP

In the privacy of your home...

YOU CAN LEARN ESP

If you use the revolutionary RYZL Method!

Unique do-it-yourself course with tapes (cassettes) — only $19.00!

First course of this kind ever published. Outcome of more than 25 years of research. Gives popular explanation of the ESP process and detailed instructions on how you can develop ESP and utilize it in everyday life. Also a method is described how you can teach ESP in others. Method was successfully tested on more than 500 persons. Now everybody can use it!

Author internationally hailed as "Creator of Psychics" in Psychic Discoveries Behind the Iron Curtain. One of his many trainees is listed in Guinness Book of World Records as the best clairvoyant ever tested.

Don't miss this unique opportunity. This valuable course can change your life! Available by mail only.

Price: $19.00 postpaid. (C.O.D.: $5.00 with order, $15.00 at delivery.)

Read other books by Milan Ryzl:
ESP in the Modern World
Hypnosis, survival, reincarnation, future of ESP. Must reading for every student of ESP. ($8.50)
Biblical Miracles, Jesus and ESP
Role of ESP in religious experience. New light shed on biblical figures. ($6.00)
Reviewed in FATE
October 1973, page 110
December 1973, page 124

Send check or money order to:
Milan Ryzl ESP Course
Box 9459, Westgate Sta.
San Jose, CA 95157

MIND EXPANSION

Using **proven** techniques of "reality-awakening," practical mysticism, ESP, "accelerated" evolution, **transcendental thinking**, esoteric sexuality. NO meditation, NO astral projection! Beyond reincarnation, beyond alpha waves. **Unlocks your NATURAL mind power.** Releases inner supra-abilities. Send for free information.

INSTITUTE OF ADVANCED THINKING
Dept. F-874
15243 La Cruz Drive, Box 606
Pacific Palisades, Calif. 90272

HISTORY OF THE SILVA METHOD

Alphagenics, a new science being investigated at the university level, deals with detection, measurement, and mental control of brain waves. Many leading scientists are now doing research in this field. Among other things, it has been stated that when a person learns to alter his brain waves mentally, he can also learn to alter the functioning of his internal organs. Medical science, we are told, could surely use mental control of brain waves for altering the function of internal organs. Such control could account for the differences between disease and health. Interestingly enough, Silva Mind Control began research in this field many years ago.

Research in mental control of brain wave function began in Laredo, Texas, in 1944. We began this research not with the intention of using the results for health purposes, but for the possibility of increasing a person's I.Q. factor. Because of research we now know more about brain waves, their frequency and energy output, than ever before. We know that we can generate more energy at a lower, more stable brain frequency than we can at a higher one. Our brain is functioning at the highest frequencies when we are at the so-called conscious state. These frequencies, known as the Beta frequencies, are typical of the five-senses type of functioning; for example, your brain is now functioning at the Beta frequency as you read. We know that the Alpha brain frequencies are lower than the Beta. We also know that the Theta and Delta are brain frequencies lower than the Alpha. The guiding concept in our research was to learn to use a lower brain frequency and apply its greater energy to make stronger impressions on brain cells, since more information can be recalled when the information has been strongly impressed. Once psychological blockage is controlled, strong impressions of information on brain cells enhance retention and recall, factors contributory to an increased I.Q. factor.

The Electroencephalograph (EEG), a very complex, delicate, and costly piece of electronic equipment, is used for brain wave detection. The high cost of EEG equipment and the difficulty in acquiring expert interpretation of its brain wave tracings prohibited us from using it in our research in Laredo. (Since then, we have equipped our laboratory with EEG equipment.) We had to find other means that would indicate and prove that the brain was functioning at lower frequencies. We proved the fact that when we are in deep slumber, the brain functions at the lowest frequency, the Delta. It was then a matter of training a subject to function somewhere in the direction of deep slumber but not in deep slumber, because a subject has no apparent conscious controls in deep slumber. Quite obviously, conscious controls are desirable so that the person can function independently of the researcher.

The next step was to prove that the brain was functioning at a different frequency. We knew that by different we meant a lower one. We went on the assumption that no brain frequency higher than the Beta existed. To prove that the brain was functioning at a different frequency, supposedly a lower one, a subject would have to do something with his body, brain, or mind that he could not normally do at higher or so-called conscious-state frequencies. In addition, the subject was required to maintain conscious awareness and controls at all times. Some of the things that subjects learned to do while at lower frequencies with conscious awareness and controls were to alter heart beat and blood pressure, to vary pain threshold, digestion, sweating, and skin temperature, and to alter blood circulation.

Since we were interested mostly in increasing the I.Q. factor and not in the health areas, we concentrated our efforts in the educational field. Our goals were: 1) when studying, to cut out distractions for greater concentration; 2) to reinforce good study habits; 3) to learn how to impress information with greater brain energy; and 4) to learn the use of keys for self-programming. While going through this research, we became attracted to a certain mental phenomenon. Subjects were sometimes answering questions that were not yet presented to them. We also found that subjects could do better with very important and valuable questions, such as emotionally involved questions.

That discovery caused us to set a new goal: to enhance that particular mental phenomenon. As research progressed, it became apparent that subjects needed to be in a special state of mind to accomplish the results we were seeking. We found that the required state of mind was not the one normally known as the conscious state of mind or Beta brain wave frequency. This Beta state of mind we named Outer Conscious Levels. We found that the state of mind required to produce the phenomenon was one of a lower brain frequency, because we became aware that the phenomenon could be produced while the subject was going in the direction of deep slumber. The special state of mind that was required to produce the phenomenon we named Inner Conscious Levels.

At that time we stopped researching to find better controls to produce higher I.Q. We were onto something more interesting. Our new project was to set up research experiments to improve the subject's so-called guessing ability. The subject was required to guess what we had in mind. This was done by giving him only bits of information and letting him fill in the details. Later subjects in the research got very proficient at guessing everything we had in mind that was relative to a problem case, and this was done without their being given any information at all.

We continued projects in the direction of improving the guessing proficiency of the subjects through special mental training. The next project was to determine whether or not a subject could be trained to give us all the information about a problem case that we had only a few details on. As soon as we were successful in getting the correct information, we started training subjects to give us information on problem cases that we knew nothing about. After this we started to shorten the training time to see how much we could shorten it and still be effective. We then worked with training groups of 20 and 30, all males, all females, mixed, and some within certain age brackets.

By this time we knew that in approximately 48 hours of class time, using special methods of mental training, everyone could learn to function with mental controls at lower brain frequencies. It is possible to know (without EEG) if a subject is functioning at lower brain frequencies after completion of his mental training by giving him a problem case that he knows nothing about. If he gives the correct information, he is there.

We can now state as fact that in approximately 48 hours we can train a group of subjects to function at lower, more stable, more energetic and very valuable brain frequencies for specific applications. Valuable end results are that not only can a subject become aware of information relative to problems, but he can also become aware of information relative to the solution of such problems. This discovery indicates that the human brain, mind and intelligence functioning at these levels have tremendous problem-solving potential. This indicates that human intelligence is not only capable of sensing information impressed on its own brain, but is also capable of sensing information on other brains at a distance. This kind of sensing, through which we can acquire information and that takes place when awareness is functioning at lower brain frequencies we call subjective communication.

CASSETTE TAPE LIST
(FOR GRADUATES OF SILVA MIND CONTROL)

Metronome Tape (Special) features both the Alpha (side 2) and Special Conditioning (side 1) Sound Effects.................. $ 7.95

MC-101-CR Review Tape With Metronome Background................. $ 7.95

MC-202-GSI Review Tape With Metronome Background................. $ 7.95

MC-303-ESP Review Tape (Part I) With Metronome Background................. $ 7.95

MC-303-ESP Review Tape (Part II) With Metronome Background................. $ 7.95

MC-404-A ESP Review Tape (Part I) With Metronome Background................. $ 7.95

MC-404-A ESP Review Tape (Part II) With Metronome Background................. $ 7.95

Electronic Metronome with Modified Frequency Output Beta, Alpha, Theta, Delta (non calibrated)................. $34.50

Silva Mind Control Monthly Newsletter................. 1 yr. $ 3.50
2 yrs. $ 6.50

SILVA MIND CONTROL INTERNATIONAL, INC.
1110 Cedar
P.O. Box 1149
Laredo, Texas 78040

Write for complete program description.

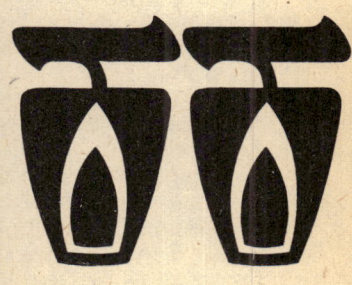

SPECIAL APM REPORT

"Mind Training" courses are immensely popular. This spreading phenomenon is analyzed by Dr. and Mrs. Elmer Green, noted biofeedback researchers at the Menninger Foundation . . . and they are concerned. Their recommendations: caution, understanding, standards, a non-profit orientation.

Note: Additional copies of this four-page presentation are available at nominal prices; for details see "Reprints" at end of presentation.

MIND TRAINING, ESP, HYPNOSIS, AND VOLUNTARY CONTROL OF INTERNAL STATES
by
Elmer and Alyce Green

In order to sharply delineate the main points of this note, it is convenient to first summarize the subjects of discussion and our understanding of them as follows:

1. Through hypnosis and through various training programs, including biofeedback, many persons can become aware of normally-unconscious processes.

2. Awareness of normally-unconscious processes is sometimes accompanied by spontaneous (and sometimes volitional) ESP phenomena.

3. Commercial mind training courses promising ESP powers are using hypnosis as the major method and, advertising to the contrary, do not give biofeedback or brain wave training, nor are the subjects necessarily in an alpha brainwave state.

4. Commercial mind training "teachers" generally deny that they use hypnosis and by denying or ignoring the risks associated with hypnotic "programming" are inducing in some persons a form of paranoid neurosis or psychosis, often related to obsession or "possession."

5. Hypnotic programming for ESP bears a similarity to some of the methods used for development of trance mediumship, especially the "possession by spirits" of low grade mediumship.

6. Awareness of normally unconscious processes can be safely taught under the guidance of a counselor, without hypnotic programming, by methods which allow each person to develop according to his own inner needs.

7. Mind training procedures should be voluntarily modified by those interested in the subject to eliminate psychic hazards. If this is not done, government agencies may summarily ban many research and training programs that otherwise, if carefully developed, might become valuable adjuncts to our education and health systems.

8. The major problems are (a) to determine what techniques are safe as well as efficient for the extension of awareness, (b) to establish standards of qualification and responsibility of teachers, and (c) to offer the benefits of awareness training programs to the public through non-profit institutions.

* * * * *

Many psychologists in the last few years have become interested in research possibilities that a few years back were considered beyond the realm of science, namely, voluntary control of normally-unconscious psychological and physiological processes. The first medical approaches to this subject in the West, starting in about 1910, sprang from the researches and developments of Autogenic Training and Psychosynthesis, beginning with Johannes Schultz in Germany and Alberto Assagioli in Italy, respectively. At about the same time, Edmund Jacobson was beginning to develop in the United States his training program known as Progressive Relaxation. In other parts of the world, new interpretations of yoga were developing, such as the Integral Yoga of Aurobindo. His *Synthesis of Yoga,* for instance, is concerned with a program for enhancement of consciousness and for control of normally-unconscious processes. The newest development along this line of self regulation of mind and body and perhaps the most applicable to Westerners in general, has resulted from research in the area of biofeedback training.

The programs mentioned above deal with one's power to modify and control, through volition, one's own mental, emotional, and physiological states, without hypnotic programming by another person; and in all of these developments (except perhaps Progressive Relaxation, which deals primarily with problems of muscle tension) parapsychological events sometimes occur. These events are not, however, the goals of training. The primary goal is self mastery, and in Psychosynthesis and in Integral Yoga the primary goal is self mastery coupled with the development of awareness of what, in Zen, is called the True Self. Unless this aspect of Self is developed, it is said, psychic powers become an "ego trip." The attainment of psychic powers may follow safely after a degree of self mastery (ego mas tery) is achieved, but if paranormal development comes first, psychological problems develop. Aurobindo's way of saying this focuses attention on what he calls the Overmind level of one's being. After achieving awareness of that, he says, one can explore in "astral" dimensions with a measure of safety. Otherwise, it is possible to become involved in psychic (pschological) entanglements and not be able to find one's way, through layers of mental and emotional confusion, back to one's center. The ancient Christian advice concerning these matters was to seek first the kingdom of Heaven, which was within, it was said, and other things would follow in due course.

These considerations seem to have an especially important meaning today because we are bombarded by newspaper advertisements of entrepreneurs who (for a fee) will develop psychic powers in us, through hypnosis. It is denied that hypnosis is the technique employed, because hypnosis is a "bad word." Instead it is called "conditioning," "programming," "brainwave training," "alpha training," etc., but nevertheless, it *is* hypnosis. On this professionals agree, though they do not always agree on how hypnosis works. The "countdown" induction procedure used in commercial mind training "programming" is a classical hypnotic technique.

Hypnosis is an extremely powerful tool for control of physiological and psychological states. It is well known that through hypnosis painless surgery can be performed, people can be made to see things that are not there, and not see things that are there, but it is not generally realized, even by professionals, that through hypnosis parapsychological sensitivity can be enhanced. Frederick Myers, in 1901, clearly summarized the major findings of hypnosis experimentation in the last century and showed that hypnosis and parapsychology are not necessarily two separate subjects. More recently, Beloff, in an analysis of the paranormal, ventures the opinion that "hypnotism may not be just a psychological phenomenon but may have a certain paranormal component as well." The points being made here are that hypnosis *can* involve the paranormal, and the paranormal is being invoked by hypnosis in some of those who take commercial mind training courses, opinions of non-investigators notwithstanding.

The question might now be raised, "So-what? What difference does it make?" This question can be answered in at least three ways, depending on whether one looks at commercial mind training (1) from a traditional *psychological* point of view, that is, treat the various phenomena that result from the program as figments of the imagination; (2) from a *psychosomatic* point of view, in which the power of mind over events inside the skin is accepted, but parapsychological events are considered to be figments of the imagination; or (3) from a *parapsychological* point of view, in which the phenomena of hypnosis are seen as consistent with research data from various psychological, psychosomatic and parapsychological studies.

But before these points of view can be considered, it is necessary to identify some of the phenomena that are claimed by commercial mind training teachers and by many of their students, namely:

(a) A person can "go down" into his own "unconscious," and while in that deep "level," can program his own physiological and psychological processes so that various diseases in him that have not yielded to standard medical treatment can be brought under control, at least temporarily.

(b) While at his deep "level," a person can become aware of physical, emotional and mental states and diseases in other people, and can correctly diagnose ailments.

(c) While at his "level," a person can learn to manipulate the physical, emotional and mental natures of other persons, sick or healthy, and thereby modify their behavior.

(d) While at his "level," a person can learn to manipulate nature so that coincidences, "accidents," or lack of accidents, can come under his control. This is, essentially, a promise of psychokinetic powers.

Now from a traditional *psychological* point of view, the above ideas are sheer nonsense, some would say "sheer madness." From that point of view, the tens of thousands who have taken mind training courses and who are convinced of the reality of some or all of the above claims, have been programmed into a serious delusional system and can be expected sooner or later, if rationality is not re-established, to develop, in consequence, some degree of neurosis or psychosis.

From a *psychosomatic* point of view it might be acceptable to hypothesize that one could learn to manipulate certain normally-unconscious psychological processes whose physiological correlates are thereby brought under control, that is, item (a) above might be accepted, but items (b) through (d) would be considered to be belief in sheer nonsense, which, if persisted in, would probably lead to mental or physical breakdown.

From the *parapsychological* point of view, none of the items listed above are at variance with data accumulated in the last fifty years indicating that such events are possible or at least worthy of hypothesis, even though not statistically probable.

In an attempt to evaluate mind training, all scientists are not equally qualified. Scientists who subscribe exclusively to the traditional psychological or the psychosomatic views are in main those who either (a) have not studied the paranormal data and literature, (b) have had no spontaneous paranormal events in their own lives (that they admit, at least), (c) have not developed their own existential sensitivities and knowledge, or (d) all or some combination of the above. A probable example of this type of "scientist" is F. U. Condon, the former head of the National Bureau of Standards. According to McConnell, Condon made the following pronouncement:

> Flying saucers and astrology are not the only pseudo-sciences which have a considerable following among us. There used to be spiritualism, there continues to be extrasensory perception, psychokinesis, and a host of others . . . Where corruption of children's minds is at stake, I do not believe in freedom of the press or freedom of speech. In my view, publishers who publish or teachers who teach any of the pseudo-sciences as established truth should, on being found guilty, be publicly horsewhipped, and forever banned from further activity in these usually honorable professions.

Opinions from such scientists, who apparently have no adequate existential or experiential base, or who have not done their homework in the field of parapsychology, or who may (in some cases) have unconscious fears of the subject, are not appropriate here. The following is written, therefore, for those who can consider the parapsychological hypothesis without doing violence to their belief structure.

To continue then from the parapsychological viewpoint, the main questions that must be raised about commercial mind training programs are (1) judged by professionals rather than entrepreneurs, what is actually happening to students in regard to psychological, psychosomatic and parapsychological events and accomplishments, (2) what are the dangers of hypnotic programming for the purpose of enhancing psychic development, (3) what is the level of responsibility of program organizers and associated teachers, (4) what mind training techniques are safe as well as efficient in bringing a person to a level of psychic development that is not inappropriate for him, (5) what is the most responsible way of presenting mind training and its various benefits to the public, and (6) how is the mind training movement to be regulated in the interest of public welfare. Concerning these questions, the following comments might be made:

Hypnotic programming as used in the commercial courses has several defects, namely: (a) Many people are psychically catapulted, so to speak, into existential realms in which they cannot protect themselves from dangers arising either from within their own unconscious, or from psychic manipulation by other persons, or from "extrapersonal" sources (dangers inherent in so called "astral" dimensions). There is not time here to review the history of spiritualism since 1849 and the psychic disasters that often resulted from dabbling in the area of trance mediumship, but mental hospitals, even today, contain many people who "hear voices." These people usually cannot turn the voices off, cannot separate fact from fiction, have lost their "reality testing" powers, and often are obliged to act out "against their will" instructions they are "given." (b) Commercial mind training students are often "programmed" in ways not appropriate to their own needs, nor at their own proper rates. What is proper for one can be disasterous for another. This hazard arises, because apart from the dangers of hypnotic penetration into "astral" levels of being, (c) many mind training teachers are incompetent to work with people in matters where psychological and physical health are at stake. For example, former salesmen who have had a few courses in hypnotic programming are not qualified to work in this very delicate area of the human psyche with its psychosomatic correlates. (d) And most seriously, psychic submission may be enhanced in "astral" dimensions rather than powers of self volition. This is the consensus of Eastern teachers who, it must be conceded, reflect much experimentation and experience over the centuries with training methods for self mastery. It is admitted that psychosomatic *self* regulation, achieved by any volitional method, is slow compared to submitting oneself to hypnotic instruction, i.e., turning the control of one's mind over to another person, but it is also maintained by the most accomplished teachers that the power of psychic self-determination is the *sine qua non* for safety in astral dimensions.

Concerning safety in "astral" dimensions, possibly the greatest specific danger associated with hypnotic submission in commercial mind training programs lies in the developing, or obtaining, of psychic "advisors." They are the male and female assistants who "know everything," who at the deep "level" of mind advise the student, and sometimes tell him what to do.

In the *mediumistic* version of the parapsychological paradigm, these advisors, however constructed or found, may serve as masks for "entities" who may attempt (now that the student has become amenable to suggestion at the unconscious level) to control the student's mental, emotional and physical behavior. The mediumistic concept will clearly be detected by mind training teachers because, if accepted, it would imply that these teachers might be responsible for serious problems in the lives of some of their trainees. The physical frontiers of our planet have presented many dangers to humans, can it be safely assumed that the inner frontier has no corresponding perils? Is it realistic to accept the assurances of commercial mind training instructors that dangers that may be associated with "territorial invasion" by humans on "astral" levels are not possible? For those who accept the possibility of "entities," is it safe to assume that only good, nice, and safe beings (like humans?) are functioning in "astral" dimensions? This would be a truly Ptolemaic assumption.

Regarding the hazards associated with the all-knowing advisors found at the deep "level," some time ago we pointed out to an acquaintance that friends of his who were students of one of the mind training programs might consider being on guard against the possibility of mediumistic-like "possession" through the agency of the advisors. The upshot of this was that these students challenged their advisors, asked them to get out of their "psychic space." Eventually we received a letter saying:

> You may be interested in knowing that after I told my two close friends . . . the warning about the assistants . . . they both went down to their workshops and told their assistants to leave. In both cases a strong but eventually successful test of wills or something took place, with the assistants becoming very ugly and hostile in the process. However, they were finally forced to leave . . . The wife later told me that before I had talked to them about it she had been having increasing trouble getting to sleep at night or going down to her levels because of the appearance of hostile and ugly faces in her mind. It had become a serious problem. Afterwards she told me that since her assistants left she was no longer bothered by the faces, that they had disappeared. So perhaps it was fortunate for them that you gave your warning.

Along this same line, one of our friends in the Bay Area, a counselor on psychological and religious problems, reports that at least a dozen of his clients are suffering from paranoid neuroses as a result of taking mind training courses. Another acquaintance, a psychiatrist who took one of the commercial courses himself, reported to us that four of the thirty who went through the program became psychotic. Two of them had to be hospitalized. In part, he attributed this result to the psychic peculiarity of the instructor. Other students with whom we have discussed the "instructor effect" have reported similar events. Apparently a kind of psychic "transference" phenomenon can occur, a kind of "psychic pollution" can take place due to the unconscious receptivity of the subject to "extra sensory projection" by the hypnotist.

Another point, Mind training teachers often maintain that no harm can be done to another person by themselves or by their students, because they are programmed with the idea that if these "powers" are used for ignoble or selfish purposes they will be lost, but this is likely to be nonsense. Post-hypnotic suggestions are notorious for their impermanence, so if real psychic "powers" are developed in students it can be assumed that hypnotically-imposed restrictions on the use of such powers will not be long lasting.

The examples given above indicate that whether one chooses to examine commercial mind training methods from either the traditional psychological point of view or from the parapsychological point of view, there is risk involved for students. We do not presume to be able to answer all the questions raised, but when over one hundred thousand persons have already been processed through such mind training programs, (including 2000 high school girls at a school in Philadelphia in October, 1972) some questions should be asked. In view of the hazards associated with hypnotic programming in commercial mind training courses, the present writers believe that hypnosis as a technique for inducing self awareness and parapsychological faculties is not adequately safe and should be discarded.

Does this mean that there is no use for hypnosis? Not at all, no more than there is no use for surgery. But even as surgery has particular use in *acute* situations, where something must be done or else unbearable pain, or permanent damage, or death may occur, so also with hypnosis. For *chronic* situations, however, those which are characteristic of most psychosomatic diseases, non-hypnotic volitional training programs such as those employing biofeedback are more desirable. For exploring in psychic domains, new and safe training methods are being developed by Dialogue House and Psychosynthesis, for example, and through research in brainwave training. Other safe methods also exist, as is well known, such as the various forms of yogic meditation. In all of these methods, both old and new, accent is placed on learning to handle psychological and physiological problems through voluntary control at a rate consistent with one's capacity for self protection.

Spiritual teachers concerned with the development of inner awareness have always excluded hypnosis as a technique, both in the East and in the West, not because it was not understood, but because it *was* understood. Self development and programming by another were considered antithetical. There is no logical reason to assume that things are now different merely because we are in the twentieth century and people are in a hurry, wish to have immediate results and perhaps even hope to get something without effort. Hypnotic programming (like LSD) has convinced many people that an inner terrain exists, and in this way it has been instrumental in drawing attention to an important dimension of human life, but it is also important that we now look at the entire area of "inner exploration" and, in as balanced a way as possible, evaluate the many programs that are being offered for penetration into hitherto arcane dimensions of the psyche. Commercialism should not enter into such a vitally important matter. Commercialism often results in (a) false and misleading use of scientific terms, such as "alpha and theta brainwave training," and distortion of what is actually accomplished by such training, (b) exaggerated claims for "powers" that can be obtained by anyone who pays the price and takes the course, (c) stressing of powers not appropriate to certain persons, such as the ability to diagnose and treat diseases, (d) undue emphasis on large enrollment in courses in order to earn more money, rather than to be of service. Large enrollment interferes with one-to-one contact between teachers and students so that whatever problems arise are unlikely to be properly handled even if the teacher had the necessary skill.

In short, commercialism in the mind training field does not lead in the direction of high responsibility and service, and this raises the very important question about the manner in which regulation can best be established in the mind training movement. We are of the opinion that if responsible control is not established quite soon by those already involved, government agencies will step in and provide regulation in the interest of public welfare.

In our estimation, a list of positive guidelines to follow in establishing an "ideal training method" might include the following items:

(1) Make it possible for each person to discover "himself" at a proper rate, that is, penetrate into the unconscious at a rate consistent with his ability to keep his feet on the ground, keep his reality testing powers intact. This means that those for whom psychic unfoldment would lead to destructive neuroses or psychoses should obtain only those insights and awarenesses which, in the usual therapeutic sense, would help integrate and bring under control various discordant sections of the personality.

(2) The student should be shielded by the training method from imperfections of the teacher that might otherwise become part of the student's "psychic atmosphere" and hinder his progress.

(3) Teachers should be ranked or evaluated according to their level of insight and awareness so that as each student progresses existentially he has a properly qualified *human* advisor with whom to talk.

(4) The student should be passed on from teacher to teacher, so to speak, as rapidly as his experiences require more advanced advice or suggestion (not analysis or programming).

(5) Training centers for self awareness should be located within access of anyone interest in participating in the program and should be established on a *non-profit* basis.

REPRINTS

Prices for additional copies of "Mind Training . . ." by Dr. and Mrs. Elmer Green are as follows: For Academy Members: 25¢/two copies; $1.00/ten copies; $5.00/seventy-five copies; 5¢/each additional copy thereafter. For Non - Members: 25¢ / one copy; $1.00/six copies; $5.00/fifty copies; 5¢/each additional copy thereafter.

All orders are postpaid. No order accepted without cash remittance in advance. Send to: The Academy of Parapsychology & Medicine
314 Second St., Los Altos, CA 94022

**INTERNATIONAL FOUNDATION
FOR PSYCHOSYNTHESIS**
Medical Plaza Suite 901
10921 Wilshire Blvd.
Los Angeles, Calif. 90024

**PSYCHOSYNTHESIS RESEARCH
FOUNDATION**
40 East 49th St., Room 1902
New York, N.Y. 10017

EAST WEST JOURNAL
Published by Order of the Universe Publications
29 Farnsworth Street
Boston, Mass. 02210
$5.00 per 12 issues U.S.
$7.00 foreign

An excellent review of psychic and spiritual community activities

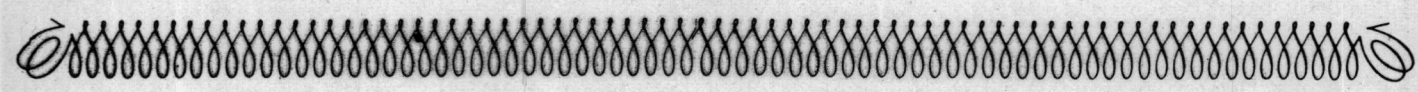

ASTRO CONSCIOUSNESS INSTITUTE FOR SELF ENLIGHTENMENT AND PEACE

The Astro Consciousness Institute offers a personalized program of self enlightenment for those individuals who desire inner control and harmony in all parts of their being — mental, emotional, physical and spiritual. Our concept of education is to train persons to become "citizens of the universe" and to help build the New Age Civilization.

Our Teaching program is precise and progressive. All ACI students begin their New Age education with Astro 6, a 6-week course based on the book, *Jonathan Livingston Seagull*. The goal here is understanding and accepting the self. We teach "energy", what it is, how to use it, and how to distinguish one's own pattern from those of others.

Astro 7, a 7-week intermediate course, has two purposes: to solidify the personal energy pattern learned in Astro 6, and to become familiar with *The Life and Teachings of the Masters of the Far East*, the underlying philosophy of the Institute. Upon the completion of this course, the student can then determine whether or not to commit himself to the New Age pattern of living.

Intensive training follows with meditation and contemplation as the keynote. The student now learns "to be" rather than "to do." This is accomplished through the inner control of personal energy outflow. It is an open-end program where the student sets his own pace.

This program does not appeal to the masses but to those few who feel there is a higher calling in life, who want to master themselves and make the necessary personal changes to achieve freedom from all bondage.

FOR INFORMATION WRITE OR CALL:

Daphne Jeffress, Master
Seattle Branch
10169 N.E. 112 Place
Kirkland, Washington 98033
Telephone: (202) 822-3372

Paul Cutright, Master
1927 South Emerson Street
Denver, Colorado 80210
Telephone: (303) 777-0700

PHENOMENON OF MAN PROJECT

The POM Project seeks to explore and to promulgate the concept of the evolution of consciousness. Through a balanced approach including intellectually-oriented as well as more intuitive-level programs, the Project assists its audiences and participants in attaining not only objective understanding but also subjective, experiential awareness of the widening dimensions of consciousness.

The point of departure for the work of the Project is the writings of Pierre Teilhard de Chardin, late French Jesuit priest and paleontologist. The "objective" side of POM's activities consists of audio-visual lecture-seminars based on the writings of Teilhard and other writers of both the East and the West, whose thought has helped to open the dimensions of Man's Future. These programs include "The Cosmic Christ," "Man, Earth and Cosmos," and "Survival." The latter is based on *"The Phenomenon of Man,"* Teilhard's best known and most widely quoted book. The lecture-seminars, to date presented to a total of over 50,000 persons, include scientifically accurate but easily understood lecture text, original and unique full-color slides, and question/answer or dialogue sessions with the audience.

More subjectively-oriented programs include weekend retreats and various formats of small-group workshops. These retreats and workshops have made use of meditative techniques, music, discussion sessions and interpersonal group dialogue.

Supplementing the "live" activities of the Project is a growing line of educational materials, including a Filmstrip Library and Tape Cassette Library based on *"The Phenomenon of Man."* Entitled "SURVIVAL," the libraries feature the masterful narration of Mr. Lew Ayres.

Inquiries about POM Project membership, published materials, and lecture or retreat sponsorship should be directed to:

Department LS4
8932 Reseda Boulevard, Suite 204
Northridge, California 91324
U.S.A.
Telephone: (213) 886-5260

What is ARICA?

ARICA, in Quechua, the pre-Incan laguage of the Andes Indians, means "Open Door."

The Arica Institute takes its name from the desert town of Arica, Chile, where in 1970, fifty Americans underwent an intensive training program in psychological development under the direction of Oscar Ichazo. Since then the Institute has become an international organization with headquarters in New York and 23 teaching houses on three continents.

Arica offers a unique training system in conscious human evolution. The trainings are intended to initiate and consolidate a process of ongoing development of the total man. Based on a coherent philosophy of man and his place in the universe, the trainings focus on developing and unifying the body, mind and emotions. The aim of the trainings is to produce greater body vitality, to eliminate negative emotions, and to replace them with positive states, to increase mental clarity, and to create a permanent higher level of awareness.

Arica recognizes that the final goal of human history is to produce a perfect society which in turn is capable of producing perfect individuals. Perfection here means the realization of our full human potential. To implement this goal, Arica uses SCIENTIFIC MYSTICISM. It is scientific because it requires no guru or belief structure. All the techniques employed are approached experimentally as hypotheses to be tested. It is mysticism because Arica affirms that the goal of humanity is unity—unity within individuals, unity with other people, and unity of the society as a whole.

The system used by Arica is based on both eastern and western techniques of development. Over 400 exercises are used, including physical exercises for integrating mind, breath, and movement, somatonic massage, relaxation techniques, meditation techniques, breathing techniques, the use of objective body positions to bring about positive emotional responses, chanting, techniques for generating and transmuting sexual energy, exercises for making objective personal contact with others, techniques for identifying and releasing negative associative patterns, the study of energy centers and the development of energy channels in the body, body awareness exercises, and individual analytic assignments. In addition there are forum presentations of theories of personality, motivation, and consciousness.

All of this work is done in a group setting. Arica maintains that the process of reaching human perfection is greatly facilitated by working in groups. The energy of consciousness increases geometrically with the number of individuals involved. By using the psycho-dynamic pressures of rapid, positive feedback, it is possible to dramatically speed up individual realization.

Arica is open to all who are interested in the development of awareness. Depending on your perspective, it can be seen as a spiritual discipline, a group psychological process, or a social alternative, offering new ways of cultural affirmation in our society. It is not a religion, nor is it therapy. Arica is a non-profit organization whose sole purpose is to teach experiential methods of human development.

Arica is an Open Center, offering hour-long programs in Psychocalisthenics, Meditation, Breathing, Relaxation, Open Path Weekends, 5-Day Programs, 9-Day Programs, and the 40-Day Intensive.

For specific times and dates, and to register for all Arica programs, contact any of our teaching houses.

Arica Institute, Inc.
24 West 57th Street
New York, New York 10019

© 1973 Arica Institute, Inc.
All Rights Reserved

Astara -- A Place of Light -- A Center of Spiritual Research and Mystical Philosophy

What is Astara?

ASTARA IS...

...A Center Of All Religions And Philosophies
...A School Of The Ancient Mysteries
...An Institute Of Psychic Research

Astara is not only a place where people meet others. It is a place where people meet ideas . . . concepts which illumine the mind. A place where faith joins hands with reason . . . where religion becomes compatible with science. A place where the wisdom of the ages combines with modern religion and philosophy to be reinterpreted in the light of today's need for intellectual understanding as well as spiritual, mental and emotional upliftment.

Those who are not satisfied with the usual religiosity find enlightenment through Astara where there are no dogmas, no creeds, no rigid ecumenical precepts. Astara is a place where TRUTH is ONE.

Astara, as a center of all religions and philosophies, fosters a reverence for all Holy Scriptures and spiritual teachings. There are many paths to the Infinite Being, and His prophets have been many, each interpreting His Word in their own way. Astara pays homage to all these enlightened mystics upon whose teachings the world's great religions and philosophies have been founded.

Astara is not a church, sect nor religion in the traditional sense. Astara embraces the mystical teachings of all, giving each person freedom to seek contact with the Infinite Being in his own way through his own Self-realization. Astara attempts to light the way to that spiritual goal which is buried deep in the heart of every man.

Astara, as a school of the ancient Mysteries, explores the wisdom teachings of ancient Egypt when the Mystery Schools flourished under the guidance of illumined Priest-Kings . . . the Mysteries of the golden age of Greece when the great philosophers lit the world with their wisdom . . . the esoteric teachings of the East, brought forth by the inspired gurus and lamas of India and Tibet.

Astara seeks out the inner meanings of Christianity . . . those teachings to which Jesus referred his select group of disciples when he said, "Unto you it is given to know the mystery of the kingdom of God . . ." Astara probes the arcane thought of Judaism, Islam, Buddhism and many another of those great spiritual movements which have touched the inner consciousness of enlightened men through the ages.

Astara, as an institute of psychic research, investigates the mental, psychic and spiritual powers of man, delving into the fascinating fields of spiritual healing, extrasensory perception, telepathy, clairvoyance and many more of the often dormant potentials possessed by each of us. Astara joins hands with science in studying the realms of mind, and suggests techniques for harnessing its power to disclose the path of intuition which leads to illumination..

• • • •

This vast storehouse of wisdom has been placed on the printed pages of the Degree Lessons, ASTARA'S BOOK OF LIFE, available to Astarian members. If you have ever pondered the questions . . .

... Who am I?
... Why am I here?
... Where did I come from?
... Where am I going?
... What is God?

these Lessons, written by Earlyne Chaney and emendated by Robert Chaney, will guide you through the realms of self into the Realms of Self . . . and Divinity.

An Astarian

In an Astarian there's no dogmatic trace
  He sees the light of God in every face,
In Mosque, Cathedral and in Synagogue,
  Wherever man may lift his cry to God.,

Wherever hearts and hands are raised in prayer,
  In every shrine, a living God is there.
He joins the Wise Men, following a star,
  And finds a Christ, a Cross, an Avatar.

In Buddha's shrine, he feels a stir within,
  He bends the knee when chants the Muezzin.

Astara

261 South Mariposa Avenue
Los Angeles, California 90004
Telephone: 387-7187

Meetings Sundays at: 11:00 a.m.

ANDERSON RESEARCH FOUNDATION INC.

As a non-profit Corporation, the Anderson Research Foundation is dedicated to research, evaluate and test almost all methods of Life Enhancement. Recognizing that no way is the only way, the Foundation takes an eclectic stance.

It sponsors research in the physical, nutritional, emotional, mental, spiritual, esoteric and other approaches to life enhancement, "accepted" and "unaccepted", scientific and unscientific, subjective and objective, Eastern and Western.

Having explored most approaches to life enhancement from acupuncture through General Semantics to Zen, ARF is now ready to apply the essence of its findings. This will be done first with a selected group of graduates of its Mind Expansion Training (MEGRIC) and later these eclectic findings, now in process of being integrated, will be applied to a workable prison reform plan. This shows promise when fully operating of solving many of the so far unsolved problems including prisoner rehabilitation, prison living conditions, recidivism, capital punishment and crime in general. Ultimately this plan has great potential for improving our whole society.

Granting that this is an ambitious project, assistance is invited. Assistance may be in the form of volunteers or workers for degrees. By arrangement with the International Studies of Humanistic Psychology (ISHP) (Hq in Switzerland), some persons contributing to this research and/or participating in ARF activities are earning degrees (BA, MA, and PhD). Free folders are available describing the degree program, the Precision Psychodrama private groups/public demonstrations, and the Mind Expansion Training.

A new 1974 policy of fewer single lectures and more courses is reflected in the Newsletter, *OLE (Operation Life Enhancement).* The Foundation's motto: *"We neither endorse nor condemn, we explore".* Monthly newsletter is sent to anyone on request. Donations to cover expenses accepted.

Dr. Laurence Anderson, Director
3968 Ingraham Street
Los Angeles, California 90005
U.S.A.
Telephone: (213) 387-9164

AUM ESOTERIC STUDY CENTER
2405 Ruscombe Lane
Baltimore, Md. 21209

YOU ARE INVITED TO BECOME A MEMBER OF AUM

The quality of our mailings has become a source of great joy for us. We intend to increase the quality of our mailings so that our members will be able to remain well-informed as to the major developments in the fields of the esoteric sciences, as well as AUM classes, guest lectures and seminars.

Also, with the help of the Savitria Press, AUM is reproducing some very rare and out-of-date prints, charts, folders and booklets that we would like to share with you. We will keep the cost of these "esoterica" at a minimum for all those who are interested, and provide these same items at no cost to those who desire to become supporting, organizational and lifetime members or patrons.

Here is a list of memberships and the benefits derived from each one. Of course all of our students and teachers are placed on our ever-growing mailing list.
Friend of AUM—All mailings and catalogues—$5 per year
Supporting Member—Mailings, posters, charts and tokens of our esteem—$10 per year
Organizational Member—Mailings, posters, charts and all AUM & Savitria publications—$25 per year
Lifetime Member—All above and admission to all future lectures at AUM—$150.00
Patron—All above with admission to all AUM lectures and classes—$1000.00

By applying for any of the above memberships in person, you also receive a reproduction of the Reverse of the Great Seal of the United States (17/ x 20/), or a "Cosmic Symbolism" poster (17/ x 22/) at no cost.

Of course all donations are tax deductable since AUM is a non-profit, tax exempt corporation . . . dedicated to sowing the Seeds of the Aquarian Age. Write for Gift Catalogue, publications list, and academic program information.

THE REVERSE OF THE GREAT SEAL OF THE USA
AMERICA'S FORGOTTEN SYMBOL

It was placed on the reverse of the one dollar bill in 1935. Our government has rejected it for various reasons. It is a mystery to them. Write to them, and you'll be surprised how little they know about its meaning. Their opinion is expressed by Prof. Eliot Norton, of Harvard. He stated it was a "dull masonic emblem". Masonic it is—dull it is not. Modern historians have unanimously rejected it, but the young are adopting it as a symbol for the return to the basic philosophy which founded America—"We reject Tyranny. We desire to live in Liberty, Fraternity, Equality."

Here are some interesting facts that are relative to the reverse side of the Great Seal that you should know, but which are not to be found in any traditional history book. The reverse of the Great Seal is a masonic emblem. Why? Because over 50 of the signers of the Declaration of Independence were Masons and Rosicrucians. This is very important, for Masonry was, and still is, very concerned with the esoteric sciences such as astrology, numerology, tarot, cabala, symbology, etc. It is known that both Benjamin Franklin and Thomas Jefferson were not only Masons, but astrologers. It is from the esoteric point of view that we should regard the reverse of the Great Seal, for the founders of this nation, as well as those who took part in the designing of the Great Seal, were esotericists and belonged to esoteric societies. There can be no doubt of this.

The eye in the triangle is the "all-seeing eye of God" in Masonry. It is spiritual vision. It is the third eye—the eye of clairvoyance. It is the eye the Bible refers to when it says, "For those who have eyes to see. . . ." It is the capstone of the Great Pyramid and hovers above it.

The Great Pyramid appears below the eye in the triangle. The Great Pyramid of Gizeh was never a tomb for a pharaoh. It is now suggested that it, like Stonehenge, is an astronomical structure from which astronomical data can be derived. Both the Masons and Rosicrucians state that the Great Pyramid was a temple for their craft, and it was for this reason that it appeared on the reverse of the Great Seal.

The two mottoes "Annuit Coeptis" and "Novus Ordo Seclorum." which mean "He prospers our undertaking" and "New Order of the Ages" respectively, are both very important. "Annuit Coeptis" states that the founders were aware that America was part of the Divine Plan, and that it was favored for a great undertaking—the creation of the brotherhood of Man. Its government was to reflect this Great Ideal. "Novus Ordo Seclorum," New Order of the Ages, refers to the rejection of a monarchical system for one of democracy. In 1776, this was a monumental break with humanity's control by government. "Ages" refers to the golden, silver, bronze, and iron ages; and one of these is the Great Year of Plato—26,000 years. The Aquarian Age is 1/12, or one part of 26,000 years. The changes taking place in the USA today reflect the coming of the Age of Aquarius, and emphasize altruism, brotherhood and synthesis, as distinct from greed, separation and division.

All of these interpretations can be drawn from the study of Masonry and Rosicrucianism. Modern historians may continue to reject them, for they are unfashionable—for the moment. Those adherents to the ancient wisdom teachings, however, find in them an understanding for our reason to be. It is sad that our present government does not reflect these ideas, as was intended. Time will alter this.
REFERENCE: The Two Great Seals of America: History and Interpretation

Robert Heironimus
Savitria Press, 1973, or AUM
$2.50

THE LOVE PROJECT
4470 Orchard Ave.
San Diego, California 92107
Write for details.

THE MOVEMENT OF SPIRITUAL INNER AWARENESS
P.O. Box 676
Rosemead, Calif. 91770

The Movement of Spiritual Inner Awareness is a spiritual organization that teaches the brotherhood of man and the Fatherhood of God. MSIA (pronounced like "Messiah") has centers of learning located all over the planet. In these centers people come together to share New Age ideas and discuss ways of making life here more exciting, while awakening higher states of awareness within themselves. Many of the ideas expressed are from a very remarkable man named John-Roger. His students have recorded his talks and seminars and made them available in cassette and written form. The subjects discussed are presented in an informal way, and because of this, they can relate to your daily life experiences.

The teachings that John-Roger expresses are part of a very ancient Mystey School. These teachings are extended to us by that which we call the Mystical Traveler Consciousness. It is a Universal Energy flowing through all life, and it extends from the Heart of God as a pure connection to all planes of existence. We are all heir to it. When you come into the guidance of this Consciousness, it can assist you in your Spiritual growth into greater freedom. In MSIA it simply cimply a matter of awakening to this freedom.

There are no laws or controls in the Movement; you progress at your own rate and awaken to your divinity in your own way. MSIA is not the only way to God, but it is a way that works; and really, the only way to God is the way that works for you.

Discourses are mailed on the first of each month. Suggested donation is $5.00 a month or $40.00 a year.

SOUL AWARENESS TAPED SEMINARS may be ordered individually or in sequence on a monthly basis. There is a suggested donation of $5.00 for each seminar tape. Tapes are available on cassette only. Please order tapes by number.

TAPES:
FNR1I Training in Awareness
JNF1I How We Let Others Control Us
13 Monitoring Yourself
KTT1I Practicing the Sound Current
LN1I Surrendering to the Soul
LB1I The Sounds of the Realms
ATM2I Handling Our Spiritual Gifts
HM2I Certainty of the Soul
ANK2I Positive Uses of Negativity
BTS2I How the Basic Self Blocks Soul Transcendence
BTK2I Getting Out of Miserable Consciousness
BNE2I Neophyte vs. the Initiate
CN2I Simran—Chanting the Sacred Tone
CB2I The Trials of the Neophyte
DNS2I Directing Energy Patterns of the Body
ETT2I Changing the Attitudes
EDV2I Keystones of Spirituality
ENL2I Finding the Knower
FV2I Peace Be Still
FNN2I The First Law of Spirit
GNK2I Matter vs. Anti-Matter
KMS2I Listen to the Heart
FNF3I The Search for a Master
KT3I The "Ideal" Seminar
KTL3I Spiritual Awakening
LTM31 Finding Oneness with Spiritual Exercise
23 Spiritual Awakening.
3 Committing Yourself to Yourself
ANR4I All Ways Use Love
CNF4I Using the Laws of Spirit
BT3I Sending the Light
ATS4I Freedom from the Tenfold Errors
KB2I Sealed Books of Consciousness
1 FNK3F The Celestial Melodies in MSIA
JTK3F Watch, Listen, Think, Do
KTR3F Unlocking Yourself
KNF3F Entering the Vision
LTN3F Micro/Macro Consciousness
CNK4F The Angel at the Gate
CS4F The Attitude and Use of Experiences
BS4F Everybody's going "Home"

Single publications deal with specialized subjects which have been presented through the MSIA teachings. The subjects are varied and represent a compilation of material from many of John-Roger's seminars. Please order publications by number.

PUBLICATIONS:
1 **The Christ Within** —The multidimensional levels of man's consciousness within Jesus the man; His expression of the Christ Consciousness as our promise of the Christ within. $2.00
2. **A Consciousness of Wealth-Creating a Money Magnet** — Keys for building a money magnet, tithing, successful care of income, precipitation of greater spiritual gifts. $2.00
3. **DREAMS** — Subconscious dream process, levels of consciousness experienced in sleep, interpretation of dreams, the spiritual potential of the sleep stat $2.00
4. **Drugs** — Effect of drugs (LSD, pills, pot, speed, etc.) on the patterns of human consciousness. $2.00
5. **The Buddha Consciousness** — The life of Buddha before, during, and after his spiritual enlightenment, his philosophy, his spiritual teachings. $2.00
6. **Disciples of Christ** — Each disciple's change in consciousness and expression, the Christ Consciousness as a working reality today. $2.00
9. **Master Chohans of the Color Rays** — Learn to work with the color frequencies and the Masters who work with them. $2.00
10. **The Path to Mastership** — Eleven keys to move your life expression into greater balance. $2.00
12. **The Sound Current** — Tones of each realm, receiving individual tones as the connection to the Sound Current, chanting the tones as an on-going path of spiritual unfoldment. $2.00
13. **Dynamics of the Lower Self** — Function of the lower self (subconscious), how it related to the conscious and high self, how to work with it in greater cooperation and understanding. $2.00
14. **Manual on Using the Light** — The "Light" which is another term for the "Holy Spirit" is one of the basic concepts of MSIA. $2.00
15. **The Spiritual Promise** — The Love and Light of Spirit is the reality of all mankind. $2.50
17. **Baraka** — Attune to the divine essence of Spirit which is extended by God to all men. $2.00

WHAT IS PSYCHOSYNTHESIS?: SOME BASIC PRINCIPLES OF THEORY AND PRACTICE

A SYNTHESIS OF MANY TRADITIONS. Psychosynthesis, as developed by the contemporary Italian psychiatrist, Dr. Roberto Assagioli, is a psychological and educational approach to development of the whole person. It may be employed in psychotherapy or in personal growth for well-functioning people who wish to more fully develop their potentials. With roots in East and West, Europe and North America, it is a true synthesis, as the name suggests, of many traditions. While most Eastern approaches have tended to emphasize the "spiritual" side of being, neglecting the personality level, and most Western approaches have focused on the "personality" side of being, paying insufficient attention to the spiritual dimensions, psychosynthesis has attempted to view man as a whole and to accord to each level its due importance. Though it does postulate in man a transpersonal essence, it holds that man's purpose in life is to "incarnate" and manifest this Self or essence as fully as possible in the world of everyday living.

THE SUPRACONSCIOUS. The concept of the higher unconscious or supraconscious is one of the key points in psychosynthesis. Like traditional psychoanalysis, psychosynthesis recognizes a primitive or "lower" unconscious—source of our atavistic and biological drives—but it also posits a supraconscious—an autonomous realm from which originate man's more highly evolved impulses: altruistic forms of love and will, humanitarian action, artistic and scientific inspiration, philosophic and religious insight, and the drive for purpose and meaning in life. The lower unconscious might be considered as representing what is "behind" for the individual and the species, while the higher unconscious points ahead to future possibilities with an invitation to become. It manifests what Jung has called the "prospective" or "forward-looking" aspect of the unconscious. Psychosynthesis maintains that man suffers not merely from repression of his basic biological drives, as Freud pointed out, but that he is equally crippled by "repression of the sublime"—by failure to live up to his highest potentials. It is concerned, therefore, not only with integration of material from the lower unconscious, but with releasing and actualizing material which is supraconscious or "above" our ordinary level of awareness. To this end, it has developed a wide range of techniques for evoking the psyche and for establishing a bridge, through the intuition, with that part of our being where true wisdom is to be found. This realm *is* accessible, in varying degrees, to the seeker, and can provide a great source of energy, inspiration, and direction.

THE SELF. One of the central tenets in psychosynthesis is the existence of the Self as an entity supraordinate to the various aspects of the personality (body, emotions, and mind), though it expresses through these. As in Jungian analytical psychology, the Self is viewed as an active center within the person through which integration takes place. A distinction is made between the "personal self"—the "I" or center of consciousness—and the "transpersonal Self," which is a deeper and more inclusive center of identity.

STAGES IN PSYCHOSYNTHESIS. The psychosynthetic process can be conceived in two stages (though these may be interwoven to some degree): the *personal* psychosynthesis in which integration of the personality takes place around the personal self and in which the person attains a level of functioning in terms of his work and relationships that would generally be considered healthy by current standards of mental health; and the *transpersonal* psychosynthesis in which the personality learns to *align* itself with and to transmit the energies of the transpersonal Self.

THE SELF AS OBJECTIVE OBSERVER. The Self may be experienced in a receptive and in an active mode. In the former, one perceives reality without distortion or defensiveness from what has been called the "fair witness" or "objective observer" position. To the extent that one is able to achieve this vantage point, the claims of the ego and its tendency to self-justification no longer stand in the way of clear vision. There are a variety of techniques in psychosynthesis to help people transcend the ego level and get in touch with this vantage point from which the most effective work on oneself can be done.

THE SELF AS INNER GUIDE. The other facet of the Self is an active, guiding, and directing one. It is as though the Self were constantly trying to point the way for us, indicating the direction in which lies our destiny and our growth, and providing us with corrective feedback when we go off course. People who have experienced this aspect of the Self often speak of the "inner voice" or the "inner guide." Many of the techniques of psychosynthesis are directed toward helping people get in touch with and learn to test their source of inner guidance. In this way, a person is freed from blind reaction to the expectations of others and to his own lower impulses and becomes able to choose a path in accordance with what is best within himself. This implies development of a sense of values and a healthy functioning of the will, both of which psychosynthesis directs itself to.

FALSE IDENTIFICATIONS. A major difficulty in learning to act from "center" is the large number of false identifications we make with partial aspects of ourselves. Thus, we may be identified with a temporary feeling such as fear or anger or depression, and loose our control and perspective. Or we may be identified with one of our "subpersonalities"—those semi-autonomous and often contradictory aspects of ourselves that follow a predictable, pre-programmed routine when evoked by a certain set of circumstances. Much of the work in psychosynthesis is aimed toward helping people to become conscious of their personalities so that they are no longer helplessly controlled by them but can learn to increasingly bring them under conscious direction of the Self. The *freedom to choose* what we want to be comes about in large measure through *disidentification* from all that is not the essential self and through *Self-identification* or experiencing our identity with the deeper center of being. Many of the techniques of psychosynthesis work with these twin principles.

METHODS EMPLOYED IN PSYCHOSYNTHESIS. There are a wide variety of methods employed in psychosynthesis to meet the diversity of needs presented by different situations and different people. Each person is treated as an individual, and an effort is made to find the methods best suited to his existential situation, his psychological type, and his developmental needs. If particular psychological functions are underdeveloped, a program is worked out to help the person develop them in a way that is harmonious and balanced in respect to the other psychological functions or aspects of the personality. In addition to the traditional Jungian functions of thinking, feeling, sensation, and intuition, psychosynthesis includes the will and the imagination, and it teaches active methods for developing all of these.

The methods used in the practice of psychosynthesis today draw on many traditions. On the one hand, there are the methods drawn from depth psychology—and "analysis" of the psychic structure is considered a first step in the psychosynthetic process, followed by and interwoven with various aspects of synthesis or "pulling things together." The methods of dream work and free association are employed when appropriate, as is the Jungian technique of "active imagination" or semi-guided fantasy. The latter technique is part of a large body of mental imagery methods which generally play an important role in the psychosynthetic process (though there are persons who have difficulty imaging who must

use other channels to contact this material). The mental imagery methods permit access in a very rapid and powerful way to the material of the unconscious which the person is ready to work on and can be used both in the analytic and synthetic stages. A number of other techniques are also used to contact and work through unconscious material. These include spontaneous movement and drawing, psychodramatic methods, and body-awareness techniques such as those employed in Gestalt therapy.
Meditative and inner dialogue techniques can also be employed to bring through material from the supraconscious.

In a group setting, psychosynthesis attempts to achieve a balance between intrapersonal and interpersonal communication. Learning to communicate with oneself in a profound way is seen as the basis for meaningful communication with others. The group process aims to help people communicate with each other in a way which is authentic, constructive, and productive of inspiration and insight for the people involved.

CANDIAN INSTITUTE OF PSYCHOSYNTHESIS, INC.
3496, avenue Marlowe, Montreal 260
Quebec

INSTITUTE OF PSYCHIC SCIENCE, INC.
2015 South Broadway
Little Rock, Ark. 72206.

The Institute of Psychic Science is incorporated nonprofit for the sole purpose of research and instruction in the field of extrasensory gifts and powers. The Institute stresses only personal development, following no special school of thought, nor affiliating with any church or organization. We explore every avenue of mind and soul enlightenment, excepting only those that seek to manipulate or control other humans. Our aim is to raise the individual to his own highest self by the development of his personal inner powers.

The Institute of Psychic Science is self-sustaining through donations of money and time, study groups in personal psychic devvelopment and a metaphysical and psychic bookstore on the premises at 2015 South Broadway, Little Rock, Arkansas.

One of the publications of the Insti Institute includes a magazine entitled *Breakthrough* which is published bi-monthly. This name is spelled with all capital letters and an exclamation point. *Breakthrough* is published primarily to instruct, uplift and inspire How-to articles which explain how one acquires the understanding and personal use of such gifts as clairvoyance, precognition, astral travel and so forth are welcome.

As part of the program for self-financing we have formed several types of memberships. BREAKTHROUGH! comes automatically with all memberships. Complimentary copies may be had for the asking. . . .

Classes at the Institute include instruction in ESP, self-hypnosis, advanced metaphysics, astrology, yoga, psychic art, astral travel, and a program of teacher training.

Research groups include weather control by the use of the mind, group travel on the astral plane using astral energies on the physical plane and a psychic rescue squad which specializes in finding lost people and objects and also exorcising trapped entities from the astral plane. Other types of research in the medical and psychological fields are being planned for the future.
Basic membership: $5.00 a year.

BREAKTHROUGH!

Institute of Psychic Science, Inc.

THE INSTITUTE OF MENTAL-PHYSICS
p.o. box 640
Yucca Valley, Calif. 92284

MENTALPHYSICS, THE ULTIMATE PHILOSOPHY

Truth is universal. The cry that grows louder in this age of growing awareness is WHERE and HOW does one find Truth? The answer of course is that Truth is Universal, the keystone to every true religion and the basis of all true philosophies. The KEY then is to not only find Truth but to recognize, understand and more importantly use Truth to build a better life, achieve greater life expression and ultimately to reach a growing Spiritual awareness which brings the peace that surpasses all understanding.

In this search for Truth, mankind has opened the doors of his mind to allow the devotion of his chosen beliefs to be heightened by the Christ-like feeling which pervades the West plus the Wisdom of the Orient and Far East. Years ahead of its time, The Science of Mentalphysics has offered this combination of ideas plus a usable, workable philosophy of life for over 46 years. Pointing out the similarities rather than the differences between religious beliefs, this ultimate philosophy chose to use one's energy to develop the total person, body, mind and spirit.

A world-wide student body attests to the practicality and success of the teachings offered in the Science of Mentalphysics. Diet, not one selected but a selected one to match the individual chemistry of each individual person. Guidance in the selection of diet, plus charts which enable one to locate his own particular chemical type and recognize the foods which are conducive to his individual health, is offered. The advice on diet selection is taught along with Pranayama (Spiritual Yoga Breaths) as one is led to build and perfect the body—a most necessary requirement to achieve . . . either physically, mentally or spiritually. A study course which does not extol a dogma or creed but offers guidelines to the understanding, testing and proving of one's own particular beliefs through USE. The study, hearing or seeing Truth in action makes Truth plausible and even believable, but to use Truth, to prove it in ones own life makes Truth a living reality. Proven Truth is not subject to doubt and can never be taken away. The mental development activates a thirst for knowledge. With open mind the student becomes a true seeker and reaches out for more and more Truth. Truth is not merely learned intellectually, but Truth becomes a real and working part of his or her life.

The Spiritual development parallels the development of body and mind, causing a balanced expression of life. The lessons lead to a better understanding of the body, the glandular system, and the true functions and requirements of the vital organs of the body. The study course leads to a better understanding of the development and use of the mind. The technique of using the Conscious Mind (which thinks, reasons, and either rejects or believes) to direct and use the subconscious mind, our great creative force within. Thought force is developed to create the desired conditions in one's life as well as "weed out" and erase 'race "race thought" all forms of negation. Negation which is in violent opposition to the laws of nature and the Divine Creative Spirit which dwells within each one.

Spiritual development, heightened by a sound and healthy body and an active, positive mind leads to the ultimate goal. Pranayama, chanting, advanced exercises which condition the body for spiritual awareness, developing physic ability, ESP, and other God given gifts that are latent in many but undeveloped. Meditation, the golden key which opens the door to true Spiritual awareness, is taught and practiced. Meditation which does usher in a feeling of tranquility and often allows the Creative Imagination to function, because of the stillness, is but the first step toward true Meditation. True Meditation comes with complete surrender of body, mind and Spirit which enables one's spirit to join the great Universal Oneness, the feeling of total pervasion as one's own Aura joins the Universal Aura and all is merged into the true reality of Universal Oneness.

The Science of Mentalphysics was founded by Edwin J. Dingle, an Englishman, who spent 21 years in the Orient. The Methods and Practices offered in his teachings are basically Tibetan for he studied under a Tibetan Llama Master during a stay in a Monastery in Tibet. He embraced the teachings and proved their worth in his own life but did not consider teaching, although his Tibetan Master predicted the time would come when he would feel compelled to teach. While lecturing on his travels and discoveries, it was brought home to him the great need for the practices and teachings he had gleaned in Tibet. Early in 1927 he began to offer the methods to a select few who made personal entreaty for the teachings. The demand grew and later in that same year he began to hold classes which were opened to the public. Noting the results in the lives of those who embraced the philosophy and practice which he westernized to meet the demands of life in the western hemisphere, he formulated his home study course which made the teaching available to more seekers.

The Philosophy grew as more and more students were brought into true understanding of who and what they were and the purpose of life as well as the ultimate expression of life to the height of one's evolutionary capabilities. The Home Study Course not only helped students to develop spiritually but to understand and appreciate Truth which had been learned intellectually but not truly understood. The teachings, rather than fitting the student for Monastery type living, enabled the highest and best to shine forth from the individual in whatever his or her chosen occupation or way of life. The Philosophy, now in its 46th year, has been used and proven by tens of thousands of students, from all parts of the world and from all walks of life.

In 1941, a Spiritual Retreat was founded by Rev. Dingle to act as a Mecca for the great and growing student body. The beautiful and modern buildings, some of which were designed by the late Frank Lloyd Wright, are harmoniously located in the beautiful high desert of Yucca Valley, California. Here students from all parts of the world gather for personal instructions in the practices and methods taught by expertly trained teachers. The pure air, reputed to be the best available on the North American Continent, enhances the breathing practices, while the quiet desert setting offers the perfect place for Spiritual progress and that quiet peace so necessary for perfect communion with the All. Before the founder, Rev. Dingle, made his transition in early 1972, he made complete plans for the continuation of this great philosophy which teaches one how to seek with self mastery and victorious living as the ultimate goal. The Science of Mentalphysics is available to all true seekers and a growing number of dedicated students vow that this will always be so.

BARKSDALE FOUNDATION

The Barksdale Foundation for Furtherance of Human Understanding is a non-profit organization devoted to helping people live happier, more effective lives. This is accomplished through achieving better understanding of how and why we get involved in emotional turmoil, and why we often have a destructive sense of inadequacy and self rejection. The primary emphasis is on assisting people to build sound self esteem and confidence in themselves and their own authority.

The basic activity of the Foundation is periodic mailings of material designed to help the reader to recognize, understand and cope with such human problems as feelings of shame, blame, guilt, remorse, inadequacy, failure, isolation, anger, resentment, anxiety, fear and rejection by self and others.

The Foundation also holds periodic seminars and workshops in Self Understanding and Building Self Esteem, perhaps the root problem of our society.

Founder and Director of the Foundation is L. S. Barksdale, formerly a successful business executive who several years ago decided to dispose of his business interests in order to devote his time and energy to sharing observations and insights that have been of tremendous help to him and his own long and troubled struggle for self understanding, emotional and physical well-being. These findings have enabled him to find inner freedom and peace of mind and also released his potential to the extent that he has achieved a happy zestful life, plus a marked success in his several business ventures, one of international prominence in its field.

Anyone interested in this material may receive it free of charge if they will send a request to Foundation headquarters.

The Foundation also maintains a free lending library of over 1000 volumes on philosophy, psychology, sociology, religion, self-discovery, self-help, extrasensory perception, etc.

L. S. Barksdale, Director and Founder
Idyllwild, California 92349
U.S.A.
Telephone: (714) 659-3858

THE INTERNATIONAL NEW THOUGHT ALLIANCE (INTA)

The International New Thought Alliance (INTA) is an organization serving as a medium through which all metaphysical schools, churches, and centers can work together. Its message is designed to lead the world into a higher consciousness, to find God in every man. New Thought Adherents envision God as an in-dwelling presence, a universal spirit permeating all nature, finding its highest expression in man.

INTA discusses this philosophy and its implications at annual congresses and interim conferences. They provide opportunities for exchange of ideas and viewpoints covering the whole spectrum of spiritual principles and laws, and their application to daily life. Cassettes are made of various inspirational speakers at these gatherings, and are distributed from Hollywood headquarters.

COMMITTEE ON COSMIC HUMANISM

This successor to the previous INTERNATIONAL COMMITTEE ON SCIENTIFIC HUMANISM focuses on the following interrelated areas:

(a) the study of the methods and the goals for the conscious control of human evolution — biological, psychological, spiritual;

(b) the formulation of subjective plans for "consciousness expansion" toward inner freedom;

(c) the development of programming for a global satellite system (Project PROMETHEUS and KRISHNA) as part of the maturation of a "planetary democracy";

(d) the discovery of laws of harmonic-union to interrelate man and the cosmos and provide a basis for communications between human beings and intelligent beings and intelligent creatures in other, extra-terrestrial systems.

(e) the publication of the SYNTHESIS SERIES of volumes.

These objectives call for the "Integration of Human Knowledge" for the purpose of learning how to convert the "power of resonant thought" into a vehicle and guiding field for the functioning of the emerging WORLD SENSORIUM.

"Cosmic Humanism is the name we give to man's ongoing search for truth. By the word *Cosmic* we indicate that our search for truth must range from nuclear physics to biochemistry, involving all the sciences. By the word *Humanism* we indicate that we must also search for truth through the whole range of life sciences, history, anthropology, psychology, the arts, and the religious expressions of mankind. A cosmology that affirms the creative principle inherent in universal operations will lead to a release of the creative capacities in man."

Executive Committee Members:
Mrs. Charles H. Babcock
Dr. Beatrice Bruteau
Dr. Oliver L. Reiser, Chairman
Prof. Keith Floyd, Co-chairman.

Oliver L. Reiser, Chairman
Emeritus Professor of Philosophy
University of Pittsburgh
Pittsburgh, Pennsylvania 15213
U.S.A.
Telephone: (412) 621-3500

In addition, INTA publicizes its ideas in all media available — radio, TV, books, and its own publication, the *NEW THOUGHT* quarterly. This magazine contains in-depth studies by noted authors in the areas of metaphysics, psychology, philosophy, self-awareness, and positive thinking. It is available by subscription from INTA headquarters.

Thus, INTA hopes to be a gathering and disseminating center for ideas and action. In this way, its spiritual message will reach and affect people the world over.

THE PSYNETICS FOUNDATION

Founded in 1962, the Psynetics Foundation now has 750 members. These men and women are "dedicated to a positive, unbiased and unprejudiced mission to discover and recognize valid and scientific principles as proclaimed by existing agencies or individuals and an open-minded search for new and advanced ideas, opinions and methods which may be accepted and used for the betterment of humanity."

The Foundation engages in study and research in an atmosphere free from tradition, dogma and doctrine to discover truths that are based on natural law and to discover the methods by which those truths may be used for the advancement and betterment of man in the physical, mental, emotional and spiritual aspects of life experiences.

Lectures, demonstrations, workshops, classes, social and recreational programs are sponsored. The Foundation operates the Psynetics Family Education Center, teaching remedial and supplementary reading and other educational skills for children and adults. It maintains a library of 1500 volumes of psychology, metaphysics, the occult, and science.

Publications include Psynetics Newsletter (monthly, no charge) and brochures which are mailed on request. The Annual Convention takes place in Orange County, California, usually in late spring.

Walter E. Tipton, General Executive Director
Bernell L. Ausmus, Associate General Executive Director
1212 E. Lincoln Avenue
Anaheim, California 92805
U.S.A.
Telephone: (714) 533-2311

74! your year of Discovery!
SSC TOURS, Box 1104
Rockville, MD 20850

A UNIQUE PROGRAM OF MEETINGS AND PRIVATE SITTINGS WITH WORLD-FAMOUS CLAIRVOYANTS, PSYCHIC MEDIUMS, AND HEALERS AT THE HEADQUARTERS OF THE RENOWNED SPIRITUALIST ASSOCIATION OF GREAT BRITAIN IN LONDON

- A WEEK LONG EXPERIENCE WITH GROUP AND PRIVATE SITTINGS
- A FULL YEAR MEMBERSHIP IN THE SPIRITUALIST ASSOCIATION
- PARTICIPATION IN ALL ASSOCIATION ACTIVITIES IN LONDON
- A VISIT TO HARRY EDWARDS HEALING SANCTUARY
- A TRIP TO THE ANCIENT STONEHENGE
- OTHER EXCITING PSYCHIC EVENTS

PLEASE SEND MORE INFORMATION
Name _____
Address _____
City _____ State, Zip _____

Transportation by **AIR-INDIA**

THE BOSTON VISIONARY CELL

The Boston Visionary Cell is an association of Neo-Platonic artists, primarily, and others from disciplines which act as supporters and consultants, for the purpose of fostering visionary art, considered as an eternal genre — otherwise known as cosmic, cosmological, magical, mystical, or occult art — in the Boston and New England area.

As individuals, we all believe in a mystical explanation for the Universe, whose forces of nature are expressed as a Macrocosm and a Microcosm — a Without and a Within of the Universe, Reason and Necessity. Also, we believe, the visionary sensibility is on the rise again in the world and will appear quite functional and necessary. In this belief we recognize, of course, the influence of many individuals and groups, but our spiritual mentor is the late Teilhard De Chardin.

The visionary sensibility has been interpreted as a revival of late nineteenth century symbolism or an entirely new phenomenon. We prefer to consider it as an essentially eternal artistic force which has time-oriented manifestations as deemed necessary by the destiny of history.

Descriptive listings of our organization occur in the: *Aquarian Unity Directory of Massachusetts;* and the *The Spiritual Community Guide for North America.*

Paul Laffoley, President
36 Bromfield Street
Boston, Massachusetts 02108
U.S.A.
Telephone: (617) 482-9044

THE AMERICAN TEILHARD DE CHARDIN ASSOCIATION INC.
867 Madison Ave.,
New York, N.Y. 10021

Founded to extend knowledge and understanding of the thought of Pierre Teilhard te Chardin, to encourage critical study of his works and promote further cevelopment of the lines of thought indicated by him.

Subscribe Now

The spiritual nation has already been born. Let's bring it down to earth. The *New Journal* will provide practical information for living in a culture that is in transition. Join us in our new monthly magazine and explore these themes: POLITICS, SEX, NUTRITION, SURVIVAL, HUMOR. The *New Journal* will feature major sections on Books, Food, and the Arts; in addition to columns on Astrology, Women, Communities, Sports, Crafts, Children.

---

new journal
145 Portland Street, Cambridge, Mass (617) 492-1800

☐ Give me a year of New Journal ($6)
☐ Make me a friend of New Journal ($25)
☐ I want New Journal for life ($100 or more)

Name _____
Street _____
City _____
State _____ Zip _____

THE ORDER OF THE UNIVERSE

The order of the universe is light, darkness, creation and separation, joy, happiness, matter and spirit. It includes everything from the great spiral galaxy to the tiniest being on earth. We are all unique versions living within the great uniqueness — the endless pattern of the order of the universe. To live is to be enfolded in the principles of change, to be formed by and in the image of this guiding force.

Each issue of *The Order of the Universe* offers practical studies based on the eternal principles of the universe. We have recently covered such topics as natural agriculture, astronomy, acupuncture, the world of spirit, the energy of sound, ancient and future worlds, and biological evolution.

To subscribe send $15.00 (foreign subscribers please include $2.00 extra) or $1.50 for a single copy to:

The Order of the Universe
62 Buckminster Road
Brookline, Massachusetts 02146

The Dialogue House program is built around its basic instrument, the Intensive Journal and its method of Journal Feedback. Based upon the writings and research of Dr. Ira Progoff, it has, since 1966, been providing a continuous and open-ended method of personal growth for an increasing number of people through public workshops and institutional programs in education, mental health, social tension areas, industry, and religion.

Ira Progroff is the author of numerous books over the past twenty years in which he developed the theoretical foundation of the program. Five of these books were reissued in paperback in 1973: JUNG'S PSYCHOLOGY AND ITS SOCIAL MEANING (1953); THE DEATH AND REBIRTH OF PSYCHOLOGY (1956); THE CLOUD OF UNKNOWING (1957); DEPTH PSYCHOLOGY AND MODERN MAN (1959); and THE SYMBOLIC AND THE REAL (1963). He is the author also of THREE CYCLES OF PROCESS MEDITATION (1972), and JUNG, SYNCHRONICITY AND HUMAN DESTINY (1973).

For further information regarding the Dialogue House Intensive Journal program and its workshop schedule in major cities, contact Dialogue House Associates, 45 West 10 Street, New York, N.Y. 10011. 212-228-9180.

Personal Paths And Teachers

o teach is to encourage an individual to draw out information that has implicit personal value. This is known as the *affective* component in all education. In a sense all of us are teachers and students at the same time. The continuous exchange of information between people must be grounded in mutual respect rather than in an anticipation of exposing another's vulnerability. Psychic development is education.

Teachers who expound theories or ideas as absolute truths while denigrating the value of alternative approaches, influence their students to adopt a similar chauvenistic attitude of intolerance and should be avoided. In such a case, the instructor is no longer helping his student to discover his own answers, but instead is limiting the student's potential for further growth by trapping him in a seductive sea of dogma and prejudice. This approach encourages followers rather than personal initiative and responsibility.

THE MASTER GAME
Robert S. DeRopp
Delta, 1968
$1.95

"This book is concerned with games and aims.

"It has been stated by Thomas Szasz that what people really need and demand from life is not wealth, comfort or esteem but *games worth playing*. He who cannot find a game worth playing is apt to fall prey to *accidie*, defined by the Fathers of the Church as one of the Deadly Sins, but now regarded as a symptom of sickness. Accidie is a paralysis of the will, a failure of the appetite, a condition of generalized boredom, total disenchantment—'God oh God, how weary, stale, flat and unprofitable seem to me all the uses of this world!' Such a state of mind, Szasz tells us, is a prelude to what is loosely called 'mental illness,' which, though Szasz defines this illness as a myth, nevertheless fills half the beds in hospitals and makes multitudes of people a burden to themselves and society.

Meta-games and Object Games

GAME	AIM
Master Game	awakening
Religion Game	salvation
Science Game	knowledge
Art Game	beauty
Householder Game	raise family
No Game	no aim
Hog in Trough	wealth
Cock on Dunghill	fame
Moloch Game	glory or victory

The Six Catches

Catch #1 Talk-Think Syndrome	Talking or thinking about the Work instead of doing it.
Catch #2 Starry-eyed Syndrome	Fanatical devotion to and belief in a teacher or system to exclusion of all others.
Catch #3 False-Messiah Syndrome	Delusion that I personally am a teacher or savior.
Catch #4 Personal-Salvation Syndrome	Delusion that I personally can be saved, enter "heaven," survive death, etc.
Catch #5 Sunday-Go-to-Meeting Syndrome	Habit of making efforts only when in presence of teacher or with other members of group.
Catch #6 Hunt-the-Guru Syndrome	Habit of wandering from teacher to teacher, without staying long enough to learn anything from any of them.

THE SPIRITUALIST ASSOCIATION OF GREAT BRITAIN
33 Belgrave Square
S.W. 1.
London, England

Write for information on spiritual healing and extensive publications list which includes *The Spiritualist Gazette*.

THE CHURCHES' FELLOWSHIP FOR PSYCHICAL AND SPIRITUAL STUDIES

The Churches' Fellowship for Psychical and Spiritual Studies is an interdenominational organisation founded in 1953, by Lt.-Col. R. M. Lester with the help of a group of clergy and laity interested in Psychical Research and its relevance to the Christian faith and life. The title 'and Spiritual' was later added in order to cover the study of Mysticism.

Studies are carried out within the framework of the Christian tradition at the regular meetings of the many local branches of the fellowship which have been formed since its inception; also by lectures, public meetings, conferences and retreats organised in the various areas. For this purpose the country is divided into regions with regional organisers and councils. The studies are helped by specialist Committees: Medical, dealing with spiritual and other forms of paranormal healing; Mental Health; Psychic Phenomena and Mysticism. There is also a Scientific Research Committee and an Educational Committee (which includes the provision of speakers for schools annd colleges). Members of most committees are also engaged in practical pastoral, field or experimental work. There is also an extensive lending library—normally housed at Headquarters but temporarily in abeyance until, as we hope, a new HQ becomes available shortly.

The governing bodies of the Fellowship are an Executive Committee and the Council which meet at least three times a year and decide on matters of policy and programme.

"*Full* membership is confined to members of Churches affiliated to the World Council, or to the British Council, of Churches, or which belong to the orthodox tradition and holds Jesus Christ as Lord and Saviour. Those interested but not falling within this category may be accepted as *Associate* members (without rights either of voting or of holding office) as the Executive may from time to time decide. Application for membership should be made to the General Secretary. The annual (minimum) subscription is £1.50 for single persons and £2.10 for married couples, Old Age Pensioners and students pay a reduced subscription. Life membership is £25. The C.F.P.S.S. publishes a Quarterly Review which is free to all members or can be bought by others for £1 (including postage) per year.

"In view of the transitory nature of our present address, our publishers have very kindly offered to forward any correspondence if it is addressed to C.F.P.S.S., c/o Rider and Co., 3 Fitzroy Square, London W1P 6JD."

The Old Fox Cottage, Hydesville, N.Y. "The Cradle of Spiritualism"

YOUR GUIDE TO OUR ASSOCIATION

FULL MEMBERSHIP : £2·10 per annum

Full Member's fee for Private Appointments, £1·88 ; Psychic Portraits, £2·00 ; Group Sittings, 47p ; Psychic Portrait Groups, 66p ; Lectures, 19p ; Demonstrations, 19p.

Only Full Members receive quarterly both "Service" and "The Spiritualist" (post free), and they can also enrol for Psychic Development Classes, fee £3·00 per session of 12 weeks (unless otherwise stated)

PATRON MEMBERSHIP : £5 per annum.   LIFE MEMBERSHIP : £15

ASSOCIATE MEMBERSHIP : £1·05 per annum.

Associate Member's fee for Private Appointments, £2·00 ; Psychic Portraits, £2·12 ; Group Sittings, 58p ; Psychic Portrait Groups, 73p ; Lectures, 22p ; Demonstrations, 22p.

Associate Members receive quarterly (post free) our "Service" magazine.

DAY MEMBERSHIP

Day Member's fee for Private Appointments, £2·63 ; Psychic Portraits, £2·66 ; Group Sittings, 72p ; Psychic Portrait Groups, 94p ; Lectures, 28p ; Demonstrations, 28p.

Visitors should note that when contemplating booking a Private Appointment or Group Sitting it is to their advantage to consider taking out Yearly Membership, as members are offered all activities at reduced fees.

THE HEYDAY OF SPIRITUALISM
Slater Brown
Pocket Books, 1972
25 cents

SPIRITUALIST CHURCH OF MONTREAL
2186 St. Catherine Street W., Montreal, Quebec.

Visitors should contact secretary in advance

THE ESSENCE OF SPIRITUALISM
Hunter Mackintosh
Spiritualists' Association of Great Britain
$2.50

THE PRESENCE OF OTHER WORLDS:
The Psychological/Spiritual Findings of Emanuel Swedenborg
Wilson Van Dusen
Harper & Row, 1974.
$6.95

THE MYSTERY TEACHINGS IN WORLD RELIGIONS
Florice Tanner
Quest, 1973
$2.45

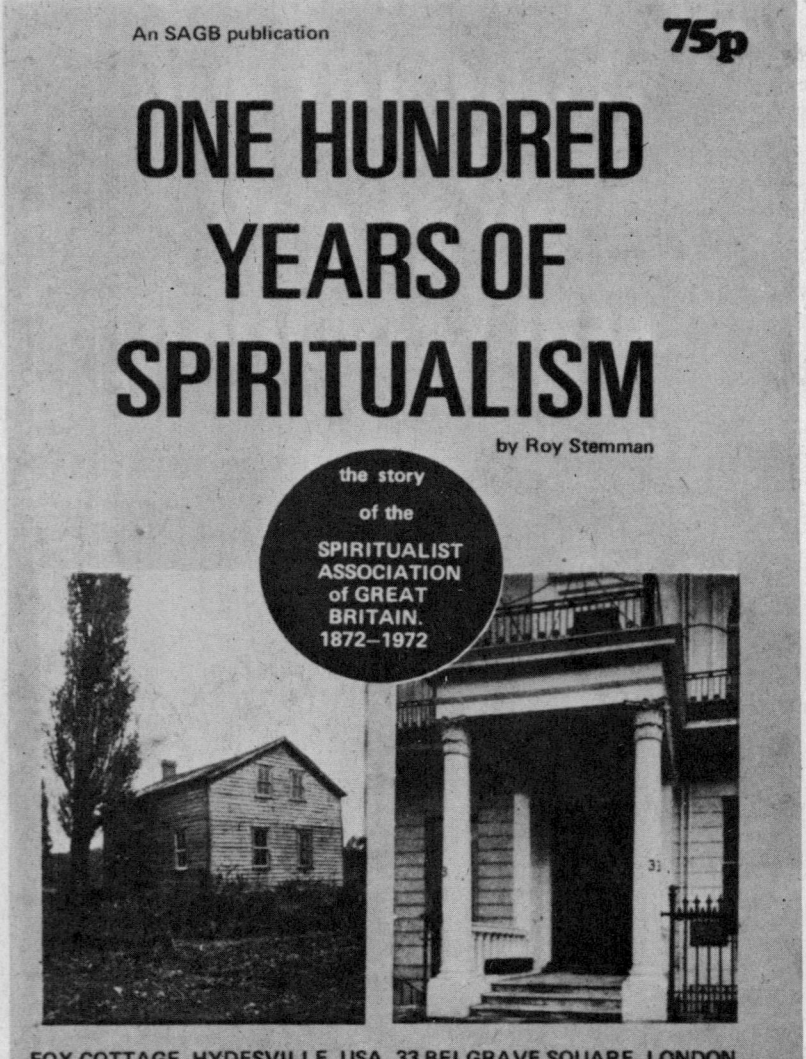

The following books are samples. While not written in an easy-going popular style, they represent an important perspective for the adventurous novice and must reading for those who are advanced in the psychic field. The Theosophical influence has been considerable. H.P. Blavatsky, *The Secret Doctrine* Volume I: *Cosmogenesis*, Volume Ii: *Anthropogenesis*
G. de Purucker, *Occult Glossary: A Compendium of Oriental and Theosophical Terms*

THE THEOSOPHICAL SOCIETY was founded in New York in 1875 by the famous Russian-born occultist Helena Petrovina Blavatsky and her American co-worker Henry Steel Olcott. The society now headquartered in Adyar, Madras, India, is dedicated to the promotion of brotherhood and the encouragement of the study of religion, philosophy and science. It stands for complete freedom of individual search and belief.

The Theosophical Publishing House of Wheaton, Illinois (P.O. Box 270) is a department of the society and is one of the largest publishers of occult literature. There are approximately 800 titles in print, 100 of which are under the Quest imprint.

Helena Petrovna Blavatsky

THE BLAVATSKY FOUNDATION
P.O. Box 1543
Fresno, Calif. 93716
To promote knowledge of the life and works of Helena P. Blavatsky

SIX THEOSOPHIC POINTS AND OTHER WRITINGS
Jacob Boehme
Ann Arbor Paperbacks, 1970
$2.25

DYNAMICS OF THE PSYCHIC WORLD: COMMENTS BY H.P. BLAVATSKY
Lina Psaltis, ed.
Quest, 1972
$1.95

VRIL: THE POWER OF THE COMING RACE
Sir Edward Bulwer Lytton
Rudolf Steiner Publications, 1972
$2.35

. . . .mankind's occult power of the future, and the kind of life and society created by its use in the interior of the earth, is the vivid picture presented in this book. Written 100 years ago by Lord Bulwer-Lytton, famous English Rosicrucian, statesman and author (see:Zanoni, a Rosicrucian Tale, another Steiner-book,), VRIL, his last book, stands as stern warning and reliable witness to his profound concern for the future welfare of mankind.

VRIL made today's science-fiction books possible and interesting, but VRIL itself was a serious and prophetic testament that man today must pay heed to, if he is to survive and become MAN.

OUR LIFE WITH GURDJIEFF
Thomas de Hartmann
Penguin, 1972
$1.65

MADAME BLAVATSKY: PRIESTESS OF THE OCCULT
Gertrude Marvin Williams
Lancer Books
$1.25

GURDJIEFF
Louis Pauwels
Weiser, 1972
$5.00

IS THERE "LIFE" ON EARTH?—AN INTRODUCTION TO GURDJIEFF
J. D. Bennett
Stonehill 1973
Available from:
Stonehill Communications Inc.
38 E. 57th St.,
New York, N.Y. 10022
$5.95

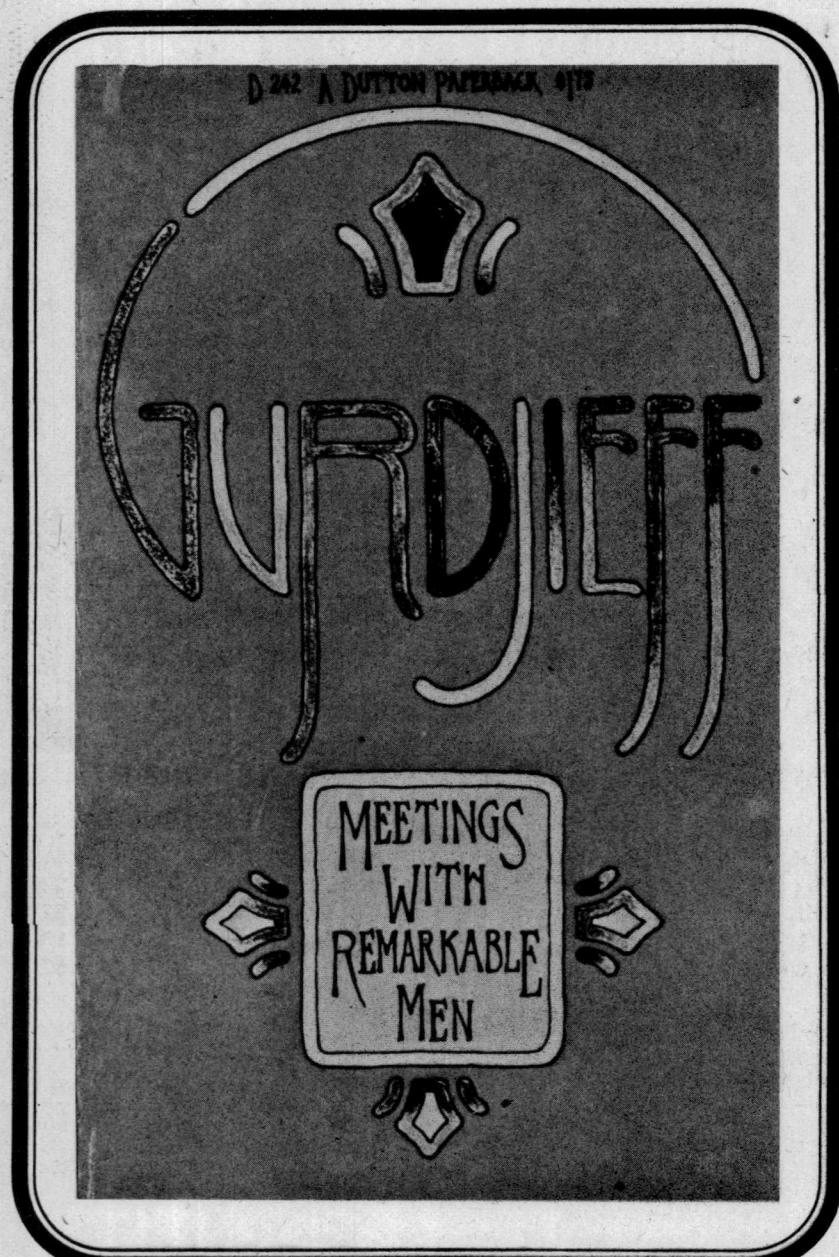

MEETINGS WITH REMARKABLE MEN
G. I. Gurdijieff
Dutton, 1969
$1.75

A NEW MODEL OF THE UNIVERSE
P. D. Ouspensky
Vintage, 1971
$2.95

Ouspensky analyzes certain of the older schools of thought—those of both the East and the West. He connects them with modern ideas and explains them in the light of recent discoveries and speculations in the realm of physics and philosophy. He explores realtivity, the fourth dimension, Christian symbolism, the tarot, yoga, dreams, hypnotism, eternal, recurrence, and various psychological theories. The book closes with a consideration of the sex problem from an entirely new point of view—that of sex in relation to the evolution of man toward superman.

Ouspensky clearly shows how ordinary knowledge is not of sufficient substance to bring about the transformation into a new man, for knowledge is not knowledge unless the part is related to the whole.

A HISTORY OF SECRET SOCIETIES
Arkon Daraul
Citadel Press, 1968
$2.25

THE Esoteric Society offers regular meetings on all aspects of the Western Esoteric tradition, including Astrology, Magic, The Qabalah, The Grail, etc. All talks led by experts (W. E. Butler, Gareth Knight, Christine Hartley, Sir John Sinclair, etc.), with refreshments and discussion. Members also receive the magazine "Esoterica" and details of other events. Full programme from: The Esoteric Society, 40 Buckingham Gate, London, S.W.I. Tel. 01-222 4683 or 828 2702

St. George Book Service

P.O. BOX 225 (W)
SPRING VALLEY, N.Y. 10977

We carry the most complete stock of books on
WALDORF EDUCATION by RUDOLF STEINER and other authors:

THE EDUCATION OF THE CHILD by R. Steiner, 50p, ppbk.	$1.00
EDUCATION AS AN ART by R. Steiner et al, 126p, ppbk.	$1.95
A MODERN ART OF EDUCATION by R. Steiner, 232p, ppbk.	$3.50
EARLY CHILDHOOD EDUCATION by E. Grunelius, 48p, ppbk.	$2.00
TEACHING OF ARITHMETIC by H.V. Baravalle, 90p, ppbk.	$3.00
THE WAY OF A CHILD by A.C. Harwood, 144p, ppbk.	$2.50

Please include 50 cents for postage & handling.
For FREE PREMIUM and CATALOG of books on Waldorf Education and the SPIRITUAL SCIENCES, send 25 cents for postage & handling.

THE CONFESSIONS OF ALEISTER CROWLEY

Aleister Crowley called himself "Beast 666" and was a self-proclaimed saint of the Gnostic Church. He became a "god" in his own temple at the age of forty-five. By that time, he was infamous in several countries as a writer, poet, painter, chess expert, master magician, mountaineer, drug addict and satyr.

Born in England in 1875, the son of a wealthy brewer, Crowley totally rejected the Victorian hypocrisy of his day and dedicated himself to a life of debauchery, evil, Satanic spells and writing, especially on such topics as sex, magic and occultism.

A notorious pleasure-seeker, Crowley truly was the hippie of his age, "doing his thing." He was banned from Italy and was forced to leave other countries, always under mysterious circumstances. Crowley was a constant user of heroin, cocaine, opium, hashish and peyote, and early in his life earned a reputation for indulging in wild sex and drug orgies which he combined with his so-called religious rites.

His reputation followed him everywhere as he traveled from country to country, practicing witchcraft and black magic with his strange group of mistresses and eccentrics.

Colorful, feared, despised and admired, Crowley brought excitement and evil with him wherever he went. He was the author of several books, treatises and poems, many of which are widely read and appreciated today.

THE CONFESSIONS OF ALEISTER CROWLEY
John Symonds and Kenneth Grant, ed.
Bantam, 1971
$1.95

THE LEGEND OF ALEISTER CROWLEY
P. R. Stephensen and Israel Regardie
Llewellyn Publications, 1970

HEALTH RESEARCH: THE ROSI CRUCIANS
Hargrave Jennings
$5.00

THE RELIGION OF THE OPPRESSED
Vittorio Lanternari
Mentor, 1965
75 cents

ROSICRUCIAN FELLOWSHIP

The Rosicrucian philosophy is a logical and sequential teaching concerning the origin, evolution, and future development of the world and man, showing both the spiritual and scientific aspects. It satisfies the mind by giving clear explanations. It provides a reasonable solution to all mysteries. But Rosicrucian Christianity does not regard the intellectual understanding of God and the universe as an end in itself. The greater the intellect, the greater the danger of its misuse. The scientific teaching is only given in order that man may believe and start to live the religious life which alone can bring true fellowship.

The Rosicrucian teachings aim to make the Christian religion a living factor in the land. It encourages people to remain with their churches as long as they can find spiritual comfort there, and gives them the explanations which creed may have obscured. To those who have already severed their connections with the church, it offers the Christian teachings from a new viewpoint so that they may again be accepted and their essential beauty recognized.

Persons from any denomination may enroll with the Fellowship without prejudice to their religious affiliation.

Anyone is eligible for membership who agrees to abide by the regulations, and who is not a hypnotist or professionally engaged as a medium, palmist, or astrologer.

Mrs. Effa Howell, Chairman
Telephone: (213) 881-2552

International Headquarters
Post Office Box 713
Oceanside, California 92056
U.S.A.

HEALTH RESEARCH: THE GOLDEN DAWN
H. Hotema
$2.00

JOURNEY TO IXTLAN: THE LESSONS OF DON JUAN
Carlos Castaneda
Pocket Books, 1974
$1.50

" 'I don't have any personal history,' he said after a long pause. 'One day I found out that personal history was no longer necessary for me and, like drinking, I dropped it.'

'I did not quite understand what he meant by that. I suddenly felt ill at ease, threatened. I reminded him that he had assured me that it was all right to ask him questions. He reiterated that he did not mind at all.

'I don't have personal history any more,' he said and looked at me probingly. 'I dropped it one day when I felt it was no longer necessary.'

"I stared at him, trying to detect the hidden meanings of his words.

" 'How can one drop one's personal history?' I asked in an argumentative mood.

" 'One must first have the desire to drop it,' he said. 'And then one must proceed harmoniously to chop it off, little by little.'

". . . 'The world around us is a mystery, he said. And men are no better than anything else. If a little plant is generous with us we must thank her, or perhaps she will not let us go.

The way he looked at me when he said that gave me a chill. I hurriedly leaned over the plants and said, 'Thank you,' in a loud voice.

". . . 'It's not enough to know how to make and set up traps,' he said. 'A hunter must live as a hunter in order to draw the most out of his life. Unfortunately, changes are difficult and happen very slowly; sometimes it takes years for a man to become convinced of the need to change. It took me years, but maybe I didn't have a knack for hunting. I think for me the most difficult thing was to really want to change.'

". . . 'What stopped inside you yesterday was what people have been telling you the world is like. You see, people tell us from the time we are born that the world is such and such and so and so, and naturally we have no choice but to see the world the way people have been telling us it is.'

"We looked at each other.

" 'Yesterday the world became as sorcerers tell you it is,' he went on. 'In that world coyotes talk and so do deer, as I once told you, and so do rattlesnakes and trees and all other living beings. But what I want you to learn is *seeing*. Perhaps you know now that *see-*

A SEPARATE REALITY: FURTHER CONVERSATIONS WITH DON JUAN

Pocket Books, 1974
$1.50

ing happens only when one sneaks between the worlds, the world of ordinary people and the world of sorcerers. You are now smack in the middle point between the two. Yesterday you believed the coyote talked to you. Any sorcerer who doesn't *see* would believe the same, but one who *sees* knows that to believe that is to be pinned down in the realm of sorcerers. By the same token, not to believe that coyotes talk is to be pinned down in the realm of ordinary men.'

"Do you mean, don Juan, that neither the world of ordinary men nor the world of sorcerers is real?"

THE ONLY DANCE THERE IS
Ram Dass
Anchor, 1974 $2.95

"How do you reconcile faith and reason? Well, as I feel it now, we have come out of a period where in the evolutionary journey of us as beings, Man evolves these great frontal lobes and this capacity for rational thought or for self-consciousness. And this is, in the Hindu system, what would be called *siddhi* or a power. That power can be used in a variety of ways. It can be used in the service of what I call the third chakra, that is, in terms of man's control over his environment, which is the way we've been doing it, which the rational mind controls. It's man over nature in the anthropological Florence Kluckhohn differentiations. She talks about societies that are man *over* nature, societies that are man *in* nature, and societies that are man *under* nature. Attachment to the siddhi of the rational mind put man in the group of man over nature. That particular way of knowing the world through the rational mind has tremendous advantages, obviously, which we have exploited as hard as we could. At the same point, it is becoming apparent that there are certain limitations to that particular device for knowing. That is, that it is in 'time' . . . it is in 'time.' takes an object and it cannot get beyond the subject-object world, the rational mind can't. It can't know itself; it's a metasystem. It is linear, for the most part and, therefore, it is tremendously limited in dealing with large numbers of variables simultaneously. Even the high-powered computer doesn't approximate.

"Now it turns out, that there are ways of knowing the universe which for the most part we have relegated to the realm of mysticism, or poetry, or romantic poetry, or falling in love. We sometimes call it 'intuitive validity' in science. That's the closest we get to it. There are ways of knowing about things that we don't know through our analytic, rational mind. But since we have committed ourselves, we have grown up. In order to survive we have become participants in a religion. If a religion is a specific faith, the faith is, faith in the rational mind. And, therefore, we as professors or as rationalists become the priests in that particular faith system, which is a faith, after all. It's faith in the fact that what you know through your senses, through your thinking mind, and through the logic of your thinking mind, that that has anything to do with anything. That's a faith. There's nothing you can do about it, because you can never get outside of the predicament of knowing, independent of that faith."

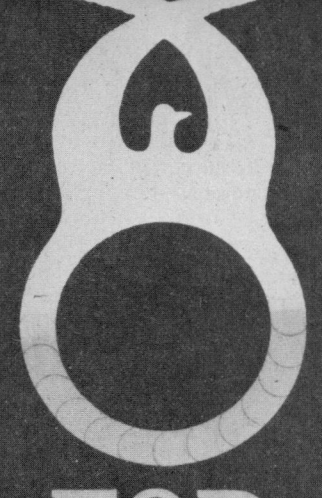

FOR FREEDOM DESTINED

Mysteries of Man's Evolution in the Mythology of Wagner's Ring Operas and Parsifal

FRANZ E. WINKLER

FOR FREEDOM DESTINED:
Mysteries of Man's Evolution in the
Mythology of Wagner's Ring Operas
and Parsifal
Franz E. Winkler
Waldorf Press, 1974
$3.95

"...When we think of the origin of man, we insist illogically on confusing the history of his purely biological being with the history of his spirit; the latter defies any attempt at investigation by methods we now call scientific. Darwin and his followers deal with the emergent evolution of visible man, while on the other hand, religion and mythology deal with the evolution of his invisible soul. In his cycle of the Ring [and in *Parsifal*], Richard Wagner uses the magic power of music, words and scenery to open man's heart to the history of the hidden essence of his own self, and to the changing forces that are active behind the sensory phenomena of man and earth."

"We have grown wise in the analysis of the material world, have expanded the scope of our perception to outer space and to the world beneath the atom. But objective *inner* experience has faded almost entirely away, and it has left us groping in the dark for the true image of ourselves. Since the beginning of history, the great leaders of mankind have tried to bring light into the gathering darkness of man's life on earth. Moses, Buddha, Jesus, Plato, Aristotle, Goethe, and Emerson are just a few of them. As a human being Richard Wagner with his glaring shortcomings of character may not fit into that illustrious group. Yet in moments of artistic inspiration, a wellspring must have opened in the soul of that strange magician, from which undoubtedly flows a wealth of long-forgotten truth, and a kind of music that can reopen the gateways of spiritual perception."

—From the book

HIGHER CONSCIOUSNESS:
The Evolutionary Thrust of Kundalini
Gopi Krishna
The Julian Press, 1974.
$7.95

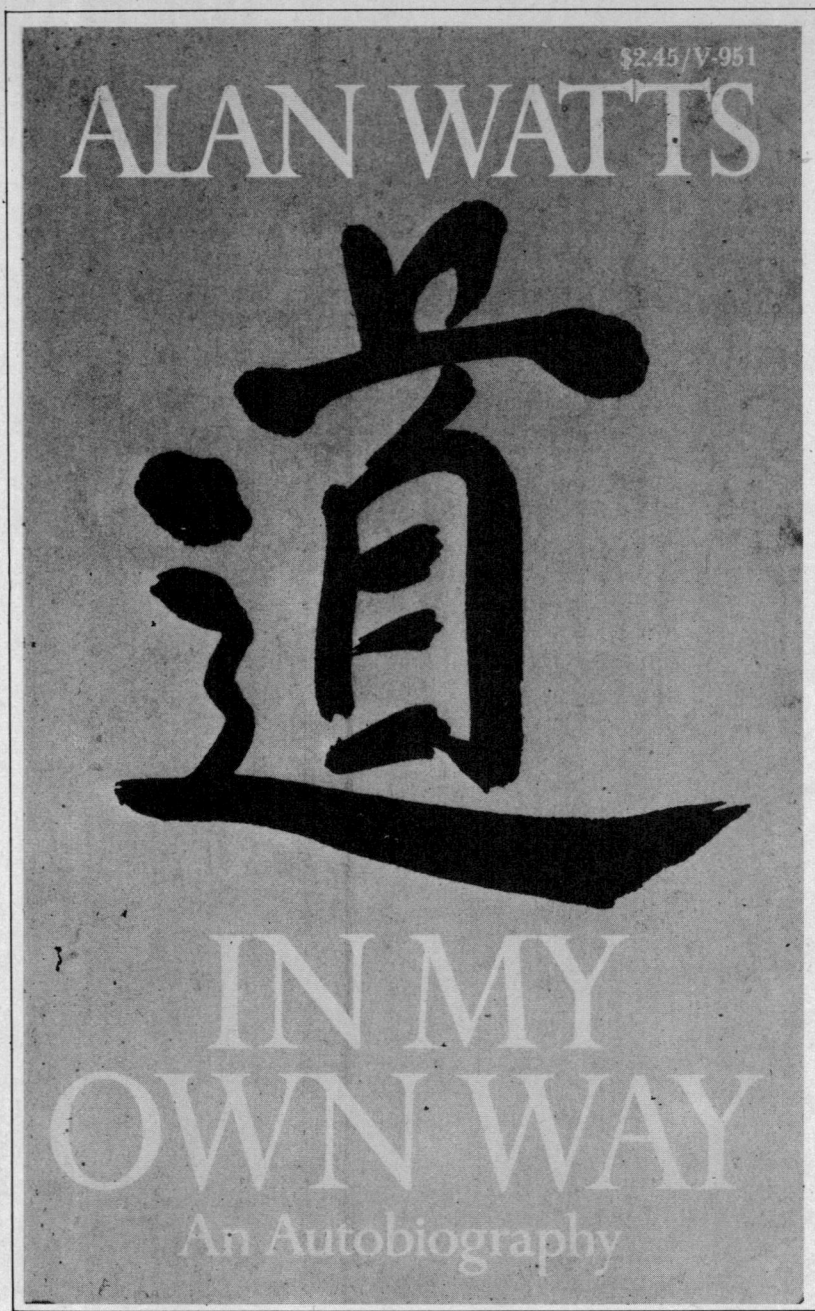

IN MY OWN WAY: AN AUTOBIOGRAPHY
Alan Watts
Vintage, 1972
$2.45

"To be or to get in your own way means all at once to fulfill yourself and to obstruct yourself, for language is full of *double entendre*—as when to cleave means both to split and to adhere, when *sacer* means both sacred and accursed, and *altus* both high and deep. I had thought originally to call this book *Coincidence of Opposites*, but the publishers, rightly, thought it too highbrow and moved me to search for something more simple and direct that would convey the spirit and style in which I have tried to live. For I am committed to the view that the whole point and joy of human life is to integrate the spiritual with the material, the mystical with the sensuous, and the altruistic with a kind of proper self-love—since it is written that you must love your neighbor as yourself.

"So I have always done things in my own way, which is at once the way that comes naturally to me, that is honest, sincere, genuine, and unforced; but also perverse, although you must remember that this word means *per* (through) *verse* (poetry), out-of-the-way and wayward, which is surely towards the way, and that to be queer—to 'follow your own weird'—is wholeheartedly to accept your own *karma*, or fate, or destiny, and thus to be odd in the service of God, 'whose service,' as the Anglican Book of Common Prayer declares, 'is perfect freedom.'"

THIS IS IT
Alan Watts
Collier, 1967
$1.50

"The most impressive fact in man's spiritual, intellectual, and poetic experience has always been, for me, the universal prevalence of those astonishing moments of insight which Richard Bucke called 'cosmic consciousness.' There is no really satisfactory name for this type of experience. To call it mystical is to confuse it with visions of another world, or of gods and angels. To call it spiritual or metaphysical is to suggest that it is not also extremely concrete and physical, while the term 'cosmic consciousness' itself has the unpoetic flavor of occultist jargon. But from all historical times and cultures we have reports of this same unmistakable sensation emerging, as a rule, quite suddenly and unexpectedly and from no clearly understood cause.

". . . The central core of the experience seems to be the conviction, or insight, that the immediate *now*, whatever its nature, is the goal and fulfillment of all living. Surrounding and flowing from this insight is an emotional ecstasy, a sense of intense relief, freedom, and lightness, and often of almost unbearable love for the world, which is, however, secondary."

ZEN IN THE ART OF ARCHERY
Eugen Herrigel
Vintage, 1953
$1.80

"In the case of archery, the hitter and the hit are no longer two opposing objects, but are one reality. The archer ceases to be conscious of himself as the one who is engaged in hitting the bull's-eye which confronts him. This state of unconsciousness is realized only when, completely empty and rid of the self, he becomes one with the perfecting of his technical skill, though there is in it something of a quite different order which cannot be attained by any progressive study of the art. . . ."

PSYCHOTHERAPY EAST AND WEST
Alan Watts
Mentor, 1963
75 cents

BEAT ZEN SUZUARE ZEN AND ZEN
Alan Watts
City Lights Books, 1959
90 cents

KEY BOOK CENTER
1223 Walnut
Boulder, Colorado
Specializes in books by Idries Shah

CARAVAN OF DREAMS
Indries Shah
Penguin, 1972
$1.25

". . . Here is a treasure-laden caravan from the Near East. In its cargo: teaching stories of the dervish philosophers and mystics, writings by Idries Shah on Mecca and on Islam, poetry, proverbs, allegories, and symbolical tales of amazing richness and variety. The collection as a whole makes delightful reading, but it also has a deeply serious purpose: to bring to the reader the spiritual essence of the Middle East and of Central Asia. For to Idries Shah the reader is like Maruf the Cobbler, who "found himself daydreaming his own fabulous caravan of riches. . . . The imagined caravan took shape, became real for a time—and arrived. May your caravan of dreams, too, find its way to you."

THE SUFI ORDER

"Beloved ones of God, you may belong to any race, caste, creed or nation, still you are impartially loved by God. You may be a believer or an unbeliever in the supreme Being, but He cares not. His mercy and grace flow through all His powers, without distinction of friend or foe." (From Volume Five of the *Sufi Message* . . . Pir O Murshid Hazrat Inayat Khan)

The activities of the Sufi Order are carried out through centers and branches in many cities across the United States and in Europe.

Pir Vilayat Inayat Khan, head of the Sufi Order in the west, may be reached, and information about his activities and the activities of the Sufi Order may be obtained, through the secretariat of the Sufi Order: c/o Shahnawaz Jamil, 408 Precita Avenue, San Francisco, California 94110, (415) 824-2300. Los Angeles Branch: 11939 Goshen Ave., L.A., Calif. 90049, (213) 826-3049.

"The greatest principle of Sufism is 'Ishq Allah Ma'bud Allah.' God is love, lover and beloved.'"

Pir Vilayat Inayat Khan
Director and President
23 Rue de la Tuilerie
92 Suresnes
France
Telephone: LONgchamp 1181

"That man has come up to his present state of development by passing through lower forms is the popular doctrine of science today. What is called evolution teaches that we have reached our present state by a very long and gradual ascent from the lowest animal organizations. It is true that the Darwinian theory takes no notice of the evolution of the soul, but only of the body. But it appears to me that a combination of the two views would remove many difficulties which still attach to the theory of natural selection and the survival of the fittest. If we are to believe in evolution, let us have the assistance of the soul itself in this development of new species.

". . . The modern doctrine of the evolution of bodily organisms is not complete, unless we unite with it the idea of a corresponding evolution of the spiritual monad, from which every organic form derives its unity. Evolution has a satisfactory meaning only when we admit that the soul is developed and educated by passing through many bodies."
JAMES FREEMAN CLARKE (1810–1888), *Ten Great Religions*

NOUMEDIA CO.
Box 750
Port Chester, N.Y. 10573
Tapes on Ram Dass, Sufism, Zen Buddhism.

ECKANKAR: THE KEY TO SECRET WORLDS
Paul Twitchell
Lancer, 1969
$1.25

"Soul, the *Atma Sarup*, is the natural body of man, which the vast majority of the species *Homo sapiens* have forgotten how to use properly in the many ages of dwelling on this planet. Spiritual teachers, saints and others have learned how to accomplish soul traveling, that is, journeying to etheric realms in the *Atma Sarup*, and have taught it to those interested in visiting the heavenly kingdoms.

". . . Therefore, the basic principle of soul travel is that man is the spirit self, that he can take charge of the soul body and can move from the visible planes into the invisible worlds at will. When he becomes proficient at this, the beneficial results are freedom, charity and wisdom. These are the God-qualities lying latent in each soul, which must be brought to soul's attention in order to unfold the true self in all its glory.

". . . That part of man which we call the soul is actually the individualized self, the true awareness of spiritual being. When the soul looks at the material side of life—that which we call matter, energy, space and time—it is said to have a negative awareness, or consciousness; but in seeking God and putting its attention on the ultimate, which we know as the positive, it is said to become spiritualized. These two qualities are the extreme poles of life, and since the purpose of life is to lift the soul upward into the highest world, the universe of all universes, man should set himself on the illuminated path as quickly as possible."

TERTIUM ORGANUM: A KEY TO THE ENIGMAS OF THE WORLD
P. D. Ouspensky
Vintage, 1970
$2.95

THE PSYCHOLOGY OF MAN'S POSSIBLE EVOLUTION
P. D. Ouspensky
Knopf, 1969
$3.95

"I maintain that cosmic religious feeling is the strongest and noblest incitement to scientific research. A contemporary has said, not unjustly, that in this age of ours the serious scientific workers are the only profoundly religious people."
ALBERT EINSTEIN, *The World As I See It*

"The most beautiful and most profound emotion we can experience is the sensation of the mystical. It is the sower of all true science. He to whom this emotion is a stranger, who can no longer wonder and stand rapt in awe, is as good as dead. To know know that what is impenetrable to us really exists, manifesting itself as the highest wisdom and the most radiant beauty which our dull faculties can comprehend only in their primitive forms—this knowledge, this feeling is at the center of true religiousness."
ALBERT EINSTEIN QUOTED IN *The Universe and Dr. Einstein* by Lincoln Barnett

TREE OF LIFE: AN INTRODUCTION TO THE CABALA
Z'ev ben Shimon Halevi
Rider, 1972
$5.95

"The Tree of Life is a picture of Creation. It is an objective diagram of the principles working throughout the Universe. Cast in the form of an analogic tree it demonstrates the flow of forces down from the Divine to the lowest world and back again. In it are contained all the laws that govern and their interaction. It is also a comprehensive view of man.

"The relative Universe hovers between two poles. All and Nothing. Either end of this fluctuating axis may be seen as Nothing or All, as both become the entry and exit points for the Absolute who stands apart from Creation. Here we have the full reality. All else is, to the ultimate observer, illusion—a cosmic drama composed and dissolved in a cyclic round of plays within plays from the subtlest reverberations in the Highest worlds to the slowest movements and changes in the coursest materiality."

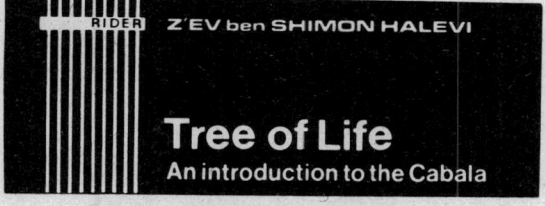

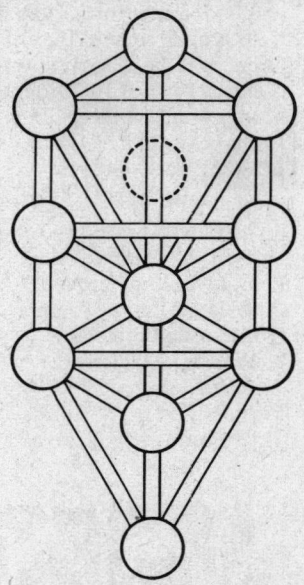

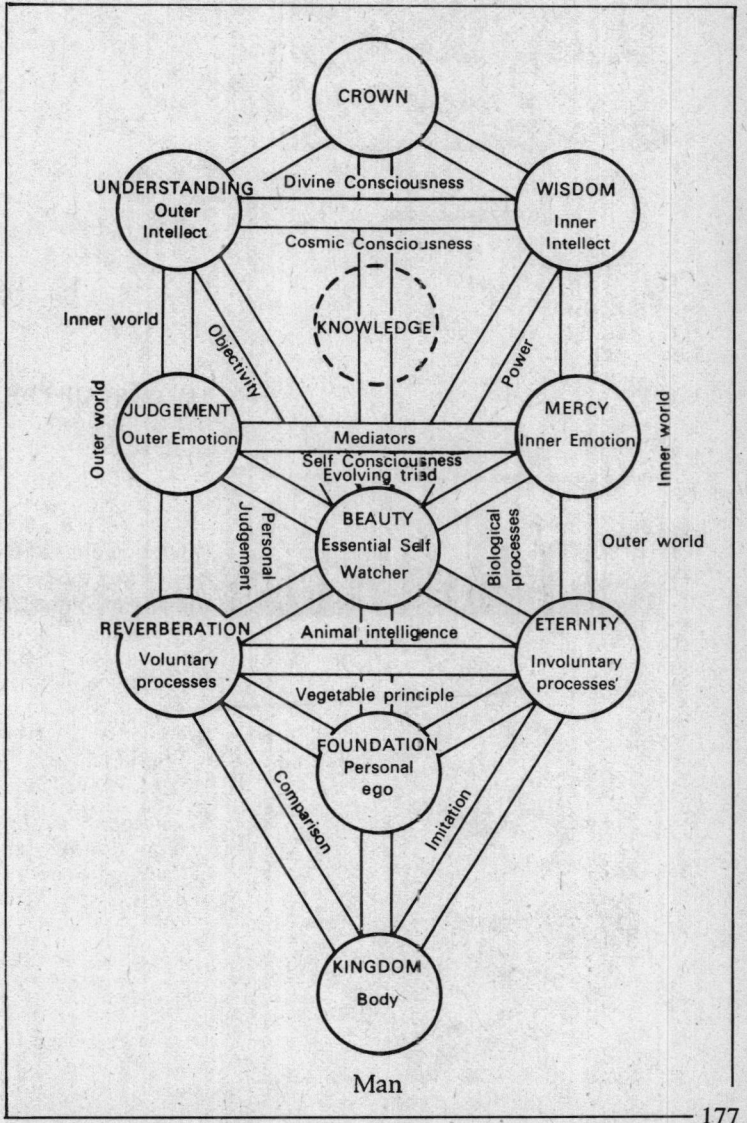

9½ MYSTICS: THE KABBALA TODAY
Herbert Weiner
Collier, 1969
$1.95

ON THE KABBALAH AND ITS SYMBOLISM
Gershorn G. Scholem
Schocken, 1973
$2.10

THE WAY OF THE SUFI
Indries Shah
Dutton, 1970
$2.25

THE SUFI ORDER

"Beloved ones of God, you may belong to any race, caste, creed or nation, still you are impartially loved by God. You may be a believer or an unbeliever in the supreme Being, but He cares not. His mercy and grace flow through all His powers, without distinction of friend or foe." (from Volume Five of the *Sufi Message* . . . Pir O Murshid Hazrat Inayat Khan)

The activities of the Sufi Order are carried out through centers and branches in many cities across the United States and in Europe.

Pir Vilayat Inayat Khan, head of the Sufi Order in the west, may be reached, and information about his activities and the activities of the Sufi Order may be obtained, through the secretariat of the Sufi Order: c/o Shahnawaz Jamil, 408 Precita Avenue, San Francisco, Calif. 94110 Los Angeles Branch: 11939 Goshen Ave., Los Angeles, Calif. 90049. (213) 826-3049.

"The greatest principle of Sufism is 'Ishq Allah Ma'bud Allah.' 'God is love, lover and beloved.' "
Pir Vilayat Inayat Khan
Director and President
23 Rue de la Tuilerie
92 Suresnes
France
Telephone: LONgchamp 1181

Spiritual Frontiers Fellowship

ITS PRINCIPLES PURPOSES and PROGRAM

SPIRITUAL FRONTIERS FELLOWSHIP (SFF) was incorporated in Illinois in 1956 by about seventy-five religious leaders and writers from all sections of the United States, to encourage and interpret to the Churches, and receive interpretation from the Churches of the rising tide of interest in mystical, psychical and paranormal experience.

SFF is **spiritual** in that it is concerned with nonphysical phenomena which relate to God, the human spirit, and the future life. It is **frontier** because it explores matters beyond the usual range of church worship and activity, the paranormal. It is a **fellowship** of those who, having accepted the validity of one or more of these phenomena, would encourage each other and ultimately the whole Church to seek for further light and greater reality in the spiritual life.

SPIRITUAL FRONTIERS FELLOWSHIP
800 Custer Avenue • Suite 1 • Evanston, Ill. 60202

THE ACADEMY OF RELIGION AND PSYCHICAL RESEARCH
(Academic Affiliate of Spiritual Frontiers Fellowship)
800 Custer Avenue
Evanston, Ill. 60202

The Academy of Religion and Psychical Research was formed in October, 1972 by an act of the executive council of SPIRITUAL FRONTIERS FELLOWSHIP. The first general announcement came at the First Academic Conference on "Religion, Psyche and the Spirit" held at Garrett Theological Seminary, November 29–December 2, 1972.

Three principal thrusts are projected for the Academy program. First, the encouragement of dialogue, idea exchange and cooperation between clergy, academics in philosophy and religion, and the researchers and scientists in parapsychology and related fields; second, to conduct an educational program for such scholars, the S.F.F. membership and general public with the goal of providing reliable information and stimulation to their spiritual life; and third, to work closely with related organizations such as the Parapsychological Association, the American Society for Psychical Research and the Academy of Parapsychology and Medicine.

To move toward these goals, the Academy plans to sponsor programs putting theologians and religious scholars in dialogue with para-psychologists and scientists in related fields. Such seminars have already been held at Garrett Theological Seminary, Evanston, Illinois; General Theological Seminary, New York City; and the School of Theology at Claremont, Claremont, California. Other seminars are already in the planning stage.

The first publication of the Academy, *A Reader's Guide to the Church's Ministry of Healing*, by J. Gordon Melton, was released in December, 1973. The *Proceedings* of the First Conference on "Religion, Psyche, and The Spirit" held at Garrett Theological Seminary, November 29–December 2, 1971, will be published in the spring and a copy sent to all Academy members.

The Academy is governed by a Board of Trustees composed of twenty-four members drawn from all areas of the theological and parapsychological disciplines. Dr. Walter Houston Clark, Professor Emeritus of the Psychology of Religion, Andover-Newton Theological Seminar, was elected the first president of the Academy. . . .

Membership in the Academy shall be of three kinds. *Academic* membership is open to academic religionists involved in teaching or research or those who have the proper terminal degrees (Ph.D., Th.D., St.D. or in some cases M.A., M.Div., and St.M.) and to teachers and researchers in fields related to psychical research. Those would include fields of parapsychology, paraphysics, pastoral counseling, humanistic psychology, etc. *Supporting* membership is open to interested persons who may wish to relate to the Academy program. The cost for these memberships is $25.00 for academic, and $15.00 for supporting. This is in line with other academic organizations. A *patron* membership has been established for anyone who wishes to contribute more substantial sums to the Academy.

Two for Now

NEW SPIRITUAL COMMUNITY GUIDE FOR NORTH AMERICA 1975-76

Introduction by Ram Dass

TEACHINGS FOR A NEW AGE:
Alan Watts, Master Subramuniya, Lama Govinda, Werner Erhard, Kahuna Ka'Ona, Swami Satchidananda, Tim Leary, and Others

COMMUNITY DIRECTORY:
Over 3,000 city-by-city listings: Yoga and Meditation Centers • Ashrams • Natural Food Stores and Restaurants • Bookstores, etc.

GUIDE TO SPIRITUAL CENTERS:
Over 100 descriptions of Major Spiritual Groups in North America.

PHOTOS. ILLUSTRATIONS. 208 pages, 5½ x 8½

A PILGRIM'S GUIDE TO PLANET EARTH 1975-76
TRAVELER'S HANDBOOK AND SPIRITUAL DIRECTORY

Introduction by Alan Watts

WHAT'S INSIDE:
INFORMATION - Thousands of Planet Earth's New Age Centers Including:
• Shrines, Temples, Churches & Monasteries • Meditation, Yoga, Zen & Growth Centers • Sites of Natural Beauty • Aquarian Schools, Publications & Communes • Vegetarian & Macrobiotic Restaurants • Health Food Stores • Lodgings • Bookstores • Celebrations & Retreats • and More

PILGRIM'S HANDBOOK - Hints and Practices to keep Body and Soul together:
• Traveler's Astrology • Money, Mail & Such • Health & Food • Meditations • Sacred Art & Music • Travel Routes • Pilgrim's Protocol, etc.

TEACHINGS - Ram Dass, Swami Muktananda, Pir Vilayat Khan, Rabbi Shlomo Carlebach, Yogi Bhajan and Others

FEATURES - Holy Places/Holy People of India • Mystical Christianity in Europe • Middle East Inner Peace • New Age Nomad • Trekking in Nepal • Lost Cities of the Andes

Photographs, Illustrations, Maps, Words, *from Pilgrims who have gone before to show the Way.*
288 pages, 5½ x 8½

ORDERING INFORMATION

( ) *A Pilgrim's Guide to Planet Earth* $4.50 _____
( ) *New Spiritual Community Guide* $3.50 _____

Please include $.35 postage for *each* book. _____

Total _____

Send to:
Spiritual Community
Dept. PK
Box 1080
San Rafael, CA 94902

Free Book and Record Catalog on Request.

SPIRITUAL COMMUNITY PUBLICATIONS

SPIRITUAL COMMUNITY

is a communications family in Marin County, just north of San Francisco, California across the Golden Gate Bridge. The dozen of us here follow different paths, but we are all dedicated to the One Work. We help channel the flow of information which links the evolving world consciousness, encouraging the further spiritual transformation of the land and its people.

We have chosen the printed word to transmit this energy. Our reference books—the Guide and the Supplement—begin and end with you. Information comes in from centers, teachers and disciples, stores and restaurants, and from our readers. This is researched, written, photographed, illustrated, designed, edited, typeset, printed and bound by individuals and groups who are themselves on the Path. By the grace of God we have now published six books, and many more are being worked on. We are developing a New-Age approach to publishing—putting out books emphasizing the spiritual aspects of travel, children, practices and teachings.

FROM SPIRITUAL COMMUNITY GUIDE
GLOSSARY

AHIMSA—non-injury, harmlessness

AJARI—teacher (Japanese)

AJNA—sixth chakra or third eye

ALLAH—God (Islamic)

ANAHATA—fourth or heart chakra

ANANDA—pure bliss

ANGA—'limb' or step in the eightfold, astanga, path of Yoga

APANA VAYU—the neg. vital force

ASAMPRAJNATA—highest state of samadhi; objectless meditation

ASANA—posture or pose

ASHRAM—Spiritual retreat

ASMITA—'I-am-ness', egotism

ASTRAL BODY—subtle body of Man

ATMAN—divine soul dormant in all beings

AURA—subtle manifestation of matter-energy seen as a glow emanating from the body

AVATAR—incarnation of God in human form, e.g. Christ, Krishna, Rama, Zoroaster, Buddha.

AVIDYA—ignorance

BABA—father

BARDO—state between death and rebirth

BHAJAN—holy songs; devotional music

BHAKTI—devotion; worship

BIJA—'seed'; one-syllable mantra

BODHI—supreme knowledge

BODHISATTVA—Enlightened Being who postpones his Nirvana to help others

BRAHMA—Divine Spirit, God

BRAHMACHARYA—sexual abstinence; 'knower of Brahma'

BUDDHI—higher intuitive intellect

CHAKRA—psychic center; center of consciousness

CHELA—student; disciple

CH'I—vital breath or energy; prana

DERVISHES—Moslem sect, associated with Sufism, known for their whirling dances

DEVA, DEVI—god; goddess

DHARMA—Cosmic Law; one's duty

DHYANA—meditation

GUNAS—three inherent characteristics of the phenomenal universe

GURU—teacher

HASIDISM—Jewish mysticism which originated in Poland in the 18th century

HATHA—ha: sun; tha: moon

HATHA YOGA—yoga through work on the body

IDA—subtle nerve in the left side of spine (moon energy)

ISVARA—the conscious principle of the universe

JAPA—repetition, especially of mantras

JIVATMAN—individual self or soul

JNANA—essence of wisdom

KABBALA—esoteric and mystical interpretations of the Jewish Scriptures

KARMA—law of cause and effect

KARMA YOGA—yoga through selfless service

KIRTAN—repetition in song of the names of God

KLESAS—sources of sorrow and problems

KOAN—Zen meditation exercise in the form of a question

KRIYA—'action'; yoga exercise

KUNDALINI—vital primordial energy at base of spine

LAMA—teacher (Tibetan)

LAYA YOGA—yoga through awakening of the kundalini

MAGI—Zoroastrian wise men or priests

MAHAT—universal wisdom

MAITHUNA—a practice of sexual intercourse in Tantric Yoga

MANAS—mental faculties

MANDALA—geometric and psychometric design used for meditation

MANTRA—recitation of sounds which have psychic effects

MARGA—spiritual path

MAYA—illusion; the phenomenal world

MISHNA—first part of the Talmud; oral interpretation of the Scriptures

MOKSHA—liberation from the wheel of death and rebirth

MUDRA—gesture of fingers, hands or limbs which affects prana

MUHLBANDH—closing of the anal sphincter

MULADHARA—first chakra at base of spine

MURSHID—guru, teacher (Sufi)

NADA—the inner, subtle sound

NADI—nerve channel

NETI-YOGA—nostril cleaning

NIRODHA—control of the thought-idea process

NIRVAKALPA—highest form of samadhi where there is no distinction between object-subject

NIRVANA—'At-one-ment' with All and Everything beyond phenomenal world

NIYAMA—moral observances (do's)

OJAS—the highest form of prana

OM—mantra indicating the principle of Brahma, or total universal energy

PADMASANA—lotus posture

PARAMAHANSA—'swan-like'; title of one high on the path.

PARATMA—supreme or collective Self

PANDIT—learned man

PINGALA—subtle nerve channel in the right side of spine (sun energy)

PRAJNA—supreme intuitive wisdom

PRAKRITI—basic substance of phenomenal universe

PRANA—life energy

PRANAYAMA—control of prana through breathing

PRASAD—consecrated food

PURUSHA—spirit contrasted to prakriti

RAJAS—energy, activity; one of the three gunas

RAJA YOGA—yoga through mastery over the mind

RINPOCHE—'Precious One'; title given to high lamas and tulkus

RISHIS—holy wise men of ancient India

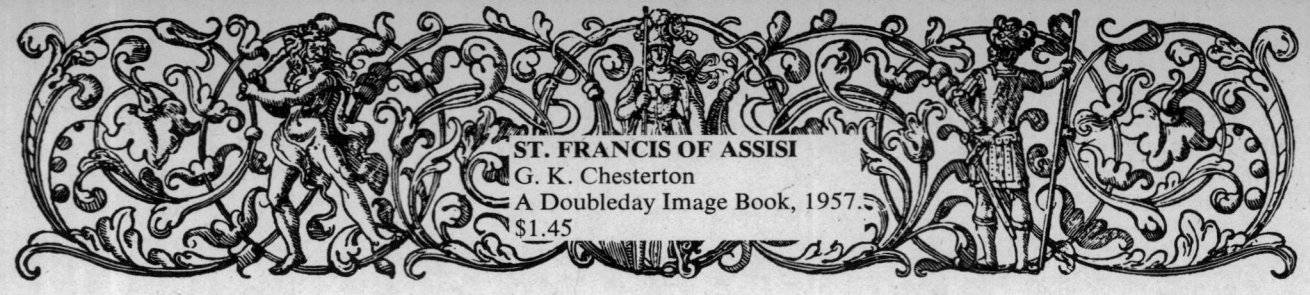

ST. FRANCIS OF ASSISI
G. K. Chesterton
A Doubleday Image Book, 1957.
$1.45

FOUNDATION OF SCIENTIFIC SPIRITUAL UNDERSTANDING, INC.
F.O.S.S.U.

The FOUNDATION OF SCIENTIFIC SPIRITUAL UNDERSTANDING was incorporated as a non-profit religious educational organization to provide a vehicle for interested individuals to explore the fundamental truths and eternal mysteries of life.

We believe that the universe is directed by an infinite consciousness who directs it in an orderly manner. We believe and teach eternal progression of the soul. Scientific Spiritual Understanding rests on education embracing the impact of physical, astral and spiritual forces.

Our main objective is to provide an opportunity for interested individuals to acquire a knowledge and understanding of the scientific spiritual laws of the universe for the betterment of their lives and the eternal progression of humanity; through the study of astrology, alchemy, extra sensory perception, esoteric psychology, philosophy, tarot and other Hermetic sciences. A knowledge of these subjects will serve as a means to a richer and fuller life for the benefit of all.

The Foundation's services include the following:

* Classes in astrology and associated sciences with certification.
* Lectures, seminars, workshops and healing ministry, meditations.
* Publications, wholesale and retail.
* Astrological books and supplies.
* "COSMOGRAPH" Quarterly (by request).

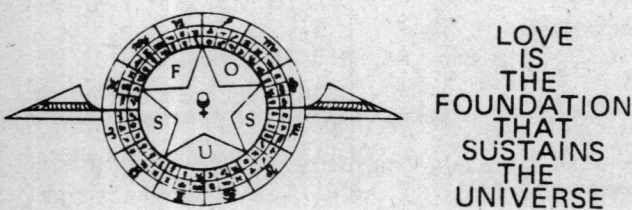

LOVE IS THE FOUNDATION THAT SUSTAINS THE UNIVERSE

Katalin B. Williams, Founder-President
Ken R. Williams, Vice-President
Janice M. Davis, Secretary
Post Office Box 93
Redondo Beach, California 90277
U.S.A.
Telephone: (213) 378-4543

AQUARIAN ARCANE COLLEGE
(Mankind Centre Australia)

Aquarian Arcane College is a subsidiary function of A.O.R.T.A.

An Order founded for the purpose of studying the Ageless Wisdom and the mysteries of the Natural and Spiritual laws of the Universe.

An AORTA ASHRAM functions as a research centre to establish the true meaning of the **DESTINY** for **HUMANITY**.

A DESTINY which is not blind fate but a purposeful unfoldment of unlimited potentials of LOVE, BEAUTY, HARMONY, JOY, the seeds of which are contained within the heart of every being, awaiting responsible preparation by all through joined cooperation.

The AORTA ASHRAM motivates the principle of BUDDHI-Love-Wisdom — and activates the desire and dedication for cooperation with the PURPOSE of the ETERNAL.

A search for the true DESTINY of MAN is not Kismet, neither is it a waiting for a Saviour to lead us to a promised land, (which can only be incidental) but a DESTINY where MAN unites with the ETERNAL, the purposeful DESTINY of the M O N A D, the Spiritual SELF, the CAPTAIN of the SOUL and the MASTER of our FATE.

Conditions for admittance as a pupil into the Aquarian Arcane College are a sincere desire or urge to help in establishing the IDEA of the NEW UNIVERSAL MAN and CIVILISATION based on UNITY in diversity among all peoples, recognition of the Oneness of LIFE, and the principle of Cooperation without distinction of Race, Creed, or Colour.

The course of instructions in the A.A.C. is of an individual nature; teacher and pupil work together in dialogue, and in this manner of communication progress results are usually much quicker. The student asks for information, the teacher selects from the vast store available for distribution from the Archives of the Order making sure not to encumber the student with unrelated material. NO FEES are required. The Order and College are non-profit Organizations.

In the immediate future the principal Project of the Aquarian Arcane College is a course in Dialogues on the New Aquarian Age Civilisation. Upon enrollment each student becomes an integral part of a Cosmic Wide Adventure where attainment is only equalled by an Infinity with unlimited Potentials.

A publication CONTACT is issued periodically. For further enquiries write:

Mr. R. T. Adamson, Secretary
Post Office Box 23
Bondi Beach, 2026, N.S.W.
AUSTRALIA

THE MANDALA SOCIETY

Our purpose is to cooperate with all individuals and all organizations seeking to raise functional being to a process that is closer to mankind's highest state of awareness.

We believe each individual can already fantasize Heaven on Earth or Nirvana or Satori.

Our purpose is to create environments where these higher states of awareness can be experienced.

The MANDALA is a symbolic art form that may be created in unlimited variations.

MANDALA represents the essence of being, the unity of life and the integration of mankind's true nature in its physical, sensory, emotional, intellectual and spiritual aspects.

Our philosophy is a way of life that can only be experienced. We have no eternal dogmas, for we feel all things will be transcended. We feel a deep respect for life mingled with awe and love.

We see expression of life as its purpose.

We are organized to provide the opportunity for each individual to experience and express his or her own uniqueness. This is accomplished through CIRCLES OF THE MANDALA. These are groups of people moving toward actualizing relationships.

We are creating a new concept of religion. The MANDALA Society has been incorporated as a non-profit religious, philosophical society dedicated to bringing about the above conditions.

David Harris
Post Office Box 23231
San Diego, California 92123
U.S.A.
Telephone: (714) 272-7330

EAST—WEST CULTURAL CENTER

A non-profit educational and religious organization inaugurated in 1953 and incorporated in 1960.

Purposes: To teach and help integrate the cultural and spiritual values of East and West in order to create greater world unity, and a more progressive creative world unity, and a more progressive creative spiritual activity in the fields of education, the living arts, philosophy, and religion.

Its Truth: The teachings of Sri Aurobindo, the Integrator of East and West, are the inspiration of the Center. His vision of a divine life on earth and his saying "The knowledge that unites is the true knowledge", are the guiding torchlights.

Activities: Open houses, lectures, classes in religion, occult arts, world-culture, Sanskrit, philosophy, dynamic yoga systems, and meditation. Dramatic and musical performances, movie and slide projection programs. Sale of books, cards, incense, mantra records, and art objects from the East, and a specialized oriental library.

MU-NE-DOWK FOUNDATION, INC.

Mu-ne-dowk Foundation, Inc. is a non-profit, non-denominational, religious and educational corporation founded by Carl and Maxine Stoelting and incorporated under the laws of the State of Wisconsin in 1967.

"Mu-ne-dowk" is the Chippewa Indian word meaning "dwelling place of the Great Spirit". It is located on 12 acres of wooded lake property, four miles from the nearest town. The Foundation supports a lodge and dormitory which provides housing for up to 45 guests.

Its space-age centered retreats are sponsored by the "Institute of Crystal Truths" — a personal spiritual movement of Maxine and Carl, with the purpose of giving crystal pure truths of the Universe to those who are attracted or directed to Mu-ne-dowk.

Our goal of 1973 of becoming One with the Universal Brotherhood has been realized through the sharing of leaders who have had personal experiences with UFO's and with other space phenomena. Dr. Dan Fry was one such leader.

Anthony Brooke is in Scandinavia bringing his New Age message to receptive audiences. He will have much to share when he comes again to Mu-ne-dowk Light Center.

Our thrust for 1974 continues to be universal in scope.

Carl and Maxine Stoelting, Founders
Box 268, Route 1
Kiel, Wisconsin 53042
U.S.A.
Telephone: (414) 894-2681; 894-2339

Wisdom-truth of all times, sages, and countries, is taught to the children through story, quotations, game, drama, music, art, dance, flag and literature of the world.

Help is given for understanding and forwarding in some practical way the work involved in the progressive construction of the first Auroville near the Sri Aurobindo Ashram in South India — A City of Human Unity and a Divine Life for people of all nations who aspire for a new and higher world of living and consciousness — truly the growing flower-child of the Sri Aurobindo Ashram in Pondicherry, South India.

Judith M. Tyberg, Founder-President
2865 West Ninth Street
Los Angeles, California 90006
U.S.A.
Telephone: (213) 386-0999

INSTITUTE OF GENERAL PSIONICS

There has been much said about the gaps that exist between people. Many have come to ignore the gaps that exist *within* the individual human that promotes the gaps between people. Gaps do exist *within* between you, your subconscious and your body. For example, you can withdraw nearly all contact and control from either the subconcious mind or the body or both. When this occurs you may develop an amnesia so that you forget that you are out of contact and control. The result is that your subconscious and the material outside world take control and you become the victim.

Our purpose is to put you back in the driver's seat, so to speak. Otherwise stated our purpose is:
1. To establish the concept of Unity between individual Human Beings and what is commonly known as God.
2. To develop and apply all necessary Methods to assist Human Beings in the Creation, Pursuit, and Accomplishment of their individual Spiritual goals.

In order to accomplish these purposes, many methods have been developed. They are of two types: 1. A system developing a common general viewpoint and a specific philosophy which is yours alone with which you can live in personal peace of mind and security. This is called the Degree Program and General Workshops. 2. A specific professional program is the Abilities Improvement and Development Engineering System (A.I.D.E.). A.I.D.E. is a Powerful system which removes the blocks that prevent you from accomplishing what you want to do. Case histories have proven that A.I.D.E. can enable you to succeed in areas where other methods have failed. This may be any endeavor from passing an important examination (such as the Bar exam), to resolving fears and doubts of a personal nature.

The result is a great increase in Personal Human Dignity which can then be granted by you in security to all others.

The Church of General Psionics (a fully non-profit organization).

Box 2186,
Palos Verdes Peninsula, California 90274
204 North Catalina
Redondo Beach, California 90277
Telephone (213) 374-4923

THE NEW AGE PRESS

The New Age Press is dedicated to the writing, publishing and dissemination of literature correlating esoteric science with the expansion of consciousness and the entry of man into the New Age. The Press was founded in 1948 as a non-profit California Corporation.

Its magazine, The New Age Interpreter, now in its 33rd year of publication, contains articles of an inspirational and philosophic nature illuminating the expansion of the New Age Consciousness.

The New Age Press publishes the extensive works of Corinne and Theodore Heline and others. These books include a seven volume set of the New Age Bible Interpretation, works on music and color in the New Age, the music of Beethoven and Wagner esoterically interpreted among others. Other subjects include: Masonry, mythology, astrology, occult anatomy, the Tarot, the Madonna and many others.

Large numbers of individuals with the New Age consciousness are now coming into incarnation in the field of physical plane existence who are earnestly seeking knowledge to guide them in their quest for a meaningful life and an understanding of the mysteries of the universe and man's place in it. It is to them that we look for the hope of the future. And it is to them that we serve in our publishing effort by continuing to make these books, guideposts on the way of attainment, available.

George Perkins, Executive Director
4636 Vineta Avenue
La Canada, Califronia 91011
U.S.A.
Telephone: (213) 790-6236

BOOK OF THE HOPI
Frank Waters
Ballantine, 1971
$1.25

LISTEN, HUMANITY
Meher Baba, D. E. Stevans,
Harper Colophon, 1971
$2.25

"There is no creature which is not destined for the supreme goal, as there is no river which is not winding its way towards the sea. But only in the human form is consciousness so developed that it is capable of expressing the perfection of its own true self, which is the Self of all.

"However, even in the human form the soul is prevented from realizing its birthright of joy and fulfillment because of the burden of *sanskaras* which it has accumulated as a by-product of its arduous development of consciousness. Like the dust that accumulates on the shoes of a traveler on foot, these *sanskaras* are gathered by the pilgrim as he treads the evolutionary path.

"In the human form, which is the crowning product of evolution, the divine life is enmeshed in the *sanskaric* deposits of the mind. The expression of the divine life is therefore curtailed and distorted by the distractions of the *sanskaras*, which weld consciousness instead to the fascinations of the false-phenomenal.

"One by one the many-colored attachments to the false must be relinquished. Bit by bit the *sanskaric* tinder feeding the deceptive flames of the separative ego must be replaced by the imperative evidence of the unquenchable flame of truth. Only in this manner can man ascend to the height of divine attainment: the endless beginning of life eternal.

"The life in eternity knows no bondage, decay or sorrow. It is the everlasting and ever renewing self-affirmation of conscious, illimitable divinity. My mission is to help you inherit this hidden treasure of the Self."

MEHER BABA

THE TAOIST VISION
William McNaughton
Ann Arbor Paperback, 1971
$1.95

THE TAO-TEH-KING SAYINGS OF LAO-TSU
C. Spurgeon Medhurst
Quest, 1971
$1.95

"One of the greatest sages of history was a man named Lao-tzu, who was born in China in the year 604 B.C. He is regarded as the founder of the system of religion known as Taoism. His writings have been preserved in a small volume of poetry entitled *Tao-Teh-King*, which translated means 'The Way and Its Power,' or 'The Book of the Way and Its Virtue.' It has also been called 'A Scripture of the Eternal and Its Characteristics,' and it was adopted as a canon in the year 666 A.D. DURING THE RULE OF THE EMPEROR KAO TSUNG OF THE T'ANG DYNASTY. BECAUSE OF ITS SUBLIME AND TIMELESS CONCEPTS, THE *Tao-Teh-King* has endured through the centuries; it has been translated into many languages, and has been the subject of numerous volumes of philosophical and speculative literature."

TAO BOOKSTORE
303 NEWBURY STREET
BOSTON, MASS., 02115

We sell metaphysical books and practical books, everything from Vajrayana Buddhism, macrobitoics or the Essene teachings to organic farming, natural childbirth, or building a tipi.

We mail order many of our books, and a lot of them are difficult to find. Write for a free catologue

THE AMERICAN INDIAN AND THE OCCULT
Christopher Dane
Popular Library, 1973
95 cents

A LOS ANGELES SPIRITUAL COMMUNITY BOOKSHOP

BUDDHISM — YOGA
ASTROLOGY — INCENSE
OCCULT — HERBS
PSYCHOLOGY — TAROT CARD
NATURAL LIVING — MEDITATION PILLOWS
MAGIC — INCENSE

THE BODHI TREE
8585 MELROSE AVENUE
LOS ANGELES, CALIF. 90069
MONDAY-SATURDAY 11—11 PM   SUNDAY 11—6 PM

TAO: THE CHINESE PHILOSOPHY OF CHANGE
Philip Rawson and Laszlo Segeza
Thames and Hudson, 1973
$5.85

"The Taoist perception of the real world differs essentially from our usual Western one. We tend to think, diagrammatically, of a world of separate things—some of them alive—arranged in an independent space. We take it for granted that these lumps of independent 'thing' 'cause' each other, 'act on' each other as they 'move about' in empty space, and pass through a series of static states of change. Even our philosophy and science limit themselves to finding substantial 'things', carefully divided from one another by definition, which will 'explain' the real world. Idealism calls them ideas, materialism calls them atoms, with their sub-atomic particles. We act on the assumption that our world is a structure assembled of solid building-bricks in many different shapes and sizes, all quite independent of the observer; each concept which denotes one of these building-bricks, its connection with others, or its activities, we take to exclude for ever its opposite or its own negative. The shapes of the building-bricks are fixed, mutually exclusive, and, by implication, unchangeable. Change happens, we assume, by one 'thing' turning into 'something else'. The way we experience and measure time is by dividing it up into countable moments, each of which is separate and, in an abstract way, identical to all others, however large or infinitely small we may choose to make them.

"Taoism sees all this as schematic, vulgar and absurd. It recognizes that, though fixed concepts referring to things and states can be extracted by human thought from the mobile reality, and can be useful, there is actually no way of reconstructing the mobility of the real by adding up fixed concepts. Therefore, the most important element—the only element that matters—is always left out of the ordinary ideas most of us have, on which we base our worlds and with which we try to come to terms with them. All static conceptualism is in the last resort impotent. . . .

". . . All the separations which men claim to decipher in the web of Tao are useful fabrications, concepts being themselves ripples in the 'mental' part of the stream. Each human being himself is woven out of a complex system of totally mobile interactions with his environment. His body is in perpetual change, not by jumps from state to state; for his aging does not correspond to minutes, hours and birthdays, but goes on all the time. . . .

". . . Two of the most important aspects of the intuition of the Tao are, first; that nothing which happens, no event or process, ever repeats itself exactly. On the ordinary human scale this is obvious, if one stops to think. Only on the microscopic scale, where invisible sub-atomic particles are isolated as 'snapshot' concepts, may they seem to repeat. But, in fact, the overall context of even such minute apparent repetitions has changed while they were happening; their nature is anyway 'vibration'. Second; this immense web consisting of rolling change does not itself change. It is the 'uncarved block' devoid of any definable shape, the 'mother', matrix of time, including both 'being' and 'not being', the present, future and vanished past—the Great Whole of continuous duration, infinite space and infinite change."

THE SECRET OF THE GOLDEN FLOWER
Richard Wilhelm and C. G. Jung
Routledge and Kegan Paul, 1972
$3.60

THE JAPANESE CULT OF TRANQUILITY
Karlfried Graf von Durkheim
Weiser, 1974
$2.95

THE WAY OF THE WHITE CLOUDS: A BUDDHIST PILGRIM IN TIBET
Lama Anagarika Govinda
Shambala Publications, 1972
$3.95

ZEN BUDDHISM
Peter Pauper Press, 1959
$1.25

STUDIES IN ZEN
D. T. Suzuki
Delta, 1955
$1.95

ZEN IN THE ART OF ARCHERY
Eugen Herrigel
Vintage, 1953
$1.80

In the case of archery, the hitter and the hit are no longer two opposing objects, but are one reality. The archer ceases to be conscious of himself as the one who is engaged in hitting the bull's-eye which confronts him. This state of unconsciousness is realized only when, completely empty and rid of the self, he becomes one with the perfecting of his technical skill, though there is in it something of a quite different order which cannot be attained by any progressive study of the art. . . .

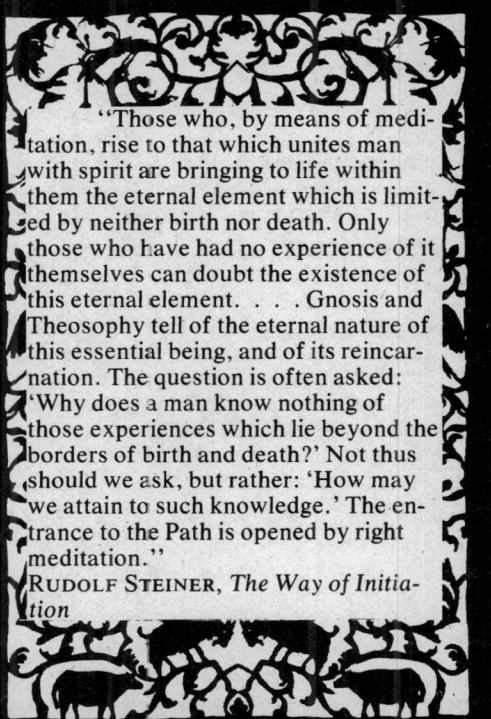

"Those who, by means of meditation, rise to that which unites man with spirit are bringing to life within them the eternal element which is limited by neither birth nor death. Only those who have had no experience of it themselves can doubt the existence of this eternal element. . . . Gnosis and Theosophy tell of the eternal nature of this essential being, and of its reincarnation. The question is often asked: 'Why does a man know nothing of those experiences which lie beyond the borders of birth and death?' Not thus should we ask, but rather: 'How may we attain to such knowledge.' The entrance to the Path is opened by right meditation."
RUDOLF STEINER, *The Way of Initiation*

FOUNDATIONS OF TIBETAN MYSTICISM
Lama Anagarita Govinda
Weiser, 1972
$3.75

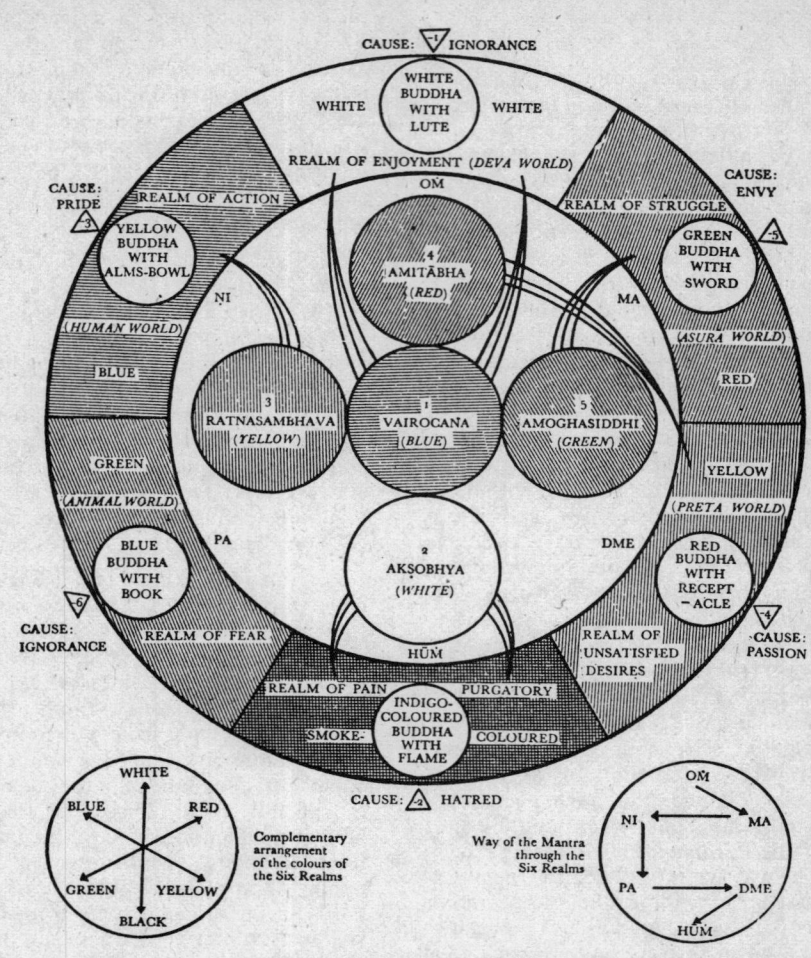

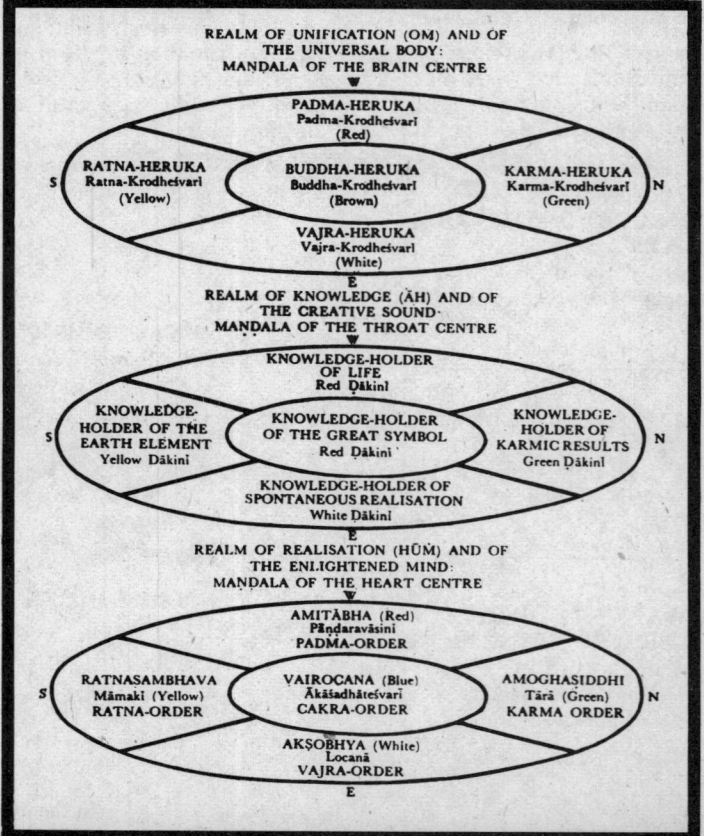

"The importance of Tibetan tradition for our time and for the spiritual development of humanity lies in the fact that Tibet is the last living link that connects us with the civilizations of a distant past. The mystery-cults of Egypt, Mesopotamia and Greece, of Incas and Ayas, have perished with the destruction of their civilizations and Mayas, for ever lost to our knowledge, except for some scanty fragments.

"The old civilizations of India and China, though well preserved in their ancient art and literature, and still glowing here and there under the ashes of modern thought, are buried and penetrated by so many strata of different cultural influences, that it is difficult, if not impossible, to separate the various elements and to recognize their original nature.

"Tibet due to its natural isolation and its inaccessibility (which was reinforced by the political conditions of the last centuries has succeeded not only in preserving but in *keeping alive* the traditions of the most distant past, the knowledge of the hidden forces of the human soul and the highest achievements and esoteric teachings of Indian saints and sages.

But in the storm of world-transforming events, which no nation on earth can escape and which will drag even Tibet out of its isolation, these spiritual achievements will be lost for ever, unless they become an integral part of a future higher civilization of humanity

Physic Centres (Cakras)		Physiological Counterparts
MAṆIPŪRA-CAKRA Navel Centre Element: 'Fire' Seed-syllable: 'RAM' Colour: Red Form: Triangle		**PLEXUS EPIGASTRICUS** (Solar Plexus) System of Nutrition
SVĀDHIṢṬHĀNA-CAKRA Abdominal Centre (4 finger-widths below the navel) Element: 'Water' Seed-syllable: 'VAM' Colour: White Form: Crescent		**PLEXUS HYPOGASTRICUS** Inner Organs of Secretion and Reproduction
In the Tibetan System combined under the name 'Sang-Nä' (*gsaṅ-gnas*)		Generative System
MŪLĀDHĀRA-CAKRA Root Centre (in the perineum). Its latent primordial force is represented by the serpent 'Kuṇḍalini', coiled round the 'Liṅgam' in the centre of the triangular 'Yoni'. Element: 'Earth' Seed-syllable: 'LAM' Colour: Yellow Form: Square		**PLEXUS PELVIS** (Sacral Plexus) which controls the outer organs of generation (represented by 'Liṅgam', the male, and 'Yoni', the female symbol of creative force (comparable to the 'libido')

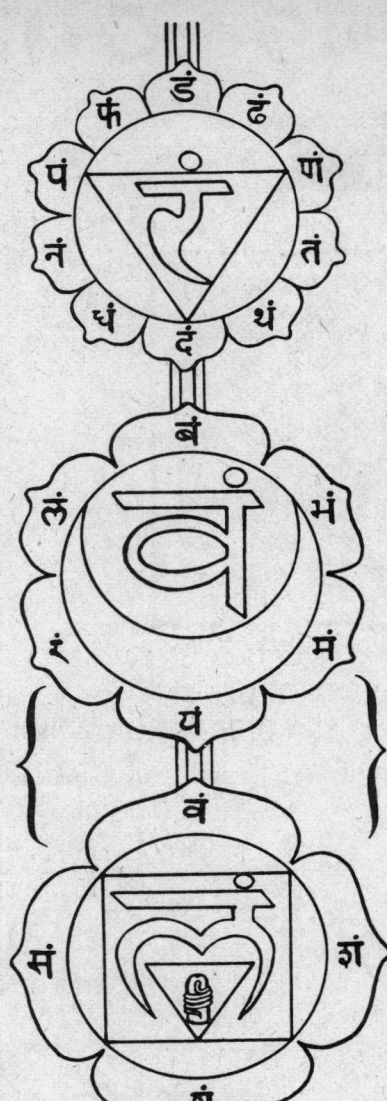

SIMPLIFIED DIAGRAM OF THE CENTRES OF PSYCHIC FORCE ACCORDING TO THE TRADITION OF THE *KUṆḌALINĪ-YOGA*

SITUATION OF THE PSYCHO-PHYSICAL CENTRES AND THE THREE MAIN CURRENTS OF PSYCHIC ENERGY IN THE HUMAN BODY

The vertical axis, corresponding to the spinal column and shown as a simple straight line, represents the *Suṣumṇā-Nāḍī*; the curved double line *Iḍā-Nāḍī*, and the opposite curved single line *Piṅgalā-Nāḍī*. We shall hear more about this in the following chapters.

THE RELIGIOUS SOUND OF TIBET

"Himalayan Mountain Flowers"

A UNIQUE ANTHOLOGY OF MONASTIC RITUALS
INCLUDING TANTRIC CHANTS, MANDALA OFFERINGS, AND INVOCATIONS.

$6.50 Mail Order/Wholesale Enquiries Welcome.

This stereo album is available from:
Dorje Ling ❖ P. O. Box 1410 ❖ Mission Rafael Station ❖ San Rafael, California 94902

ORIGINAL $1.65

A CATALOG OF THE WAYS PEOPLE GROW
SEVERIN PETERSON

PATANJALI'S YOGA AIKIDO PSYCHODRAMA
ASTROLOGY GESTALT THERAPY MYSTICISM
CONTEMPLATION DREAMS CONSCIOUSNESS
TAROT BREATHING THERAPY MEDITATION
ENCOUNTER GROUP YOGA THEATER GAMES
T-GROUPS ALEXANDER TECHNIQUE ZEN
HASIDISM SYNANON SENSITIVITY TRAINING
ANALYTICAL PSYCHOLOGY T'AI CHI CH'UAN
GROWTH CENTERS HATHA YOGA HYPNOSIS
BIOENERGETIC ANALYSIS FAMILY THERAPY
SOCIETY OF FRIENDS   MOVEMENT IN DEPTH
STRUCTURAL INTEGRATION YOGA PRECEPTS
HUMANISTIC PSYCHOLOGY ESP PRAYER
SHAMANISM TRANSCENDENTAL MEDITATION
SHELDON'S TYPES HARA INNER IMAGERY
PSYCHOTHERAPY SENSORY AWARENESS

A CATALOGUE OF THE WAYS PEOPLE GROW
Severin Peterson
Ballantine, 1971
$1.65

J. KRISHNAMURTI: think on these things
D. Rajagopal, ed.
Perennial Library, 1964
$1.25

"Most of us cling to some small part of life, and think that through that part we shall discover the whole. Without leaving the room we hope to explore the whole length and width of the river and perceive the richness of the green pastures along its banks. We live in a little room, we paint on a little canvas, thinking that we have grasped life by the hand or understood the significance of death; but we have not. To do that we must go outside. And it is extraordinarily difficult to go outside, to leave the room with its narrow window and see everything as it is without judging, without condemning, without saying, 'This I like and that I don't like'; because most of us think that through the part we shall understand the whole. Through a single spoke we hope to understand the wheel; but one spoke does not make a wheel, does it? It takes many spokes, as well as a hub and a rim, to make the thing called a wheel, and we need to see the whole wheel in order to comprehend it. In the same way we must perceive the whole process of living if we are really to understand life."

TAOIST YOGA: ALCHEMY AND IMMORTALITY Lu K'uan Yu
Weiser, 1970
$3.50

YOGA: A SCIENTIFIC EVALUATION
Kovon Behanan
Dover, 1964
$2.50

KARMA YOGA AND BHAKTI-YOGA
Swami Vichananda
1970
$3.50
Write to:
Swami Nikhilananda
Ramakrishna-Vivchenanda Center,
17 East 94th Street,
New York, N.Y.

PSYCHO-YOGA: THE PRACTICE OF MIND CONTROL
Dr. B. Edwin
Citadel Press, 1967
$1.95

BABA
Arnold Schulman
Pocket Books, 1973
$1.25

"The writer heard of Baba during his first stay in India and through a friend, an Indian novelist, had arranged to meet him.

"Baba, in his early forties, was slightly over five feet tall. He wore a bright orange silk dress that hung loosely down to his chunky bare feet; but the first thing one noticed was his Afro-electric hair standing straight out from all parts of his head like a black, kinky halo five or six inches wide. His coloring was the soft beige of a Brahmin. He spoke gently and with great sweetness to each of the seven people in the room, but did not reveal anything about anyone's past or future. He confined his remarks to platitudes about God, love, and devotion. Then, just before Baba ended the audience, he materialized a ruby ring, which he gave to the novelist, and a handful of ashes, which he gave to a woman in the group. Baba was talking to someone else on the other side of the room when suddenly he had stopped in the middle of a sentence and turned to the woman.

"'I will cure your appendicitis,' he said, as he materialized the ashes. 'Take this in water three days.'

"She had suffered an attack of appendicitis the night before and was in great pain. No one had mentioned her attack.

"She followed his instructions and three days later, when the pain had completely disappeared, she had two reputable doctors in another town examine her thoroughly. Neither of them could find any trace of appendicitis."

SWAMI SATCHIDANANDA: HIS BIOGRAPHY
Sita Weiner
Bantam, 1972
$1.95

"The hour before dawn is the blackest time of night. A great change has already begun. We are living now amongst violence and confusion but we are on the brink of a great age of spirituality. Whenever we take a young plant from its nursery and re-plant it elsewhere, the plant withers. Many of the leaves fall off. But that doesn't mean it is dying. Till it gets rooted, the plant shakes a bit and trembles. But it must face that shaking and overcome it, because it can't come to full growth in the nursery itself. Young people today are being transplanted into another area altogether, and so we see this shaking. We see it all over the globe. But I see a very bright future. All the shaking will cease. Slowly, slowly, we are getting re-rooted, in the right place, with the right ideas. Consciousness is everywhere expanding. And America is going to lead the way. It is time for the West to show the East. There is great peace here and love. And we can spread this peace everywhere, all over the world. The West has realized the superficiality of the material life. The West is crying for true knowledge and is getting it. I have a great hope. There is great awakening. The whole world is going to enjoy the peace through you people. Day by day I see it progressing. All these calamities, all these wars, will come to an end. And we will all soon be enjoying the bliss of that peaceful sunshine, no doubt."

BHAGAVAD-GITA: AS IT IS
A. C. Bhaktivedanta Swami Pradhupada
Collier, 1971
$4.95

A masterpiece of scriptural literature, Bhagavad-gita is a sacred "song" in the form of a battlefield dialogue between the Lord Sri Krsna and Arjuna, his friend and disciple. Krsna, acting as Arjuna's adviser, instructs him in the science of self-realization, teaching him how to live as a devotee of the Lord and thus to reach the eternal spiritual world while continuing to perform his earthly duties.

AUTOBIOGRAPHY OF A YOGI
Paramahansa Yogananda
Self-Realization Fellowship, 1972
$1.95

"The science of *Kriya Yoga*, mentioned so often in these pages, became widely known in modern India through the instrumentality of Lahiri Mahasaya, my guru's guru. The Sanskrit root of *kriya* is *kri*, to do, to act and react; the same root is found in the word *karma*, the natural principle of cause and effect. *Kriya Yoga* is thus 'union (*yoga*) with the Infinite through a certain action or rite *kriya*.' A yogi who faithfully practices the technique is gradually freed from karma or the lawful chain of cause-effect equilibriums. " '. . . *Kriya Kriya Yoga* is an instrument through which human evolution can be quickened.' Sri Yukteswar explained to his students. "The ancient yogis discovered that the secret of cosmic consciousness is intimately linked with breath mastery. This is India's unique and deathless contribution to the world's treasury of knowledge. . . .

". . . The *Kriya Yogi* mentally directs his life energy to revolve, upward and downward, around the six spinal centers (medullary, cervical, dorsal, lumbar, sacral, and coccygeal plexuses), which correspond to the twelve astral signs of the zodiac, the symbolic Cosmic Man. One-half minute of revolution of energy around the sensitive spinal cord of man effects subtle progress in his evolution; that half-minute of *Kriya* equals one year of natural spiritual unfoldment.

"The astral system of a human being, with six (twelve by polarity) inner constellations revolving around the sun of the omniscient spiritual eye, is interrelated with the physical sun and the twelve zodiacal signs. All men are thus affected by an inner and an outer universe. The ancient rishis discovered that man's earthly and heavenly environment, in a series of twelve-year cycles, push him forward on his natural path. The scriptures aver that man requires a million years of normal, diseaseless evolution to perfect his human brain and attain cosmic consciousness.

"One thousand *Kiryas* practiced in 8½ hours gives the yogi, in one day, the equivalent of one thousand years of natural evolution: 365,000 years of evolution in one year. In three years, a *Kriya Yogi* can thus accomplish by intelligent self-effort the same result that Nature brings to pass in a million years. The *Kriya* shortcut, of course, can be taken only by deeply developed yogis. With the guidance of a guru, such yogis have carefully prepared their body and brain to withstand the power generated by intensive practice.

". . . *Kriya Yoga* has nothing in common with the unscientific breathing exercises taught by a number of misguided zealots. Attempts to hold breath forcibly in the lungs are unnatural and decidedly unpleasant. *Kriya* practice, on the other hand, is accompanied from the very beginning by feelings of peace and by soothing sensations of regenerative effect in the spine.

"The ancient yogic technique converts the breath into mind-stuff. By spiritual advancement, one is able to cognize the breath as a mental concept, an act of mind: a dream breath."

THE COMPLETE ILLUSTRATED BOOK OF YOGA
Swami Vishnudevananda
Pocket Books, 1971
$1.50

SOUNDS OF THE SPIRIT

INSIDE by Paul Horn EPIC
Celestial flute music recorded on location inside the Taj Mahal, India on April 25, 1968. $3.88

MUSIC AND GIBRAN
by Rosko VERVE/FORECAST
Contemporary interpretation of Kahil Gibran, author of THE PROPHET, as formerly heard on the syndicated LOVE FM radio program. The background sounds are performed by a Middle-Eastern ensemble. $3.88

GRAIL AND THE LOTUS
by Robbie Basho TACOMA
Beautiful guitar folk-ragas of East and West, weaving magical tapestries of Knights and Eastern saints. $5.98

RAGA by Ravi Shankar APPLE
Motion picture soundtrack music by Ravi Shankar, the world's foremost sitar player. $3.98

BANGLA DESH
by Usted Ali Akbar Kahn
CONNOSIEUR SOCIETY OF AMERICA
India's premier sarod player offers a solo, personal tribute to the courageous people of Bangla Desh. $5.98

BLIND WILLIE JOHNSON 1927 - 1930 RBF
A collection of lively and moving spirituals by one of the pioneers of the blues guitar. $5.98

SATYA SAI BABA CHANTS THE BAJANS WORLD PACIFIC
Devotional songs led by Satya Sai Baba, an Avatar of the Age, at a Holy Festival in India with 15,000 chanting devotees. $5.00

COMANCHE PEYOTE SONGS VOLS. 1 & 2 INDIAN HOUSE
A contact high, sharing the religious experience of Comanche Indian members of the Native American Church, through Morning Songs of night-long Peyote Ceremonies. $5.98 ea. $10.00

SOUNDS OF INDIAN AMERICA PLAINS AND SOUTHWEST
INDIAN HOUSE
Ceremonial songs and dances of thirteen tribes of the Plains and Southwest, recorded at the 48th Indian Tribal Ceremonial in Gallup, New Mexico. Introductory notes and 7 pages of full color photos included. $5.98

REAL RELAXATION
by Gladys Ruth Kanter
This recorded program is moderated by a teacher of yoga and creative movement. It contains both a daily and bedtime relaxation program based on the Jacobsen Progressive Relaxation Method. $6.00

IF MAN BUT KNEW
by Habibiya ISLAND
Journey to the center of the Heart is channeled through Western Sufi musicians. $5.00

HAPPY BIRTHDAY by Peter Townsend and Friends
A reflection of the inward search for Truth inspired by a Master of Love, Meher Baba. Peter Townsend, of the WHO, produced this record magazine package, consisting of original songs by Peter and other English musicians; included is a thirty-page pictorial magazine dedicated to Meher Baba. $5.00

I AM by Peter Townsend & Friends
The second musical dedication to Meher Baba produced by Peter Townsend. This record-magazine package includes a 48-page magazine produced by the aritst of TOMMY; and songs including "Parvardigar," the master prayer of Baba. $5.95

YOU THE PEOPLE by Rev. Cecil Williams GLIDE
"Put your bodies where your minds are!" Experiencing Christ through Joy at a recorded Sunday celebration with Rev. Cecil Williams at Glide Memorial Presbyterian Church in San Francisco. $5.95

BUDDHIST DRUMS, BELLS AND CHANTS LYRICHORD
Zen, Nembutsu, and Yamabushi chants, recorded on location in the temples of Kyoto, Japan. $5.95

A BELL RINGING IN THE EMPTY SKY NONESUCH
by Goro Yamaguchi
Music of the shakuhachi bamboo flute, traditionally the musical instrument of Japanese Zen monks and reformed Samurai. $2.95

TIBETAN RITUAL MUSIC
LYRICHORD
Chanting and instrumental worship by Lamas and monks of the four great orders of Tibetan Buddhism recorded in monasteries. $5.95

TIBETAN BELLS ISLAND
The transcendental experience of Tibetan Buddhist rituals. $3.88

THE RADHA KRSNA TEMPLE
APPLE
Mantric songs to the Lord Krishna by the devotees at the Radha Krsna Temple in London. Produced by George Harrison. $3.88

SPIRITUAL COMMUNITY RECORDS
P. O. Box 1080
San Rafael, California 94902

Dear Spiritual Community:
Please send me the records I have listed.

Name
Address
City
State _____ Zip
Please Print

Please enclose 25¢ for shipping & handling for one record; 10¢ per additional record.

No. Copies	Title	Price	Total

Grand Total
Calif. residents please add 5% sales tax
Shipping & Handling
Payment Enclosed

The whole manifestation in all its aspects is a record upon which the voice is reproduced; and that voice is a person's thought.

from COSMIC LANGUAGE
by Hazrat Inayat Kahn

THE HIDDEN TEACHING BEYOND YOGA and THE WISDOM OF THE OVERSELF
Paul Brunton
Weiser

YOGA AND WESTERN PSYCHOLOGY
Geraldine Coster
Harper Colophon, 1972
$2.45

COSMIC CHANTS
Paramahansa Yogananda
Available from:
Self-Realization Fellowship
3880 San Rafael Avenue
Los Angeles, Calif. 90065
1973
$3.00

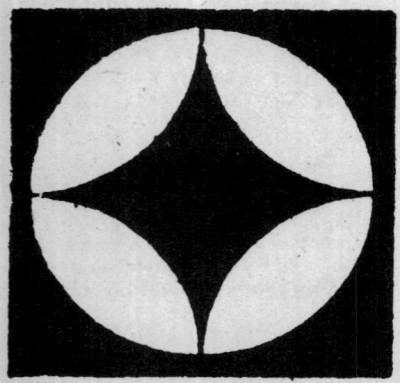

AVAILABLE FROM:
YES! INC.
1039 31st St., N.W.
Washington, D.C. 20007

RECORDS & CASSETTES
Unless otherwise noted, the selections listed are stereo record albums.
ARICA INSTITUTE. *ARICA AUDITION ALBUM*, $6.75. A two-record set. The music on the first 3 sides is arranged to accompany one of the basic exercises of the Arica training, "listening with the soles of the feet." Directions are given for each selection. The 4th side consists of a 6-part mantram. A reprint on Arica from *Psychology Today* is included.

BURCHETTE, WILBURN. GUITAR GRIMORE, $4.98. Burchette's 2nd record: "transcendental vibrations on the impro guitar for spells, rites, incantations, rituals and ceremonial magic."

HOW TO MEDITATE: A GUIDE TO SELF DISCOVERY
Lawrence Leshan
Little, Brown and Company, 1974
$5.95

METAPHYSICAL MEDITATIONS
Paramahansa Yogananda
Self-Realization Fellowship, 1971

——— WILBURN BURCHETTE OPENS THE SEVEN GATES OF TRANSCENDENTAL CONSCIOUSNESS, $5.00. One of our most popular records. "Listeners who wish to 'raise their vibration' and elevate their present level of awareness can find no better aid to the realization of both goals than this album."—Brad Steiger. The music was created and played by Burchette and he designed the unique impro guitar on which it is played.

DASS, BHAGVAN. *AH!*, $6.00. Singing/chanting and instrumental offerings by an American saddhu. Bhagvan Dass is the young American hippy who led Ram Dass to his Guru in India. "The voice is the ultimate instrument because you don't have to take it with you. Anywhere you go it's always there... all you have to do is open your heart and say AH!" A 2-record set, some sections we found quite moving, and some we grew bored with.

DAVIS, ROY EUGENE. *HOW TO EXPERIENCE YOUR GOD NATURE THROUGH MEDITATION*, $5.00. The first side includes a talk on meditation and practical instructions; side 2 is designed to lead the listener into a meditational state. The record ends with chanting in Sanskrit and English. Cassette or record same price.

GASKIN, STEVEN. *PRAISE—BLAME* and *AT COSMOS PARK, COLUMBIA, MISSOURI*, $3.00/each. Cassettes of public talks given by Steven.

KRISHNAMURTI, J. *DIALOGUES* $10.95. This is a double cassette consisting of questions and answers as Krishnamurti is interviewed by Prof. J. Needleman, a religious historian. Many topics are covered.

———. *MIND IN MEDITATION*, $5.50. Cassette also available for $6.55.

———. *OJAI*, 1972, $10.95. A double cassette of talks with students, mainly questions and answers.

———. *A RELIGIOUS LIFE*, $6.55. Cassette of a talk in Amsterdam, 1969.

———. *THIS LIGHT IN ONESELF*, $5.50. Cassette also available for $6.55.

———. *THOUGHT BREEDS FEAR*, $5.50. Cassette also available for $6.55.

KRIYANANDA, SWAMI. *SONGS OF THE SOUL*, $5.00. A selection of devotional songs in the Indian mode. Some are favorite traditional songs in Hindi, Bengali, and Sanskrit. Others are English compositions by Swami Kriyananda. Swamiji was a close disciple of Yogananda, and is the founder of Ananda Cooperative Community in Calif. Members of the community sing along with him on a few selections. This is one of our favorite records.

———. *YOGA FOR SELF AWARENESS*, $9.00. Swamiji sings, reads and leads yoga exercises and meditations. 2 record set.

MUKTANANDA, SWAMI. *GURU GITA*, $4.95. A recitation of the dialogue between Lord Shiva and Parvati, in which Shiva replies to Parvati's question: How can one attain all powers and all realizations? The format is a Sanskrit prayer and Muktananda does not have the most melodious voice. Listening to it takes intense concentration. It is definitely not a pretty, joyous sound.

PRABHAVANANDA, SWAMI, *WHAT IS RELIGION*, $4.95. Readings from selected lectures on religion, renunciation, self-surrender, worship and meditation, grace and self-effort, and perfection. more on Swami Prabhavananda see the Indian Phil. section.

RAM DASS, BABA. *THE EVOLUTION OF CONSCIOUSNESS*, $7.50 A 3-record set of a Darshan held by Ram Dass on 31 March 1969. This is the original recording used to create the core book of *Be Here Now*. Includes a 30-min. chanting meditation.

———. *HERE WE ALL ARE*, $6.50. "These records (3), originally recorded on tape at a gathering at the Univ. of British Columbia (summer, 1969), concern a series of experiences which led me from the role of a Harvard Univ. prof. and psychologist. . . through my work in psychedelics and association with Timothy Leary and then on to India where I met my Guru and became Ram Dass. The lecture. . . . included reflections on the system of Yoga (Ashtanga or Raja) I was being initiated into, as well as a consideration of the implications of this Yoga for us in the West."

THE RELIGIOUS SOUND OF TIBET, $5.95. A collection of Tibetan Buddhist chants and hymns recorded at monasteries on the Tibetan border (1969-70). Very intense, powerful sounds.

SAI BABA, SATHYA. *BHAJANS*, $4.00. Cassette, recorded at his Temple, 60 min.

———. *DISCOURSE AND DIVINE MATERIALIZATION*, $6.00. 90-min. cassette.

———. *CHANTS THE BHAJANS*, $5.00.

———. *DISCOURSE ON MEDITATION*, 4.00. Cassette, 60 min.

THE SUFI CHOIR, $4.95. This is our favorite record; we especially like the second side and the haunting Jai Ram chant. It was the background music for the joyous movie, *Sunseed*.

The Sufi Choir are followers of Sufi Sam Lewis and they are well known performers in the San Francisco area. The songs are in Sanskrit, Hebrew, Arabic, and English

YOGANANDA, *CHANTS & PRAYERS*, , 5.00. $5.00. recording of the voice of Paramahansa Yogananda singing devotional chants in English and Bengali.

———. *I WILL BE THINE ALWAYS*, $4.95. 9 selections from Cosmic Chants, sung by nuns of the Self-Realization Order.

———. *IN THE LAND BEYOND MY DREAMS*, $5.00. Selections from *Cosmic Chants*, arranged for the organ by a monk of the Self-Realization Order.

———. *WHEN THY SONG FLOWS THROUGH ME*, $5.00. Selections from Yogananda's *Cosmic Chants* sung by monks of the Self-Realization Order.

THE SUMMIT LIGHTHOUSE
Box A
Colorado Springs, Colo. 1-30714 80901

THE SUMMIT LIGHTHOUSE

The Summit Lighthouse is a unique nondenominational religious and philosophical organization founded in Washington, D.c., in 1958 by Rev. Mark L. Prophet. Its program for unlocking the creative potential of the individual makes it one of the fastest growing organizations of its kind in the world today. With international headquarters in Colorado Springs, the organization serves a large membership in over fifty countries.

As a multifaceted humanitarian activity, The Summit Lighthouse seeks the betterment of mankind and the resolving of all human problems by assisting individuals and nations to realize their intrinsic worth and capability.

The Summit teachings point to truth wherever it is found. Contemporary revelation, combined with the philosophies world. of Jesus, Buddha, Zoroaster, Lao Tse, and other great spiritual leaders, provides a framework for spiritual growth free from dogma and narrow-mindedness.

The Summit maintains its own graphic arts department and printing plant in Colorado Springs. Each year it publishes numerous books, pamphlets, and weekly publications which it distributes around the wo d.

For those pursuing a deeper understanding of religious philosophy, The Summit Lighthouse sponsors the Ascended Master University in Santa Barbara. Highlighting the 5-quarter curriculum is a course in new-age psychiatry taught by Elizabeth Clare Prophet, founder and president of the university. An active student body of over two hundred develop a working knowledge of such subjects as Alchemy, Golden Age astrology, new-age healing, Christic meditation, esoteric chemistry and physics. Established in 1971, AMU will embark on a building project to accommodate the expanding student body.

For younger students Elizabeth Clare Prophet founded Montessori International in 1970 to provide a well-rounded education for children from preschool age through grade nine. Montessori International is considered one of the best private schools in the state of Colorado.

Recently The Summit Lighthouse started a spiritual community in northern Idaho. Located on a 340-acre farm overlooking Lake Coeur d'Alene, the community is being built as an ideal retreat completely self-sufficient and designed for the maximum preservation of the natural environment.

The Summit Lighthouse also owns and operates a health-food store, bakery, and restaurant in Colorado Springs known as the Four Winds. With its outstanding vegetarian cuisine, the Four Winds was awarded the only health-food concession at Expo '74 in Spokane, Washington.

One of The Summit's most rapidly growing enterprises is Lanello Reserves, Inc. This privately owned corporation specializes in the sale of precious metals, emergency food supplies, outdoor survival equipment, and reverse osmosis water purifiers. Lanello Reserves also handles an extremely fine line of gold and silver art objects.

INTERNATIONAL REGISTRY OF WORLD CITIZENS
United States Center

The International Registry of World Citizens provides both opportunity and incentive to individuals to record their commitment to the belief that desperately needed permanent world peace will not come by nationally administered deterrence by violence or threats of violence, or by bilateral or multinational treaties, alliances or pacts but rather by democratically conceived and administered world government.

Registrants of the IRWC believe that the best way to implement this commitment is by pledging to try at all times and in all places to demonstrate their recognition of their responsibilities as members of the world community by carrying their IRWC Identity Card, wearing the IRWC button, and being prepared to explain, advocate and non-violently defend the IRWC proposition that world peace requires adequate democratic world government.

IRWC registrants recognize all men and women as fellow-citizens of the world, whatever their race, color, creed, politics or nationality, and they accept their responsibility as members of the world community to contribute to the development of world citizenship and the establishment of world law.

The Registry was established in Paris, France, in 1949 and in 1952 a World Council for the Peoples' Constituent Assembly was formed by a group of Nobel Peace Prize winners, diplomats, scientists and academicians from ten countries. They were aware that: (1) in the absence of supranational law, nations are obliged to resort to force to defend their interests; (2) war is the absurd "final solution"; (3) adequate world institutions are required to satisfy the fundamental needs of mankind while eliminating catastrophic wastes; and (4) scientific and technical progress make it possible to organize a world community of justice and abundance in which fundamental liberties could be guaranteed to all. These world citizens pledged to hold an ongoing series of democratically conducted elections to a Peoples' World Assembly Committee of Delegates. Meetings and elections on a biennial basis have been held since 1969 in furtherance of the eventual formation of such an Assembly, and in support of mundialization.

Mundialization is a political action wherein an institution, or a municipality, county, province, state or nation, in an official Declaration by its people, or their elected representatives, sets forth: (1) their conviction that security and welfare are matters of mutual interest; their wish to cooperate in holding a Peoples' World Assembly and establishing a world-rule of law; (3) their desire to withhold public funds from military budgets and use them for world-wide efforts related to Item (2) above; (4) their conviction that their portion of the earth is world territory and an irrevocable part of our whole world community; and (5) their recommendation to other comparable political constituencies to join in the official issuance of such a Declaration as an expression of planetary solidarity.

For more information or Applications for world citizen registration write:

Alfred C. Williams, Director, U.S. Center
P. O. Box 27044
San Francisco, California 94127
U.S.A.

International Centre
55, Rue Lacepede
Paris 5
France

Scientology Answers

Man has asked a great many questions about himself.

Such questions are "Who am I?" "Where do I come from?" "What is Death?" "Is there a Hereafter?"

Any child asks these questions, yet Man has never had answers that long satisfied him.

Religions have various answers to these questions and they belong in fact in the field of religious philosophy, since this is the area of Man's knowledge that has sought to answer them.

Answers have varied through the ages and race to race and this variation alone is the stumbling block which brings disbelief into faiths. Old religions fade because people no longer find their answers to the above questions real.

The decline of Christianity is marked by modern cynicism about a Hell where one burns for an eternity and a Heaven where one plays a harp forever.

Materialistic sciences have sought to invalidate the entire field by shrugging the problem off with the equally impossible answers that one is merely meat and all life arose by spontaneous and accidental combustion from a sea of ammonia. Such "answers" sound more like pre-Buddhist India where the world was said to be carried on seven pillars that stood on seven pillars which stood on a turtle and, in exasperation to the child's question as to what the turtle stood on, "Mud! And it's mud from there on down!"

It is the nature of Truth that if one knows it, even more things get understood. The disease and decay of Asia tends to invalidate their concepts as Truth and in the West, war, where soldiers saw "Gott Mit Uns" on the slain enemy belt buckles tended to end the domination of the churches of those times — for God could not be on both sides of such Devil's work, or so the soldiers reasoned.

Even Christ's great commandment of "Love thy neighbour" seems to have less force today in a world of income tax, inflation and the slaughter of civil populations in the name of peace.

So, without in any way condemning or scorning any man's beliefs. Scientology arose from the ashes of a spiritless science and again asked — and answered — the eternal questions.

That the answers have the force of truth is attested by the results. Instead of the sickness or religious India, Scientologists are seldom ill. Instead of internal warfare such as the riots of Alexandria, Scientologists live in relative harmony with each other and have skills that restore relations rapidly.

The world tends to attack new things and Scientology has had its share from vested interest groups and governments but it keeps rising eventually victorious from each clash without bitterness.

Various interesting results proceed from the practice of Scientology and one's ability to handle his problems is markedly bettered.

One does not have to study Scientology very long to know that one does not have to die to find out what he is or where he is going after death, for *one can experience* it all for himself with no persuasion or hypnotism or "faith."

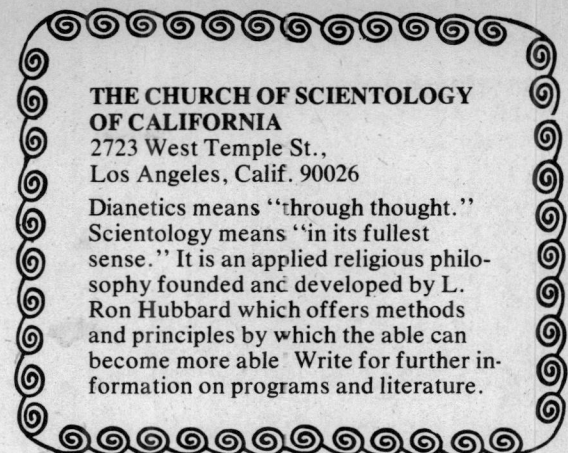

THE CHURCH OF SCIENTOLOGY OF CALIFORNIA
2723 West Temple St.,
Los Angeles, Calif. 90026

Dianetics means "through thought." Scientology means "in its fullest sense." It is an applied religious philosophy founded and developed by L. Ron Hubbard which offers methods and principles by which the able can become more able. Write for further information on programs and literature.

So Scientology is different mainly because one doesn't have to *believe* in it to have it work. Its truths are of the order of "Is this black?" "Is this white?" You can see for yourself something is black if it's black and that something is white when it's white.

No tricks of logic are needed to prove any point and Scientologists only ask people to look for themselves.

Scientology can achieve positive invariable results. Given the same conditions, one always gets the same results. And anyone given the same conditions can obtain the same results.

What has happened is the *superstition* has been subtracted from spiritual studies. And today this is a very acceptable state of affairs to Man.

The ultimate freedom depends on knowing the ultimate Truth. Truth is not what people *say* it is, it is what it *is*. And Truth, quite remarkably, sets one free, just like philosophers have said down the ages.

What the philosophers did *not* say was how free can one get? And that is the surprise contained in Scientology for everyone who walks the Road to Truth — one *can* be totally free.

Naturally this makes no friendly news to the person who wants slaves and Fascistic, Capitalistic and even some more liberal creeds forbid that utterly, for who could be a master, so they think, where no slave wears his chains? They miss the point entirely, for who *has* to be a master?

When you yourself hold the Truth the shadows by which you are bound tend to slither away.

And when you at last know for yourself in your own experience that Scientology does have the answers, and when you have applied them, you have the result all philosophers, savants, sages and saviours have always dreamed of — and freedom as well.

As much of Scientology is true for you as you know of it, those who know it only by name react to the hope of it. And as one advances upon the road, one knows more and more of it and is more and more free. Unlike so many promises made to man and which have made him fear disappointment, Scientology delivers. It may be over a rough road. It may be over a smooth one. But Scientology eventually delivers all it says it can.

And that is what is new about it and why it grows. No other religion ever given Man delivered. They all waited until after the end for one to find his harp or his Nirvana.

For the first time in all the ages there *is* something that within one lifetime delivers the answers to the eternal questions and delivers immortality as well.

Scientology is an applied religious philosophy, the study of knowledge in its fullest sense.

MATAGIRI
Mt. Tremper
New York 12457.

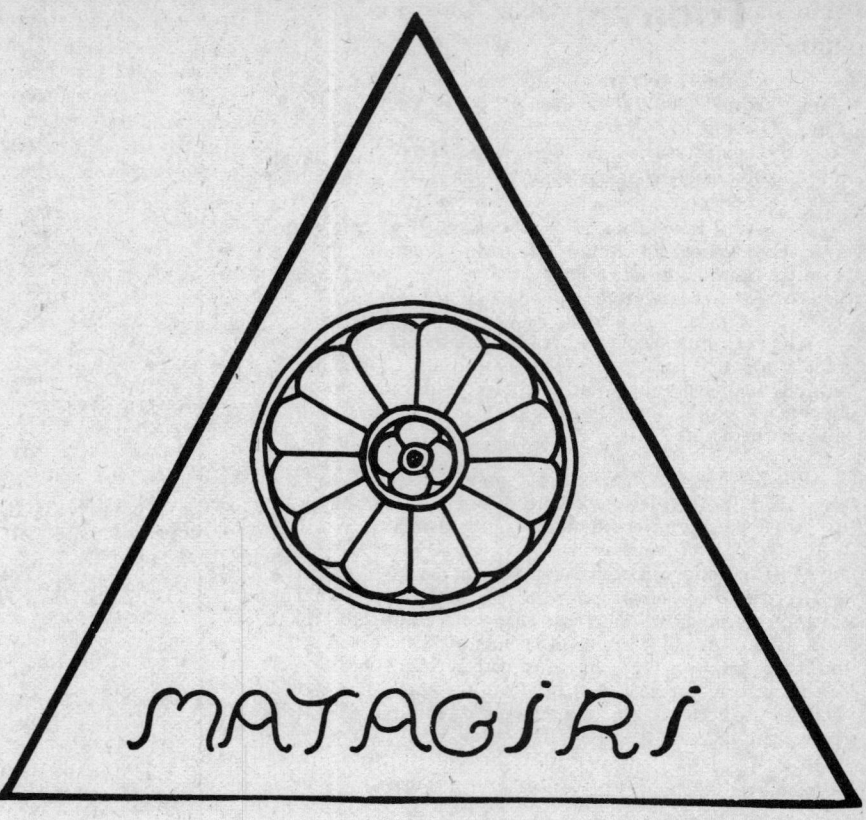

"IT IS ONLY RATHER RECENTLY THAT A NECESSITY BEGAN TO ARISE OF A COLLECTIVE REALITY THAT WOULD EMBRACE ALL WHO HAVE DECLARED THEMSELVES—I do not mean materially but in their consciousness—to be disciples of Sri Aurobindo and have tried to live his teaching. Among them all there has arisen the necessity of a true common life, which is not based merely upon altogether material circumstances, but which represents a deeper truth and is the beginning of what Sri Aurobindo calls a supramental or gnostic community."

These remarks of the Mother, spoken in the 1950s, express the primary purpose of Matagiri.

Inspired in 1962 and established in 1968, Matagiri is located on 42 wooded acres near Woodstock, New York. There is an extensive library of the works of Sri Aurobindo, the Mother and their disciples, and related works, as well as Ashram periodicals, tapes of the Mother's music, reading and talks, and the music of disciples; slides and photographs of Sri Aurobindo, the Mother, the Ashram and Auroville.

Matagiri is also a representative of the Sri Aurobindo Books Distribution Agency, a center for the dissemination of information about the teaching of Sri Aurobindo, the Sri Aurobindo Ashram and Auroville, a new city now being built in India as an expression of the vision of Sri Aurobindo. In addition, it is an outlet for such Ashram products as incense, handmade paper, hand-marbled silks and other items.

VISITORS

Visitors are welcome. Accommodations are limited and simple, so reservations must be made in advance. Rooms are usually shared. As Matagiri is not a retreat, much of a typical day is devoted to work done in a spirit of consecration and detachment.

daily schedule

6:45 a.m.—reading from the works of Sri Aurobindo or the Mother
7:30 a.m.—breakfast
8:00 a.m.—work
11:30 a.m.—lunch
12:30 p.m.—work
5:30 p.m.—dinner

SRI AUROBINDO

Sri Aurobindo was born in Calcutta on 15 August 1872. At the age of seven he was sent to England to be educated. During a brilliant academic career at St. Paul's and Cambridge he mastered Greek, Latin, English and French and became familiar with German, Italian and Spanish. In 1893 he returned to India and entered the Baroda State service. In England he made up this deficiency. He learned Sanskrit and several modern Indian languages and assimilated the spirit of Indian civilization and its forms past and present. These were years of self-culture, literary creation and silent political activity. It was here that he had his first major spiritual experience, that of the silent Brahman.

In 1906 he gave up the Baroda service, went to Bengal and openly joined and took a leading part in the movement for India's liberation. He advanced complete independence as the national goal and revolutionized tthe moderate stand of the Congress party. In 1908 the British Raj implicated him in the Alipore Conspiracy case. During a one-year period of detention, much of it in solitary confinement, he practiced yoga. He had the realization of the cosmic consciousness and the vision of Sri Krishna everywhere. After his acquittal, as his inner life was pressing upon him for an exclusive concentration, he withdrew from the political field.

Sri Aurobindo came to Pondicherry in 1910. After a period of silent yoga, in 1914 he started a philosophical monthly, *Arya*, in which most of his major works— *The Life Divine*, *The Synthesis of Yoga*, *Essays on the Gita*, *The Secret of the Veda*, *The Human Cycle*, *The Ideal of Human Unity*, *Foundations of Indian Culture* —first appeared, in serial form. Throughout his life he continued to write poetry and to work on his masterpiece, the epic poem *Savitri*.

In 1926 he had a mjor siddhi in his yoga and withdrew from outward activity, turning over the operation of the Ashram and the sadhana of his disciples to the Mother, his spiritual collaborator. At the same time he kept a close watch on all that was happening in India and the world and answered hundreds of letters from disciples and aspirants.

In December 1950 he left the body. Since then his work has been continued by the Mother.

Auroville Today

The city spreads along the borders of Pondicherry and Tamil Nadu and lies about 152 kilometres southeast of the city of Madras, on the Bay of Bengal. Planned to house 50,000 Auroville is concentric in shape with a diameter of 3 kilometres. The city centre is 6 kilometres from the sea and a green belt encircles the town.

Established to experiment in a new order of living, Auroville was founded near the former French settlement of Pondicherry in February 1968 at a ceremony which was attended by international representatives.

The town is divided into four zones, residential, cultural, industrial and international corresponding to four fundamental aspects of man's activity. The new city is a unique psychological, educational and architectural experiment to reorient and recreate human activity on a surer and more harmonious basis.

Auroville is conceived as a living organism which will evolve together with its inhabitants. This demands great plasticity in its construction with structures which can be altered or adapted according to the developing needs of the town, the zone and the individual.

Centre for Meditation

The four zones converge upon a central point where the Matrimandir is located. This is the heart of the town marked by a huge golden sphere. This is a centre for meditation, not according to any denomination but according to each individual's inner urge towards communion.

The Matrimandir, which is under construction, will be encircled by twelve carefully laid out gardens. Engaged in construction work are, in addition to hundreds of local people, a number of young volunteers from various countries who are part of this remarkable international scene.

The Foundations

Auroville has arisen from the philosophical teaching of Sri Aurobindo and his spiritual collaborator known to millions in India and overseas as the Mother of the Sri Aurobindo ashram at Pondicherry. The ashram has, today, 2,000 inmates who come from all over the world and belong to many religions.

Sri Aurobindo, who lived from 1872-1950 has been described by Romain Rolland as the most complete synthesis of the genius of Asia and Europe. The Mother, now in her mid-nineties, is the inspiration and presiding spirit of Auroville. She is French by birth and met Sri Aurobindo in 1914 at Pondicherry, then a French possession. She wrote more than half a century ago that there should be "a place of peace, concord, harmony, where all the fighting instincts of man would be used exclusively to conquer the causes of his sufferings and miseries, to surmount his weakness and ignorance, to triumph over his limitations and incapacities..."

To a considerable extent this vision was realised at the ashram but in time its scope expanded and, in 1964, at the world conference of the Sri Aurobindo Society held at Pondicherry, the idea of the city of Auroville crystallised.

From its inception Auroville has won the support of many institutions and governments including UNESCO but financial assistance has also come from unexpected sources. Private individuals contributed and help came from welfare organisations in India and abroad.

But the more interesting contributions have been the individual ones like young John Fisher, the son of a General, who heard about Auroville when it was launched, drove from Kathmandu, where he happened to be, to Pondicherry, put his money and his vehicle to work and saw, to his satisfaction the completion of the first road to the site.

Agriculture

Research is underway to improve the quality of the soil by using organic fertilizer and even organic pesticides. Synthetic products are avoided. As scarcity of water was a major problem Aurovillians dug deep-bore wells which now irrigate land which was barren. Young scientists are working on the possibility of irrigation using sea water.

Afforestation has been undertaken and thousands of saplings have been planted to prevent soil erosion and provide a green belt around the city. Flowers introduced from a variety of climatic regions flourish in an experimental botanical garden.

Aurofuture

Planning and research for the building of Auroville is carried out by Aurofuture, composed of a team of architects, engineers and urban designers, the Auroville Planning Group and the Auroville Centre for Environmental Studies. The city, which will not conform to any particular architectural design, has architects and engineers from France, Italy, Germany and America in addition to India. They are at work in Aurofuture evolving expressions and forms to give substantial shape to the essence of this unique city.

Multi-national Community

Auroville's present population is small but represents sixteen countries. They live in communities in temporary houses according to their work and inclinations. One of the communities, named Aspiration, will soon enlarge into an advanced colony accommodating 2,000. This will form a model for the city of Auroville. The population of Aspiration live in simple, beautifully designed hexagonal cottages. All the civic services necessary for the communal living have been set up including a health centre.

Exhibition Pavilion

The largest structure approaching completion, Bharat Nivas, will house a permanent cultural exhibition from each Indian state. In addition the pavilion will have an auditorium, an institute for teaching Indian languages, a library, a restaurant and accommodation for staff and students. Several other countries will also set up permanent pavilions.

International University

Completed three years ago the novel architectural design of the educational complex has put into substance the university's objectives of new adventures in ideas and experimentation.

The university is expected to grow into an international institution with faculties providing free advanced education. The centre of integral culture, Mandala, will concentrate on the study of the inter-relation among various branches of learning. Research will be conducted for the development of spheres of consciousness beyond the mind as well as possibilities of prenatal education.

Industrial Zone

Located at a distance from the residential area, the industrial zone will combine functional architectural design with beauty of form and colour. A beginning for Auroville's industries has already been made with a printing press, a polyester unit presently engaged in making decorative objects, panels and roofings for buildings and a handmade paper mill. The Aurofood factory, situated on the outskirts of the city, was established by a philanthropist.

THE ESSENTIAL AUROBINDO
Sri Aurobindo
Edited by Robert McDermott
Schocken, 1973
$2.95

SRI AUROBINDO INTERNATIONAL CENTER AND ASSOCIATION FOR AUROVILLE
140 West 58th Street
New York, N.Y. 10019

Please enclose $1.25 to cover the cost of handling and shipping for each item ordered. C.O.D. orders in Canada only.
Address all orders and inquiries to

SIVANANDA ASHRAM YOGA CAMP
8th Avenue, Val Morin, P.Q., Canada

Situated 45 miles north of Montreal, on 60 acres of wooded land, the camp overlooks beautiful rolling hills with lush vegetation dotted with small lakes.

The facilities for Yogic practices are the best imaginable. Still more popular with the campers is the open-air platform for exercises. It is close to the artificial lake and overlooks Lac Raymond and a Laurentian mountain range behind which campers see the sun rise while flocking to the hall for meditation early in the morning. The pure Laurentian air adds to the benefits of the Yogic postures and especially of the breathing exercises.

The Krishna temple, inaugurated during the summer of 1971, with its atmosphere loaded with pure vibrations will satisfy the keenest expectations of the devotional type of campers.

A large swimming pool is lodged on the camp ground, in complete privacy. A perennial underground spring from the mountain constantly flows into the filtered water. Besides the swimming pool there are a number of other provisions for group recreation such as, hiking, volleyball and other games. For animal lovers there are horses at the Ashram. To show the campers who come from all parts of the North American continent the beauties of the Laurentian mountains, a picnic trip to Mont Tremblant, the highest mountain of the Laurentians, is undertaken during almost every camp session.

During the winter months there is ample opportunity for skiing and skating. The camp has its own ski slope and poma lift. Ski instructors are available and ski equipment may be rented at the village of Val Morin.

The original Finnish Sauna of the camp is an attraction not only during the summer but also during the winter.

Coming out from the sauna bath, courageous campers roll in the snow, which, due to the increased blood circulation, gives them an additional feeling of well-being.

Another asset greatly appreciated by campers is the absolutely pure spring water supplied from an 80 foot deep artesian well.

ACCOMMODATIONS
Except for married couples, campers will share rooms either in the main lodge or in the registration building. Each room in the lodge has its own private bath with hot and cold water. The registration building is provided with bath facilities on each floor. Accommodations are comfortable but not luxurious.

FOOD
Vegetarian food, not necessarily "health food," is served at the camp. This food is most conducive to perfect health and spiritual progress. Vegetables, grains, fruit and some dairy products form the menu.

COST
All Sivananda Centers and Ashrams are founded on the great Master Swami Sivananda's principle that true Yoga can neither be bought nor sold and thus have no profit motive. None of the workers are paid. All expenses of building, operation and maintenance are met by donations from the campers. It has unfortunately become necessary to request a minimum donation of fifteen dollars per day to cover costs. Any additional voluntary contribution will be greatly appreciated, and will go towards improvements and expansion as well as paying off the mortgages.

YOGA KIRTAN......................$5.00
Chanting of Sanskrit Mantras led by Swami Vishnudevananda and recorded at the Yoga Camp. Also included is the translation and meaning of the chants.

YOGA HOME EXERCISES......$6.00
Includes all basic exercises and relaxation as taught by Swami Vishnudevananda. Wall chart with photographs of the postures and step-by-step instructions also included.

INDIAN CLASSICAL MUSIC...$5.00
"Sounds of Swami Vidyananda" Contains Sanskrit chants and Indian classics by a foremost Vidyananda." player.

Available from:
SIVANANDA ASHRAM YOGA CAMP
    8th Avenue
    Val Morin
Quebec, Canada

SATHYA SAI BABA CENTER AND BOOK STORE
7720 Sunset Blvd.
Los Angeles, Calif. 99046

Write for mail order list of books, cassettes, records, etc.

❖❖❖❖❖❖❖❖❖❖❖❖

SHAMBALA BOOKSELLERS 2482 Telegraph Avenue
Berkeley, Calif. 94704

Large selection of books on Oriental Religion and Western Mysticism. Publishes a bimonthly guide, Codes Shambala, of its books in stick. Sample is 25 cents. One year—$1.00.

From: Brochure Published and Distributed by **SWAMI VISHNU-DEVANANDA** and the Sivananda Yoga Vadanta Center, H.Q., 8th Avenue, Val Morin, Province of Quebec

Yoga Vedanta Crossword Puzzle

ACROSS
1. Tasmai Sri ———————— Namah
6. Intellect
9. Repetitive prayer
11. Prostrations
14. OM——— Hrim Kleem
15. Guru bead
16. Victory
19. Beyond all knowledge
21. Astral nerve tube
24. Fierce goddess
25. The first
26. Impurity
28. Krishna's dance with the gopis
29. Existence. Know——dge, Bliss
31. Man's Soul
34. Hatha Yoga purification technique
36. Concentration
37. Discrimination
39. Bija mantra
40. Highest guna
41. "Union"
43. The Creator
44. Spiritual singing
47. Epic of Ram
48. Hatha Yoga lock
52. What a yogi wants to raise
54. Lord's play
55. Charmer of the gopis
56. Indian sweet of semolina
57. Moderate diet
59. Ceremony of Light
62. Consort of Parvati
63. Individual soul

DOWN
2. Lord Siva
3. Dispassion
4. One who leads from darkness to light
5. The Pranava
6. Seed mantra
7. Consort of Shankara
10. Yoga posture
11. Vital energy
12. One without a second
13. Wandering holy man
17. Lord of death
18. Second chakra
20. Born of inertia
22. Muslim name for God
23. Chosen image
24. Lust
27. Prem
30. Servant of God
32. Cosmic illusion
33. Name
35. "That"
37. Right inquiry
38. Law of action and reaction
40. Superconscious state
42. Story of Krishna and Arjuna
45. Perfect bliss
46. Goddess
49. Heart chakra
50. Headstand
51. Mind
52. Mudra for Divine Nectar
53. A spiritual plane
58. King
60. Vrind ———an
61. Austerity

EARTH RELIGION NEWS
300 Henry Street,
Brooklyn, N.Y. 11201.

Subscription: $8.00 for 12 issues
A pagan tabloid newspaper dedicated to the practice and study of paganism.

CHURCH OF ALL WORLDS
Box 2953
St. Louis, Mo. 63130

The Church of All Worlds offers a religious position uniquely suited to the enlightened, inquiring modern mind. In harmony with the principles and conclusions of science, receptive to the values and wisdom of the ancients and the great religions of humanity, sensitive to the deep psychological and spiritual needs of mankind, the Church of All Worlds is the free, growing, and unifying religion that today's and tomorrow's world so urgently needs.

The Church of All Worlds is Neo-Pagan: a modern Earth Religion—an orientation chosen because of its traditional associations with Life and the processes of Nature, which we consider the appropriate religious orientation for the now emerging Aquarian Age. As Western "civilization" has been to a great degree the product of two thousand years of Piscean Age Christianity, so do we envision a new whole-Earth culture of transformative religious ecology to become the product of the next two thousand years of aquarian age Neo-Paganism. In common with many other Neo-Pagan religions, CAW presents a life-affirming religious philosophy for the joyous unification of eros, ethos and ecos; of cult, culture and cultivation.

We consider the Church of All Worlds to be radically evolutionary in concept, rather than merely revolutionary. We see the evolution of Life on Earth as moving towards a point of actualization (Teilhard de Chardin's "Omega Point") whereby the entire planet will come to share a single vast global consciousness. We see mankind as being instrumental in the course of that evolution from this point forward. As humans are the only creatures on the planet capable of disrupting entire eco-systems, it becomes our manifest responsibility through our unique freedom of choice to prevent such systems from being disrupted. We are not antitechnology or science, but recognize that certain scientific and technological advances, such as ecology, geology, astronomy, psychology, archaeology, cybernetics, astrophysics, communications and the technology of the bio-renaissance are positively evolutionary and in harmony with the accelerating advance of emerging planetary consciousness. What we stand opposed to technologically is the senseless use of industrial technology to wreak havoc with the planetary eco-system in the name of the Biblical injunction that Man is to have "dominion over the Earth." We perceive our role not as dominion, but as responsible stewardship.

Applying evolutionary concepts to each individual, we agree with Erich Fromm that the purpose of life is "to become what we potentially are." We identify strongly with the concepts of human self-actualization identified by Abraham Maslow and found in current current transpersonal psychology and ethics. rejecting utterly concepts of predestination and inherent sin, we affirm the ultimate freedom and responsibility appropriate to conscious entities, which we express in the phrase, "Thou Art God" as used by Robert Heinlein. This implies that each one of us must define our own specific purpose. There is no excuse; no shelter from the awesome responsibility of total freedom.

Recognizing that all life on Earth comprises a single vast living Entity, which has been intuitively conceptualized as a feminine Divinity from time immemorial, we are in harmony with our Pagan ancestors who worshipped The Goddess: Mother Earth: Mother Nature. Thus we also affirm mystically and mythically the Pantheistic conceptualization of immanent Divinity inherent in all living entites, as synergic Living Nature, for we define Divinity as the highest level of aware consciousness accessible to each living Being, manifesting Itself in the self-actualization of that Being. Hence, "Thou Art God" applies equally to a person, a tree, a grasshopper, or a planet. As Neo-Pagans, we are concerned, not with life after death, but with life after birth. We have no dogmas of immortality, but accept the possibility of death as the termination of life, and perhaps an evolutionary necessity for the birth of new life. We see the dead as being returned to the elements of the Earth, from which their energy and matter will eventually be recycled and reconstituted into the energy and matter of other life forms. Other than our ecological responsibility of returning to the Earth that which we have taken from Her, we are not concerned with dying but with living.

We are concerned with improving the quality of that life, to which end we agree with population ecologists that its quantity (in sheer numbers of people) must be drastically reduced. Thus we are strongly supportive of the various measures of population control advocated by Zero Population Growth, including full legalization of abortion. We greatly fear that if humanity does not choose to limit its numbers by reducing births, Nature will do it for us by increasing deaths.

The word "religion" means "relinking." The basic commitment of the Church of All Worlds is to the re-integration or re-linking of people with themselves, their fellow humans, and with the whole of living Nature. In company with all other Pagan peoples, we create no artificial demarcations between the sacred and the secular, for we recognize that religion must ultimately be an entire way of life, not merely some acts performed once a week in a ritual. We are committed to developing and promulgating an organic, vitalistic philosophy of life and its expression in an organ culture. Since this involves the questions of "What is the good life?" and "What are the ethics and morals of the good human, living the good life, in order to achieve happiness, fulfillment, and harmony within and without his or her self?"

To this end then, the Church of All Worlds devotes itself to those who need or want the help and understanding of others through the processes of unlearning and learning. It is our aim to offer assistance through any personal expansion programs found to be effective. Further, we intend to remain openminded and receptive to new ideas, interests and goals, and learn to live responsibly and responsively with each other.

We are involved with every conceivable aspect of the emerging Aquarian Age culture, from religious service and mythology to family relations and child rearing; from education to ecology; from psychic development to space travel; from astronomy to astrology; from the sexual to the sensual; from intentional communities to world government. "Nothing short of everything will ever really do."

Since we are concerned with the emergent evolution of a total new culture and lifestyle, and since we perceive no distinction between the sacred and the secular, we consider every activity to be essentially a religious activity For us, taking our cans and bottles to the recycling center is as much a religious duty as meditation. And so are composting our garbage, growing organic vegetables, protecting animals, practicing birth-control eating natural foods, using bio-degradable detergents, physical exercise, psychic training, study, and celebration of the seasons. We hold weekly religious services, sensitivity sessions, encounter groups, council meetings, study-discussion seminars, pot-luck dinners, and just plain good time parties. We celebrate the eight seasonal Festivals with feasting, sharing, music and ritual. We come together for work parties to publish our magazines, fix up old houses, help in farm work, or whatever is needed. We go on camping trips, travel around the country, speak to other interested groups upon request. In all, we recognize that the essence of a religion is in the living of it.

If these concepts and principles appeal to you, and you would like to become better acquainted with the Church of All Worlds, we suggest you subscribe to our magazine, *Green Egg*, which is at present the most comprehensive publication of Neo-Paganism in the U.S. Not only the CAW but many other groups are featured and discussed, as are ideas and discoveries of mind-rending impact. A full third of the magazine is devoted to a Readers' providing providing feedback and interchange on many controversies. *Green Egg* is published eight times a year and runs to 48-56 pages per issue. A contribution of $1.00 per copy or $6 a year ($1.25 a copy or $8 a year outside the U.S.) is requested to cover our expenses. Our other magazine, *The Pagan!* is an annual. It is much fancier in layout and design, and is oriented towards the general public. A truly beautiful collection of Pagan writing and artwork, the latest issue is available for $1. If all this material turns you on, we will be happy to meet you and get to know you—so drop us a line!

The Church of All Worlds is dedicated to the celebration of Life, the maximal actualization of Human potential, and the realization of ultimate individual freedom and personal responsibility in harmonious eco-physic relationship with the total Biosphere of Holy Mother Earth.

Thou art God(ess)!

TIM ZEU

CALIFORNIA INSTITUTE OF ASIAN STUDIES

California Institute of Asian Studies is a graduate school specializing in Asian culture and civilization and also in comparative studies East and West. It is a center of higher education of Cultural Integration Fellowship, Inc., which includes such other subsidiaries as the Center of Universal Religion (San Francisco Ashram), East-West Research and Publication Center, Yoga and Meditation Center, and the Center of Integral Education for Children. The Fellowship was founded in San Francisco in 1951 with a view to promoting intercultural understanding, human unity and world peace.

In April 1968, the Institute fulfilled the legal requirements of Section 29007(a) (3) of Division 21 of the California Education Code in order to operate as a graduate school and qualify students for M.A., Ph.D. and Th.D. degrees. It has now fulfilled the requirements of Section 29007.5 of the aforesaid Education Code for the issuance of such diplomas as: *Teacher of Asian Culture, Yoga Teacher and Counselor, Meditation Therapist, Minister of Humanistic Religion, and Counselor on Asian Affairs.*

The Institute is fortunate to have an excellent faculty including such internationally noted thinkers as: Dr. Haridas Chaudhuri, author of *Philosophy of Integralism, Integral Yoga,* and others; Dr. Framroze A. Bode, author of *Songs of Zarathustra* and others; Dr. Auil K. Sarkar, author of *Changing Phases of Buddhism* and others; Dr. Peter Kwan, professor of Chinese Philosophy; Bishop Nippo Syaku, professor of Japanese Buddhism; Lama Kunga Rimpoche, professor of Tibetan Mysticism; and others.

Special research and publication programs of this unique Institute include: The Integral Perspective in Philosophy, Religion, Mysticism, Art, Psychology, Psychotherapy, Education, Methodology, and International Relations; Parapsychology and Meditation Therapy; Spiritual Alternatives to Drug Use; Transpersonal Psychology and the Psychonuclear Energy; and Integral Humanism.

Dr. Haridas Chaudhuri, Founder-President
3494 - 21st Street
San Francisco, California 94110
U.S.A.
Telephone: (415) 648-1489 or 863-0663 or 752-9890

NEMETON WILL STRIKE AGAIN!

FOUR TIMES A YEAR

Nemeton erupts from the depths of the earth with articles by well known authors, attacks on the patriarchal establishment, and news of Pagan revivals in the Western Hemisphere!!!

SEND TO

NEMETON • P.O. BOX 13037 • OAKLAND • CALIFORNIA • 94661

Premiere edition of NEMETON $1.50 ☐

Songs for the Old Religion $2.50 ☐

Subscription to NEMETON Magazine ☐ $5.00 (4 issues)

Gift subscription to NEMETON Magazine ☐ $5.00 (4 issues)

Begin my subscription with issue #_____ ☐
next issue ☐

Begin gift subscription with issue #_____ ☐
next issue ☐

INVOCATION TO A PAGAN DIVINITY
George Galavaris
A Magic Flute Publication
Order From:
The Carlyle Book Distributor Regd.
Box 41
Montreal 304, Quebec, Canada

The eight stories in this collection are the expression of a powerful sensitivity attempting to probe the mists of experience whose importance is only half glimpsed in the obscure passage of time. A variety of techniques are used to express the complex relation of the individual to time and experience, dream, and reality, fact and memory. Impressions, mood, atmosphere, and a plastic handling of language create word-paintings that reveal a particular view of "reality." Pagan divinities and Christian heroes, the mystic and the commonplace, symbol and sensory experience — all are poetically united.

George Galavaris, a distinguished scholar, is Professor of Art History at McGill University in Montreal.

PART FOUR: DIMENSIONS OF HEALING

To heal is to restore a state of harmony between mind, body and spirit. While this belief can be found in early medical philosophies dating back to practitioners of the Hippocratic school, modern medicine has instead focused on the machine-like circuitry of the body. An increasing awareness of the limitations of this neglect is emerging as scientific research reveals the complementary nature of mind and body as parts of an underlying reality.

Roads To Health

How many roads to health are there? Perhaps the numerous ritualistic cross-cultural attempts to heal are merely a window dressing for a basic unified process which aims towards the restoration of a harmonious state, unique to each individual. To give oneself up to someone designated as a healer requires a great act of faith. A major reason to attempt to develop one's sensory awareness is that it may encourage a greater desire to become more directly involved in one's own healing process. Without this personal involvement, healing effects can at best be temporary. Health can be seen as a state of existence to which one must *continually* aspire.

CEPTAR

CENTER FOR PREVENTIVE THERAPY AND REHABILITATION INC

1143 New Hampshire Avenue, N.W.
Washington, D.C. 20037
Telephone: (202) 785-1235

Dear Doctor:

A new facility has been established in Washington, D.C., to help meet the needs of your difficult cases—hypertension, migraines, breast cancer detection, arteriosclerosis, etc.

The Center for Preventive Therapy and Rehabilitation (CEPTAR), offering services which are non-destructive and non-toxic, is located in the heart of Washington near several major medical centers. Our Technical Director, Carl Schleicher, Ph.D., reports the availablility of the following services:

BIOFEEDBACK TRAINING, under the supervision of Boris Vern, M.D., enables your patient to learn independent control over his own physiological processes, such as blood pressure, skin temperature, heart rate, etc. It is natural, safe, and effective. Such control can be taught through a series of courses which are primarily designed to alleviate essential hypertension, migraines, and headache pain. The cost of this service ranges form $10 to $40 per visit.

CEPTAR is pleased to announce the capable assistance and participation of the Stress Transformation Center in providing clinical services specifically oriented towards stress control and tension reduction. According to a recent article in Internal Medicine News (May 15, 1974), biofeedback therapy aims at the patient's gaining control over his bodily processes and transferring that control into everyday life. It is further reported that clinical applications of biofeedback include such conditions as sleep-onset insomnia, tension headaches, migraine headaches, and asthma.

In addition to providing biofeedback therapy, CEPTAR also conducts training in biofeedback to members of the medical and dental community, builds and evaluates state-of-the-art biofeedback equipment, and leases or sells biofeedback equipment to those obtaining medical-user authorization.

THERMOGRAPHY, under the direction of John Stauch, Ph.D, is an assessment of the body's infrared radiation. Study of heat patterns is most helpful in early detection of arteriosclerosis, breast cancer, arthritis, stroke, etc. Thermography requires only a few minutes for scanning and photography, and a report will be sent to you within 24-48 hours. The cost of this service varies from $25 to $75, depending upon purpose and need.

Future services of the Center for Preventive Therapy and Rehabilitation will include advanced bioelectric neuromuscular devices for rehabilitation and improving sensory functions. These services are designed to relieve these stresses and disabilities prevalent in today's world and to contribute to the well-being of the handicapped person.

We at CEPTAR are happy to make this unique combination of services available for your use, and welcome your personal inspection of our facilities. CEPTAR clinical services qualify for most medical insurance plans. Call (202) 785-1235 for referrals of your patients or for further information on current or future CEPTAR services. Also enquire about CEPTAR biofeedback research programs and charity treatment schedules.

John G. Normyle, D.D.S.
President

Howard Lutz, M.D.
Medical Director

CURRENT OPINION

Metapsychiatry

By Dr. Stanley R. Dean
*Clinical Professor of Psychiatry,
University of Miami School of Medicine, Miami,
and University of Florida School of Medicine, Gainesville, Fla.*

Transcultural psychiatry has become increasingly interested in shamanism and psychic healing. These and many other psychic phenomena are relevant to psychiatry and could greatly expand our frontiers of knowledge about the human mind. As a result, psychic research has begun to develop a new thrust and direction that deserves greater psychiatric attention than ever before. It is true that serious studies have been made of extrasensory perception in the past. They served an important need in a statistical, psychological, and philosophical way. The big difference now is in the emphasis on the practical uses of psychic research—i.e., its technological application to psychiatry, sociology, and other behavioral sciences.

I have recently taken the liberty of introducing a new and, I believe, much needed word into psychiatric nomenclature—"metapsychiatry" (see the *American Journal of Psychiatry*, September, 1973). Metapsychiatry is a term born of necessity to designate the important but hitherto unclassified interface of psychiatry and mysticism.

Metapsychiatry encompasses not only parapsychology but also all other suprasensory, suprarational, and so-called supernatural manifestations of consciousness that are in any way relevant to the thory and practice of psychiatry. Metapsychiatry can be conceptualized as the base of a pyramid whose three sides are psychiatry, parapsychology, and mysticism.

Considerable evidence has been presented for the existence of psychic phenomena, and now the current need is to establish the scientific basis of such phenomena, their relevance to psychiatry, and their development for the betterment of mankind.

My premise is that psychic research is a legitimate concern of psychiatry, the specialty which, by its very nature, is best qualified to assess validity and expose fallacy in matters of the mind.

Before the turn of the century Dr. Richard Maurice Bucke, president of the antecedent American Psychiatric Association, published a book entitled *Cosmic Consciousness* in which he developed the theory that a seemingly miraculous higher consciousness, appearing sporadically throughout the ages, was a natural rather than an occult phenomenon. He felt that cosmic consciousness was latent in all of us and was, in fact, an evolutionary process that would eventually raise all mankind to a higher level of existence. He predicted that psychic research would eventually become a major concern of psychiatry. Dr. Bucke was ahead of his time, but his book is being rediscovered and acclaimed.

Taking my cue from Dr. Bucke, I reason that the developing human mind harbors a rudimentary awareness of cosmic evolution, more manifest in some than in others, that may ultimately evolve into an aggregate understanding of the origin and nature of the universe. I suggest the phrase "Psychogeny recapitulates cosmogeny" to summarize that concept, comparing it with the well-known embryological aphorism "Ontogeny recapitulates phylogeny."

Today's professional and lay literature is replete with studies on extrasensory perception, biofeedback, transcendental meditation, psychedelic experiences, and the role of telepathic communication in parent-child and patient-doctor relationships. Alleged photography of halolike bioenergetic emanations has provided fertile ground for the re-evaluation of religion in scientific terms. There are new concepts of thought as a form of energy with universal field properties, which like other energy fields—e.g., magnetic and gravitational—are amenable to scientific investigation.

In order to give greater emphasis to the relationship between psychiatry and psychic phenomena, I and some of my colleagues are in the process of organizing an American Metapsychiatric Association (A.M.P.A.) which, though psychiatrically oriented, will be open to all behavioral scientists and responsible laymen. Our activities will be guided by the proposition that phenomena that are empirically validated should be as carefully considered as those that are scientifically proven. Our goal throughout will be to replace sensationalism with logic, common sense, and professional responsibility. We welcome all inquiries.

A THEORY OF DISEASE
Arthur Guirdham
Neville Spearman
$5.00

"If we look back over the history of the philosophy of medicine in Europe since the age of Aristotle, I think we can summarise by saying that the first theories of disease insisted on some intrinsic and determining factor in the personality of the individual. After the lapse of centuries, and following several ephemeral flirtations with other hypotheses of disease, we are returning to a conception of morbidity based on, and in its varying manifestations coloured by, the innate and vulnerable nature of the individual. . . .

"My aim in this book is to carry the personality theory of disease a stage further. I am not concerned with the elucidation of further personality types each with its correlated group of diseases. I am endeavouring to advance the theory that the very formation of personality, inevitable though this may be, is in itself conducive to morbidity or, more specifically, that our own perception of our striving, harassed and perpetually threatened individuality is an invitation to our own disintegration

LIFE AND DEATH AND MEDICINE
Special issue, *Scientific American*
September, 1973
$1.00

MAGIC, MYTH AND MEDICINE
John Camp
Taplinger, 1974
$8.50

. . . examines folk medicine from many countries, traces its origins and development and describes its surprising survival. . . .

IMMUNOLOGY: THE MANY-EDGED SWORD
Harold M. Schmeck
George Braziller 1974
$2.95

THE STORY OF X-RAYS: FROM RONTGEN TO ISOTOPES
Alan Ralph Bleich
Dover, 1960
$2.35

METAPSYCHIATRY
From *Medical Tribune and Medical News*
Vol. 14, No. 46, 1973

Write to: STANLEY R. DEAN, M.D.
2121 North Bayshore Drive
Miami, Fla. 33137

PSYCHIC APHORISMS
A personal compendium of psi beliefs and theories

1. Faith is not fantasy; it is a form of precognition that has divined for countless years what science is just beginning to understand.

2. Science and mysticism are fraternal twins, long separated, but now on the verge of reunion.

3. Psychogeny recapitulates cosmogeny—i.e., the developing mind includes an innate awareness of the origin and meaning of the universe.

4. Evolution is not homogenous, but proceeds in two divergent streams: mental and physical; mental evolution is far ahead of physical.

5. The ultraconscious state bridges the evolutionary gap and produces cosmic awareness.

6. Psi power is latent in all, and an experiential reality to many.

7. Thought is a form of energy; it has universal "field" properties which, like gravitational and magnetic fields, are amenable to scientific research.

8. Thought fields, like the theoretical "tachyon," can interact, traverse space and penetrate matter more or less instantaneously.

9. Thought fields survive death and are analogous to soul and spirit.

10. Thought fields are eternal; hence, past existence (reincarnation) is as valid a concept as future immortality.

11. Psychic research is on a par with other important courses of study; it should be included in academic curricula and lead to degrees and doctorates.

12. A new age is dawning—the Psychic Age—on the heels of the Atomic Age and Space Age.

HEALING YOURSELF
Naboru Mora Moto
Avon, 1973
$3.95

THE EPIC OF MEDICINE
Felix Murti-Ibanez, M.D.
Bramhall House, 1962

THE JOURNAL OF THE AMERICAN SOCIETY OF PSYCHO-SOMATIC DENTISTRY AND MEDICINE
published quarterly
Available from 2802 Ramade Avenue
Brooklyn, N.Y. 11224

Objectives of the society

The objectives of the American Society of Psycho-somatic Dentistry and Medicine to inculcate in the practices of those professional practitioners of hypnosis a strong desire to advance in both thinking and practice for the ultimate benefit of their patients.

AMERICAN MEDICAL-PSYCHIC RESEARCH ASSOCIATION
135 Madison Avenue, N.E.
Albuquerque, N.M. 87123
Founded to bring people from all healing fields together
Write for details.

PREVENTION: THE MAGAZINE FOR BETTER HEALTH
Rodale Press, Inc.
33 East Minor Street
Emmaus, Pa. 18049
Subscription $6.85 a year.
Monthly.

ART: ITS OCCULT BASIS AND HEALING VALUE
Eleanor C. Marry
New Knowledge Books, 1961
$6.50

HEALING STONES
Doris M. Hodges
Hiawatha Publishing Company, 1973
$2.00

MEDICAL RESEARCH PROGRAM

Located at 4018 North 40th St., Phoenix, Arizona, the A.R.E. Clinic, Ltd. is an outgrowth of the Medical Research Division of the Edgar Cayce Foundation, which, since 1968, has sponsored annual medical symposia on "Concepts in Physiology and Therapy as Found in the Edgar Cayce Readings." Several published papers and original research in the Cayce readings have come from the Foundation's effort, making available to physicians interpretations of the concepts of physiology and therapy found in the nearly 9,000 "physical" readings.

A Physician's Reference Notebook has been published and made available to all the doctors who are cooperating in the Foundation's research program. Some 35 different illnesses here are discussed, with emphasis on patterns of physiology as Cayce "saw" them active in the human body, bringing about physical abnormalities. His concepts of therapy were also found to be patterns of treatment, and are discussed and correlated in the commentaries in the Reference Notebook. These also are in the Circulating Files of the Association, which are available to members on loan. The Circulating File Service is part of the research program of the Edgar Cayce Foundation and brings together the work of physicians scattered across the United States and elsewhere.

The Clinic, under the leadership of the Director of the Medical Research Division of the Foundation, has been designed to care for patients at an out-patient level, although living quarters for a limited number of out-of-town patients are near the Clinic and next door to the Southwest A.R.E. Branch Office. Reading material from the library is obtainable at the out-patient residence, including much in the way of an expanding group of indexed Edgar Cayce readings.

The Clinic resulted from the incorporation of the medical practices of William and Gladys McGarey, both M.D.'s, in conformance with Arizona law. Future plans include expansion of its present staff. It is designed to enlarge upon the current program of research, emphasizing the clinical aspect, and stimulating more of the academic and laboratory research which underlies the work with actual disease processes. Specific research projects, which involve the medical mind and talents, are being encouraged as part of the internal function of the Clinic. Funding of such projects is part of the program of the Edgar Cayce Foundation and of the Association, as those funds become available.

EDGAR CAYCE ON HEALING
Mary E. Carter and William A. McGarey, M.D.
Paperback Library, 1972
95 cents

Patient care at the Clinic is designed to utilize the best of modern medical knowledge as it conforms with the ideals expressed in the Cayce readings, and to apply at a research level the concepts of physiology and therapy found in the readings in approaching the problems of the patient in question. Such ideals, such concepts are touched upon in many of the readings:

BORN TO HEAL
Ruth Montgomery
Popular Library, 1973
$1.50

THE ACADEMY OF PARAPSYCHOLOGY AND MEDICINE
314 Second Street
Los Altos, Calif. 94022

The Academy of Parapsychology and Medicine, founded in 1970, is a non-profit educational organization established to increase man's understanding of the physical and biological sciences, metaphysics, and religion as they relate to the healing of mental and physical ills. It fosters scientific research in these fields and, through its events and publications, brings the findings of such studies to the professional community and interested laymen.

The Academy is entirely free of ties with established educational, political, or ecclesastical organizations.

In May of 1969 the Lockheed Management Association and three institutions of higher learning in the San Francisco Bay Area jointly sponsored a symposium on the medical aspects of parapsychology. This was the first serious attempt to present publicly a representative sampling of the professional research being conducted on paramedical healing. Except for one session, which was co-sponsored by the Santa Clara County Medical Society exclusively for physicians, the symposium was open to both professionals and the general public. The enthusiastic response to this symposium revealed that an unsuspected degree of interest existed in the whole field of paranormal and unorthodox healing.

The following year a group of physicians and scientists, committed to the belief that a common but as yet little understood rationale lies behind all healing experience, founded The Academy of Parapsychology and Medicine.

In October 1971 another symposium was organized to explore "The Varieties of Healing Experience." This time The Academy co-sponsored the event with the Lockheed Management Association. Public response was even greater than the first time, filling the largest auditorium available in the area, with hundreds turned away, confirming the impressions drawn from the earlier meeting and moving the directors of The Academy to plan a more active program of public events and publication, begun in 1972.

The Academy of Parapsychology and Medicine is founded on an idea that is as old as man: that spirit and matter are somehow one, and that it is the essential purpose of man to seek meaning behind all human experience if the true nature of healing is to be found.

Modern medicine is increasingly coming to recognize the importance of the effect that the mind and the emotions have on the economy of man's physical well-being. Psychosomatic medicine has established the significance of this interdimensional relationship. The religions of all cultures and times have posited man's spiritual nature as the essential dimension of man and the ground wherein all negative conditions may be transmuted.

That man is a mulitidimensional being whose experience and ultimate purposes are inextricably and meaningfully related, and that that meaning is made manifest in patterns of health and disease is a fundamental belief of The Academy.

The Academy also believes that medicine must adopt a new view of man: one which recognizes the unity of body, mind, and spirit, and the importance of the interrelationship of these dimensions in health and disease; that all physical and mental disease is directive experience in human development, and that it must be viewed as a manifestation of conditions existing on subtler levels—whether mental, emotional, or spiritual; that the treatment of disease must be directed at the whole man, and that no lasting healing of the physical body can be achieved where the mental, emotional and spiritual elements have been untouched.

Membership

Membership in the Academy of Parapsychology and Medicine is open to all who wish to support or participate in the activities and pursuits of the organization. The following categories of membership are available to all applicants.

Associate Membership
Yearly Dues $15

Associate members will receive the APM Report, advance notification of public Academy events, reduced registration fees and reduced rates on all materials or publications produced by the Academy as a part of its regular on-going program.

Participating Membership
Yearly Dues $25

Participating members in addition to receiving the privileges of the Associate member will have access to all project materials, whether published in the Journals of the Academy or in special project reports to be issued periodically. Participating membership will provide the medical, paramedical and scientific community an opportunity to be in closer touch with the Academy's projects.

Sponsoring Membership

Three classes of Sponsoring membership are offered:

Contributing Sponsor	Yearly Dues $100
Sustaining Sponsor	Yearly Dues $500
Principal Sponsor	Yearly Dues $1,000

A Sponsoring member (Sponsor) will receive all rights and privileges of Participating membership.

THE LIFE AND DOCTRINES OF PARACELSUS
Franz Hartmann, M.D.
Health Research, 1963
$5.50

"A physician who knows nothing more about his patient than what the latter will tell him knows very little indeed. He must be able to judge from the external appearance of the latter about his internal condition. He must be able to see the internal in the external man. . . .

"nature—not man—is the physician. . . .

"a physician must be a *Philosopher*; that is to say, he must dare to use his own reason and not cling to antiquated opinions and book-authorities. He must above all be in possession of that faculty which is called Intuition, and which cannot be acquired by blindly following the footsteps of another; he must be able to see his own way. There are natural philosophers and there are artificial philosophers. The former have a knowledge of their own; the latter have borrowed knowledge from their books. If you wish to be a true physician, you must be able to do your own thinking, and not merely employ the thoughts of others. What others may teach you may be good enough to assist you in your search for knowledge, but you should be able to think for yourself, and not cling to the coat-tail of any authority, no matter how big-sounding the title of the latter may be."

HIPPOCRATES HEALTH
INSTITUTE
25 Exeter St.
Boston, Mass. 02116

THE SECRET OF LIFE
Georges Lakhovsky
Health Research, 1970
$5.00

"The fundamental principle of Lakhovsky's scientific system may be summed up in the axiom 'Every living being emits radiations.' Inspired by this principle Lakhovsky was able to explain such diverse phenomena as instinct in animals, migration of birds, health, disease, and in general, all the manifestations of organic life.

"According to Lakhovsky, the nucleus of a living cell may be compared to an electrical oscillating circuit. This nucleus consists of tubular filaments, chromosomes and mitochondria, made up of insulating material and filled with a conducting fluid containing all the mineral salts found in sea-water. These filaments are thus comarable to oscillating circuits endowed with capacity and self-inductance and therefore capable of oscillating according to a specific frequency. "In the light of Lakhovsky's theories the fight between the living organism and microbes is fundamentaly a 'war of radiations.' If the radiations of the microbe win, the cell ceases to oscillate, and death is the ultimate result. If, on the other hand, the radiations of the cell gain the ascendant, the microbe is killed and health is preserved. Broadly speaking, health is equivalent to oscillatory equilibrium while disease is characterised by oscillatory disequilibrium. This general principle has given rise to a vast number of experiments covering the whole field of biology.'

MAN, MEDICINE AND ENVIRONMENT
Rene Dubos
Mentor, 1969
$1.25

"Like animals, primitive man had health instincts to help him overcome or minimize the effects of accidents or disease. In addition to these instincts, he must early have recognized some direct and obvious cause-and-effect relationships between certain empirical practices and the improvements of wounds or the alleviation of symptoms. Also, many forces he regarded as mysterious because they were indirect or outside the range of his conscious apprehension affected the health of primitive man. Magic thus early became an essential component of his attitude toward the causation and control of disease. Medicine therefore had dual nature from its very beginning. It included the empirical knowledge of effective procedures and belief in magical influences. Even today, medicine men in primitive populations supplement their practical skill in surgical techniques and the use of drugs with a large variety of weird practies based on the tribal lore. Throughout history, and whatever the level of civilization, the structure of medicine has been determined not only by the state of science but also by the prevailing attitudes toward disease. These in turn are influenced by religious and philosophical beliefs. This is just as true of the most evolved urban and industrialized societies as it is of the most primitive populations. Like his Stone Age ancestors, modern man lives by myths . . .

"The fundamental philosophy of Hippocratic medicine is that diseases are not caused by capricious gods or irrational forces, as primitive people are wont to believe. They constitute natural phenomena developing in accordance with natural laws."

Hippocrates Health Institute

Located at 25 Exeter Street, Boston, Massachusetts 02116, U.S.A., is the educational subdivision of Rising Sun Christianity. HIPPOCRATES HEALTH INSTITUTE is a philanthropic, nonsectarian, non-profit, tax-exempt organization, incorporated under the laws of the District of Columbia, U.S.A. As an applied environmental study center the Institute was founded to share the discoveries of more than a decade of research in nutrition and ecology. Here, the young, the elderly, the novice and the professional learn how to regenerate the human body, survive ecological crises, and initiate patterns of peace and well-being in their lives.

Ann Wigmore, D.D. - Founder

Ann Wigmore has written four published books and many periodicals and booklets about health, animals, children, indoor gardening, etc. She has taught the LIVE FOOD gospel for many years. Dr. Ann has set her life's work to improve the health of suffering human beings. She bears a burning desire to see the "Temple of the Soul" – the human body – perfected to house the spark of God.

Victor Kulvinskas, M.S. – Director

Four years ago, Victor at age 30 retired from his career, teaching college mathematics and consulting in computer programming, to pursue a program of natural living. Like many others of our New Age, he discarded drugs, cigarettes, coffee and plastic foods. Overcoming many critical ailments, he has seriously, objectively studied nutrition and spiritual disciplines. Now an author and lecturer, Victor's documented, scientific research will soon be published. Available for lectures, LIVE FOOD banquets and workshops.

THE DIMENSIONS OF HEALING
A Symposium.
The Academy of Parapsychology and
Medicine, 1972
$10.00

THE DIMENSIONS OF HEALING

PREFACE   4

I. INTRODUCTION
   New Developments in Personal Awareness   5
      by Captain Edgar Mitchell, U.S.N.

II. THE DIMENSIONS OF HEALING
   1. The Triune Approach to Healing of the Edgar Cayce Readings   13
      by Herbert B. Puryear, Ph.D.
   2. Healing by Unconventional Methods   22
      by Olga Worrall, Ph.D.
   3. Laboratory Evidence of the "Laying-On-of-Hands"   29
      by Bernard Grad, Ph.D.
   4. The Healing Potential of Psychosomatic Integration   35
      by Haridas Chaudhuri, Ph.D.
   5. How to Make Use of the Field of Mind Theory   41
      by Elmer E. Green, Ph.D.
   6. The Search for a Common Denominator in Medicine and Healing   54
      by Andrija Puharich, M.D.
   7. Consciousness, Radiation, and the Developing Sensory System   61
      by William A. Tiller, Ph.D.
   8. A Possible Technology of Acupuncture   86
      by Kendall L. Johnson
   9. Acupuncture and Body Energies — A Bridge in Understanding   93
      the Healing Process by William A. McGarey, M.D.
   10. High Voltage Photography Applied to Psychic Healing   102
      by Douglas Dean, M.Sc.
   11. The Influence on Enzyme Growth by the "Laying-On-of-Hands"   110
      by Sister M. Justa Smith, Ph.D.
   12. Photographic Evidence of Healing Energy on Plants and People   121
      by Thelma S. Moss, Ph.D.
   13. Total Personality Inventory and Hypnotherapy   132
      by Robert Bradley, M.D.
   14. The Role of the Mind in Cancer Therapy   139
      by Carl Simonton, M.D.
   15. Panel Discussion   146

III. INTRODUCING ACUPUNCTURE TO WESTERN MEDICINE
   The Western Physician and Acupuncture   159
      by William A. McGarey, M.D.
   Basic Energy Systems in Acupuncture   168
      by Andrija Puharich, M.D.

THE VARIETIES OF HEALING EXPERIENCE
Exploring Psychic Phenomena in Healing.

Transcript of the Interdisciplinary Symposium of October 30, 1971. The Academy of Parapsychology and Medicine, 1972
$5.00

The Varieties of Healing Experience

Exploring Psychic Phenomena in Healing

SATURDAY, OCTOBER 30, 1971

AFTERNOON SESSION

"PARAPSYCHOLOGY AND MEDICINE IN PERSPECTIVE"
Jack H. Holland, Ph.D., *Moderator*

"HEALING AND YOUR I.Q.—THE RELATIONSHIP OF THE ELEMENTS OF SPIRITUAL MIND HEALING"
Raymond K. Lilley, D.D.

"BIOFEEDBACK for MIND-BODY SELF-REGULATION: HEALING AND CREATIVITY"
Elmer Green, Ph.D.

"THE WORK OF THE BRAZILIAN HEALER ARIGÓ"
Henry K. Puharich, M.D.

EVENING SESSION

"RADIONICS, RADIESTHESIA AND PHYSICS"
William A. Tiller, Ph.D.

"RUSSIAN PARAPSYCHOLOGY AND THE CAYCE CONCEPTS OF HEALING"
William A. McGarey, M.D.

"THE NEED FOR THE ACADEMY OF PARAPSYCHOLOGY AND MEDICINE"
Robert A. Bradley, M.D.

MASSAGE: THE ORIENTAL WAY
Katsusuke Serizawa
Wehman Bros., 1972
$3.95

ACUPUNCTURE THERAPEUTICS: AN INTRODUCTORY TEXT
Frederick F. Kao with the collaboration of John J. Kao
$5.95
Available from:
P.O. Box 555
Garden City, N.Y. 11530
$5.95

ACUPUNCTURE: THE CURE OF MANY DISEASES
Dr. Felix Mann
(Foreword by Aldous Huxley)
Tao Books and Publications Inc.
$2.25
Available from: 31 Farnsworth Street
Boston, Mass. 02210

ACUPUNCTURE SUPPLIES
Books - Charts, etc.

Chinese - Japanese - Ryodoraku and American Systems

Manual and Electrical
Traditional and Western
Needles and Needle-less

DOCTOR'S SUPPLY
24028 UNION Dept. EW
Dearborn, Michigan 48124

free literature on request

ACUPUNCTURE: WHAT CAN IT DO FOR YOU!
A special report from the editors of *Enterprise Science News*
$1.00
Available from: 230 Park Avenue
New York, N.Y. 10017

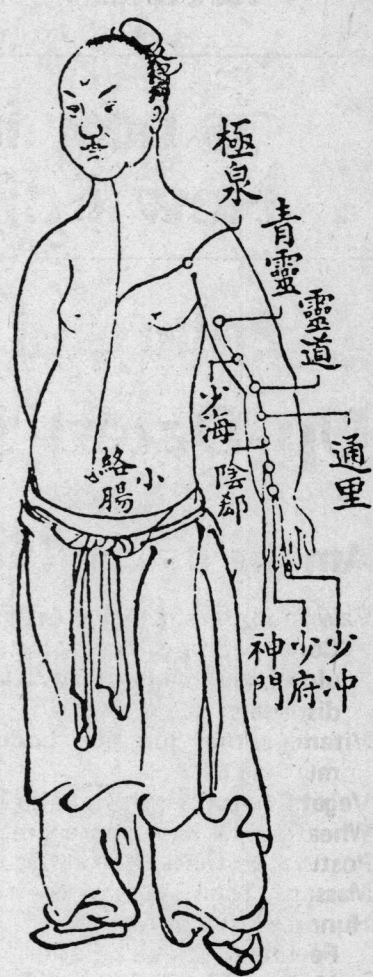

**THE ARM LESSER YIN
(Heart) MERIDIAN**

THE PUZZLE OF PAIN
Ronald Melzack
Penguin, 1973
$3.25

"The obvious biological value of pain as a signal of tissue damage leads most of us to expect that it must always occur after injury and that the intensity of pain we feel is proportional to the extent of the damage. Actually, in higher species at least, there is much evidence that pain is not simply a function of the amount of bodily damage alone. Rather, the amount and quality of pain we feel are also determined by our previous experiences and how well we remember them, by our ability to understand the cause of the pain and to grasp its consequences. Even the culture in which we have been brought up plays an essential role in how we feel and respond to pain."

THE WHEEL OF HEALTH: THE SOURCES OF LONG LIFE AND HEALTH AMONG THE HUNZA
G. T. Wrench
Schocken, 1972
$1.75

Is it really necessary that illness and ailments play such a tremendous part in the lives of citizens of modern civilized countries? If not, upon what does health primarily depend?

Dr. Wrench found the answers in the work of Dr. Robert McCarrison, who had been Director of Nurtrition Research in India and who had studied for many years the Hunza people of northwest India, whom he came to regard as the healthiest people in the world. Many of the Hunzas lived to be more than 100; cancer was unknown and they rarely suffered degenerative diseases. The Wheel of Health is a presentation of the Hunza way of health. It describes their diet and their methods of food cultivation and establishes the connection between healthy soil, healthy food and healthy people: namely that together these form the wheel of health.

MAGICAL MEDICINE: A NIGERIAN CASE-STUDY
Una Maclean
Penguin, 1974
$1.95

". . . The real value of African medicine . . . lies not in its materials but in the methods and concepts which underlie their use. It is characterized by its ability to supply meaningful answers to questions which are relevant to patient and practitioner alike."

This Marvelous Personal Testament
to the 'Natural Way'

is now in a New Edition

Enlarged & Up-Dated $3.00
(SOFT COVER)

Among its contents:

Raw food treatment for Arthritis, Asthma, Constipation, Emphysema, Over-weight, ulcers, and many other maladies & disorders...

Vitamins, their function, bodily needs, multiple uses...

Vegetarianism — why and how...

Wheatgrass — how to prepare and use...

Posture, Exercise, Relaxation, & Sleep...

Massage, Zone Therapy, & Acupuncture

Hundreds of tips for
Feeling & Looking Better,
More vibrant living...

Recipes and Menus by the dozen for exciting dishes and tasty, nutritious meals...

Pet Care, Ecology, Natural Cosmetics...

BE YOUR OWN DOCTOR —
Nature's Way is the Organic Way
by Ann Wigmore D.D. N.D.

ANN WIGMORE, D.D., N.D.
Founder-Director of the
HIPPOCRATES HEALTH INSTITUTE,
Author of "Why Suffer — The Wheatgrass Story" and other popular books,
Pamphlets & Articles on health
in the Hundreds!

BIOTONIC THERAPY: THERAPEUTIC USE OF ENERGY
Maryla de Chrapowicki
C.W. Daniel Company Ltd., 1952
$2.50

MAGNET DOWSING or THE MAGNET SUDY OF LIFE
Benoytosh Bhattacharyye
Firma K. L. Mukhopadhyay, 1967
2.75

HEALING AND REGENERATION THROUGH COLOR
Corinne Heline
J. F. Rowny Press, 1972
$1.95

OF MEN AND PLANTS
Maurice Messegue
Bantam, 1974
$1.75

Messegue has used flowers, vegetables and herbs to cure people of diseases such as asthma, rheumatism, arthritis, eczema, etc.

AMERICAN INDIAN MEDICINE
Virgil J. Vogel
Ballantine, 1973
$1.95

... shows the effect of Indian medicinal practices on white civilization, describes Indian theories of disease and methods of treatment. ...

COUNTRYWIDE TOUR

Boston Center of the Healing Arts is continuing its countrywide tour for June, July, August September -- presenting programs on "Healing with Massage and Natural Medicine," based on the principles of Acupuncture and Oriental Medicine. For further information, tel. (617) 522-0908, or write Boston Center of the Healing Arts, One Park Place, Boston, Mass., 02130 -- Attention: Stephen Uprichard or Lino Stanchich.

WE ARE ALL HEALERS
Sally Hammond
Ballantine, 1974
$1.95

OCCIDENTAL INSTITUE OF CHINESE STUDIES
P.O. Box 1010, Station B
Weston, Ontario, Canada

"Many researchers have commented that there may be a relationship between the workings of acupuncture and some of the phenomena observed in the field of parapsychology. They feel that acupuncture is more closely related to the 'psychic' form of healing, rather than the physical forms of healing, and as such may belong more to the realm of the 'spiritual' healer rather than the medical doctor.

"Current psychic researchers see acupuncture as a sort of 'missing link' between the physical plane and the psychic or paranormal plane, in that it is something that seems to 'put it all together.' Acupuncture for them relates or ties together many of the concepts of metaphysics, parapsychology, life energy theory, and so on, to the physical world or plane."

ABOUT THE INSTITUTE
occidental Institute of Chinese Studies was conceived in 1971 as it became apparent that acupuncture would be accepted in North America. The Institute's prime purpose is to put before the English speaking people a simple and comprehensive amount of information on the subject of acupuncture, sufficient to enable anyone interested in this ancient system of healing to practice the art; or at least make a very good beginning in it therapeutically.

Secondly, it aims to promote the establishment of acupuncture as recognized therapeutic practice in North America and to propagate the cause of acupuncture on this continent. Along with this, an important aspect is the establishment of standards for future practitioners of acupuncture (other than physicians, etc.).

Thirdly, to conduct and participate in research projects to find out exactly how and why acupuncture works, and the best ways to use it clinically; as well as gather research information from all possible sources, acting as an acupuncture resource center and clearinghouse of information for our students and graduates.

In championing for positive action we are no less than promoting a *"bill of rights"* for the sick, the maimed, the aged, the aged, the handicapped, or those otherwise in need of health care. We feel anyone has a right to be treated using the best available method consistent with his personal interest, regardless of whether or not it might step on some toes or upset an established medical order. After all, in medical care, an essential service, only one thing is of importance: RESULTS!

The Institute's acupuncture activities are directed by Dr. Walter D. Sturm, Ph.D., Master of Acupuncture (Nevada). Dr. Sturm is an experienced educator and has years of background in teaching, including by means of the home study method. He holds a Doctor of Philosophy degree in Chinese studies and is a member of the prestigious International Society of Acupuncture in Paris, France. Some of his other professional affiliations are: The German Acupuncture Association, German Society for Electro-Acupuncture, National Acupuncture Research Society (New York), Acupuncture Research Institute (Calif.), Participating Member in The Academy of Parapsychology and Medicine (U.S.A.) and the Kyoto Pain Control Institute (Japan). He has spent years reducing the problem of teaching this subject by correspondence to its simplest and most effective form. The course and, to a great extent, this Institute are the result of his work and efforts.

ABOUT THE COURSE
Contrary to popular belief, Oriental medicine, if taught properly, is not all that complicated or difficult to learn. The course hopefully will disperse these beliefs by training along current modern therapeutic applications of acupuncture, in addition to lessons dealing with classical Chinese theories. We present three approaches to acupuncture therapy: symptomatic (treatment by known combinations and formulas); needle and non-needle electronic methods; and treatment according to traditional Chinese methods. Graduates can then take their choice in practice.

Quite early in the course you will have a treatment method explained to you, other than the "needle," this being acu-pressure (finger pressure at the acupuncture points) and meridian massage. Thus, early in the course you will be able to put your knowledge to practical use and practice on yourself, without any risk of accidents with the needles. Acu-pressure and meridian massage are the simplest of all methods, requiring no instruments or equipment of any kind. They are almost as effective as any other, and in many instances are preferable, especially when treating the very old, very young, or "needle-nervous" patients. Some elementary self-treatment forms of these are already popular, such as *Shiatsu* and *Do-IN*.

Inaddition, this course introduces to North America the new, "needle-less" electronic acupuncture techniques, so popular and commonly used in Europe today. This involves stimulation of acupuncture points directly with very mild positive or negative electronic current (not to be confused with stimulation of the needles themselves with electronic current). Thus, it is not necessary to puncture the skin with needles in order to obtain the desired results. This method, along with acu-pressure and meridian massage, may be employed in clinical practice, in place of needles, or until such time as the "legality" of needle use is settled.

The acupuncture "needle techniques" are purposely postponed to later in the course. This helps the student by not offering him too early the temptation to "try sticking a needle in," before being sufficiently aware of what he is doing. Moxibustion is also covered fully. By the conclusion of the course you will have more complete acupuncture treatment formulas than have so far ever been published.

The course uses the "college method of learning." In colleges knowledge is imparted by verbal lecture—we give it in written lecture form. The lectures (lessons) each have their own assignments and question papers for you to complete and send to the Institute for marking, grading and comments, after which they are returned to you for review. We make extensive use of the *"Clinique"* (Clinical Critique) method whereby the student is given an illness problem along with all pertinent facts, and must then tell us how he or she would go about treating it.

The course, in two volumes (custom binders supplied) is a major new work of *over 500 pages*, constantly revised and updated It is fully illustrated with many large diagrams and charts. students' questions are answered if appropriate to the lessons, and full consideration is given their problems. Resident training is not offered at this time, however, weekend seminars for advanced students and graduates are offered throughout Canda and the United States. These cover advanced aspects of acupuncture that are impossible to teach in a written format, such as those of pulse diagnosis and the needle Canada manipulative skills.

YOGA AND MEDICINE: THE MERGING OF YOGIC CONCEPTS WITH MODERN MEDICAL KNOWLEDGE
Steven F. Brena, M.D.
Penguin, 1973
$1.25

"We could look at our body as a highly sophisticated machine in which two great systems can be distinguished: an outer system and an inner system. Through the former, man is connected and interrelates with the external world, which is his outer environment; we can call this organization a 'Somatic system' or a 'system of relation.' The inner system, on the other hand, provides for the vital functions and maintains and sustains our life; we can call it 'vegetative' or 'visceral system.' Through this delicate visceral organization, man keeps his 'inner environment' balanced, this expression meaning a good functioning of the sets of cells and tissues that make up the human body."

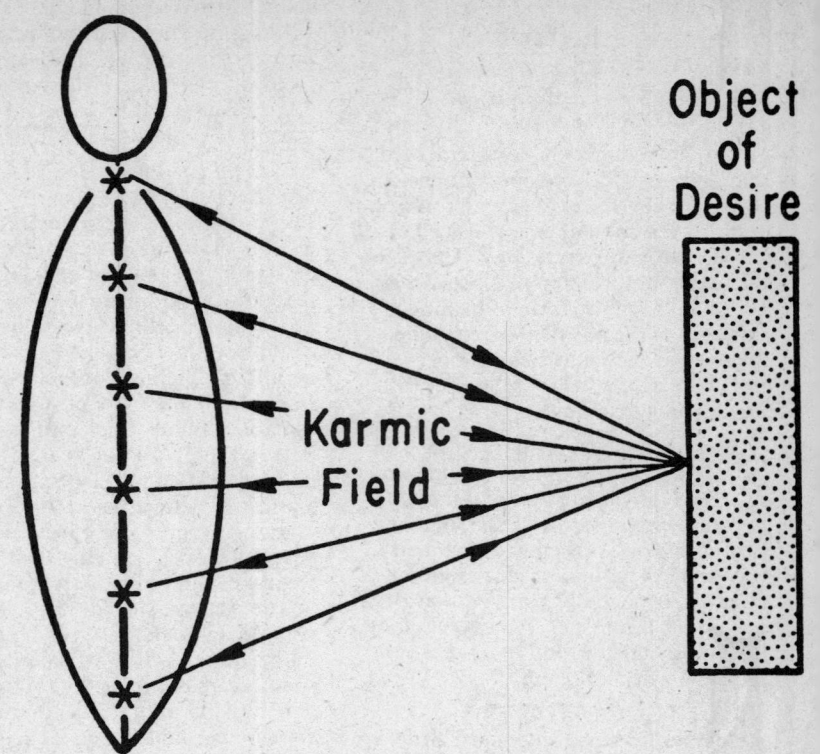

Reinforcing the karmic field

When we perform an action in response to a desire, the waves of energy triggered by it hit the object of our desire and rebound back to us. With repeated "back-firing," one or more of our *Chakras* will soon become involved in the rebounding waves and consequently it will become bound to the object, as if magnetically attracted to it. The links between ourselves and the desired object will be compounded according to the number of the *Chakras* involved, each one reinforcing the Karmic field. The end-result is that we have lost our freedom so far as that particular object is concerned, because we are conditioned by it. We express this slavery in affirmations such as "I want it with all my heart," "I feel it in my stomach," "It moves my heart," and so on.

Contemporary medicine is well aware of these phenomena. They have been identified and investigated as emotional expressions, sustained mainly through the activity of the sympathetic system (see Chapter One).

Learning how to gain control of the *Chakras* through *prāṇāyāma* and *pratyāhāra*, the Yogi is actually capable of permanently breaking the links with all objects of desire, and merge free in Cosmic Consciousness.

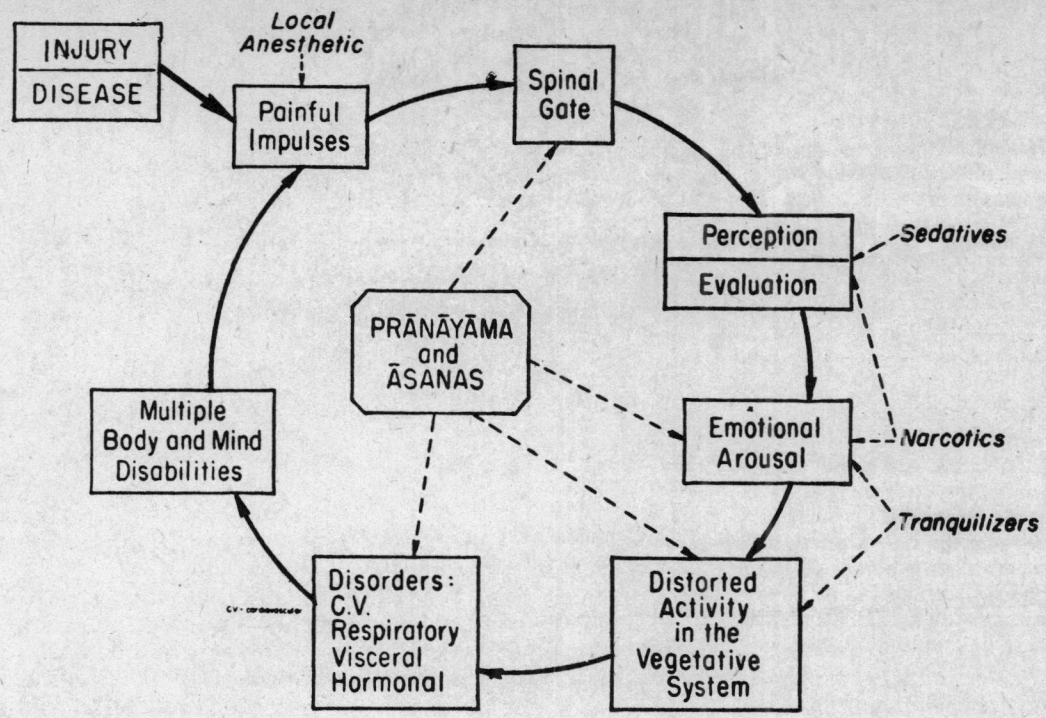

The vicious cycle of chronic illness

Painful impulses, on reaching the brain after having been modulated through the "spinal gate," are perceived and evaluated, and trigger an emotional arousal. If not properly checked through an orderly rational and volitional control, the emotional reaction may induce and sustain abnormal activities within the vegetative system, mostly sympathetic (*see also* Chapters One and Seven). As a consequence, various disorders in the heart, arteries and veins, hormones, and other various viscera are produced; each one in turn induces further mental and physical disabilities. A vicious circle of pain and sickness is generated in this way, with more painful impulses further deteriorating the emotional stability of the sufferer.

Sedative drugs probably act in reducing the perceptive evaluation of the painful impulses. Narcotics and tranquillizers slow down and dull both the emotional arousal and the consequent sympathetic distorted activities. All these drugs, however, act in negative ways, practically poisoning the nervous structures into inactivity. *Āsanas* and *prāṇāyāma*, on the other hand, act upon the same nervous stations in positive ways, bringing the emotional responses to pain under the control of cognition and volition, and rehabilitating the neuro-vegetative system to function properly again. Moreover, *prāṇāyāma* can gain control of the "gate," consequently breaking through whatever vicious circle of chronic illness that might have been generated.

ACUPUNCTURE
Mark Duke
Pyramid House, 1972
$6.95

PULSE DIAGNOSIS
Using their first three fingers, acupuncturists sense the pulses of the twelve internal organs on the radial artery, as shown. "Superficial" pulses are taken by applying light finger pressure. "Deep" pulses require heavy pressure. Each of the twelve pulses reveals up to twenty-seven different qualities, each an indication of a specific illness or disease.

CHINESE DOCTORS believe that there are twelve different pulses in the body, each associated with a vital organ. They believe that they can distinguish various pulses, and from what they learn discover the seat of an illness—the Yin-Yang imbalance. Western doctors insist that there is one pulse and that it reveals only a small amount about the internal condition of the body. . . .

"Acupuncturists depend on the pulses they feel to reveal the exact nature of any illness in the body. They believe that the pulses are never wrong. While symptoms may lead to more than one organ, or even to none at all, the pulses are specific and undeniably correct.

"Taking the pulse in Chinese medicine differs completely from the common experience Western people have in their doctors' offices. The acupuncturist does not merely pick up your wrist, count the beats he feels against a clock, and jot down the result on your medical record. A traditional Chinese physician will study the pulses for between ten minutes and three hours. He will attempt to discern, in each of the twelve pulses, up to twenty-seven different qualities, all of which date back to the classic texts on medicine. Acupuncturists find, classify, and judge more than three hundred distinct characteristics in a patient's pulse, while Western doctors take note of a total of three."

> "The superior doctor prevents illness; the mediocre doctor cures imminent illness; the inferior doctor treats actual illness."
> —Chinese Proverb

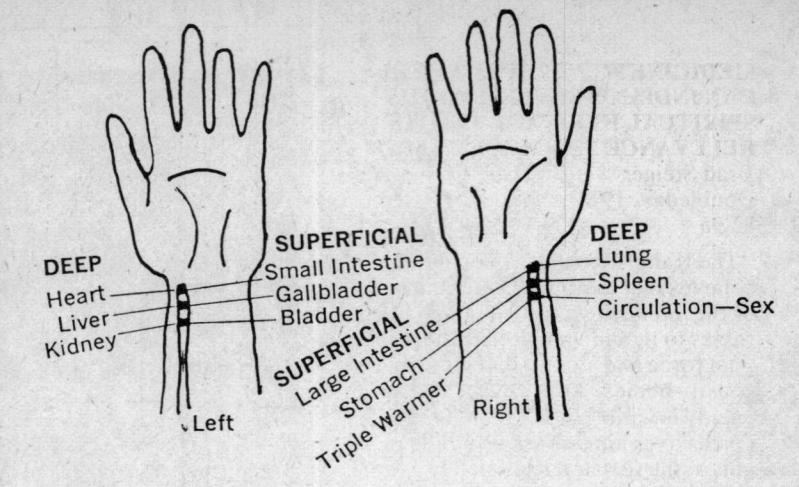

PULSE DIAGNOSIS
Using their first three fingers, acupuncturists sense the pulses of the twelve internal organs on the radial artery, as shown. "Superficial" pulses are taken by applying light finger pressure. "Deep" pulses require heavy pressure. Each of the twelve pulses reveals up to twenty-seven different qualities, each an indication of a specific illness or disease.

CHINESE MEDICINE
Georges Beau
Avon, 1972
$1.25

"Man is a summary of the universe, a microcosm (from the Greek *mikros kosmos*, 'small world') in relation to the macrocosm (*makros kosmos*, 'great world'). Being an integral part of the whole, and at the same time a miniature version of it, he is subject to the same universal laws. The same idea of a relation between the life of the heavenly bodies and that of earthly organisms is also found in astrology and other divining arts. The belief that events on earth are influenced by the heavenly bodies has been held all over the world . . .

"For the ancient Chinese, all knowledge was summed up in three terms: Yang, Yin, and Tao. The word *yang* originally meant 'sunlight,' or what pertained to it; *yin* meant 'absence of light' and therefore 'shadow' or 'darkness. . . .

"The dualistic theory of Yang and Yin is cosmic in scope, since the sky and the sun are Yang, while the earth and the moon are Yin. All living beings contain both principles. Yang is masculinity, activity, spendor, and hardness. It is left and black. The number that corresponds to it is one, and the other odd numbers are Yang. Yin represents what is feminine, passive, plain, and soft. It is the void. It is right and white. Its number is two, and all the other even numbers are Yin.

"This opposition extends to the seasons. Since the ancient Chinese lived in the northern hemisphere, they regarded the south as the cardinal point of heat and associated the north with cold. . . .

From this correlation between the seasons and the cardinal points, it followed that summer was paired with the south and winter with the north; spring was paired with the east because the sun rose there, and autumn with the west because that was where the sun set. . . .

"Each human being represents a harmonious combination of celestial and earthly principles. Any disturbance of that balance is manifested in physiological disorders, recognizable by certain irregularities in the rhythmic pulsations of the energy that circulates through the body. By pulse examination, among other means, the traditional Chinese physician detects these anomalies. Treatment consists in restoring balance by enabling the body to increase or decrease the amount of one of the elements within it, depending on whether it is suffering from an excess or a deficiency."

MEDICINE POWER: THE AMERICAN INDIAN'S REVIVAL OF HIS SPIRITUAL HERITAGE AND ITS RELEVANCE FOR MODERN MAN
Brad Steiger
Doubleday, 1974
$2.95

"The Kahuna, Witch, Medicine Man believes that the spirits enter the body of the intended victim, or attach themselves to it, and vampirelike, absorb his vital force and store it in their own ghostly bodies. As the mana of the enemy is withdrawn, a numbness comes over him, which generally begins at the feet and rises slowly over a period of three days to knees, hips, and finally to the heart. Once the numbness has encircled the heart, the enemy will soon be dead.

"When the victim has expired, the satiated spirits withdraw, taking with them their newly absorbed charges of mana. Upon their return to their master, the practitioner, they are commanded to play about the lodge until they have dissipated the vital force which they have stolen from the victim. Such spirit recreation finds its release in poltergeistic activities, in which objects are tossed about in violent explosions of energy.

"If the intended victim should be rescued through the paranormal prowess of another practitioner, the invading spirits might be directed back to the one who chants the death prayer with fatal results. In order to prevent such a boomerang of the death curse, the skilled practitioner who looks for longevity in his craft will always observe a ritual cleansing. In certain cases, the more cautious practitioners will demand that the person who has employed them to send out a curse take an oath that the named victim is truly deserving of such drastic punishment. Should another practitioner, or the spiritual strength of the intended victim himself, thereby accomplish a reversal of the curse, the client alone will be held accountable by the enraged familiar spirits."

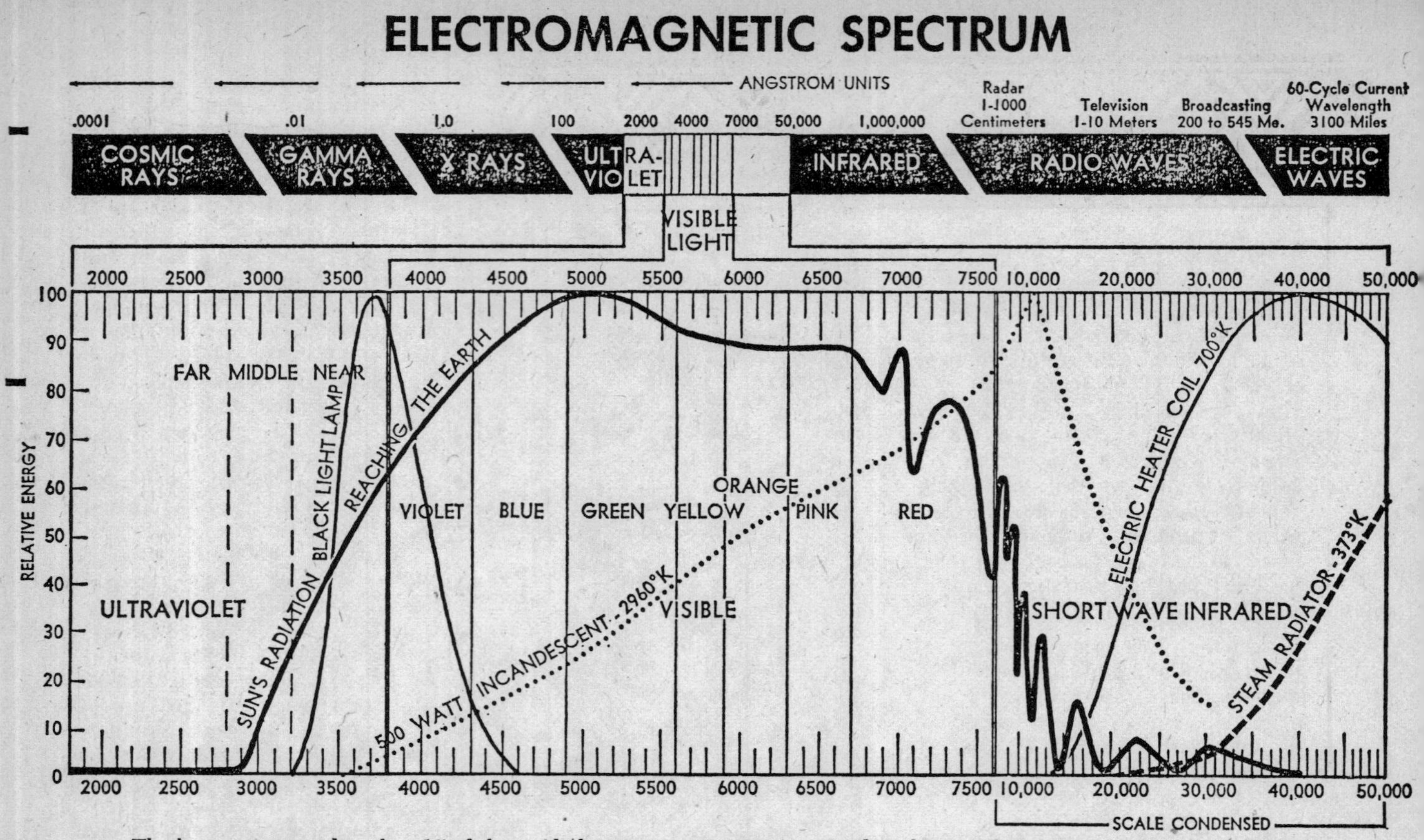

ELECTROMAGNETIC SPECTRUM

The human eye sees less than 1% of the total electromagnetic spectrum. Little is known about the mysterious light sources at either end of the visible spectrum—the ultraviolet, infrared, and so-called background radiation—but evidence now seems to indicate that they exert a profound influence on the physical and mental health of animals, plants and man.

HEALTH AND LIGHT: THE EFFECTS OF NATURAL AND ARTIFICIAL LIGHT ON MAN AND OTHER LIVING THINGS
John N. Ott
Devin-Adair, 1973
$7.50

"Ever since the research of William Rowan in the '20s we have known that seasonal changes in the lengths of daylight and darkness have a significant effect on bird migration as well as upon mating periods for some species. Out of such studies, also, have grown the poultry industry's programs of lengthening short daylight hours in winter by means of artificial light in order to increase egg production. The response of the hens is due to the light energy entering the eyes and stimulating the pituitary gland. This has given rise to strong evidence that the endocrine system of mammals responds to particular wavelengths of *visible light* as well as other areas of the *total spectrum*, including the longer wavelengths of ultraviolet that penetrate the atmosphere...."

"As man has become more industrialized, living under an environment of artificial light, behind window glass and windshield, watching TV, looking through colored sunglasses, working in windowless buildings, the wavelength energy entering the eye has become greatly distorted from that of natural sunlight."

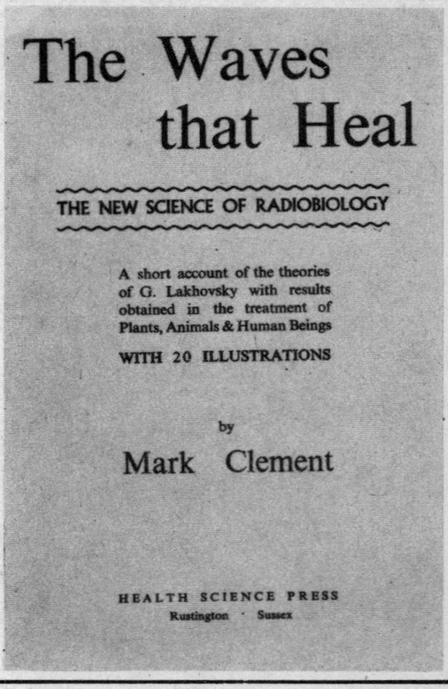

THE WAVES THAT HEAL: THE NEW SCIENCE OF RADIOBIOLOGY
Mark Clement
Health Science Press, 1965
$1.50

THE INSTITUTE FOR RELIGIOUS PSYCHOLOGY
4-11-7 Inokashira
Mitaka-shi
Tokyo, Japan

In 1962, having received a Doctoral Degree in philosophy and psychology from the Tokyo University of Education and having attained a high level of spiritual realization through many years of yoga procatice and religious asceticism, Dr. Hiroshi Motoyama founded the Institute for Religious Psychology in an effort to bring together the worlds of religious experience and scientific research. His aim was to utilize the latest technological theories and instrumentation, to verify those religious and psychic truths discovered through the centuries by yogis and great spiritual souls. He felt Parapsychology and the study of the mind-body correlation to be the most appropriate means for clarifying the mechanism through which psi-ability and religious realization manifest, and for distinguishing between psychopathological and paranormal phenomena. Such an approach, he thought, would also be very helpful in devising a safe and efficacious method through which each individual could carry on his own religious practice, suitable to his particular nature, so as to create peace and harmony in his own life, and make evolution in his mind. The Institute has therefore carried out the triple function of: (1) undertaking high-level scientific research of physiological-psychological processes, (2) teaching appropriate methods of yoga and zazen practice for mental-spiritual evolution, and (3) giving consultations on physical and mental health problems, and those difficulties met in religious development. In addition, the Institute, along with "The International Association for Religion and Parapsychology," publishes a monthly newspaper of its activities, a highly professional journal appearing quarterly, and maintains a full-time acupuncture clinic.

The Institute, a three-story reinforced concrete building, is located on the grounds of Tama Mitsu Shrine in beautiful Inokashira Park, MiTaka City, only 25 minutes from central Tokyo by public train. The Institute is staffed by about 10 people, Japanese and foreign, and in addition to Dr. Motoyama has two full-time researchers.

Motoyama's Apparatus for Measuring the Condition of the Meridians and the Corresponding Internal Organs of the Living Body (pat. 599776)

The 14 major meridians, each corresponding to a particular internal organ, terminate at the tips of the fingers and toes at points called "seiketsu" points. With this machine, especially designed and perfected electrodes, capable of measuring skin current, capacity, and potential, are placed at the 28 seiketsu points and an electrical stimulation of 3 volts is given. The machine is then able to measure resistance of skin current value before, during, and after polarization caused by the electric stimulation. One can thereby measure the basic situation of the living body *before* (the only machine to date that can do this) polarization is induced by the electrical stimulation necessarily given during measurement. It can also determine how strong the defensive reaction is to the given stimulation, as the body reacts to maintain "homeostasis." In this way it is possible to detect whether an abnormal or unbalanced situation exists in any meridian or internal organ, and determine whether such an altered state is functional or constitutional. (An attached computer provides for rapid diagnosis—the whole process takes 5 to 10 minutes—and contains in its memory bank, the criteria for determining normal or abnormal functioning of meridians and internal organs.) It can also determine whether such an unbalanced situation is caused by an excess or deficit of "Ki" (vital energy) and whether a particular meridian is excessively excited or weak.

Thus this machine can be used in acupuncture treatment to determine exactly which point of which meridian must be treated and how much stimulation should be given. Hospitals have found it very useful for a general screening of the body to determine which part might be affected by such things as tumors or cancer, and which internal organs may be functioning abnormally, thus being able to predict what illnesses a person might acquire in the future. The machine can be used in carrying out a variety of physiological experiments, and can indicate the daily or seasonal biorhythm of the body, whether a person's nervous system is primarily sympathetic or parasympathetic, and whether a person has any chakras awakened and working, thus capable of manifesting psi-ability.

This machine is now on sale in Japan and abroad. For more information, please contact: San-ei Instrument Co. Ltd., Nishi-Okubo 2-223-2 Shinjuku, Tokyo or The Institute for Religious Psychology. A 200 page book is available on the use of this machine entitled: *How to Measure and Diagnose the Function of Acupuncture Meridians and the Corresponding Internal Organs.*

ARIGO: Surgeon of the Rusty Knife

The astounding story of the Brazilian peasant who mystified the medical profession with his surgical and healing powers

by John G. Fuller — Author of *Incident at Exeter*

Afterword by Henry K. Puharich, M.D.

ARIGO: SURGEON OF THE RUSTY KNIFE
John G. Fuller
Thomas Y. Crowell Co., 1974
$7.95

"It is an established *fact* that Ze Arigo, the peasant Brazilian surgeon-healer, could cut through the flesh and viscera with an unclean kitchen- or pocket-knife and there would be no pain, no hemostasis—the tying off of blood vessels—and no need for stitches. It is a *fact* that he could stop the flow of blood with a sharp verbal command. It is a *fact* that there would be no ensuing infection, even though no antisepsis was used.

"It is a fact that he could write swiftly some of the most sophisticated prescriptions in modern pharmacology, yet he never went beyond third grade and never studied the subject. It is a fact that he could almost instantly make clear, accurate, and confirmable diagnoses or blood pressure readings with scarcely a glance at the patient.

"It is a fact that both Brazilian and American doctors have verified Arigo's healings and have taken plicit color motion pictures of his work and operations. It is a fact that Arigo treated over three hundred patients a day for nearly wo decades and never charged for his services. "It is a fact that among his patients were leading executives, statesmen, lawyers, scientists, doctors, aristocrats from many countries, as well as the poor and desolate. It is a fact that Brazil's former President, Juscelino K Bitschek, the creator of the capital city of Brasilia and himself a physician, brought his daughter to Arigo for successful treatment. It is a fact that Arigo brought about medically confirmed cures in cases of cancer and other fatal diseases that had been given up as hopeless by leading doctors and hospitals in some of the most advanced countries in the Western world.

Spiritual Healing

The idea that a person can act as a vehicle to transmit energy from a higher universal force to another is central to spiritual healing. Healing can be conveyed through prayer or the transference of one's energy, which serves to activate the healing process. This ability appears to require a great love for one's fellow man, and a "sense of mission" devoid of ambition or self-interest. Spiritual healing was once believed to be primarily a process of heightening an individual's suggestibility; PSI researchers are now examining what suggestibility may in fact mean. Research in electrophotography, for example, has revealed that the energy patterns around a healer's fingertips change as the healing process begins. Because of the pioneering nature of this research, such results at this stage must be viewed as inconclusive. The disparaging attitude reflected in the use of such terms as "suggestibility" will hopefully be replaced by a less prejudiced attitude amenable to revealing the dynamics of healing.

EXPLORE YOUR PSYCHIC WORLD
Ambrose A. Worrall and Olga N. Worrall, with Will Oursler
Harper & Row, 1970
$4.95

... is a product of the deeper search as carried on by the Commission for the Study of Healing. ... It is based on a series of six sermons on spiritual healing conducted by Olga and Ambrose Worrall in the fall and winter of 1967–68.

PSYCHIC SURGERY
Tom Valentine
Henry Regery, 1973.
$6.95.

Examines . . . increasing reports of "healers," many of them the Philippine Islands, who claim the phenomenal ability to perform psychic surgery. These practitioners claim that the human body is opened for surgery without the use of instruments; only the bare hands of the healer touch the patient. The psychic surgeon uses no anaesthetic The patient remains fully conscious but feels no pain. . . .

HINTS FOR HEALERS
Ursula Roberts
Available from:
The secretary of Ursula Roberts
Sunny Gardens Road
Hendon, London N.W. 4 1SL
10 new pence or $1.00

FAITH HEALING
Louis Rose
Penguin, 1971
$1.25.

AN OUTLINE OF SPIRITUAL HEALING
Gordon Turner
Warner Paperback Library 1972
$1.25

DRUM AND CANDLE
David St. Clair
Doubleday, 1971
$3.00

THE SPIRITUAL HEALER HEALER: THE JOURNAL OF SPIRITUAL HEALING AND PHILOSOPHY
Monthly, $5.7

Order from:
The Healer Publishing Company, Burrows Lea
Shere, Guilford
Surrey, England

"WONDER" HEALERS OF THE PHILIPPINES
Harold Sherman
DeVorss & Company, 1974.
$5.25

ERNEST HOLMES MEMORIAL RESEARCH FOUNDATION
P.O. Box 75127
Los Angeles, Calif. 90075

Research into spiritual healing to "further refine, improve and discover new techniques of spiritual healing that everyone can use."

Write for details.

NOW AVAILABLE!
CASSETTE RECORDINGS OF ALL THE TALKS

SCIENCE OF MIND SYMPOSIUM
"SCIENTIFIC APPROACH TO SPIRITUAL HEALING"

Each speaker is introduced by
Master of Ceremonies Robert Young
(TV's Dr. Welby)

(A) Cleve Backster, CELLULAR CONSCIOUSNESS
(B) Robert N. Miller, Ph.D., SCIENTIFIC EVIDENCE FOR THE EFFECTIVENESS OF PRAYER
(C) O. Carl Simonton, M.D., MEDITATION AND CANCER
(D) Gloria Swanson, RECOLLECTIONS OF THINGS SPIRITUAL
(E) Marcel Vogel, Ph.D., THOUGHT AND MOLECULAR STRUCTURE
(F) Olga Worrall, Ph.D., SCIENTIFIC STUDIES OF UNCONVENTIONAL HEALING

SINGLE CASSETTES $5   SET OF ALL SIX $25

Please designate by letter the cassettes of your choice

MAIL YOUR ORDER TO:
Science of Mind, P.O. Box 75127, Los Angeles CA 90075

BECOME INVOLVED!
BECOME AN ACTIVE MEMBER OF THE

ERNEST HOLMES MEMORIAL RESEARCH FOUNDATION

—a continuing program of scientific research into spiritual healing, to further refine, improve, and discover new techniques of spiritual healing that everyone can use.
At least $250,000 is needed to develop the first five-year plan. You can share in this endeavor. (All gifts are tax deductible).

MEMBERSHIP CATEGORIES:
☐ FOUNDER ($500 or more)*
☐ SUSTAINING ($250 or more)*
☐ SUPPORTING ($100 or more)*
☐ DONOR (Less than $100)

*YOU WILL RECEIVE THE SIX CASSETTE TAPES OF THE SYMPOSIUM TALKS AS A GIFT

MAKE CHECKS PAYABLE TO:
ERNEST HOLMES MEMORIAL RESEARCH FOUNDATION
MAILING ADDRESS: P.O. Box 75127, Los Angeles CA 90075

THE HEALING INTELLIGENCE: HOW YOUR INNER POWERS WORK AND HOW THEY CAN BE REAWAKENED
Harry Edwards
Hawthorn, 1965
$2.50

"'Absent healing' is healing from a distance. The only thought. that of thou t. The healer may know the patient's name, where he lives, the nature of the sickness, and that is all—but even this information is not essential. "Absent healing is as effective as contact healing. In my work absent healing has become the major part. The 6,000 citations given in my book *The Evidence for Spiritual Healing* mainly concern recoveries resulting from the absent healing method. On average no day passes without some supernormal healings being recorded. The absent healing work has grown continuously. This is the result of success in healing the sick, often when medical science could do no more. My post averages half a million letters a year. If there was not appreciable success it would have frittered away. . . .

"Medical science does not know a great deal about the purposes, operation, or functions of our ductless glands. There is supporting evidence and some medical admissvn of the existence of one, which I will call the 'psychic gland.' . . .

"The spiritual evolution of a person is partially determined by the way he conducts his life. Our genes are influenced and conditioned by our personal qualities, and as these are passed on from parent to child we evolve in personally, individually, and, in a more general way, racially.

NEW LIGHT ON THERAPEUTIC ENERGIES
Mark L. Gallert
James Clarke & Co. Ltd., 1966
$5.00

"The concepts of scientific research as developed by the Western world in recent centuries, with the emphasis on established principles and the efforts to fit newly observed facts into those principles insofar as possible, has had the effect of encouraging the study and use of certain types of energy—namely, those with widespread uses in material or non-organic science, such as heat, steam, short-wave, etc. and has had the effect of discouraging the study and use other types of energy. Physics has dealt mainly with non-organic uses of energy, and has attempted to explain organic application of energies in the light of the principles of non-organic uses of energy. It is our view that this has led to many misconceptions and blind spots in the study of the energy of human and animal organisms.

It is becoming apparent, from research in various fields, some of which are outlined in this book, that the characteristics of the living organism embrace more types of energy than has previously been realized, and include some energy types that have not entered into the field of non-organic science.

wilhelm Reich
the evolution of his work

DAVID BOADELLA

With Appendices by Myron Sharaf, Roger du Teil, Nic Waal, Ola Raknes & A. S. Neill

$3.95

WILHELM REICH: THE EVOLUTION OF HIS WORK
David Boadella
Henry Regnery, 1973
$3.95

ETHER, GOD AND DEVIL/COSMIC SUPERIMPOSITION
Wilhelm Reich
Farrar, Straus and Giroux, 1973
$3.80

PAMPHLET ON WILHELM REICH
Write to:
Eden
Box 34
Careywood, Idaho ID 83809

WILHELM REICH AND ORGONOMY
Ola Raknes
Pelican, 1970
$1.45

WILHELM REICH VS. THE U.S.A.
Jerome Greenfield
Illustrated,
W.W. Norton & Co. $10

ORGONE, REICH AND EROS: WILHELM REICH'S THEORY OF LIFE ENERGY
W. Edward Mann
Simon and Schuster, 1973
$8.95 also available in paper edition

THE JOURNAL OF ORGONOMY
Published semiannually in May and November by
Orgonomic Publications
P.O. Box 565, Ansonia Station
New York, N.Y. 10023
Single Issue: $3.00   Foreign: $3.50
Subscription: $6.00   Foreign $7.00

BACK ISSUES OF THE JOURNAL OF ORGONOMY
NOTE: Some issues are out of print. Those marked with an asterisk are still available from Orgonomic Publications, Inc. (address above). All back issues are now available from University Microfilms, 300 North Zeeb Road, Ann Arbor, Mich. 48106, in microfilm (Vols. 1-6, $12) or Xeroxed (8c per page with a $3 minimum order).

Some major articles:

Vol. 1, Nos. 1 & 2, 1967: "The Basic Antithesis of Vegetative Life," Part I, by W. Reich; "Wilhelm Reich" by E. F. Baker, M.D.; "United States of America v. Wilhelm Reich," Part I, by D. Blasband, A.B., LL.B.; "The Cult of Orgonomy" by N. M. Levy, M.D.

Vol. 2, No. 1, 1968: "The Basic Antithesis of Vegetative Life," Part II, by W. Reich; "United States of America v. Wilhelm Reich," Part II, by D. Blasband, A.B., LL.B.; "From Reich to Where?" by A. S. Neill; "Emotional Expression as Resistance in Therapy" by N. M. Levy, M.D.

Vol. 2, No. 2, 1968: "The Orgasm as an Electrophysiological Discharge" by W. Reich; "The Biopathic Diathesis" by R. A. Dew, M.D.; "Mass and the Gravitational Function" by C. F. Rosenblum, B.S.

Vol. 3, No. 1, 1969: "Experimental Investigation of the Electrical Function of Sexuality and Anxiety (Part I)," by W. Reich; "A Further Study of Genital Anxiety in Nursing Mothers," by E. F. Baker, M.D.; "The Biopathic Diathesis (Part II)," by R. A. Dew, M.D.

Vol. 3, No. 2, 1969: "Experimental Investigation of the Electrical Function of Sexuality and Anxiety (Part II)" by W. Reich; "Problems of Atmospheric Circulation (Part I)" by R. A. Blasband, M.D.; "The Electroscope (Part I)" by C. F. Rosenblum, B.S.

Vol. 4, No. 1, 1970: "The Impulsive Character" by W. Reich; "Orgonomic Functionalism in Problems of Atmospheric Circulation (Part II. The Drought)" by R. A. Blasband, M.D.; "The Electroscope (Part II)" by C. F. Rosenblum, B.S.

Vol. 4, No. 2, 1970: "The Impulsive Character (Part II)" by W. Reich; "Problems of Atmospheric Circulation (Part III. On Desert)" by R. A. Blasband, M.D.; "The Red Shift" by C. F. Rosenblum, B.S.; "The Biopathic Diathesis (Part IV)" by R. A. Dew, M.D.

Vol. 5, No. 1, 1971: "The Impulsive Character (Part III)" by W. Reich; "Development of a Cancer Biopathy" by M. Herskowitz, D.O.; "Intolerance of Aggression—A Case History" by C. Konia, M.D.

Vol. 5, No. 2, 1971: "The Impulsive Character (Part IV)" by W. Reich; "The Orgasm Reflex: A Case History" by W. Reich; "The Two Aspects of Orgone Therapy" by N. M. Levy, M.D.; "On Armor, War, and Peace," by P. Mathews, M.A.; "Thermal Orgonometry" by R. A. Blasband, M.D.

Vol. 6, No. 1, 1972: "The Impulsive Character (Part V)" by W. Reich; "A Case of Masochism" by E. F. Baker, M.D.; "Thermal Effects of the Reich DOR-Buster" by C. Konia, M.D.; "The Temperature Difference: Experimental Protocol" by C. F. Rosenblum, B.S.

Vol. 6, No. 2, 1972: "The Carcinomatous Shrinking Biopathy" by W. Reich, M.D.; "The Biopathic Diathesis (Part V: The Pulmonary Biopathies)" by R. A. Dew, M.D.; "An Analysis of the U.S. Food and Drug Administration's Scientific Evidence Against Wilhelm Reich" by R. A. Blasband, M.D. and C. F. Rosenblum, B.S.

Vol. 7, No 1, 1973: "The Natural Organization of Protozoa from Orgone Energy Vesicles," by W. Reich; "Schizophrenia—Dynamics and Treatment," by E. F. Baker, M.D.; "The Rise of the Psychopath," by B. Koopman, M.D., Ph.D.

Vol. 7, No. 2, 1973: "The Natural Organization of Protozoa from Orgone Energy Vesicles," by W. Reich; "An Appreciation of Reich," by L. Wyvell; "Orgonomic Morphology," by N. C. Hale; "Gastrointestinal Peptic Ulcer," by R. A. Dew, M.D.; "The Passive-Feminine Schizophrenic," by C. Konia, M.D.

THE MYSTERY OF HEALING
The Medical Group
Theosophical Research Center, London
Quest, 1968.
$1.45

"From the point of view of this study, all chronic systemic diseases are psychosomatic. This is to say that the cause of disharmony in the body is an *interior* disharmony, registering as physical disease, or ill-health; the psychic and somatic elements thus appearing as two sides of a single entity. With increasing frequency, medical circles are recognizing that physical disorders which resist attempts at treatment may often have their origin in the psyche, and are not accessible to physical treatment alone. The association of peptic ulcers with sudden mental shock, or prolonged anxiety, is well established, while many cases of chronic colitis are known to have a psychological origin. Similarly, severe malfunctions of the heart, chronic skin diseases, and general muscular weakness are often traced to emotional conflict, and can only be cured by resolving the latter.

"Modern medicine has tended to concentrate so exclusively upon the elaborations of physical detail, and has assembled such a vast array of more or less important material concerning the physical mechanism, that the real significance of the inner man, the consciousness that uses the body, has often failed to be recognized. Psychological medicine, which has received so much greater recognition in recent years than hitherto, constitutes a healthy healthy.

"The modern emphasis on preventive aspects of medicine in such matters as diet, hygiene, environment and working conditions is admirable as far as it goes. But it is still far too much engrossed with seeking immunity from specific diseases by means of shortcuts, such as the use of prophylactic innoculations, and too little with probing the fundamental causes and applying commonsense methods which promote what is already being described as 'positive health.'"

Radionics And Medical Radiesthesia

Radionics and medical radiesthesia are systems of medicine involving the use of a variety of instruments that enable an individual to focus his mind on and rectify a patient's condition. It has been speculated that this technique may involve a latent ability in all individuals to somehow make direct contact with the energy blueprints of others and through a strong mental focus stimulate a healing process. While these practitioners use a large variety of increasingly sophisticated instruments, and offer numerous theories to explain how the process seems to work, the central underlying agreement is that the mind of the operator is central to the entire process.

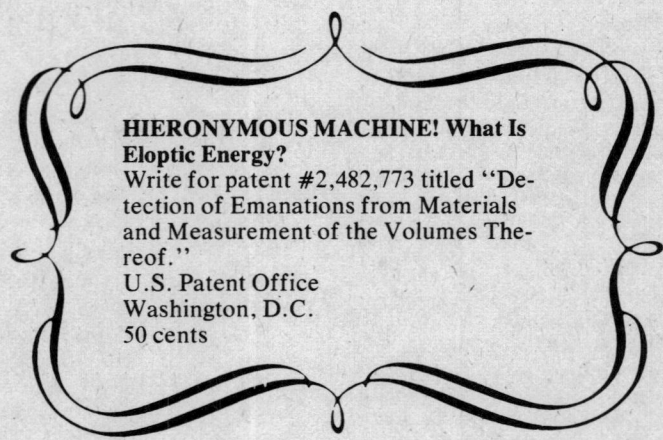

HIERONYMOUS MACHINE! What Is Eloptic Energy?
Write for patent #2,482,773 titled "Detection of Emanations from Materials and Measurement of the Volumes Thereof."
U.S. Patent Office
Washington, D.C.
50 cents

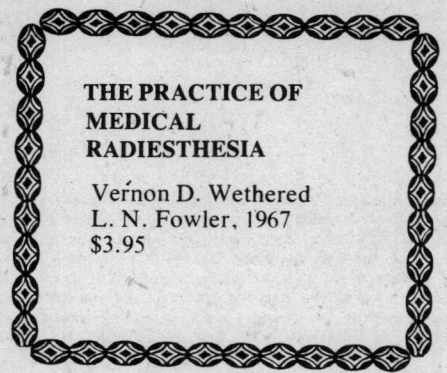

THE PRACTICE OF MEDICAL RADIESTHESIA

Vernon D. Wethered
L. N. Fowler, 1967
$3.95

The work of George De La Warr can be explored in:

MATTER IN THE MAKING
Langston Day in collaboration with George De La Warr
Vincent Stuart, 1966
$6.50

and

NEW WORLDS BEYOND THE ATOM
Langston Day and George De La Warr
EP Publishing, republished in 1973
$7.00

First published 1956
pp. 176

What kind of world would we discover beyond the atom?

A clue to this problem is contained in this book which describes fascinating research work carried out in the fifties by the Delawarr Laboratories, Oxford, work which revealed new forms of radiation previously unknown to Science.

The discoveries are a step away from the gross materialism which still fetters scientific thought towards a new standpoint bridging the world of matter and new worlds of subtle influences. They are the birthcry of a fresh and highly important branch of science.

They throw light on some of the enigmas of Physics and Biology, such as the origin of shapes and forms in Nature, the means whereby vital energy passes to living things, and the mystery of the creation of matter out of an apparent void.

They are also likely to affect our daily lives in a variety of ways. Instruments have been invented which make use of these radiations for diagnosis and therapy, the stimulation of the growth of crops and the destruction of pests by a broadcasting technique, the detection of metals and minerals, and the analysis of foods and other substances. A camera which has undergone exhaustive tests is able to photograph the flower which is due to grow from a seed, and the clinical condition of a patient who may be hundreds of miles distant.

DELAWARR LABORATORIES LIMITED
Raleigh Park Road
Oxford, England

Write for current publications list. Back issues of *Mind and Matter* (the original journal of the Mind and Matter Trust) and *The Radionic-Magnetic Centre Newsletters* are available. Also papers by the late G. W. De la Warr.

This survey of the activities of Delawarr Laboratories is primarily written for those who are interested in what has come to be known as 'fringe medicine' and in particular Radionic therapy, Chromotherapy, Magnetic and Vibration therapy. The directors of the Company realise that many people who have been to the Laboratories may find themselves in possession of this small brochure and will already know something about the structure of the Laboratories and its activities. We should like these people to bear with us if what is contained herein is already known to them.

One of the most important things concerning the structure of the Company is the Board of Directors and there has been a great deal of confusion in the past regarding the Board caused mainly by claimants to directorship of this Company. In 1954 the Company was registered as a limited liability company, the directors being Mr. G. Warr, Mr. G.W. de la Warr, Mrs. M. de la Warr. There have only been three changes of directors; the first occasion at the death of Mr. G. Warr, the second occasion occurring when Miss A. de la Warr and Miss D. de la Warr were elected to the Board, the third change being upon the death of Mr. G.W. de la Warr on 31st March, 1969.

The present Board of Directors consists of Mrs. M. de la Warr as the Managing Director, and Mrs. E.A. Hudak (née de la Warr) and Mrs. D. Di Pinto (née de la Warr). Apart from the late Mr. Warr and the late Mr. G.W. de la Warr there have been no other directors at any time during the life of the Company.

Generally speaking, the Company operates on a triple programme basis, which is to say that it has three principal disciplines. Perhaps the most important side of the work of the Laboratories is the Radionic practice which has been operated by Mrs. de la Warr since approximately 1943 and which is responsible for the organisation of treatment for an average of 200 patients at a time. The Practice operates on the basis of Radionic therapy but patients who need supportive and supplementive therapy receive Colour therapy, Vibration therapy (particularly in the case of músculo-skeletal conditions) and Magnetic therapy principally concerned with altering blood chemistry and relieving vasomotor conditions such as hay fever and bronchial asthma.

These treatments are given by properly qualified staff and Radionic therapy is the particular responsibility of one technician who is required to change the treatment 'rates' on approximately 150 instruments, six times a day.

The second discipline which has occupied a great deal of the Laboratories' time and resources, is research; both original and corroborative. Corroborative research is necessary in order to bring the findings of other research workers in line with the work carried out at the Laboratories and a long sequence of research of this nature has been carried out using the theories of the late Dr. Albert Abrams as a hypothesis. Since the inception of the Laboratories, the director of research was Mr. G.W. de la Warr who accepted complete responsibility for the initiation and implementation of the research programme.

Original research is carried out into methods of bringing about changes in organic and inorganic substances using unconventional equipment and instrumentation based on original hypotheses. Into this category comes methods of 'treating' human beings and animals and increasing either the growth rate or the yield or both, of plant life. Research under this classification is primarily concerned with bringing about changes in organic and inorganic substances with an intermediate vehicle such as a blood specimen in the case of human beings; a hair sample in the case of animals and soil and seed samples in the case of plant life.

Other original research is carried on into the problem of endeavouring to bring about changes in inorganic substances which eventually will bring about changes in organic substances such as subjecting pure distilled water to magnetic fields in an endeavour to create energy fields within the distilled water which would be inimical with the energy fields of true substances. Thus it is considered feasible to subject distilled water with the energy field of Vitamin C (ascorbic acid) and feeding this 'energised' water to Laboratory animals under controlled circumstances in order to determine whether or not such animals become deficient in Vitamin C so as to produce scorbutus. The same hypothesis is utilised in the subjection of a neutral substance such as vermiculite (which is a chemically stable micaceous substance capable of absorbing up to 25 times its own weight in water) with very weak magnetic fields designed to impart the energy fields of plant macro elements. Although of course the substance remains chemically the same, research has shown that under certain circumstances it is possible to obtain an increase in growth rate or yield if the plant is grown in this substance which has been 'treated' whereas of course under ordinary circumstances, since the material is completely chemically stable, it neither dissolves nor breaks down and therefore liberates nothing, not even oxygen, into water.

The third discipline is concerned with the manufacture of special and original instruments necessary for research projects, which means that a design and development programme go hand in hand with the workshop production and the instrument department also makes a range of standard Radionic therapy instruments, both for diagnosis and treatment, together with Colour therapy instruments as well as making Magnetic therapy and Vibration therapy instruments for ethical distribution.

In general, the Company does not employ a qualified doctor as a medical adviser although during the period of from 1954 to 1960 a Dr. A. Taylor-Smith and a Dr. J. Ritchie and a Dr. Ashraf Kazmi became medical advisers to the Laboratories in the order as shown above. No person has been employed as a medical adviser since 1960.

In the last twenty-five years, sixty-three technical papers have been published, together with three hard-back books entitled *New Worlds Beyond the Atom*, *Matter in the Making* and *Biomagnetism*. The first two titles were written in collaboration with Mr. G. Langston Day and the third book was written in collaboration with Dr. Douglas Baker.

Delawarr Laboratories have also carried out a great deal of research on the controversial subject of what has come to be called 'thoughtography'. During the formative research years, some 12,000 photographs were taken between 1950 and 1960 and many of the technical papers written by Mr. de la Warr described this particular line of research.

In general, the Laboratories have not worked with collaborators except where large-scale agricultural experiments have been carried out through the courtesy of a farmer possessing fields in reasonable juxtaposition to enable control sampling to be carried out. All the original research work was carried out by the Laboratorie on their own premises involving only members of the staff employed by the Company. There were two notable exceptions to this in the latter stages of the work when a Mr. John Rawson and a Mr. Tony Broad did work under the Laboratories' guidance, in their own homes and using apparatus supplied in basic detail by Delawarr Laboratories and set up and constructed by these two gentlemen. There never have been any other collaborators in this particular field.

The present organisation of the Company shows two divisions other than the parent company and these two divisions are Sonic Therapeutics Ltd. and the Radionic-Magnetic Centre Organisation. This last organisation was formed to enable some form of participation to take place on the part of the large number of persons who display interest in the work of the Laboratories and in fringe medicine in general. Thus the Radionic-Magnetic Centre Organisation is responsible for disseminating information to these persons who become members of the Organisation and pay an annual subscription. The Organisation mounts an annual general meeting, the theme of which is different every year and invites notable scientists and guest speakers according to the current theme. This membership is open to any person but does not, of course, give that person a right to vote at meetings of the parent company nor does it give a person the right to control any part of the business of Delawarr Laboratories Ltd.

The Laboratories are contained in three separate blocks of buildings, arranged in an estate of approximately 1¾ acres. The main block consists of a reception and secretary's office, the consulting room, the accounts room, the two principal treatment rooms, the publications office, the board room and an annexe containing the dispensary and a research room. The second block proximal to the first block contains the instrument-making section, workshop and carpentry shop, together with the outside maintenance staff room. The third block which is situated approximately 100 yards away from the central blocks, consists of the physics laboratory, the chemistry laboratory, the central records library, an electronics room, metal store and two dark rooms. The central records library contains approximately 1,100 volumes of technical and reference books covering the fields of anatomy, physiology, biology, chemistry, physics, bacteriology, zoology, and parasitology, crystalography, horticultural chemistry and practice, mathematics, photography and laboratory techniques. It also contains records of all patients passing through the practice within the last 10 years filed in alphabetical order, year by year since 1957.

The Company of necessity, gives instructions in the use of the diagnostic instrument and has also published a standard manual of Radionic practice which has been available for sale. This manual sets out the standard recommendations for carrying out any diagnosis, extracting information at consultations, setting down the information as a result of the analysis and writing the summaries of reports and the supporting letters subsequent to the analysis being carried out. The manual also includes short sections on fundamental electricity such as would be used by physiotherapists and Radionic practitioners and gives a certain amount of historical data regarding Radionic therapy. The Company maintains correspondence with several eminent physicists, physicians and scientists, both in this country and abroad and has entertained at the Laboratories, guests from America, Sweden, Denmark, Spain, South Africa, New Zealand, Australia, Bahamas, Ghana, Canada, Venezuela, Greece, Germany, France, Italy, Belgium, Netherlands, Norway, Finland, India and Pakistan.

February, 1971

FRINGE MEDICINE
Brian Inglis
Faber and Faber, 1964
$3.50

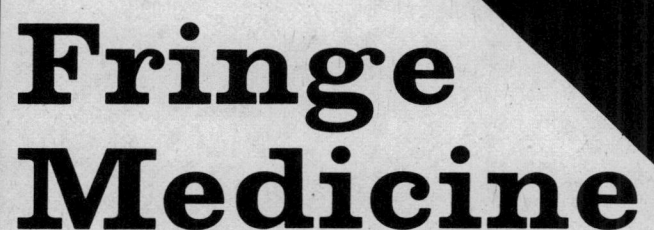

Disillusionment has been growing recently with orthodox medicine: not only in Britain, but in Europe and America. The successive triumphs of medical science, since Pasteur showed the way, have proved to be less remarkable than they seemed: although many diseases have been banished, and others rendered relatively harmless, the problem of disease remains.

Inevitably there has been an increase of interest in 'fringe medicine' – a term at first used derisively, but now treated with more respect, and applied to a wide range of clinical techniques not taught in orthodox medical schools. Some of their practitioners, for example the homeopaths, have acquired a precarious foothold in the National Health Service; others, like osteopaths and chiropractors, flourish outside it.

'This book will cause a healthy scandal. It is a frontal attack on the narrow-minded orthodoxy of the medical establishment and a spirited defence of the unorthodox methods practised on its fringes. Among these the author includes nature cures and herbalism; homeopathy, osteopathy, and chiropractice; acupuncture; psychotherapy and hypnosis; faith healing and radiesthesia . . . the author's main argument . . . is of vital importance to us all.' Arthur Koestler in *The Observer*

. . . This book cannot be dismissed as a bright and indiscriminate diatribe by a writer with a natural sympathy for the bizarre and a feverish reaction to authority. It is the work of an extraordinarily gifted and constructive mind. I would hazard that some of the ideas he expresses may well become part of the basic currency of medicine. If any doctor resents the author's opinions he should at least reflect that Mr Inglis has remarkable insight into the problems of the profession.' Arthur Guirdham, a psychiatrist, in the *Yorkshire Post*

THE PATTERN OF HEALTH: A SEARCH FOR GREATER UNDERSTANDING OF THE LIFE FORCE IN HEALTH AND DISEASE
T. Westlake, M.D.
Shambalah Publications Inc., 1973
$2.95

"This book is an account of a search for a greater understanding of the true nature of health and disease and particularly of health. It may indeed be said to form a sort of pilgrimage which led into unknown regions of medicine and allied subjects, where it was difficult to keep a sense of direction, to find the right path, and to distinguish between the truth and error.

"As the search went on it was found that the concepts of health and disease seemed to alter; indeed I was finally led right out of the material field into regions where I had to abandon my preconceptions and reorientate my ideas. But it was at this point that light began to be thrown on the whole subject, and a consistent and coherent picture of health and disease began to emerge.

"As will be seen, the thread which enabled me to find my way through the maze was provided by one clue, the supersensory force—Vis Medicatrix Naturae (the healing power of Nature)—a force which has kept on being discovered in all its various forms by so many workers both in the past and in the present, and which has been given so many different names and yet is, in my opinion, one and the same vital force of aspect of it. . . .

"Medicine during the long period of the Indian, Chinese, Greek and Arabian civilizations, culminating in the great Persian physician Avicenna (980–1037), had its roots in religion and philosophy; it remained one with the other sciences, and disease was approached through the front door of health. But with the coming of the Renaissance medicine first threw off religion, and, two centuries later, philosophy as well, becoming increasingly materialistic as it became purely scientific.

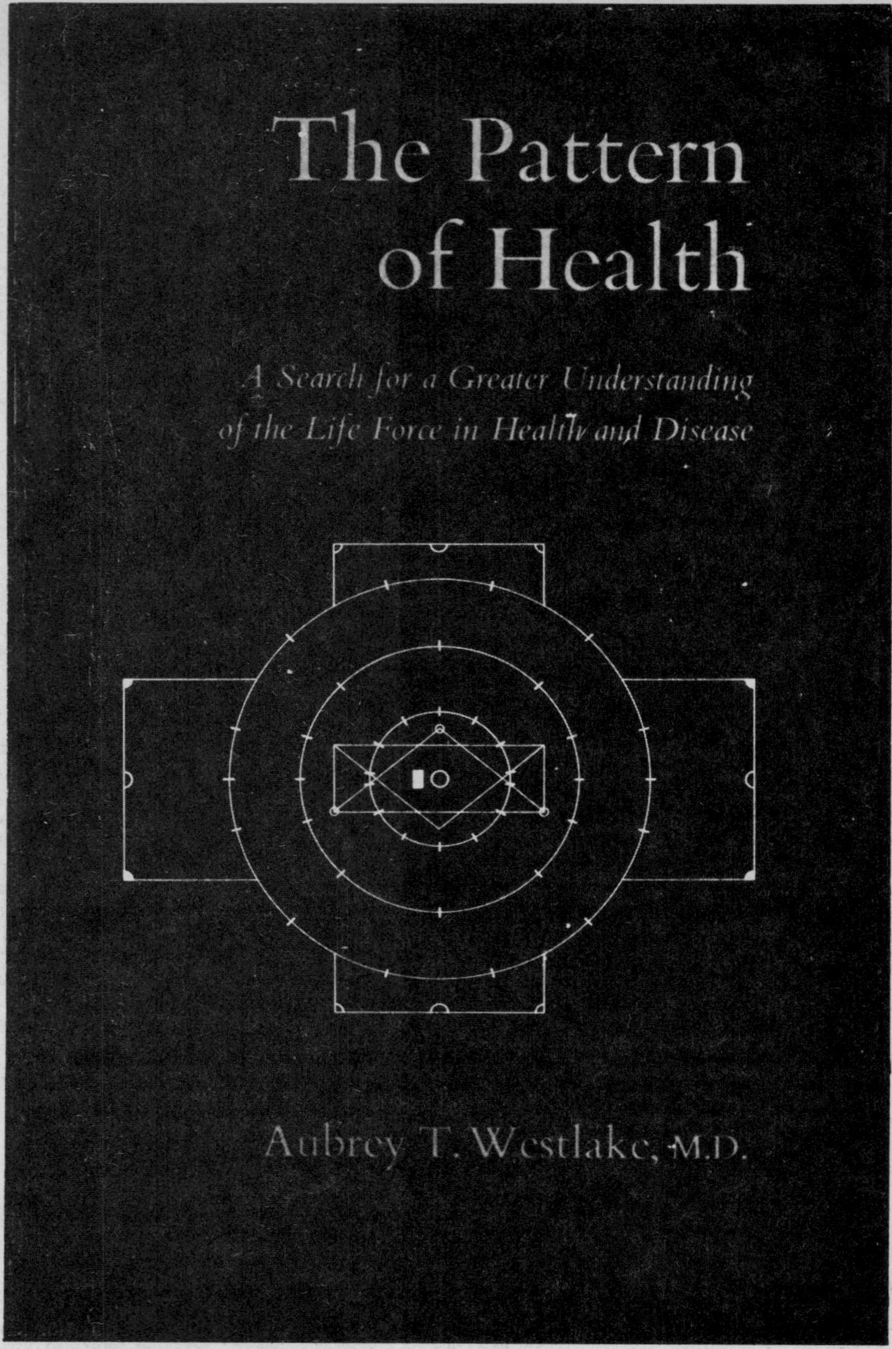

THE DIVINATION OF DISEASE: A STUDY OF RADIESTHESIA
H. Tomlinson
Health Science Press
$6.50

"This book is an attempt to give to professional colleagues an outline of the use of the pendulum in the detection and treatment of disease. Whilst a medical training is, I think, essential to the practice of the science to the best advantage, it is nevertheless true that any person, given average intelligence and application, can master and use the technique. There is nothing at all in the various divining processes which cannot be learnt, though the road thereto may be hard to travel.

"Divining processes fall into two main groups—namely Dowsing and Radiesthesia. Dowsing deals especially with the divining in the earth's crust of water, ores, minerals and other objects, and the instrument mostly used is called a divining rod. This is either a forked twig, or two pieces of whalebone joined at one end to form a V, or other modifications of this."

PRINCIPLES AND PRACTICE OF RADIESTHESIA: A TEXTBOOK FOR PRACTITIONERS AND STUDENTS
Abbe Mermet
Nelson, $6.50

"A. All bodies without exception are constantly emitting undulations or radiations.

"B. The human body enters these fields of influence and becomes the seat of nervous reactions, of some kind of current, which flows through the hands.

C. If an appropriate object, such as a rod or a pendulum, is held in the hand, the invisible flux is made manifest in the movements given to this object, which acts as a kind of indicator. . . .

A pendulum may be defined as any body suspended by a flexible link. In principle, anything held up in the air by a flexible link is capable of balancing freely.

2. SUBSTANCE

"The pendulum may be made of metal, wood, ivory, glass, marble, or liquid contained in a flagon, or any other heavy body. A watch answers the purpose quite well but using it that way puts it out of order either by shaking its spring or by magnetising it. It is preferable to use a neutral substance such as wood, glass, or ivory, or else the substance itself that one is searching for. Some radiesthetists use a hollow instrument in which fragments of the substance searched for are placed.

3. SHAPE
"The shape has the advantage of being less affected by winds. . . . WHO CAN BE A RADIESTHETIST!

"This question is often asked. The required talent is by no means rare but the gifted individual is not aware of it. It would seem that about three men out of four possess this gift in the latent state, and all that is necessary is to develop it. Sme reveal themselves to be radiesthetists at the first attempt, sometimes while ndertaking an experiment for fun. Others need guidance.

AN INTRODUCTION TO MEDICAL RADIESTHESIA AND RADIONICS
Vernon D. Wethered
C.W. Daniel, 1974
$2.75

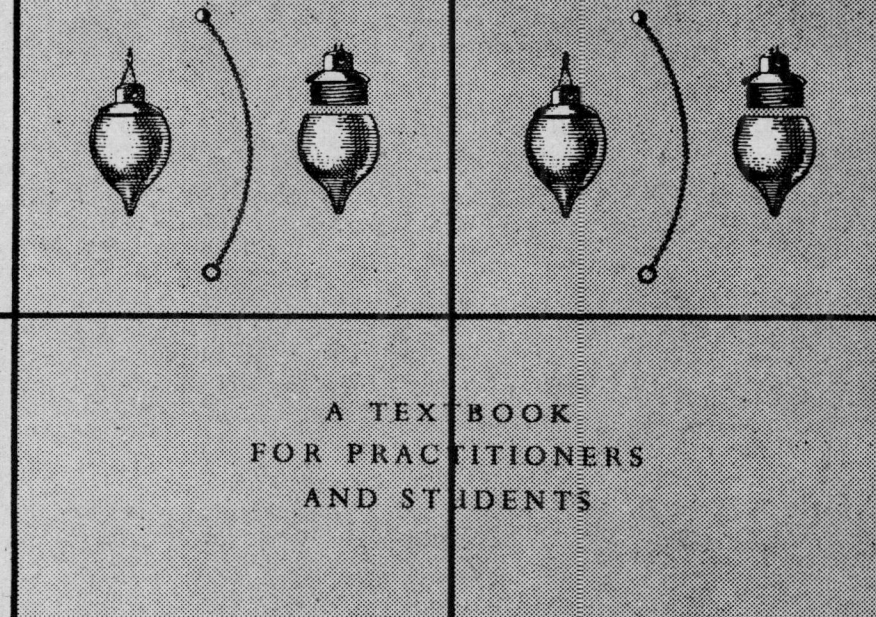

FROM:
William Tiller
"Radionics, Radiesthesia, and Physics"
From the Academy of Parapsychology and Medicine Symposium,
"The Varieties of Healing Experience"

"A basic idea in radionics is that each individual, organism or material radiates and absorbs energy via a unique wave field which exhibits certain geometrical, frequency and radiation-type characteristics. This is an extended force field that exists around all forms of matter whether animate or inanimate.

"Think of a current of vitality that flows through the etheric circuit which links the seven chakras—these being at the location of the spleen, the base of the spine, the navel, the heart, the throat, the forehead, and the top of the head. These are very essential organs in the etheric body. In the physical body we have another current of vitality, and it links up the seven major endocrine centers. These are, from the bottom, the gonads, the lyden (cells of Leydig), the adrenals, the thymus, the thyroid, the pineal, and the pituitary.

"Try to visualize these bodies as two transparencies superimposed one on the other and think of the connecting circuits just as simple loops of parallel wires. Think of the chakra/endocrine pairs, which are located in the same places in the body, as boxes attached to these loops. Think of these boxes as having three segments—that relating to the etheric on the left, that relating to the transfer between the etheric and the physical in the middle and that relating to the endocrine on the right. The function of these chakra/endocrine pairs is very much like that of power receiving stations and transmitting stations in our vehicles. Both power and information are tapped from a cosmic or environmental source into the etheric. It is transduced into a different form into the physical, is used to function in life and, in transmuted form, is radiated through the endocrine/chakra unit back into the environment. The currents in the individual circuits provide important energies for various parts of the body. In principle, we can think of great energy streams flowing through space and passing through our bodies unabsorbed and unnoticed unless we tune the chakras to couple with this power source and transduce some of its energy into the etheric system.

". . . the device contains two ports, one designated as male and the other female, for containing the witness of the patient. The witness is generally a spot of the patient's blood on a piece of filter paper. The device contains a bar magnet that is rotated to tune the device into overall resonance with the basic wave field of the patient. It contains a series of dials upon which a frequency (or set of ratios) is set that has been previously determined to be the mapping transform for the particular gland or condition under question; i.e., it allows the proper phase-resonance to the individual's wave field to be made. It contains a dial to indicate the effectiveness of operation of the gland or the degree of advancement of the condition. (The abnormality present may be manifest in the energy body and not yet materialized in the physical body, so that one must be careful in the interpretation of this reading.) Finally, it contains a cavity covered with a rubber membrane that serves to provide a yes-/no response to a particular mentally held question.

"The procedure for obtaining this response is to drag one's fingers repeatedly across the membrane without pressing so hard that the rubber bunches up and folds and makes a 'sticking' sound. The *no* response to a held thought is that nothing special happens as the membrane is rhythmically rubbed. The *yes* response to a held ought is that friction between the finger and the membrane seems to increase and the 'stick' condition is ob-

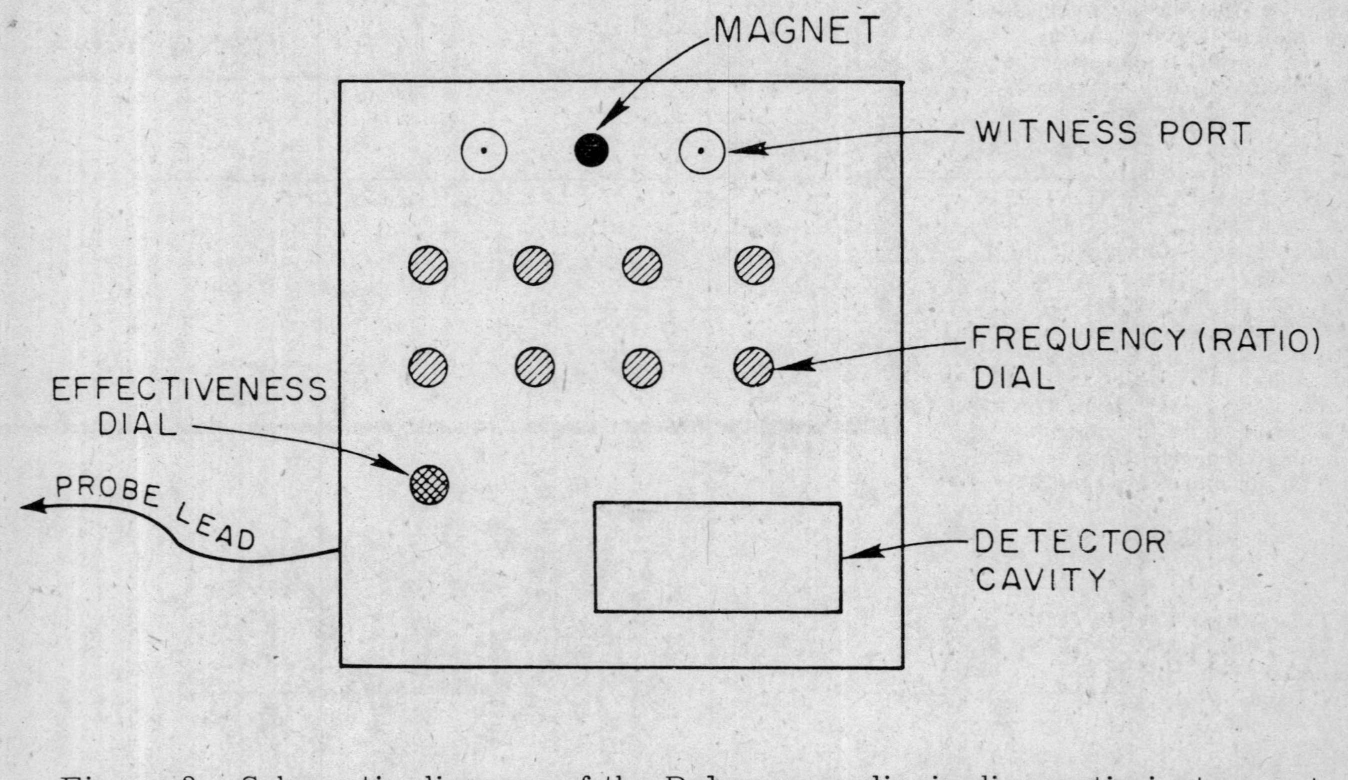

Figure 3. Schematic diagram of the Delawarr radionic diagnostic instrument.

tained; i.e., the membrane folds or flaps...."

"The technical 'Is of device operation for a health diagnosis is to first place the witness in the proper well of the instrument by finding the response to the mentally held question "Is this the proper well for this patient?" Next the magnet is slowly rotated by hand into its C.R.P. for that patient where a stick occurs to the mentally held question 'Is this the correct magnet rotation for this patient?' Next, one takes a sheet on which is written the most troublesome symptoms and, with all frequency dials set at zero and the effectiveness dial at 10, one either uses the cursor or the probe lead to touch each question in turn to see where one obtains a stick to the mentally held question 'Is this the symptom of primary importance?' After finding the major symptom, one tracks down the general location of the more important conditions supporting this symptom, followed by a more precise location, followed by the cause or causes of the trouble in terms of specific bacterium, mineral imbalance, psychological conditions, etc. Proceeding in this way, one can resolve the causes to the point of being able to prescribe particular remedies for the patient.

"In principle, if one maintains a healing attitude of high unconsciousness, it seems possible with this procedure to obtain any of the information obtainable by a first-rank psychic like Edgar Cayce."

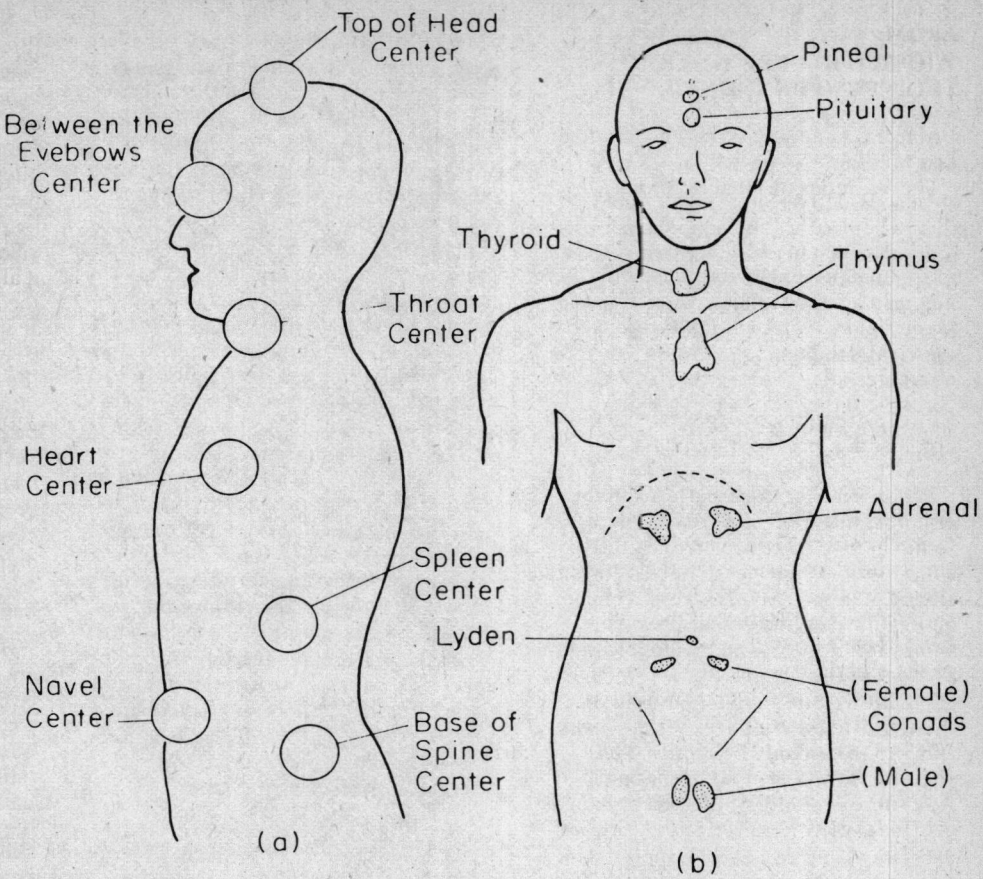

(a) Location of the 7 major chakras at the etheric level of substance,

(b) location of the 7 major endocrine glands at the physical level of substance.

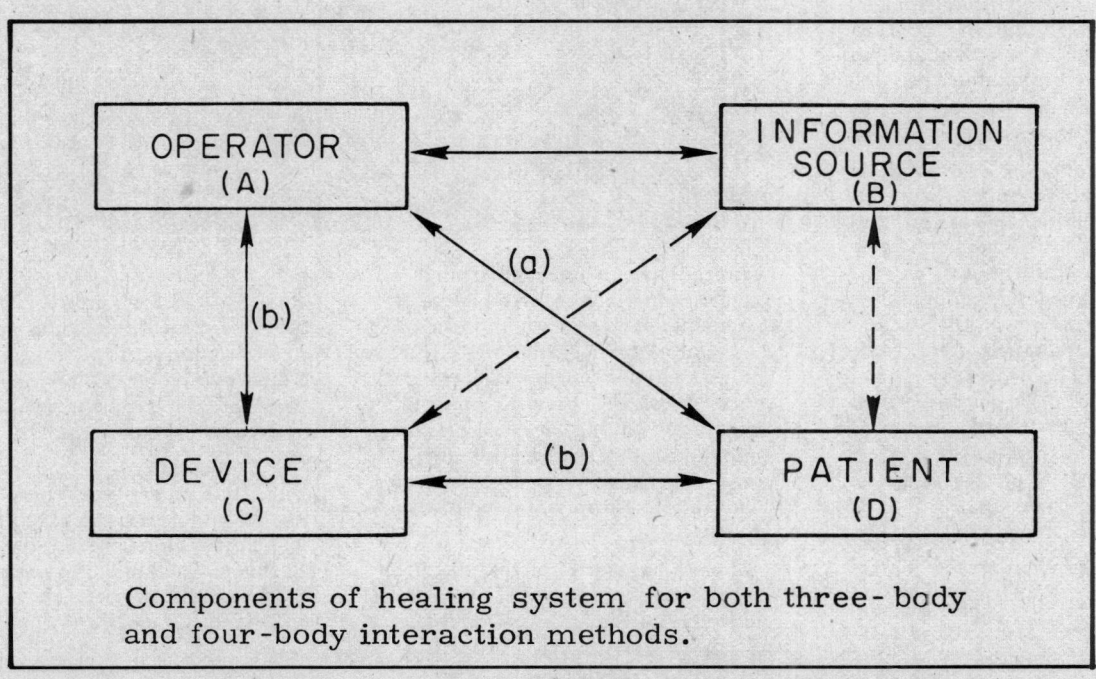

Components of healing system for both three-body and four-body interaction methods.

235

REPORT ON RADIONICS, SCIENCE OF THE FUTURE: THE SCIENCE WHICH CAN CURE WHERE ORTHODOX MEDICINE FAILS
Edward W. Russel
Neville Spearman, 1973
$10.35

"An accepted definition of a field is this: when something happens at one point in space because something else happened at another point, with no visible means by which the 'cause' can be related to the 'event', the two events are said to be connected by 'field.' . . .

"Burr's great discovery shows that disorganisation precedes—and is the cause of—disease. For he demonstrate that abnormal voltage-patterns in the organizing L-field of the body are often found before there are any physical symptoms. Abnormal voltages, for instance, can sometimes give warning of malignant growths before physical symptoms appear—an invaluable aid to doctors of the future. . . . "Since organization is the product of mind or thought—in the broadest sense—*disor*ganization can only be rectified by something akin to mind or thought. And there is plenty of evidence that this is not only possible but quite common. . . .

"Dr. Leonard J. Ravitz, Jr., a pupil of Burr, has demonstrated electronically that mind or thought has a *measurable* influence on the L-field of the human body—in other words, that mind can affect at least the electromagnetic organizer of the body. For, as far back as 1948, he discovered that it is possible to measure ty depth of hypnosis with a sensitive voltmeter because hypnosis changes the L-field. In other experiments he has also found that the state of the mind is reflected by voltage-patterns in the field; and that it is possible to detect emotionally unstable people by the erratic voltages of their fields.

"Such experiments show that mind, thought or memory—subtle, little-understood phenomena—can produce effects on the L-field *which can be measured electrically*. So it is easy to understand that negative thoughts—such as anxiety, worry or grief—can have a bad effect on the L-field. Normally the L-field controls the organization of the body but, if it is partly disorganized or upset by the influence of the mind, we would expect adverse effects on the body. That, probably, is how 'psychosomatic' illnesses are caused. . . .

"Science has shown us that all matter is composed of the basic elements in different proportions and arrangements. It has also shown that the elements themselves are composed of similar sub-atomic particles in different numbers and arrangements. The differences, therefore, between one kind of matter and another or between one element and another are merely *differences of arrangement—or of organizations in space—of common basic components*.

"Physics has shown us that the difference between one form of electromagnetic energy and another—between light-waves or radiowaves, for instance—is merely one of frequency or the number of wave-cycles per second. In other words, the difference between light-waves and radio waves or between red light and blue is merely one of *organization in time* . . . .

"Radionics, then—in which thought plays such an important part—is closer to reality in its treatment of diseases than purely chemical or biological methods. For it makes a *direct* attack on *disorganization*, which is the primary cause of disease."

A SHORT LIST OF
BOOKS and PUBLICATIONS

Published by or available from The Radionic Association at Field House.

Books:

"Radionics and the Subtle Anatomy of Man" by David Tansley, D.C.
(Health Science Press, £1.25 U.K. postage and packing 10p)

"New Light on Therapeutic Energies," by Mark Gallert, N.D.
(James Clark, £1.50, U.K. postage and packing 18p)

"A Theology of Harmony" by H. W. Heason
(Regency Press, £1.25, U.K. postage and packing 18p)

"Adventures in Healing" by Parnall Bradbury
(Neville Spearman Ltd., £1.50, U.K. postage and packing 18p)

"A Theory of Disease" by Arthur Guirdham, B.Ch., L.M.S.A.A., D.P.H.
(Neville Spearman Ltd., £1.75, U.K. postage and packing 18p)

"Design for Destiny" by Edward Russell, O.B.E.
(Neville Spearman Ltd., £1.75, U.K. postage and packing 18p)

"New Worlds beyond the Atom" by L. Day and G. de la Warr
(£2.25, U.K. postage and packing 18p)

"Blueprint for Immortality" by H. S Burr, Ph.D
(Neville Spearman Ltd., £2.10, U.K. postage and packing 18p)

"Report on Radionics" by Edward Russell, O.B.E.
(Neville Spearman Ltd., £2.95, U.K. postage and packing 20p)

Pamphlets and Journals:

"An Introduction to Radionics" (4p, U.K. postage and packing 4p)

"Memorandum and Articles of Association of the Radionic Association"
(25p, U.K. postage and packing 5p)

"Radionic Quarterly" (current issue 65p, back numbers 45p, U.K. postage and packing 5p. Annual subscription £2.50 Sterling; £3.00 in overseas currency)

Monographs:

"Question and Answer: The Use of the Pendulum" by Jane Wilcox
(15p, U.K. postage and packing 4p)

"Radionics and the Human Force Field" by David Tansley, D.C.
(30p, U.K. postage and packing 4p)

"Radionics and the Electric Patterns of Life" by David Tansley, D.C.
(20p, U.K. postage and packing 4p)

"The Pattern of Telepathic Communication" by Father Andrew Glazewski
(20p, U.K. postage and packing 4p)

"Radionics, Radiesthesia and Physics" by William A. Tiller, Ph.D.
(40p, U.K. postage and packing 5p)

"A Basic Pattern of Forces Underlying Human Existence"
by D. R. Milner, D.Sc., F. Inst. P. (15p, U.K. postage and packing 4p)

Overseas purchasers are requested to make reasonable allowance for the extra cost of mailing orders overseas, surface mail.

Cheques and Postal Orders should be crossed and made payable to
THE RADIONIC ASSOCIATION LTD.

WHY JOIN THE RADIONIC ASSOCIATION/

If you are one of the increasing number of people searching for true health and a comprehension of Universal Law in an age of "scientific" technology, if you are concerned with research, or are simply interested in any of the various forms of Extra Sensory Perception, then the Association Membership of the Radionic Association, whether you are a professional or a layman, would be of great value to you.

Apart from being the professional body representing qualified Radionic Practitioners, one of the main aims of the Association is to cater for the many and varied interests of its members, who include doctors and scientists, practitioners of various healing techniques and many laymen, all of whom are willing to pool their knowledge for the advancement of what Rudolf Steiner called the "Spiritual Science" of the New Age. Radionics leads inevitably from physics to metaphysics, from psychology to parapsychology, from philosophy to religion and the subjects studied by the Association cannot be confined within the limits of the conventional classifications of knowledge. The Association seeks to foster a friendly atmosphere in which the questions of newcomers and the contributions of those with greater experience are equally welcome.

Meetings and Conferences

General Meetings are held by the Association every two months, usually in London on Saturday afternoons, to which members may bring guests.

The annual week-end conference of the Association has reached and maintained a high standard. It is held in March and it is now the established custom to select a definite theme and invite distinguished outside speakers as well as members to take part.

The Journal and Other Publications

Lectures and reports of proceedings are published in the Association's *The Th Radionic Quarterly*, which is issued free to members and is the Association's main publication. Two pamphlets are published for those information about Radionics and other publications are available dealing with training and the constitution of the Association.

Training

In 1962 the Association founded The Radionic Trust, another company limited by guarantee, which runs the School of Radionics. The School provides Introductory Courses for those who wish to acquaint themselves with the rudiments of Radionics and Training Courses for those who wish to practice Radionics professionally and acquire the qualifications conferred by the Association, whether for treatment of humans, animals, plants or soil.

Enquiries

Enquiries should be addressed to The Secretary, The Radionic Association, Field House, Peaslake, Nr. Guildford, Surrey, GU5 9SS.

Subscriptions

Entry fee . . . 1.00
    Fellows . . . 7.00
    Members . . . 6.50
    Licentiates . . . 5.00
    Associates . . . 5.00
    Journal only . . . 2.50

RADIONICS AND THE SUBTLE ANATOMY OF MAN
David V. Tansely, D.C.
Health Science Press, 1972
$4.40

"If one examines the history and development of radionics from the pioneering work of Dr. Albert Abrams and Ruth Drown, to the latest experimental work at the de la Warr Laboratories, a curious paradox emerges.

Radionics professes to be a method of diagnosis and therapy, which is primarily concerned with the utilization of subtle force fields and energies, for the purpose of investigating and combating the causes of disease whch which ravage and the other kingdoms of nature. However, in discussions or articles, in the methods of diagnosis and treatment, and in the rate books which provide the very core of radionic therapeutic measures, one finds continual reference to the physical organic systems of man, and precious little of practical value regarding the probability of underlying force fields which might govern and determine the health of the physical form. . . .

"Regular radionic diagnostic procedure is a long and something process, somethi entailing protracted periods of tiring work, which frequently leave the practitioner drained of energy. These physically orientated methods, dealing as they do with the organic systems, cannot in the final analysis arrive at the cause of disease. It is essential to determine the conditions existing in the force centres and the subtle bodies, in order to get near to the cause of imbalances in the human force fields.

The Seven Major Spinal Chakras

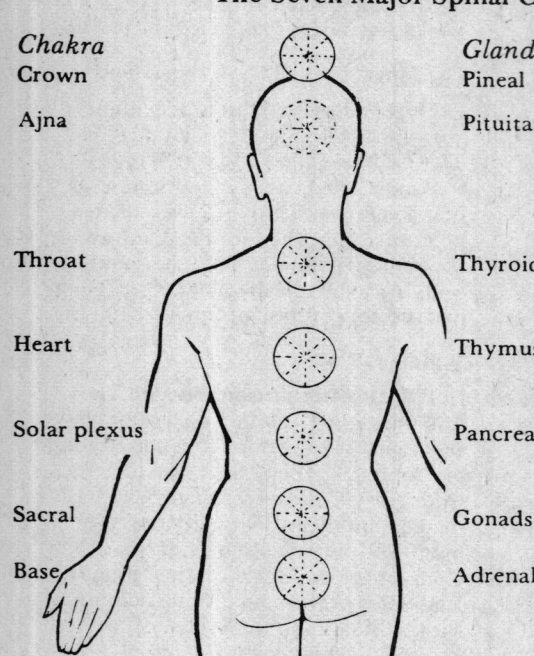

Chakra	Gland	Area Governed
Crown	Pineal	Upper brain. Right eye.
Ajna	Pituitary	Lower brain. Left eye. Ears. Nose. Nervous system.
Throat	Thyroid	Bronchial and vocal apparatus. Lungs. Alimentary canal.
Heart	Thymus	Heart. Blood. Vagus nerve. Circulatory system.
Solar plexus	Pancreas	Stomach. Liver. Gall bladder. Nervous system.
Sacral	Gonads	Reproductive system.
Base	Adrenals	Spinal column. Kidneys.

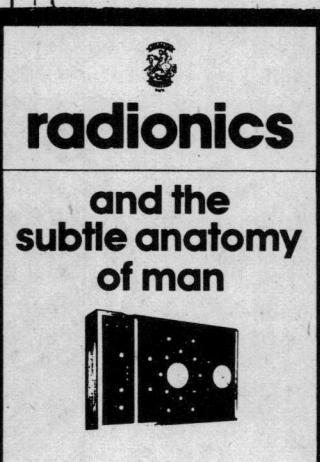

The Seven Planes and Man's Subtle Anatomy

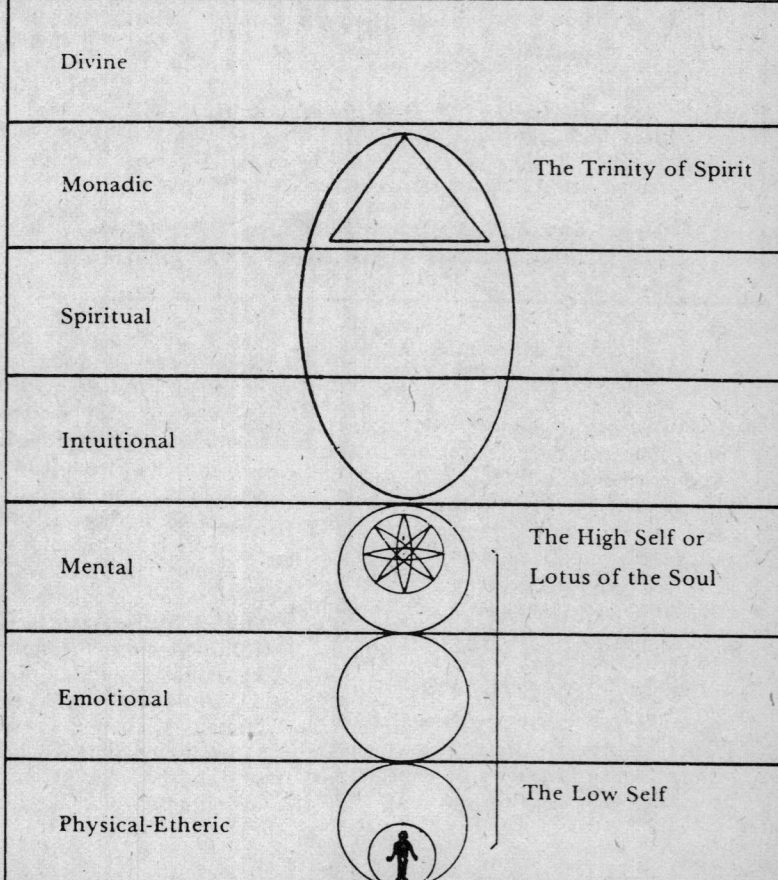

PART FIVE: MYSTERIES OF TIME AND SPACE

Many people have great difficulty in understanding how certain human behavior such as the ability to prophecy can be *possible* since it simply does not fit into time schemes that govern everyday life. Investigations of PSI which have incorporated an understanding of recent developments in physics have produced an intriguing body of speculation on how time-space can accommodate the seemingly impossible.

Time And The Multi-Dimensional Self

ne of the more intriguing ideas coming from PSI literature is that there is no past, present or future as we know it but rather that the "self" operates simultaneously at different levels of reality. One aspect of self may exist in what we would call the past and another in the future and so on. According to Jane Roberts' medium personality called Seth, " . . . everything in the universe exists at one time, simultaneously. The first words ever spoken still ring through the universe and in your terms, the last words ever spoken have already been said, for there is no beginning. It is only your perception that is limited."

THE EDUCATION OF OVERSOUL 7
Jane Roberts
Prentice-Hall, 1973
$6.95

" 'In your *what* state of development? Don't you *see*, seven?'

"Her words rang through Seven's mind, and in some indescribable way his mind expanded. Barrier after barrier previously invisible and unfelt dropped away, until Seven's comprehension itself encompassed everything he saw or knew or perceived. His consciousness circled the analogy in the sky—and he went *through* it, finding that all these times were different appearances of one inexpressible experience in which all Happening Out of Itself kept newly, freshly Happening."

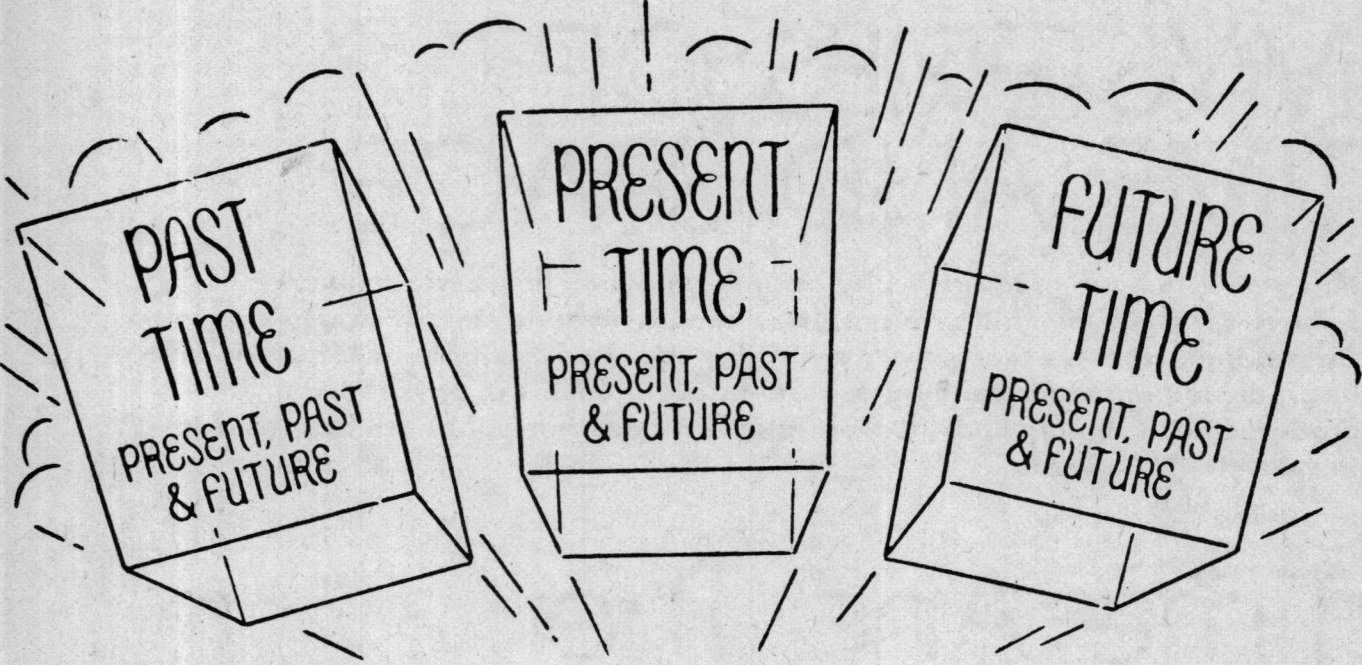

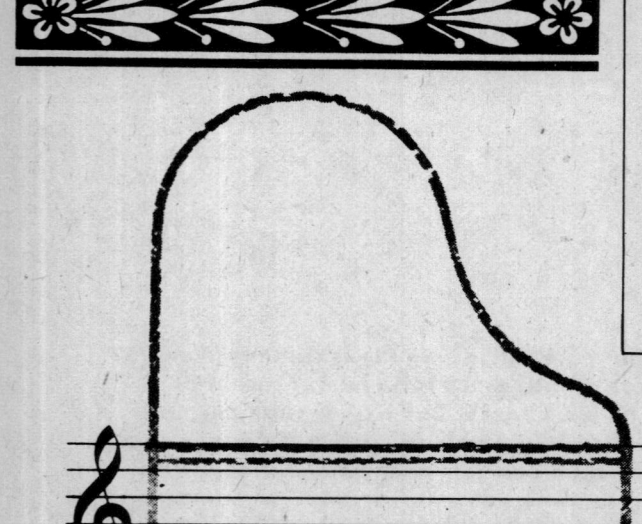

just published
The Rosemary Brown Piano Album
Seven pieces, inspired by Beethoven, Schubert, Chopin, Schumann, Brahms and Liszt. Available from your local music dealer; or in case of difficulty, direct from us. Price **60p**

Novello, music for everyone
NOVELLO
Borough Green, Sevenoaks, Kent

> *Homo duplex, homo duplex!* The first time that I perceived that I was two was at the death of my brother Henri, when my father cried out so dramatically, 'He is dead, he is dead!' While my first self wept, my second self thought, 'How truly given was that cry, how fine it would be at the theater.' I was then fourteen years old.
> This horrible duality has often given me matter for reflection. Oh, this terrible second me, always seated whilst the other is on foot, acting, living, suffering, bestirring itself. This second me that I have never been able to intoxicate, to make shed tears, or put to sleep. And how it sees into things, and how it mocks!
>
> Alphonse Daudet

MANY MANSIONS
Gina Cerminara
Signet, 1967
95 cents

A DICTIONARY OF ANGELS: INCLUDING THE FALLEN ANGELS
Gustav Davidson
Free Press, 1967
$4.95

THE PRESENCE OF OTHER WORLDS: FINDINGS OF EMANUEL SWEDENBORG
Wilson van Dusen
Harper & Row, 1974
$6.95

A WORLD BEYOND
Ruth Montgomery
Fawcett, 1972
95 cents

. . . is the account of a monumental journey of one misunderstood eighteenth-century man through the depths of his own mind to spiritual worlds.

TIME ZONE,
Satty,
Straight Arrow Books, 1973
$5.95

"There is a time in the span of civilizations when creative energy and the human spirit are wholly, if briefly focussed. When this occurs culture in all its manifestations reaches its zenith. The moment passes; civilizations decline, only to be replaced by others. This process of life appears cyclic. Communities become tribes, turn into nations and become empires which, like suns, radiate their energy to the limits of their power, then decay and finally vanish, leaving behind only traces. This cycle, which may continue until our sun—or our planet—fails us, is the principal concern of my book.

"*Time Zone* tells a story using printed images derived from past and present. This visual vocabulary is more universal and intelligible than a verbal language and can be experienced on many levels. A tale told in such a language is timely since we live in an age when visual forms are the dominant vehicle of communication through the pervasive use of electronic and printed media. An enormous barrage of images has been indiscriminately disseminated, presenting a confusing vision of the world that forces even innocent children into a neurotic life experience.

"The experience of receiving all this bewildering information creates an unhealthy emotional environment which, like the physical environments man creates, appears subject to the balancing process of nature. Since Man is a part of nature, he must continually re-examine his role in relation to the natural experience.

"We are at a critical turn: for the artificial emotional environment we have created is not in balance, has not been defined, nor has the extent of its influence been determined. If this condition continues we may unconsciously be triggering a form of mass insanity and premature decay, signs of which are already visible. Understanding this may help us clarify our reality so we can find a way to complete a natural cycle.

"Towards this understanding—a new beginning—this book is dedicated."

MYSTERIES OF TIME AND SPACE
Brad Steiger
Prentice-Hall
$7.95

SYNCHRONICITY: AN ACAUSAL CONNECTING PRINCIPLE
C. H. Jung
Princeton/Bollingen
Paperback Edition 1973
$2.45

"Jung's only extended work in the field of para-psychology aims, on the one hand, to incorporate the findings of 'extrasensory perception' (ESP) research into a general scientific point of view and, on the other, to ascertain the nature of the psychic factor in such phenomena. While he had advanced the 'synchronicity' hypothesis as early as the 1920's, Jung gave a full statement only in 1951, in an Eranos lecture; the following year (he was seventy-seven) he published the present monograph in a volume with a related study by the physicist (and Nobel winner) Wolfgang Pauli. Together with a wealth of historical and contemporary material on 'synchronicity,' Jung describes an astrological experiment conducted to test his theory.

" 'The concept of synchronicity indicates a meaningful coincidence of two or more events, where something other than the probability of chance is involved. Chance is a statistical concept which "explains" deviations within certain patterns of probability. Synchronicity elucidates meaningful arrangements and coincidence which somehow go beyond the calculations of probability. Pre-cognition, clairvoyance, telepathy, etc. are phenomena which are inexplicable through chance, but become empirically intelligible through the employment of the principle of synchronicity, which suggests a kind of harmony at work in the interrelation of both psychic and physical events.' *The Journal of Religious Thought.*"

THE FUTURE OF TIME: MAN'S TEMPORAL ENVIRONMENT
Henri Yaher et al., ed.
Anchor, 1972
$5.45

THE SENSE AND NONSENSE OF PROPHECY
Eileen J. Garrett
Berkley, 1950
75 cents

"What woman, conventional or otherwise, wouldn't like to hear that there is a handsome stranger in the offing ready to offer love, laughter, new and richer delights? Who shall blame Madame Zoola if she notes the display of riches and calculates that for a good prognostication she can earn a hundred dollars as easily as one? If she asks—and gets—the hundred dollars, her stage will begin to take on a new pattern; the settings will be more elaborate, a few added magical symbols will grace her parlor; the horoscope, the dream book and the tea-leaf reading will be discarded in favor of higher things.

"Thus, in Madame Zoola's case it is money that makes all the difference. Madame Zoola may —probably does— have a marked psychic gift. But it is a gift which she has allowed to atrophy; instead of it she uses unctuous flattery, ambiguous phrases, and half truths. . . .

". . . Who is at fault? Neither the seeker nor the giver. In the present mechanistic age of instruction, without basic education of a religious or philosophic nature, everyone is obsessed with the idea that he must get to the top in a hurry. Hard work is regarded as a fool's game. . . .

". . . Look into a crystal ball. What do you see? You see exactly what I see—nothing. Nothing, that is, that isn't already in your mind.

"'The crystal is clouded.' Why? Because you are unsure, either because your impressions are not coming to the surface quickly, or because your mind is working too hard.

"Crystal gazers—if they are at all good—are usually more genuine psychic than most other occult specialists. The lines, mounts, and shape of a hand, the spots on a tarot card, or even a mass of soggy tea leaves give at least some picture—some tangible evidence—to both reader and sitter so that the seer will be able to talk about *something* vaguely connoted in the 'magic symbols' until a message of sorts has been prepared. But the crystal itself contains no magic symbols.

"The crystal ball, although it has great historical significance, as we shall see later, is nothing but a stage property, mysterious and pretty, that adds glamour to the most ordinary seance. It has value in that it encourages greater concentration; by gazing steadfastly into the crystal the medium succeeds in shutting out the noise of the outside world, and sometimes even succeeds in achieving a slight trance. This is why many hypnotists—not the best of them, to be sure—use a crystal ball or a bright coin when trying to induce trance in their subjects.

"But the waves that come through to the subject have nothing to do with a crystal ball. During a seance the subject's subconscious is in control. His unconscious mind is working like radio, like a sensitive receiving instrument; it is incapable of thought, for conscious thought is like static to this frame of mind. But with deep concentration, even rather insensitive people are often capable of remarkable flashes of perception."

EGO AND ARCHETYPE
Edward F. Edinger
Penguin, 1973
$3.45

MAN AND HIS SYMBOLS
Carl G. Jung, ed.
Laurel, 1972
$1.25

POSSIBILITY OF EXPERIMENTAL STUDY OF THE PROPERTIES OF TIME
N. A. Kozyrev, May 2, 1968
Write to National Technical Information Service
Springfield, Va. 22151.
Ask for J P R S-45238, title, date and author

DURATION AND SIMULTANEITY
Henri Bergson
Bobbs-Merrill, 1965
$1.75

THE PHENOMENOLOGY OF INTERNAL TIME-CONSCIOUSNESS
Edmund Husserl, edited by Martin Heidegger,
Translated by James S. Churchill
Indiana University Press, 1966
$1.95

THE PROPHECIES OF NOSTRADAMUS
Erika Cheetham
Capricorn, 1973
$8.95

"Nostradamus, sixteenth-century French physician and astrologer, foresaw the events of his own and future times with remarkable clarity. From the first publication of his work *(The Centuries)* in 1555, the clairvoyant's prophecies have been coming true with startling regularity: the execution of King Charles I, the abdication of King Edward VIII, Hitler's rise and fall, the assassination of the Kennedy brothers, the Cuban missile crisis, etc. Kings, dictators, industrialists and heads of state have long heeded the seer's prophetic quatrains, and even now many of his miraculous forecasts remain to be borne out in history."

THE PHILOSOPHY OF TIME: A COLLECTION OF ESSAYS
Richard M. Gale, ed.
Doubleday-Anchor, 1967
$1.75

LAST HOUDINI SEANCE
Recording of 1936 Seance. Available on tape, reel or cassette. If reel, specify speed.
From:
64-1 Twin Lakes,
Mystic Island, N.J. 08087
$4.95

THE UNOBSTRUCTED UNIVERSE
Stewart Edward White
Dell, 1970
95 cents

"Betty," the author's wife, was a world-renowned psychic researcher. But it was only after death that Betty was able to open the channel through which the author, in forty actual witnessed conversations with his wife, was able to obtain this completely detailed factual report on what life after death really consists of and what it means to all of us.

AN EXPERIMENT WITH TIME
J. W. Dunne
Faber and Faber, 1967
$1.95

PATTERNS OF PROPHECY
Allan Vaughan
Hawthorn Inc., 1973
$7.95

"I wondered if there might be a common cause, some transcendental plan of life that preexists and guides our individual destinies. Jung spoke of synchronicities clustering around an archetypal situation. But perhaps he was only noticing particularly emotional or important (to the person) situations that exhibited more of these coincidences than overage situations. Certainly the defini tion of archetype blurred in my mind as I studied events. Everything, in some way, was archetypal. There was nothing really new under the sun.

"From the angle of the individual, his own inner 'blueprints' might incorporate countless archetypal situations, many different archetypal roles—the father, the warrior, the hunter, the lover, and so on. Certainly in my case the predicted events had greater than usual emotional significance, more coincidences clustering around them than usual. And in the background there seemed to lurk some general patterns of life that hooked them all together. In my life, then, these general patterns that tended to repeat were my individual archetypes that made up my individual 'blueprint' of life. Some writers have referred to this inner "blueprint" as the *superconscious* level of the psyche, to distinguish it from repressed and forgotten memories of the subconscious. The superconscious would seem to be the source of prophecy—and perhaps life itself.''

TIME AND ITS MYSTERIES: EIGHT LECTURES GIVEN ON THE JAMES ARTHUR FOUNDATION
New York University
Harlow Shapley, intro.,
Collier, 1962
95 cents

THE VOICES OF TIME: A COOPERATIVE SURVEY OF MAN'S VIEWS OF TIME AS EXPRESSED BY THE SCIENCES AND BY THE HUMANITIES
T. M. Frazer, ed.
George Braziller, 1966
$12.50

THE FIFTH DIMENSION
Vera Stanley Adler
Rider, 1970
$4.75

THE FATIMA PROPHECY: DAYS OF DARKNESS, PROMISE OF LIGHT
Ray Stanford
The Association for the Understanding of Man, 1972

PREDICTIONS FOR 1974
Warren Smith, ed.
Award Books, 1973
$1.25

THEY FORESAW THE FUTURE: THE STORY OF FULFILLED PROPHECY
Justine Glass
Berkley, 1970
$1.25

PROPHECY IN OUR TIME
Martin Ebon
Wilshire Book Co., 1968
$2.50

PREDICTIONS FOR 1974
By renowned psychics from around the world
Compiled and edited by Warren Smith
AWARD BOOKS AQ1184 $1.25

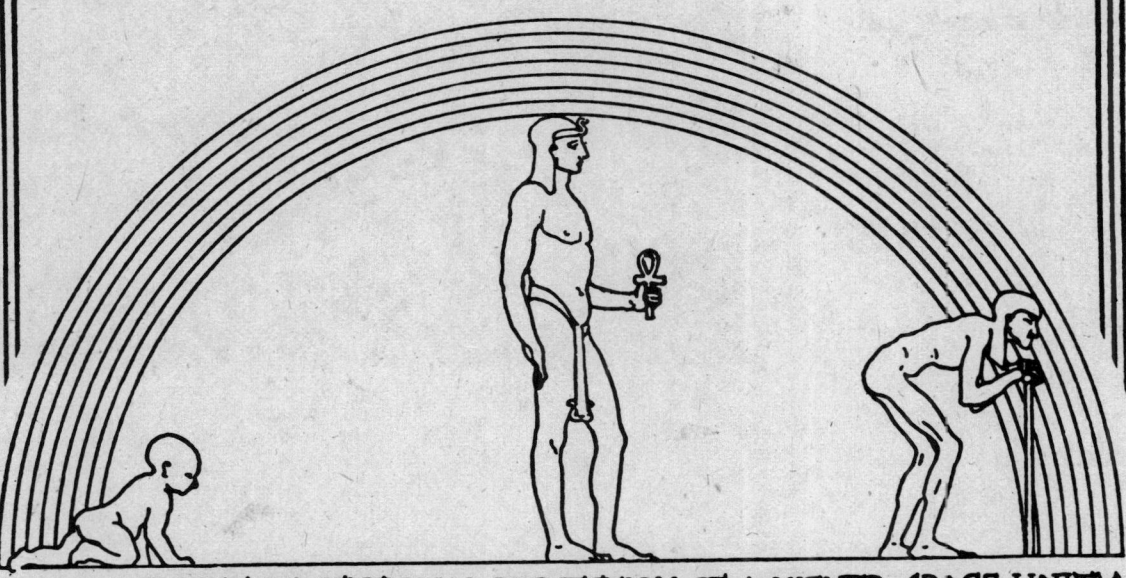

A PRIMER OF HIGHER SPACE: THE FOURTH DIMENSION
Claude Brayden
Omen Press, 1972
$2.25

WINGED PHARAOH
Joan Grant
Berkley Medallion, 1969
95 cents

FAR MEMORY: THE AUTOBIOGRAPHY OF JOAN GRANT
Joan Grant
Avon, 1969
75 cents

RETURN TO ELYSIUM
Joan Grant
Avon, 1969
75 cents

"During the last twenty years, seven books of mine have been published as historical novels which to me are biographies of previous lives I have known. . . . From early childhood, often to my extreme discomfort, I was sometimes aware beyond the usual range of the five senses. I tried to ignore the implications of this awareness, but it was too insistent; so in an attempt to understand what was happening I laboriously trained the faculty of far memory. This book describes, among other things, how I did so and what happened to me as the result."
JOAN GRANT, preface to *Far Memory*

Painter and Poet

"I have been here before,
 But when or how I cannot tell;
I know the grass beyond the door,
 The sweet keen smell,
The sighing sound, the lights around
 the shore.
You have been mine before,—
 How long ago I may not know:
But just when at that swallow's soar
 Your neck turned so,
Some veil did fall,—I knew it all of
 yore."

DANTE GABRIEL ROSSETTI, *Sudden Light*

THE BEST NOVEL OF TELEPATHY & REINCARNATION EVER WRITTEN!

WINGED PHARAOH
JOAN GRANT

"Joan Grant's novels have caused considerable comment and wonder, especially her *Winged Pharaoh*, because without scholarly study she disclosed an unusually accurate knowledge of ancient times."
JOSEPH HEAD and S. L. CRANSTON, *Reincarnation: An East-West Anthology*.

Reincarnation is frequently regarded as an Oriental concept incompatible with Western thinking and traditional belief. This encyclopedic compilation of quotations from eminent philosophers, theologians, poets, scientists, and other thinkers of every period of Western culture, and the thoroughly documented survey of reincarnation in the world religions, will serve to dispel this idea. In no sense dogmatic, the ideas presented are stimulating, challenging and inspiring. Both adherents and dissenters to the rebirth theory are represented.

This book was highly acclaimed when it was first published in a hard cover edition in 1961. It was listed in the annual report of the famous Bodleian Library, Oxford University, England, as among their sixty-nine "Chief Donations" received 1961-1962.

REINCARNATION: AN EAST-WEST ANTHOLOGY
Joseph Head and S. L. Cranston, ed.
Quest, 1970
$2.25

THE SEARCH FOR BRIDEY MURPHEY
Morey Bernstein
Lancer, 1965
$1.25

ARTHUR FORD: THE MAN WHO TALKED WITH THE DEAD
Allen Spraggett and William V. Rauscher
Signet, 1973
$1.50

SCIENTIFIC EVIDENCE OF THE EXISTENCE OF THE SOUL
Benito F. Reyes
Quest, 1970
$2.45

LIFE, DEATH AND PSYCHICAL RESEARCH: STUDIES ON BEHALF OF THE CHURCHES' FELLOWSHIP FOR PSYCHICAL AND SPIRITUAL STUDIES
Canon J. D. Pearce–Higgins and Rev. G. Stanley White, ed.
Rider, 1973
$6.75

THE EDGE OF THE UNKNOWN
Sir Arthur Conan Doyle
Berkley, 1968
75 cents

HERE AND HEREAFTER
Ruth Montgomery
Fawcett, 1968
75 cents

THE LIFE BEYOND DEATH
Arthur Ford
Berkley, 1971
$1.25

UNFINISHED SYMPHONIES: VOICES FROM THE BEYOND
Rosemary Brown
Pan, 1973
$1.25

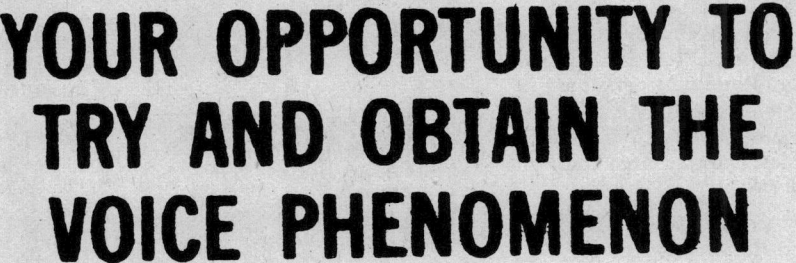

YOUR OPPORTUNITY TO TRY AND OBTAIN THE VOICE PHENOMENON

OWN PLUG-IN AERIAL

EXTERNAL AERIAL MAY ALSO BE PLUGGED IN

SWITCH FOR DIODE OR MICROPHONE OPERATION

£5.00 inc. P&P

DIODE UNIT

Fitted with two D.I.N. sockets. Just plug in your tape recorder and microphone.

Sent with instructions for use. Send your remittance of £5 to:

KHARA, 36 CASTLETON ROAD WIGSTON, LEICESTER

APPARITIONS
G. N. M. Tyrell
Collier, 1969
95 cents

In this classic of psychical research, George N. M. Tyrell submits that "ghosts" are subjective and telepathic, created in the regions of the personality outside the field of normal consciousness. Basing his theories on a vast collection of psychical data, and substantiating his arguments with more than sixty dramatic, well-documented case histories, he establishes a clear relationship between the phenomena of sensory hallucinations and modern psychology.

"The absence of memory of any actions done in a previous state cannot be a conclusive argument against our having lived through it. Forgetfulness of the past may be one of the conditions of an entrance upon a new stage of existence. The body which is the organ of sense-perception may be quite as much a hindrance as a help to remembrance. In that case casual gleams of memory, giving us sudden abrupt and momentary revelations of the past, are precisely the phenomena we would expect to meet with. If the soul has pre-existed, what we would a priori anticipate are only some faint traces of recollection surviving in the crypts of memory. . . .

"Stripped of all extravagance and expressed in the modest terms of probability, the theory [of metempsychosis] has immense speculative interest and great ethical value. It is much to have the puzzle of the origin of evil thrown back for an indefinite number of cycles of lives: to have a workable explanation of Nemesis, and of what we are accustomed to call the moral tragedies and the untoward birth of a multitude of men and women."
WILLIAM KNIGHT (Scottish philosopher and professor),
"Doctrine of Metempsychosis," Fortnightly Review
September, 1878

"Were an Asiatic to ask me for a definition of Europe, I should be forced to answer him: It is that part of the world which is haunted by the incredible delusion that man was created out of nothing, and that his present birth is his first entrance into life."
ARTHUR SCHOPENHAUER, *Parega and Paralipomena*

BREAKTHROUGH
Konstantin Raudive
Lancer Books, 1971
$1.75

. . . is the authentic document of electronic communications with the dead—the universe of human spirits. Already a source of heated debate in established scientific circles, the findings of Dr. Konstantin Raudive and his colleagues constitute the most revolutionary and thorough experimental research ever to be conducted in any area of psychic phenomena.

Using tape recorders, diodes and radio receivers, Raudive was able to hear—when the tapes were replayed—the actual voices of persons who had died—persons who were communicating to him from a "world" whose existence had been, until this time, a purely metaphysical construct. Voices of men and women from Raudive's personal life were interspersed with voices of well-known persons such as C. G. Jung, Ortega y Gasset, Garcia Lorca and Fyodor Dostoevsky.

For an LP record of voice phenomena recorded by Raudive, write to:
    Vista Productions
    64a Lansdowne Road,
    London, W11 2LR, England
    $3.00/air mail add $2.00

PREMONITION BUREAUS
To register a premonition, write to:
Premonitions Registry,
Toronto Society for Psychical Research,
10 North Sherbourne Street,
Toronto 5, Ontario, Canada

Central Premonitions Registry,
Box 482 Times Square Station,
New York, N.Y.

The Southern California SPR,
send premonitions to:
Carolyn Jones
4325 East Broadway
Long Beach, Calif. 90803

YANKEE GHOSTS
Hans Holzer
Ace, 1966
60 cents

SOME CANADIAN GHOSTS
Sheila Hervey
Pocket Books, 1973
$1.50

STRANGE GUESTS
Brad Steiger
Ace, 1968
95 cents

A GAZETEER OF BRITISH GHOSTS
Peter Underwood
Pan, 1971
$1.25

AN EXPERIENCE OF PHANTOMS
D. Scott Rogo
Taplinger, 1974
$8.50

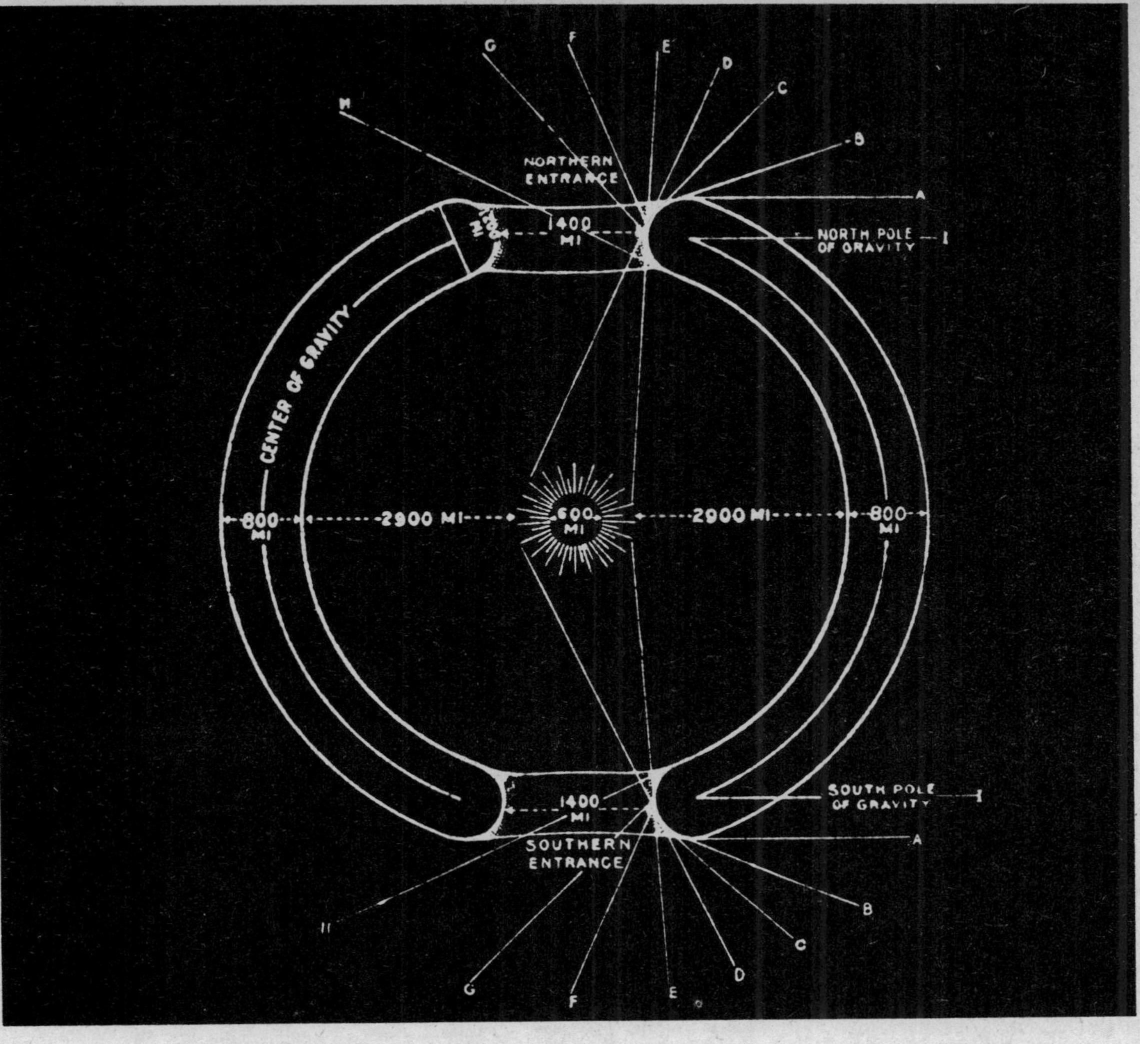

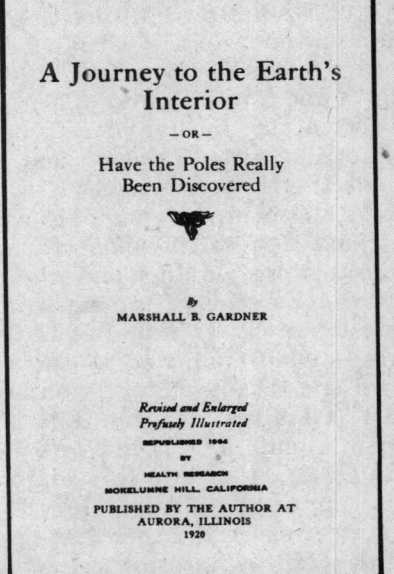

Diagram showing the earth as a hollow sphere with its polar openings and central sun. The letters at top and bottom of diagram indicate the various steps of an imaginary journey through the planet's interior. At the point marked "D" we catch our first glimpse of the corona of the central sun; at the point marked "E" we can see the central sun in its entirety.

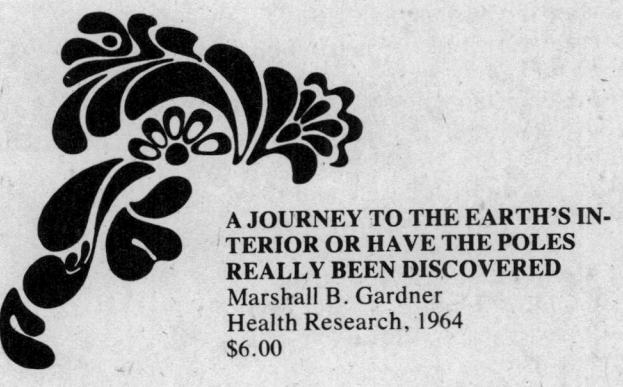

A JOURNEY TO THE EARTH'S INTERIOR OR HAVE THE POLES REALLY BEEN DISCOVERED
Marshall B. Gardner
Health Research, 1964
$6.00

The Hollow Earth

The Hollow Earth, Dr. Raymond Bernard, 105 pages, $3.50 p.p., Health Research, P.O. Box 70, Mokelumne Hill, Ca. 95245.

This book is based upon the discoveries of Rear Admiral Richard E. Byrd, U.S. Navy. Certain statements made by Admiral Byrd, before, after, and during his explorations remain difficult to intrepret without assuming that the earth is something more than just a solid, spherical ball. The following statement was made by Admiral Byrd: "That enchanted Continent in the Sky, Land of Everlasting Mystery!" and "I'd like to see that land beyond the (North) Pole. That area beyond the pole is the center of the Great unknown!" It is reported that Byrd flew 1,700 miles beyond the North Pole and 2,300 miles beyond the South Pole. All of this flying was done, apparently, without coming back to civilization, and below them, during the trip, was vegetation, forests, and animal life! Certainly, one would not expect this at the North Pole. Admiral Byrd's statement is one of grandeur and not one that would be attributed to traveling only over ice.

The Hollow Earth theory deals with the concept that the earth is, in truth, a hollow ball and one can gain entrance to the earth's interior by means of openings at the North and South Poles. The theory states that anyone flying directly north will not ultimately reach the North Pole, but will enter an opening at the pole where a transtition will be made from cold to warm weather and where the vast interior of the earth will be contacted. It is believed that this is what happened to Admiral Byrd and that he actually explored 1,700 miles into this region when he entered at the North Pole and 2,300 miles into this region entering at the South Pole. The theory goes on to state that the earth's hollow interior is heated by a central, smoky sun.

Furthermore, the vegetation and animal life in the interior of the earth grows much larger than on its exterior and that a great and highly evolved civilization of giant men inhabit the interior of our own planet. They are said to be descendents of the Atlantians, a great scientific race that once lived on the continent of Atlantis that was destroyed more than 11,500 years ago. It is further stated that it is this race of beings that fly the saucers that have so frequently been seen in our skys and which are reported to come from other planets.

Long before the explorations of Admiral Byrd, however, several other men independently explored a part of this world. A gentleman by the name of Marshall Gardner published a book in 1906 claiming that the earth was hollow and drew some excellent pictures to illustrate his concepts. Some of these pictures are reprinted in the Hollow Earth. Another person, William Reed, also published a book in 1906 giving scientific proof that there is a large opening at the poles from which the interior of the earth can be reached.. The name of his book was, The Phantom of the Poles. Several death bed accounts given by old sailors who claim to have entered this massive interior world have been recorded and they agree with each other almost completely, even tho the individuals telling the stories were unknown to each other and often coming from different countries. The most noteworthy account is given in a book called The Smoky God, written by Willis George Emerson and published by **HEALTH RESEARCH.** This is the facinating story of an old Norseman sailor, Olaf Jansen, and it tells of his exciting exploration of the inner world.

Yet, the evidence of this inner world does not stop here. In nearly all the ancient writings and scriptures of the eastern peoples, there are references to this inner world (Agharta) and to the marvelous flying ships (saucers) which come from it. For example, the Mongols of Russia have deep legends and beliefs about the Gods who come from the center of the earth. The Hindu books, such as the Ramayana, and the Mahabrarata speak of Godlike emissaries coming from the inner earth on flying ships. As a matter of fact, the word Agharta is of Buddhist origin and refers to the subterranean world.

If you wish to learn more about this inner world, read the book The Hollow Earth by Dr. Raymond Bernard and published by Health Reasearch in Mokelumne Hill, California. This book gives many exciting facts, both scientific and historical that will not fail to fascinate you if not convince you of the existence of this marvelous inner world. Dr. Bernard has done a wonderful job in compiling all available evidence that relates to this inner world and presents it in a logical, consistent and entertaining manner that will not fail to amuse lovers of knowledge and thrills alike. I strongly recommend the book, The Hollow Earth to all open minded readers who wish to know more about the history of some of the world's legends and the origin of flying saucers.

—Henry Monteith

IS THE EARTH HOLLOW?

We have scores of books which say it is! Hundreds of highly educated personalities over a long period of time have reached this conclusion. Who knows? Don't reject until you investigate! See: *Lost Continents Beyond the Poles* By Jack Scaparro (SAGA, The Magazine For Men); October 1947 issue of *The National Geographic Magazine*. This magazine clearly shows photographs of some of the South Pole area which happens to be TROPICAL; Federal Report prepared by the Brookings Institution for NASCA & the books below:

HOLLOW EARTH By Dr. Raymond Bernard, Ph.D.	$3.50
AGHARTA - THE SUBTERRANEAN WORLD By Dr. Raymond Bernard. 8½ x 11 Mimeo.	3.00
AGHARTA By Dr. Robert Ernst Dickhoff - Illustrated, offset printing.	3.50
FLYING SAUCERS FROM THE EARTH'S INTERIOR By Dr. Raymond Bernard - Ills., Mimeo	3.00
A JOURNEY TO THE EARTH'S INTERIOR - Marshall Gardner - 465 pages, facsimile	6.00
INTERMERE By William Alexander Taylor - 148 pages, facsimile, spirals	2.50
TELAH SPEAKS! Partana Vegan - 47 pgs.	1.50
THE SMOKY GOD - Willis George Emerson - 176 pages, illustrated, facsimile	3.00
PARADISE FOUND - William F. Warren - The Cradle of the Human Race - 505 pages	6.00
ETIDORHPA Or The End of Earth by John Uri Lloyd - 386 pages, facsimile	5.50
THE PHANTOM OF THE POLES By William Reed	5.00
THROUGH THE EARTH By Clement Fesandie (1898) 237 pages, facsimile	5.00
THE PERFECT WORLD By Ella Scrymsour. Fantasy Novel. 391 pages, facsimile	4.00
BARON TRUMPS MARVELOUS UNDERGROUND JOURNEY By Ingersoll Lockwood - 253 pages	5.00

Available from: HEALTH RESEARCH, Box 70, MOKELUMNE HILL, CALIFORNIA 95245. (Include Postage)

THIS HOLLOW EARTH
Eric Norman
Lancer, 1972
95 cents

THE UNDER-PEOPLE
Eric Norman
Award Books, 1969
75 cents

THE HOLLOW EARTH
Raymond Bernard
Dell, 1969
$1.50

HEALTH RESEARCH—THE HOLLOW EARTH: THE GREATEST GEOGRAPHICAL DISCOVERY IN HISTORY REGARDING THE ASTROLOGICAL HOUSES: THE SPECTRUM OF INDIVIDUAL EXPERIENCE
Dane Rudhyar
Doubleday, 1972
$2.95

IS IT TRUE?
The Underground World of Supermen Discovered by Admiral Byrd . . . Under the North Pole . . . and Kept Secret by U. S. Government

Dr. Raymond Bernard, A.B., M.A., Ph.D., noted scholar and author of "THE HOLLOW EARTH," says that the true home of the flying saucers is a huge underground world whose entrance is at the North Polar opening. Dr. Raymond Bernard believes in the hollow interior of the Earth lives a super race which wants nothing to do with man on the surface. They launched their flying saucers only after man threatened the world with A-Bombs.

Admiral Byrd, says sources quoted by Dr. Bernard, led a Navy team into the polar opening and came upon this underground region. It is free of ice and snow, has mountains covered with forests, lakes, rivers, vegetation and strange animals. But the news of his discovery was suppressed by the U.S. government in order to prevent other nations from exploring the inner world and claiming it.

Now Dr. Bernard in his book "The Hollow Earth" leads you through this subterranean world to meet the civilization which occupies an underground area larger than North America! Beneath the 800 mile crust of the Earth is the greatest discovery in human history inhabited by millions of super intelligent beings. If you are ready for information that not many people can handle, order this book today. Send $5.95 today and we'll pay all postage and handling charges!

CAN YOU EXPLAIN THE FOLLOWING?
- Why does one find tropical seeds, plants and trees floating in the fresh water of icebergs?
- Why do millions of tropical birds and animals go farther North in the wintertime?
- If it is not hollow and warm inside the Earth at the Poles, then why does colored pollen color the Earth for thousands of miles?
- Why is it warmer at the Poles than 600 to 1000 miles away from them?
- Why does the North Wind in the Arctic get warmer as one sails North beyond 70° latitude?

Mystic Arts Book Society—Dept. F-9
1615 Hillside Avenue
New Hyde Park, N.Y. 11040

Please send me "The Hollow Earth" by Dr. Bernard.
☐ I enclose $5.95. Ship postpaid.
Name ....
Address ....
City .... State .... Zip ....

STRANGE CREATURES FROM TIME AND SPACE
John A. Keel
Fawcett, 1970
75 cents

"No matter where you live on this planet, someone within two hundred miles of your home has had a direct confrontation with a frightening apparition or inexplicable 'monster' within the last generation. Perhaps it was even your cousin or your next-door neighbor. There is a chance—a very good one—that sometime in the next few years you will actually come face to face with a giant hair-covered humanoid or a little man with bulging eyes, surrounded by a ghostly greenish glow.

"An almost infinite variety of known and unknown creatures thrive on this mudball and appear regularly year after year, century after century. Uncounted millions of people have been terrified by their unexpected appearances in isolated forests, deserted highways, and even in the quiet back streets of heavily populated cities. Whole counties have been seized by "monster mania," with every available man joining armed posses to beat the bushes in search for the unbelievable somethings that have killed herds of cows and slaughtered dogs and horses.

". . . We have a theory. It is not very scientific but it is based upon the known facts. These creatures and strange events tend to recur in the same areas year after year, even century after century. This, in itself, indicates that the creatures somehow live in those areas which we call 'windows.' West Virginia had many unusual creature reports before 'Motherman' appeared in 1966. Either everyone in West Virginia is slap-happy, a theory we vehemently contest since we have visited that state five times in the past three years, or else there is some place in the back hills where these things are hiding out."

CHARLES FORT: PROPHET OF THE UNEXPLAINED
Damon Knight
Doubleday, 1970
$6.95

A BIOGRAPHY OF THE AMERICAN ICONOCLAST—WHO DARED TO EXPLAIN CENTURIES OF STRANGE OCCULT PHENOMENA —INCLUDING UFO's, BLACK RAIN AND LOST PLANETS.

THE BOOK OF THE DAMNED
Charles Fort
Ace, 1941
75 cents

"A procession of the damned.

"By the damned, I mean the excluded.

"We shall have a procession of data that Science has excluded.

"Battalions of the accursed, captained by pallid data that I have exhumed, will march. You'll read them—or they'll march. Some of them livid and some of them fiery and some of them rotten.

"Some of them are corpses, skeletons, mummies, twitching, tottering, animated by companions that have been damned alive. There are giants that will walk by, though sound asleep. There are things that are theorems and things that are rags: they'll go by like Euclid arm in arm with the spirit of anarchy. Here and there will flit little harlots. Many are clowns. But many are of the highest respectability. Some are assassins. There are pale stenches and gaunt superstitions and mere shadows and lively malices: whims and amiabilities. The naive and the pedantic and the bizarre and the grotesque and the sincere and the insincere, ". . . I profound and the puerile.

. . . I conceive of one inter-continuous nexus, in which and of which all seeming things are only different expressions, but in which all things are localizations of one attempt to break away and become real things, or to establish entity of positive difference or final demarcation or unmodified independence—or personality or soul, as it is called in human phenomena—. . . ."

INTERNATIONAL FORTEAN ORGANIZATION (INFO)
Write for information to:

INFO
P.O. Box 367
Arlington, Va. 22210

WILD TALENTS
Charles Fort
Ace, 1932
95 cents

LO!
Charles Fort
Ace, 1941

NEW LANDS
Charles Fort
Ace, 1941
60 cents

ODDITIES
Rupert T. Gould
Paperback Library, 1969
95 cents

Scientific proof that there is a large opening at the poles from which the interior of the earth can be reached. The name of his book was, *The Phantom of the Poles*. Several death bed accounts given by old sailors who claim to have entered this massive interior world have been recorded and they agree with each other almost completely, even though the individuals telling the stories were unknown to each other and often coming from different countries. The most noteworthy account is in a book called *The Smoky God*, written by Willis George Emerson and published by

This is the fascinating story of an old Norseman sailor, Olaf Jansen, and it tells of his exciting exploration of the inner world.

Yet, the evidence of this inner world does not stop here. In nearly all the ancient writings and scriptures of the eastern peoples, there are references to this inner world (Agharta) and to the marvelous flying ships (saucers) which come from it. For example, the Mongols of Russia have deep legends and beliefs about the Gods who come from the center of the earth. The Hindu books, such as the Ramayana, and the Mahabarata speak of God-like emissaries coming from the inner earth on flying ships. As a matter of fact, the word Agharta is of Buddhist origin and refers to the subterranean world.

If you wish to learn more about this inner world, read the book *The Hollow Earth* by Dr. Raymond Bernard and published by Health Research in Mokelumne Hill, California. This book gives many exciting facts, both scientific and historical that will not fail to fascinate you if not convince you of the existence of this marvelous inner world. Dr. Bernard has done a wonderful job in compiling all available evidence that relates to this inner world and presents it in a logical, consistent and entertaining that will not fail to amuse lovers of knowledge and thrills alike. I strongly recommend the book *The Hollow Earth* to all open minded readers who wish to know more about the history of some of the world's legends and the origin of flying saucers.
—HENRY MONTEITH

Ancient Mysteries

ately, we have witnessed a great proliferation of books arguing that numerous planetary enigmas can be explained by the theory of our planet having been visited by superior beings. Several theories describing how they may have "paninseminated" the human species have been advanced. While a number of these books have been severely criticized for their selective omission of data, they have undoubtedly served a valuable function in challenging some of our inadequate appraisals of human history. It should also be pointed out, however, that the perspective presented by these books about our past is suspiciously much too *linear*. New understanding of time-space may demand that we look at these enigmas from the standpoint of the existence of a simultaneous past, present and future.

IMMANUEL VELIKOVSKY
PENSEE
P.O. Box 414
Portland, Oregon 97207

In 1950 Velikovsky was pronounced a heretic and his unorthodox theories banned from discussion at scientific gatherings.

On February 25, 1974, the American Association for the Advancement of Science will conduct a pioneering symposium on his work.

Many things have happened during the last 24 years. *Pensee* is one of them.

We don't claim to know how much of Velikovsky's work is correct. But a burgeoning number of scientists and scholars in all fields are making the effort to find out. And the results so far have been startling enough to guarantee that the Velikovsky debate will be the number one scientific issue during the coming year.

If you wish to follow the debate, a subscription to *Pensee* is a must. Here are a few of the features you can expect in forthcoming issues:

- Full coverage of the AAAS symposium.
- A report on the discussions at NASA's Langley Research Center during Velikovsky's December visit there at the invitation of the Center's scientific staff.
- Excerpts from *The Torrid Love Affair of Mars and Moon*, a new book in preparation by Professor Alfred De Grazia (editor of *The Velikovsky Affair*).
- Lively debate between Velikovsky and his critics.
- Analyses of the latest space probe data from the moon, Mars, and Venus—are their surfaces scarred by catastrophes during the first and second millennia, B.C.?
- A report on Velikovsky's participation in the 1974 Philosophy of Science Association convention.
- China's dragon—participant in the catastrophe of 1500 B.C.?
- An archaeologist's view of the Queen of Sheba and the Land of Punt.

EARTH IN UPHEAVAL
Immanuel Velikovsky
Laurel, 1955
95 cents

". . . increased radioactivity coming from outside this planet or from the bowels of the earth could be the cause of the spontaneous origin of new species. Should an interplanetary discharge take place between the earth and another celestial body, such as a planet a planetoid, a trail of meteorites, or a charged cloud of gases, with possibly billions of volts of potential difference and nuclear fission or fusion, the effect would be similar to that of an explosion of many hydrogen bombs with ensuing procreation of monstrosities and growth anomalies on a large scale.

". . . Numerous catastrophes or bursts of effect radiation must have taken place in the geological past in order to change so radically the living forms on earth, as the record of fossils embedded in lava and sediment bears witness.

"How would this understanding of evolution meet the facts, and especially those facts that always appeared to be in discord with the theory of natural selection?

". . . Natural selection had its role, too, but not in procreating new species; it was a decisive factor in the survival or dying out of new forms, in the struggle for existence, not only between individuals, races, species, and orders but also against the elements. In natural selection all those forms were weeded out that could not meet competition or the rapidly changing conditions of a world in upheaval.

"The origin of new species from old could be caused by the processes that can be duplicated in laboratories—by thermal or chemical, all of which must have taken part in natural catastrophes of the past, and could have played a role in building new species, as the case of new plants in the bomb craters appears to indicate.

"The theory of evolution is vindicated by catastrophic events in the earth's past; the proclaimed enemy of the theory of evolution is the teaching of uniformity, or the non-occurrence of any extraordinary events in the past. This teaching, called by Darwin the mainstay of the theory of evolution, almost set the theory apart from reality."

On June 10, 1895, Immanuel Velikovsky was born in Vitebsk, Russia. He learned several languages as a child, performed exceptionally well in Russian and mathematics at the Medvednikov Gymnasium after moving to Moscow, and graduated with a gold medal in 1913. He then traveled to Europe, visiting Palestine, France, and taking premedical courses at the University of Edinburgh.

Having returned to Russia before the outbreak of World War I, Velikovsky enrolled in the University of Moscow, and received a medical degree in 1921. Then he left Russia for Berlin, where he married Elisheva Kramer, a young violinist. He edited the *Scripta Universitatis*, for which Albert Einstein prepared the mathematical-physical section.

From 1924 to 1939 Velikovsky lived in Palestine, practicing psychoanalysis—he had studied under Freud's pupil Wilhelm Stekel in Vienna—and editing *Scripta Academica Hierosolymitana*. In 1930 he published the first paper to suggest epileptics are characterized by pathological encephalograms. Some of his writings appeared in Freud's *Imago*.

After reading *Moses and Monotheism*, Velikovsky conceived the possibility that Pharaoh Akhnaton, the real hero of Freud's book, was the legendary Oedipus (a thesis later argued in his book, *Oedipus and Akhnaton*). In 1939 Velikovsky took a sabbatical year, traveling with his family to New York only a few weeks before World War II tore Europe apart. For eight months he worked on *Oedipus and Akhnaton* in the libraries.

In April, 1940, Velikovsky was first struck by the idea that a great natural catastrophe had taken place at the time of the Israelites' Exodus from Egypt—a time when plague occurred, the Sea of Passage parted, Mt. Sinai erupted, and the pillar of cloud and fire moved in the sky. Velikovsky wondered: Does any Egyptian record of a similar catastrophe exist? He found the answer in an obscure papyrus stored in Leiden, Holland—the lamentations of an Egyptian sage, Ipuwer.

WORLDS IN COLLISION
Immanuel Velikovsky
Laurel, 1950
95 cents

The Ipuwer document, Velikovsky became convinced, parallels the Book of Exodus, describing the same natural catastrophe, the same plagues. As a result he began to reconstruct ancient Middle Eastern history, taking this catastrophe—which brought the downfall of the Egyptian Middle Kingdom—as a starting point from which to synchronize the histories of Egypt and Israel. He titled his work *Ages in Chaos*.

The cause of the catastrophe terminating the Middle Kingdom remained unexplained. One afternoon, in October, 1940, Velikovsky noticed an important fact: the Book of Joshua describes a destructive shower of meteorites occurring before the sun "stood still" in the sky. Could this be coincidence, or were the ancients recording a cosmic disturbance that must have shaken the entire Earth and might have been related to the upheavals approximately 50 years earlier during the Exodus? A survey of other sources around the world convinced Velikovsky that a global cataclysm had indeed overtaken the Earth, and that Venus played a decisive role in that cataclysm. For 10 years he researched and wrote *Ages in Chaos* and *Worlds in Collision*. He had by now taken up permanent residence in the United States.

In 1950 after more than a dozen publishing houses rejected the two manuscripts, Macmillan published *Worlds in Collision*. Even before its appearance, the book was enveloped by furious controversy. Macmillan, intimidated by threats from academicians and scientists—the people who write and buy its textbooks—transferred the book to Doubleday. *Worlds in Collison* was then the number one bestseller in the nation. . . .

AGES IN CHAOS, Vol. I: FROM THE EXODUS TO KING AKHNATON,
Immanuel Velikovsky,
Doubleday, 1952
$8.50

IMMANUEL VELIKOVSKY RECONSIDERED—HOW MUCH OF YESTERDAY'S HERESY IS TODAY'S SCIENCE?
Pensee, Special Issue, Student Academic Freedom Forum,
May 1972, Vol. 2, No. 2
$2.00

THE DESTRUCTION OF ATLANTIS—RAGNAROK: THE AGE OF FIRE AND GRAVEL
Ignatius Donnelly
Rudolf Steiner Publication, 1971
$2.45

COSMIC MEMORY' ATLANTIS AND LEMURI
Rudolf Steiner Publication, 1959
$1.95

"The Atlanteans also had for example, the capacity to control the life force in a certain way. They constructed their wonderful machines through this force. But on the other hand, they had nothing of the gift for story-telling which the peoples of the fifth root race possess. There were as yet no myths and fairy tales among them. The life-mastering power of the Atlanteans first appeared among the members of our race under the mask of mythology. In this form it could become the basis for the intellectual activity of our race. The great inventors among us are incarnations of 'seers' of the Atlanteans. In their inspirations of genius is manifested what has as its basis something that was like life-producing power in them during their Atlantean incarnation. Our logic, knowledge of nature, technology and so forth, grow from a foundation which was laid in Atlantis. . . ."

THE ATLANTEANS is a group of people dedicated to finding a deeper understanding and compassion of life through meditation, philosophy and healing based on the occult traditions of Atlantis. Bimonthly magazine, regular newsletter, comprehensive meditation courses and teachings, four Festivals of Isis, healing classes for members, varied social activities and public meetings which are held as follows: Centre Branch, Cheltenham—Fridays 8 p.m. at House of Isis, 42 St. George's Street; Bristol—Mondays 8 p.m. at Oakfield Road Church Hall, Clifton; London—Bromley—Mondays 8 p.m. at St. Mary's Church Hall, College Road. Further details including sample magazine and Diary of Events from the Atlanteans, House of Isis, 42 St. George's Street, Cheltenham GL50 4AF.

ATLANTIS: THE ANTEDILUVIAN WORD
Ignatius Donnelly
Rudolf Steiner Publications, 1971
$2.45

"This book is an attempt to demonstrate several distinct and novel propositions. These are:

"1. That there once existed in the Atlantic Ocean, opposite the mouth of the Mediterranean Sea, a large island, which was the remnant of an Atlantic continent, and known to the ancient world as Atlantis.

"2. That the description of this island given by Plato is not, as has been long supposed, fable, but veritable history.

"3. That Atlantis was the region where man first rose from a state of barbarism to civilization.

"4. That it became, in the course of ages, a populous and mighty nation, from whose overflowings the shores of the Gulf of Mexico, the Mississippi River, the Amazon, the Pacific coast of South America, the Mediterranean, the west coast of Europe and Africa, the Baltic, the Black Sea, and the Caspian were populated by civilized nations.

"5. That it was the true Antediluvian world; the Garden of Eden; the Gardens of the Hesperides; the Elysian Fields; the Gardens of Alcinous; the Mesomphalos; the Olympos; the Asgard of the traditions of the ancient nations; representing a universal memory of a great land, where early mankind dwelt for ages in peace and happiness.

"6. That the gods and goddesses of the ancient Greeks, the Phoenicians, the Hindoos, and the Scandinavians were simply the kings, queens, and heroes of Atlantis; and the acts attributed to them in mythology are a confused recollection of real historical events.

"7. That the mythology of Egypt and Peru represented the original religion of Atlantis, which was sun-worship.

"8. That the oldest colony formed by the Atlanteans was probably in Egypt, whose civilization was a reproduction of that of the Atlantic island.

"9. That the implements of the 'Bronze Age' of Europe were derived from Atlantis. The Atlanteans were also the first manufacturers of iron.

"10. That the Phoenician alphabet, parent of all the European alphabets, was derived from an Atlantis alphabet, which was also conveyed from Atlantis to the Mayas of Central America.

"11. That Atlantis was the original seat of the Aryan or Indo-European family of nations, as well as of the Semitic peoples, and possibly also of the Turanian races.

"12. That Atlantis perished in a terrible convulsion of nature, in which the whole island sunk into the ocean, with nearly all its inhabitants.

"13. That a few persons escaped in ships and on rafts, and carried to the nations east and west the tidings of the appalling catastrophe, which has survived to our own time in the Flood and Deluge legends of the different nations of the old and new worlds."

THE EGYPTIAN BOOK OF THE DEAD
E. A. Wallis Budge
Dover, 1967
$3.95

". . . Embodying a ritual to be performed for the dead, with detailed instructions for the behavior of the disembodied spirit in the hands of the gods, it served as the most important repository of religious authority for some three thousand years. Chapters were carved on the pyramids of of the Fifth Dynasty, texts were written in papyrus, and selections were painted on mummy cases well into the Christian era. . . ."

THE MUMMY
E.A. Wallis Budge
Collier, 1972
$2.95

LOST CITIES AND VANISHED CIVILIZATIONS
Robert Silverberg
Bantam, 1974
95 cents

IN SEARCH OF ANCIENT GODS: MY PICTORIAL EVIDENCE FOR THE IMPOSSIBLE
Erich von Däniken
Putnam, 1974
$8.95

GODS AND SPACEMEN IN THE ANCIENT EAST
W. Raymond Drake
Signet, 1968
$1.50

"Occultists, Yogis and psychics like Swedenborg believed in countless inhabited worlds in various stages of evolution; many planets were apparently allied into associations grouped into Galactic Federations and possibly ever greater organisations. To our sardonic minds this conception smacks of science-fiction with its inter-planetary wars and galactic rivalries, yet behind the phantasy lies Cosmic Truth. Occult traditions hint at Adepts and Masters dwelling on Earth, who in secrecy and silence direct the evolution of our planet; they are said to maintain telepathic or astral communication with Avatars on neighbouring worlds, all are subordinate to Celestials on the Sun, who probably obey some great Intelligence controlling the Galaxy, Himself obedient to yet Higher Entity ascending through a Hierarchy approaching the infinite, ineffable Absolute. There is reason to believe that some of these Super-Beings have appeared on Earth by incarnation, astral manifestation or landing from spaceships; here they have taught Man cosmic truths, the arts and crafts of civilisation, and prompted human evolution in accordance with the divine plan."

THE MOUND BUILDERS
Robert Silverberg
Ballantine Books, 1970
$1.50

Includes Pompeii, Homer's Troy, Knossos of Crete, Babylon, Chichen Itza of the Mayas, Angkor-City in the Jungle.

". . . a young man of 24 dreamed of finding Priam's Troy, Homer's Troy, and proving forever that the great poems of Homer were based on historical happenings.

"He was Heinrich Schliemann, born in 1822 in the little village of Ankershagen, Germany. His father was a poor but well-educated clergyman, who amused young Heinrich by telling him stories of ancient Troy, tales of Hector and Achilles, Agamemnon and Priam. Heinrich heard these stories over and over again until they became part of him. He retold them to his playmates. In his imagination, he stood with Achilles outside the walls of Troy; he relived with Odysseus the 10-year journey home to Ithaca . . .

"Homer had depicted a society of much earlier times as one that boasted a thousand ships and splendid palaces and cities. Had all the majesty of Homeric Greece been swallowed up by Time? It was simpler to believe that Homer had been inventing than to think that Greece had once been great, had lapsed back into darkness for hundreds of years, and then once again had attained power and glory. Agamemnon and the rest were pure legends, these skeptics said.

"But Schliemann refused to hear them. He had all the evidence he needed. Homer's descriptions of shields and ships and chariots were too accurate to be mere works of imagination. No one, Schliemann insisted, could have visualized a mythical society in such vivid detail. Troy was real! It *had* to be!"

MYTHS AND SYMBOLS IN INDIAN ART AND CIVILIZATION
Heinrich Zimmer
Edited by Joseph Campbell
Bollingen Series—Princeton, 1963
Series 6
$2.95

STRANGE DISAPPEARANCES
Elliott O'Donnell
University Books 1972
$7.95

IMPOSSIBLE POSSIBILITIES
Louis Pauwels and Jacques Bergier
Stein and Day, 1971
$6.95

"Like all other cultures, our own is a conspiracy. A bevy of petty divinities who derive their power solely from our unprotesting acquiescence and constantly deflect our gaze away from the fantastic aspect of reality. The conspiracy causes us to renounce of our own free will the realization that there is another world within the world inhabited by us, another man inside the man known to us. It is imperative for us to break out of this pact, to leave the circle of conspirators. The only way to achieve this is to use differently the knowledge available to us, to establish fresh connections between the various branches of knowledge, to look at the facts of life with eyes cleared of the hypnosis of traditional values—in short, to conduct ourselves in the realm of the intellect like intelligent beings who came from elsewhere with the sole aim of seeking revelation. If we do behave in this way, the fantastic will always reveal itself to us simultaneously with the real."

ETERNAL MAN
Louis Pauwels and Jacques Bergier
Mayflower, 1973
$1.95

FROM SPHINX TO CHRIST: AN OCCULT HISTORY
Edward Schure
Rudolf Steiner Publications, 1970
$1.95

THE VEIL OF ISIS or MYSTERIES OF THE DRUIDS
W. Winwood Reade
Health Research
$4.00

MORNING OF THE MAGICIANS
Louis Pauwels and Jacques Bergier
Avon, 1971
$1.25

ONE HUNDRED THOUSAND YEARS OF MAN'S UNKNOWN HISTORY
Robert Charroux
Berkley, 1970
95 cents

LEGACY OF THE GODS
Robert Charroux
Berkley, 1974
$1.25

THE GODS UNKNOWN
Robert Charroux
Berkley, 1972
$1.25

ASPECTS OF ANTIQUITY
M. D. Finley
Penguin, 1972
$1.35

SECRET OF THE ANDES
Brother Philip
Corgi, 1973
$1.25

THE BAFFLING WORLD, NO. 1, 2 and 3
John Godwin
Bantam, 1971
No. 1 75 cents Nos. 2 and 3 95 cents

MYSTERIES OF EASTER ISLAND
Francis Maguire
Tower, 1973
95 cents

IN SEARCH OF ANCIENT MYSTERIES
Allan and Sally Landsburg Bantam,
Bantam 1974
$1.50

WE ARE NOT THE FIRST
Andrew Tomas
Bantam, 1973
$1.25

Rediscovery of Science

Scientific and Technological Ideas	Known in Antiquity	Rediscovered
Atomic theory	Uluka Kanada (*c.* 500 B.C.) Democritus (460-361 B.C.) Leucippus (b. *c.* 480 B.C.) Epicurus (341-270 B.C.)	Boyle (1661) Dalton (1805)
Theory of relativity	Heraclitus (*c.* 540-475 B.C.) Zeno of Elea (5th century B.C.)	Einstein (1916)
Transmutation	The alchemists (1st century B.C.—1st A.D.)	Rutherford (1919)
Age of the earth	Life-span of the universe 4.32 billion years (the *Mahabharata* and the *Puranas*)	4.6 billion years (20th century)
Formation of the solar system	The *Popul Vuh* Wang Chung (A.D. 82)	Kant (1755) Laplace (1796)
Evolution	Anaximander (*c.* 611-547 B.C.) Book of Manu (*c.* 200 B.C.)	Darwin (1859)
Earth as a planet	Pythagoras (6th century B.C.) Anaximander (611-547 B.C.) Heracleides of Pontus (388-315 B.C.)	Copernicus (1473-1543)
The moon shining by reflected light	Parmenides (b. *c.* 544 B.C.) Plutarch (1st century A.D.)	Galileo (1610)
The moon's connection with tides	Posidonius (135-50 B.C.)	Kepler (1571-1630)
Planets beyond Saturn	Democritus (5th century B.C.) Anaximenes (5th century B.C.) Seneca (1st century A.D.)	Uranus (1781) Neptune (1846) Pluto (1930)
Sunspots	Chinese astronomers 2,000 years ago.	Galileo (1610)
Jupiter's four largest moons, phases of Venus, seven satellites of Saturn	Babylonian priests (*c.* 2000 B.C.)	Galileo (1610) Cassini, Huygens, Herschel, Bond (17th-19th century)

Scientific and Technological Ideas	Known in Antiquity	Rediscovered
Milky Way—a cloud of stars	Democritus (5th century B.C.)	Galileo (1610)
Meteorites—stones from space	Diogenes of Apollonia (5th century B.C.)	Academy of Sciences, Paris (1803)
Extraterrestrial space	*The Epic of Etana* (2700 B.C.), *The Book of the Dead* (c. 1500 B.C.), The Book of Enoch (2nd century B.C.)	Gagarin (1961)
Music of the spheres	Pythagoras (6th century B.C.)	Radio astronomers Jansky-Reber (1930s-1940s)
Electric batteries	Babylon batteries (2,000 years old)	Volta (1800)
Aviation	Daedalus (2500 B.C.), Emperor Shun (2258-2208 B.C.), Ki Kung Shi (1766 B.C.), etc.	Wright brothers (1903)
Turbo-jet engine	Heron (1st century B.C.)	Von Ohain (1939) Whittle (1941)
Space travel	Orbiting the earth (the *Surya Siddhanta*, 2,000 years old)	Sputnik I (1957)
Robots and computers	Daedalus' automatons (2500 B.C.), Antikythera computer (65 B.C.), etc.	Wiener (1950s)
Plumbing and sanitation	Knossos (2000 B.C.), Mohenjo Daro, Harappa (2500 B.C.)	19th century
City planning	Mohenjo Daro, Harappa (2500 B.C.)	Paris, Washington (17th-18th centuries)
Vaccination	The *Vedas* (1500 B.C.)	Jenner (1749-1823)
Penicillin	Egypt (c. 2000 B.C.)	Fleming (1928)
Existence of America	Plato (4th century B.C.) Seneca (1st century A.D.) The *Vishnu Purana* (200 A.D.)	Bjarni and Ericson (c. 1000) Columbus (1492)

THE GOLD OF THE GODS
Erich Von Daniken
Souvenir Press, 1973
$8.25

This gold figure, 20 ins. high, has normal human proportions, but only four fingers and four toes on hands and feet. The serious scientific explanation? An adding machine! Were the Incas so stupid as to make a whole figure just to represent a 'four'? Really this is the 'Star God'

MYSTERIES FROM FORGOTEN WORLDS
Charles Berlitz
Laurel, 1973
$1.25

"The structive potential of scientific technology is no secret to the generations of man now inhabiting a planet menaced not only by the dangers inherent in an unstable cosmos, but also by disasters and possibly final doom paradoxically brought about by our own advances in science and by our own growing understanding of the universe. The thought suggests itself, therefore, that, given the long-time presence on this planet of a civilized race before the apparent start of our own civilization, a race, moreover, whose mental ability, as calculated by estimated brain capacity, in measuring surviving skulls of the Cro-Magnon man, was equal or *superior* to our own, the descendants of this, or a more or less contemporaneous race may have developed a science, which while not analagous to ours and taking perhaps a different road, might have nevertheless arrived at the same final impasse."

THE ANCIENT ENGINEERS
L Sprague de Camp
Ballantine, 1974
$1.75

THE MYSTERIES OF ANCIENT EGYPT   HERMES/MOSES
Edouard Schure
Rudolf Steiner Publications, 1971
$1.75

ATLANTIS: FACT OR FICTION
Edgar E. Cayce
A.R.E. Press
Professional Study Series No. 2, 1972
$1.25

THE COMING OF THE GODS
Jan Sendy
A Brkeley Medallion Book, 1973
$0.95

LOST ATLANTIS
James Bramwell
Freeway Press, 1973
$1.75

ATLANTIS RISING
Brad Steiger
A Dell Book, 1973
$0.95

ARE THE VON DÄNIKEN THEORIES REALLY TRUE?

WAS EARTH ONCE VISITED FROM OUTER SPACE? DID ALIEN BEINGS WALK OUR PLANET? A MAJOR NASA ENGINEER REVEALS SOME ASTONISHING FACTS!

THE SPACESHIPS OF EZEKIEL BY JOSEF F. BLUMRICH

THE SPACESHIPS OF EZEKIEL
Joseph F. Blumrich
Bantam, 1974
$1.95

Ezekiel begins his book with the description of the final phase of a spaceship's descent from a circular orbit to the earth and of its subsequent landing. This narrative is accompanied by a description of the main parts of the sp ecraft. Remarkable is that in describing his last encounter with a spaceship, he explicitly stresses its apparent identity with the one he had seen twenty years earlier.

Ezekiel also peaks of the commanders of the spaceships; he hears them talk, he observes their movements; on one occasion he witnesses a peculiar event involving the participation of a ground crew summoned by the commander. He takes part himself in flights in these spaceships; two flights take him to temples whose location and significance are still unsolved mysteries.

The key to the clear understanding of Ezekiel's report lies in a very careful analysis of his description of the components of the spacecraft and of their function, carried out in the light of today's knowledge of spacecraft and rocket technology. This method proved successful very quickly. Further and increasingly detailed investigations and comparisons have shown that Ezekiel's descriptions are amazingly accurate. The amount and accuracy of detail reflected in his record lead to the conclusion that he must have possessed extraordinary gifts of observation and an almost photographic memory. This made it possible not only to develop a simple sketch, but also to express dimensions, weights, and capabilities in figures. Thus, for the first time, it became possible to free an ancient report on spaceships from its disguising pictures and to transpose it into the language of engineers. This breakthrough made it further possible to interpret occurrences which had seemed to have no real meaning.

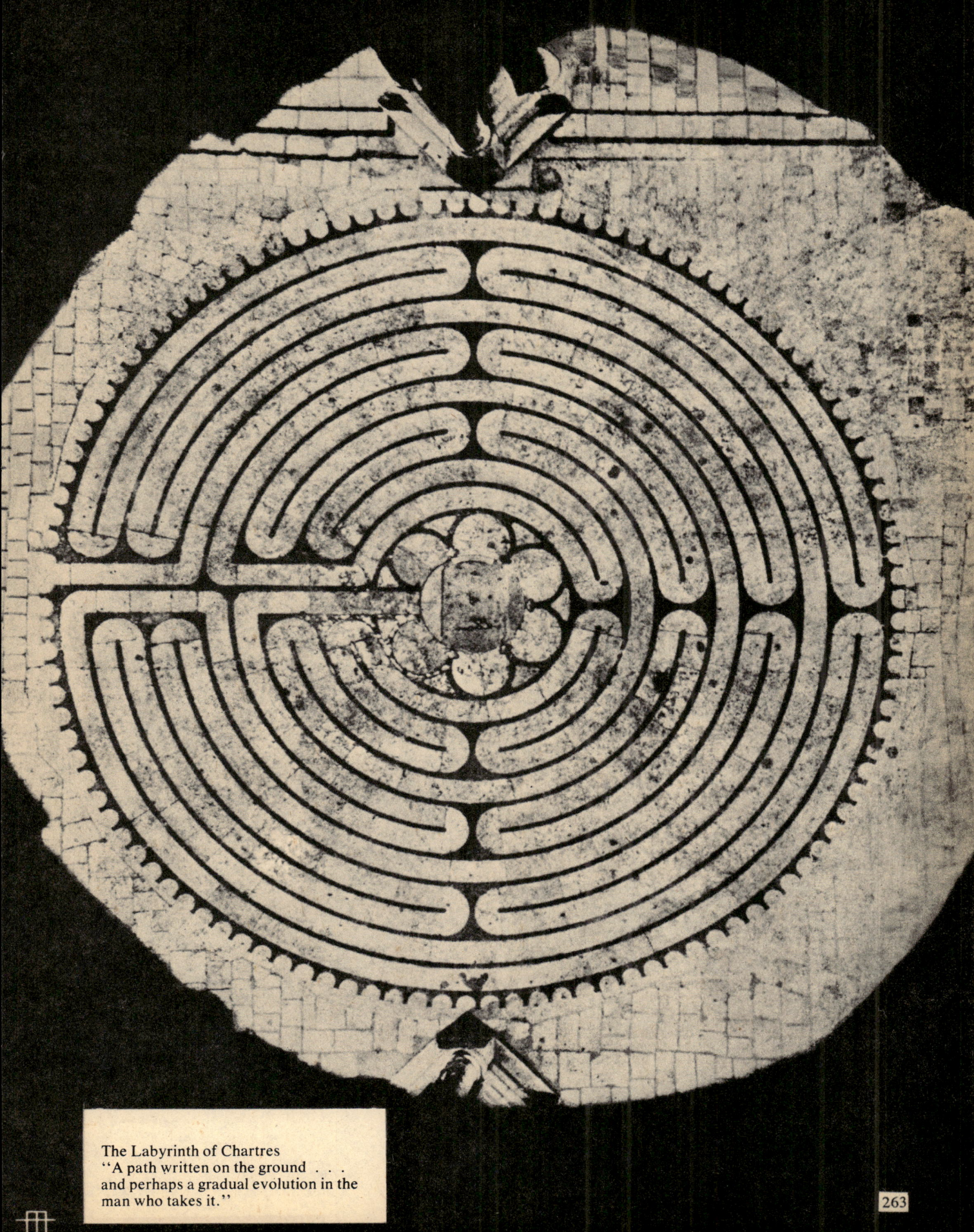

The Labyrinth of Chartres
"A path written on the ground . . .
and perhaps a gradual evolution in the
man who takes it."

the mysteries of chartres cathedral

LOUIS CHARPENTIER
translated by Sir Ronald Fraser

Is the cathedral of Chartres the lineal successor of Dolmens under which the Druids fitted their novices for initiation? Is it, through the Order of the Knights Templar and by the knowledge of the Cisterians, the direct lineal successor of the Pyramids and the Temple of Solomon?

RESEARCH INTO LOST KNOWLEDGE ORGANISATION

THE MYSTERIES OF CHARTRES CATHEDRAL
Louis Charpentier, translated by Sir Ronald Fraser.
Available from:
Thorsons Publishers Ltd.
37/38 Margaret Street
London W. 1., England

ALPHA: THE MYTHS OF CREATION
Charles H. Long
Collier, 1963
$1.50

"Alpha brings together in one fascinating volume the great primitive myths of creation, with a vivid commentary that explores their significance as an expression of cosmic orientation. Grouped into five basic categories— emergence myths, world-parent myths, creation from chaos and from the cosmic egg, creation from nothing and earth-diver myths—these ancient attempts to explain the earth's origins represent cultures as diverse as the Maori and the Babylonian, the Brahman and the Huron, the Hebrew and the Tahitian."

THE CRYSTAL SKULL
RIchard Gavin
Pocket Books, 1974
$1.25

What unknown hand carved it 12,000 years ago? Does it really have the power of life and death?

In 1927, while searching for the lost civilization of Atlantis, archaeologists discovered in the ruins of a Mayan city the most extraordinary—and perhaps the oldest—object ever fashioned by the hand of man.

It is a perfect replica of a human skull exquisitely carved and polished from single piece of quartz crystal. It is clearly the product of a sophisticated civilization—yet its age has been estimated at 12,000 years!

The skull's eyes flicker as if alive. Observers have reported strange sounds, odors and light effects emanating from it. Its influence is said to have caused violence, physical injury, even death.

REVELATION, The magazine for psychic and spiritual studies. Subscription 56p. Specimen copy 14p from The Revelation Society, P. Carman, 6 St. Annes Road East, St. Annes, Lancs FY8 IUL.

STONEHENGE VIEWPOINT
A quaterly. 12 issue subscription is $3
Order from:
Annular Publications
25 West Anapamu Street,
Suite 5,
Santa Barbara, CA 93101

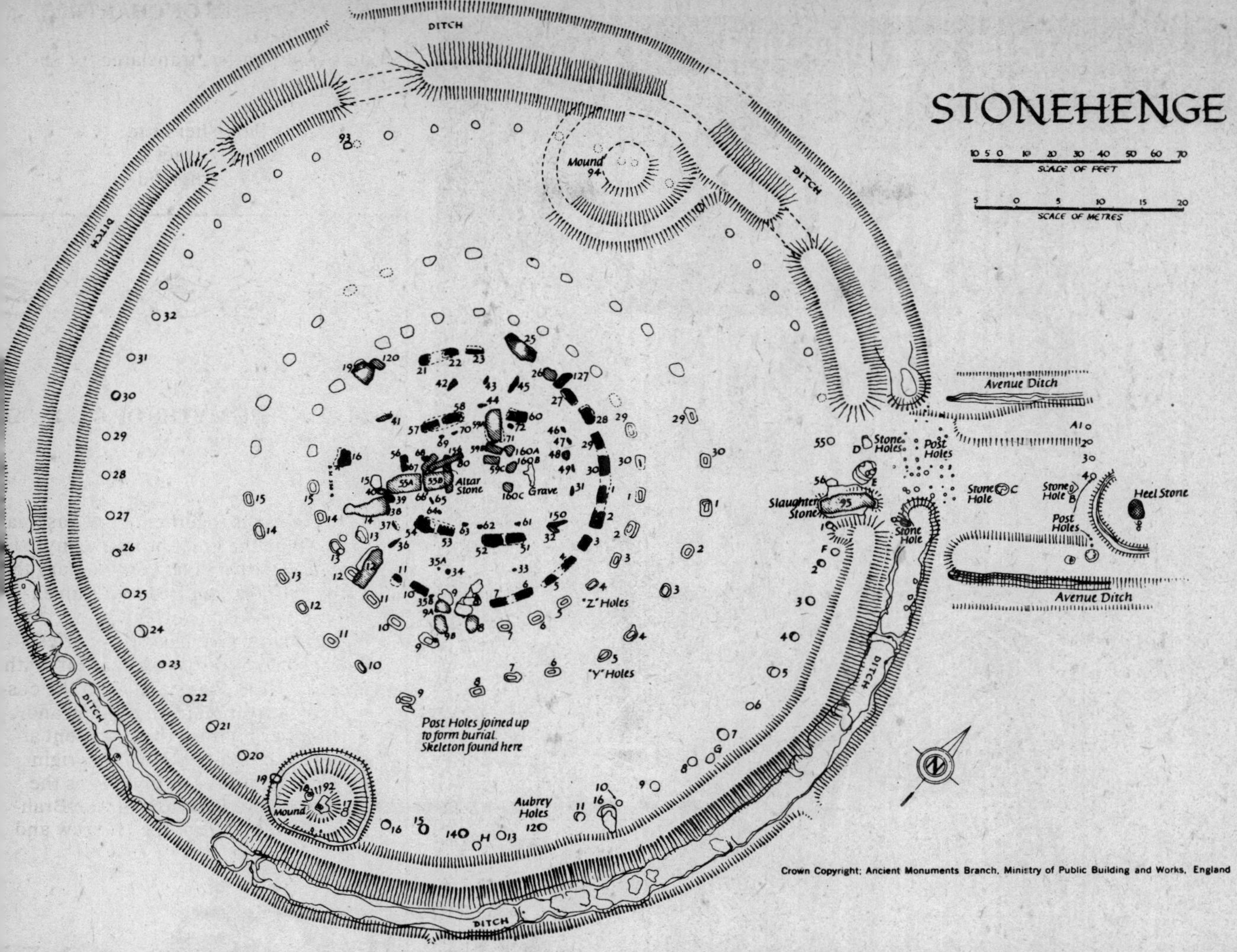

STONEHENGE

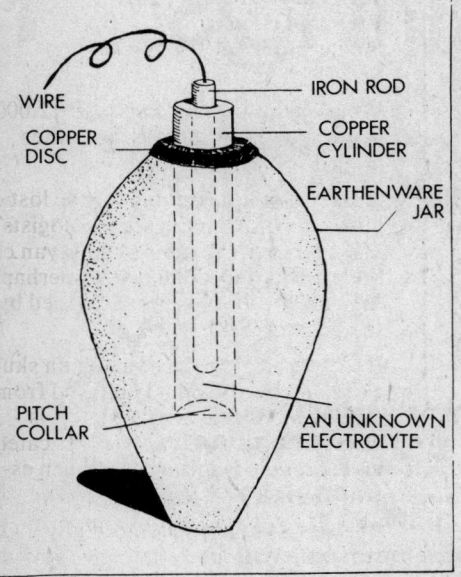

This electric cell invented in ancient Babylon proves that electricity was known to antiquity. (Author's diagram)

THE HOME OF THE GODS: ATLANTIS FROM LEGEND TO DISCOVERY
Andrew Thomas
Berkley, 1972
$1.25

STONEHENGE DECODED
Gerald S. Hawkins in collaboration with John B. White
Delta, 1965
$1.45

"There can be no doubt that Stonehenge was an observatory; the impartial mathematics of probability and the celestial sphere are on my side. In form the monument is an ingenious computing machine, but was it ever put to use! As a scientist I cannot say. But in my defense a similar skepticism can be turned toward other probers of ancient humanity. Do we need to see lip marks on a drinking cup, blood on a dagger and sparks from a flint striking pyrites to convince us that these things were indeed used?

"This investigation was carried out at the Smithsonian Astrophysical Observatory, Harvard College Observatory, Boston University, and at the site of Stonehenge and the surrounding English countryside.

ATLANTIS REVISITED
STEREO LP
AVAILABLE FROM:
  CHANNEL 1 RECORDS
  120 East Flamingo Road
  Suite 250
  Las Vegas, Nev. 89109
  $6.65

Strange Sightings And Extraterrestrials

hile it is tempting to believe that UFOs may be vehicles from distant star-systems, more PSI investigators are speculating that these sightings as well as those of strange creatures such as the Big-Foot and the Loch Ness monster may be "psychic" in nature as manifested extensions of man's psyche. A greater understanding of the multi-dimensional aspects of the mind may underscore the arrogant and naive statements of well-known astronomers that UFO sightings are unlikely because of the great distances between stars.

HEALTH RESEARCH: HOMECOMING OF THE MARTIANS AN ENCYCLOPAEDIC WORK ON FLYING SAUCERS (a limited edition)
Published 1964
Copyright Dr. Robert Ernst Dickhoff
$3.00

PURSUIT "Science is the pursuit of the unexplained."
Available from Society for the Investigation of the Unexplained, founded by Ivan T. Sanderson, devoted to the investigation of things that are customarily discounted.

Membership to the society is $10.00 a year, and runs from January 1 to December 31. Members receive our quarterly journal *Pursuit* and annual report and auditor's report and all special Society publications for that year. You don't have to be a professional or even an amateur scientist to join.

Quarterly publication, available from The Society for the Investigation of the Unexplained, Columbia, New Jersey, 07832.

THE TRUTH ABOUT FLYING SAUCERS
Aime Michel
Pyramid, 1974
$1.25

FLYING SAUCER REVIEW
Annual subscription U.K. and overseas 2.10; U.S. and Canada $5.40
International journal devoted to the study of unidentified flying objects, available from The Editor, Flying Saucer Review, 21 Cecil Court, Charing Cross Road, London WC2N 4HB England.
Bimonthly publication
FLYING SAUCER REVIEW, an international journal established in 1955, is a bimonthly magazine of 32 pages (excluding covers) printed by quality litho on fine art paper. It is produced in collaboration with an international team of jesearchers researchers the global problem of unidentified flying objects. Its aim is to study every aspect of the subject scientifically and objectively, and to keep readers up-to-date with the international UFO scene.

The FSR team of writers and consultants includes C. Maxwell Cade, AInstP, FRAS, AFRAeS, CEng, FIEE, FIERE (Author of *Other Worlds Than Ours*); linguistics and anthropological expert Gordon Creighton, MA, FRAI, FRGS, FRAS; design engineer R. H. B. Winder, BSc, CEng, AMI-Mech E; aeronautics historian Charles H. Gibbs-Smith, MA, FMA, Hon. Companion RAeS; Dr. Bernard Finch, MRCS, LRCP, DCh, FBIS; science journalist and broadcaster Aime Michel (author of *The Truth About Flying Saucers, Flying Saucers and the Straight-Line Mystery*); aviation writer Derek D. Dempster (joint author of *The Narrow Margin' Margin*, authoritative history of the Battle of Britain); Dr. Berthold E. Schwarz, consultant psychiatrist. Other contributors include Dr. Jacques Vallee (author of *Anatomy of a Phenomenon, Challenge to Science*—in collaboration with Janine Vallee—and *Passport to Magonia*); Dr. J. Allen Hynek, Northwestern University astronomer and former Civilian Scientific Consultant on UFOs to the US Air Force.

FSR is taken by readers in more than 60 countries, and by many Governmental bodies and learned institutions. . . .

FSR CASE HISTORIES

These Supplements (same size and format as FSR, but half the number of pages, i.e., 16 pages plus covers) were first issued in October 1970 and are devoted entirely to UFO and occupant reports and investigations into such reports. Numbers 2 to 16 are still available at 24 pence each (65 cents) by surface mail. From Supplement 19 onwards they will however appear not more than three times per year and will be identical with FSR not only in size and format but also the number of pages (32 plus covers). Subscription will be for **six issues,** and will thus cost the same as FSR, i.e. 2.40 ($6.60) postfree home and abroad by surface mail; single copies 40 pence ($1.10) by surface mail. For AIRMAIL add: USA, Canada, S. Africa, Argentina, Brazil and rest of Western Hemisphere, 1.60 ($4.20.) Australia, New Zealand, etc., add 2.00. For Middle East, add 1.20.

SPECIAL ISSUES

UFO PERCIPIENTS. Includes a remarkable study of the effects on a doctor and his baby son of a UFO encounter—with photographic evidence! Price 40 pence; overseas 45 pence or US $1.20.

UFOs IN TWO WORLDS. Includes the Rev. N. E. G. delightful account of the experiences of missionaries, teachers and Papuan natives during the wave of 1958/59. Price 60p. or $1.80.

UFO ENCOUNTERS. Deals with Contact, "Contactees, and photography, with interesting overlaps. Price 40p. or $1.20.

NOTE. THE HUMANOIDS. This famous FSR classic, Special Issue No. 1, is no longer available from us in its original edition. But a new hard-cover edition, price 1.50 (plus 10% for postage in U.K., 20% for overseas) can be ordered direct from Compendium Books at the address given below. This book is a *must* for every student of the subject, and is being translated into several languages. It gives 168 cases, many of them in great detail, in which the occupants of landed UFOs have been seen or encountered, often at very close quarters.

For other books on UFOs, Forteana, Parapsychology, Comparative Religion, and related topics, apply likewise to Compendium Books direct.

METHOD OF PAYMENT: Overseas subscribers should remit by check on a London bank, banker's draft on a London bank, by Dollar check, or by International Money Order (Mandat de Poste International). All remittances should be made payable to FSR Publications Ltd.
Flying Saucer Review is available for $7.50 per year by surface mail. Add $4.20 per year for airmail.

UFO NEWSCLIPPING SERVICE
WRITE TO'

UFO RESEARCH COMMITTEE
3521 S.W. 104th Street
Seattle, Wash. 98146
Service Cost: $4.00 per month

CATALOG ON FLYING SAUCER TAPES, RECORDINGS, PHOTOS AND SLIDE SETS

AVAILABLE FROM:

UFO INTERNATIONAL
P.O. Box 552
Detroit, Mich. 48232
35 cents

SPACEVIEW: EXPLORING THE OUTER SPACE OF UFOs AND THE INNER SPACE OF MAN
6 issues, $3.95
Available from Suite 103, Goodhue Building
Beaumont, Texas 77701
12 issues for $6.95

HAD ENOUGH OF UFO & OCCULT MAGAZINES THAT NEVER SEEM TO GET PRINTED! Read CAVEAT EMPTOR—now in its third year of regular publication! CAVEAT EMPTOR is the magazine on UFOs, the Occult and the Aquarian Age that dares to be different! $3.00 for 6 issues from G & G Steinberg, Box 688PR, Coatesville, Pa. 19320.

FLYING SAUCERS HAVE LANDED! See secret government documents—Actual photo of outer space humanoid—Weird crafts from other planets. Order ALIENS AMONG US, $2.00. ESP, 303 5th Avenue (130P), New York, N.Y. 10016.

FLYING SAUCER SLIDE SETS
ALL SLIDES ARE IN FULL COLOR

Producer	Title	Price
BLAZS SLIDE SET NO. 1	AFSCA Review - Part 1 (Reviews highlights of AFSCA magazine issues 4-12.) Gabriel Green. 1898 San Francisco sighting. Veloz UFO. Saucer news clippings. Fry Saucer. Contactees. Sick Miller's contact. Giant Rock Airport. Anderson star. Integratron. Ackerman saucer. (35 color slides with taped narration. Playing time: 37 min.)	17.75
BLAZS SLIDE SET NO. 2	AFSCA Review - Part 2 (Reviews highlights of AFSCA magazine issues 13-18). Chief Standing Horse. News Clippings. Reinhold Schmidt story. Moon Probe. Keenes boy sighting. Wilcox contact. Reeves story. Renton saucer. (33 color slides with taped narration. Playing time: 53 min.)	16.75
BLAZS SLIDE SET NO. 3	AFSCA Review - Part 3 (Reviews highlights of AFSCA magazine issues 19-23.) Canberra sighting. News clippings. Crowe sighting. Heflin saucer. Renaud Korendian contacts. Paul Villa pictures. (36 color slides with taped narration. Playing time: 30 min.)	18.25
BLAZS SLIDE SET NO. 4	Saucer Book Review (Reviews contents of selected saucer books.) Fry -"White Sands Incident". Bethrum - "Aboard A Flying Saucer". Kraspedon - "My Contact with Flying Saucers". Girvin - "The Night Has A Thousand Saucers". Reeve - "Flying Saucer Pilgramage". Rowe - "A Call at Dawn". Lee - "Why We Are Here". Keyhoe - "Flying Saucers, Top Secret". King - "You Are Responsible" and "The Nine Freedoms". Menger - "From Outer Space to You". Stranges - "Flying Saucerama" and "My Friend from Beyond Earth". (34 color slides with taped narration. Playing time: 40 min.)	17.25
BLAZS SLIDE SET NO. 5	Interplanetary Carriers and Venusian Scouts (Compilation) Adamski Sets 1-2, Menger sets 1-2, Allingham set. (36 color slides with taped narration. Playing time: 30 min.)	18.25
BLAZS SLIDE SET NO. 6	Saucer Drawings Panorama (Compilation) Saucer Drawings sets 1-3. (26 color slides with taped narration. Playing time: 30 min.)	13.25
BLAZS SLIDE SET NO. 7	UFOs and Flying Clouds (Compilation) Pentagon set. UFO sets 1-2. Cloud set 1-2. (36 color slides with taped recording. Playing time: 18 min.)	18.25
BLAZS SLIDE SET NO. 8	Flying Saucer Odities (Compilation) Odity set 1-4. (34 color slides with taped narration. Playing time: 30 min.)	17.25

PLEASE ADD 50¢ PER SLIDE SET FOR POSTAGE AND HANDLING

FLYING SAUCER PICTURE SETS

PICTURE SETS (3 1/2 x 5 color prints with fact sheet.) Description	Price

ADAMSKI SET NO. 1 (1) Interplanetary carrier and one scout, (2) Interplanetary carrier and two scouts, (3) Interplanetary carrier and five scouts, (4) Interplanetary carrier and six scouts, (5) Interplanetary carrier, (6) Submarine type interplanetary carrier, (7) Diagram of Venusian interplanetary carrier, (8) Diagram of Saturnian laboratory interplanetary carrier. Color added. Rating: Excellent.   2.90

ADAMSKI SET NO. 2 (1) Saucer with moon in background, (2) Flying saucer, (3) Venusian scout hovering, (4) Venusian scout side view closeup, (5) Venusian scout landing gear, (6) Saucer disappearing over desert, (7) Diagram of Venusian scout ship, (8) Diagram of Saturnian scout. Color added. Rating: Excellent.   2.90

AFRICAN SET (1) Rhodesian saucer, (2) Saucer over city, (3) Saucer top view, (4) Saucer top view (enlargement) (5) Saucer in flight, (6-7) Klarer saucer. Color added. Rating: Good.   2.55

ALLINGHAM SET (1-2) Saucer in clouds, (3-4) Saucer landing, (5) Saucer on ground, (6) Martian walking away. Color added. Rating: Very good.   2.20

BRAZIL SET (1) Saucer enlargement, (2-5) Saucer over sea, (6) Saucer over tree, (7) Saucer bottom. Color added. Rating: Very good.   2.55

CLOUD SET NO. 1 (1) Flying cloud over housing development, (2) Flying clouds over cars, (3) Flying clouds over hills, (4) Flying cloud over houses, (5) Flying clouds over boys, (6) Reserve Sheriff W. A. Ackerman, (7) Flying cloud over giant rock. Color added. Rating: Excellent.   2.55

CLOUD SET NO. 2 (1) Cylindrical cloud, (2) Cloud near moon, (3) Cloud over building, (4) Cloud over peak, (5-6) Cloud behind rocks, (7) Cloud over hills. Color added. Rating: Excellent.   2.55

DRAWINGS SET NO. 1 (1) Flying Saucer, (2) Saucer from Jupiter, (3) Crescent-winged craft, (4) Disc near ground, (5) Saucer rising, (6) Korendian craft on ground, (7) Korendian craft in flight, (8) Trent saucer. Color added. Rating: Excellent.   2.90

DRAWINGS SET NO. 2 (1) Saturn spaceship, (2) Grounded saucer, (3-4) UFO over city, (5) Jupiter saucer, (6) Flying top, (7) Pyramid saucer, (8) Wheel saucer. Color added. Rating: Very good.   2.90

DRAWINGS SET NO. 3 (1) Venusian scout, (2) Martian saucer, (3) Japanese saucer, (4) Fry saucer, (5) Venusian saucer, (6) Dexter saucer, (7) Saragfulus carrier, (8) Van tassel saucer. Color added. Rating: Very good.   2.90

FRY SET (1-5) Approaching spacecraft, (-7) Flying top. Color added. Rating: Excellent.   2.55

HEFLIN SET (1-4) Heflin saucer. Color added. Rating: Very good.   1.50

PLEASE ADD 15¢ PER PICTURE SET FOR POSTAGE AND HANDLING

UFO MAPS
SATISFACTION GUARANTEED

Map (A)   shows the UFO concentration of activity in three different categories in the continental U. S. The three catalogs are graphically shown so as to give the viewer instant tabulation of UFO sightings at a glance. A must for all UFO enthusiasts.

Map (B)   shows the most famous 100 UFO sightings from 1947 - 1967 in the continental U. S. Each sightings in each state, as well as possible straight and/or curve line theories of flight by UFO's.

Map (C)   shows the most published 50 UFO landings recorded in UFOlogical history in the continental U. S. Each landing shows immediately the location to the viewer for quick, easy reference. Designed for the UFO researcher.

Map (D)   shows where UFO occupants or aliens, monsters, etc. were seen in the continental U. S. This map also indicates if a UFO was near the occupant at the time of the contact or not. An excellent too for UFOlogical research.

Map (E)   shows the most fantastic UFO landing in the world. This map will help to pick out in an instant the 75 world UFO landings UFO researchers should have this at their finger tips.

Map (F)   shows the major and minor UFO organizations of the world. Great for the student UFO researcher who needs, at a moments notice, the number of UFO organizations of any consequence in each country of the world.

Map (G)   shows the "Angel Hair Falls" in the continental U. S. from 1947 to 1967. This map ideally indicates to the hard-core UFO researcher the Angel Hair Falls at a glance.

Map (H)   shows the "Angel Hair Falls" throughout the world from 1947 to 1967. This map ideally indicates to the hard-core UFO researcher the Angel Hair Falls at a glance.

Map (I)   shows the "Magnetic Effects Cases" in the continental U. S. from 1947 to 1967. This map will be a powerful tool to the hard-core researcher.

Map (J)   shows the "Magnetic Effects Cases" throughout the world from 1947 to 1967. This map, along with other world maps in this series, is a must for all UFO researchers.

— all 10 ONLY $2.95

ALL MAPS MOUNTED ON HEAVY PAPER-BOARD SUITABLE FOR FRAMING. EACH MAP IS 8½"X11". Prices apply to residents in U. S., Canada, and Mexico.

ORDER FROM: SPACEVIEW
Suite 103, Goodhue Building
Beaumont, Texas 77701

THE UFO EXPERIENCE: A SCIENTIFIC INQUIRY
J. Allen Hynek
Ballantine, 1974
$1.00

THE REPORT ON UNIDENTIFIED FLYING OBJECTS
Edward J. Ruppelt
Ace, 1956
75 cents

INTELLIGENT LIFE IN THE UNIVERSE
I. S. Shklovskii and Carl Sagan
Delta, 1966
$2.95

"In primitive times, when very little was understood about the nature of living systems, the most routine biological activities, such as the germination of a seed or the flowering of a plant, were attributed to divine intervention. In the early years of the Industrial Revolution, when advances in celestial mechanics gave something close to a complete understanding of the positions and motions of the heavenly bodies, the concept arose that living systems may be nothing more than a particularly intricate kind of clockwork. But when early investigations failed to unveil the clockwork, a kind of ghostly mainspring was invented—the 'vital force.' The vital force was a rebellion from mechanistic biology, an explanation of all that mechanism could not explain, or for which mechanisms could not be found. It also appealed to those who felt debased by the implication that they were 'nothing more' than a collection of atoms, that their urges and supposed free wills arose merely from the interaction of an enormously large number of molecules, in a way which, although too complex to use predictively, was, in principle, determined.

"But today, we find no evidence for a vital force; indeed, the concept is very poorly defined, a kind of universal catch-all for anything we cannot explain. The opposite tack—that all living systems are made of atoms and nothing else—has proved a particularly useful idea. An entire new science of molecular biology has made startling progress and achieved fundamental insights starting from this assumption. And there is nothing debasing in the thought that we are made of atoms alone. We are thereby related to the rest of the universe; and if we are made of the same stuff, more or less, as everything else, then elsewhere there may be things rather like us."

MYSTERIOUS FIRES AND LIGHTS
Vincent H. Gaddis
Dell, 1968
75 cents

"The suggestion that some UFOs may be animals—i.e., life-forms or animate creatures indigenous to rarified atmospheres or possibly space itself—may seem fantastic at first. Actually it is a logical theory that answers many questions about the behavior of some UFOs and strange lights.

". . . Ordeals by fire, to establish the guilt or innocence of a suspected person, have been historical customs and still exist today in certain primitive cultures. According to Sir William Blackstone, the famed English legal writer, the ordeal of the Middle Ages consisted of either picking up a piece of red-hot iron, or walking barefoot and blindfolded over red-hot ploughshares laid lengthwise at unequal distances. If the subject was burned, he was judged guilty; if unhurt, he was innocent.

". . . There have been luminous persons and magnetic persons. There have been electrically charged persons displaying psychokinesis, and victims of certain diseases whose discharged life-energies produced rapping sounds on bedroom walls and furniture. These are elementary manifestations of man's electrodynamic nature, which is more spectacularly evidenced in poltergeist phenomena.

". . . Spontaneous combustion deaths, although rare, may be more frequent than is generally imagined. In the United States we are usually told that the victims fell asleep while smoking, but in the British Isles, it seems, these cases are reported more accurately. Eric Frank Russell, the English writer, recorded nineteen victims, six of them men, during 1938, simply by checking several newspapers daily. Some of these occurrences that baffled physicians and coroners are of special interest."

THE JOURNAL OF BORDERLAND RESEARCH.

BSRF No. 1 Published by Borderland Sciences Research Foundation, Inc., PO Box 548, Vista, Calif. 92083. Edited by the Director, Riley Hansard Crabb, Doctor of Metaphysics in the Society of St. Luke the Physician.

The Journal is published six issues a year with the assistance of the Associates, at the Director's home, 1103 Bobolink Drive, Vista. It is printed, 36 pages an issue. The Foundation was incorporated under California law, May 21, 1951, # 254264, and has been in continuous existence since then. Address all correspondence to the PO Box. *The Journal is included in the Foundation membership of $7.50 a year. Single copies and back issues of the Journal are now $1.50 each.* If you don't care to join you may receive the Journal by donating $7.50 a year or more to the Foundation. The Director's wife, Ms. Judith Crabb, is office manager and Secretary-Treasurer.

PURPOSES OF BSRF: This is a nonprofit organization of people who take an active interest in unusual happenings along the borderland between the visible and invisible worlds. In the words of the late Meade Layne, founder and director of BSRA from 1946 to 1959: "BSRA publications are scientific in approach but employ few technical expressions. They deal with significant phenomena which orthodox science cannot or will not investigate. For example: The Fortean falls of objects from the sky. Teleportation, Radiesthesia, PK Effects, Underground Races, Mysterious Disappearances, Occult and Psychic Phenomena, Photography of the Invisible, Nature of the Ethers and the problem of the Aeroforms (Flying Saucers). In the year 1946 BSRA obtained an interpretation of the phenomena which since has come to be known as the Etheric or 4-D interpretation, and which has not been radically altered since that time. This continues to be the only explanation which makes good science, sound metaphysics and common sense."

The chief present concern of the Foundation is to make this kind of unusual information available as a public service at reasonable cost. Headquarters acts as a receiving, coordinating and distributing center. An important part of the Director's work is to give recognition, understanding and encouragement to people who are having unusual experiences of the borderland type and/or are conducting research in any of the above fields. For consultation on borderland problems, or for Spiritual healing through prayer, write or phone 714-724-2043 for help or for an appointment. Donations and bequests toward Foundation research programs and expenses are welcome.

The 28-page list of BSRF publications is available from Headquarters for $1.00 in coin or stamps. This includes mimeo brochures on borderland subjects, tape recordings of Mr. Crabb's lectures and of members of the Inner Circle, talking through trance-medium Mark Probert. Write to BSRF, PO Box 548, Vista, Calif. 92083.

NATIONAL INVESTIGATIONS COMMITTEE ON UFO'S
Write for information:
7970 Woodman Avenue #114
Van Nuys, Calif. 91402

CENTER FOR UFO STUDIES
P.O. Box 11
Northfield, Ill. 60093
Formed by Dr. J. Allen Hynek
Call toll-free (800-621-7725) to report UFO sighting.

INCIDENT AT EXETER
John G. Fuller
Berkley, 1966
75 cents

AERIAL PHENOMENA RESEARCH ORGANIZATION
3910 East Kleindale Road, Tucson, Ariz. 85712

Publishes a bimonthly newsletter detailing UFO reports worldwide.

You can send your UFO photographs for analysis.

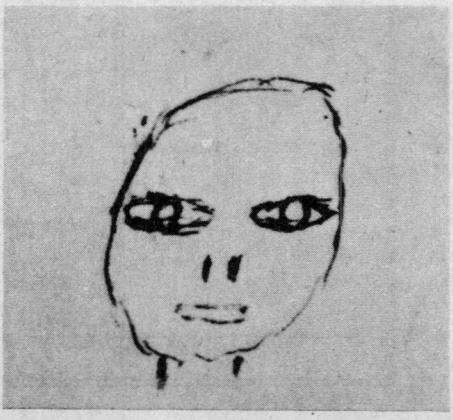

Barney Hill, under hypnosis, drew the above sketch of the "leader" of the alleged abductors. Later, while he was listening to the tape recording of his own account of the incident, he seemed to go into a trance-like state, and drew the more finished sketch below. The eyes were elongated, he said, and the lips appeared to have no muscles.

THE INTERRUPTED JOURNEY
John G. Fuller
Berkley, 1966
$1.25

On the night of 19-20 Sept. between 20/001 and 10/0100 Mr. and Mrs. Hill were traveling south on Route 3 near Lincoln, N.H. when they observed, through the windshield of their car, a strange object in the sky. They noticed it because of its shape and the intensity of its lighting as compared to the stars in the sky. The weather and sky were clear at the time.

A. Description of Object

"**1.** Continuous band of lights—cigar shaped at all times, despite changes in direction. Neither of the Hills recalls whether they mentioned the disc shape of the craft at close range.
"**2. Size:** When first observed it appeared to be about the size of a nickel at arm's length. Later when it seemed to be a matter of hundreds of feet above the automobile it would be about the size of a dinner plate held at arm's length.
"**3. Color:** Only color evident was that of the band of lights when comparable to the intensity and color of a filament of an incandescent lamp. [Blarney, who felt impelled at this time to understate everything, shied away from giving his full impression of the of the craft.]"

A Journal of the Mystery of Uri Geller

By Andrija Puharich

"... AP: 'May I have permission to ask my list of questions?'

This is Hoova. Yes, we heard, and will answer what we can.

"AP: 'What is the history of Hoova in the evolution of the human race on this earth?'

"We first interfered with the human race twenty thousand years ago. We came on a planned mission from our own solar galaxy, and our first landing place on earth was at the place you were at in Israel, at the Oak of Mamre in Hebron where Abraham met us. That is the origin of the legend of the ladder to the gods, because they saw us come out of our craft on a ladder device. However, we found traces of the presence of other visitors from other spaces who had been on earth millions of years earlier. But we found man in much the same animal condition that you see him in today.

"AP: 'When was the last time that you actively tried to upgrade the quality of man's self and of his civilization?'

"We give advice actually about once every six thousand years. The last time that we did this was six thousand years ago to the Egyptians. Our advice is usually given gently and is not too strong, and we do it more for our own purposes than for man's benefit.

"... It is obvious that I am personally convinced that superior beings from other spaces and other times have initiated a renewed dialogue with humanity. But it is equally obvious that my case for this conviction can be carried into the heart of every person largely by the sense of truth my words carry, and not on the basis of objective proof. It is my hope that as Uri continues his research efforts at the hands of science, and as he carries personal testimony to people, the truth of what he and I say will take hold. And of course, it is up to the Nine and their various controllers and messengers to decide who shall be witness to their presence."

A JOURNAL OF THE MYSTERY OF URI GELLER
Andrija Puharich
Anchor, 1974
$7.95

"... The letter said in summary: 'His son saw Uri Geller, a 23 year old stage performer, do some amazing things for a group of students and their professors. He made it clear that his son does not believe in these things as being paranormal. His son thinks some kind of a trick is involved, but nobody knows the trick, not even the magicians.'

"His son's friend had held a gold ring clenched in his hand while Geller held his left hand over this hand for about thirty seconds. When his son's friend opened his hand, the ring was split.... ."

SYMPOSIUM ON UNIDENTIFIED FLYING OBJECTS: Hearings Before the Committee on Science and Astronautics, U.S. House of Representatives, Ninetieth Congress, Second Session, July 29, 1968, No. 7. U.S. Government Printing Office, Washington, 1968.

"Today the House Committee on Science and Astronautics conducts a very special session, a symposium on the subject of unidentified flying objects' the name of which is a reminder to us of our ignorance on this subject and a challenge to acquire more knowledge thereof.

"We approach the question of unidentified flying objects as purely a scientific scientific problem, one of unanswered questions. Certainly the rigid and exacting discipline of science should be marshaled to explore the nature of phenomena which reliable citizens continue to report.

"A significant part of the problem has been that the sightings reported have not been accompanied by so-called hardware or materials that could be investigated and analyzed. So we are left with hypotheses about the nature of UFO's. These hypotheses range from the conclusion that they are purely psychological phenomena, that is, some kind of hallucinatory phenomena; to that of some kind of natural physical phenomena; to that of advanced technological machinery manned by some kind of intelligence, that is, the extraterrestrial hypotheses.

CONTENTS

STATEMENTS

Dr. J. Allen Hynek, head, Department of Astronomy, Northwestern University, Evanston, Ill

Prof. James E. McDonald, Department of Meteorology, University of Arizona, Tucson, Ariz.

Dr. Carl Sagan, associate professor of astronomy, Center for Radiophysics and Space Research, Cornell University

Dr. Robert L. Hall, head, Department of Sociology, University of Illinois, Chicago, Ill

Dr. James A. Harder, associate professor of civil engineering, University of California

Dr. Robert M. L. Baker, Jr., senior scientist, System Sciences Corp., 650 North Sepulveda Boulevard, El Segundo, Calif.

PREPARED PAPERS

Dr. Donald H. Menzel, Harvard College Observatory

Dr. R. Leo Sprinkle, Division of

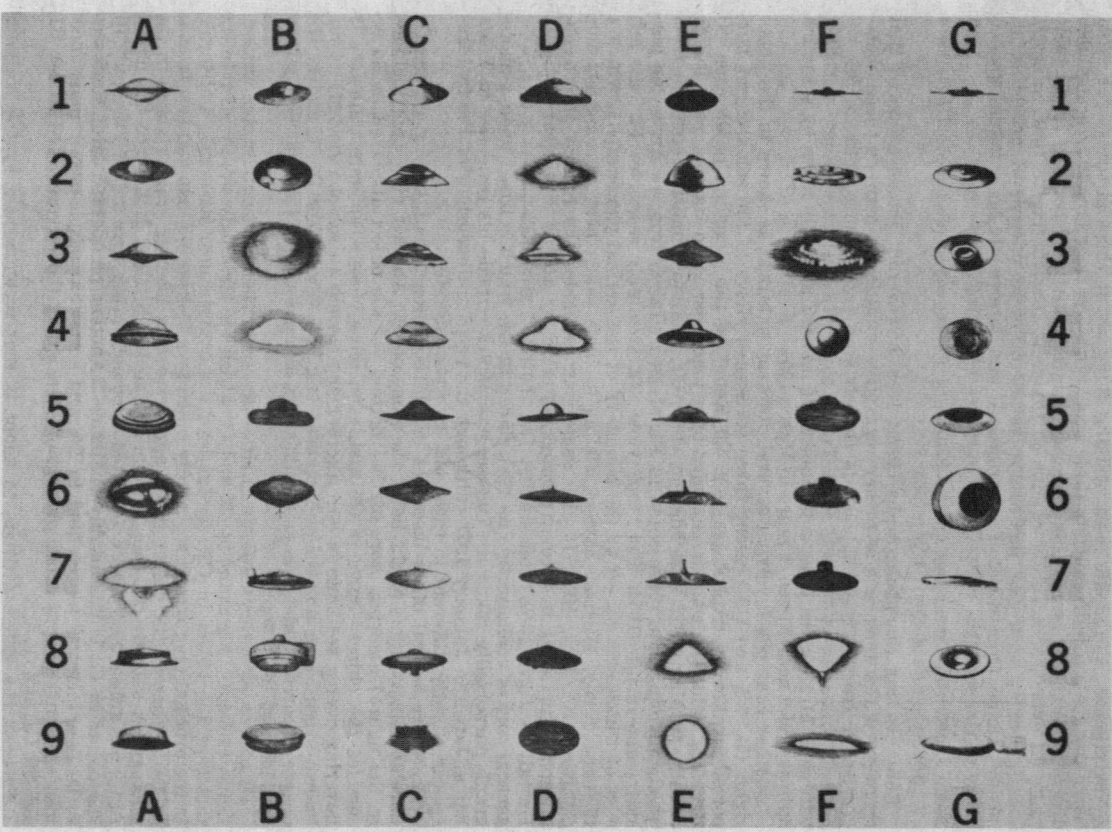

The array is intended only to convey some idea of the variety of shapes that have appeared, it does not give an adequate impression of the relative frequencies with which the different shapes have appeared. In fact, the images most commonly appearing in my total sample show either a small point, formless blob, or fuzzy ellipse of light in a night sky, or else a dark, more or less distinct ellipse (like that shown in D9) against a lighter sky. With very few exceptions, such as the rocket- or "cigar"-shaped object with "exhaust trail" (G9), which allegedly was photographed over Peru in 1952, the more well-defined objects appear to be some variant of the "saucer" or "domed disk."

INSIDE THE FLYING SAUCERS
George Adamski
Warner Paperback Library, 1973
75 cents

"As I have told you, I do have witnesses to one of my journeys in a space craft. Both are scientists who hold high positions. Once they are able to make a statement the picture will change overnight. However, the way things are nowadays with everything classified as security, for the time being they must remain in the shadow. When they believe that they can release the substantiation they have without jeopardizing either the national defense or themselves, they have said that they will do so through the press. How soon that will be, your guess is as good as mine. But because they were with me at the request of the Brothers, some things are moving in behalf of both the Brothers and the general public that otherwise could not have been started. And much as we would like to, we cannot speak of these things yet because good intentions can have bad reactions. Anything acted upon prematurely can ruin the best beginnings."

FLYING SAUCERS ESOTERIC—discussion meetings, London (and elsewhere). Details from Viewpoint Aquarius, c/o Fish Tanks Ltd., 49 Blandford Street, London, W.1. 935 3719. Two sample copies of 30 page magazine 50p.

UFOS—Friends or Foes? Shocking facts! Stamp brings details. EDEN, Box 34P, Careywood, Idaho 83809.

UFO MAGAZINE NEWS BULLETIN contains UFO reports every issue. $1.00 for four issues; 3403 West 119th, Cleveland, Ohio 44111.

BEHIND THE FLYING SAUCER MYSTERY
George Adamski
Warner Paperback Library, 1974
95 cents

STRANGE WORLDS
A magazine focusing on UFOs and unexplained happenings

Order From:
Strange Worlds
Dept. FT, Box 688
Cootesville, PA. 19320
$4.00 for 6 issues
$7.00 for 12 issues
$13.00 for 24 issues

PLANET IN TROUBLE: THE UFO ASSAULT ON EARTH
Jerome Eden
Exposition Press, 1973
$7.50

ALIEN FROM SPACE ... THE REAL STORY OF UNIDENTIFIED FLYING OBJECTS
Major Donald E. Keyhoe
Doubleday, 1973
$7.95

INVISIBLE RESIDENTS
Ivan T. Sanderson
Avon, 1973
95 cents

"Basically, the dozen or so apparently unrelated matters that we have discussed would seem to have nothing much more in common than that they all have something to do with water. There is, nonetheless, an underlying unity, but this comes to light only when we review them together as possible aspects of and evidence for an over-all concept. This, moreover, is simply that there is an underwater 'civilization' (or civilizations) on this planet that has been here for a very long time and which was evolved here, and/or that there are intelligent entities who have been coming here from elsewhere, probably for a very long time, and which prefer to use the bottom of the hydrosphere, and possibly also the surface layers of the lithosphere below that, on or in which to reside and from which to operate. . . .

"Now, we *presume* that we are the only form of what we call 'intelligent' life on this planet, and since we live in the atmosphere, we *assume* that being the only form of intelligent life, no other such intelligence could evolve or exist in water. This notion has, however, been considerably shaken recently by the investigation of the mental abilities of the cetaceans (porpoises, dolphins, and whales), but panic has been held to a minimum by the observation that these fine creatures don't have hands and that 'intelligence,' as we think of it, is founded on technology, which in turn calls for the employment of what we call heat in order to invent and carry on metallurgical procedures. However, we can weld metal under water and we can mix concrete that sets under water, so it would seem that a technological civilization is not impossible in a liquid, and especially in such a delightfully inert one as water.

UNINVITED VISITORS
Ivan T. Sanderson
Cowles, 1967
$6.95

"Here is such a chart of: *What Could They Be?*
  I. INANIMATE
    A. *Natural*
      1. Nonmaterial—energy packets, as in bolides
      2. Nonsolid—gaseous, as in clouds
      3. Solid—like meteorites
    B. *Artificial*
      1. Self-contained items—like artificial satellites
      2. Transports—like freighters
      3. Auxiliary devices (manned)—like airplanes
      4. Auxiliary devices (robotic)—like space probes
      5. Missiles—like bullets and ICBM's
  II. ANIMATE
    A. *Natural*
      1. Life-forms indigenous to space
      2. Life-forms indigenous to atmospheres
      3. Life-forms indigenous to solid bodies
    B. *Artificial*
      1. Domesticated natural life-forms
      2. Genetically created life-forms
      3. Biochemically created life-forms

". . . This theory has come to be known among the more specialized aficionados as the Wassilko-Serecki Theory, in deference to an Austrian titled lady of that name who devoted a fortune and untold time to backing any person or group with proper scientific training who expressed a desire to try and investigate properly any facet of life that did not conform to established belief or understanding. The Wassilko-Serecki Theory is simply that *some* UAO's could themselves be life-forms, indigenous to space and "feeding" on pure energy.

Counseling and Testing, University of Wyoming

Dr. Garry C. Henderson, senior research scientist, Space Sciences, General Dynamics

Dr. Stanton T. Friedman, Westinghouse Astronuclear Laboratory

Dr. Roger N. Shepard, Department of Psychology, Stanford University

Dr. Frank B. Salisbury, head, Plant Science Department, Utah State University

". . . In seeking explanations for UFO reports, I like to weigh witness-accounts in terms of eight principal UFO hypotheses:

"1. Hoaxes, fabrications, and frauds.

"2. Hallucination, mass hysteria, rumor phenomena.

"3. Lay misinterpretations of well-known physical phenomena (meteorological, astronomical, optical, aeronautical, etc.).

"4. Semi-secret advanced technology (new test vehicles, satellites, novel weapons, flares, re-entry phenomena, etc.).

"5. Poorly understood physical phenomena (rare atmospheric-electrical or atmospheric-electrical effects, unusual meteoric phenomena, natural or artificial plasmoids, etc.).

"6. Poorly understood psychological phenomena.

"7. Extraterrestrial devices of some surveillance nature.

"8. Spaceships bringing messengers of terrestrial salvation and occult truth."

LIMBO OF THE LOST
John Wallace Spencer
Bantam, 1973
$1.50

"One of the most frustrating, perplexing mysteries of the oceans is most generally known as the 'Bermuda Triangle,' or, as John Spencer most aptly puts it, the 'Limbo of the Lost,' This particular geographic location has become a kind of hole in the water through which have disappeared an unbelievable number of ships and planes.

The author presents a well-researched and documented compilation of airplanes and ships that have disappeared in this vast triangle of Atlantic Ocean, which includes such islands as the Azores, Cuba, Jamaica, Haiti, Dominican Republic, Puerto Rico, West Indies, Bahamas, and hundreds of small islands.

"Well over a thousand people and more than a hundred planes and ships have mysteriously disappeared there, without a trace—no debris, survivors, lifeboats, or oil slicks. Most often the ships' current position and time of arrival was radioed. After that, nothing. No further communication of any kind."

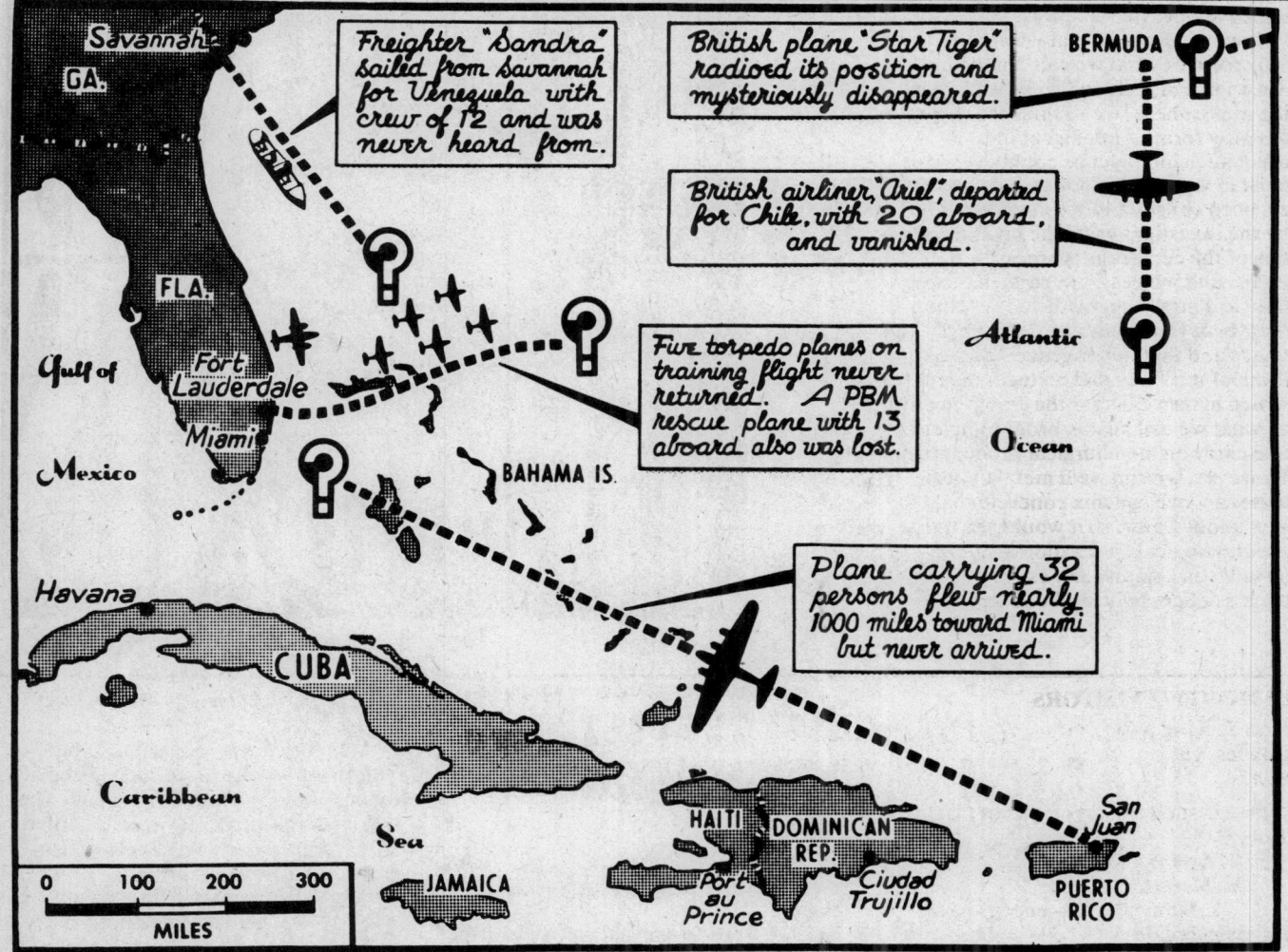

Map showing last recorded position of 9 planes and 1 ship lost in "The Devil's Triangle."

CHARIOTS OF THE GODS?
Erich Von Daniken
Bantam, 1970
$1.25

Cave drawings in Kohistan, France, North America, and Southern Rhodesia, in the Sahara and Peru, as well as Chile, all contribute to our theory. Henri Lhote, a French scholar, discovered at Tassili, in the Sahara, several hundred walls painted with many thousands of pictures of animals and men, including figures in short elegant coats. They carry sticks and indefinable chests on the stick Next to the animal paintings we are astonished by a being in a kind of diver's suit. The great god Mars—so Lhote christened him—was originally more than 18 feet high; but the "savage" who bequeathed the drawing to us can scarcely have been as primitive as we should like him to be if everything is to fit neatly into the old pattern of thought. After all, the "savage" obviously used a scaffolding to be able to drawin proportion like that, for there have been no shifts in ground level in these caves during the last millennia. Without overstretching my imagination, I got the impression that the great god Mars is depicted in a space or diving suit. . . .

* * * If our own space travers happen to meet primitive peoples on a p planet one day, they too will presumably seem like "sons of heaven" or "gods" to them. Perhaps our intelligences will be as far ahead of the inhabitants of these unknown and as yet unimagined regions as those fabulous apppions from the universe were ahead of our primitive ancestors. But what a disappointment if time on this as yet unknown landing place had also been progressing and our astronauts were not greeted as "gods" but laughed at as beings living far behind the times!

WAS GOD AN ASTRONAUT?

All over the world there are fantastic ruins and improbable objects which cannot be explained by reference to conventional theories of archeology, history and religion.

Why are the world's sacred books full of descriptions of gods who came down from the sky in fiery chariots and who always promised to return? How could an ancient Sanskrit text contain an account which can only be of a journey in a spaceship, complete with a graphic description of the force of gravity?

What possible explanations can be found for a huge block of rock the size of a four-story house, weighing some 20,000 tons, complete with steps, ramps and decorations? Then what titanic forces could have turned it upside down? Do maps found in the seventeenth century really outline the coast of Antarctica which within historical memory has never been free of a massive ice cap?

THE COSMIC CONNECTION: AN EXTRATERRESTRIAL PERSPECTIVE
Carl Sagan
Doubleday, 1973
$7.95

"The change in the climate of opinion about extraterrestrial life was reflected in 1971 by a scientific conference held in Byurakan, Soviet Armenia, and sponsored jointly by the Soviet Academy of Sciences of the U.S.S.R. and the National Academy of Sciences of the United States. I had the privilege of chairing the U.S. delegation to this meeting. The participants represented astronomy, physics, mathematics, biology, chemistry, archaeology, anthropology, history, electronics, computer technology, and cryptography. The group, which included two skeptical Nobel laureates, was marked for its crossing of national as well as disciplinary boundaries. The conference concluded that the chances of there being extraterrestrial communicative societies and our present technological ability to contact them were both sufficiently high that a serious search was warranted. . . ."

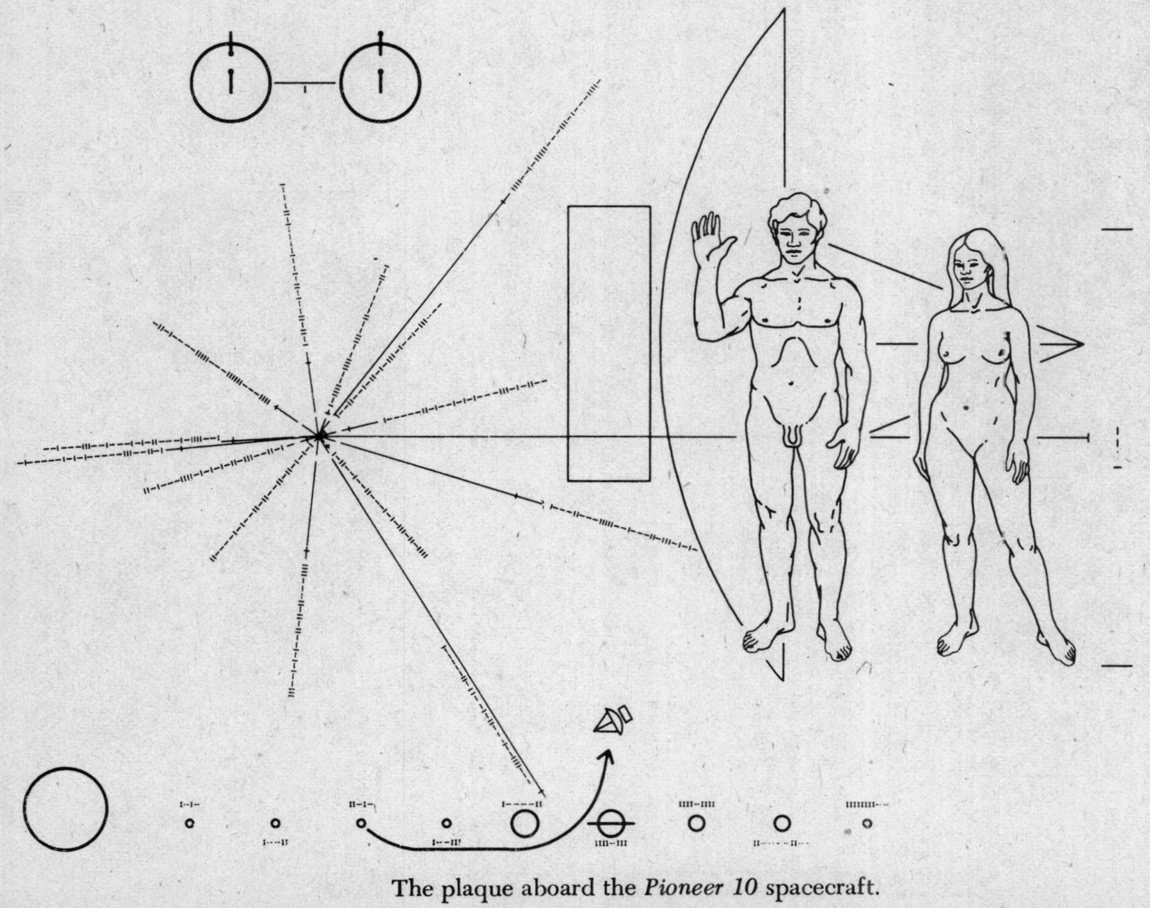

The plaque aboard the *Pioneer 10* spacecraft.

BEYOND EARTH: MAN'S CONTACT WITH UFOs
Ralph Blum and Judith Blum
Bantam, 1974
$1.50

"CAVETT: . . . on my left Carl Sagan, Professor of Astronomy at Cornell. He is a bit of a skeptic but is interested in the subject of whether there's life on other planets, even though—
(Turning to Sagan)
—you may not believe in UFOs. Have I misrepresented you there?

"SAGAN: No, I think that's fair. Belief is a serious question in science. Certainly there's nothing we know which would *exclude* the possibility of intelligent life on planets other than the ones in the solar system. But it's tough to travel between the stars, because the stars are ex*tremely* far apart. For example Pioneer 10 is the fastest space craft that we've ever launched, and it will be our first interstellar space craft to leave the solar system—it's travelling so fast that it will travel the distance to the nearest star in *only* eighty thousand years. That's our fastest space craft. Our slower ones take longer, of course. . . .

"(A ripple of laughter from the audience)

"CAVETT: What's the most convincing evidence that there may be life somewhere else?

"SAGAN: Well, there's certainly no—despite what I've heard so far—
(Chuckle)
today—there's no direct evidence I would say that forces us to believe that there's life elsewhere, much less intelligent life elsewhere. There's an awful lot of places. And there's an awful lot of time. And the molecules which make up life are littering the Universe. There's also the kind of Copernican tradition of how remarkable it would be if we happened to be living on the only inhabited planet—the chances are just enormous against that. The sun is one of maybe two hundred billion stars that make up the Milky Way Galary . . . And our galaxy is one of billions of other galaxies, so you have an e*nor*mous weight of numbers.

Pascagoula UFO occupant, as described by Charles Hickson to Tony Accurso, artist for the "Dick Cavett Show."

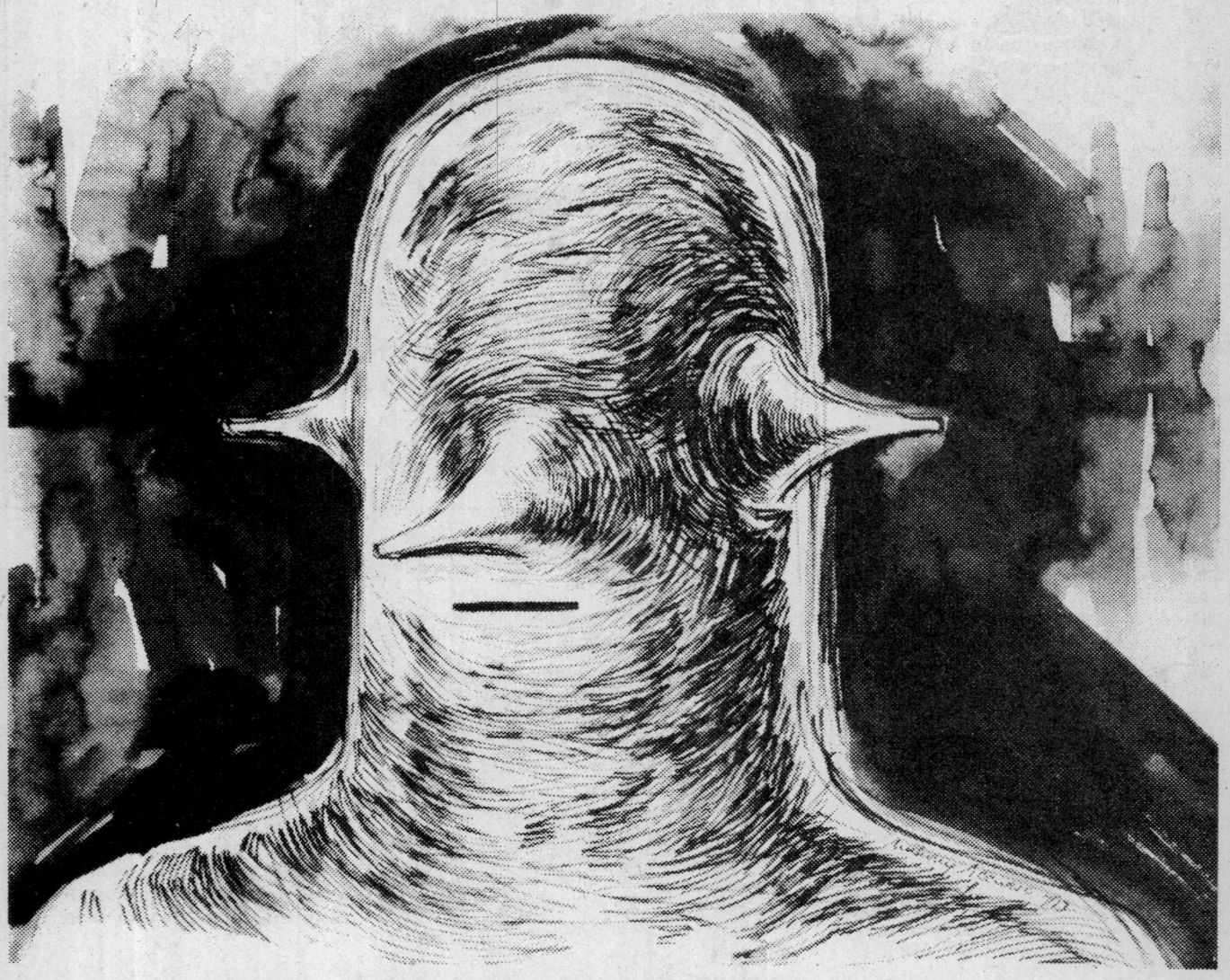

(Shifts to a light, dismissing tone)

"Now the UFO thing is very *interest*ing. There's no doubt, as Al Hynek said, about the emotional validity of some of the experiences that we've heard. The question is: what does it take to have belief?

"Perhaps a better question would be: What does it take to suspend disbelief, if only in the interest of scientific curiosity?

"For a start, it would help if men of Carl Sagan's stature didn't pretend on national television that the whole universe must be shackled by the limitations of *our* scientific knowledge. That 80,000-years-to-get-there ploy is a load of horsefeathers! The loud unspoken implication is: because *we* can't get to Proxima Centauri yet, no one in the universe is sufficiently advanced to get here."

REVELATION
Brad Steiger
Prentice-Hall, 1973
$7.95

"After exhaustive research and interviews, I am convinced that the soul-igniting mechanism of the gifts of Spirit did not cease with the prophets and saints of antiquity. I contend that the Divine Fire—the transfer of thought, spirit, and power from an Infinite Intelligence to a finite, human intelligence—is a vital, continuing process which observes no denominational boundaries and employs a spiritual-psychic mechanism that is timeless and universal. . . .

". . . So many revelators had mentioned being stunned, even blinded, by a brilliant light that seemed to beam down on them from the sky or that seemed suddenly to surround them. I wanted to know what my interviewees believed was the source of the 'blinding light' that so often signaled the onset of revelatory experience.

". . . I am writing about a transfer of thought and spirit from what we call God, or one of his messengers, to a recipient who feels compelled to share his revelation, or other spiritual gift, with his fellows. I am writing about the 'missionary' element in illumination that inflames the recipient with the desire to 'go quickly and tell,' to put his visions and dreams into practical application and help others discover for themselves the universal spiritual truths.

". . . Literally dozens of revelators throughout the world claim to be receiving direct communications from entities who identify themselves as beings from other worlds. In UFO research there is the phenomenon of the 'contactee,' one who claims special knowledge through direct communication with the occupants of what he is told is an extraterrestrial spacecraft. Again, we may be observing the evidence of an intelligence that presents itself to percipients in a manner that they will find most acceptable."

REVELATION
THE DIVINE FIRE

An Investigation of Men and Women Who Claim to be in Spiritual Communication with a Higher Intelligence
BY BRAD STEIGER

Here is an amazing monster safari, spanning five continents, in search of the legendary Loch Ness Monster and all his fabulous brethren wherever they are at home beneath the waves. Exploring that shadowy boundary where science meets the mysterious, a young investigator trained in anthropology and literature marshals compelling evidence of the existence and nature of the lake monsters that have stealthily inhabited the world's freshwater lakes for centuries.

While watchers sweep the skies for UFO sightings, and Erich von Däniken searches the past for traces of early astronauts, Peter Costello pursues elusive creatures like Scotland's "Nessie" —so famous that a permanent spotting station has been established by the lake to collect year-round data on the monster's habits. No creature out of the past has so consistently caught and held the imagination of scientist and general public alike as has the lake monster, its undulating coils and giant size belying its essentially gentle temperament. But the Loch Ness animal is not unique—the author introduces Idaho's "Slimey Slim," Sweden's "Storsjö Animal," Ireland's "Pooka" and "Piast," and Canada's "Ogopogo." Evidence of their existence is buttressed with eyewitness reports, rare photographs and drawings of the animals by their awed encounterers, plus a log of every onshore monster sighting recorded from the 1870's to the present.

IN SEARCH OF LAKE MONSTERS is the first work consistently to trace reports of all lake monsters from Scotland to Utah, British Columbia to Sweden, the jungles of Africa and New Zealand and taking in Patagonia and Siberia on the way. It offers intriguing evidence these fabulous creatures *do* exist.

IN SEARCH OF LAKE MONSTERS
Pete Costello
Coward, McCann & Geoghegan
1974

ON THE TRACK OF THE SASQUATCH, JOHN GREEN, AVAILABLE FROM:
CHEAM PUBLISHING LTD., BOX 99, AGAZZIZ, BRITISH COLUMBIA, CANADA. $3.40

What would you do if you were driving alone on a country road and saw a hair-covered human-shaped monster cross in front of your car?

Would you tell your wife what you saw?

Would she believe you?

Would you tell your friends?

Would they believe you?

Would you tell the police, or the people at a university?

Would you expect to be believed there?

If you think about those questions I expect you will note that there are few, if any of them to which you can answer "yes" with any degree of confidence. The people who know you well would ask what you had been drinking, or at best they might take you seriously enough to start worrying about you. The authorities would be polite to you, but they wouldn't do anything and they would be glad to see you go.

Right there is the key to the whole problem of the Sasquatch. No matter how often they are seen--and I expect that far more people see them than would see, for instance, wolverines--the information doesn't go anywhere. It doesn't add a weight of accumulated testimony because it doesn't accumulate at all.

We learn at our mother's knee that giants are only in fairy tales. Our religion teaches that only man is made in God's image. Scientists are sure that no advanced primate but man ever lived in North America. The result is a solid wall of rejection that goes far beyond scepticism.

The strange thing is that there is nothing about the Sasquatch that is particularly remarkable. An elephant is a far more unlikely animal, and a duckbill platypus even more so. Descriptions, photographs, footprints, all indicate that the Sasquatch is just a big primate of the same family as man and the anthropoid apes which has made the same adaption that man did for walking on only two legs. People ask what it could find to eat, but that isn't much of a problem. It shares its habitat with moose, elk and bears that are of similar size and far more numerous. Gorillas, which are just about as big, get along on a strictly vegetable diet.

The Sasquatch doesn't enjoy the same choice of fodder, but it also eats meat. The origin of such a creature is no problem either. Teeth and jawbones of something quite similar have been found in China. It lived 500,000 years ago, and has been described as being bigger than a gorilla but walking erect--a pretty good thumbnail description of what people have been seeing in North America all along. How it got here is also no problem. Man and a lot of types of animals are believed to have reached North America via a land bridge from Siberia. Gigantopithecus, as he has been labled, could easily have tagged along.

One question that is not answered to my satisfaction is how the Sasquatch population spends the winter. It is not too many years ago since trappers roamed the remote areas every winter, yet I know of relatively few reports of the big footprints being found in snow. It does happen, but not nearly as often as it seems to me reasonable to expect. There are several possibilities. Perhaps the creatures are few enough in numbers to come down to the sea coast in winter and avoid most of the snow. If they were going to migrate in that way, however, it would seem more likely that they would clear right out of the country and go south. They don't do that, or at least not all of them do, since footprints are sometimes found in the snow in northern B.C. right in the middle of winter. Perhaps they just made note of the trappers' regular routes and stayed well away from them. The most fascinating possibility is that they might hibernate as the bears do. It would be quite a thing for science to be able to study how one of man's nearest relatives was able to turn himself off and live for months without eating.

Another matter for speculation is the susceptibility of the Sasquatch to human diseases. All the apes can catch smallpox and tuberculosis, the white man's chief weapons in taking over North America from the Indians. It seems logical to suppose that the Sasquatch too would be hard hit by the introduction of these killers and that there may have been a long period when their numbers were greatly reduced.

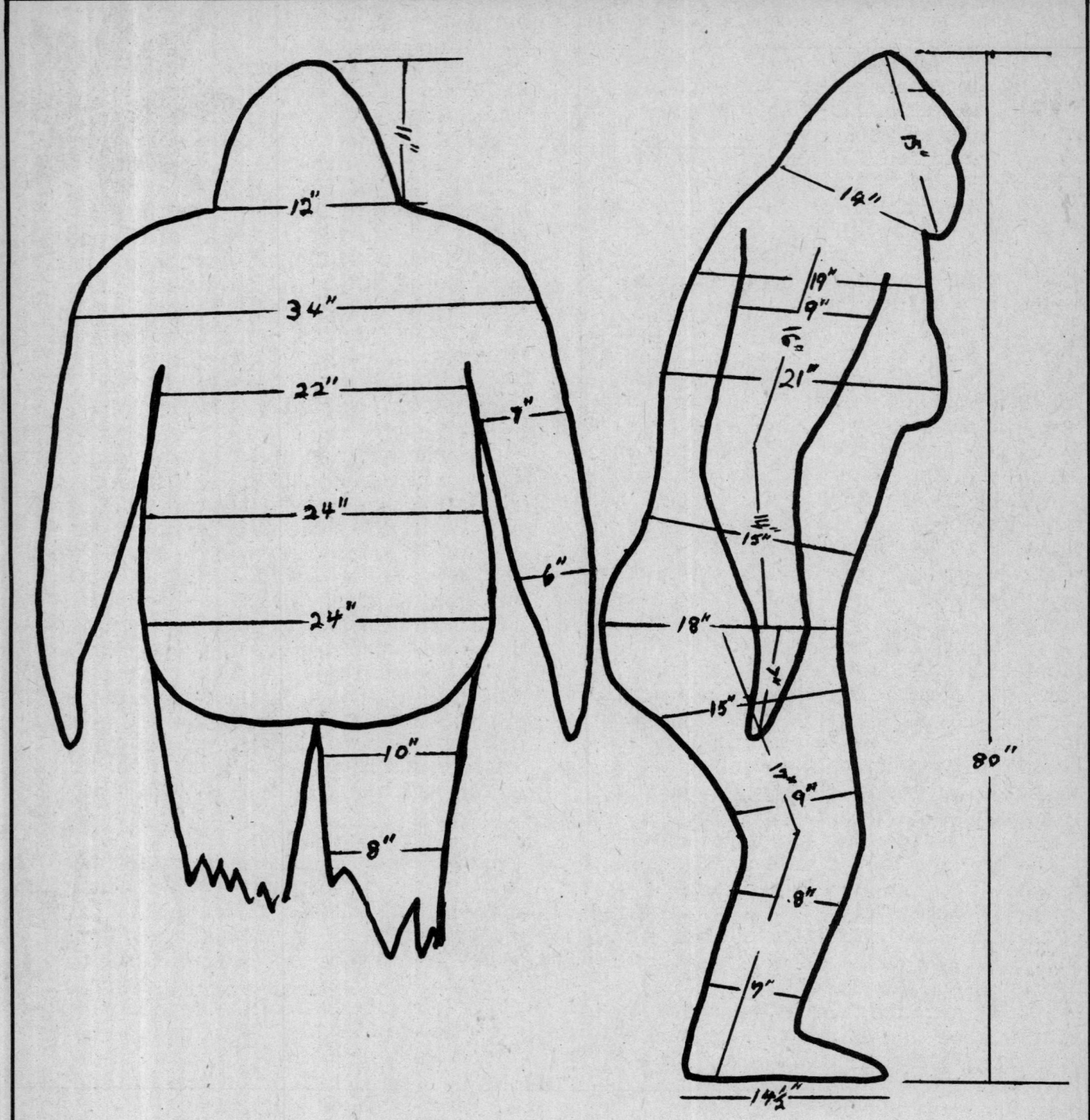

DIMENSIONS OF THE PATTERSON SASQUATCH

The measurements above are taken from Roger Patterson's movie of a Northern California Sasquatch, using the known length of the footprint, 14 1/2 inches, as a standard. Since the picture is blurred and the creature has a fur coat of unknown thickness, the measurements are not exact. Position of joints is estimated from the motion of the limbs. Measurements from the back are considerably less exact than from the side, as this view of the creature in the film is at a much greater distance. The approximate height is verified by comparisons made at the spot where the film was taken.

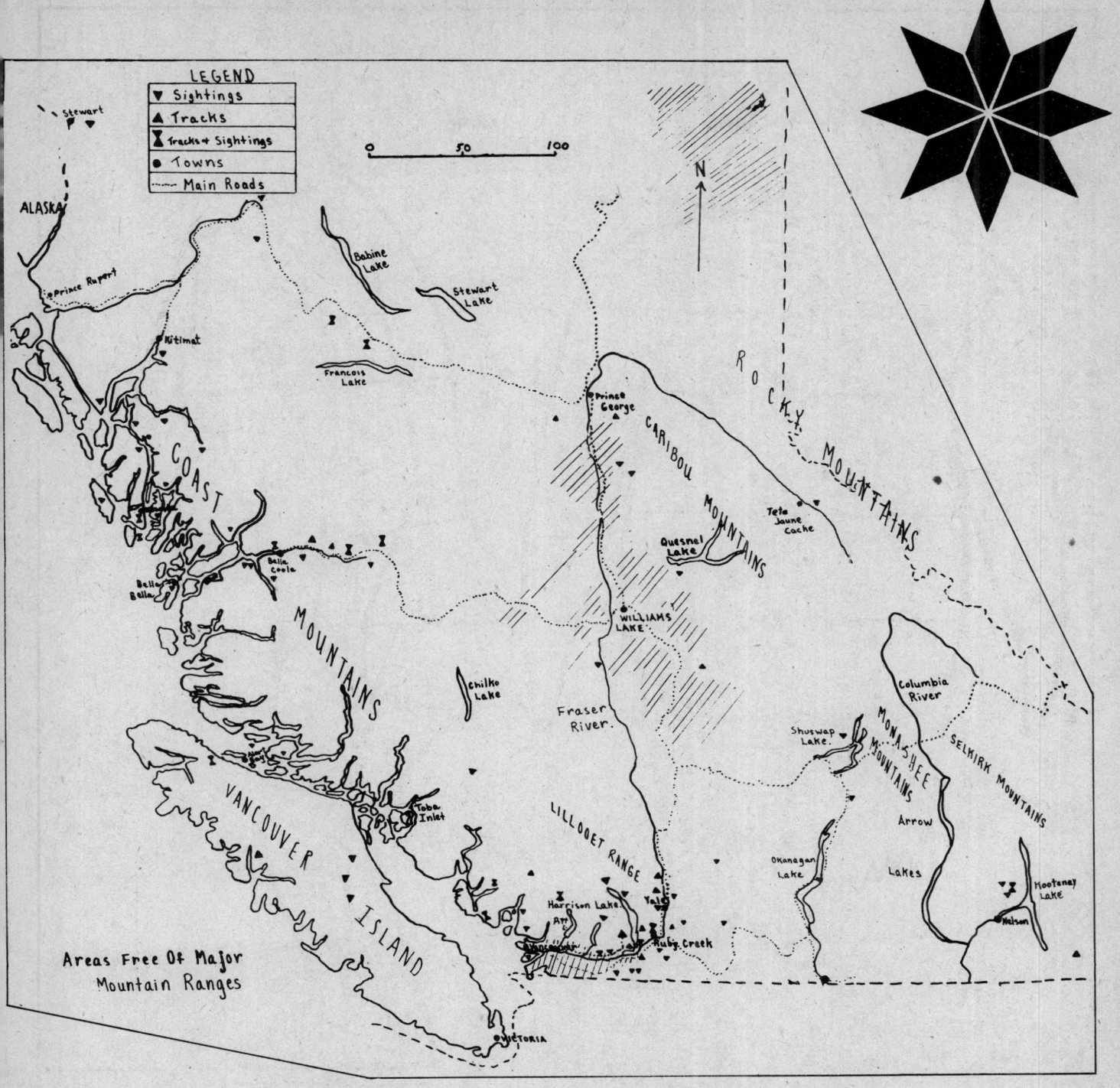

SIGHTING AND TRACK REPORTS IN BRITISH COLUMBIA

The maps in this book are intended only to give a general impression of the number and location of Sasquatch reports known to the author. Locations are not precisely plotted, nor have all the incidents shown been investigated. A secondary purpose is to indicate the amount of mountainous area. Only main roads are shown, but it should be noted that crossing the Coast Range in British Columbia and in some other substantial blocks of mountains there are very few other roads, if any. Concentration of reports along the road and water routes indicates not that the Sasquatch are concentrated in such locations but that there is where there are people to see them. Humans occupy only a very small percentage of the area of British Columbia. There are hundreds of thousands of square miles where man is only a very occasional visitor.

Slightly smaller than life size, this picture of a 13-inch footprint gives some idea of the depth to which the big footprints sink in packed, wet sand. Note that at the bottom of the picture a human boot makes only a slight surface impression.

PART SIX:
THE POWER OF THE MIND

The power of the human mind is not a toy to be played with indiscriminately. We are only beginning to develop a better understanding of the power of thought which an individual can unleash against himself or others. Good intentions can inadvertently produce bad effects when a person is not well enough informed of the implications of any given process.

There is also a growing belief that each individual is involved in a continuous communication process. People are inclined to believe that they can enter and step out of any communication at will, but there is evidence to indicate that this may not be the case. Information from a wide variety of communication networks may possibly be tapped at other levels of the self. That information can be broadcast to and be internalized by an individual without his awareness is a fact already established and exploited in subliminal advertising. A more conscious awareness of this kind of process may enable a person to achieve greater control of what he broadcasts and receives.

JADOO
John A. Keel
Pyramid, 1972
$1.25

WRITE TO:
Burchette Brothers Productions
P.O. Box 1363
Spring Valley, Calif. 92077

Ask for price list and information on the Psychic Medication home study course.

A NEW STEREO RECORD ALBUM OF MYSTICAL MUSIC

FOR MAGICAL PRACTICES AND MYSTIC MEDITATION

MAGIC, WHITE AND BLACK
Franz Hartmann, M.D.
Newcastle Publishing Company, 1971
$3.45

VOODOO IN HAITI
Alfred Metraux
Shocken, 1972
$3.95

RELIGION AND THE DECLINE OF MAGIC
Keith Thomas
Penguin, 1971
3 pounds

Telepathic Power, Magic, And The Power Of Symbols

uman beings communicate symbolically and as a result certain symbols have been endowed with particular powers. Passed from generation to generation they acquire a life of their own and can serve as strong focal points for generating human desires. Hex signs are a good example. An experienced Hexenmeister, knowing a thought to be a thing, sends out a symbolic telepathic blueprint of what he desires to be interpreted by the subject at the subconscious level. Practitioners of black magic similarly may create a mental image or link and charge it with enough energy to reach their victim. It is believed that a thought form of equal strength may neutralize such an attempt.

Legendary Penna. Dutch Hex Signs

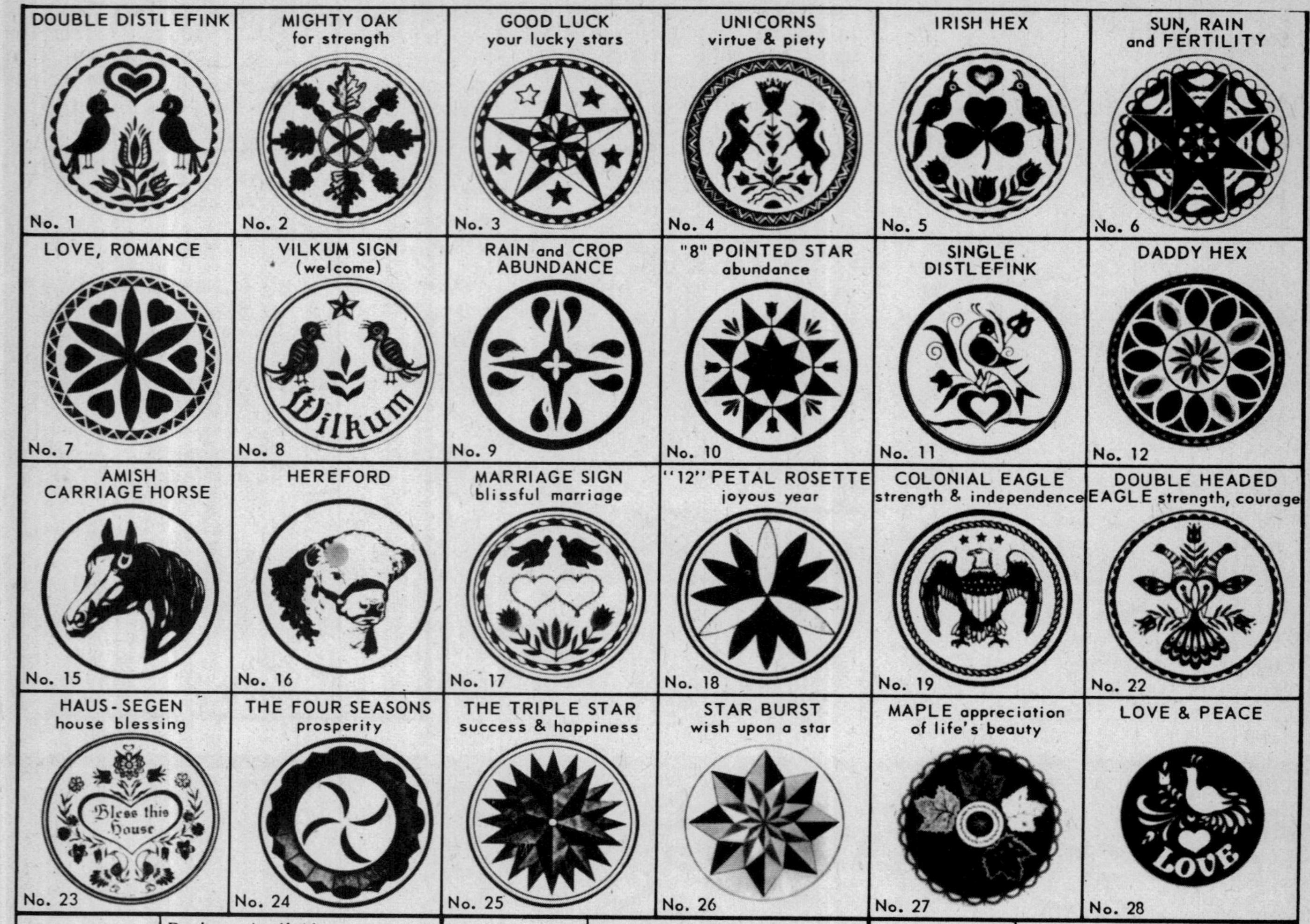

No. 1 DOUBLE DISTLEFINK	No. 2 MIGHTY OAK for strength	No. 3 GOOD LUCK your lucky stars	No. 4 UNICORNS virtue & piety	No. 5 IRISH HEX	No. 6 SUN, RAIN and FERTILITY
No. 7 LOVE, ROMANCE	No. 8 VILKUM SIGN (welcome)	No. 9 RAIN and CROP ABUNDANCE	No. 10 "8" POINTED STAR abundance	No. 11 SINGLE DISTLEFINK	No. 12 DADDY HEX
No. 15 AMISH CARRIAGE HORSE	No. 16 HEREFORD	No. 17 MARRIAGE SIGN blissful marriage	No. 18 "12" PETAL ROSETTE joyous year	No. 19 COLONIAL EAGLE strength & independence	No. 22 DOUBLE HEADED EAGLE strength, courage
No. 23 HAUS-SEGEN house blessing	No. 24 THE FOUR SEASONS prosperity	No. 25 THE TRIPLE STAR success & happiness	No. 26 STAR BURST wish upon a star	No. 27 MAPLE appreciation of life's beauty	No. 28 LOVE & PEACE

| Size 8" Price $1.00 ea. | Designs Available — 1-2-3-4-5-6-7-8-9-10-11-12-15-17-18-19-22-23-25-26-27-28 | Size 16" Price $2.00 ea. | Designs Available — 1-2-3-4-5-6-7-8-9-10-11-12-15-17-18-19-22-23-24-25-26-27-28 | Size 24" Price $5.00 ea. | Designs Available — 2-4-5-6-7-8-9-10-11-12-15-16-18-19-22-26 |

HISTORY — Hex Signs are a part of the legend and superstition of the early Pennsylvania Dutch settlers. They painted them on their large soaring barns, dower chests, birth and marriage certificates. Illustrated history and meaning sheet furnished with each Hex Sign.

Jacob and Jane Zook's Craft Shops
PARADISE • LANCASTER COUNTY • PENNSYLVANIA • 17562

NINE MILES EAST OF LANCASTER ON U.S. 30 - Tel.: Area Code 717 687-6333

**STRANGE EXPERIENCE:
THE AUTOBIOGRAPHY OF A
HEXENMEISTER**
Lee R. Gandee
Prentice-Hall, 1971
$6.95

"My Zachariah achariah Lee could command rain so well he could stop a shower at will, or bring up one in a few hours. Now *there* was a Hex! But one day he grew angry because lightning had struck his favorite shade tree and almost frightened his great-grandson to death, so he stepped to the edge of the porch, shook his fist at the clouds, and cried, ''Bust my tree and scare a little boy, damn you! This is old Zach; let's see you flash one at *me* once!' A Hex should not say such things. The lightning obeyed him; he was killed instantly.

". . . Binding however, implies more than idle thinking. To truly *bind*, there must be concentration and emotional intensity. In pow-wow, the concentration comes from remembering the odd incantations and the gestures, and the emotion is faith. In a black Hex, the concentration comes from the incantation and the ritual, and the emotion either from fear (of the devil and his demons) or from horror induced by some act of the ritual. In idle-minded hypochondria, disease is induced by the fear that one will develop the symptoms, by fear of contagion, and by some strong emotion—hate, envy, greed, or whatever—held simultaneously, though not necessarily in connection with the contemplation of disease.

". . . All my experience suggests that "magic" power is derived from the action of the mind at the subconscious level. A symbol is more potent than a naturalistic representation simply because a realistic drawing is interpreted mainly at the conscious level. I am left quite unmoved by all pictures of the Crucifixion that show the scene as it was, or might have been. The only one which ever reached down to the level of my subconsciousness showed it as it could *never* have been—on a German hilltop, with somber fir trees and brooding hillsides, but not a living soul—only the dead Christ and the dead malefactors, all forsaken equally. Even though the details were all but photographic in their realism, that paint painting a symbol. In fact the realism was the strongest symbol, for that is how it *is* with the crucified!

"In solitude and secrecy, the mind thinks in symbols—as is proved best by the graffiti found in public latrines. There the subconscious turns to sex, protesting that sex is as natural and necessary as defecation or urination. So if the repressed individual is responsive to the subconscious, and has a pencil or pen, he draws sexual symbols on the wall. Here he reverts to the most primitive pattern of thought, seeing the part as the whole, and drawing stylized sketches. If any body is represented, usually the genitals are greatly exaggerated, as in African fetishes and idols. It is quite revealing that such symbols drawn in college and art-school washrooms are not noticeably different from or superior in technique to those scribbled by truck drivers, coal miners, or stevedores. Below the belt all men are brothers, and so are they below the level of the conscious mind. For thousands of generations, man's subconsciousness has used symbol as the language of instinct and emotion and the phallic symbols made by prehistoric man are so like those made yesterday by your neighbor's son that they could be interchanged without exciting professional comment.

". . . A hex knows a thought to be a *thing*—a form with an electronic force field, so when he arranges his motifs what he really is doing is sending out into the universe a telepathic blueprint image of what he wishes materialized. Nature is so constituted that the image tends to be materialized and sent back. To be a witch, one must be able to send *sustained* images *far enough* out to attract enough energy to effect the materialization, and to draw this basic rosette sign with concentration pushes the signals across the entire universe, which, like Diriac's ocean, is without resistance. Space is no obstacle to telepathy.

"Internally, any structure (the universe or an atom) has certain lines and points of balance. In a Hex sign these are connecting alternate points around the circumference to the points opposite. In a six-segmented circle, these lines form two equilateral triangles so arranged as to have six equidistant points arranged around an internal hexagon. To surround oneself mentally with these six lines is to establish oneself within the strongest balance in the universe.

MENTAL RADIO
Upton Sinclair
Collier, 1971
$1.95

The book that inspired the modern scientific investigation of extrasensory phenomena is the account of the experiments of Upton Sinclair's wife, Mary Craig Kennedy. It explains step by step the methods she used for spontaneous concentration and relaxation—how to let yourself go in every muscle, every tense spot in the body and how to be conscious and unconscious at the same time. This is the method by which she found it possible to receive telepathic messages, to see pictures on hidden cards and symbolic pictures of the contents of books.

TELEPATHIC IMPRESSIONS: A REVIEW AND REPORT OF THIRTY-FIVE NEW CASES
Ian Stevenson, M.D.
University Press of Virginia, 1970
$6.50

THOUGHTS THROUGH SPACE
Harold Sherman and Sir Hubert Wilkins
Fawcett, 1973
95 cents

It all began when a group of Russian fliers crashed on the Alaskan side of the North Pole. The Russian government commissioned Sir Hubert Wilkins, famed Arctic explorer, to find and rescue them.

Just prior to leaving on the mission, he met Harold Sherman, who impressed him with his mental powers and knowledge of telepathy. They agreed to try this method of thought transference during Wilkins' rescue mission.

Wilkins and Sherman, though 3,400 miles apart—one encamped on the snow-swept Arctic tundra, the other living in a Manhattan apartment—kept in mind-to-mind contact three nights a week for six months!

THE NEW GOLDEN BOUGH: A NEW ABRIDGEMENT OF THE CLASSIC WORK BY SIR JAMES FRAZER
Dr. Theodore H. Gaster, ed.
Mentor, 1964
$1.95

SPIRIT MAGIC
Alice Wellman
Berkeley-Medallion, 1973
95 cents

EXPERIMENTS IN MENTAL SUGGESTION
V. V. Vasiliev
Institute for the Study of Mental Images, 1963
1 pound and 5 pence

THIS WORLD AND THAT: AN ANALYTICAL STUDY OF PSYCHIC COMMUNICATION
Phoebe D. Payne and Laurence J. Bendit
Quest, 1969
$2.00

BEYOND TELEPATHY
Andrija Puharich
Anchor Press, 1973
$2.50

"Dr. Rudolf von Urban, Dr. Alexander Pilcz, and some colleagues made a study of the Indian Rope Trick. They were interested in the problem of mass hallucination and it was their idea that the Indian Rope Trick would serve as a good experiment for their purposes. They collected several hundred people and a Fakir to put on the show. All of the observers, including the scientists, saw the Fakir throw a coil of rope in the air and saw a small boy climb up the rope and disappear. Subsequently dismembered parts of this small boy came tumbling down to the ground; the Fakir gathered them up in the basket, ascended the rope, and both the boy and the Fakir came down smiling. It is astonishing that several hundred people witnessed this demonstration and agreed in general on the details as described. There was not a single person present in the crowd who could deny these facts. However, when the motion pictures of this scene were developed subsequently, it was found that the Fakir had walked into the center of the group of people and thrown the rope into the air, but that it had fallen to the ground. The Fakir and his boy assistant had stood motionless by the rope throughout the rest of the demonstration. The rope did not stay in the air, the boy did not ascend the rope. In other words, everyone present had witnessed the same hallucination. Presumably the hallucination originated with the Fakir as the agent or sender. At no time in the course of the demonstration did the Fakir tell the audience what they were going to see. The entire demonstration was carried out in silence. In view of this fact we must assume that the hallucination was telepathically inspired and therefore extended to the several hundred people present as receivers of this delusion."

THE OCCULT REICH
J. H. Brennan
Signet, 1974
$1.50

"The swastika is one of mankind's oldest symbols, and apart from the cross and the circle, probably the most widely distributed. It is shown on a pottery fragment from Greece dating back to the eighth century B.C. It was used in ancient Egypt, India, and China. The Navaho Indians of North America have a traditional swastika pattern. Arab-Islamic sorcerers used it. In more recent times, it was incorporated in the flags of certain Baltic States.

"Early Christian missionaries to India, who found it on the head of Vishnu idols, called it the 'devil's sign.' In fact, in its original form, it was rather the reverse, a symbol of the sun and therefore of life. Buddhists thought of it as 'the accumulation of lucky signs possessing ten thousand virtues, being one of the sixty-five mystic figures which are believed to be traceable to every one of the famous footprints of Buddha.'" The very name is derived from the Sanskrit *svastika* meaning good fortune and well-being.

". . . Krohn produced designs for the actual form in which the Nazis came to use the symbol—with one important difference. It was this difference—and Hitler's reaction to it—which give us our first (although by no means our only) clue to the fact that the Third Reich was not merely a magical state, but a deliberately black magical or Satanic state."

THE CHALLENGE OF CHANCE: A MASS EXPERIMENT IN TELEPATHY AND ITS UNEXPECTED OUTCOME
Alister Hardy, Robert Harvie, Arthur Koestler
Random House, 1973
$8.95

In the autumn of 1967, on seven consecutive Monday evenings, 200 people met at Caxton Hall, Westminster, London, to participate in a series of visual experiments arranged by Professor Sir Alister Hardy. The form of the experiments was relatively simple. Volunteers were placed in enclosed cubicles so that they could see nothing outside. At the other end of the auditorium a picture or photograph was flashed on a screen, and the volunteers were then asked either to sketch what they imagined the illustration to be, or to describe it briefly in words.

The remarkable results are fully described and illustrated in this book, and they lead inescapably to some startling... conclusions. The original object was to investigate the possibility of telepathy, but quite unexpectedly, "simultaneous coincident thoughts," which were quite *unconnected* with those pictures employed in the tests, emerged from the people participating. Could they be attributed to telepathy?

Determined to subject these "coincidences" to the most searching scientific scrutiny, Sir Alister enlisted the services of Robert Harvie, a psychology graduate of London University with a training in statistical methods. The two men devised a series of unprecedented tests of the raw material that Hardy had gathered, and these convinced them that even if it played a part, telepathy was not the *whole* story. The coincidences in the controls were just as striking as those in the original experiment. Were they the result of mere chance? And just what do we mean by chance? That is the challenge in the title of this book.

At this stage the two scientists approached Arthur Koestler, whose *Roots of Coincidence* had made a plea for an open-minded approach to the subject of parapsychology, avoiding the opposite dangers of rigid materialism and superstitious credulity. It is in this spirit that the three authors of *The Challenge of Chance* have approached the whole field of coincidence, telepathy, precognition and related subjects. The result is a speculative book which reaches to the very frontiers of these fascinating problems—from a detailed and meticulous survey of the theory of random numbers (is there such a thing as "randomness"?) to the clusters of baffling personal coincidences which happen to all of us from time to time.

The Challenge of Chance may be the first book to be written jointly by a Fellow of the Royal Society and a Fellow of the Royal Society of Literature—with a psychologist providing the bridge between the two cultures. Sir Alister's introduction and description of the experiments and Mr. Harvie's statistical analyses are subjected by Mr. Koestler to a detailed examination which begins where *The Roots of Coincidence* left off. He concludes that the deterministic, mechanistic view of the world no longer has validity, and that materialism cannot claim to be a scientific philosophy. But though the speculations contained in this book only lift a corner of the curtain on the mysteries of causality and acausality, they point to the direction in which further research must proceed.

TALISMANS

TALISMANS

TALISMAN: Something, as a ring or stone, bearing engraved figures or symbols supposed to bring good luck, keep away evil, etc. Anything supposed to have magical powers, a charm.

AMULET: A charms, something worn, often around the neck, as a remedy or protection against evils or mischief. Amulets were common in earlier days. They consisted of stones, metals, or plants, and sometimes of words, characters, or sentences, arranged in a particular order.

Amulets and talismans are symbols which promise the unknown; they bring the intangible within our grasp. A wedding ring, a rabbit's foot, a crucifix—each is a symbol which we have made represent our dreams, our hopes. The influence of gems, stones, and metals on the physical, mental, and spiritual conditions of man was once a highly developed science. Vibratory forces from certain objects unite with similar forces within individuals, permitting them to receive and transmit healing vibrations, realize their desires, or obtain nourishment for soul development. Whatever the symbol, whether it is a number, a ring, stone, a necklace, a parchment seal, a certain color . . . it is only used to help us attune with the creative forces. It is intended to help us find strength in directing our destiny.

If you believe in the powers of talismans, we offer a magnificent collection from which you can select the ones you wish to put to the test. Our selection is so varied you will find one—or several—to fit the objective you have in mind . . . love, success, safety, protection, knowledge, wisdom. . . .

A truly worthy amulet does not have to be hand made at exorbitant prices. It is not the one who makes the talisman which gives it its magnetism and power. It is the possessor, the wearer, who imparts to the talisman that personal psychic energy, inherent in each individual, wherein lies trmendous protection, great persuasion, and our principal lines of contact and influence with others. It is the wearing of the talisman close to one's body which charges or magnetizes the inanimate symbol into a powerful positive or negative force. After you have made or purchased an amulet for a particular purpose, it should be worn and handled by you alone. Do not let others wear it, borrow it, or even touch it . . . keep it pure and clean and safe with only your own personal mystic powers flowing between your inner self and the talisman you have chosen.

Available from:
INTERNATIONAL IMPORTS
Box 2010
Toluca Lake, Calif. 91602

THE SORCERER'S HANDBOOK
Wade Baskin
Citadel Press, 1974
$4.95

THE MAGIC AND POWER OF SYMBOLS
Marguerite Haymes
Award, 1970
75 cents

MAGIC, SCIENCE AND RELIGION
Bronislaw Malinowski
Doubleday-Anchor, 1954
$1.25

TABOO
Franz Steiner
Pelican, 1967
95 cents

THE WORLD OF MAGIC
Ernesto de Martino
Pyramid, 1972
$1.45

MAGIC, SUPERNATURALISM AND RELIGION
Kurt Seligmann
Pantheon, 1971
$3.95

HIPSHER'S OCCULT SUPPLY HOUSE
419 E 33rd
Kansas City, Mo. 64109

Specialists in witchcraft and voodoo supplies

A HISTORY OF MAGIC
Jerome-Antoine Rony
Tower Book
95 cents

THE BOOK OF TALISMANS, AMULETS AND ZODIACAL GEMS
William Pavitt
Wilshire Book Company, 1974
$3.00

MAGICIANS, WIZARDS AND SORCERERS
Daniel Cohen
Lippincott, 1973
$4.95

INTERNATIONAL IMPORTS
BOX 2010-PL • TOLUCA LAKE, CALIF. 91602

LARGEST MAIL ORDER SOURCE FOR ALL OCCULT SUPPLIES!

Magical / Metaphysical / Psychic / Spiritual

TALISMANS

Ancient occult texts reveal that talismans are effective against all perils of Air, Earth, Fire, and Water; they can be used against all kinds of illnesses, terrors, and fear, and as a protection against all forms of magic and sorcery. We make no magical claims for any items offered, but if you believe in the powers of charms, we offer a most extensive collection of quality talismans.

EGYPTIAN SCARAB

A charm which, from time immemorial, has been prized as an emblem of the Great Creator of the Universe. It figures on all their ancient buildings, ruins and temples and has been discovered by the thousand in the tomb of Tutankhamen. Scarabs were worn by the living and buried with the dead. It is a favorite Egyptian talisman for good luck and protection against misfortune. We offer a variety of these amulets so that you may choose the ones most suited to your budget and preference.

1275 - SCARAB NECKLACE - The design on the left above is $1\frac{1}{4} \times 1\frac{1}{2}$", antiqued silver finish pewter on 24" neckchain . . . . $ 3.50

The center design above is 1/2 x 3/4" electroplated gold finish, and is available in any of the following pieces.

2387-N	Necklace . .	8.50	2387-P	Pins (Set of 2) . . 8.50
2387-B	Bracelet . .	7.50	2387-C	Cuff Links 8.50
2387-T	Tie Clip . .	6.00	2387-R	Ring (Adjustable) . 6.00

The design on the right above is 3/8 x 5/8" and is available in either sterling silver or 14 Karat gold.

2467 - Scarab Necklace in Sterling Silver . . . . $ 24.50

2468 - Scarab Necklace in 14 Karat Gold . . . . $ 89.50

International Imports
Box 2010
Toluca Lake, Calif. 91602

Talismanic Magic

SOLOMON, King of Israel. Son of David and Bathsheba, Solomon was a King, the son of a King, the wise son of a wise father, a righteous man's righteous child. Solomon was born in the year 986 B.C., and reigned over Israel for forty years. Fortune seemed to favor this great king and his land prospered, his kingdom and his fortune grew, and peace prevailed all through his lands. Many Biblical stories are told of his miraculous powers and prophetic ability. Writings attributed to him are the Book of Proverbs, Ecclesiastes, the Song of Solomon, and the Wisdom of Solomon. Solomon promises us that we can obtain information, bring up facts from the sub-conscious, destroy our enemies, understand the voices of nature, heal diseases, and obtain treasures.

The six amulets we offer are all of antiqued silver finish pewter, about 1½" in diameter or width and will add much interest to any talismanic collection.

2159 - HEXAGRAM OF SOLOMON . . . . $ 3.00
Worn as a protection against misfortune, this is designed to make the spirits obedient to the wearer's wishes and desires.

1147 - MAGIC CIRCLE OF SOLOMON -
. . . . $ 3.00
Solomon himself allegedly wore this design as a protection against evil spirits.

1860 - MAGIC DISC OF SOLOMON. . $ 3.00
This is the form of the Magic Ring which is held before the face to protect the wearer from all stinking fumes and from the flaming breath of evil spirits.

2446 - MAGIC TRIANGLE OF SOLOMON . . . . . $ 3.00
Solomon reputedly bound and command all evil spirits with the wearing of this talisman.

2161 - PENTAGRAM OF SOLOMON
. . . . $ 3.50
The five-pointed star is the universal symbol of man (his head plus the four limbs of the body and likewise the four fingers plus the thumb of the hand). Also symbolic of the five senses — seeing, hearing, tasting, smelling, and touching. Worn on the breast, this talisman is said to protect the possessor from all dangers and all harmful or malicious spirits.

2158 - SOLOMON'S SEAL . . . . $ 3.50
With this Secret Seal, King Solomon is claimed to have gained the love of all manner of persons and was victorious in battle for neither weapons, nor fire, nor water could hurt him.

Voodoo Dolls...

International Imports
Box 2010
Toluca Lake, Calif. 91602

The magic menagerie

All types of dolls are used in Voodoo practice — cloth, clay, wax, straw, or just a flat image cut from paper. Practitioners believe one should work with one doll for one purpose — if the object of the "spell" or the objective changes, a new doll must be used. A doll should have a name tag attached and adorn it, if possible, with a bit of clothing or an object belonging to the person the doll is to represent. No magical claims are made for any of our dolls, and they are offered as curios only. All dolls are about 6" tall and come packaged with name tag, pin, cord, and description of How to Voodoo with Dolls.

4030 - **RED DOLL** (Love, romance) Handmade cloth, Haitian designed

4032 - **GREEN DOLL** (Luck, money, gambling) "

4033 - **YELLOW DOLL** (Dispel evil influences) "

4034 - **PINK DOLL** (Success, attraction) "

Only $1.50 ea

1777 - **MINI DOLLS** - Tiny 1¼" hand made dolls, imported from South America. 3 dolls with pins, tags, and How to Voodoo with dolls . . . $1.00

DOLL MAGIC

Each "Spell Kit" is complete with the detailed ritual to be followed and all supplies necessary, including the appropriate color doll to use.

3062 - ATTRACT MONEY or WEALTH $5.00

3063 - TO BREAK A HEX or SPELL $6.00

3065 - FINDING A LOVER $5.00

THE SPEAR OF DESTINY: THE OCCULT POWER BEHIND THE SPEAR WHICH PIERCED THE SIDE OF CHRIST
Trevor Ravenscroft
Putnam, 1973
$8.95

"For 2,000 years the Spear of Destiny, since it pierced the side of Christ, has been invested with amazing occult powers.

This book records this legend and its continuing fulfilment in the decline of the Roman Empire, the Dark Ages and the twentieth century. It tells the story of the chain of men who possessed the spear from Herod the Great to Adolph Hitler, and how they sought to change the face of history by wielding its occult powers for good or evil. . . ."

AMULETS CHARMS AND TALISMANS
Deborah Lippman and Paul Colin
M. Evans, 1974
$4.95

"The world was an extremely vital place for early man. Everything possessed an animate, natural power invisible to the human eye. This force, or mana, is the power by which magic works. The mana in any object can be intensified or deployed by means of certain words or rituals. Some things naturally possess more mana than others; these came to be employed as amulets. These natural amulets were of a variety of materials: herbs, stones, or dried lizards to name just a few. They were chosen because of ther unusual form or color (e.g. perforated or sparkling stones) or because they came from an animal whose characteristics man wished to emulate. The parts of the body with which animals killed their prey were regarded as very potent magical objects.

"In addition to merely finding natural objects endowed with mana, man began to create his own charms. The Egyptians were the first to make amulets of durable materials, but other civilizations weren't far behind. The most common form of manmade amulets were small models of animals and medallions or lockets containing sacred inscriptions. Amulets are usually graphic representations of divine powers or symbolic signs. Early amulets tended to embody religious principles in graphic symbolic forms. These amulets not only absorbed local religious deities but incorporated and called upon as many deities as possible, without regard to any existing or nonexisting connections between these gods.

"By and large, amulets can be broken down into two classes: the personal or individual, and the general. The personal amulet is the one that protects man from disease, increases strength and virility, and protects from a specific danger such as plague or lightning. These amulets should be carried or worn in contact with the skin or the specific part of the body they are designed to protect. The general amulets work in a sphere of influence and are designed to protect towns, homes, etc. Early civilizations usually constructed mammoth sphere of influence amulets that were placed upon the walls of their cities.

"A talisman is virtually the same thing as an amulet except that it is intended for a very specific purpose, and an amulet is of a more general nature. Also, an amulet is endowed with special powers of protection or the ability to bring good fortune. It cannot do harm, while a talisman can be constructed for evil purposes.

". . . Most amulets are constructed according to the principles of contagious and sympathetic magic. Sympathetic magic works according to the Law of Correspondences and homeopathy. That is, like cures like and like things produce like effects. Belief in this law causes Tyrolese hunters to wear eagle feathers when they wish to gain the keen eyesight of this bird, and other cultures to use green (the color of vegetation) stones as amulets for fertility. The Law of Correspondences further states that all causation here on earth is a reflection of True processes. Certain natural objects and symbols are representations of spiritual truths. These symbols can be employed to achieve certain results on the mundane level. Into this category also falls the use of the names and signatures of gods and spirits. The name of the god contains the essence and power of its being and an amulet bearing the signature of this name brings the wearer into direct contact with the power of the deity and allows for its invocation. Contagious magic works on the principle that things which were once in contact magically retain a bond with each other. Such things as articles of clothing, locks of hair, and nail parings are materials commonly employed. Thus, by acting with or upon a part, the whole is effected. ". . . Many people believe that there are individuals who can injure or kill with a glance. Throughout small European towns, the inhabitants wear protective amulets against the Evil Eye. Mothers shoo their children inside when a person believed to be a "fascinator" walks by. These people inflict untold harm, especially upon babies and small animals. Sometimes they do this without even wanting to; and many sad stories are told about people forced to leave their homes and families for fear of gazing upon them with the Evil Eye."

How To Make Amulets, Charms & Talismans

What They Mean & How To Use Them

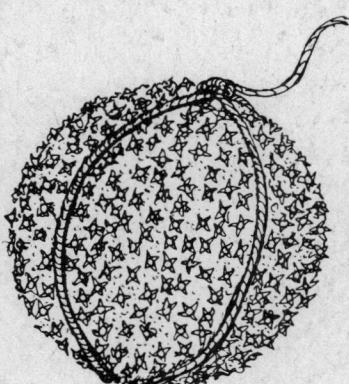

by Deborah Lippman & Paul Colin

THE COMPLETE BOOK OF VOODOO
Robert W. Pelton
Berkley, 1972
95 cents

"Voodoo is a powerful religious concept that cannot be understood or correctly utilized, unless one sincerely believes. It is a force working only from within the individual practitioner—never from without. Those on the outer fringes rarely get to know certain basic Voodoo secrets. Those who seriously practice this mystical religious art will not reveal these secrets.

"Many people, including scholars, claim Voodoo is a combination of black magic, snake worship, licentious sexual orgies, unspeakable brutality, and cannibalism—yet Voodooists observe all important religious holidays of the Christian year. . . .

". . . Thought hought transference of a houngan or a mambo is one of Voodoo's most powerful weapons. It is best utilized in the successful casting of a wanga on an enemy. Distance seems to have absolutely no bearing on how well a hex, curse, or crossing works. Seems rather fantastic and farfetched? It may well be, yet innumerable reports verify the fact that knowledgeable Voodoo practitioners actually can accomplish this very thing.

"Voodoo dolls are most commonly used hexing another individual. It must always be remember that it is not the doll itself, for *it* is merely the medium which represents the intended victim. And the doll is the means by which thought transference is successfully transmitted. The doll is the means by which direct contact is established between the priest or priestess and the person to be made ill, wounded, or even sometimes killed. The actual act is the end result of powerful concentrated thoughts.

"The best Voodoo dolls (most powerful and effective) *must* be made by the Voodooist who intends to cast a specific spell on someone. It must be created out of a number of items carrying the intended victim's vibrations—personal things which are used or worn by the individual, or a part of the victim's physical being. An item of clothing should be used for the doll's outer covering. Try to get something recently worn by the victim (a shirt, shorts, socks, etc.)."

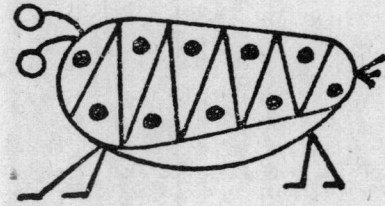

Loa Guede-masaka—protects wearer against poisoning.

Loa Ezili-Freda-Dahomey—leads wearer to sensual pleasures.

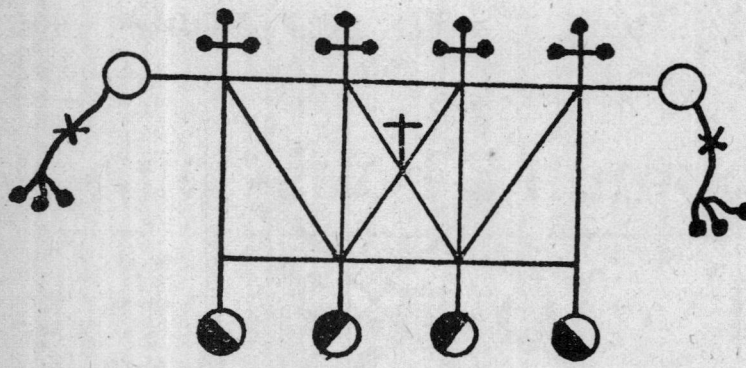

Loa Danh—brings wearer and associates tremendous wealth.

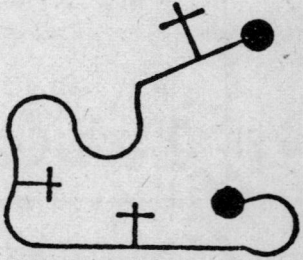

Loa Bakulu-Baka—protects wearer from death hexes.

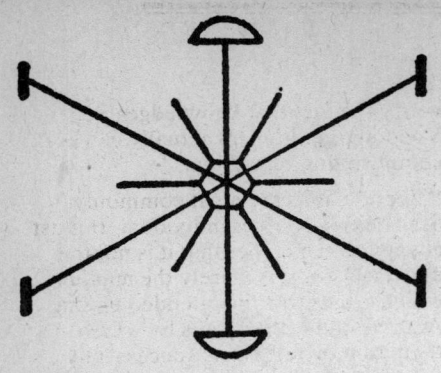

Loa Marinette—protects against all sickness.

Loa Zaca Tonerre—protects interests of the poor.

Loa Guede-Nimbo—helpful in all areas of life. A very lucky talisman.

Loa La-Sirene—aids in the seduction of the opposite sex.

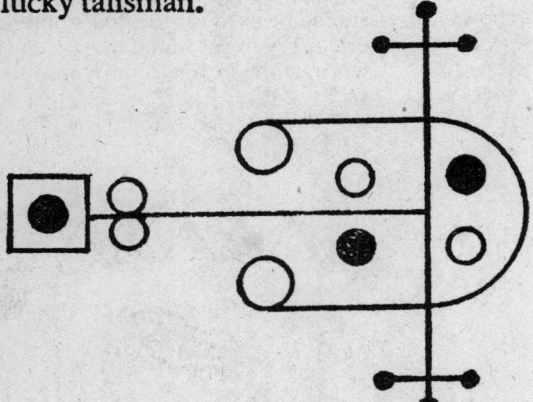

Loa Avrada—assists wearer in childbirth and pregancy.

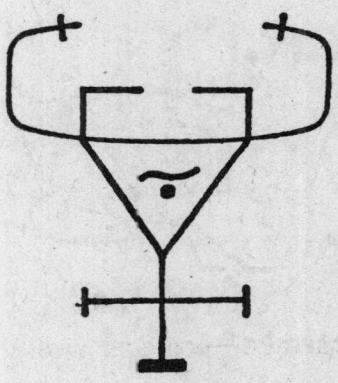

Loa Aizan—protects wearer from all evil spirits.

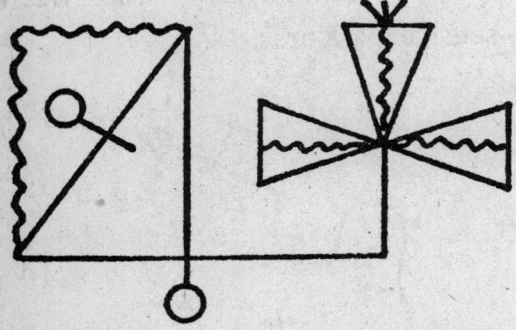

Loa Loco—gives healing power to wearer.

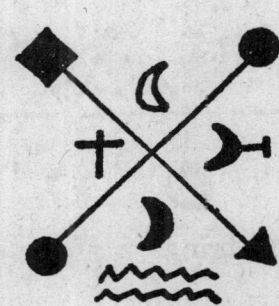

Loa Bossu-trois-cornes—protects wearer from all war injuries and accidents.

PSYCHIC SELF-DEFENSE:
A Study In Pathology and Criminality
Dion Fortune
Samuel Wiser, 1973.
$6.00

For the first time a professed Occultist explains how to detect psychic attacks and provides detailed instructions for defense against them.

This book includes revelations concerning Black Lodges, the methods employed in making a psychic attack, motives for psychic attack the physical aspect of it and defense.
Dion Fortune also deals with Vampirism, the pathology of non-human contacts, projection of the etheric body, and substances employed in Black Magic.

Witchcraft And Demonology

t is extremely unfortunate that many members of the psychic community shy away from attempting to consider and study the underlying beliefs in witchcraft. This may be partly due to a deeply ingrained prejudice clouded by ill-defined religious perspectives as well as an inability to view human rituals within a much wider cultural perspective. However, like any other system, witchcraft is open to severe abuse. Due to the wide misinterpretations of its aims and the often mysterious and ominous reputation surrounding its practice, it may be just that more difficult to develop a clear appraisal of what it can offer.

A witch in her dominion. Behind her stands the symbolic source of her power, a huge, shadowy male figure silhouetted against the sun, bearing in his left hand a horned moon and in his right a star. In front of the witch are her imps, a cat and a hare. Around her various figures and objects represent aspects of the witch's role in the community—influencing for example the weather, and fertility and health in humans, livestock and nature, and consulting the stars for a glimpse of the future.

WITCHCRAFT, by Erich Maple.

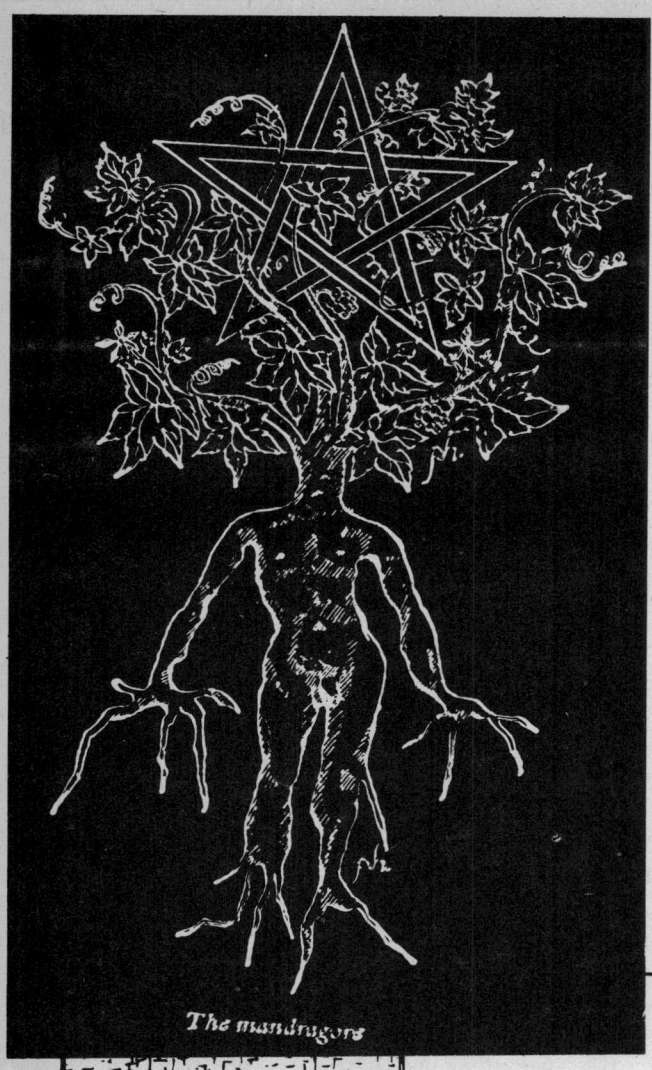
The mandragora

The Most Complete Line Of
Occult Supplies

Candles - Oils - Incense - Herbs

Special Discount to
Witches - Mediums - Spiritualists
Send 25c for Catalog

Wholesale - Retail

Fulton Religious Supply Co.

1304 Fulton St.
Bklyn. N.Y. 11216

PAUL HUSON, *Mastering Witchcraft: A Pictorial Guide For Witches, Warlocks & Covens,* Berkley
—illustrations done by Paul Herdsen,

An execution of witches in England

A HISTORY OF THE DEVIL
William Woods
Putnam 1974
$6.95

THE BLACK ARTS
Richard Cavendish
Capricorn, 1968
$2.45

"The driving force behind black magic is hunger for power. Its ultimate aim was stated, appropriately enough, by the serpent in the Garden of Eden. Adam and Eve were afraid that if they ate the fruit of the Tree of the Knowledge of Good and Evil they would die. But the serpent said, 'Ye shall not surely die: for God doth know that in the day ye eat thereof, then your eyes shall be opened and *ye shall be as gods*, knowing good and evil'. In occultism the serpent is a symbol of wisdom, and for centuries magicians have devoted themselves to the search for the forbidden fruit which would bring fulfilment of the serpent's promise. Carried to its furthest extreme, the black magician's ambition is to wield supreme power over the entire universe, to make himself a god.

"Black magic is rooted in the darkest levels of the mind, and this is a large part of its attraction, but it is much more than a product of the love of evil or a liking for mysterious mumbo-jumbo. It is a titanic attempt to exalt the stature of man, to put man in the place which religious thought reserves for God. In spite of its crudities and squalors this gives it a certain magnificence.

". . . In this unified magical universe mysterious forces are at work, moving beneath the external fabric of things like the invisible currents of the sea. Their effects are all around us, but most of us do not recognize their true nature. The universe is man on a huge scale and the impulses which move man—love, hate, lust, pity, the urge to survive, the urge to dominate—are found on a much greater scale in the universe. For instance, all things contain a greater or lesser amount of 'life-force', an immensely powerful drive which impels life to continue. It shows itself in the instinct of self-preservation, in the urge to survive—the struggle of everything in Nature to cling to life even in cruel and hopeless conditions—and in the universal urge to procreate, to ensure life's continuation by reproducing one's own kind. Magicians also see a force of violent destructive energy in the universe, which is a greater counterpart of man's destructive impulses and lies behind every form of savagery, bloodshed, warfare and havoc. These forces are named for gods and planets. The life-force is called the force of the sun, because the sun's light and heat are necessary for the existence of all life on earth. The violent destructive force is named for Mars, the Roman god of war.''

THE SATANIC CHURCH
208 South Taylor
Oak Park, Ill. 66302

. . . One of the major beliefs of the Church is to continually expand our minds, by the utilization of the knowledge of the ancients; which encompasses:
The age old study of witchcraft. . . .

The complete understanding and practice of the Art of Demonology. . . .

A thorough knowledge of astrology and herbology. . .

With these, and all other related philosophies any member can learn to harness nature and the elements to his advantage. By this control he will be able to shape his destiny, and the destiny of others.

We also believe in reincarnation of the soul, thru which the understanding of the Satanic Religion's Doctrine unfolds.

A part of the Doctrine we are sure you would be interested in, is the degrees that are available to you. The Church offers the Chela, which is the novice, or initiate, sufficient knowledge to progress to an active member. Once active, this member has the opportunity to enter into the Ministry if so desired.

You now have the opportunity of becoming a Chela in the Satanic Church by enclosing a check for fifteen dollars; which entitles you to your membership card. You will also receive your Church medallion and an informative newsletter which will be sent to you on a quarterly basis. With your membership courses are offered to you in the following subjects on cassette tapes:

Witchcraft, the history and precepts of . . . Psychometry . . . Tarot . . . Palmistry. . . Crystal Ball grazing . . . image and Voodoo magic. . . .

MALLEUS MALEFICARUM
Montague Summers, trans. Heinrich Kramer and James Sprenger
Avon, 1971
$1.95

"The most famous of all books about witchcraft, *Malleus Maleficarum* was written in 1486 by two Dominican monks. At once, and for the next three centuries, it became the indispensable handbook and ultimate authority for the Inquisition; for every judge, magistrate and priest, Catholic and Protestant, in the struggle against witchcraft in Europe.

INTERNATIONAL IMPORTS
Box 2010
Toluca Lake, Calif. 91602

RECORDS
THE SATANIC MASS—First time on record! Anton LaVey, first High Priest of the Church of Satan, recites a number of invocations to Satan, to the conjuration of lust, and to the conjuration of destruction. Included also are readings from The Satanic Bible. A great party piece, a soul-searching document, or a blasphemous production—depending on your own individual outlook and point of view—$6.00

WITCHCRAFT AND MAGIC—An Adventure in Demonology told by Vincent Price. Secrets of magic and witchcraft revealed—how to make love potions, charms, spells and curses, raising the devil, invoking demons and unseen forces, how to become a practicing witch, witch tortures, the witches' sabbat, the magic bloodstone, and much more! 104 minutes of information for use, study and entertainment. A 2-record set—$8.50.

PSYCHIC MEDITATION—WITCHCRAFT MUSIC RECORDS.
Free Brochure (Dealers Welcome)
Transcendentalist
Box 1363, Spring Valley, Calif. 92077.

CATALOGUE
Write to:
Marlar Publishing Co.
Publishers and Distributors
Box 17038
Minneapolis, Minn. 55417

"It covered the powers and practices of witches, their relationship with the Devil, their detection, the setting up and conduct of Courts to try them, the use of torture, methods of punishment. The Inquisition, the burnings, the torture, mental and physical, of the crusade against witchcraft; these are notorious. And behind every blood-stained act lay this book; at once justification and instruction manual.

RECORD SALE

WITCH OR WARLOCK?

TWO-RECORD SET!

The only record of its kind on the market!

BARBARA, THE GRAY WITCH tells all!

ESP – EXORCISM – RITUALS – VOODOO – OUIJA BOARD – SPIRITS ... and MORE !!

Order # 1332 – BARBARA, The Gray Witch $7.95

2 Records

Save more than $4.00 on an album that can change your life.

You may have been born a witch or warlock and do not know it! Up until the release of the album "Barbara, The Gray Witch," the only way your witchcraft abilities could be measured was by contacting a coven of witches and warlocks. But now for the first time, these tests are made available to the public. You can now test yourself in the privacy of your home. "Barbara, The Gray Witch" also exposes secret experiments designed to measure your witchcraft potential—even if you're just an interested mortal. Almost 90-minutes of non-stop witchcraft information ... including 6 of the most hauntingly, beautiful chants ever recorded! It's all yours on "Barbara, The Gray Witch." This album is an "under-the-counter" best seller at $11.98. But if you mail the coupon below today, you'll receive this fascinating stereo two-record set for just $7.95. That's right! However, only a limited number of these albums can be sold at more than $4.00 below the manufacturer's list price—so order today!

Three ESP tests which can lead you into telepathy ✦ How to check your psychic phenomena abilities by logging your dreams ✦ How to use the Ouija Board more effectively in contacting "earth-bound" spirits ✦ How to call forth a spirit from the other life — by yourself and in your own home ✦ What rewards can you expect from witchcraft ✦ Which realm to practice—black, white or gray ✦ How to contact a coven ✦ How to furnish your witchcraft room ✦ What it would be like practicing witchcraft in a modern society ✦ The christening and purification rituals in the black realm ✦ How a black coven calls forth Satan and his demons ✦ How black witches and warlocks get imps and cadavers, and how these evil spirits work ✦ What is the real strength behind tarot cards ✦ How white covens use voodoo to rid the neighborhood of undesirables ✦ Why the gray faith is called the modern realm of witchcraft ✦ How to perform the rewarding prosperity ritual in your own home ✦ How a gray witch or warlock can continue a love affair beyond death ✦ And how to exorcise an evil spirit.

The Satanic Mass

FIRST TIME ON RECORD! Authentic Satanic ceremony conducted by Anton LeVey, first High Priest of the Church of Satan.

INVOCATIONS TO SATAN

READINGS FROM THE SATANIC BIBLE ... the SATANIC BEATITUDES ...

Order # 6660 – THE SATANIC MASS $6.00

WITCHCRAFT AND MAGIC, An Adventure in Demonology told by VINCENT PRICE..

How to Make Love Potions
Charms, Spells and Curses
How to Become a Practicing Witch
The Witches' Sabbat
And much more!
104 minutes of information

Raising the Devil
Invoking Demons
Witch Tortures
The Magic Bloodstone
To use, Study, and Entertain
Two-Record Set

Order # 2063 – WITCHCRAFT AND MAGIC – The 2-Record Set $8.50

SPECIAL SAVING

Get ALL THREE ALBUMS described above and save $2.45 over our individual prices..

Order # 3036 – 3 Albums (Barbara, The Gray Witch, a two record set) – (The Satanic Mass) – and (Witchcraft and Magic, a two-record set) .. LIMITED TIME OFFER $20.00

INTERNATIONAL IMPORTS
BOX 2010 - TOLUCA LAKE, CALIF. 91602

The New Broom

A JOURNAL OF WITCHCRAFT

Published Quarterly

$4.00 per year

P.O. Box 1646 * Dallas, Texas 75221

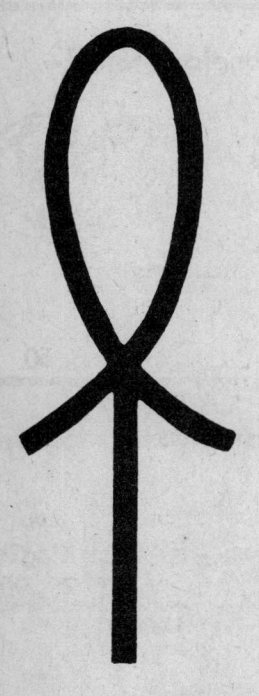

WITCHCRAFT

Learn the theory and practice of **WITCHCRAFT**. Obtain serenity and fulfillment. Send $1.00 for Serenity Guide, protective pentacle and course information.

A NON-PROFIT ASSOCIATION

CHURCH AND SCHOOL OF WICCA
Route 2
Salem, Missouri 65560

Earth Religious Supplies, Inc.

Pagan & Witchcraft Supplies
Herbs, Books, Jewelry & Paraphernalia

85 Atlantic Avenue
Brooklyn, NY 11201
Mail order catalog $1.00 (no currency)

1974 OCCULT digest
MAIL ORDER CATALOGUE FOR ALL OCCULT SUPPLIES
Available from:
International Imports
Box 2010
Toluca Lake, Calif. California 91602.

THE WARLOCK SHOP
Herbs, witches' supplies, books, occult curios
300 Henry Street
Brooklyn, N.Y. 11201

THE BUCKLAND MUSEUM OF WITCHCRAFT AND MAGIC
6 First Avenue
Bay Shore, N.Y. 11706.

THE HOUSE OF WICCA
(Museum) at 378 Florida,
Buffalo, N.Y. 14208. 14208

UNDERGROUND JOURNAL OF OCCULT
Send $1.00 to—
Box 7374, Riverdale Station,
Hampton, Va. 23366

WITCHCRAFT SUPPLIES
Write for catalogue to:
Tyrad Company
Box 17006
Minneapolis, Minn. 55417

OCCULT SUPPLIES
Cauldron
P.O. Box AQ-403
Rego Park, N.Y. 11374
Catalogue 25 cents

WITCHES
T. C. Lethbridge
Citadel Press, 1972
$2.45

The investigation of an ancient religion involving the worship of Diana—the Witch Cult—laying as much stress on the consorts of the goddesses as on the lady herself.

SALEM POSSESSED: THE SOCIAL ORIGINS OF WITCHCRAFT
Paul Boyer and Stephen Nissenbaum
Harvard University Press, 1974
$10.00

DIARY OF A WITCH
Sybil Leek
Signet 1968
$0.75

EROS AND EVIL
R. E. I. Masters
Lancer, 1969
$1.75

WITCHCRAFT
Pennethorne Hughes
Pelican, 1965
$1.25

THE DEVIL IN LEGEND AND LITERATURE
Maximillian Rudwin
The Open Court Publishing Co., 1959
$3.95

THE SATANIC BIBLE
Anton Szandor LaVey
Avon, 1969
$1.25

MASTERING WITCHCRAFT
Paul Huson
Berkley, 1970
$1.25

SONGS FOR THE OLD RELIGION
$2.50
written by pagans, sung by pagans
Send to Nemeton
P.O. Box 13037,
Oakland, Calif. 94661
Just songs, not an album

THE DEVIL IN MASSACHUSETTS
Marion L. Starkey
Anchor, 1969
$1.95

THE HISTORY OF WITCHCRAFT AND DEMONOLOGY
Montague Summers
Routledge and Kegan Paul, 1973
$8.95

LETTERS ON DEMONOLOGY AND WITCHCRAFT
Sir Walter Scott
Ace, 1970
$0.75

DEVILS AND DEMONS: A DICTIONARY OF DEMONOLOGY
J. Tondriau and R. Villeneuve
Pyramid, 1972
$1.95

WITCHCRAFT AT SALEM
Chadwick Hansen
Signet, 1969
$1.25

Possession, Poltergeists And Exorcism

We contend that movies such as The Exorcist serve to obscure the complex dynamics of what may be involved in actual cases of possession. An attempt to show what a possessed individual may look like should not be accompanied by shallow innuendo. Such approaches contribute to a sensationalistic attitude towards anything associated with psychic phenomena and further fires popular misconceptions and irrational media-created fears of the unknown. The idea that demonic forces from the bowels of hell have focused on an individual in order to claim another victim, reflects a prevalent theological inability to focus more attention on how this behavior may reflect the uncontrolled eruptions of repressed dimensions of an individual's "self."

A creative focus on presenting PSI occurrences within an enlightening educational context rather than with an eye on crass commercial exploitation would contribute significantly to the gradual erosion of damaging fears of PSI phenomena and to the development of a more sophisticated, critical perspective.

EXORCISM: FACT NOT FICTION
Martin Ebon, ed.
Signet, 1974
$1.25

"I have assembled a variety of exorcism cases that range widely in approach and subject matter. The most detailed is a case of exorcism in Iowa in 1928. It has elements of the traditional-religious and the modern-psychological and is a prime example of interaction between victim and exorcist. There is a definite tendency, and we can observe it in many settings, for an apparently possessed person to fall quickly in line with the conceptions of the exorcist: if he expects demons to talk through them, demons they will produce. The German authority T. K. Oesterreich states in his book *Possession: Demoniacal and Other* that certain 'methods of treatment' create the conditions they are supposed to eliminate. Exorcisers, then, sometimes create demons to be exorcised. I find a striking similarity between the relationship of the hypnotist to his subject and the exorciser to a 'possessed' person. Self-dramatization, serious emotional imbalance, a psychological 'opening up' to outside influences—sometimes through drugs or psychophysiological exercises—can be factors leading to symptoms of possession. We know too little about psychosomatic factors, even in such illnesses as headaches, stomach pains, or skin rashes, to speak with any sort of certainty about possession cases. But there exists a strong element of cultural expectation; of that we can be sure. And I do not doubt that the right kind of exorcism, performed within the appropriate setting, can indeed 'drive out' an emotional and psychophysiological illness that may dramatize itself in a personalized manner."

ECSTATIC RELIGION: AN ANTHROPOLOGICAL STUDY OF SPIRIT POSSESSION AND SHAMANISM
I. M. Lewis
Pelican, 1971
$1.50

"This book explores that most decisive and profound of all religious dramas, the seizure of man by divinity. Such ecstatic encounters are by no means uniformly encouraged in all religions. Yet it is difficult to find a religion which has not, at some stage in its history, inspired in the breasts of at least certain of its followers those transports of mystical exaltation in which man's whole being seems to fuse in a glorious communion with the divinity. Transcendental experiences of this kind, typically conceived of as states of 'possession', have given the mystic a unique claim to direct experiential knowledge of the divine and, where this is acknowledged by others, the authority to act as a privileged channel of communication between man and the supernatural. The accessory phenomena associated with such experiences, particularly the 'speaking with tongues', prophesying, clairvoyance, the transmission of messages from the dead, and other mystical gifts, have naturally attracted the attention not only of the devout but also of sceptics. For many people, in fact, such phenomena seem to provide persuasive evidence or experience." the existence of a world transcending that of ordinary everyday experience.

POLTERGEIST
William G. Roll
Signet, 1972
$1.25

THE MIND POSSESSED: A PHYSIOLOGY OF POSSESSION, MYSTICS AND FAITH HEALING
William Sargent
Lippincott, 1974
$7.95

THE COFFEE TABLE BOOK OF WITCHCRAFT AND DEMONOLOGY
Paul Huson, ed.,
Putnam, 1973
$12.50

THE ORDER OF EXORCISM FROM THE RITUALE ROMANUM SET FORTH BY ORDER OF THE SUPREME PONTIFF, PAUL V [1605-21]

(The 1947 New York edition of the *Rituale Romanum* (with an introduction by Francis, Cardinal Spellman) reproduced verbatim the rite as printed by Maximilian van Eynatten in 1619, and included in the *Thesaurus Exorcismorum,* from which the following abstract is translated.)

The priest, robed in surplice and violet stole, one end of which is placed round the neck of the possessed person, bound if he is violent, sprinkles those present with holy water. Then the service begins.

1. The Litany.
2. Psalm 54 ("Save me, O God, by thy name").
3. Adjuration imploring God's grace for the proposed exorcism against the "wicked dragon" and a caution to the possessing spirit to "tell me thy name, the day, and the hour of thy going out, by some sign."
4. The Gospel (John i; and/or Mark xvi; Luke x; Luke xi).
5. Preparatory prayer.

Then the priest, protecting himself and the possessed by the sign of the cross, placing part of his stole round the neck and placing his right hand on the head of the possessed, resolutely and with great faith shall say what follows.

6. First Exorcism:

"I exorcize thee, most vile spirit, the very embodiment of our enemy, the entire specter, the whole legion, in the name of Jesus Christ, to ✠ get out and flee from this creature of God ✠✠

"He himself commands thee, who has ordered those cast down from the heights of heaven to the depths of the earth. He commands thee, he who commanded the sea, the winds, and the tempests.

"Hear therefore and fear, O Satan, enemy of the faith, foe to the human race, producer of death, thief of life, destroyer of justice, root of evils, kindler of vices, seducer of men, betrayer of nations, inciter of envy, origin of avarice, cause of discord, procurer of sorrows. Why dost thou stand and resist, when thou knowest that Christ the Lord will destroy thy strength? Fear him who was immolated in Isaac, sold in Joseph, slain in the lamb, crucified in man, and then was triumphant over hell.

(*The following signs of the cross should be made on the forehead of the possessed.*) "Depart therefore in the name of the ✠ Father, and of the ✠ Son, and of the Holy ✠ Ghost; give place to the Holy Ghost, by the sign of the ✠ Cross of Jesus Christ our Lord, who with the Father and the same Holy Ghost liveth and reigneth one God, for ever and ever, world without end."

7. Prayer for success, and making the signs of the cross over the demoniac.
8. Second Exorcism:

"I adjure thee, thou old serpent, by the judge of the quick and the dead, by thy maker and the maker of the world, by him who has power to send thee to hell, that thou depart quickly from this servant of God, N., who returns to the bosom of the Church, with fear and the affliction of thy terror. I adjure thee again (✠ *on his forehead*), not in my infirmity, but by the virtue of the Holy Ghost, that thou depart from this servant of God, N., whom Almighty God hath made in his own image.

DELIVER US FROM EVIL, Don Basham, Chosen Books, 1972, $2.50

DELIVER US FROM EVIL

The Story of a Man Who Dared to Explore the Censored Fourth of Christ's Ministry

By DON BASHAM

"Let me give you a word of advice," says a woman the author meets early in this book. "The Deliverance Ministry is nothing to fool around with."

The Reverend Don Basham couldn't have agreed more. The idea of demons or demon-possession was repulsive to him. Yet Don Basham found himself drawn reluctantly into the subject as time and again he was confronted by stark evidence that people he met and knew were inhabited by what the Bible describes as "evil spirits." As, slowly, step by reasoned step, he moves from disbelief in demons to acceptance of their reality, you will find yourself reading a detective story, a logical putting together of clues, a fascinating, true-life adventure. What emerges is a factual picture, the truth behind the stories that millions of readers have read in fictional form in books such as the enthralling *The Exorcist*.

Finds Answers to Personal Problems

Don Basham is a Christian living in today's scientific and pragmatic age. He has spent years counseling people with chronic, recurring problems, their debilitating emotions and addictions. In the course of his work, he was utterly amazed to learn that taking authority over a demon could achieve in an instant what months of personal counseling often failed to do. And so, deliverance became not a fearful thing to him, but a thing of hope and reassurance. In these pages you will find something more than eerie laughs and strange, sinister happenings; you will find actual people being healed of ailments, or freed from anxiety, or released from the tyranny of tobacco and alcohol. Don Basham makes clear that the ministry he now understands so well means more than deliverance *from* evil, it means delivery *into* health and well-being.

POLTERGEIST
A special issue of Psychic observer
Vol. XXXII, No. 3, 1971
50 cents

"Sometimes poltergeist and haunting are used interchangeably, but generally poltergeist is reserved for disturbances which are physically violent. In poltergeist cases there are often daily movements and breakage of plates, knickknacks, furniture, and other movable household effects, whereas in the typical haunting case such incidents are more rare and more spread out in time if they occur at all. Poltergeist disturbances are also generally of fairly short duration, rarely lasting more than a couple of months, and often less. Hauntings, however, may go on for years. The typical poltergeist case has no reference to hallucinatory experiences, such as seeing ghosts and hearing footsteps. Reports of such experiences, however, are common in hauntings.

"Investigations of poltergeists are generally conducted in a private house or business—that is, away from the home base of the investigatior, his own research laboratory. As a rule, therefore, he cannot impose all the precautions and controls that are possible in experimental work, and he often has to labor under a great deal of uncertainty. Poltergeist studies are not for the person who craves a neat and well-controlled research design. My task, as I have seen it, has been to collect as many observations as I could, under as good conditions as possible, given the circumstances, in the hope that some regularity or pattern would emerge in the data which would point to an explanation. This could then be put to the test in future field studies and, hopefully, in controlled experimentation. . . ."

EXORCISM: THE REPORT OF A COMMISSION CONVENED BY THE BISHOP OF EXETER, edited by Dom Robert Petitpierre, O.S.B., 1972. $1.75
Available from:
Holy Trinity Church
Marylebone Road
London NW1 4DV, England.

EXORCISM

EDITED BY
Dom Robert Petitpierre
O.S.B.

THE FINDINGS OF A COMMISSION CONVENED BY THE BISHOP OF EXETER

EXORCISM

At a time when there is increasing, and too often unhealthy, interest in witchcraft, magic, and the occult, it is important that the Church should have a clear mind about the spiritual casualties so often involved and how to deal with them. A commission was appointed by the Bishop of Exeter to inquire into the history and practice of Exorcism as a function of the Christian ministry and their report is printed here, supported by an introductory essay on "Exorcism in the New Testament" by Fr J. Crehan, S.J., and by a number of forms of service and prayer for the various occasions of exorcism and spiritual healing. Edited by Dom Robert Petitpierre (an Anglican Benedictine monk, who has experience in these matters, and has on occasion made broadcasts about them) this book will bring welcome help not only to the clergy but also to doctors, psychiatrists, social workers, and others concerned with these problems.

CONTENTS

Members of the Commission

Foreword by the Bishop of Exeter

Exorcism in the New Testament
by Fr J. H. Crehan, S.J.

Report on Christian Exorcism

APPENDIX I
A Note on the Occurrence of Exorcism Prayers in the Book of Common Prayer

APPENDIX II
The Exorcism and Blessing of a Place

APPENDIX III
The Exorcism and Blessing of a Person

APPENDIX IV
A Form for Blessing Holy Water

APPENDIX V
Suitable forms of Prayer and Exorcism

APPENDIX VI
Forms of Service for the Ministry of the Laying on of Hands and for the Anointing with Oil for the Sick

DEFINITION

Christian exorcism is the binding of evil powers by the triumph of Christ Jesus, through the application of the power demonstrated by that triumph, in and by his Church. The New Testament not only assumes the existence of non-human powers of evil, it asserts repeatedly the fact of the triumph of Christ Jesus over them. The prominence given in the gospels to the exorcisms done by our Lord is evidence of this, as is also the close association with them of the word *exousia*.

It will be as well at the outset to note that in Christian usage the verb *to exorcize* applies strictly only to demons. It is possible to speak loosely about exorcizing persons or places, but what is meant is the exorcizing of the demonic forces of evil *in* those persons or places. Exorcism is an exercise of *exousia*: it commands and binds. This, as noted below, must never be applied to humans as such. And in dealing with places it is well to exorcize *over* the place, in order to release it from the domination of any evil powers that may be there. Such exorcism should of course always be associated with prayer and a blessing. . . .

THE FORMS OF EXORCISM

(a) All forms in ordinary use should contain, in the context of either prayer or command, an order to the demon (i) to depart, (ii) to harm no one and, most importantly, (iii) to depart to its own place, there to remain for ever.

(b) The form of exorcism may take the form either of a prayer to Almighty God, or of a command in the name of Christ to the powers of evil. It would seem that older formulae were usually addressed to God, but the earliest on record is the word *Exi!* (*Get out!*) addressed to a demon by a nun. Later formulae, since the seventh century, are on the whole in the command form accompanied by a rich use of the names of God.

(c) The Lord's prayer itself is a form of exorcism. It begins with an invocation of the holy name, and ends with the petition for deliverance from the evil one. It is very suitable for use with that intention by the laity, either in times of personal temptation or when in a group which is involved in a tense and potentially evil situation.

(d) It should be noted that exorcism can be and has been carried out by any Christian, and even by non-Christians, in the name of Christ.[6] But since it is always advisable to follow every exorcism with a blessing, on the principle of not leaving the house empty,[7] it is best to have a priest present, and therefore it is logical that the priest shall himself be the chief exorcist where there is not a bishop so acting.

(e) The external technique of exorcism consists in the recital of the formula, accompanied by some appropriate action at the operative clause in the formula. The most usual action is the sprinkling of holy water (prepared with the appropriate prayers): the sign of the cross: or a deep exhalation (an ancient form of invoking the Holy Spirit) over the affected person.

MAIL ORDER EXORCISM

Satan Is the Pusher-Man

If churches today have anyone to thank for increased attendance, it's Satan. The recent popularity of demonic possession has given some preachers just the boost they need to attract borderline cases who fancy they have fallen under an evil influence. Churches, particularly throughout the South, are thriving on exorcism sermons and have been importing demon specialists who can up the ante in nightly collection plates.

Most of the devil specialists have been exorcists-come-lately, but some old-time preachers have been waiting for just such an opportunity. Mail-order evangelists appear to be the biggest beneficiaries of the devil business and two in particular are C. S. Lovett and Morris Cerullo.

Lovett runs an organization called Personal Christianity in Baldwin Park, California; and Cerullo, who calls himself the world's foremost "Christian Jew," conducts worldwide crusades from his home office in San Diego.

Lovett rushed into the devil sweepstakes with his "Resist Satan Special," a personal protection kit selling for $4.97 (reg. $6.85 value). The special consists of three paperback books that teach one how to deal with the Evil One via a four-point plan. Lovett's mail-out (headed in stark red-and-black type) asks: "Has Satan Injured Your Family—Yet?" He relates how the inspiration came to him when an alarmed family sought his aid when their son had been jailed for possession of "marihuana [sic] and attacking a young girl." Unaccountably, Lovett makes his pitch with a drawing of a young couple "making out" in a convertible and he equates "sex ignorance" with "Satan ignorance." He further advises that "love for Jesus affords no anti-Satan protection."

Cerullo mounted a larger offensive against dark forces. His first step was to field a "witchmobile," a fearsomely illustrated travel trailer exhibiting the terrible results of witchcraft, including a "genuine human skull."

His research also led him to publish a 28-page tabloid which "contains a wealth of information on both the occult scene and carries an informative supplement on drug abuse." The newspaper covers an astonishing range of subjects and at last reveals the truth about the I Ching, Jeanne Dixon, Yoga, Voodoo, Crystal Gazing, and a

© August 15, 1974, "Rolling Stone."

dozen other subjects familiar to witches. Cerullo's tabloid also advertises his definitive book on the occult. *The Back Side of Satan* covers all you need to know about this worrisome Lucifer business: "Charge-a-voodoo-hex on Master Charge," "How California's Professional Witch Hunters Work," "Teenagers Dying through Witchcraft Experimentation," "Influence of Witchcraft on Movies and Music," and "The Role of the Occult in the Manson Murders." It's illustrated with "revealing photos taken at occult meetings."

A bonus to the tabloid is a two-page dictionary divided into the "Jargon of the Occult" and "Dopers Jargon." If your children or loved ones use any of the following terms, you might want to summon the witchmobile: "Cosmic consciousness: to be in tune with the Universe, an expression used by people spaced out by drugs or meditation"; "Yoga: exercise and meditation opening mind to dark powers"; "Crash pad: place where user withdraws from amphetamines"; "Fuzz: the police"; "Pig: policeman"; "Flush: initial feeling after injecting a drug like methamphetamine"; "Flip: become psychotic"; "Cop: to obtain heroin"; "Heavy: significant or highly emotional"; "Make it: to buy narcotics"; Re-entry: return from a trip"; "High: under the influence of drugs"; "Split: to leave or to flee"; "Piece: a pistol, revolver; "Clean: addict not currently using drugs."

Additionally, Cerullo provides the following, extremely valuable chronology of an "LSD Trip": "Illusions and hallucinations occur, increase in blood pressure and blood sugar and heart rate, impaired memory and attention span, impulses toward violence and suicidal acts, possible damage to retina of eye, can alter chromosome structure, possible permanent brain damage, severe muscle spasms can break bones, personality changes and psychosis, homicidal attempts occur, can create psychological dependence, loss of sanity—become a vegetable."

If that is not enough to put your foot on the right path, Cerullo directs your attention to the following chronology of suffering undergone by "marijuana addicts": "Impairs judgment and memory, alters reality by lowering blood glucose, causes psychological dependence, affects entire intestinal tract, causes irritability and confusion, can cause coma, causes inflammation of mucous membrane, time and space perception are altered, loss of motivation and ambition, anxiety reactions and panic states, can cause psychotic breakdowns, causes hilarity and carelessness. Note: Marijuana is also known as weed, pot, M, grass, hemp, jive, rope, Indian hay, Mary Jane, loco weed, giggle smoke, hashish, joint, stick, reefer, ashes, Sweet Lucy, hay and roach."

If you think that little of the above has anything to do with witchcraft, guess again. Cerullo has found that members of the occult control much of this nation's drug traffic. So, remember: What you consider to be a harmless "stick" of "Sweet Lucy" may be the first step toward demonic possession. Be advised.

Rolling Stone, August 15, 1974.

—Chet Flippo

PUBLISHERS LISTED IN PSI: THE OTHER WORLD CATALOGUE

Abelard-Schuman Ltd.,
450 Edgeware Road,
London W2 1EG, England.

Ace Publishing Corp., Ace Books, Ace Star,
1120 Avenue of the Americas
New York, N.Y. 10036.

American Society for Psychical Research,
5 West 73rd Street,
New York, N.Y. 10023.

Ann Arbor Paperbacks,
Box 146
611 Church St.
Ann Arbor, Michigan

A.R.E. Press
Box 595
Virginia Beach, Virginia 23451

Arrow Books Ltd.,
178–202 Great Portland Street,
London, W.1., England.

Award Books,
235 East 45th Street,
New York, N.Y. 10017.

Avon Books–Discus,
959 Eighth Avenue,
New York, N.Y. 10019.

Ballantine Books Inc.,
201 East 50th Street,
New York, N.Y. 10022.

Ballantine Books–Mockingbird Books,
Department CS,
36 West 20th Street,
New York, N.Y. 10003.

Bantam Books Inc.,
666 5th Avenue,
New York, N.Y. 10019.

Berkely Publishing Corporation,
Berkely Medallion
200 Madison Avenue,
New York, N.Y. 10016.

The Bobbs–Merrill Co. Inc.,
4300 West 62nd St.
Indianapolis, Indiana 46206

The Bolen Company,
680 Beach Street,
San Francisco, Cal. 94109.

Borderland Sciences Research Foundation,
P.O. Box 548,
Vista, Cal. 92083.

George Braziller,
1 Park Avenue,
New York, N.Y. 10016.

Chosen Books
Washington Depot
Connecticut, 06794.

The Citadel Press,
120 Enterprise Avenue,
Secaucus, New Jersey, 07094.

James Clarke & Co. Ltd.,
31 Queen Anne's Gate,
London, S.W. 1., England.

Collier Books,
866 Third Avenue,
New York, N.Y. 10022.

Coronet Communications, Inc.,
Paperback Library,
P.B.L. Occult,
315 Park Avenue S.,
New York, N.Y. 10010.

Coward, McCann & Geoghegan Inc., Popular Library,
200 Madison Avenue,
New York, N.Y. 10016.

Cowles Education Corporation,
LOOK Building,
488 Madison Avenue,
New York, N.Y. 10022.

Thomas Y. Crowell Co.,
666 Fifth Avenue
N.Y., N.Y. 10019

CSA Printers & Publishers,
Lakemont,
Georgia, 30552.

H.S. Dakin,
3456 Jackson Street,
San Francisco, Cal. 94118.

The C.W. Daniel Co. Ltd.,
60 Muswell Road,
London, N.10, England.

Darshana International,
Moradabad–19,
India.

Dell—Laurel, Delta, Delacorte Press,
1 Dag Hammarskjold Plaza,
New York, N.Y. 10017.

The Devin–Adair Co.,
1 Park Avenue,
Old Greenwich, Conn. 06870.

DeVorss & Co.,
1641 Lincoln Boulevard,
Santa Monica, Cal. 90404.

Doubleday–Anchor Books,
277 Park Avenue,
New York, N.Y. 10017.

Dover Publications, Inc.,
180 Varick Street,
New York, N.Y. 10014.

E.P. Dutton & Company Inc.,
201 Park Avenue S.,
New York, N.Y. 10003.

East West Journal,
31 Farnsworth Street,
Bsoton, Mass. 022110.

Educational Research Institute,
P.O. Box 4203,
North Hollywood, Cal. 91607.

El Cariso Publications,
P.O. Box 176
Elsinore, California, 92330.

EP Publishing Ltd.,
East Ardsley,
Wakefield,
Yorkshire, England.

ESPress, Inc.,
5605 Sixteenth Street,
N.W. Washington, D.C. 20011.

M. Evans and Co. Inc.,
216 E. 49th Street,
New York, N.Y. 10017.

Faber and Faber Ltd.,
24 Russell Square,
London, W.C.1., England.

Fawcett Publications—Fawcett Crest Books,
Fawcett Building,
Greenwich, Conn., 06830.

Frederick Fell Publishers, Inc.,
386 Park Avenue South,
New York, N.Y. 10016.

L. N. Fowler & Co. Ltd.,
15 New Bridge Street,
London, EC4V 6BB, England.

W.H. Freeman and Co.,
660 Market Street,
San Francisco, Cal. 94104.

Freeway Press,
220 Park Avenue South,
New York, N.Y. 10003.

Garrett Publications,
29 West 57th St.
N.Y., N.Y.

Gordon and Breach, Science Publishers, Inc.,—Interface Books,
1 Park Avenue,
New York, N.Y. 10016.

Gordon and Breach, Science Publishers, Inc.,—Interface Books,
1 Park Avenue,
New York, N.Y. 10016.

Granada Publishing Ltd.—Mayflower Books,
Frogmore,
St. Albans,
Herts. AL2 2NF, England.

Grove Press, Inc.,
53 East 11th Street,
New York, N.Y. 10003.

Harper & Row—Harper Torchbooks, H. Colophon, Perennial,
49 East 33rd Street,
New York, N.Y. 10016.

Harper & Row—Harper Torchbooks,
H. Colophon, Perennial,
49 East 33rd Street,
New York, N.Y. 10016.

Hawthorn Books Inc.
260 Madison Avenue
New York, N.Y. 10016

Health Research,
70 Lafayette Street,
Mokelumne Hill, Cal. 95245.

Houghton Mifflin Company,
2 Park Street,
Boston, Mass. 02107.

Hutchison & Co. Ltd.,
3 Fitzroy Square,
London, W.1., England.

Indiana University Press,
10th and Morton Streets,
Bloomington, Ind., 47401.

Institute for the Study of Mental Images,
Church Crookham,
Hampshire, England.

Alfred A. Knopf—Borzoi Books,
201 East 50th Street,
New York, N.Y. 10022.

Lancer Books,
1560 Broadway,
New York, N.Y. 10036.

J.B. Lippincot Co.,
E. Washington Square,
Philadelphia, Pa. 19105.

Llewellyn Publications,
St. Paul, Minnesota 55165.

Lyle Stewart Inc.,
120 Enterprise Avenue,
Secaucus, N.U. 07094.

Macalester Park Publishing Co.,
1571 Grand Avenue,
St. Paul, Minnesota 55105.

Macfadden-Bartell Corp.;—Macfadden Books,
205 East 42nd Street,
New York, N.Y. 10017.

The Macmillan Co.—Collier Books,
866 Third Avenue,
New York, N.Y. 10022.

Manor Books Inc.,
329 Fifth Avenue,
New York, N.Y. 10016.

The MIT Press,
Cambridge,
Massachusetts 02142.

Thomas Nelson,
30 East 42nd Street,
New York, N.Y. 10017.

New Age Press Inc.,
4634 Vineta Avenue,
La Canada, Cal. 91011.

New American Library—Signet, Signet Mystic, Signette, Mentor, Classic, Plume & NAL Books,
1301 Avenue of the Americas,
New York, N.Y. 10019.

Newcastle Publishing Co. Inc.,
1521 No. Vine Street,
Hollywood, Cal. 90028.

The Noonday Press,
19 Union Square West,
New York, 10003.

Octopus Books Ltd.,
59 Grosvenor Street,
London W.1., England.

Omen Press,
P.O. Box 12457,
Tucson, Ariz. 85711.

Oxford University Press, Inc.—Galaxy Books,
200 Madison Avenue
N.Y., N.Y. 10016

Pan Books Ltd.,
33 Tothill Street,
London, S.W.1., England.

Parapsychology Foundation Inc.,
29 West 57th Street,
New York, N.Y. 10019.

The parapsychology Press,
P.O. Box 6847,
College Station,
Durham, North Carolina, 27708.

Parker Publishing Co. Inc.,
Department GC—501,
West Nyack, N.Y. 10994.

Penguin Books Inc.—Pelican,
2110 Ambassador Road,
Baltimore, Maryland 21207.

Pinnacle Books, Inc.,
275 Madison Avenue,
New York, N.Y. 10016.

Pocket Books/Simon & Schuster,
1 West 39th Street,
New York, N.Y. 10018.

Prentice-Hall Inc.,
Englewood Cliffs,
New Jersey, 07632.

Princeton University Press—Bollingen Series,
Princeton, New Jersey 08540

Pursuit, Journal for the Study of the Unexplained,
R.D., Columbia,
New Jersey, 07832.

G.P. Putnam's Sons—Capricorn Books,
200 Madison Avenue,
New York, N.Y. 10016.

Pyramid Communications, Inc.—Pyramid Special Books,
919 Third Avenue,
New York, N.Y. 10022.

Quadrangle/The New York Times Book Co.,
330 Madison Avenue,
New York, N.Y. 10017.

Random House—Vintage Books,
201 E. 50th Street,
New York, N.Y. 10022.

Regency Press (London and New York) Ltd.,
43 New Oxford Street,
London, W.C.1., England.

Henry Regnery Co.,
114 West Illinois Street,
Chicago, Illinois, 60610.

Rider & Company,
3 Fitzroy Square
London, W.1., England.

J.F. Roun Y Press Publishers,
Santa Barbara, Cal.

Routledge & Kegan Paul Ltd.,
68-74 Carter Lane,
London, EC4V 5ELL, England.

Rudolf Steiner Publications,
151 North Moison Road,
Blauvelt, N.Y. 10913.

Saucerian Books,
Box 2228,
Clarksburg, West Virginia.

The Scarecrow Press, Inc.,
Metuchen,
New Jersey.

Schocken Books,
67 Park Avenue,
New York, N.Y. 10016.

Charles Scribner's Sons,
597 Fifth Avenue,
New York, N.Y. 10017.

Self-Realization Fellowship,
388 San Rafael Avenue,
Los Angeles, Cal. 90065.

Shambala Publications Inc.,
1409 Fifth Street,
Berkeley, Cal. 94710.

Simon and Shuster,
Rockefeller Center,
630 Fifth Avenue,
New York, N.Y. 10020.

The Society for Psychical Research,
1 Adam and Eve Mews,
London, W.8., England.

Society of Rosicrucians Inc.,
321 West 101st Street,
New York, N.Y. 10025.

Neville Spearman,
112 Whitefield
London, England

The Spiritualist Association of Great Britain,
33 Belgrave Square,
London, SW1X 8QL, England.

Stein and Day,
7 East 48th Street,
New York, N.Y. 10017.

Straight Arrow Books,
625 Third Street,
San Francisco, Cal. 94107.

Taplinger Publishing Co.,
200 Park Avenue South,
New York, N.Y. 10003.

Thames and Hudson,
30 Bloomsbury Street,
London, WC1B 3QP, England.

The Theosophical Publishing House (London) Ltd.,
64 Great Russell Street,
W.C.1., England. and Wheaton, Illinois, USA.

Theosophical University Press,
Pasadena, California.

Tower Publications Inc.,
185 Madison Avenue,
New York, N.Y. 10016.

Transworld Publishers Ltd.—Corgi Books,
Cavendish House,
57–59 Uxbridge Road,
Ealing, London, W.5., England.

Universal Publishing and Distributing Corp.—Award Books,
285 East 45th Street,
New York, N.Y. 10017.

University Books,
120 Enterprise Avenue
Secaucus, N.J. 07094

University Press of Virginia,
Charlottesville,
Virginia.

U.S. Government Printing Office,
Washington, D.C.

The Viking Press, Inc.—Esalen Books,
625 Madison Avenue,
New York, N.Y. 10022.

Vincent Stuart Publishers Ltd.,
45 Lower Blegrave Street,
London, S.W.1., England.

Warner Books Inc.—Warner Paperback,
315 Park Avenue South,
New York, N.Y. 10010.

Weidenfield & Nicholson—World University,
5 Winsley Street,
London, W.1., England.

Samuel Weiser Inc.,
734 Broadway,
New York, N.Y. 10003.

Wilshire Book Company,
12015 Sherman Road,
North Hollywood, Cal. 91605.

The World Publishing Co.,
110 East 59th Street,
New York, N.Y. 10022.

Zebra Publications Inc.,
275 Madison Avenue,
New York, N.Y. 10016.